Oracle Press™

Oracle9*i* DBA 101

About the Authors

Marlene Theriault has been an Oracle DBA for over 19 years and has worked with Oracle products since version 2.0 of the Oracle RDBMS. She is coauthor of the new book *Oracle Security Handbook* with Aaron Newman (Oracle Press, 2001). Ms. Theriault is also the author or coauthor of four other Oracle Press books: *Oracle8i Networking 101*; *Oracle9i DBA Handbook* and *Oracle8i DBA Handbook* with Kevin Loney; *Oracle DBA 101* with Rachel Carmichael and James Viscusi; and she coauthored *Oracle Security* with William Heney (O'Reilly and Associates, 1998). An award-winning speaker, Ms. Theriault has presented technical papers and tutorials at Oracle conferences throughout the world. She and her husband, Nelson, are avid recreational walkers. She can be reached at mtheriault@mindspring.com.

Rachel Carmichael has been an Oracle DBA for over 10 years. She chairs the DBA Special Interest Group and is the meeting agenda coordinator for the New York Oracle Users Group, is both Chauncey and OCP certified, and has presented at various international and national conferences. She has coauthored three Oracle Press books: *Oracle SQL and PL/SQL Annotated Archives* (1998), with Kevin Loney, *Oracle9i Instant PL/SQL Scripts* (2001), with Megh Thakar and Kevin Loney, and *Oracle DBA 101* (2000), with Marlene Theriault and James Viscusi. She can be reached at wisernet100@yahoo.com.

James Viscusi has been working with relational database products for over 12 years and specifically with Oracle for the last 8 years. He currently works with Oracle Corporation in the High Availability Group. He has presented at several conferences worldwide, including Oracle Open World, IOUG-A, and many East Coast Regional Users Groups. Mr. Viscusi is coauthor of *Oracle DBA 101* (2000), with Marlene Theriault and Rachel Carmichael. He is also a husband, father of two children, and volunteers as an emergency medical technician.

Oracle Press™

Oracle9*i* DBA 101

Marlene Theriault, Rachel Carmichael,
and James Viscusi

McGraw-Hill/Osborne

New York Chicago San Francisco
Lisbon London Madrid Mexico City
Milan New Delhi San Juan
Seoul Singapore Sydney Toronto

McGraw-Hill/Osborne
2600 Tenth Street
Berkeley, California 94710
U.S.A.

To arrange bulk purchase discounts for sales promotions, premiums, or fund-raisers, please contact **McGraw-Hill**/Osborne at the above address. For information on translations or book distributors outside the U.S.A., please see the International Contact Information page immediately following the index of this book.

Oracle9*i* DBA 101

1234567890 CUS CUS 0198765432

ISBN 0-07-2224746

Publisher
Brandon A. Nordin

Vice President & Associate Publisher
Scott Rogers

Acquisitions Editor
Jeremy Judson

Project Editor
Madhu Prasher

Acquisitions Coordinator
Athena Honore

Technical Editors
Joseph S. Testa and Jay Norton

Copy Editor
Judith Brown

Proofreader
Cheryl Applewood

Indexer
Valerie Robbins

Computer Designers
Elizabeth Jang, Lucie Ericksen, Mickey Galicia

Illustrators
Michael Mueller, Lyssa Wald

Cover Series Design
Damore Johann Design, Inc.

This book was composed with Corel VENTURA™ Publisher.

In memory of my aunt, Mollie C. Robbins,
September 4, 1911 – January 30, 2002

To my mother, Lillian Mona Siegel, age 93,
who just keeps on truckin' along

And to my family, who continue to
support me in all that I do.

—Marlene Theriault

To Peter, always. And dragonflies.

—Rachel Carmichael

To Sara and James, who were patient
when Daddy had to be "busy"
and still manage to delight me daily

and

To Sandi, who understood why and covered for me
when I needed it most.

—James Viscusi

Contents at a Glance

PART IV
Tuning Your World

PART V
Appendixes

Contents

PART IV
Tuning Your World

PART V
Appendixes

Acknowledgments

Acknowledgments from All of Us

Thanks to everyone at Osborne/McGraw-Hill. You have all worked very hard to make this book a reality and have done a marvelous job: Scott Rogers, Jeremy Judson, Madhu Prasher, Athena Honore, Judith Brown, and the rest of the staff involved. Special thanks to Jeremy, who found ways to squeeze out extra pages for us to fill.

Joe Testa has been a valued friend of both Rachel's and Marlene's for several years, and his technical review has been both expert and invaluable. Thank you so much, Joe, for juggling the technical review along with raising a family and maintaining a full-time job. You are amazing! While we're on the subject of technical review, we'd like to thank Jay Norton, of Oracle Education, for providing excellent insights. His expertise has made this book much more accurate. Thanks Joe and Jay for helping to keep us straight!

Acknowledgments from Marlene Theriault

In the original *Oracle DBA 101*, I wrote that it was perhaps the easiest book for me to be involved with writing both because it was a book that I had wanted to write for a very long time and because my coauthors were so wonderful. I summed up my feelings with "In any event, this book has been a joy to be involved in from start to finish. The effort put forth by everyone involved has been stellar." I can only echo those words—only more so—in this edition. The writing flowed easily, and this book came together in record time thanks to the efforts of everyone involved.

My thanks, as always, go first and foremost to Rachel Carmichael, who has been my beloved friend and one of my writing partners for many years. We've shared both great and not so great times together and come through them all with a greater appreciation, understanding, and love of each other. I am sure that no matter what life may throw at either one of us, the other will be there to soften the blow and provide guidance and support. Words cannot express what her friendship has meant and continues to mean to me.

I am very grateful that Jim Viscusi has been a special friend to me for so long. The longer I know him, the more I value his support, advice, help, and friendship. His contribution to this book has been significant, and I thank him wholeheartedly for being willing to take precious time away from his family to be involved with this task. Jim, you ARE the best!

Scott Gossett and John Hough, of Oracle Education, were always there to answer a question or provide needed guidance, and I truly value their contributions as well. Other Oracle employees (all valued friends) who contributed to this book are Edward Montes, Cathy Lockwood, and Sue Hornbuckle. I rely on you all to help keep me straight.

My thanks continue to go to Kevin Loney, who has provided opportunities to help me enhance both my knowledge and career. Kevin, you are truly both a wonderful, patient mentor and even better friend.

I'd like to personally thank Bert Spencer and Carl Dudley for their continued contribution to the European Oracle user community and, more importantly, for their friendship. There are several people who continue to be both my personal top Oracle gurus and, more importantly, very special friends. These are the folks that I turn to first when I have a question, need special insights, or am in a quandary and need help and advice: Dan Hotka, Michael Ault, Eyal Aronoff, Robert Freeman, Dan Peacock, Bill Thater, Matt Reagan, Darryl Hickson, and Aaron Newman. You guys have never let me down!

Friends play a vital part in helping to bring a book to completion, and I must thank Roz Croog for always being there to help and support me.

As always, I must thank my husband, Nelson, for seeing me through seven books! Without him to keep everything running smoothly and, more importantly, helping to keep me sane and grounded, I could not do any of this. And, finally, thank you to my family, especially my son, Marc Goodman, and daughter, Jean Cahill, for being there to buoy my spirits and provide amazing guidance and wisdom.

Acknowledgments from Rachel Carmichael

In September 1990, never having seen an Oracle database, I became the Oracle DBA. (We need a DBA. "Poof!" You're the DBA.) The memory of those first frantic months, desperately trying to learn enough, to understand the workings of the database, will never leave me and, in part, is the reason for this book. In March 1991, I attended the first East Coast Oracle user's conference, where I met Marlene Theriault. She's been stuck with me ever since. In 1996, at IOUW in San Francisco, Kevin Loney introduced Marlene and me to James Viscusi, and Jim has been stuck with us ever since.

Updating a book may be even harder than writing one, something I didn't think possible. Finding ways to make room for new information was painful, and I thank Marlene and Jim for the blood, sweat, and tears as we reworked (and reworked!) the contents.

I would like to thank the wonderful people of Oracle Users Resource, who put on the ECO conference each year from 1991 to 2000. You gave Marlene and me a home. Most especially I want to thank Tony Ziemba, who urged me every year to present and who eventually had to hire me so he could *tell* me to present, and Mike LaMagna, who ran the DBA seminar. Mike finally just gave in to the inevitable and allowed Marlene and me to take over the seminar each year. It was at these seminars that we began the DBA 101 course, the basis of this book.

My special thanks to Joe Testa, tech editor and friend, for starting the oracle-l-ot list, which fills my inbox but kept me sane and laughing through this process.

I spend a good deal of time hanging out on the ORACLE-L email listserv. The people on this list have taught me that as little as I think I know, I have a great deal to give. And no matter how much I have learned, there is always something new. My thanks to Jared Still, the list owner, who gives me a forum to learn and to help others.

There are others, too, who contributed by valiantly running scripts over and over as I attempted to find just the right code for various examples. My thanks and extra hugs go to Dan Peacock, Bill Thater, Jeff Stevenson, and Kevin Lange.

I want to thank Kevin Loney, who got me started on this writing merry-go-round by inviting me to coauthor the *Oracle SQL & PL/SQL Annotated Archives* with him. One of these days I may forgive him for that! His belief in my abilities and his willingness to correct my misunderstandings have made me a much better DBA.

Jim Viscusi has been a friend for a number of years. He has always been available to help me solve problems, both personal and professional, spending time he doesn't have to spare, to answer my questions. He has been there with advice, friendship, and support at all turns. His contributions to this book have been invaluable, and I am indebted to him for so much.

My friendship with Marlene Theriault began in the middle of a sentence with talks about Oracle and has expanded to fill every area of my life. She has been there for me at every moment, encouraging me, supporting me, and urging me to grow and develop. We've gone through good and bad times together, and I am not sure there are words adequate enough to express what she means to me. I love her dearly and am grateful every day for her friendship.

I owe a good deal to my family and friends, who put up with my distraction and lack of time while we were writing this. Mom and Dad, I could not have survived the last few years without your help. I love you. And Tigger, who sat beside me as I wrote, reminding me of priorities by insisting on cuddling, purring, getting "scritches," and occasionally "contributing" by walking over the keyboard. I miss him daily.

Finally, and always, my love and thanks go to Peter. I will live with the lessons he taught me forever.

Acknowledgments from James Viscusi

This book is about helping people start something new. In your case it is being an Oracle DBA. My first steps on this road would not have been nearly as successful without a willingness to try something new and without support from many sources, only some of which I can thank here.

I first met Marlene Theriault at Oracle Open World in 1996, and the more I have gotten to know her, the more impressed I have become. Marlene's success in life is extraordinary by any standards, but I admire it even more knowing some of the paths she has had to travel along the way. She handled the job of leading this project with grace and style and always had an encouraging word along the way—even when she was busy juggling her own commitments—making my part in the process that much more rewarding. To my gentle, preprogrammed nag, my sincere thanks for keeping me honest to my own commitments without ever bruising our friendship along the way.

Meeting Rachel and Marlene on the same night is like winning the lottery twice in the same day! Over the years, Rachel has always been a good friend to turn to, professionally and personally. She has always had one of the best qualities in a friend—the ability to know when to give advice and when to just listen. I'm grateful for her friendship and our many conversations over the years—none of which were casual!

Kevin Loney's name shows up all through these acknowledgments and with good reason. I cannot thank Kevin enough for his encouragement while we worked together and for asking me to present with him at Open World. In that act, Kevin's actions embodied the spirit of this book. His willingness to take on a "partner" and his support and encouragement of my beginning efforts set me on the path to be a better DBA and led inevitably to my contributions here.

I'm deeply indebted to many people at Oracle who took the time to share their experiences and in many cases their friendship. One who deserves special recognition is Anjo Kolk, performance guru and the person who exposed me to some of the philosophies behind tuning databases. Thanks as well to Andy Tremayne for many days and nights of conversation and debate on how to build practical experience into a set of diagnostic questions. Many thanks to my current workmates who were willing to share and collaborate when the topic of performance came up: Steve Andrew, Karl Daday, Ray Dutcher, Susan Kim, Vijay Lunawat, Roderick Manalac, Erhan Odok, Sameer Patkar, Stefan Pommerenk, Hector Pujol, Kevin Reardon, and Lawrence To. This time around, a special thank you to Shari Yamaguchi, who continually astounds me with a combination of boundless energy and an unfailingly positive attitude, for her help and support while I did this update.

A special nod to Bruce Costa for long years of friendship and advice and a swift kick in the tail when required. My completing any contributions at all is in part due to a long night of conversation and advice that could be best boiled down to, "Sit down, shut up, and write!"

In the end, it was my family who was the most consistent source of support. Thanks to my parents, who were always supportive and willing to pitch in whenever things got really hectic. Most importantly, special thanks to my wife, Sandi, who helped in so many ways. Whether it was reading drafts, listening to me rant, or just knowing when to bring me a cup of coffee and shut the door, she was there through this entire process. I'm grateful for her support in more ways than I can ever fully express. She's earned all the "spoiling" I can provide.

Getting Started

new•bie *n*

/n[y]oo'bee/ (Originally from British public-school and military slang variant of "new boy") An inexperienced user of a system.

Beginnings are scary. Whether it's starting in a new school, beginning a new job, or learning a new skill, despite the exciting prospect, there's always an element of fear, a feeling of being overwhelmed, of "How will I ever manage to learn it all?" We call this feeling the "New Kid on the Block" syndrome, and it applies to every new venture we begin. We are all, always, newbies about something.

In 1991, Rachel Carmichael was a brand-new Oracle DBA, without having ever seen or worked with Oracle before. And although Marlene Theriault had been working with Oracle for a while, the new release, version 6, was an almost complete rewrite of the database, making her a newbie all over again. Fortunately for them both, in March of that year, a small group of people, incorporated as Oracle User Resources, held their first-ever East Coast Oracle (ECO) conference in Washington, D.C. The conference was titled "A Wizard's Gathering."

Standing in the hotel registration line, Marlene found herself in conversation with the woman next to her. That woman was Rachel. Neither one of them can remember how that conversation started or what it was about, but there is one thing that both of them are very sure of. That conversation started in the middle of a sentence! And they haven't stopped talking since.

Over the next few years, with very few other resources available, they used snail mail and phone calls to help one another learn each new release of Oracle—all the time wishing that someone else could help them learn the new things so they didn't constantly feel overwhelmed.

As their knowledge grew, they began to give back to the Oracle community, presenting at conferences and trying to help the newer newbies. At the IOUW conference in 1996, Kevin Loney, a friend and, later, coauthor with both Marlene and Rachel, introduced them to Jim Viscusi. The three kept in touch via email, answering each other's questions, expanding each other's knowledge. And Marlene and Rachel always went "home," to ECO, to present and help each year.

In 1997, the two of them put together a workshop called "DBA 101: A Refresher Course." The workshop was turned into a paper and was presented at several conferences. The response was tremendous. And they realized that the best way to help as many people as possible was to turn this presentation into a book. Fortunately, Osborne/McGraw-Hill agreed with them, and now you hold the results in your hands. Jim, with his detailed knowledge of performance tuning and Oracle database administration, was a natural choice to be the third member of this book's writing team.

As you may have noticed by now, this is not a "normal" book introduction. So far, it does not have one word about "Here's what this book contains" or "Here's what this book is (or isn't)." You see, we wanted you to get a brief introduction to who we are and how this book came into being. We felt it was important for you to get a sense of who we are and how we write. You'll be getting more glimpses of "us" as you read.

Okay, here's a little bit "about this book." The style you see here is the style we've used throughout the book. Our goal was to write a book that Marlene's 93-year-old mother could read and (mostly) understand. This book is not your typical Oracle textbook, but does contain many advanced concepts in what we hope is an easy-to-understand form.

So, keep in mind that everyone is a newbie at times, there is no such thing as a dumb question, and please do sit back and enjoy the ride as we help you learn just what is involved in becoming an Oracle DBA.

PART I

Defining Your World

CHAPTER 1

About Being an Oracle DBA

e've heard it said that "Nobody knows exactly what an Oracle database administrator *really* does, but every company is very sure they need at least one or, probably, two or more of them." Even as late as a couple of years ago, if you asked a group of Oracle database administrators (DBAs), "How many of you grew up saying, 'When I grow up, I want to be an Oracle DBA'?" there would be no hands raised. More recently, the same question will produce several hands waving in the air. High school students are becoming more aware of the industry need for trained Oracle professionals and are entering college with the intent of becoming Oracle DBAs. More and more people interested in changing careers are looking toward Oracle technology as a great (and potentially lucrative) field in which to work.

In this chapter, we will examine not only what a database is but also what an Oracle DBA is and does. We'll show you the possible tasks that you could spend your days doing and give you a brief overview of SQL*Plus—the most basic interface you use to interact with an Oracle database.

How You "Talk" to a Database

In order to communicate with an Oracle database, you must be able to "speak" the language that an Oracle database understands. Originally, that language was called User Friendly Interface (UFI). UFI was a very early and limited language, and you could not do much more than basic database actions. You could perform the following basic tasks:

- Insert, which allowed you to put information into your database
- Update, which allowed you to modify existing information
- Select, which allowed you to look at the information stored in the database
- Delete, which allowed you to remove information from the database
- Perform mathematical operations
- Perform some limited date manipulations

As the language evolved, it was renamed Structured Query Language, or SQL (pronounced "see-quel"). Over the years, SQL has become the standard that you use to speak to a database. We realize that a basic understanding of SQL is necessary to help you understand the scripts and other code that we will be presenting in this book. Teaching you SQL is outside the scope of this book, and if you find that you are having trouble understanding the scripts and code and how they work, we recommend you look for a basic book on SQL to study. At the end of this chapter, we will go over some of the basic things that you can do within SQL*Plus to customize your interaction with the database and format your data output.

What Is an Oracle DBA, and What Does One Do?

So, what *is* an Oracle DBA? To answer this question, we'll have to look at what an Oracle database is. Or, better yet, let's talk first about what a general database is. Take just a minute to look around you. How many databases do you see? Well, if you are sitting in a room that has any books or magazines lying around, you can count each of them as a database of sorts. Loosely stated, a *database* is a collection of information. A dictionary is a collection, or database, of words, while a cookbook is a database of recipes. If you have a telephone book, you have a database of names and their associated telephone numbers and addresses.

Now, let's take this one step further and think about what electronic databases you have in your home. If you have a speed dialer on your phone, you have a database of numbers that you frequently call. Likewise, a caller identification box would be a database of people who call you frequently. If you have cable television, usually one or more channels show the television program schedule. Wow, there's yet another database to count. My gosh, you're surrounded by them! If you own and use a personal digital assistant (PDA), such as a Palm Pilot, you carry a multipurpose database around with you.

A Banking Example

If you have an account at a bank and use their automatic teller machine (ATM), you are interacting with a database that holds your account information. You might have a checking account, a savings account, a money market account, some kind of loan account—to buy a car or a house—a Christmas fund, and even an individual retirement account (IRA), all at the same bank. The database that stores all the information about all of your accounts might even be an Oracle database.

What happens when you can't get to your specific bank branch and you need money? You can usually use a "fast cash" machine at a grocery store or go to an ATM at another bank branch, and not necessarily another branch of your specific bank. The machine that you use can tap into several different systems to interact with many different banks and enable you to get money from your personal account remotely. Pretty amazing!

The mechanism that lets you get money from your account is actually one or more computer programs made up of lists of commands or instructions that tell a computer what to do. Once you have inserted your card in the ATM and entered your personal identification number (PIN) for the account, a group of computer programs (called an application) present information and ask you questions to perform the following actions:

- Determine what action you want to take—in this case, withdraw cash
- Find out how much cash you want
- Compare how much money you are requesting with how much you have available
- Determine whether you have enough money to remove some and still have whatever minimum amount is required by your bank to keep the account solvent
- Dispense the requested amount to you if you have enough money available

The programs that have been run to perform all of these tasks are written to interact with a database. The programs ask for information, or *query*, the database during some of the steps listed here. When you insert your card into the machine and are prompted for your PIN, the program checks the information on the magnetic strip on the back of the card to determine that the PIN you have entered matches the value stored on the strip. After the program has obtained the inputs from you for what action you want to perform and how much money you want, the database is queried to find out your account balance. The program takes the following actions:

- Verifies whether the card has been reported as stolen
- Does the math to verify that you have sufficient funds for the transaction
- Checks to make sure the transaction will not exceed your daily withdrawal limit
- Updates your account to show a withdrawal has occurred
- Modifies the balance to reflect the withdrawn amount plus any service charges your bank imposes on ATM withdrawals
- Modifies your old balance to reflect your new balance
- Dispenses the money to you

How does the program know it has located the correct account? What information is stored in the database? Where exactly is it stored? What mechanisms are used to ensure that your account information is really yours? We'll look at the answers to these questions in the next section.

Storing the Information

The pieces of information that the bank's database would need to store for your account might be

- Your name
- Your address
- Your telephone number
- A way to uniquely identify your account (account number)
- A way to verify you are who you say you are (mother's maiden name, perhaps)
- The amount of money you have available

You can probably think of other pieces of information that might also be required. Taking a look at the composition of the information, we see that your name actually might have up to five parts:

- A salutation, such as Mr., Mrs., Ms.
- First name
- Middle name or middle initial
- Last name
- A suffix, such as Junior, or a number (the first, second, third, etc.)

Your address could have the following parts:

- Street number
- Street name
- Apartment number
- City
- State
- Zip code

In other words, each area of information could be broken down into smaller pieces. A database is used to organize and store the pieces of information.

So, What's an Oracle Database?

Oracle Corporation has produced a set of very complex software programs that enable people to build and populate databases with all kinds of information. Since the information is defined based on the relational model, the databases are referred to as relational database management systems (RDBMS). In Chapter 2, we will begin to tell you how the Oracle software is used to handle and organize the information.

As Oracle's products have matured, the databases have become bigger and more complex. Controlling the configuration and performance has become almost an art form that requires both skill and knowledge on the part of the people who administer the databases. The status and tasks required of an Oracle DBA have changed and matured as well.

Now we've established what a database is and have a brief definition of what an Oracle database is. Let's take a few minutes to examine whether you have what it takes to be an Oracle DBA.

This "test" assumes you have been out in the work world for some period of time. If you have not worked for a living yet, try to think about a comparable situation that you have been through. After you've had a chance to mull over your answers to the following questions, we'll look at the possible evolution of a DBA from junior DBA through expert.

Do You Have What It Takes to Be a DBA?

This bit of humor was circulating around electronic mail a while ago. We don't know who wrote it, but it's a fun twist on an old joke:

CIOs leap tall buildings in a single bound
Are faster than a speeding bullet (rats, missed him again)
Are more powerful than a locomotive
Talk to God

Sr. Managers leap short buildings with a running start
Are faster than a BB gun
Are more powerful than a streetcar
Ask God questions

Midlevel DBAs can clear a single-story house most of the time
Can outrun the arrows that users shoot at them, with a head start
Get run over by bicycles
Beg God not to notice them

Junior DBAs trip over the stoop
Wonder why there are holes in their body
Say "Look at the choo-choo"
Make God mad by asking, "What happens if I turn off the server?"

Senior DBAs run through buildings
Eat the bullets
Throw the locomotive at the users
Are Oracle Gods (or Goddesses)!

Below are some questions to ask yourself to determine whether you have the proper personality and mind-set to enjoy being a DBA. We've included some of our perspectives on the interpretation of the questions. Remember that this is all for fun (with just a little bit of reality thrown in), so relax and enjoy it. Please realize, too, that if some of these questions seem too negative, there is really a positive side to each one. We'll try to show you the positive in each of these questions.

What It Takes to Be a DBA

Are you able to function at top efficiency with little or no sleep—possibly for days at a time?

It was suggested that the above question might be better stated as "four days at a time." The truth is that DBAs are often called upon to work nonstop to recover a database that has crashed, regardless of how long that might take. Somehow, your users tend to view their ability to interact with a database as having precedence over your personal schedule. Generally, companies will expect you to do whatever is necessary to "get the job done," and if that includes working around the clock to solve a problem, you'll probably work around the clock. The other side of the coin is that if you are a really thorough DBA who takes pride in your work, you will probably *want* to work around the clock, even if your boss says to you, "Hey, take a break and come back in the morning." Rachel's manager literally had to force her to go home one night (day? Eternity!) after a database crash. Yes, she successfully recovered the database.

The status of being known as "the person to rely on" in an emergency is both a blessing and a curse. Although you may end up working some long hours, you will usually earn management's loyalty and respect and much higher salary than your fellow employees, and you have the satisfaction of knowing that you truly are needed in your company.

Do you like getting phone calls in the middle of the night that *aren't* a wrong number?

If something goes wrong with your database, it won't matter to your users whether it is day or night. They will want the database back up and available as soon as possible. If you are running a database that must be available 24 hours a day, you will probably be expected to respond whenever you are called. We've all spent some number of nights blearily answering the phone and then getting up to fix the problem.

On the other side, you can often work from home if the need arises, and your management will usually give you compensation time for the extra hours that you have worked.

Do you enjoy being the "invisible" person in your organization, that is, until something goes wrong?

It's sad but true… as long as everything is running smoothly and at an optimal performance level, no one notices you. That situation can quickly change if something breaks. Suddenly, you are the most important, most visible person in your organization, that is, until the problem gets fixed.

Over time, the role of the DBA has changed some, and most of us are no longer quite as "invisible" as we once were. If you are doing a really good job of keeping your databases tuned and sized correctly, you may be called upon to participate more fully in the decision-making processes for design and implementation. By keeping your databases tuned and protected, you will have ensured that you have the time to participate in other areas of the database arena.

You might also want to learn to "toot your own horn" occasionally and be sure to let your management know that you interceded to avert a problem *before* it became a real showstopper. It's perfectly all right to keep your boss up to speed on your activities by saying something like, "I just noticed we were switching redo log files too often, so I added additional log files and increased the size of all of them before it became a problem for our users."

Do you enjoy life under a microscope?

As stated above, when something breaks, you are suddenly under severe scrutiny. Marlene can remember having a downed production system two weeks after her database "went live" that took several hours to recover. When it came time to recover the database, she looked up to find 12 people hovering around her doorway just watching her typing. Fortunately, the database was recovered with no lost data, and she was "hero for a day."

Do you enjoy long lines of people outside your door?

No, this doesn't refer to the prior question.

There will usually be a steady stream of DBAs and developers stopping by your office to get questions answered, disk space allocated, help with problems, or just general moral support. You really need to like people and believe that anyone stopping by your door is a user who needs assistance. You also should be able to pick up where you left off with what you were doing, even if it is several hours later!

Do you enjoy spending time filling out electronic iTARs in the off chance that a human being will actually pick them up, read, and respond to them in a "timely manner?"

Truly, Oracle World Wide Support has improved radically over the years. Calls to support were a way of life for DBAs. Now, Oracle encourages you to use electronic submittals to report problems and ask for support. You have to have great faith in the system to believe that the question you are posing or the problem you are describing is going to receive a valid response in short order.

Regardless of the version of software you are running or the platform you are running on, you may have to interact with support on occasion, and you really need to have both patience and a sense of humor to survive. You also have to realize that the first person who responds to your problem may be only the messenger and not the one who will eventually help you to find a solution. That situation seems to be improving too.

The good news is that Oracle World Wide Support can usually help you find the answers you need to get your job done more efficiently. There is wonderful information available on Oracle's support home page and through their MetaLink Web site. More and more, Oracle Support is relying on MetaLink, their Web-based support application, to provide your first line of support. MetaLink contains a wealth of information, and you can often find the answer to your question or the solution to your problem by searching the site without having to file a request for support.

Do you love solving puzzles that make no sense?

Well, the last time we said, "But that makes absolutely no sense," we had found a bug... err... undocumented feature... in a product. Solving problems and troubleshooting go hand in hand with being a DBA. We are often called upon to work through very fascinating (to us) problems or questions.

We've found that if you enjoy doing crossword puzzles or word problems or love to watch and puzzle through mysteries, you will make a wonderful DBA. The mind-set that enjoys puzzle solving will also enjoy DBA tasks.

Is your favorite weekend meal Twinkies and Coca-Cola, and do you view pizza as a seven-day-a-week healthy meal plan?

In most companies, the only time that upgrades, maintenance, or changes can be made to a system are over weekends, late at night, or very early in the morning. If you work for a company that has databases running seven days a week 24 hours a day ("24 x 7 shops"), the times that you can get your very necessary work done are even more limited. Unfortunately, the jobs usually require you to be there to make sure everything goes smoothly. The good news is that most companies now do have vending machines that are restocked on a fairly frequent basis—or we would have starved to death years ago. Hey, lots of pizza places deliver late at night. Every good DBA we know has a wide collection of take-out menus from places that deliver.

As with working odd hours when something goes wrong with your database, doing maintenance on off-hours will usually earn you compensation time to use when something important comes up for you to do outside of work. Things tend to balance out either with higher pay raises or time off when you need it. Most companies do recognize that you are making extraordinary efforts on their behalf and do reward you for the extra effort.

Do you love being on a perpetual *steep* learning curve?

In industry, most professionals have a very predictable learning curve. After graduation from college, the learning curve will be very steep. Over time, the curve tapers off and levels off in most careers. Later, the curve may actually start sliding down hill, and many people end up trudging along in a nonproductive and boring job. Not so with an Oracle DBA!

Just as you begin to feel that you have truly grasped the workings of your current release (or even before that happy point in time), Oracle comes out with a new, much more complex version, and you get to start all over again. It's great. You need never be bored. You can also never learn it all, so there is always something to do or study. How wonderful to know that you will continue to learn and grow over your entire career!

Do you enjoy the challenge of moving between different computer platforms?

More and more companies are finding that they need different computer platforms for different types of work. It's not unusual to find Oracle installed on several different flavors of Unix (each with its own little quirks) and several Windows boxes or other platforms—all in the same shop.

Do you believe that you'll have enough time to teach yourself <fill in the blank> (possible choices: XML, 9i, PL/SQL, Built-in Packages, Java, etc.)?

In other words, are you the eternal optimist who believes that you will have time on your hands just to read or study? Do you love the thought that you will always have choices in what direction you want to learn and grow? Although there are times when you will be too busy even to think about stopping to learn something new, there will also be times when you will be able to just sit, read, experiment, and learn.

You may be encouraged to try out different software and evaluate various tools to help make your job easier. If you are the typical Oracle DBA, you will end up having a whole list of things that you want to learn about or work with. As we said earlier, there is just no way to know it *all*. The software changes too rapidly to ever completely catch up with all of the latest, greatest features. Ah, but isn't the chase exciting? And, the more you learn and grow, the more in demand your skills and you will be. There is something to be said for not ever having to fear unemployment.

In most work environments, DBAs are often forced to learn things on the fly. They are generally people who love to "tinker" and find ways to solve problems on their own. Many DBAs have been known to take the approach, "I wonder what would happen if…" and then go about finding out what happens. (Usually we don't crash the database when doing this!)

Reading the documentation is done in small "sips," since there is rarely enough time to read complete chapters at one sitting. It is quite common to grab a manual, search for the topic of interest, read enough to figure out what's wrong in the situation you are currently troubleshooting, fix the problem, and set the manual aside. This approach can lead to a very real problem: you end up with incomplete knowledge and information.

If you were able to answer yes to some of the questions presented here, then you will love being a DBA.

Types of DBAs

You can look at the database administrator's changing roles and tasks within organizations in several different ways. Today's DBA may end up specializing in one area of administration or performing a subset of tasks within all of the following areas:

- The systems or operational DBA, who monitors all of the instances and servers and makes structural changes to the databases themselves, such as adding users, tablespaces, and so on
- The architectural DBA, who works closely with an application development team to provide an optimal database solution
- The application DBA, who does more coding in PL/SQL or Java (for Oracle8i/9i), HTML, WebDB, and other database programming methods to provide either end-user solutions or foundations for other applications development
- The data DBA, who specializes in data integrity and cleansing issues, primarily within a data warehouse or data mart environment

A data modeler understands the requirements, the process flow, and all entities within a business and creates a data model to reflect these things. It is often the responsibility of the data DBA to convert the data model into a physical database.

Because the beginning DBA will usually start out performing basic database tasks, we will emphasize the systems DBA's tasks here.

We have attempted to present as thorough a list of tasks as possible. Tasks that may be unique to your company's environment may not appear here. There may also be tasks presented that are viewed as inappropriate for a DBA to perform in your organization. The tasks are not presented here in order of priority or with complete detail. Throughout the book, we will try to ensure that the tasks listed here are covered in enough detail to enable you to perform them effectively.

The Tasks

Your top priorities as a database administrator are to ensure optimal performance of the databases and monitor the resources available for the various database systems to assure reliability, accessibility, and recoverability. The general health and well-being of the databases are of prime concern.

The normal scope of your functions can include (but is not limited to) the following set of tasks. Don't worry if you do not understand some of the tasks mentioned below; they are explained in later sections. The purpose here is for you to become familiar with the various terms and tasks that a DBA may perform.

Software Installations/Upgrades

In the software installation and upgrade area, you will need to

- Stay abreast of the most current releases of Oracle software and compatibility issues with the appropriate operating systems as well as intra-Oracle software compatibility.
- Determine whether a new release is stable enough to consider placing it on the development system for testing and integration with your application.
- Create an environment area for new release installation.
- Verify (on a high-level basis) the proper functioning of the new software release.
- Plan and coordinate the testing of the new release for each database and each application area.
- Plan, coordinate, and execute the implementation of the upgrade on the development system for all applications once the software has been tested and certified against all the applications on all of the databases in development.
- Plan, coordinate, and execute the implementation of the upgrade on the production system once the software has been verified for all applications.
- Log Technical Assistant Requests (TARs), as necessary, against a new or upgraded version of the RDBMS, and arrange for, apply, and verify patches when they are needed and available.

You might also have to monitor and advise management on licensing issues.

Database Actions

By "database actions," we mean those tasks you perform that directly change the composition and configuration of your database. You might need to

- Determine the space (disk storage) requirements for a proposed database, working with the developers and system administrator.
- Allocate the space for and build the database per Oracle's Optimal Flexible Architecture standards within the available hardware configuration.
- Determine and implement the backup/recovery plan for each database, both while in development and as the application moves to production, and coordinate that plan against database availability requirements.
- Monitor and coordinate updates of the database recoverability plan with the site's disaster recovery plan.
- Monitor the database performance while the application is in development on an ongoing, database-by-database basis, to identify potential performance problems before getting to a production status.
- Provide an ongoing tuning process for a database once an application goes into production, for example, adjust shared pool size, database block buffers, log buffers, and so on, as needed.
- Monitor table and tablespace growth and fragmentation on a periodic basis to ensure that space allocation does not become a critical issue.
- Maintain an ongoing configuration map for each database on both development and production, including any links to other databases.
- Test the backup/recovery plan for each database on a regular basis, coordinating the test with the site's disaster recovery plan testing.

System Issues

- We use the term "system issues" to specify the actions that you take at the operating system level that directly or indirectly affect your database. These actions affect the environment in which your database exists. Verify on a daily basis that nightly (or periodic) backups have run successfully; examine all appropriate logs (alert logs, startup logs, shutdown logs, tuning information, etc.); verify that all databases that should be up and running are available and accessible.

- Perform housecleaning tasks as required, such as purging old files from the Oracle software areas, ensuring that archive logs have enough disk space (if applicable), and so on.
- Perform ongoing database performance tuning, and work with the system administrator on operating system-specific performance issues related to the Oracle databases, such as system patches that may be required or system parameters that may need adjustment.
- Monitor the space used by each database and space availability on a systemwide basis, and generate future capacity plans for management's use.
- Coordinate upgrades of system software products to resolve any Oracle/operating system issues/conflicts.
- Research, test, and recommend for purchase tools related to Oracle database administration, or propose tools for development in-house.

Education Issues

By "education issues" we mean those actions that ensure that you, as the DBA, are not the only person who knows what is available in the latest releases of the database.

- Disseminate Oracle information to the developers and users when appropriate.
- Train backup DBAs, operation center staff, and other appropriate staff.
- Attend training classes and user group conferences to stay on top of the latest information and newest products interacting with Oracle.
- Subscribe to and read trade journals such as *Oracle Magazine*.
- Subscribe to and participate in Internet listservs and usenet groups to collect information from your peers.

Developer Issues

Most DBAs live in a world where they either directly or indirectly interact with the developers who are writing applications that use their databases. By "developer issues" we mean those actions that help the development team accomplish their goals. Know enough about the Oracle tools' normal functional behavior to be able to determine whether a problem is tools based or application based.

- Be able to log Technical Assistant Requests (TARs), apply patches, and coordinate with developers to verify that a patch has corrected a problem without causing other problems.
- Assist developers with database design issues and problem resolution, including knowledge on how to run and understand the output from both TKPROF and the Explain Plan utilities to tune the SQL queries.

Security Issues

Unless the database is accessible, it's not going to be particularly useful. At the same time, not all users should be allowed to see all the data in the database. By "security issues" we mean developing and maintaining processes and procedures that control the access to your database.

- Set and maintain user and DBA passwords for all databases, and document same.
- Create user and developer accounts, and distribute appropriate privileges as needed to approved people by authority of approved people, and document same.
- When appropriate, use Oracle's audit facilities to monitor table/user activities.
- Develop, document, and maintain change control procedures to prevent unauthorized changes to database objects.

Database Standards

By "database standards" we mean a set of policies that make the maintenance of the database simpler by defining naming conventions, general practices, and repetitive procedures.

- Define, document, and maintain database standards for the organization to ensure consistency in database creation, schema definitions, and tablespace, table, constraint, trigger, package, procedure, and index naming conventions.
- Create naming conventions for SQL*Net files (listener.ora, tnsnames.ora, etc.) for ease of installation, configuration, and maintainability.
- Where appropriate, write and distribute procedures (both step-by-step narratives and actual code) for tasks that must be performed frequently.
- Define standards for database documentation.
- Create a "Database Administrator's Handbook" of documentation on all customized code and procedures, and keep the documentation as current as possible.

A Logical Progression

A truth must be pointed out before we examine the growth path of a DBA. Just as with any other occupation, some people will easily grow into expert DBAs and some never will. There is a slogan being used by a newspaper in the Washington, D.C., area to the effect that "If you don't get it, you don't GET it"© (© The Washington Post). This is also true in the area of Oracle database administration. We have seen bright, gifted computer people who just never "got" how to be an effective DBA. They never made it past the tasks listed in the first section below, "In the Beginning...".

The progression presented here is based on our observations of the way many DBAs have developed in companies in which we have worked. As a most junior-level DBA, you will tend to spend a great deal of time learning the basics of doing your job. As you become adept at the basic skills, you will begin to have enough time to progress into more advanced concerns. When you have reached a level of having several years as a working DBA, you will probably have progressed to a point where others around you will do the lower-level functions so that you can devote more time to the advanced topics. We believe the progression represents a set of mind-sets, and as a person becomes more senior, he or she reaches new levels of awareness about the functionality of an Oracle database and the care that it requires.

In the Beginning...

As a new DBA you will spend most of your time learning to perform and performing the most "necessary" tasks. These tasks can include building and maintaining one or more databases. You will need to learn how to create users and create and grant roles to those users. When you have a problem and there is no senior DBA around to ask, you will need to call Oracle Support Services. You will need to learn how to log Technical Assistant Requests (TARs). Performing installations of Oracle software, relinking the software, and applying patches to the software are all tasks that you will learn. A big part of your education will be learning how to read and understand what the Oracle documentation is *really* saying (not an easy feat), learning how to find things out for yourself within the database, and sharpening your SQL skills.

Over Time...

As you become more experienced, you will spend time developing and testing an effective backup/recovery plan. You will begin to see areas that you can automate and will start to write scripts to perform your daily tasks through batch jobs so that you will be free to spend more time monitoring database growth and performance. You will tend to spend more time performing developer and user support functions. As you gain knowledge about your database, you will spend more time learning to tune the database—developing a daily routine to check the health of your databases. Although you might be permitted to attend conferences and Oracle user group meetings as a junior DBA, you will begin to gain much more from conferences as your base of knowledge and reference grows. As new versions of Oracle are released, you will want to attend Oracle classes on the latest version so that you can begin to evaluate the impact of the new features on your systems. You will start to develop more effective problem-solving and troubleshooting approaches.

As Your Experience Grows...

Once you become a more senior DBA, you will tend to stay abreast of current releases and learn the tricks involved in determining what version is stable enough to use. You will plan, coordinate, and migrate databases to new releases. You will have developed a toolkit of scripts to help you monitor your databases effectively. You will be able to advise your upper-level management on licensing issues. One of your most important tasks will be to create an effective site disaster recovery plan and ensure that your backup and recovery strategies work well. You will usually maintain configuration maps and documentation on your databases. You will be expected to disseminate information, train backup DBAs and operations staff, and coach and mentor others. You may become involved with database design. Because of your advanced knowledge, you may be called upon to define and maintain database standards; write and distribute procedures. You will monitor space use and space availability and generate capacity plans for management. You will research, test, and recommend tools for database administration and development. You may be expected to call to management's attention areas of potential trouble (for example, version versus platform compatibilities).

Things You Need to Know About SQL*Plus

We are going to assume that you have done a little reading in the documentation Oracle provides and have learned how to start a SQL*Plus session. While this may seem as if we are asking you to jump headfirst into the deep end of the pool, we do use the SQL*Plus formatting tools throughout the book, and we want you to be able to understand the basics so that you can concentrate on what we are doing later on.

My goodness, look at the stars tonight! Aren't they beautiful? The night is so clear and just cool enough to be pleasant. Let's do a bit of stargazing before we go any further. Hmm, what will we use to look more closely at the stars? Oh, you say that you have a pair of binoculars? That will be great. We have a telescope we can set up, too. There! That should do it. We can now do some stargazing with our eyes, your binoculars, or our telescope. If we were really intent on examining the stars more closely, we could even go to an observatory and look through their telescope, the one that's much more powerful than ours. There are many products that you could buy to enhance your ability to see the stars well.

As you can see from our stargazing experience, there are many different ways that you can look at something and many different tools that you can use to "do the job." Some tools will give you a more in-depth view than others or show you different aspects of the object that you are trying to view. There are even additional products that you can buy to enhance your ability to see into one area or another. This is all true of an Oracle database as well.

In this section, we are going to explore some aspects of SQL*Plus. As we said earlier, there are many great books on the market from which you can learn SQL. In this section, we will concentrate on how to use SQL*Plus commands to obtain formatted reports of your database activity. So, let's get started with a look at SQL*Plus.

In the beginning, back around version 2.0, Oracle supplied a tool called the User Friendly Interface (UFI, pronounced "youfee"), which you could use to execute commands and see into the database. As database products became more popular, standards were written, and slowly, all of the database manufacturers began to adopt a standard database language called Structured Query Language, or SQL (pronounced "see-quel"). Oracle Corporation then developed the program called SQL*Plus to allow you to manipulate SQL commands and PL/SQL blocks as well as to perform a number of calculations and reporting functions. PL/SQL is Oracle's proprietary Procedural Language that extends SQL.

SQL*Plus is provided with every current version of the database. Although there are a great many excellent third-party tools available that allow you to query the database and give you a graphical interface as well, SQL*Plus is still a valuable tool. First, it's free. Second, it allows you to develop ad hoc queries and reports quickly and easily.

Oracle provides you with a statement buffer so that you can edit the command you just issued to modify the format or the output. You are also provided with commands to set up your environment and format your reports. With the release of Oracle9i, Oracle replaced the Server Manager tool with SQL*Plus as the means to do database startup and shutdown for all platforms. Therefore, it's a good idea to become familiar with this tool. We can't include every command available, but we're going to "hit the highlights" and include some of the ones we use most often.

Accessing SQL*Plus

Before we can tell you about the commands we use within SQL*Plus, we need to help you get into the tool itself. From the command line, you start SQL*Plus by typing

```
sqlplus <username>/<password>
```

For Windows platforms, you can also access SQL*Plus from the Start | Programs | Oracle menu.

If you were going to connect to the HR database as a user named JAMES with the password THEBEST, at the command line, you'd type

```
sqlplus james/thebest@hr
```

You can leave off the username and/or the password, and Oracle will prompt you for them. The advantage of this is that anyone looking over your shoulder will not be able to see your password when you type. Also, it avoids the added security risk (with Unix) that someone may view your .history file to try and get your Oracle password. You can connect to a remote database using an Oracle Net connect string. For Windows-based platforms, you access SQL*Plus either from the DOS prompt or from the Start menu, and a window will pop up with prompts for username, password, and connect string. If you are connecting to your default database, no connection string is necessary.

There is a specialized login used for startup, shutdown, and anything else you need to do as the most privileged account. At the command line you would type

```
sqlplus "/ as sysdba"
```

When you log on to your computer, the operating system runs a script or set of scripts (autoexec.bat for PCs, .profile or .login for Unix, login.com for VMS) to set up your environment. Oracle also runs scripts to set up your SQL*Plus environment. If you have commands that you want executed for every user who accesses SQL*Plus, such as changing the prompt to show which database they have logged on to, you put these commands in a global login script, called glogin.sql. This script should be placed in the ORACLE_HOME/sqlplus/admin directory on non-Windows platforms and in the ORACLE_HOME\sqlplus\admin directory for Windows-based platforms. The environment commands you place in this script will be executed for every user who logs on to the database via SQL*Plus. You can put SQL, PL/SQL, and SQL*Plus commands in this script.

Just as your system administrator might have certain environment variables she wants set every time you log on to the server, you may have environment variables that you want set only for your own session. You set them by creating your own version of the login script and accessing it after the global login script has been run. You can do the same within SQL*Plus, setting up a customized environment just for yourself. To set up this environment, you need to create a login.sql file and place it either in the local directory from which you access SQL*Plus or in a directory that is part of an operating system–dependent path. Oracle will look first for glogin.sql and execute it if it is found, and then look for the login.sql file and execute it. As with the glogin.sql file, you can put SQL, PL/SQL, and SQL*Plus commands in the login.sql file.

Here is a sample glogin.sql file:

```
--
--  SQL*Plus Global Login startup file.
--
--  This is the global login file for SQL*Plus.
--  Add any sqlplus commands here that are to be
--  executed when a user invokes sqlplus
--  Used for the SHOW ERRORS command
column Line/Col format A8
column Error    format A65  WORD_WRAPPED
set term on echo on
set numwidth 10
set pagesize 10
set linesize 132
```

And a sample login.sql file:

```
-- My personal login.sql
--
set numwidth 9
set linesize 100
set pagesize 24
col User new_value usernm
set term off echo off
select User from DUAL;
set sqlprompt &usernm>>
set term on echo on
```

When you first log in with these two scripts, you will see

```
SQL> set pagesize 10
SQL> set linesize 132
SQL> set numwidth 9
SQL> set linesize 100
SQL> set pagesize 24
SQL> col User new_value usernm
SQL> set term off echo off
QC_USER>>
```

The prompt has been changed to the username of the user logging in to SQL*Plus, and some of the global environmental settings have been overridden. One thing to note about the glogin.sql and login.sql scripts is that they are only executed when you first log in to SQL*Plus. If you reconnect to another user from within SQL*Plus itself, without going back to the operating system, the scripts will not be reexecuted.

Okay, now that you know how to get into SQL*Plus, let's go inside and see what you can do once you get there! Remember that while we are going to separate the commands into the following different areas, many of the commands are used in all of these areas.

- Commands that establish your environment
- Information-gathering commands
- Report generation commands

Environment Commands

In the previous section, we showed you some of the commands you can include in the various login scripts. Let's take a look at these commands, as well as a few others, and see what they actually do.

```
--
--   SQL*Plus Global Login startup file.
--
--   This is the global login file for SQL*Plus.
--   Add any sqlplus commands here that are to be
--   executed when a user invokes sqlplus
--   Used for the SHOW ERRORS command
column Line/Col format A8
column Error    format A65  word_wrapped
set term on echo on
set numwidth 10
set pagesize 10
set linesize 132
```

In the global login script, we first use the SQL*Plus command **column** and its associated subcommands **format** and **word_wrapped**. The **column** command lets you define the attributes of a column in a query result. The **format** subcommand tells Oracle how to format the display of the column. The column named Line/Col will be displayed with 8 characters, while the column named Error will be displayed with 65 characters on the line. If the value of the column is greater than 65, the data within the column will wrap to the next line. The **word_wrapped** subcommand tells Oracle to left-justify each new line and to remove any initial blanks, tabs, or newline characters on each line. A variation of the **word_wrapped** subcommand is the **wrapped** subcommand, which tells Oracle either to wrap the data onto a new line or truncate it at the column width. You can also change the heading of a column using the **heading** subcommand. For example, you might feel that the column Name would be more meaningful if it was displayed as "EMPLOYEE NAME." You would use the **column** command as follows to change the heading:

```
column Name heading 'EMPLOYEE NAME'
```

We'll see the **column** command quite a bit as we explore our most-used SQL*Plus commands.

The **set** command has a number of subcommands that can be used with it. Here, we are using the **termout** and **echo** commands, and enabling them. **Termout** controls the display of the output generated by commands, while **echo** controls whether each command in a script file is listed as it is executed. Turning them both on means that you will see all the commands as well as their output. Hmm, did you notice something here? Although the actual command name is **termout**, in the script it is referred to as "term." Many of the SQL*Plus commands have abbreviated forms, and the only way to tell if they do (and what they are) is to read the manual.

In the login.sql script, we use the **column** command again, this time with another subcommand, **new_value**. Here, it is used to specify a local variable that will "hold" the value of that column so we can use it later. In this script, we are telling Oracle to save the value of the User column so we can reuse it. User is a system-defined environment variable that Oracle fills with the username you used to log in with. To get the value, you can select it from the DUAL pseudo-table, which really just fills in values from either memory or the operating system. Finally, we use another **set** subcommand, **sqlprompt**, to change the default prompt of SQL to the username.

```
-- My personal login.sql
--
set numwidth 9
set linesize 100
set pagesize 24
col User new_value usernm
set term off echo off
select User from DUAL;
set sqlprompt &usernm>>
set term on echo on
```

The other **set** subcommands we are using here are **numwidth**, **pagesize**, and **linesize**. **Numwidth** defines the default display width of numeric columns. If you do not override the default numwidth, either by explicitly setting the column width with the **column... format...** command or by issuing another **set numwidth** command, any numeric column will be displayed using the default numwidth. If the value to be displayed is less than the default number of characters, Oracle will fill in spaces. If it is greater than the default, but there is enough room, Oracle will display the value using exponential format. Finally, if the value is greater than the default, and there is not enough room to display using exponential format, Oracle will fill the display with #, to indicate that the value has overflowed the column width. Let's take a look at an example of this.

```
SYSTEM>>set numwidth 10
SYSTEM>>select File_Name, Bytes
  2        from DBA_DATA_FILES
  3       where Tablespace_Name = 'SYSTEM';

FILE_NAME                            BYTES
------------------------------ ----------
D:\ORANT\DATABASE\SYS1ORCL.ORA   62914560
D:\ORANT\DATABASE\SYSOORCL.ORA   52428800

SYSTEM>>set numwidth 7
SYSTEM>>select File_Name, Bytes
  2        from DBA_DATA_FILES
  3       where Tablespace_Name = 'SYSTEM';

FILE_NAME                         BYTES
------------------------------ -------
D:\ORANT\DATABASE\SYS1ORCL.ORA 6.3E+07
D:\ORANT\DATABASE\SYSOORCL.ORA 5.2E+07

SYSTEM>>set numwidth 5
SYSTEM>>select File_Name, Bytes
  2        from DBA_DATA_FILES
  3       where Tablespace_Name = 'SYSTEM';

FILE_NAME                       BYTES
------------------------------ -----
D:\ORANT\DATABASE\SYS1ORCL.ORA #####
D:\ORANT\DATABASE\SYSOORCL.ORA #####
```

The **pagesize** subcommand defines the number of lines of output that will be displayed before a page break is inserted and the headers are repeated. You can use this subcommand to format your screen display or to format the number of lines on a report, as you will see a bit later in the "Reporting Commands" section. In addition, there is a neat trick you can use **pagesize** for. If you issue the command **set pagesize 0**, Oracle will remove all page breaks from your output, as well as any column headings that would normally be displayed. Why is this useful? Well, while Oracle provides you with the SQL*Loader utility to load flat-file data into the database, there is no such utility to extract flat-file data. So you can use SQL*Plus and the **set pagesize 0** command to generate an ASCII list of the rows of your table or tables. We use it as part of our backup strategy, to make sure we list every file in the database that should be backed up. The flat file of file names that we generate is used as input to our backup scripts. That way, we never have to worry that we forgot to update the backups when we add a new datafile to the database!

The **linesize** subcommand defines how wide the display will be before Oracle wraps the line to the next line. Depending on whether you are displaying to the screen or printing in different orientations, you may want to make it larger or smaller. The default value is 80; the maximum value is operating system dependent.

A few other environment commands you should know about are listed here:

- **show** Just as **set** defines some of the environment variables, **show** displays the current settings of your environment. In addition to all the variables defined by **set**, you can display the page titles, username, errors, and error codes, as well as the Oracle release.

- **clear** Clears the SQL buffer, any breaks and compute settings, and the screen display.

- **define** Allows you to define local variables. If you have a constant that you want to use, such as a carriage return that you want to include in various displays, you can use the **define** command to set the value.

- **undefine** Just as you use **define** to set values, you use **undefine** to clear the values of variables. **Undefine** can also be used to clear the values of implicitly defined variables. To define an implicit variable, use the & character before the variable name, and Oracle will prompt you for a value.

- **set arraysize** Tells Oracle the number of rows to return in a single call to the database. While the maximum value is 5000, setting the array size to greater than 100 usually has no additional effect on performance. The larger the array size setting, the more memory Oracle will need for each fetch.

- **set maxdata** Sets the maximum total row width that SQL*Plus can process. It is used in conjunction with the **arraysize** command, and the larger the value of maxdata, the lower the array size should be set. (This is no longer supported in 8.0 but still can be set using the **set** command.)

- **set autocommit** Controls when Oracle commits pending changes to the database. If you set this to on, Oracle will automatically issue a commit after each successful insert, update, delete, or PL/SQL block. The default value is off, which means you must manually commit your changes by issuing the **commit** command.

- **set pause** Controls the scrolling of output to your screen. Setting pause on will cause the screen display to stop and wait for you to press ENTER before displaying the next page.

- **set colsep** Defines the text to be displayed between columns. You can use this to set off columns. This sets the value to be displayed between all columns.
- **set recsep** Just as **colsep** defines the separator string to be displayed between columns, **recsep** defines the line to be displayed between each row of output.
- **set timing** Used to collect and display data on the amount of computer resources used to run one or more commands or blocks of PL/SQL or SQL code. **Timing** collects data for an elapsed period of time, saving the data on commands run during the period in a timer. To delete all timers, you use the **clear timing** command.

Information-Gathering Commands

Now that the environment has been set up, let's see what you can do to get information about the results of SQL commands you've run as well as the definitions of objects within your database.

Wouldn't it be great if you could get trace information about the SQL statements you're running, as you run them? Guess what! You can, by using some of the informational commands available in SQL*Plus.

Some commands give you information either about your database or about what is going on within your session. The **show errors** command will display the compilation errors of any procedure, function, or package that you attempt to create or compile. In the example below, an error within the procedure prevents it from compiling. The error message that is returned, however, is not very explicit. By using the **show errors** command, you can retrieve more information about the error, which can help you to debug the problem quickly.

```
SYSTEM>>create procedure qc_user.validate_date
  2  as valdate date;
  3  begin
  4  select sydate into valdate from DUAL;
  5  end;
  6  /

Warning: Procedure created with compilation errors.

SYSTEM>>show errors
Errors for PROCEDURE QC_USER.VALIDATE_DATE:

LINE/COL ERROR
-------- -----------------------------------------------------
4/1      PL/SQL: SQL Statement ignored
4/8      PLS-00201: identifier 'SYDATE' must be declared
```

In the listing above, the **show errors** command returns two rows. The first tells you that line 4 of the procedure contains a SQL statement that has been ignored because of an error. The second tells you what the error on that line is. The information retrieved by the **show errors** command can also be queried from the DBA_ERRORS view.

If you just type **show errors** at the prompt, SQL*Plus will display the errors for the most recently created or altered stored procedure. To display the errors for a particular stored program, use the expanded form of the command:

```
show errors <type> <stored program name>
```

You can display the errors for functions, procedures, packages, package bodies, and triggers.

The next SQL*Plus informational command can be used in conjunction with the **show errors** command to retrieve the line that has an error, so that you can review the problem and correct it. The **list** command, with a line number, will display the individual line. If you do not supply a line number, the entire SQL statement will be displayed. To continue the example above:

```
SYSTEM>>list 4
  4* select sydate into valdate from DUAL;
SYSTEM>>
```

At this point, you can edit the line, using the **change** command, and retry the compilation.

Hmm, this seems to be a good time to talk briefly about the **change** command. The **change** command is a single-line editor, which allows you to substitute a new character string for an existing one. You type the **change** command, followed by a nonalphanumeric separator character, then the string you want to replace, the same separator character, and finally, the new string. To correct the problem above, you would type

```
SYSTEM>>change /sydate/sysdate
  4* select sysdate into valdate from DUAL;
SYSTEM>>
```

You can now reexecute the command, and it will compile. When you use the **change** command, the default will be the last line you entered. In our example, the line we modified is the fourth line in a list of six lines used. Let's go back to the command before this last one to see how we told Oracle which line we wanted to edit.

```
SYSTEM>>list 4
  4* select sydate into valdate from DUAL;
SYSTEM>>
```

See! We first told Oracle to display the fourth line in our listing. The asterisk next to a number indicates the line Oracle is currently pointing to. In this case, the 4 has an asterisk after it, so we know Oracle is pointing to the correct line. Now, let's do this exercise again using a bit of "shorthand." Since we already know where our error is in this example, we'll go right to the problem line:

```
SYSTEM>> 4
  4*   select sydate into valdate from DUAL;
SYSTEM>> c/sydate/sysdate
  4*   select sysdate into valdate from DUAL;
SYSTEM>> l
  1  create procedure qc_user.validate_date
  2      as valdate date;
  3   begin
  4  select sysdate into valdate from DUAL;
  5     end;
  6* /
```

There are three things of interest in this listing. We did not use the subcommand **list** for the line number but merely typed in the number of the line we wanted Oracle to point to. We did not type the full command **change** but used only its abbreviated form. Finally, we again used the abbreviated form of a command (**list**) to ask Oracle to list the entire set of commands in our procedure. Oh, look at the line Oracle is now pointing to. Yep, it's line 6.

If you find that the SQL in your list contains multiple errors, single-line editing can be rather tedious. The SQL*Plus command allows you to edit your SQL statements using an editor. This can be done via **define _editor = <editor>**. Within Unix, you could use the vi editor, and NT's default editor is Notepad. Also, within Unix, setting the environment variable **editor** has the same effect.

The final information-gathering command we want to talk about is the **describe** command. This command is used to display information about tables and views. Suppose you want to create a report on the information in one of your tables. (We'll tell you how to create reports in the next section.) Before you can begin to format your report, you'd need to know what information is in your table, right? By doing a **describe** on the table, you can see what the column names are, how wide the columns are, and which of the columns must not be null.

```
SYSTEM>>describe EXTGROW
 Name                                Null?    Type
 ----------------------------------- -------- ----
 SEGNAME                             NOT NULL VARCHAR2(81)
 SEGOWN                              NOT NULL VARCHAR2(30)
 GROWDATE                            NOT NULL DATE
 SEGTYPE                                      VARCHAR2(17)
 SEGTBS                                       VARCHAR2(30)
```

```
EXTS                                      NUMBER
NEXTEXT                                   NUMBER
TBSFREE                                   NUMBER
HWM                                       NUMBER
TOTBYTES                                  NUMBER
USEDBYTES                                 NUMBER
CONTIGFREE                                NUMBER
FREEPCT                                   NUMBER
TBSEXTS                                   NUMBER
```

Looking at this, you know that you will probably have to reformat some of the columns or each of the rows of the report won't fit on one line. Okay, now that we know what the EXTGROW table looks like, let's see how we'd run a report on the information in this table.

Reporting Commands

One of the things you want when creating a report is for the report to be readable. It doesn't matter how good the information you are including is, if the report has lines wrapping all over the place, no one is going to use it. SQL*Plus has a number of report formatting commands to help you create readable, informative reports.

We're going to create a report on the EXTGROW table, building the report section by section as we explain the commands we are using. Let's start by defining the display environment.

```
set pagesize 50 trimspool on linesize 250 verify off feedback off
set echo off term off
```

Some of these commands we've discussed in earlier sections. We've decided to set the number of lines per page to 50 and the number of characters on each line to at most 250. We've also decided not to display the commands to the screen and not to display the output to the screen. By turning **echo** and **term** off and spooling the output to a file, the file will contain a report without any extraneous lines. Notice that we did not use five separate commands preceded by the keyword **set**, but we ran the five commands together in one line. You can group your **set** commands like this to save space.

We are using several new **set** subcommands for this report. The subcommand **trimspool on** tells Oracle that trailing blanks on the output line should be trimmed off, so that if the line does not fill all 250 characters we defined for linesize, we won't get blanks filling in the empty spaces. If you use a variable name prefixed by an ampersand (&) in Oracle, you will be prompted for the value of the variable and will see the old and new values of this variable. By using the **verify off** subcommand, you tell Oracle not to prompt you and not to tell you what you entered. The **feedback off** subcommand tells Oracle not to display a row count at the end of the report.

The next section of the report prompts for the values to use later in the where clause of the select statement.

```
accept free_pct prompt 'Enter maximum percentage free: '
accept grow_date prompt 'Enter date to report on: '
accept tbsname prompt 'Enter tablespace to report on: '
```

The **accept** command, with its subcommand **prompt**, lets you create a report that is somewhat dynamic, as the contents are determined at runtime by the values input when you run the script. You could also prompt the user for the values by simply using the variable name with & in front of it at the point in the script where you need the value, but when you do that, you cannot choose the prompting text. The **accept** command allows you to request the information with a prompt that is clearer to the user.

We've seen and explained the **column** command in earlier sections of this chapter. However, we're using some new subcommands here, and they need to be explained. The **format** subcommand allows you to format numeric data as well as alphanumeric data. When you format a numeric column, you can have Oracle display the number with commas and periods as well as minus and plus signs. The *SQL*Plus Reference Manual* has a complete list of all the possible format masks for numeric columns. The other column subcommand we are using is **heading**. We mentioned this subcommand earlier when we first talked about the **column** command, but we didn't tell you very much about it. By default, if you do not specify a heading for a column, Oracle will use the name of the column as the heading, displaying it in all capitals, with underscores if they are in the name. Also by default, Oracle will truncate the column heading name to the number of characters you have defined in the **format** subcommand, or the length of the column itself if you don't define a format. This can lead to a somewhat ambiguous set of headings, and you can use the **heading** subcommand to override the default headings and have your report display more meaningful names.

```
col Segname format a30 heading 'OBJECT'
col Segown format a10 heading 'OWNER'
col Segtype format a5 heading 'TYPE'
col Segtbs format a15 heading 'TABLESPACE'
col Exts format 9999 heading 'OBJEXTS'
col Nextext format 9,999,999,999 heading 'NEXT EXTENT'
col Tbsfree format 9,999,999,999 heading 'TOTAL TBS FREE'
col Hwm format 9,999,999,999 heading 'HIGHWATER MARK'
col Totbytes format 9,999,999,999 heading 'TOT ALLOC SPC'
col Usedbytes format 9,999,999,999 heading 'USED SPACE'
col Contigfree format 9,999,999,999 heading 'LARGEST FREE'
col Freepct format 999.99 heading '% FREE'
col Tbsexts format 9999 heading 'TBSEXTS'
```

The next two commands work in conjunction with each other. The **compute** command tells Oracle what computation to make and when. The computation is displayed every time the **break** command takes effect. In this example, you are not only telling Oracle to sum up the Nextext column and display the sum every time the Segtbs column changes value, but also to suppress the printing of the Segtbs column until the value changes. In addition, the total sum will be displayed at the end of the report. Any break location that does not have an action associated with it by a **compute** command will not actually cause a break, but will suppress the printing of the column information until the information changes. In this example, Oracle will only print the values of the Tbsfree, Contigfree, Tbsext, and Segown columns when their contents change from the last time they were displayed. The Segtbs column will also print only once per value; but in addition, when the value changes, the sum of the Nextext column will be displayed, because of the **compute** command, and a blank line will be inserted into the report, because of the **skip 1** clause.

```
compute sum of Nextext on Segtbs
break on report on Segtbs skip 1 on Tbsfree on Contigfree on Tbsexts on Segown
```

Careful use and combination of the **break** and **compute** commands can make for a very complex, very readable report.

The final section of the script contains the actual query statement as well as the final formatting commands for the output.

```
select Segtbs,  Tbsfree,  Contigfree,  Tbsexts, Segown,  Segname,
       Segtype,  Hwm,  Totbytes,  Usedbytes, Exts,  Nextext,  Freepct
  from EXTGROW
 where Freepct < &free_pct and Growdate = to_date('&grow_date','YYYYMMDD')
   and Seqtbs like upper('%tbsname%')
 order by Seqtbs, Segown, Segname

set concat +
spool spacerpt_&grow_date.log
```

Oracle normally uses a period to terminate a substitution variable—any variable name prefixed by &. Another useful feature of SQL*Plus is the double ampersand (&&). It is used to avoid being prompted for a value multiple times when that value occurs in several places within the report or query.

If you didn't reset the concatenation symbol, the **spool** command, which tells Oracle the name of the file to write the output to, would create a file named spacerpt_<growdate>log, with no extension. The **set concat** command tells Oracle that for the next command, you are replacing the concatenation symbol of a period with the symbol in the **set concat** command. This allows you to create an output file named spacerpt_<growdate>.log. Did you notice that there was a blank line right before the **set concat** statement? That blank line lets Oracle know that you have ended the SQL command but are not ready to run it. By putting the blank line after the statement, we are able to have the **spool** command after the SQL statement so that the statement itself doesn't show up in the report.

Now, let's take another look at the script, all in one piece, and look at the results when we run this script.

```
set pagesize 50 trimspool on linesize 250 verify off feedback off
set echo off term on
accept free_pct prompt 'Enter maximum percentage free: '
accept grow_date prompt 'Enter date to report on: '
accept tbsname prompt 'Enter tablespace to report on: '
set term off
col Segname format a30 heading 'OBJECT'
col Segown format a10 heading 'OWNER'
col Segtype format a5 heading 'TYPE'
col Segtbs format a15 heading 'TABLESPACE'
col Exts format 9999 heading 'OBJEXTS'
col Nextext format 9,999,999,999 heading 'NEXT EXTENT'
col Tbsfree format 9,999,999,999 heading 'TOTAL TBS FREE'
col Hwm format 9,999,999,999 heading 'HIGHWATER MARK'
col Totbytes format 9,999,999,999 heading 'TOT ALLOC SPC'
col Usedbytes format 9,999,999,999 heading 'USED SPACE'
col Contigfree format 9,999,999,999 heading 'LARGEST FREE'
col Freepct format 999.99 heading '% FREE'
col Tbsexts format 9999 heading 'TBSEXTS'
compute sum of Nextext on Segtbs
break on report on Segtbs skip 1 on Tbsfree on Contigfree on Tbsexts on Segown
select Segtbs,  Tbsfree,  Contigfree,  Tbsexts, Segown,  Segname,
       Segtype,  Hwm,  Totbytes,  Usedbytes, Exts,  Nextext,  Freepct
  from EXTGROW
 where Freepct < &free_pct
   and Growdate = to_date('&grow_date','YYYYMMDD')
   and Seqtbs like upper('%tbsname%')
 order by Seqtbs, Segown, Segname

set concat +
spool spacerpt_&grow_date.log
/
TABLESPACE       TOTAL TBS FREE   LARGEST FREE TBSEXTS OWNER      OBJECT
TYPE  HIGHWATER MARK  TOT ALLOC SPC     USED SPACE OBJEXTS     NEXT EXTENT  % FREE
--------------- -------------- -------------- ------- ----------
------------------------------ ----- -------------- -------------- --------------
USERS               603,635,712     66,314,240     327 TEST        IDX_MSGS_IN
INDEX
                     327,680        327,680        8          40,960      .00
                                                                   IDX_MSGS_OUT
INDEX
                   2,621,440      2,621,440       60          40,960      .00
                                                                   MSGS_IN
TABLE
    44,998,656    14,049,280     14,049,280      332          40,960      .00
                                                                   MSGS_OUT
TABLE
    15,351,808    52,510,720     52,428,800      224       1,048,576      .16
************** ************** ************** ******* **************
                                                    --------------
sum                                                      1,171,456
```

Unfortunately, the listing is so wide that it will still wrap from one line to the next. However, you can imagine just how unreadable the report would be if the repeated column values were not suppressed! If you print this file using the landscape orientation of your printer, the rows will appear on a single line each, because we reset the line size to a wide enough value.

There are several other SQL*Plus commands you can use to make your reports more sophisticated. The **ttitle** command and the associated **btitle** command allow you to set a header and footer for each page. You can set a variable to contain the date, using the **new_value** subcommand of the **column** command, and insert that into the header or footer on the page. Notice that we added yet another subcommand to the **column** command, the **noprint** subcommand. This command tells Oracle not to display the results of the query. We use that to set the value of the variable today_date that we will use later in the report.

```
btitle off
ttitle off
set pagesize 10 linesize 30 heading off
col today new_value today_date noprint
select Sysdate today
  from DUAL;

ttitle center 'Tablespace Listing'
btitle left 'Page: ' format 999 sql.pno right today_date
select Tablespace_Name
  from DBA_TABLESPACES;

      Tablespace Listing
SYSTEM
USER_DATA
ROLLBACK_DATA
TEMPORARY_DATA
TESTTBS
Page:    1            05-SEP-99
```

The SQL*Plus commands **repheader** and **repfooter**, new in Oracle8, use the same variables and subcommands as **ttitle** and **btitle**, but they are displayed only once per report, rather than once on each page. You can use them to create a title page and end page for your reports.

The last commands we want to talk about are subcommands to the **set** command:

- **serveroutput** Controls whether to display the output of stored procedures or PL/SQL blocks in SQL*Plus. PL/SQL programs display output via the Oracle-supplied DBMS_OUTPUT package. You must issue the command **set serveroutput on** to see the results of calls to DBMS_OUTPUT from your PL/SQL program. The maximum number of characters you can display is 1 million.

- **newpage** Sets the number of blank lines printed before the top title on a page. A zero value will put a formfeed at the beginning of every page.
- **embedded** Controls where each report begins on a page. Setting **embedded** to off forces each report to start at the top of a new page. If you want reports to print immediately after one another, set embedded to on.

Now that we've given you an idea of what it means to be a DBA, and taught you some basics about accessing a database, let's go on to see just what makes up a database.

CHAPTER 2

Oracle Database Layout

hen you were little and learning to read, did you find it difficult? There were the physical alphabet blocks that you looked at and handled, but it was hard to relate that to the intangible concept of letters and words. You might even have learned a song to help remember the letters of the alphabet, but picturing what each letter looked like could be problematic. How about learning to tell time? You could look at a clock to see what time it was. You could keep track of hours, minutes, and seconds. But, when you were just starting out, relating the hands on the clock and the clock face to the concept of time passing might have been challenging.

The alphabet and the clock are both physical representations of logical entities. The alphabet provides the foundation for the words you read, while the clock measures the passage of time in seconds, minutes, and hours.

Within an Oracle system, you have both physical and logical entities. In this chapter, we are going to talk about the various objects and entities that make up an Oracle system. Some people find these concepts a little hard to understand, so hang on to your hat because this is liable to be a bumpy ride!

Logical vs. Physical Objects

Let's pretend for a moment that you are a file clerk in a large company. Your company sells hardware supplies to the general public. Almost daily, deliveries of various forms of hardware are received from your suppliers. Your job is to take all the invoices describing the items that your company has received and all the bills that have been paid and file them together in a large black filing cabinet.

Gee, what would you do if your boss needed to know how many skingwattles were delivered from the XYZ Company last March? You'd have to go through the various folders in the cabinet until you located the folder for the XYZ Company. Removing the folder from the cabinet, you'd have to locate all of the bills for the month of March and then add up each purchase of skingwattles listed in the invoices. Sounds like a pretty tedious job, doesn't it?

"Wouldn't it be wonderful," you might ponder after working for many hours to compile your report, "if all the invoices and bills were together in one easy-to-access electronic location that everyone could get to?" Companies have spent millions of dollars because they agree with you that storing all of their business information in a central electronic repository makes wonderful sense. But how do you store the data, and what do you use to see the information?

Oracle Corporation has for many years supplied computer software to accomplish both the task of storing information and the means to view it. In the case of information storage, Oracle supplies tools that enable you to build one or more databases. To view information, Oracle provides several tools that developers can use to build software *applications*—groups of computer programs that help you to view and interact with the information stored in your database. Oracle also provides applications for several different forms of information tracking that you can buy "off the shelf." For this book, we will concentrate on the database side of the Oracle product set. As a DBA, this is the software you will interact with most of the time, and this is the software you will "take care of."

To help you understand the differences between the logical and physical entities that we are going to be talking about in this chapter, we introduce these concepts by looking at three different "worlds":

- The human world
- The computer hardware world
- The database world

An object can be physical in one world but logical in another. Confusing? Let's look at some examples of the different worlds to see how this nomenclature works. In Table 2-1, we have listed the three worlds and some of the objects in those worlds. You can see that in our human world, we have what we consider to be solid objects and perceptions or concepts. You can touch and hold a pencil or a piece of paper because it has three dimensions and a solid composition. You can see a dream with your mind's eye and can hold on to it with your mind but not with your hands.

In the computer world, you can touch a computer, its disks, and all of its physical components. If you use a monitor screen, you can see the directories and files on the disks, but you can't hold them in your hands.

In the database world, you can hold the CD-ROM disk that you receive from Oracle. Now, here's where the tricky part comes in. Files appear as "logical" in our computer world, but in the database world, they are thought of as "physical." This is one case where an object has crossed over from the logical to the physical when it went from one world to another. We know, it's kind of a hokey concept and hard to really pin down, but consider that through a database's software, you can really

Type of World	Physical Example	Logical Example
Human world	Filing cabinet, paper, pencils	Thoughts, dreams
Computer world	Disk, CPU	File on disk, computer program
Database world	Datafile, redo log file, control file	Table, view, index, tablespace

TABLE 2-1. *The Three Worlds Example*

touch the objects that we refer to as physical. So, in the database world, files on a disk are considered as physical, and there are objects inside the database that we think of as logical, such as tables, views, and indexes.

To begin our exploration of the composition of an Oracle database, let's look at the so-called physical pieces. Because we are talking about computers, even some of what we refer to and view as physical objects can't be picked up and carried around individually. Just keep in mind that these different worlds exist, and let's go from there.

Physical Objects

Although we are not here to teach you about basic computer hardware, we need to look briefly at the general composition of a computer to understand how and where Oracle fits into the picture. A computer is composed of a multitude of different pieces. If you were to take a computer apart—and please don't try this at home without a net—you would find an assortment of

- Computer chips
- Resistors
- At least one central processing unit (CPU)
- An internal disk on which you can store computer programs or data
- Possible external disks connected to the computer for more storage
- Memory modules
- Many other components

Okay, so there are lots of electronic components that make up a computer. The disks—both internal and external—are used to store information in a measure known as a *byte*. The bytes are grouped together in operating system *blocks* of (usually) 512 bytes. So, you could say that 512 bytes make up a block of operating system space. Oracle also measures its storage in bytes and blocks, but you get to pick the size of an Oracle block from several choices when you create the database. In Oracle9i when you use the Oracle Database Configuration Assistant to create a database, you are given the opportunity to declare the default database block size that you want to use. Along with the block size that you establish as the default for your database, with the release of Oracle9i, the database can also support up to four other block sizes in the same database. We'll look more closely at Oracle block sizing and database creation in Chapter 7.

There is also operating system software associated with your computer. In the next section, we'll look at the structure of some software components.

About Operating Systems

Operating systems vary depending on the type of hardware you are using. Oracle Corporation offers versions of the Oracle software for a variety of operating systems and computers.

The operating system (OS) is a layer between the computer hardware and computer software. The OS understands how to speak to a disk drive when the software issues a command such as "write to this file." There are many different operating systems, and some computer hardware is designed to work properly with only certain kinds of operating systems. Oracle software may not be available for some of the operating systems or for various versions of the same operating system. The general areas in which information is stored are called *directories*, and the information is stored in *files* within a directory. In Figure 2-1, you can see the top-level directory structure for a Windows 2000 installation of Oracle RDBMS v9.0.1.

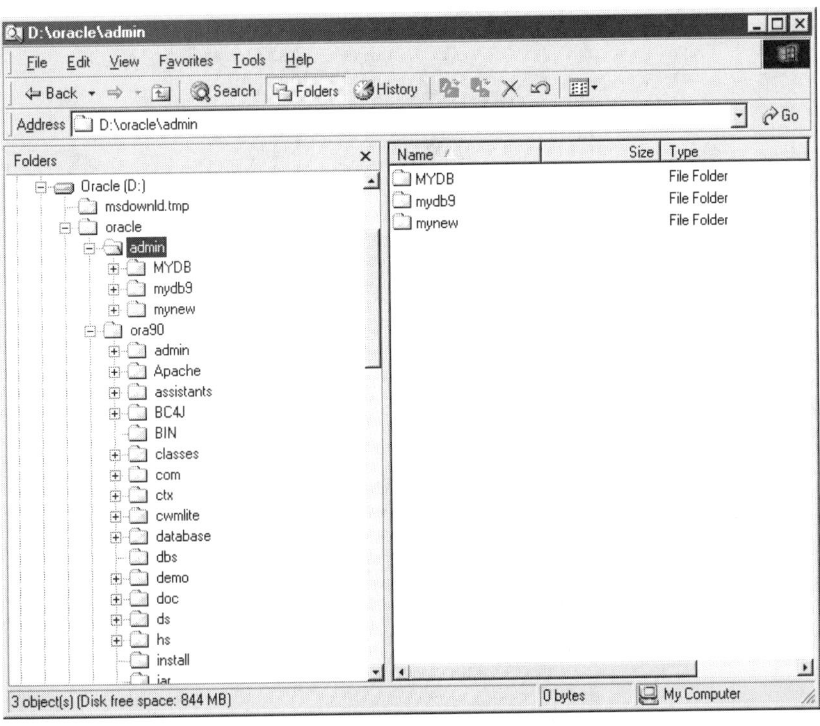

FIGURE 2-1. *Top-level directory structure on Windows 2000*

On a Windows system, the directory indicators, or *icons*, look like the folders you might use to file papers in a filing cabinet. The files within a directory are displayed on the right side of the screen. Each file has an icon that shows you its function.

If you are using a Unix operating system, the directory structure will be displayed with file names but no icons. The following listing displays a directory listing for a Unix system.

```
$ ls -l $ORACLE_HOME
total 96
drwxr-xr-x   6 oracle   dba          512 Jun 26  2001 Apache/
lrwxrwxrwx   1 oracle   dba           22 Jun 26  2001 JRE >/home/oracle/jre/1.1.8/
drwxr-xr-x   5 oracle   dba          512 Jun 26  2001 assistants/
drwxr-xr-x   2 oracle   dba         3584 Jun 26  2001 bin/
drwxr-xr-x   3 oracle   dba          512 Jun 26  2001 classes/
drwxr-xr-x   2 oracle   dba          512 Aug 10 07:35 dbs/
drwxr-xr-x   3 oracle   dba          512 Jun 26  2001 demo/
drwxr-xr-x  10 oracle   dba          512 Jun 26  2001 ds/
drwxr-xr-x   7 oracle   dba          512 Jun 26  2001 hs/
drwxr-xr-x   3 oracle   dba          512 Jun 26  2001 install/
drwxr-xr-x   2 oracle   dba          512 Jun 26  2001 jar/
drwxr-xr-x   8 oracle   dba          512 Jun 26  2001 javavm/
drwxr-xr-x   5 oracle   dba          512 Jun 26  2001 jdbc/
drwxr-xr-x   7 oracle   dba          512 Jun 26  2001 jis/
drwxr-xr-x   2 oracle   dba         1024 Jun 26  2001 jlib/
drwxr-xr-x   6 oracle   dba          512 Jun 26  2001 jsp/
drwxr-xr-x  15 oracle   dba          512 Jun 26  2001 ldap/
drwxr-xr-x   3 oracle   dba         3072 Jun 26  2001 lib/
drwxr-xr-x   4 oracle   dba          512 Jun 26  2001 md/
drwxr-xr-x  13 oracle   dba          512 Jun 26  2001 network/
drwxr-xr-x   3 oracle   dba          512 Jun 26  2001 oci/
drwxr-xr-x   3 oracle   dba          512 Jun 26  2001 ocommon/
drwxr-xr-x   4 oracle   dba          512 Jun 26  2001 oracore/
drwxr-xr-x  13 oracle   dba          512 Jun 26  2001 ord/
drwxr-xr-x   7 oracle   dba          512 Jun 26  2001 otrace/
drwxr-xr-x   4 oracle   dba          512 Jun 26  2001 owm/
drwxr-xr-x   8 oracle   dba          512 Jun 26  2001 plsql/
drwxr-xr-x   8 oracle   dba          512 Jun 26  2001 precomp/
drwxr-xr-x  13 oracle   dba          512 Jun 26  2001 rdbms/
drwxr-xr-x   6 oracle   dba          512 Jun 26  2001 relnotes/
-rwxr-xr-x   1 oracle   dba         5816 Jun 26  2001 root.sh*
drwxr-xr-x   3 oracle   dba          512 Jun 26  2001 slax/
drwxr-xr-x   5 oracle   dba          512 Jun 26  2001 sqlj/
drwxr-xr-x   7 oracle   dba          512 Jun 26  2001 sqlplus/
drwxr-xr-x   8 oracle   dba          512 Jun 26  2001 syndication/
drwxr-xr-x  10 oracle   dba          512 Jun 26  2001 ultrasearch/
drwxr-xr-x   3 oracle   dba          512 Jun 26  2001 wwg/
drwxr-xr-x   8 oracle   dba          512 Jun 26  2001 xdk/
```

What you will notice from comparing the Windows directory structure shown in Figure 2-1 and the Unix structure above is that although the basic structure for a directory is different, the contents seem to be very similar. In reality, for Oracle software, there are many files with the same names across all of the different operating systems. A file called pupbld.sql on a Windows system will be identical to a file with the same name on a Unix system. That's one of the great things about Oracle software. There are consistencies across the different operating systems that you, as a DBA, can rely on.

Windows and Unix both have a text interface, which means you can "talk" to the operating system through text commands. In a Windows environment, you use a DOS window, while for Unix you use a command line. Windows and Unix also have a graphical interface (Explorer, XWindows). However, because most people use the Windows graphical interface and the Unix command line, we are displaying them here in these formats.

How Oracle Fits In

Where does Oracle fit into all of this? Well, for one thing, Oracle takes advantage of the various components of any operating system to help perform its processing. Oracle uses the computer's disks to store many different types of files and many different types of information. These files are viewed as physical objects because you can copy them from one disk to another or even copy them onto tapes and carry them to another computer with the same operating system.

Oracle Software

Among the files that make up an Oracle system is the Oracle Corporation-supplied software that you will use to build and manage your databases. This software is made up of different files that serve various functions.

When you install the Oracle software, you will be given the option of letting Oracle create a small demonstration database for you. If this is the first time you are installing this version of the Oracle software, you will want to let Oracle create a database so you will have an area in which you can explore and learn the new features and just generally "play." Allowing Oracle to create a database during installation will also give you your first chance to use the Oracle Database Configuration Assistant. Remember, the best way for you to learn to be an Oracle DBA is to practice and experiment with a database that you can safely mess up or even destroy.

Oracle's "Physical" Composition

In Chapter 7, we'll look more closely at installing the Oracle-supplied software. For now, you just need to remember that the Oracle software will "live" on a computer disk on your system in files within directories.

When you create an Oracle database, there are two types of files that Oracle uses to store information. The information about the database structure (the *metadata*) is stored in one set of files and your company's actual data in another form of files. There are three types of physical files associated with an Oracle database: control files, redo log files, and datafiles. Although not part of the database, there are informational log files, such as the alert and trace log files associated with each database, as well. In addition, parameter files—used to initialize Oracle's memory area—are necessary to start the database but are not actually part of it. A sixth type of file—backup files that are copies of the datafiles—may also exist for the database but, again, are not an actual part of it.

- **Datafiles** contain the actual data that you think of when you hear the word *database*.
- **Parameter files** contain the initialization parameters that you can modify to tell Oracle how to create the memory area it will use to manage the database.
- **Control files** map the physical files of a database to the logical tablespaces and online redo log files in the database dictionary as well as maintain information Oracle needs to ensure that your database is consistent.
- **Redo log files** contain enough information to allow Oracle to reconstruct or back out transactions should the database be shut down before the changes have been written to the disk files.
- **Alert and trace log files** contain information about the health of the database and provide warnings when problems occur.
- **Backup files** contain copies of the database files that can be used to recover both structural and datafiles.

The database metadata is stored within the Oracle data dictionary, which itself is stored within a physical datafile. Information is stored in the data dictionary about the logical entities that make up the database, such as tables, views, synonyms, triggers, and procedures, and the locations of the physical objects, such as the datafiles, control files, redo log files, and log files. In the following sections, we'll talk about the various types of files in more detail.

Datafiles

If you let Oracle create a small demonstration database for you when you install the Oracle-supplied software and you look at the directory structure, you will find several files associated with your new database. Figure 2-2 shows a Windows

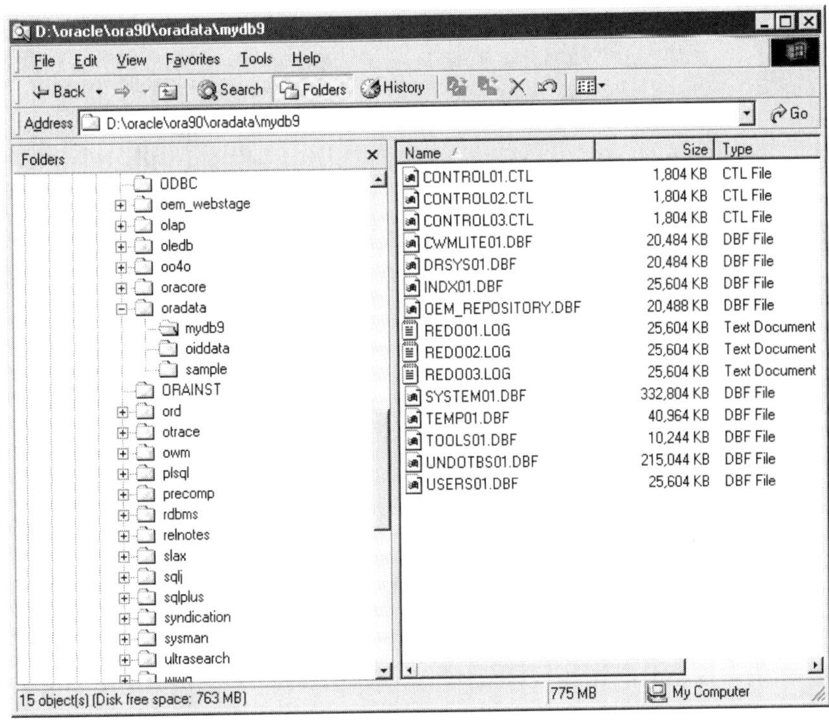

FIGURE 2-2. *Windows directory structure with files for MYDB9*

directory structure with a list of file names for a new database called MYDB9. Yes, each database you create will have a name and a *system identification name,* or SID. This system identification name is usually, but not always, the same as the database name. As of Oracle8i, a database can also have a *service name.* A service name is used as a unique identifier for an instance but can be any name you choose to assign. The service name can match the database name but doesn't have to do so.

A database is used to store and manipulate data in a logical way. When a database is up, several Oracle processes are running in the background. We'll talk more about these processes in Chapter 7. These processes make up the instance and allow the data to be accessed. Oracle uses a SID and/or service name to differentiate between instances and to ensure the correct processes, and in turn the correct data, are being manipulated. An Oracle instance is composed of these processes and the memory area that Oracle maintains (called the SGA, or system global area). A database, on the other hand, is the collection of physical files that contain the information you are storing.

There can be many datafiles within a database, and Oracle uses each datafile to store information. Oracle writes to the datafiles using a binary format, so you can't really read or modify the contents of a datafile yourself. Datafiles are the physical areas of database storage. Most DBAs use a standard convention for naming their database files so they can easily tell the type of file and its specific use. In the list of files in Figure 2-2, you can see that several different file *extensions*, or ending names, are used:

- .CTL for control files
- .ORA for parameter files
- .LOG for redo log files
- .DBF for datafiles

Looking again at Figure 2-2, you can see that the beginning of each name shows the function or object with which the file is associated. A number is used after the beginning of the name to uniquely identify a file. The following list shows some commonly used names that are association with various database file types.

- **CON** Configuration parameter file
- **CRTL** Control file
- **DAT** Datafile in which company information might be stored
- **IDX** Datafile in which index information might be stored
- **INIT or SPFILE** Initialization parameter file
- **LOG** Redo log file
- **RBS** Rollback or undo segment datafile
- **SYS** System datafile
- **TMP** Temporary segment datafile
- **TOOL** Datafile in which application tool information might be stored
- **USR** Datafile in which user information might be stored

If you saw the file name TmpMydb3.dbf in a directory, you would immediately be able to guess that the file was the third datafile used for temporary segment information for the MYDB database. Please realize that the convention we are showing here is just one of many that you could use. There are no set rules for naming your tablespaces, tables, indexes, and other objects. We recommend, however, that you use a consistent naming approach when working with the various Oracle files. You will then be able to easily identify the associations between the objects and their intended use. Consistent naming conventions will help make your life much easier!

At the very lowest physical level, an Oracle database is composed of database blocks. The database blocks are used to store all of the database data. As a DBA, you will determine the Oracle database block size when you create a database. The size is set using the parameter **db_block_size**. You'll put this parameter either in the initialization parameter file or config.ora file. Once you create a database with a specific block size, the size cannot be changed unless the database is rebuilt. Because the block size is "cast in concrete," you will need to be careful when you select a database block size so that you will enhance and help optimize the performance of the application that will use the database. On modern, memory-rich systems, database block sizes of 4, 8, 16, or even 32 kilobytes are within reason. So, how do you decide what size to make your database blocks? In Chapter 7, we'll look more closely at how to size your database blocks to best match the performance requirements for your database.

In an Oracle database, an *extent* is a contiguous allocation of database blocks. An extent is dedicated to a specific table, cluster, index, temporary segment, or rollback segment. An extent is created whenever a segment is created or a current segment is not large enough to hold information that is being inserted. A *segment* is a collection of extents that make up a single table, index, temporary segment, or rollback segment. Table 2-2 shows the relationship between the logical and physical constructs in the database. We'll be looking at this table again later on, in Chapter 7.

Parameter Files

In the previous section, you saw that there are two different files with a file extension of .ORA. In the explanations, you saw that the .ORA extension is used to indicate a parameter file—either an initialization parameter file or a configuration parameter file.

Logical Construct	Physical Implementation
Instance	Database
Tablespace	Datafiles
Tables/indexes/rollback and temporary segments	Segments
Extents	Blocks

TABLE 2-2. *Relationship of Logical to Physical Database Constructs*

These files are used to tell Oracle that you want to change the value that Oracle would normally use as its default for a specific parameter when the database is started. These parameters are used to influence how Oracle will perform its various tasks. When you use an init.ora file, any modifications you make to the file will not take effect until the database is shut down and restarted. In other words, the values in an init.ora file are static in nature.

Historically, most nondefault configuration parameters have been placed in either the init.ora or config.ora files for Oracle's use when the database is started. One of the ongoing problems with having a static initialization file is that if you change configuration parameters dynamically (as you've been able to do since Oracle's version 7), the changes are only in effect until the database is shut down. Once the database is restarted, unless you manually filter the changes back to the initialization file, you lose your modifications.

Oracle now provides a new approach and new file known as the SPFILE (Server Parameter file) to store the initialization parameters. The physical file is stored by default in the $ORACLE_HOME/dbs directory on some Unix systems and in ORACLE_HOME\database on a Windows system, and is named using the convention SPFILE<database_name>.ORA. For example, the SPFILE for the MYDB9 database would be called spfileMYDB9.ora.

You cannot directly edit an spfile.ora file, but you can modify its contents interactively by issuing commands that modify dynamic system parameters. We'll look more closely at the SPFILE composition and uses in Chapter 7.

The Initialization Parameter File

When you create a database, Oracle creates a sample, default init.ora file. If you do not modify any values in the Oracle-supplied file, Oracle will use all default settings when it starts your database. Why do you care what values are used? Well, you care because the parameters influence how quickly users can obtain information from your database—otherwise known as database performance. Let's face it. If you have to sit in front of a computer screen waiting for information to be returned from a database, and you sit for more than about 45 seconds, you will feel like you've been waiting for several minutes! It's human nature to believe that more time has gone by than really has when you're waiting for a response. As a DBA, you want the information to be retrieved from your database as quickly as possible, especially if it's the president of the company waiting for the data. So, you will end up being vitally interested in how quickly your database is returning information.

There are many other parameters in the initialization file that you can modify for purposes other than performance tuning. We'll talk more about the other parameters as we get into the software installation information in Chapter 7. Just as a piece of inside information, even though the actual initialization file that will be created for a database named mydb9 will be named initMYDB9.ora or spfileMYDB9.ora, in DBA-speak, the initialization file is referred to as the init.ora file or SPFILE. The same applies to the config.ora file discussed next. Oh, and the file is really talked about as the "init dot ora" file, SPFILE, or "config dot ora" file. Go figure!

The Configuration Parameter File

The configuration file, which is generally named config.ora or config<DB_NAME>.ora, is used for instance-specific information. This file is a text file that is called or activated by the init.ora or SPFILE file. The init.ora file will contain a parameter called **ifile**, which stands for "include file." The **ifile** parameter will be set equal to the location of the config.ora file, and points to a file whose contents should be included in the initialization parameter file when it is read by Oracle. The value will look something like the following for a Windows location:

```
ifile=c:\orant\database\config.ora
```

You may not even have or need a configuration file on your system for your database, and that's okay. You may have multiple configuration files in your init.ora, each one setting the parameters for various database options. A configuration file will contain values for parameters that generally do not change in your database.

Oracle provides an extra-cost option that enables you to have more than one instance on different machines attach to a single database on a shared file system. This option is called the Oracle Real Application Clusters (RAC) option. If you have this option and are performing parallel server operations, you will use a configuration file to hold the configuration for each specific instance that attaches to your database. We'll talk more about the nomenclature of *instance* versus *database* in Chapter 7. For now, just keep in mind that the information you usually store in a configuration file consists of the following:

- Location of the control files
- Name of the database
- Oracle block size for the database
- Location of the dump files for users and for the instance

Since there is more than one instance connecting to a single database, the elements listed in the configuration file can be very different for each instance. Of course, if there is only one instance connected to a database, all of this information can be stored in the init.ora file, and no config.ora file is really necessary.

If you are using an SPFILE in place of an init.ora file, you can store your configuration information for each instance within one SPFILE. At the risk of sounding like a broken record, we'll tell you more about how to store multiple instances' information in one SPFILE in Chapter 7. And, yes, Chapter 7 is really going to be jam-packed!

Log Files

Marlene and her husband are avid recreational walkers who participate in an international walking sport called Volksmarching. One of the programs that they have completed is to walk at least 10 kilometers (6.2 miles) in each of the 50 United States. Various Volksmarching clubs throughout the United States have created measured and mapped walks that anyone can go to and walk almost any day of the year. These walks are known as Year Around Events or YREs. While Marlene and Nelson were participating in this program, Marlene kept track of the following information:

- Name of the city and state in which they walked
- Name of the club that sponsored the walk
- Weather conditions
- Date the walk was completed
- Distance walked
- Time it took to complete the walk
- Any interesting or noteworthy sights along the trail

All of the information collected gives a very good view of the experiences along the trail and provides a record of some wonderful adventures. You could say that Marlene kept a "Volksmarch walking log."

Oracle creates two different forms of logs: informational logs and internal activity logs. Each log type keeps track of a different form of database activity. Here are lists of the different types of logs that are created and a notation of what type of information each log contains. We'll look more closely at each of the different logs in Chapter 7.

The informational logs that are generally created by an Oracle database at various times include

- **Database startup log** Can be created each time a database is started
- **Database shutdown log** Can be created each time a database is closed and shut down
- **Alert log** Created when the database is first created to log various database events and updated with all subsequent database events

- **Trace files** Created when a database or process system error occurs, a user requests a SQL trace of his or her session, or the DBA requests a dump of the control file to a readable trace file
- **Oracle Net Listener log** Created or written to each time a listener event occurs

The log files that are created and used by Oracle for its own internal activity tracking include

- **Redo log files** Used to track data changes for recoverability
- **Control files** Used to track the location of database files on the system
- **Archive log files** (if archive logging is enabled) Used for database recovery

All of these logs will be discussed more thoroughly in Chapter 7.

Backup Files

Think for a moment about car or household insurance that you purchase to ensure that if something happens to your possessions, you will be able to replace them. Making copies—called *backups*—of the Oracle files and their contents helps you ensure that you will be able to replace your company's data if an accident or hardware failure occurs. Your data could be lost in several different ways. Any one of the following kinds of events could occur:

- Hardware failure
- Software failure
- Natural disaster, such as a flood or fire
- Human error

In each of these cases, if you do not have a copy of your database with the most current data available, your company could lose large amounts of both time and money replacing the lost information.

Oracle provides many useful options to help you protect your data. In most cases, the options you choose to back up your database will generate files that will be stored on your computer disks. The command procedures you will use to create the backups will also be stored on physical disks.

In Chapter 11, we'll tell you more about your backup options and how they work.

Logical Database Objects

In the preceding sections, you have been introduced to the physical files associated with an Oracle database. It's now time to learn about the logical files. As we mentioned in the earlier section, "Oracle's 'Physical' Composition," the information about the contents of the logical files is all stored in the data dictionary. In the following sections, you will see how the contents of the data dictionary correspond to the contents in the database physical files.

Tablespaces

One of the most difficult concepts to understand about an Oracle database is a *tablespace*. It's also one of the most difficult to explain! Think for a minute about your last trip to a library. The library was filled with books, magazines, videocassettes, music CDs, newspapers, possibly artwork, and reference materials. In other words, the library contained a wide assortment of different kinds of information. Well, a tablespace is the logical representation of stored information. There is a direct correlation between a tablespace and the datafiles that store the data. When you create a tablespace, you tell Oracle the location for the initial datafile with which the tablespace will be associated. You also tell Oracle the size of the datafile. There are many parameters that you can use to describe how your new tablespace will "look."

Managing tablespaces involves many considerations and issues. In Chapter 8, we'll look at tablespace composition and management in depth.

Tables

Whether you realize it or not, you have already been looking at potential Oracle database table structures both in this chapter and in Chapter 1. Sneaky, aren't we! So, what is a database *table*? Is it like my kitchen table at home—the one where I keep piling all those magazines I get and intend to read some day? Well, sort of. In a way, a database table is more like a storage cabinet with drawers. Each drawer can be of a different size or the same size, and you can put something in each drawer, or the drawer can be left empty for a period of time (or forever). A table is a location where you put similar pieces of information of various sizes.

Creating a Table

Remember back in Chapter 1 when we were talking about the information that a bank needs in order to keep track of your transactions? We listed the following information about your name:

- A salutation, such as Mister (Mr), Mistress (Mrs), Miss (Ms)
- First name
- Middle name or middle initial
- Last name
- A suffix, such as Junior (Jr) or a number (the first, second, third, etc.)

Technically, for our table, each drawer is called a *column*. Each complete customer name is called a *row*, and the cabinet is called a table. Once you have decided on the components you need for your table to be able to store the customer names, you must decide what size each column needs to be. Let's assign some tentative sizes (we'll count each alphabetical letter as one character) to each column in the proposed customer names table, as shown in Table 2-3.

This particular table only has alphabetical letters. Can you have numbers in your column sizes? What about calendar dates? Of course! You can have many different *data types*, and there are wonderful SQL language books that can tell you all about the different types.

Column	**Size**
Salutation	5 characters
First Name	15 characters
Middle Name	15 characters
Last Name	25 characters
Suffix	10 characters

TABLE 2-3. *Sizing a Table's Columns*

For now, the only data types we'll talk about are the character ones so that we can develop our table. Most documentation will tell you that there are three different ways to define a character data type: CHAR, VARCHAR, and VARCHAR2. In reality, as of Oracle8, only two of these types are actually used: CHAR and VARCHAR2. Even if you tell Oracle that you want to use, or *declare*, a column as VARCHAR, Oracle will automatically convert your declaration to VARCHAR2. So, what's the difference between CHAR and VARCHAR2?

If you have a column that you say will be 15 characters long and the value that you want to store in the column is only 5 characters long, what will happen? If the column is declared as CHAR, Oracle will insert blank characters onto the end of the value so that there are actually 15 characters stored. If the column is declared as VARCHAR2, Oracle will only store the 5 actual characters, with no blanks "padded on to the end." If you have a million rows in your table, the amount of storage space required could be drastically different depending on how the columns are defined. There are times that you will want the complete column length held for data, and you will want to use CHAR. Most of the time, you will probably use VARCHAR2.

Naming Tables and Columns

The next step you will take to create the customer names table is to decide what names you will give each column. There aren't a lot of hard-and-fast rules for naming tables and columns, but it's nice to have meaningful names so you can recognize the purpose that each name represents. You could choose a name for your table such as CUSTOMER_NAMES or CUST_NAMES. If you decide to really cut back the number of letters used, you might choose CST_NMS, but, as you can see, the more letters you drop, the less meaningful the name becomes. For this table, let's go with CUST_NAMES. Oracle table and column names can have a maximum of 30 characters.

Now, let's think about the column names and their data types. How about:

```
Salut          varchar2(5)
First_Name     varchar2(15)
Middle_Name    varchar2(15)
Last_Name      varchar2(25)
Suffix         varchar2(10)
```

That looks pretty good. The names are short enough to be easily typed and used but long enough to be meaningful.

Table Creation Code

You have the table name, the column names, their data types and sizes. You have enough information and are now ready to actually create your first, small, simple table. The command you will use is as follows:

```
create table CUST_NAMES
 (Salut  varchar2(5),
  First_Name varchar2(15),
  Middle_Name varchar2(15),
  Last_Name varchar2(25),
  Suffix  varchar2(10))
```

To let Oracle know that you've completed your command and want the program to perform the requested task, you use either a semicolon (;) or a slash (/). Let's go ahead and run the table creation script in an Oracle v9.0.1 database and see what happens.

```
create table CUST_NAMES
 (Salut  varchar2(5),
  First_Name varchar2(15),
  Middle_Name varchar2(15),
  Last_Name varchar2(25),
  Suffix  varchar2(10))
/

Table created.

describe CUST_NAMES;

Name                                              Null?    Type
------------------------------------------------- -------- ------------
SALUT                                                      VARCHAR2(5)
FIRST_NAME                                                 VARCHAR2(15)
MIDDLE_NAME                                                VARCHAR2(15)
LAST_NAME                                                  VARCHAR2(25)
SUFFIX                                                     VARCHAR2(10)
```

Once the table is created, you can store information in it by writing

```
insert into CUST_NAMES
(Salut, First_Name, Middle_Name, Last_Name, Suffix)
values ('MR','ROGER','BUNNY','RABBIT',NULL);
```

There are three interesting things to look at in the last statement:

- All of the column names are listed in the insert statement.
- There is no owner listed in the table name because the owner of the schema is doing the insert. If another person were doing the insert, an owner would need to be designated in the insert statement in the form owner.table_name.

- All of the name values are capitalized to make comparisons easier in future queries.
- The word "NULL" is used to show that there is no value for the Suffix column.

This is a very simple table without any rules enforced. We'll talk more about owner references in the "To Role or Not to Role" section later in the chapter.

Enforcing Business Rules

What are some of the rules you might want to enforce on a table and why? You might want one or more of the following rules enforced to ensure the consistency of the data being entered:

- Every customer's name must include at least a first name and a last name.
- The only values that can be used in the Salut column are DR, MS, MR, MRS, REV.
- The only values that can be used in the Suffix column are JR, SR, I, II, III.

To impose the rules, you can use an Oracle feature called a *constraint*. There are two different categories of constraints available: table constraints and column constraints. If you want to ensure that the information is consistent across the entire table, you use a table constraint. For example, if you need a way to uniquely identify each row in a table, you can use a constraint that says, "Each row must have a column with a unique number in it for identification purposes." You create a *primary key constraint* to enforce that rule across the entire table. If you want to ensure that the contents of a column only contain specific information (such as our Salut or Suffix columns), you use a constraint that checks the value being added to the column to ensure that only the permitted values are accepted. You use a column-level *check constraint*.

Within the categories of table and column constraints, different types of constraints are available to ensure that your business rules are enforced. Here is a list of some of the available constraints:

- **Primary key constraint** Table constraint used to ensure unique rows across a table
- **Foreign key constraint** Table constraint used to ensure consistency across tables
- **Unique column constraint** Column constraint used to ensure unique values in a column

- **Null constraint** Column constraint used to allow or disallow the absence of a value in a specific column
- **Check constraint** Column constraint used to ensure that only specific values will be allowed for storage in a column

In earlier versions of Oracle, you would have to write application code to enforce these business rules. With the addition of constraints in later versions of Oracle, you can now use the database to enforce these rules both efficiently and effectively.

More Complex Tables

So far, all you've seen is a very simple table and some rules that you can apply, called constraints, to help you enforce your company's business rules. However, there are many different kinds of tables that you could use in Oracle8i and 9i to help you manage and administer your data.

Here is a list of some other table types that you can use:

- **Partitioned tables** Used to spread a large table over a set of smaller tables for ease of maintainability and more efficient data retrieval
- **Advanced Queue tables** Used to integrate a message queuing system within the database
- **Index-Organized tables** (also called Index-Only) Used to store index columns as a table to aid in faster data retrieval
- **Nested tables** Used to store multiple columns of data within one column of a table
- **Object tables** Used to enable the creation of object types that more closely represent their composition in the real world
- **Temporary tables** Used to store table data for one or more processes on a temporary basis

More information about these table types can be found in the *Oracle9i DBA Handbook*, by Kevin Loney and Marlene Theriault (Osborne/McGraw-Hill, 2001).

Indexes

Just as you have many more databases around you than you realized, you have many indexes as well. You probably use indexes already as a way to quickly find information you need. Think about a cookbook. The recipes are often grouped by type of meal (breakfast, lunch, dinner, etc.). Suppose you wanted to find recipes using chicken. Well, you could read the whole book, checking each and every recipe's ingredient list for the word "chicken." Of course, if your family will be home in an hour and you need to find a recipe to make for dinner, this isn't going to be useful, unless this is a very short cookbook! To quickly go to the recipes that have chicken in them, of course, you turn to the back of the book, where you can look up the word "chicken" and find a list of recipes and pages. Much faster, and you might even have time to relax before dinner.

Let's look at some other indexes. The catalog at the local library is actually several indexes. The catalog lists books by author (first index), subject (second index), and title (third index). And a book may appear several times within the same index, perhaps because it has several authors or because it can be listed under many subjects. (This book, for example, could be listed in the author index three times.) Even the shelves holding the books are a kind of index. If you are in the fiction section, the racks of shelves will have ranges of letters of the alphabet attached to them. This way, if you know the author you are looking for, you can move quickly to the section where his books can be found. You may have to look through several shelves to find the book you want, but it's still faster than looking through every book in the library.

So how do we translate this concept to a database? Let's look again at the hardware company we discussed earlier in this chapter. The company has converted that filing cabinet system to a computerized one and now has a database that stores its invoice information. One of the tables in the database has information about the invoices the company sends out. The invoice table has to have the following pieces of information:

- Customer name
- Customer account
- Customer address
- A shipping address if it is different from the customer's address
- Date of the invoice
- List of products
- Quantity sold
- Price per individual product
- Total charges

Without indexes, you have to look at every row in your table. The action of examining every row in a table is known as a *full table scan*. If your boss wants you to tell him the total skingwattles sold to the XYZ Company between March and April, you will have to look at each and every invoice row in the invoice table, decide if it is for the XYZ Company, and then look at the date and product on the invoice before deciding whether or not to count this invoice. Hmm… looks like you haven't come very far in getting the system to be easier and more friendly to interact with yet. As long as you don't have many invoices, looking at every one of them is not a problem. But if your company is doing well, you are going to have lots and lots of invoices, and it may take more time than your boss is willing to wait to come up with the information.

Now let's add an index to the invoice table. We could add one on customer, and then you would only have to look at the invoices sent to the XYZ Company. But what if your boss wants to see the total of skingwattles sold, and doesn't care which customer you sold them to? In that case, the index on customer is not going to help. Just as the library has many indexes, and a single book can appear in more than one of them, so a database can have many indexes on a single table. And the indexes don't have to be on only one column in the table. So you can have an index on customer, and another one on product, and a third on date, or you can have each of those indexes plus an index that is made up of both customer and product information, or customer, product, and date information. In other words, you can mix and match columns in a table to have multiple indexes to perform different jobs.

However, keep in mind that you don't want a bunch of indexes on a table just to have indexes. You really do want to have good business reasons to have an index. While indexes can help you find information faster, having too many of them can slow you down when it comes to adding data to your database. Every time you add a new row to a table, you have to add a row to each and every one of the indexes for that table. So the more indexes you have, the slower your database may respond when you add data.

Database Triggers

In order to shoot a gun, you must pull the trigger. The effect of pulling the trigger is as follows:

1. The trigger causes a hammer to strike the firing pin.
2. The firing pin strikes the percussion cap, which causes a minor explosion.
3. The minor explosion causes a major explosion that propels the bullet out of the chamber through the barrel.

What does shooting a gun have to do with an Oracle database? In the same way that pulling a trigger of a gun causes specific actions to occur, "firing" a database trigger causes Oracle to take specific actions in the database. For example, let's say that every time the Salary column of the PAYROLL table is modified, you want to capture the name of the person making the change and the day on which the change occurs. You want to save this information to the PAYROLL_AUDIT table. Oracle provides various forms of *triggers* that you can use to capture information or load other tables with data as needed.

There are four different types of triggers:

- Data Manipulation Language (DML) triggers on tables
- "Instead of" triggers on views
- System triggers on databases that fire for each event for every user in the entire database
- Schema triggers on schemas that fire for each event for a specific schema

Triggers can be written to fire on DML statements such as insert, update, or delete. They can be written to fire on Data Definition Language (DDL) statements such as create, alter, or drop. They can also be written to fire when a specific database action occurs, such as database shutdown or startup. Triggers can be created to take action before or after a behavior occurs. You can even have a trigger that takes effect whenever a user connects to the database, known as an **on logon** trigger. In our PAYROLL_AUDIT example, you want to capture the information after the payroll record is modified, so you would use an "after update" trigger.

You can have triggers that will fire when data is inserted, updated, or deleted from a table, and you can have the trigger fire either before or after the action has occurred. Triggers can be created to fire for every row that is affected as well as only once per statement. You can also have an "instead of" trigger that can be used to modify data through a view. Coupled with the "instead of" trigger, you can use the parameter **for each row** to tell Oracle that you want the action applied to each row in the table that is affected by the trigger. Remember though, that if the trigger action fails to complete, the entire change will fail.

Views

When you use a camera to take a picture, you use a viewfinder to isolate only the area you want to capture on film. If you look out over a horizon, you will see the full scope of the scenery. When you look through the camera's viewfinder, you see only a narrow portion of the whole scene.

An Oracle view works much the same way as a viewfinder on a camera. It is a mask laid over a table or tables to change the picture the user sees when accessing the data. A view can be created by selecting columns from a larger table, or a view can be written to restrict the number of rows or type of data returned from a select. You can define a view that joins several tables together, with complicated selection criteria, so that you can optimize the access path to the data.

Why use views? If a complicated query is run often, it is simpler to access a view with a simple select statement than it is to constantly rewrite the statement. Should the query change, you only have to change the view definition, rather than change the SQL in every program that has this query. You can control access to data with the where clause in a view, limiting your user's access to certain columns or rows.

Oracle also decides whether or not to parse a SQL statement by first checking to see if the statement already exists in the SQL area of the system global area (SGA). The statement must match *exactly*, down to capitalization and spacing. By using views to store complicated queries that are run often, the statement does not have to be reparsed, saving time and increasing database performance. We'll talk more about the SQL area and the SGA in Chapter 6.

Materialized Views

Originally, Oracle used a mechanism known as a *snapshot* to capture a picture of data frozen at a particular time much as a photograph is a picture of something in the world, frozen in time. An Oracle snapshot was a picture of a table or set of tables that was captured at a point in time. Snapshots were copies of data in one database that had been copied to another database.

Unfortunately, snapshots were very limited. In Oracle8i, the concept of a materialized view was introduced, and in Oracle9i, materialized views have completely replaced snapshots. Materialized views enable the storage of summary data known as *aggregate data* like sums or counts of items. When applied to a data warehouse environment, materialized views really shine. Also, if you enable the mechanism known as *query rewrite*, Oracle will transparently rewrite appropriate queries to use the materialized views instead of the underlying tables—thus speeding transaction processing substantially.

Why use materialized views?

If some of your users want to do reporting on the data and don't need an up-to-the-minute picture of the database, you can move the reporting functions to another database and keep your main database for online activity. This allows you to tune each database for better performance based on the workload each database has.

Another great way to use materialized views is if you have an application in one database that relies on having the latest information from another database, but stored in a little different format. For example, let's say you have personnel location information in Database A and need pieces of that information in Database B. In Database A you have all of each employee's data, while in Database B you only need the employee's name, room number, and phone number. An employee's location could change from one day to the next, so you need the information refreshed on a daily basis to keep the locations current. Materialized views are a perfect way to accomplish this task.

Rollback Segments and Undo Tablespace

Think about a bank and how it handles a transfer of money from one account to another. The money is first taken from one account and then added to another account—a single transaction in which both parts must be completed or else both must be wiped out. If for some reason the money can't be added to the second account after it is removed from the first account, what happens? The money can't just disappear. The books have to balance. The bank program (or database program) has to hold the previous balance of the account somewhere so that it can "roll back" the removal of the money if it has to and replace the account balance with the original amount. In an Oracle database, the information about the previous balance will be held in a rollback segment so that Oracle can keep track of the *before image*, or appearance of the data, in case the transaction is not completed.

How does a rollback segment work? As your program begins to change data in the database, Oracle is changing the physical blocks that contain that information. Before writing the changed information into the data block buffers in the SGA, or to disk, Oracle first assigns your transaction to a rollback segment and makes a copy of the original information in the rollback segment. So if you change your mind and cancel the transaction, the original information is there and can be written back to the disk. If you have a very large transaction, Oracle will expand the rollback segment by adding extents, just as it expands a table when you add information to it. We'll talk more about the data block buffers and the SGA in Chapter 6.

As you can see in Figure 2-3, Oracle views a rollback segment like a circle and expands the circle by adding extents if your transaction needs more space. Oracle will only "wrap" back to the beginning of a rollback segment and reuse the extents in it if the first extent in the rollback segment no longer has a transaction in it.

Using rollback segments also enables Oracle to allow other users of the database to access the table you are changing. Oracle builds a consistent view of the data from the rollback segment, so someone accessing a table while you are in the middle of an update will see a picture of the data in the table before you began your changes. Even if you commit the changes to the database, Oracle will attempt to continue providing a consistent picture to the other user by continuing to read from the rollback segment.

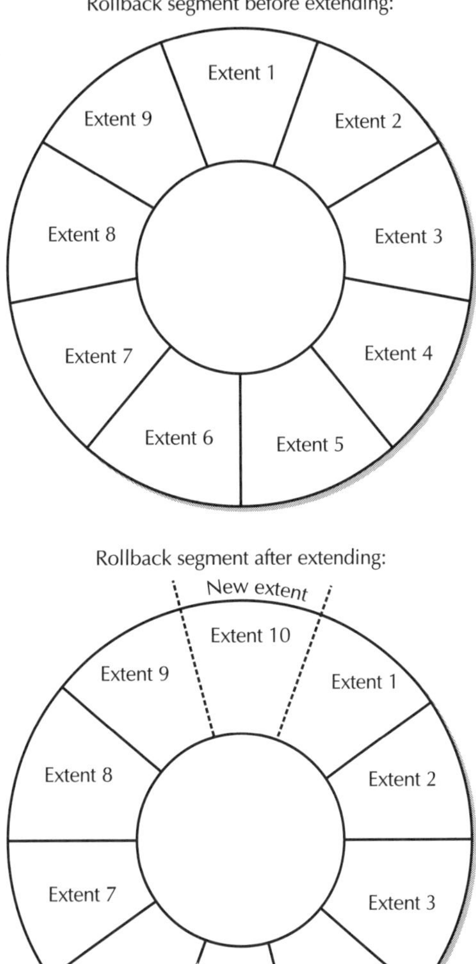

FIGURE 2-3. *Rollback segment before and after extending*

Rollback segments take up physical space in the database, usually in a tablespace that has been reserved exclusively for them. Why reserve a separate tablespace just for rollback segments? Well, the rollback segments are accessed by many transactions and can grow quickly if a lot of data is being changed, so they can take up a lot of the free blocks in a tablespace, leaving little room for the tables. And they can also shrink back to their original size, either automatically by setting a parameter called **optimal** when you create them, or by the DBA manually issuing a **shrink** command. This extension and shrinkage can cause fragmentation in the tablespace and, if other data is stored there, could cause the database to be unable to allocate space when it needs to.

To further simplify the tracking and management of undo information, in Oracle9i an automatic undo management feature has been introduced to enable all change tracking to be done automatically within the database in an Undo Tablespace. With automatic undo segment management, you no longer have to create, drop, or alter rollback segments. You still do have the ability to use rollback segments instead of the new Undo Tablespace if you want to do so, but you cannot use both at the same time.

To enable Undo Tablespace management, you set the parameter UNDO_MANAGEMENT in the initialization parameter file to AUTO; otherwise set the value to MANUAL to use rollback segments. If you opt to use the automatic Undo Tablespace approach, there will be one tablespace created in the database called UNDO_TABLESPACE. You cannot have more than one "active" Undo Tablespace within a database at a time. If you have enough space, you could have an extra large file available but offline.

Let's look at the automatic undo management design. There will always be one SYSTEM undo segment within the SYSTEM tablespace whether you use automatic or manual segments. With rollback segments, you create several static segments of a specific size. With undo segments, Oracle creates and maintains the undo segments automatically and internally as they are needed. The only allocation that you do is to tell Oracle the size to make the overall Undo Tablespace.

To create an Undo Tablespace when you create your database, you use the following syntax:

```
create database MYDB9
. . .
undo tablespace <tablespace_name>
datafile 'D:\oracle\ora90\oradata\mydb9\undotbl01.dbf'
size 200M;
```

If you do not specify an Undo Tablespace clause in your database creation statement and UNDO_MANAGEMENT is set to AUTO, the system will create a tablespace called SYS_UNDOTBS, and AUTOEXTEND will be set to ON with an initial size of 10M. We recommend that if you are going to enable Undo Tablespace, that you specify a tablespace name, include the DATAFILE description (the only argument allowed), and set a specific limiting size instead of letting Oracle do things for you.

To create an Undo Tablespace after database creation, create the tablespace and *then* put the UNDO_TABLESPACE parameter in the initialization parameter file to specify the name of the tablespace to use on database startup; just as you would use ROLLBACK SEGMENTS= for rollback segments brought online at database startup.

```
create undo tablespace UNDO_TBLSP
datafile 'D:\oracle\ora90\oradata\mydb9\undotbl01.dbf'
size 200M;
```

Once the tablespace is created, you can shut down the database, put the UNDO_TABLESPACE parameter in the initialization parameter file, and restart the database.

You can alter an Undo Tablespace to add a datafile, rename the datafile, bring the datafile online/offline, or begin or end backup. In order to drop an Undo Tablespace, the tablespace cannot be currently in use. This means that there cannot be any uncommitted transactions. You can use the V$TRANSACTION view to verify whether or not there are any transactions of interest.

There is also an UNDO_RETENTION parameter that you can set to tell Oracle the amount of undo to retain (in seconds). The default value is 900 seconds. If you do not specify sufficient space in the Undo Tablespace to support all of the transactions, you can end up with Oracle overwriting data, which could lead to an ORA-1555 "Snapshot too old" error. You can use the V$UNDOSTAT view to produce a histogram of how well the system is performing. You can take the information you gain from V$UNDOSTAT to determine the size for UNDO_RETENTION as follows:

```
Undo space = (UNDO_RETENTION value in seconds * Undo blocks per second
      * database block size)  + Overhead for metadata
```

If UNDO_RETENTION is set to 3600 seconds (one hour) and the transaction rate is 20 undo blocks per second with a 4k block size, the required undo space would be

```
Undo space = 3600 * 20 * 4096 = 2.95 GB
```

Pretty scary amount of space to use just for undo information, huh!

You can switch from one Undo Tablespace to another by using

```
alter system set UNDO_TABLESPACE=<new_tablespace_name>;
```

Once you've switched from one tablespace to the other, you can drop the old tablespace as soon as all active transactions have completed.

The other available parameter used with Undo Tablespace is UNDO_SUPPRESS_ERRORS to suppress errors when you are attempting to execute manual operations such as "alter rollback segment online" while in automatic mode. The values are TRUE and FALSE, and the default is FALSE.

Temporary Segments

Have you ever alphabetized a stack of cards? If the stack was small enough, you could hold all the cards in your hands while putting them in order. But if the stack was large, you wouldn't be able to hold them all at once. In order to make it easier on yourself, you might first separate the cards into two piles, one for the letters A–L and the other for M–Z. Then you would take the piles and break them down even further, A–G, H–L, M–R, and S–Z. You would keep breaking the piles into smaller piles, until you had few enough cards in a pile to hold in your hands while ordering them. Each of the piles you made was temporary, used only for holding the cards until you could get to that pile and put it in order or break it down further. Once you had finished sorting the cards, the piles disappeared.

For certain database actions, Oracle needs to build a temporary staging area to contain the data from the intermediary steps of the processing. Creating an index, selecting data using "union" or "group by" or "order by" clauses, or doing a join on columns that do not have an index will cause Oracle to sort the data and use this staging area. As part of your initialization parameter file, you can set aside a section of memory in the process global area (PGA) called the **sort_area_size**, for sorting. The PGA is allocated for each user process connecting to the database. If Oracle can fit everything it needs to sort into this memory area, it will not use a temporary segment.

If, however, the data being manipulated is larger than the **sort_area_size**, Oracle will write chunks of the data to disk, allocating temporary segments. Temporary segments are allocated in the tablespace defined as the temporary tablespace for the user running the query. Each database user can have a different temporary tablespace assigned to him or her.

Once Oracle is done with the operation that needed the temporary segments, they are released back to the free space of the tablespace. To help speed performance, Oracle allows you to designate the contents of a tablespace as TEMPORARY. If you do this, the temporary segments are not immediately released, but stay available for reuse by another operation. Tablespaces defined as TEMPORARY cannot contain anything other than temporary segments. You can't create a "temporary" table or other object in a tablespace that has been marked as TEMPORARY, even though you are sure the table you are creating will only exist for a little while. Once a tablespace has been marked as TEMPORARY, Oracle will not allow you to create anything other than temporary segments there.

With 8i, Oracle also allowed you to create a new type of tablespace, a truly temporary tablespace. These tablespaces use tempfiles instead of datafiles to hold the temporary segments. They must be created as locally managed, and do not generate any redo or rollback, so they are ideal for standby databases or read-only tablespaces. We'll talk more about tempfiles in Chapter 3.

Roles

Do you remember playing make-believe when you were young? You'd go outside with your friends, and suddenly the neighborhood was the Old West, and you and your best friend were cowboys. You took on the role of "cowboy," and with that role came the ability to ride a horse, rope a cow, and shoot a six-gun. You had gunfights and shoot-outs and generally had a great time. Or maybe you daydreamed yourself into your favorite television show. There you were, the dashing young doctor saving lives, or the heroic police officer fighting crime, or the graceful ballerina dancing across the stage. The characters you became had defined abilities and actions they could perform.

As you grew, the roles you played changed. You became a student. Perhaps you participated in after-school activities or became an athlete. In order to get spending cash, you took an after-school or summer job and worked as a baby-sitter or in the local fast-food restaurant or as a lifeguard. You were then playing many roles at once, but each one you played was played individually—one at a time.

These roles can also be made up of other roles. The lifeguard might also teach swimming, so "swimming teacher" becomes a subrole of lifeguard. What never changes about these roles is that with each role comes a set of abilities, privileges, and actions that you can perform, just by stepping into the role. So a role can be defined as a set of actions and rights granted to the person adopting that role.

Now, let's go back to the hardware company and your job as a file clerk. If you've come to the conclusion that file clerk is a role, you're right. A person filling the file clerk role needs access to the invoices that the company receives from its suppliers. A person filling the role of accounting clerk needs access to the invoices from suppliers and to the invoices the company has sent to its customers. This means the accounting clerk role is actually made up of the file clerk role and some additional rights and actions.

In Figure 2-4 we see that the manager role has the ability to function as both the file clerk role and the accounting clerk role. In addition, some actions can't be done by either role, but only by the manager role.

How do we translate the actions we perform and privileges we have in our roles in life to a database? Well, the file clerk action of looking up invoices could be moved to a computer, with all the invoice information stored in a database. When you automate the work that people do, or just move some of the paperwork to a computer, you are defining roles in a database.

With version 6, Oracle introduced the concept of database roles. Roles were designed to make it easier to administer user system and object privileges. You can grant and revoke privileges to the application objects (tables, views, packages, procedures, etc.) without directly granting them to each user who needs them. So, how and why would you want to use roles, and what are their advantages and drawbacks? In the next section, we'll try to answer these questions for you.

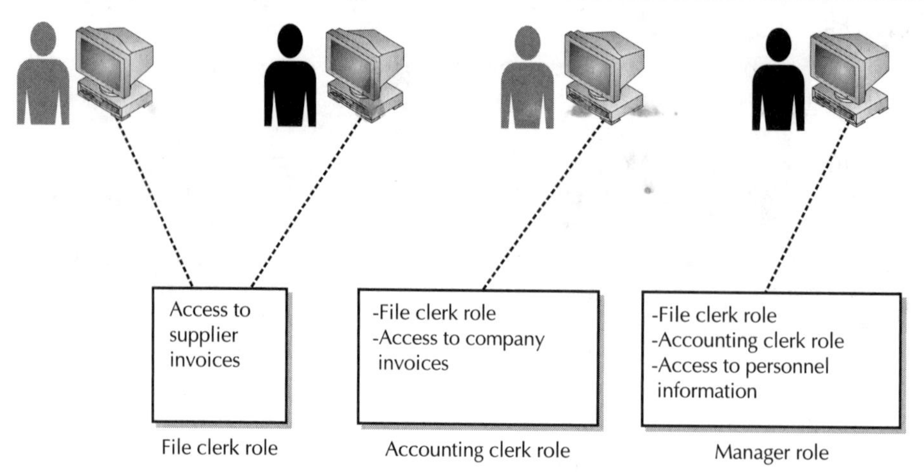

FIGURE 2-4. *Assignment of roles*

To Role or Not to Role

Why use roles rather than grant privileges directly? Let's look at an example. If you have an application with 100 objects, and you have 100 users, you need to make 10,000 grants (100 grants each for 100 users). If one user leaves, you have to revoke 100 grants to maintain security. And if you add a new object, you need to grant access to it to 100 users. Magnify this by multiple tables and multiple users, and you end up spending all your time just granting access to objects. Now complicate this even further by assuming that your users fall into different categories, and each category of user should have access to only some of the objects. How do you ensure that users get access to only those objects that they should?

To help control this problem, Oracle introduced roles. Rather than grant privileges to users directly, you grant privileges to a role and then grant the role to users. Now, when you add a new object, you only have to grant access to the role, and all users who are granted that role automatically inherit that access. And when a user leaves, you don't have to revoke access at all.

Sounds perfect, doesn't it? Before you rush out and create roles for everything and grant them to all your users, you should be aware of a few drawbacks to using roles. First, roles cannot own objects. Why is this important? Well, if you do a "**select distinct Object_Type from DBA_OBJECTS**," one of the object types that is returned is SYNONYM. So roles can't own synonyms. Why is that important?

A synonym is an alias for an object. When you reference an object in your program, unless you own the object or there is a synonym defined for it, you need to reference the object using the syntax "object_owner.object_name"

(MARLENE.CUST_NAMES instead of CUST_NAMES). This can become a problem as you move programs and procedures from one database to another and the owner of the object changes. You would have to remember to change your code everywhere you reference the object and remember who the owner is in that particular database. If you create a synonym for the object, you only need to refer to the object by its synonym in your program. You can create a synonym of the same name in different databases, and they can refer to different objects, or different object owners, or both. So your program does not have to change.

Now back to why it's important that a role can't own a synonym. This means that the only way you can allow a role to access an object is by either hard-coding the owner of the object into every object access or creating public synonyms. A public synonym is a synonym that is available to everyone, not just you. And the problem with public synonyms is that if you have two applications in your database, and each one has a table named HOLIDAYS that contains different data for each application, you can't create the same public synonym name for the two tables.

Second, you can't create stored procedures, functions, or packages using the access privileges you get from a role. So all your developers will have to have access granted directly. Because of this restriction, it's generally a good idea in production to have a single userid that owns all the objects and the procedures that access the objects.

Advantages of Roles

Managed properly, roles can make your life a good deal easier. Let's go back to the hardware supplies company example we used earlier. Your management has decided to keep all information in one database, so you have data about the invoices, your inventory, and even personnel information in the database. As a file clerk, you need access to the invoices, and you may, or may not, need information on the remaining items in stock. But you do *not* need personnel information. In fact, it's illegal for you to have it. So how does your company allow you access to the data you need and keep you from the data you aren't supposed to see?

You can define separate roles, one for a file clerk (CLERK) and one for personnel (PAYROLL) and assign access to the invoices and inventory data to CLERK and access to the employee information to PAYROLL. Then the DBA assigns you the role CLERK, and you can see the information you need to do your job. If there is only one file clerk in the company, you don't need a role. But as we discussed before, what if there are many people working as file clerks? And what if there are many additions to the objects that a file clerk needs to work with? Tracking all the changes and making sure each object is assigned to the proper person and that each person is assigned all the objects they need becomes a full-time job! And what if you change jobs within the company and now need access to the personnel information? The DBA would have to ensure that he or she revokes all the privileges you had to the file clerk data and then add all the privileges you will need for the personnel data. It's easy to miss either revoking one or adding one. But if the privileges have been grouped into roles, the grants and revokes become single statements.

Packages, Procedures, and Functions

Once you have your data in your tables in your database, you need a way to get the data back out to your users. You could give them each a list of all the SQL statements they would need to use in order to retrieve the data. However, that is awkward and someone would inevitably either mistype the statements or need to manipulate the information in a way that can't be done using SQL alone.

Oracle has provided a procedural language extension to SQL, called PL/SQL, that you can use to mix SQL statements with programming constructs such as loops. This allows you to write programs that can be stored within the database. These programs are stored in the database already compiled and parsed and will execute faster than if they are called from outside the database.

There are several forms of stored programs, all of which are written in PL/SQL and stored within the database. Each type of program can take input and return output. Functions always return a single value to the caller, while procedures can return none, one, or more values. With version 7.0, Oracle added a new form of stored program—a package. Packages are made up of combinations of procedures and functions and allow you to group related functions, procedures, and cursors as a single program unit.

Sequences

Going back to when you were young, think about when you went to a movie theater. You purchased a ticket, and when you entered the theater, the attendant ripped the ticket in half and gave you one half and kept the other. Each ticket had a number on it, and each ticket was unique. In this way, the theater could keep track of exactly how many tickets were sold and ensure that they did not sell more tickets than they had seats in which people could sit.

People have bank accounts with an account number, books have an International Standard Book Number (ISBN), Oracle has TAR (Technical Assistant Request) numbers. Each of these numbers is used to identify the object they are assigned to, because there is no other way to uniquely identify these things.

In the hardware company, you need a way to uniquely identify your customers, your suppliers, your invoices, and your employees. You need to ensure that information about one customer and her bills is not connected to information about any other customer. What steps would you need to take to assign a unique number to each customer, supplier, invoice, or employee? You could keep a table somewhere that contained a number. Each time you needed a new, unique number, you could have your program do the following steps:

1. Lock the row in your unique number table so that no one else could read or change the number until you were done looking at and using it.
2. Select the current number to assign to your customer.
3. Add one to the number in the table to make it unique and different from the number you just selected.
4. Unlock the record so someone else who needed a unique number could use the table.

The problem with this method is that it's time consuming, resource intensive, and if the person who requested the number goes to lunch in the middle of the work, everyone waits while the number table is locked. This is not an efficient solution.

Oracle provides sequences as a way around this problem. Sequences are unique number generators, providing sequential numbers that can be used to uniquely identify rows in a table. They are not linked to a table, so you can define one sequence to generate all the numbers in your database, or you can have multiple sequence generators to serve different purposes.

If you don't need every number in the sequence (for customer numbers that just have to be unique), you can tell Oracle to *cache* (or save) numbers from the sequence into memory. This means that while you may lose numbers when the database shuts down, you can retrieve a sequence number more quickly. For numbers that must be sequential (invoice numbers), you can define the sequence to read from disk for each number. Information about sequences is stored in a single data dictionary table in the SYSTEM tablespace, so it is always available. Once a number has been generated from the sequence, it will never be generated again unless the sequence has been created to cycle back to the beginning.

Privileges

Now that you have all the information stored in your database, and you have defined the various roles that people will play in your application, you need to grant access to the objects and privileges to do certain things within the database. Oracle distinguishes between privileges to manipulate data and privileges to perform actions. Privileges to manipulate data are called *object privileges*, and privileges to perform actions are called *system privileges*.

Object privileges include the following rights:

- Look at rows and columns in your tables and views (select)
- Add new rows (insert)
- Update existing rows (update)

- Delete information (delete)
- Execute stored programs (execute)

System privileges allow you to perform actions that affect the overall state of the database. System privileges enable you or your users to change the structure of the database. A few simple privileges are as follows:

- Create a table, index, view, snapshot
- Drop a table, index, view, snapshot
- Create a session in the database in order to connect to the database to perform work

We'll look more closely at system privileges in a minute. For now, let's consider why you need privileges on objects in your database.

Why not make everything accessible to everyone and allow any user to modify system structures? Not all data should be available to every user. If you store personnel information in your database as well as business data, you want to ensure that only those people authorized to look at personnel information have access to it. You don't want an employee to be able to look at another employee's salary or medical information, nor do you want someone to be able to update his or her own payroll, vacation, or sick leave accrual records.

Another form of information that you might not want everyone to have access to is your company-private information. At the April 1999 International Oracle User Group (IOUG-A Live) conference, a DBA described how a contractor who had been hired to work on his database copied company-private information and then left the company and used the copied information to win a contract at a lower bid. Although this is totally unprofessional, it might be difficult to prove the information was removed and used against the company.

Let's first talk about object privileges. These are rights you give to other users to access your objects. You can grant different privileges to different users, letting some only select data and others change it. You can also grant access to other users **with grant option** to allow them to grant access for you. This allows you to keep ownership of all objects within a single schema, create a role for administration of access (DATASEC), grant access to all objects with grant option to DATASEC, and grant the DATASEC role to your data center operations staff. By granting a privilege with grant option to someone else, it allows you to keep access to the owner schema restricted and yet allows others to grant access to the application objects.

For example, if Rachel grants Marlene select privilege on the CUST_NAMES table **with grant option**, Marlene can grant select on the CUST_NAMES table to Ross. Now Marlene and Ross can both see what's in the CUST_NAMES table. But what happens if Rachel changes her mind and decides that Marlene should no longer be able to see this table? Rachel can *revoke* select from Marlene. Gee, what happens to Ross's ability to select from the table? Well, Ross loses his ability to select from the table as soon as Marlene loses her privileges. You will need to remember the ramifications of revoking privileges from someone who has had grant option on an object because of this ripple effect.

Now let's talk about system privileges. These privileges allow you to connect to the database, to affect database objects such as rollback segments and tablespaces, and to create user objects such as tables, views, indexes, and stored procedures. Like object privileges, you can pass on the ability to grant these privileges to another user or role, with the **with admin option**.

If you grant a privilege to someone else **with admin option** and then revoke the privilege from that person, anyone who has been granted privileges through that option would still retain his or her privileges. That sounds kind of confusing, so let's look at an example. Marlene grants **create table with admin option** to Rachel. Rachel then grants **create table** to Ross. Marlene decides that it was not a good idea to grant Rachel this privilege, so she revokes the privilege from Rachel. Guess what? Ross will still have the **create table** privilege!

You will need to take your time and use care as you decide who should have the ability to create objects and who should be able to perform work or grant privileges in your databases.

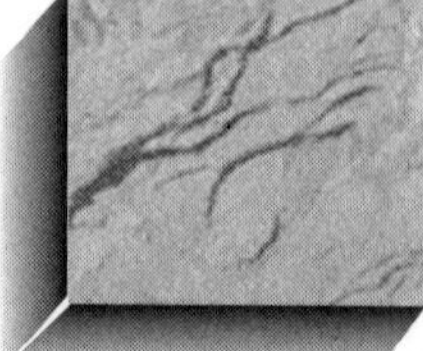

CHAPTER 3

How to Look at the Database

ave you ever been frustrated when you asked how to spell a word and your folks said, "Look it up in the dictionary." Well, gee, how can you look it up to see how to spell it if you don't know how to spell it in the first place! Right? We still feel that way! Anyhow, over a period of years, you learned how to use a dictionary effectively; even for words you don't know how to spell. You should now feel pretty comfortable with the idea of "looking it up."

Throughout the book, we are going to refer to the data dictionary views that Oracle provides, which contain information about the composition of the database (the metadata). In this and the next three chapters, you'll learn how you can use the data dictionary views, specifically the DBA_ views (pronounced "DBA underscore"), as well as a special set of fixed and virtual memory views called the V$ views (pronounced "Vee dollar"), to help you in your daily work. Now, let's get started.

The Data Dictionary Views

Oracle has provided a set of dictionary views for you to use to look up information about various areas of interest in the data dictionary. A specific naming convention is associated with the dictionary views and three different categories of views, as follows:

- USER_ views
- ALL_ views
- DBA_ views

The naming convention gives you a hint as to what information you can see in each of these categories of views. When users look at the USER_ views, they see only the objects that are owned specifically by each of them. When you look at the ALL_ views, you see the objects to which you have access that are owned by yourself or other users. The DBA_ views are available to users with DBA privileges and show both more information and information about every object in the database. They are a superset of the USER_ and ALL_ views.

In the next few chapters, we are going to concentrate on the most commonly used data dictionary views and explain them in more detail, grouping them by the way we use them. In this chapter, we'll concentrate on how to look at and get information about the database, looking at how we organize and store the data in the database. In Chapter 4, we'll continue to look at how to get information about the database, using the V$ views. Next, in Chapter 5, we'll take a look at how to protect the database from unauthorized users or changes. Finally, in Chapter 6, we'll investigate the V$ views that help us to manage the performance of the database. For a complete list of all the default DBA_ views available in Oracle9i, look in the *Oracle9i Database Reference* manual. You can create other useful DBA_ views by running some of the catxxxxx.sql and dbmsxxxx.sql scripts located in your rdbms/admin directory. We'll tell you about the catalog.sql and catproc.sql scripts, used to set up the basic DBA_ views, in Chapter 7, when we talk about how to set up and build a database. You can run catblock.sql to create the DBA_ views to look at locks and locking in your database, or run catdbsyn.sql to create private synonyms for the DBA_ views. The dbmsxxxx.sql scripts create packages that you can use to manipulate your database environment.

The DBA_ Views

As a DBA with full privileges on the system, you can use the DBA_ views to see the complete information about objects in the database. But how do you know what the data dictionary view names are? Or if you get a new version of the RDBMS, how will you know what's been added or what's changed? Good questions!

In Oracle8.1.6 there are 151 views that start with DBA_, and in Oracle9.0.1 there are 243. What does this mean? Well, for one thing, it means that Oracle did a lot of work enhancing the database between versions. And it means there are a lot of new views for you to learn about that have been created to support the new features for each new version. So we're back to the question of how do you know what's been added.

Oracle provides a view (yes, another one!) called DICTIONARY. If you do a **describe** on this view, you'll see that it lists table names and comments about these tables. In reality, the contents of DICTIONARY are all views. This view contains descriptions of all the data dictionary views and the V$ views that we will discuss in this chapter and Chapters 4, 5, and 6. You should always create a test database for each new version of Oracle so that you have a place to test out the differences. We'll tell you how to build a database in Chapter 7, when we talk about Oracle installations. For now, just remember that you can do a **select Table_Name from DICTIONARY** in both your current database and the test database, and then compare the two lists to see what's new (assuming that one database is a different version than the other).

```
SQL>  describe DICTIONARY
Name                             Null?    Type
-------------------------------- -------- ----------------------------
TABLE_NAME                                VARCHAR2(30)
COMMENTS                                  VARCHAR2(4000)
```

Okay, that tells you what's new. How do you know what's been changed? Unfortunately, that's not quite as easy. We're going to tell you now and will continue to say: you are going to have to read the documentation. For every DBA_ view that you use frequently, take a few minutes and read through the new documentation on that view. Oracle may have added new columns (as they did to the DBA_DATA_FILES view between versions 7.x and 8.0), or they may have changed the default values for some of the columns in the views. The only way you can be sure is to read the documentation.

Before we begin talking about the individual views, let's take a quick look at the ones we'll be discussing in this chapter. Table 3-1 contains a list of the views along with a short description of each one.

Although this list is in alphabetical order, we'll talk about the views in logical groups, as they relate to each other. And now, on to some of the DBA_ views we use most often.

View	Description
DBA_CONS_COLUMNS	Information about accessible columns in constraint definitions
DBA_CONSTRAINTS	Constraint definitions on all tables
DBA_DATA_FILES	Information about database datafiles
DBA_EXTENTS	Extents composing all segments in the database
DBA_IND_COLUMNS	Columns composing indexes on all tables and clusters
DBA_INDEXES	Description for all indexes in the database
DBA_OBJECTS	All objects in the database
DBA_ROLLBACK_SEGS	Description of rollback segments
DBA_SEGMENTS	Storage allocated for all database segments
DBA_TAB_COLUMNS	Columns of user's tables, views, and clusters
DBA_TABLES	Description of all relational tables in the database
DBA_TABLESPACES	Description of all tablespaces
DBA_TEMP_FILES	Information about database temporary files (tempfiles)
DBA_UNDO_EXTENTS	Information about the undo extents

TABLE 3-1. *DBA_ Database Layout Views*

DBA_TABLESPACES

In Chapter 8 we are going to spend a good deal of time talking about tablespaces and how to manage them. The view DBA_TABLESPACES contains information and descriptions of all the tablespaces in the database. In this and the next few sections, we're going to show you how to find out more detailed information about your database's physical layout and how you can combine these views with others to find out more about the layout of your database. Table 3-2 contains a list of all the columns in this view and what they represent.

Column	Description
TABLESPACE_NAME	Tablespace name
BLOCK_SIZE	Tablespace block size
INITIAL_EXTENT	Default initial extent size
NEXT_EXTENT	Default incremental extent size
MIN_EXTENTS	Default minimum number of extents
MAX_EXTENTS	Default maximum number of extents
MIN_EXTLEN	Minimum extent size for the tablespace
PCT_INCREASE	Default percent increase for extent size
STATUS	Tablespace status: ONLINE, OFFLINE, or READ ONLY
CONTENTS	Tablespace contents: PERMANENT or TEMPORARY
LOGGING	Default logging attribute
EXTENT_MANAGEMENT	Extent management tracking: DICTIONARY or LOCAL
ALLOCATION_TYPE	Type of extent allocation in effect for this tablespace
PLUGGED_IN	YES—the tablespace is plugged in; NO—it is not plugged in
SEGMENT_SPACE_MANAGEMENT	Segment space management tracking: AUTO or MANUAL

TABLE 3-2. *DBA_TABLESPACES View*

In versions of Oracle prior to 8.0, the recommendation was to group objects in tablespaces by type—indexes in one tablespace, tables in another—and to place the datafiles that made up those tablespaces on different disks. Beginning with Oracle8.0 the focus changed, and Oracle's Center of Expertise began to recommend that you group data along the lines of size. You would have one tablespace for small objects, one for medium-sized objects, and one for large objects (sounds a bit like Goldilocks and the Three Bears, doesn't it?). This recommendation was designed to free the DBA from dealing with space issues in the database. While anything that frees us from routine, repetitive work is good, we still think you should take this a step further and separate data and index tablespaces within the differently sized groups. This entails extra tablespaces to manage, but can speed up recovery, as it's usually faster to re-create an index than to recover it.

With each later release of the software, Oracle moved more and more towards releasing the DBA from the task of disk monitor. Let's take a look at how you can see that through this view.

The first column after the tablespace name is Block_Size. Before 9i, once you created the database and chose an Oracle database block size, you couldn't change it without rebuilding the database. If you chose the wrong block size, or if the application requirements changed, you would either have to live with your choice and the problems it generated or find time and space to rebuild the database with a new block size. In 9i, Oracle gives you the ability to set different block sizes for different tablespaces. This column tells you the block size you chose for this tablespace. If you don't specify a block size when you create the tablespace, Oracle will use the default block size you specify in your initialization parameter file. The SYSTEM tablespace is always created with the database default block size.

The next set of columns in the view deal with the default storage for any objects created in this tablespace. Initial_Extent, in combination with Min_Extents, determines how much space Oracle will allocate when you create an object in this tablespace. If you have an initial extent size of 8192000 (1000 blocks in a database with an 8K block size), and minimum extents of 5, how many blocks will Oracle allocate when you create an object without a storage clause? If you said 5000 blocks, you're absolutely right.

We'll talk more about Max_Extents, Next_Extent, and Pct_Increase a little later. For now, you need to remember that these values determine the size the object can grow to, by limiting the number of extents (Max_Extents) and by determining how large each succeeding extent will be (Next_Extent and Pct_Increase). These columns are used when you ask Oracle to manage the tablespace through the data dictionary. Min_Extlen was introduced in Oracle8 to help control fragmentation. As a DBA, you should be concerned about tablespace fragmentation. If the objects you place in your tablespace have extent sizes that are not multiples of each other, your tablespace can become very fragmented as these objects are dropped or truncated. Eventually, you can end up with a tablespace that has lots of free space, but much of it will be unusable because the extent sizes are not multiples of one another. The space in the tablespace will end up looking like a moth-eaten coat, and the free extents will be too small to be usable. Min_Extlen lets you set a minimum extent size for the objects in that tablespace, and all objects that are created must have extent sizes that are multiples of this minimum.

While Min_Extlen, used properly, did a great deal to relieve fragmentation in a tablespace, Oracle added new features in succeeding releases to help even more. With the release of Oracle8i, the DBA could now create tablespaces that were "locally managed" (referred to generally as LMTs). Rather than have Oracle manage the disk space through the data dictionary, you could opt to manage it yourself. If the Extent_Management column is set to LOCAL, Oracle will manage the space allocation within the datafiles of the tablespace using a bitmap in the header of the datafile, rather than using the data dictionary tables. This improves performance, as Oracle no longer has to do additional reads to allocate or free space. If you decide to manage your tablespaces yourself, you can then specify either to have uniform extents (extents all the same size) or to have Oracle manage the extent sizes, and this is reflected in the Allocation_Type column. Any tablespace that is created as an LMT does not need to have free space coalesced.

Plugged_In refers to transportable tablespaces and will be discussed in detail in Chapter 8. The final column, Segment_Space_Management, is new in Oracle9i. Just as you can have Oracle manage the space allocation within the tablespace using a bitmap or using the data dictionary, you can now have the space allocation within each table or index in the tablespace managed using a bitmap (automatic) or using free lists (lists of data blocks that have space available for inserting rows—manual). Free lists were the only way space was managed prior to Oracle9i and are the default. You can only use the automatic segment space management feature in tablespaces that are locally managed.

Let's try an example and see what happens when we attempt to create a tablespace.

```
create tablespace TESTTBS
datafile '/usr/local/ora9/oradata/test9i/testtbs01.dbf' size 10M
blocksize 8K
extent management local uniform size 80K
segment space management auto
/
```

We told Oracle to create a tablespace with a block size of 8K and to let us manage the extents, by creating extents of a uniform size of 80K. If you notice, we didn't specify a default storage clause. Let's see what Oracle thinks it should be.

```
select *
  from DBA_TABLESPACES
 where Tablespace_Name='TESTTBS';
```

```
TABLESPACE            BLOCK_SIZE       INITIAL_EXTENT          NEXT_EXTENT       MIN_EXTENTS
---------- ------------------- ------------------- ------------------- ----------------
        MAX_EXTENTS           PCT_INCREASE           MIN_EXTLEN STATUS    CONTENTS  LOGGING
------------------- ------------------- ------------------- --------- --------- --------
EXTENT_MAN ALLOCATIO PLU SEGMEN
---------- --------- --- ------
TESTTBS                       8192                81920                81920                1
         2147483645                      0            81920 ONLINE    PERMANENT LOGGING
LOCAL      UNIFORM   NO  AUTO
```

Hmm, Oracle took the uniform extent size we specified and made that the initial and next extent values. That makes sense, since we said that we want every extent to be of a uniform size. The good thing about this is, we won't have to worry about fragmentation in this tablespace, every extent allocated will be the same size, and there will be no "holes" that we can't fill.

The remaining columns were added to the view with the introduction of Oracle8. Status lets you know whether the tablespace is online, offline, or read-only. An offline tablespace is part of the database but cannot be accessed by any user. A read-only tablespace is one that you can only select from. Contents tells you whether the contents of the tablespace are permanent or temporary. If the contents of a tablespace are temporary, you cannot have any objects in that tablespace. Oracle will use that tablespace and create a single temporary segment for sorting that is shared by all users and will not drop this temporary segment once the sort operation is done. This can improve the performance of your application if it does a lot of sorting, since the temporary segments will not have to be allocated for each sort.

Logging has to do with whether the DML (Data Manipulation Language) and DDL (Data Definition Language) operations are written to the redo logs. Why would you *not* want to log something? Well, sometimes it's faster to re-create an object than to recover it from the log files. It is usually faster to re-create an index than it is to do recovery to restore it. Not all DML and DDL operations can be done without logging. For more details on which operations can be done without logging to the redo logs, check the *Oracle SQL Reference* manual.

DBA_DATA_FILES

The DBA_DATA_FILES data dictionary view, described in Table 3-3, holds the information about the physical files that make up the tablespaces and the database.

Datafiles are the foundation of the database. Without the physical files, there is nowhere to place the data. This view can be used to see the layout of your files on disk, and it can quickly show you if you have put datafiles from "competing" tablespaces (such as rollback segment and system tablespaces) on the same disks. In combination with other data dictionary views, you can see the fragmentation within

Column	Description
FILE_NAME	Name of the database file
FILE_ID	ID of the database file
TABLESPACE_NAME	Name of the tablespace to which the file belongs
BYTES	Size of the file in bytes
BLOCKS	Size of the file in Oracle blocks
STATUS	File status: AVAILABLE or INVALID
RELATIVE_FNO	Relative file number
AUTOEXTENSIBLE	Autoextensible indicator
MAXBYTES	Maximum file size in bytes
MAXBLOCKS	Maximum file size in blocks
INCREMENT_BY	Autoextension increment
USER_BYTES	Corresponding number of bytes
USER_BLOCKS	Number of blocks that can be used by the data

TABLE 3-3. *DBA_DATA_FILES View*

your datafiles and tablespaces, as in the scripts we use for daily monitoring that we discuss in Chapter 9.

The columns File_Name and File_ID both contain unique information. No datafile name can be repeated, and no File_ID (assigned by Oracle) can be either. So why does Oracle have both columns, when each one is unique? Well, the underlying database tables that these views are built on have indexes on them so that Oracle can return the information to you quickly. In general, it's a better idea to index a numeric column than it is to index a character column. So even though both columns are unique, and there is some extra space "wasted" to store the File_ID, ORACLE includes that column to improve performance. We'll see this repetition of unique columns in other data dictionary views as well.

The File_ID column is a number, unique within the database, that identifies the datafile. Oracle's documentation will refer to this number as the *absolute file number.* The absolute file number is used as a foreign key in other data dictionary views, notably DBA_EXTENTS and DBA_ROLLBACK_SEGS. These views can be joined to the DBA_DATA_FILES view to provide more information about the object allocation and rollback segments in your database. The Bytes and Blocks columns define the total size of the datafile. When you create a tablespace or add another datafile to an existing tablespace, you must give Oracle the size of the datafile. This is the amount of space that will be initially allocated at the operating system level for this datafile. Unless you have turned autoextend on for this datafile, this is the maximum size the datafile will be. Blocks are always defined in Oracle blocks.

Status refers to whether the datafile is available or invalid. A datafile is invalid if that file in the tablespace was dropped. Why would you drop a datafile? Suppose you have a corrupted datafile, and you do not have a valid backup of that file so you cannot perform media recovery. The database will not open, as the files are not consistent. Oracle will allow you to mount the database and alter the database to drop the datafile. You use the statement:

```
alter datafile '<datafile_name>' offline drop;
```

When you issue this statement, you are telling Oracle that you will drop the associated tablespace as soon as you can. Once you have issued this statement and opened the database, you will not be able to do anything else with the tablespace to which the datafile belongs except drop it. You will not even be able to alter the tablespace offline because Oracle already views it as offline. If you check the Status column of that datafile before you drop the tablespace, it will be INVALID. You should immediately drop the tablespace and take a backup of the database.

Relative_Fno is the relative file number for the datafile within that particular tablespace. While the File_ID is the absolute (or unique) file number within your database, the relative file number is unique only within a tablespace. So several tablespaces can have datafiles with the same Relative_Fno, but the File_ID of each of these datafiles will be different. For the first 1021 datafiles in the database, the relative file number will be the same as the absolute file number. Once you have more than 1022 datafiles in your database, Oracle begins to reuse the relative file numbers across different tablespaces. You cannot have more than 1022 datafiles in a single tablespace. Oracle has added the Relative_Fno column to all the DBA_ views that contain both the datafile's File_ID and the tablespace name.

Autoextensible, Max_Bytes, Max_Blocks, and Increment_By all refer to the ability to automatically extend the size of a datafile. Autoextensible is a YES/NO flag to indicate whether the datafile can automatically extend. Max_Bytes and Max_Blocks are the maximum size the file can extend to, in both bytes and Oracle blocks. Increment_By is the amount to extend each time the datafile needs more space, expressed in Oracle blocks.

If you allow Oracle to create the default database as part of the installation, be sure to check the Autoextensible column for the datafiles that are created. Several of the tablespaces are created with autoextend on, and you should know which ones they are and disable autoextend where appropriate.

The query below selects all information about the datafiles in the SYSTEM tablespace.

```
select *
  from DBA_DATA_FILES
 where tablespace_name ='SYSTEM';
```

There are two datafiles in the SYSTEM tablespace. The first one can autoextend, the second cannot. Each time the first one extends, Oracle will allocate another 5120 Oracle blocks (in this case 1M, as this database has a 2K block size) of physical disk space, up to a maximum allocation of 200M for the datafile. If Oracle attempts to autoextend the datafile and cannot get the physical space, the transaction causing the extend will fail.

```
FILE_NAME                              FILE_ID TABLESPACE_NAME      BYTES     BLOCKS
----------------------------- --------- --------------- --------- ---------
STATUS     RELATIVE_FNO AUT  MAXBYTES MAXBLOCKS INCREMENT_BY
--------- ------------ --- --------- --------- ------------
D:\ORANT\DATABASE\SYS1ORCL.ORA           1 SYSTEM          62914560     30720
AVAILABLE              1 YES 209715200    102400         5120

D:\ORANT\DATABASE\SYS0ORCL.ORA           5 SYSTEM          52428800     25600
AVAILABLE              5  NO         0         0            0
```

User_Bytes and User_Blocks are used to define how much space the data can take up in a datafile. The values are displayed in both byte and block format. To better understand how the values for User_Bytes/User_Blocks work, let's take a look at the entry for the USERS tablespace in our Oracle9i demonstration database. We happen to know that this tablespace has objects in it.

```
FILE_NAME                                          FILE_ID TBS                BYTES
--------------------------------------------- -------- ---------- ----------
    BLOCKS STATUS      RFNO AUT  MAXBYTES  MAX BLKS  INCR_BY  USR BYTES  USR BLKS
---------- --------- ----- --- --------- --------- -------- ---------- ---------
/usr/local/ora9/oradata/test9i/users01.dbf           7 USERS        26214400
      3200 AVAILABLE     7 NO          0         0        0   26148864      3192
```

Okay, we see that the total number of blocks available in this tablespace is 3200, with 3192 blocks available for data. Therefore, we can assume that the 8 blocks that are not available are being held (reserved) by Oracle for some other use. Hmm. Do you wonder how much space has been allocated so far in this datafile? Just out of curiosity, let's take a look. We'll use the DBA_SEGMENTS view (we'll talk about it in more depth next) to get the total number of bytes and blocks that have been allocated for objects currently in the USERS tablespace.

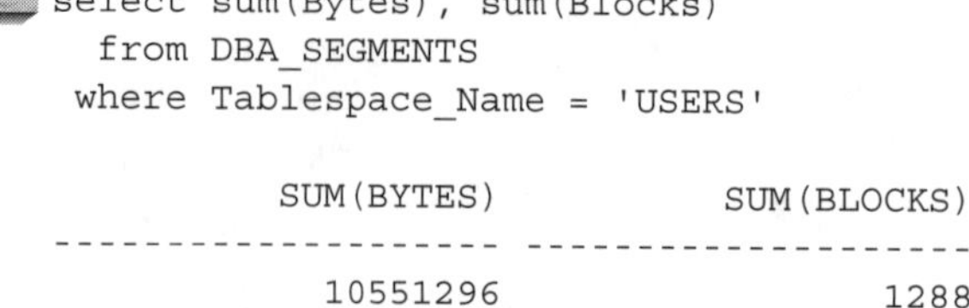

```
select sum(Bytes), sum(Blocks)
  from DBA_SEGMENTS
 where Tablespace_Name = 'USERS'

          SUM(BYTES)          SUM(BLOCKS)
-------------------- --------------------
            10551296                 1288
```

If you look back at the values in User_Bytes and User_Blocks compared to Bytes and Blocks allocated, it's pretty obvious that neither column reflects any space that is being used in the datafile by current data; only the limits that have been set. So what were those 8 blocks being reserved for? Well, this is a locally managed tablespace, and those 8 blocks are where Oracle places the bitmap to manage the allocations in this tablespace.

DBA_SEGMENTS

The DBA_SEGMENTS view, described in Table 3-4, contains information about storage allocated for all database segments.

So far in this chapter, we've talked about the physical world of the database in large terms, describing the tablespaces and datafiles and the space in them. Now we're going to talk a little about the things that go into the datafiles and use up that space.

Every object in the database that can take up space is called a *segment*. You can see the storage information about the segment by querying the DBA_SEGMENTS view. Every segment is created in a tablespace and may also be created in a partition. Each table, index, rollback segment, and so on, will have an Initial_Extent that defines the size of the first chunk of blocks allocated for that segment. The Next_Extent, in combination with the Pct_Increase defined, will determine the size of each succeeding chunk that is allocated. Well, almost. The initial and next extents requested in the storage clause may not actually be the amount of space allocated for that segment, since Oracle will round the bytes allocated up to a multiple of a database block. And, even then, if the tablespace has a minimum extent length defined, the initial and next extent values stored in this view may not reflect the sizes of the extents allocated. In fact, if you are using locally managed tablespaces, Oracle will accept the storage clause you give it, but will use the tablespace storage values, not the ones you specify. So why look at this view if the information may not be accurate? In Chapter 8, in the section "Creating Objects in the Database," we will show you how to calculate what the size of the segment should be, based on the Initial_Extent, Next_Extent, Pct_Increase, and number of

Column	Description
OWNER	Username of the segment owner
SEGMENT_NAME	Name of the segment
PARTITION_NAME	Object partition name
SEGMENT_TYPE	Type of segment
TABLESPACE_NAME	Name of the tablespace containing the segment
HEADER_FILE	ID of the file containing the segment header
HEADER_BLOCK	ID of the block containing the segment header
BYTES	Size in bytes of the segment
BLOCKS	Size in Oracle blocks of the segment
EXTENTS	Number of extents allocated to the segment
INITIAL_EXTENT	Size in bytes of the initial extent of the segment
NEXT_EXTENT	Size in bytes of the next extent to be allocated to the segment
MIN_EXTENTS	Minimum number of extents allowed in the segment
MAX_EXTENTS	Maximum number of extents allowed in the segment
PCT_INCREASE	Percent by which to increase the size of the next extent to be allocated
FREELISTS	Number of process freelists allocated to this segment
FREELIST_GROUPS	Number of freelist groups allocated to this segment
RELATIVE_FNO	Relative file number of the segment header
BUFFER_POOL	Name of the default buffer pool for the appropriate object

TABLE 3-4. *DBA_SEGMENTS View*

extents allocated (the Extents column). If the segment is not the size you think it should be, you, as a proactive DBA, should be looking to see why it isn't. The fastest way to know if things are not quite the size you expect them to be is to look at the values in the DBA_SEGMENTS view.

In addition, Oracle gives you the ability to decide in which buffer pool within the SGA to place the segment, by specifying the Buffer_Pool when the segment is created or altered. The buffer pools determine whether the data blocks of this segment are retained in memory or flushed as they are no longer needed. Why keep the data blocks in memory? Let's go back to the XYZ Company for a moment. They have a list of products they manufacture, and each product has a product code attached to it. Every time an order is placed, the person taking the order has to look up the product code for that product in the table. If that table is kept in memory, the lookup will be much faster. The other side of this is that the customer information probably does not have to stay in memory, because it is not likely that the customer will call back several times in a single day to place orders. As more blocks are moved into the Keep buffer pool, the older ones will still be flushed to disk. So setting the buffer pool to KEEP on a table still doesn't ensure you won't have to read from disk at some point.

You can use the script below to check how close the segments in your database are to reaching their maximum extents.

```
select Owner, Tablespace_Name, Segment_Name, Extents, Max_Extents,
       (Extents/Max_Extents)*100 Usedpct
  from DBA_SEGMENTS
 where Owner not in ('SYS','SYSTEM')
   and Segment_Type not in ('ROLLBACK','DEFERRED ROLLBACK','TEMPORARY')
 order by Tablespace_Name, Owner, Extents
/

OWNER      TABLESPACE SEGMENT_NAME       EXTENTS  MAX_EXTENTS  USEDPCT
---------- ---------- --------------- --------- ------------ --------
JAMES      TESTTBS    TEST1                   5          500    1.000
RACHEL     TESTTBS    ABC                     5          500    1.000
MY_SCHEMA  USER_DATA  PRIMATES                1          500     .200
MY_SCHEMA  USER_DATA  PRIMATES_PK             1          121     .826
QC_USER    USER_DATA  FREESP                  1          121     .826
QC_USER    USER_DATA  TOY                     1          121     .826
QC_USER    USER_DATA  STUDENT                 1          121     .826
QC_USER    USER_DATA  ABC                     1   2147483645     .000
QC_USER    USER_DATA  PRIMATES                1          500     .200
```

It seems that none of the segments is close to reaching its maximum extent, which is good. But wait a minute. One of the segments has a very unusual Max_Extents of 2147483645. What's that all about? Well, starting with version 7.3, Oracle added a new feature to the storage clause—the ability to create a segment with a **maxextents unlimited** subclause. Since Oracle has to store some number in the Max_Extents column, they chose 2147483645, which is the numeric value of 2GB. Anytime you see a segment with a Max_Extents value of 2147483645, you know that it has actually been created with **maxextents unlimited**.

DBA_EXTENTS

The DBA_EXTENTS view, described in Table 3-5, lists the extents composing all segments in the database.

In the prior section, we looked at DBA_SEGMENTS and the storage allocation parameters you define when you create a segment. The DBA_EXTENTS view is a more detailed look at the segments, with information about each extent that has been allocated for a particular segment. What is an extent? An *extent* is a contiguous number of data blocks allocated for storing data.

The information in the DBA_EXTENTS view is a road map of the segment. There is a parent-child relationship between the DBA_SEGMENTS and DBA_EXTENTS views, with one row in DBA_EXTENTS for every extent allocated to the segment. Each row contains the Segment_Name, Owner, Segment_Type, and Tablespace_Name, which in combination can be used to link the rows in the DBA_EXTENTS view back to the DBA_SEGMENTS view. Other columns in this view are the Extent_ID, unique within the segment, indicating the order in which that extent has been allocated; the File_ID and Block_ID, which locate the extent within the datafile; and the Bytes and Blocks columns, which are the amount of space allocated for this extent, expressed in both bytes and database blocks.

Column	Description
OWNER	Owner of the segment associated with the extent
SEGMENT_NAME	Name of the segment associated with the extent
SEGMENT_TYPE	Type of the segment
TABLESPACE_NAME	Name of the tablespace containing the extent
EXTENT_ID	Extent number in the segment
FILE_ID	Name of the file containing the extent
BLOCK_ID	Starting block number of the extent
BYTES	Size of the extent in bytes
BLOCKS	Size of the extent in Oracle blocks
RELATIVE_FNO	Relative file number of the first extent block
PARTITION_NAME	Object partition name (Set to NULL for nonpartitioned objects)

TABLE 3-5. *DBA_EXTENTS View*

Why drill down to this level of detail? As we discuss in Chapter 9, as a proactive DBA, you need to monitor not only the number of extents allocated to a segment, but also the size and growth of these extents. If you have set a non-zero percent increase for a segment, you will want to keep a close eye on the last extent size allocated, so that you can ensure there is enough space in the tablespace for the next extent to be allocated when needed.

Another reason to check on the number of extents in a segment has to do with the way Oracle releases extents back to the database when you drop or truncate a table or index in a dictionary managed tablespace. As the extents are released, information about the extent is removed from an internal used-extent table and added to an internal free-extent table. Releasing a lot of extents causes a lot of activity at the data dictionary level. So if you have a lot of extents allocated to the segment, it won't cause a performance impact when you access the data, unless you try to release that space. We know of a DBA who had to drop a table with 10,000 extents. He was patient and waited it out until the bitter end—ten hours later!

Do you remember your parents asking you, "If everyone jumped off a bridge, would you jump too?" Just because you are able to do something, it's not always a good idea to do it. Although Oracle allows you to set the maximum number of extents to "unlimited," in practice it's a good idea if you try to keep the actual maximum number of extents to under 4096. If your table or index is growing that large, you should make it a candidate for movement to a tablespace that has a larger extent size.

Let's take a look at a segment with more than one extent:

```
select *
  from DBA_SEGMENTS
 where Segment_Name ='TSTTAB'
/

OWNER      SEG_NAME   PART_NAME  SEG_TYP TBS_NAME   HDR_FILE   NDR_BLK
---------- ---------- ---------- ------- ---------- -------- ---------
     BYTES     BLOCKS   EXTENTS  INIT_EXT  NEXT_EXT    MIN_EXT     MAX_EXT
---------- ---------- --------- --------- --------- ---------- -----------
 PCT_INCR FREELISTS FREEL_GRPS REL_FNO BUFF_POOL
--------- --------- ---------- ------- ----------
RAC9I      TSTTAB                TABLE   USERS             7       137
  10485760       1280        10   9502720                    1  2147483645
                    1          1       7 DEFAULT

select *
  from DBA_EXTENTS
 where Segment_Name = 'TSTTAB'
/

OWNER   SEGNAME PARTNM SEG_TYP TBS_NAME EXT_ID   FILEID BLK_ID    BYTES   BLKS REL_FNO
------- ------- ------ ------- -------- ------ -------- ------ -------- ------ -------
RAC9I   TSTTAB         TABLE   USERS         0        7    137  1048576    128       7
RAC9I   TSTTAB         TABLE   USERS         1        7    265  1048576    128       7
```

```
RAC9I    TSTTAB          TABLE   USERS          2         7     393  1048576      128          7
RAC9I    TSTTAB          TABLE   USERS          3         7     521  1048576      128          7
RAC9I    TSTTAB          TABLE   USERS          4         7     649  1048576      128          7
RAC9I    TSTTAB          TABLE   USERS          5         7     777  1048576      128          7
RAC9I    TSTTAB          TABLE   USERS          6         7     905  1048576      128          7
RAC9I    TSTTAB          TABLE   USERS          7         7    1033  1048576      128          7
RAC9I    TSTTAB          TABLE   USERS          8         7    1161  1048576      128          7
RAC9I    TSTTAB          TABLE   USERS          9         7    1289  1048576      128          7
```

Did you notice anything about this segment? If you look at the Block_ID column in the select from the DBA_EXTENTS view, you see that the blocks are contiguous. This is an unusual occurrence in an active database, so why did it happen? Checking the DBA_SEGMENTS information, you can see that the extents value is 10. So all the extents were allocated at the same time. If your tablespace is very fragmented, you may still see the extents placed all over the tablespace, wherever Oracle can find the room for them.

DBA_ROLLBACK_SEGS

The DBA_ROLLBACK_SEGS view, described in Table 3-6, contains information about the rollback segments available to the database.

Have you ever rearranged the furniture in your living room and then decided the change made the room look terrible and put everything back where it originally was? When you make changes to the data in the database, Oracle keeps a copy of the old version of the data in case you change your mind and want to put everything back the way it was. Oracle uses a special database object called a *rollback segment* to store the old versions of the data blocks. In addition, Oracle uses the information in a rollback segment to present a consistent picture of the original data to other users, so that you don't stop everyone from working if you start to make changes and then go out to lunch! Until you commit your changes, anyone else trying to access that data will read the changed blocks from the rollback segments.

Because rollback segments store copies of the before image of the columns being changed, they also take up physical space in the database. Oracle's special DBA_ view DBA_ROLLBACK_SEGS lets you quickly see the information about your rollback segments. Most of the information in this view can be extracted from the data dictionary by querying the DBA_SEGMENTS and DBA_EXTENTS views we discussed earlier in this chapter. As you can see from the select statement and results below, a rollback segment, like any other segment, has a Segment_Name, Owner, Initial_Extent, Next_Extent, Min_Extent, Max_Extent, and Pct_Increase defined. Also like any other segment, it is created and takes up space in a tablespace, shown in the Tablespace_Name column. Unlike other segments, a rollback segment has a unique Segment_ID column, which can be joined to the Usn column of the V$ROLLSTAT view (which will be discussed in detail in Chapter 6) to give you dynamic information about your rollback segments. In addition, a rollback segment must have a minimum

Column	Description
SEGMENT_NAME	Name of the rollback segment
OWNER	Owner of the rollback segment
TABLESPACE_NAME	Name of the tablespace containing the rollback segment
SEGMENT_ID	ID number of the rollback segment
FILE_ID	ID number of the file containing the segment header
BLOCK_ID	ID number of the block containing the segment header
INITIAL_EXTENT	Initial extent size in bytes
NEXT_EXTENT	Secondary extent size in bytes
MIN_EXTENTS	Minimum number of extents
MAX_EXTENTS	Maximum number of extents
PCT_INCREASE	Percent increase for extent size
STATUS	Rollback segment status
INSTANCE_NUM	Rollback segment owning parallel server instance number
RELATIVE_FNO	Relative file number of the segment header

TABLE 3-6. *DBA_ROLLBACK_SEGS View*

of at least two extents, although it can have more, and a percent increase of zero (or null for the special undo segments we will discuss in the next section). The first of the extents allocated for a rollback segment is the *header block* and is used by Oracle to store information that tracks the transactions accessing this rollback segment and the extents the transaction is using. In the File_ID and Block_ID columns, Oracle maintains information about the location of the header block.

```
select Segment_Name, Tablespace_Name, Owner, Initial_Extent,
       Next_Extent, Min_Extents, Max_Extents, Pct_Increase, Status
  from DBA_ROLLBACK_SEGS
/
SEGMENT    TABLESPACE           OWNER         INITIAL      NEXT  MINEXT  MAXEXT  PCT STATUS
---------- -------------------- ---------- --------- --------- ------- ------- ---- -------
SYSTEM     SYSTEM               SYS            57344     57344       2     505    0 ONLINE
_SYSSMU1$  UNDOTBS              PUBLIC        131072                 2   32765      ONLINE
_SYSSMU2$  UNDOTBS              PUBLIC        131072                 2   32765      ONLINE
_SYSSMU3$  UNDOTBS              PUBLIC        131072                 2   32765      ONLINE
_SYSSMU4$  UNDOTBS              PUBLIC        131072                 2   32765      ONLINE
_SYSSMU5$  UNDOTBS              PUBLIC        131072                 2   32765      ONLINE
```

```
_SYSSMU6$  UNDOTBS          PUBLIC       131072                  2  32765       ONLINE
_SYSSMU7$  UNDOTBS          PUBLIC       131072                  2  32765       ONLINE
_SYSSMU8$  UNDOTBS          PUBLIC       131072                  2  32765       ONLINE
_SYSSMU9$  UNDOTBS          PUBLIC       131072                  2  32765       ONLINE
_SYSSMU10$ UNDOTBS          PUBLIC       131072                  2  32765       ONLINE
RB1        RBS              SYS         1048576    1048576       2    505     0 OFFLINE
RB2        RBS              SYS         1048576    1048576       2    505     0 OFFLINE
```

So you can get the same storage information from DBA_ROLLBACK_SEGS that you can from DBA_SEGMENTS. Why create a separate view? Unlike any other type of segment, a rollback segment can be created with a status of ONLINE or OFFLINE and, if you are using Oracle's Parallel Server (renamed to Real Application Clusters in Oracle9i), can be owned by an individual instance (the Instance_Num column).

What's the difference between ONLINE and OFFLINE, and how is the status set? A rollback segment that is online is one that is available for the database to use. There will be information about your online rollback segments in the V$ROLLSTAT and V$ROLLNAME views, which you can use to tune the performance of your database. If you are not using automatic undo management, you can bring an existing rollback segment online by either specifically listing it in your initialization parameter file or config.ora file using the parameter **rollback_segments**, or by using the command **alter rollback segment <rollback segment name> online**. When you create a rollback segment, it is created as offline by default, but you can override this on the **create** command line.

Did you notice something interesting in the results above? Some of the rollback segments are owned by PUBLIC and have unusual names. When you use automatic undo management (AUM), Oracle creates the rollback segments for you and names them _SYSSMU#$. Oracle decides how many undo segments to create based on the **sessions** parameter in the database initialization parameter file. You cannot create manually managed rollback segments if you are using AUM.

Rollback segments that are listed in one of the initialization parameter files are considered private rather than public. A *private* rollback segment is available only to the instance that names it in the parameter file, while a *public* one is available to any instance. The only time there is a difference between private and public rollback segments is when you are using Real Application Clusters. If you are using RAC, each instance can create both private rollback segments that can only be seen by that instance and public rollback segments that are available to all the instances. You identify rollback segments as private by naming them in your initialization parameter file using the **rollback_segments** parameter. No two instances can identify the same rollback segments as private.

In the listing, one of the rollback segments is in the tablespace SYSTEM. When you create a database, Oracle automatically creates a rollback segment named SYSTEM and reserves it for its own use. If you are going to manage your rollback segments yourself, you should create a separate tablespace for your rollback segments and then create the rollback segments. Rollback segments expand and can fragment your SYSTEM tablespace if you create them in it. You should not list the SYSTEM rollback segment in the **rollback_segments** parameter list because you do not want any process but Oracle's to access the SYSTEM rollback segment.

DBA_UNDO_EXTENTS

The DBA_UNDO_EXTENTS view, described in Table 3-7, contains information about the undo extents used with automatic undo management. You can have either rollback segments or undo segments online and active in the database, but not both at the same time. This view is new in Oracle9i.

In Chapter 2, we told you about a new feature in Oracle9i, automatic undo management. With this feature, you can now choose to let Oracle manage the undo process rather than monitoring the rollback segments yourself. You can set a retention time, which tells Oracle to hold onto the information in the undo extent for that amount of time. This lets you implement another new feature, flashback query, so that you can extract the SQL that was run in that time period. You can then undo a change that was run by mistake.

Column	Description
OWNER	Owner of the undo tablespace
SEGMENT_NAME	Name of the undo segment
TABLESPACE_NAME	Name of the undo tablespace
EXTENT_ID	ID of the extent
FILE_ID	Number of the file containing the extent
BLOCK_ID	Start block number of the extent
BYTES	Size of the extent in bytes
BLOCKS	Size of the extent in blocks
RELATIVE_FNO	Relative file number of the segment header
COMMIT_JTIME	Commit time of the extent expressed as Julian time
COMMIT_WTIME	Commit time of the extent expressed as wallclock time

TABLE 3-7. *DBA_UNDO_EXTENTS View*

The undo extents, like rollback segments, belong to a particular tablespace. Unlike rollback segments, you can have only one Undo Tablespace in use in a database, and you cannot create the undo extents ahead of time. Oracle will create the undo extents for you, based on the **sessions** parameter in your initialization parameter file. The space information columns in this view are similar to those in DBA_ROLLBACK_SEGS and DBA_SEGMENTS, and we have described them in the section on DBA_SEGMENTS. The last two columns, COMMIT_JTIME and COMMIT_WTIME, are the interesting ones here.

Unlike rollback segments, which can be reused and whose extents can be overwritten once the transaction commits, the undo segments do not get reused until the committed transaction has been held for the **undo_retention** period or the Undo Tablespace runs out of space. Under normal conditions, the undo information will be held for the retention time. The commit time columns contain the timestamp of the commit for this transactional information. The commit time plus the retention time tells you when the undo segment will be reused.

You need to be very careful when setting the retention time, taking into account not only how long your users want to be able to undo changes but also the number and size of changes in any given time period. You can easily run out of space if there is an unusually large volume of activity.

DBA_OBJECTS

The DBA_OBJECTS view, described in Table 3-8, contains information about the objects in the database.

What is an object? In simple terms, an object is anything that a user can own. Wait a minute, how is that different from a segment? Well, a segment is an object that takes up physical space in the database; but there are other types of objects, such as views, synonyms, sequences, and stored programs, that can be owned by a user but don't take up physical space. So all segments are objects, right? Not exactly. There are three special types of segments—temporary segments, rollback segments, and undo segments—that take up space in the database but do not appear in a list of object types. These segments cannot be directly accessed by any user and so are not considered objects.

Okay, now that we've confused you just a bit, let's take a look at the DBA_OBJECTS view and see if we can make things a bit clearer. When you look at the columns in the view, you see that, like segments, objects have an Object_Name, Owner, and Object_Type. Unlike segments, however, there is no tablespace associated with the object. Think about a synonym. A synonym is merely another name for something and doesn't take up space. If it doesn't take up space, it doesn't need a tablespace. The Object_ID, like the IDs in some of the other DBA_ views, is a number that uniquely identifies this object.

Column	Description
OWNER	Username of the owner of the object
OBJECT_NAME	Name of the object
SUBOBJECT_NAME	Name of the sub-object (for example, partition)
OBJECT_ID	Object number of the object
DATA_OBJECT_ID	Object number of the segment that contains the object
OBJECT_TYPE	Type of the object (for example, TABLE, INDEX)
CREATED	Timestamp for the creation of the object
LAST_DDL_TIME	Timestamp for the last DDL change (including GRANT and REVOKE) to the object
TIMESTAMP	Timestamp for the specification of the object
STATUS	Status of the object
TEMPORARY	Can the current session only see data that it places in this object itself?
GENERATED	Was the name of this object generated by the system?
SECONDARY	Is this a secondary object created as part of icreate for domain indexes?

TABLE 3-8. *DBA_OBJECTS View*

There are three dates associated with an object. Created is the date the object was created. Last_DDL_Time is the date of the last DDL change to the object, and Timestamp is the last time someone changed the object. Hmm, isn't that the same thing? No, not quite. Timestamp will be updated only when the object itself is changed, such as changing the definition of a view; while Last_DDL_Time will be updated then as well, but will also be updated when a grant or revoke is done on the object. One of the authors spent a few worried hours trying to figure out why it seemed as if everything in her database had been changed overnight before she realized what the difference was between the two columns! She had granted access to all the objects to a new user.

Status is either VALID or INVALID. In the case of objects that are stored programs or views, the status will be INVALID if the program does not compile properly or if an object that the stored program accesses is changed. If you want to find all the stored programs that are invalid, you can run the following script:

```
select Owner Oown, Object_Name Oname, Object_Type Otype
  from DBA_OBJECTS
 where Object_Type in
     ('PROCEDURE','PACKAGE','FUNCTION','TRIGGER','PACKAGE BODY','VIEW')
   and Owner not in ('SYS','SYSTEM')
   and Status != 'VALID'
 order by 1,4,3,2
/

OOWN       ONAME           OTYPE
---------- --------------- ---------------
ORDSYS     ORDIMG_PKG      PACKAGE BODY
QC_USER    INSTRIG         TRIGGER
```

The column Generated indicates that the object name has been created by Oracle itself. While there is nothing wrong with letting Oracle create the name of the object, it is generally not a good idea to do so. When you generate object names yourself, you can create meaningful names that link the objects together, such as PK_<tablename> for the primary key of a table. This allows you to quickly see object relationships.

When you let Oracle name the object, the Generated column value is Y, while the object that you explicitly name has a Generated column value of N. At this time, Oracle uses the naming convention of prefixing all names it generates with "SYS_C." This convention may change in future releases, and if it does, you will still be able to use the new column Generated to find out which objects have been named by Oracle.

DBA_TEMP_FILES

The DBA_TEMP_FILES data dictionary view, described in Table 3-9, holds the information about the physical files that make up the temporary tablespaces in the database.

At first glance, there doesn't seem to be any difference between the DBA_DATA_FILES view we discussed earlier and this one. And, in fact, the columns are identical. There is, however, a major difference. Physical disk files that are associated with datafiles in the database must be backed up, while physical disk files associated with tempfiles do not need to be backed up.

With the release of Oracle7.3, you were able to create tablespaces for user sorting with the Contents set to "temporary" using the command **create tablespace ...... temporary**. A tablespace created this way uses datafiles, and these files have to be backed up, even though they can never contain permanent data. With Oracle8i, a new type of tablespace was introduced, the TEMPORARY tablespace, created with the command **create temporary tablespace ..... tempfile ....** This tablespace is created with locally managed files, called tempfiles. Tempfiles are still permanent files on disk; the name refers only to their function within the database. These files do not generate any sort of redo information when used, so you do not need to include them in a backup.

Column	Description
FILE_NAME	Name of the database tempfile
FILE_ID	ID of the database tempfile
TABLESPACE_NAME	Name of the tablespace to which the file belongs
BYTES	Size of the file in bytes
BLOCKS	Size of the file in Oracle blocks
STATUS	File status: AVAILABLE or INVALID
RELATIVE_FNO	Relative file number
AUTOEXTENSIBLE	Autoextensible indicator
MAXBYTES	Maximum file size in bytes
MAXBLOCKS	Maximum file size in blocks
INCREMENT_BY	Autoextension increment
USER_BYTES	Corresponding number of bytes
USER_BLOCKS	Number of blocks that can be used by the data

TABLE 3-9. *DBA_TEMP_FILES View*

DBA_TABLES

In the earlier sections of this chapter, we talked about the DBA_ views that let you see the physical world of the database. In the following sections, we are going to talk about the way your data is logically laid out and stored, in tables, indexes, and constraints. The DBA_ views we'll be talking about in these sections are like a road map or atlas. You can use these views to "drive" from one location to another, gathering information along the way about the data stored in the database. As with the physical world views, the logical data map shows the structure of the data and not the data itself.

A table is the basic logical building block for the database. The physical representation of a table is a segment, but while a segment and the extents that make up a segment define the space that a table takes up within the datafiles, a table and its columns represent the actual information you are storing within the database.

DBA_TABLES contains descriptions of all the relational tables in the database. If you use the **analyze** command when viewing the table, the view will also contain statistics that the Cost Based Optimizer can use when choosing an execution plan. We'll talk more about the Cost Based Optimizer in Chapter 13. Table 3-10 shows the columns in this view and what the columns represent.

Column	Description
OWNER	Owner of the table
TABLE_NAME	Name of the table
TABLESPACE_NAME	Name of the tablespace containing the table
CLUSTER_NAME	Name of the cluster, if any, to which the table belongs
IOT_NAME	Name of the index organized table, if any, to which the overflow entry belongs
PCT_FREE	Minimum percentage of free space in a block
PCT_USED	Minimum percentage of used space in a block
INI_TRANS	Initial number of transactions
MAX_TRANS	Maximum number of transactions
INITIAL_EXTENT	Size of the initial extent in bytes
NEXT_EXTENT	Size of secondary extents in bytes
MIN_EXTENTS	Minimum number of extents allowed in the segment
MAX_EXTENTS	Maximum number of extents allowed in the segment
PCT_INCREASE	Percentage increase in extent size
FREELISTS	Number of process freelists allocated to this segment
FREELIST_GROUPS	Number of freelist groups allocated to this segment
LOGGING	Whether logging is enabled (YES or NO)
BACKED_UP	Has table been backed up since last modification?
NUM_ROWS	Number of rows returned by the **analyze** command
BLOCKS	Number of blocks below the high-water mark
EMPTY_BLOCKS	Number of empty (never used) data blocks in the table
AVG_SPACE	Average available free space in the table
CHAIN_CNT	Number of chained rows in the table
AVG_ROW_LEN	Average row length, including row overhead
AVG_SPACE_FREELIST_BLOCKS	Average free space of all blocks on a freelist
NUM_FREELIST_BLOCKS	Number of blocks on the freelist

TABLE 3-10. *DBA_TABLES View*

Column	Description
DEGREE	Number of query servers used for a full table scan
INSTANCES	Number of instances across which the table is to be scanned
CACHE	Whether the table is to be cached in the buffer cache
TABLE_LOCK	Whether table locking is enabled or disabled
SAMPLE_SIZE	Sample size used in analyzing this table
LAST_ANALYZED	Date of the most recent time this table was analyzed
PARTITIONED	Whether this table is partitioned
IOT_TYPE	If this is an index organized table, then IOT_TYPE is IOT or IOT_OVERFLOW. If this is not an index organized table, then IOT_TYPE is NULL
TEMPORARY	Whether the table is temporary
SECONDARY	Is this table object created as part of icreate for domain indexes?
NESTED	Is the table a nested table?
BUFFER_POOL	Name of the default buffer pool for the appropriate object
ROW_MOVEMENT	Whether partitioned row movement is enabled or disabled
GLOBAL_STATS	Are the statistics calculated without merging underlying partitions?
USER_STATS	Were the statistics entered directly by the user?
DURATION	If temporary table, then duration is SYS$SESSION or SYS$TRANSACTION, else NULL
SKIP_CORRUPT	Whether skip corrupt blocks is enabled or disabled
MONITORING	Whether to gather statistics for the number of rows altered by DML statements
CLUSTER_OWNER	Owner of the cluster, if any, to which the table belongs
DEPENDENCIES	Should we keep track of row-level dependencies?

TABLE 3-10. *DBA_TABLES View* (continued)

Each table is uniquely defined by a combination of Owner and Table_Name. Multiple users can have tables with the same name, and these tables do not need to be identical.

Because tables do take up physical space, they can be created with a storage clause. The Tablespace_Name column has the information about the tablespace that contains this table. The Initial_Extent, Next_Extent, and Pct_Increase columns all have to do with the sizing of the first and all subsequent extents within the table, while Min_Extents and Max_Extents contain information about the initial and maximum size of the table. We recommend that you do not set these when you create a table, but rather let the values default to those defined for the tablespace in which you place this table.

Init_Trans and Max_Trans deal with the number of concurrent transactions that can access each data block in the table at a time. Once the Max_Trans number of transactions is accessing the data block, any other users attempting to access the block will have to wait. The Freelists column is the number of process freelists for that table. A *process freelist,* also known as a freelist, is simply a list of free data blocks within the extents within the table. The default for this column is 1. Prior to the release of Oracle8.1.6, once you established the freelist value for a table, it could not be changed dynamically. In other words, once you set the value, you were stuck with it. The only way to change this value was to drop and re-create the table with a larger freelist size declared. With the release of Oracle8.1.6, you could dynamically alter the number of freelists. The Freelist_Groups column is used mainly with the Oracle Parallel Server (RAC in Oracle9i) and is the number of freelists to be created for use by the various instances that are part of the Parallel Server. We'll talk more about freelists in Chapter 12.

Pct_Free is the percentage of the block that should be reserved for overflow on updates. If you have a table that is rarely updated, or where the columns are static sizes, you can set Pct_Free to a very low number. Pct_Used determines when Oracle will begin inserts into the block again. Pct_Used is not checked until the block has first reached the Pct_Free number. If you have set Pct_Free to 10, then when the block is 90 percent full, Oracle stops inserting new rows into it. If you have also set Pct_Used to 70, Oracle will begin inserting rows into the block again once it is less than 70 percent used.

The Num_Rows, Blocks, Empty_Blocks, Avg_Space, Chain_Cnt, Avg_Row_Len, Sample_Size, and Last_Analyzed columns are all filled when you analyze a table. The Cost Based Optimizer uses the information stored in these columns to determine the best way to access the data in the table.

```
select Num_Rows, Blocks, Empty_Blocks, Avg_Space,
       Chain_Cnt, Avg_Row_Len, Sample_Size, Last_Analyzed
  from DBA_TABLES
 where Table_Name='ALBUM'
/
```

```
NUM_ROWS  BLOCKS EMPTY BLKS AVG_SPACE CHAIN_CNT AVG_ROW_LEN SAMPLE_SIZE LAST_ANAL
-------- ------- ---------- --------- --------- ----------- ----------- ---------
  512844   43624         55      1333         6         574           0 19-JAN-02
```

In the output to this query, you can see that there are 512,844 rows stored in the ALBUM table. The rows are using 43624 blocks of space, and there are 55 empty blocks available. By analyzing a table, you can gather important information about that table's current state and its potential for running out of space. Looks like this table is pretty close to full and will need to extend soon!

The User_Stats column, introduced in Oracle8i, indicates whether the optimizer statistics have been inserted by the user. Why would you want to insert your own statistics? Well, if you don't have enough room in your test database to keep a complete copy of production, your testing can be inaccurate. If you can insert the production statistics, even if you don't have all the production data, you can get a more accurate gauge of what the execution plan and performance will be. Oracle decides how best to access the requested data by parsing the query and following an execution plan.

Buffer_Pool determines whether the data blocks of this table are retained in memory or flushed as they are no longer needed. With version 8, Oracle introduced the concept of multiple buffer pools. You can assign a table to one of three buffer pools: KEEP, RECYCLE, or DEFAULT. The size of these buffer pools is set in the initialization parameter file by the parameters **buffer_pool_keep**, **buffer_pool_ recycle**, and **db_block_buffers** (**db_block_buffers** is replaced by **db_cache_size** in Oracle9i). Tables assigned to the KEEP buffer pool will have their data blocks kept in memory, while those assigned to the RECYCLE buffer pool will have their data blocks flushed from memory more quickly. Data blocks in the DEFAULT buffer pool will be kept or flushed based on their position in the LRU list. The LRU, or Least Recently Used, list is used by Oracle to determine which blocks can most easily be flushed from memory and written back to disk.

Cache indicates whether the table is to be cached in the buffer cache. A cached table has its data blocks placed at the most recently used end of the LRU list in the buffer cache when a full table scan is performed. This keeps the data in the table in the SGA longer and is useful for small lookup tables. Logging has to do with whether the creation of the table (and any indexes created because of table constraints) and subsequent direct-load changes to the table are logged to the redo logs. Although you can improve load performance by not logging changes, you should back up the database immediately after a nologging load, or you will not be able to do recovery. Tables that are cached cannot have logging turned off.

The Degree column is used in conjunction with the parallel query option and specifies the number of query servers to use when doing parallel queries on the table.

DBA_TAB_COLUMNS

DBA_TAB_COLUMNS contains information on the columns of all tables, views, and clusters in the database. If you analyze the table, both the DBA_TABLES and DBA_TAB_COLUMNS views will also contain statistics that the Cost Based Optimizer can use to determine the execution plan. Table 3-11 shows the columns in this view and what the columns represent.

Column	Description
OWNER	Owner of the table, view, or cluster
TABLE_NAME	Table, view, or cluster name
COLUMN_NAME	Column name
DATA_TYPE	Data type of the column
DATA_TYPE_MOD	Data type modifier of the column
DATA_TYPE_OWNER	Owner of the data type of the column
DATA_LENGTH	Length of the column in bytes
DATA_PRECISION	Decimal precision for NUMBER data type; binary precision for FLOAT data type; NULL for all other data types
DATA_SCALE	Digits to the right of decimal point in a number
NULLABLE	Does the column allow NULL values?
COLUMN_ID	Sequence number of the column as created
DEFAULT_LENGTH	Length of default value for the column
DATA_DEFAULT	Default value for the column
NUM_DISTINCT, LOW_VALUE, HIGH_VALUE, DENSITY, NUM_NULLS	These columns remain for backward compatibility with Oracle7. This information is now in the {TAB|PART}_COL_STATISTICS views.
NUM_BUCKETS	Number of buckets in histogram for the column
LAST_ANALYZED	Date of the most recent time this column was analyzed

TABLE 3-11. *DBA_TAB_COLUMNS View*

Column	Description
SAMPLE_SIZE	Sample size used in analyzing this column
CHARACTER_SET_NAME	Name of the character set: CHAR_CS, NCHAR_CS
CHAR_COL_DECL_LENGTH	Declaration length of character type column
GLOBAL_STATS	Are the statistics calculated without merging underlying partitions?
USER_STATS	Were the statistics entered directly by the user?
AVG_COL_LEN	Average column length in bytes
CHAR_LENGTH	The maximum length of the column in characters
CHAR_USED	C if the width was specified in characters, B if in bytes
V80_FMT_IMAGE	Is column data in 8.0 image format?
DATA_UPGRADED	Has column data been upgraded to the latest type version format?

TABLE 3-11. *DBA_TAB_COLUMNS View* (continued)

The DBA_TABLES view gives you the storage and physical layout of the table, while the DBA_TAB_COLUMNS view gives you the layout of the information stored within the table. Information about each column of your table is stored in a single row within this view. Even the columns of the view itself are stored within this view!

The Owner, Table_Name, and Column_Name columns make up the unique key of this view. It's possible for the same table name to be owned by different users, or for the column names to be reused between tables. In fact, an easy way to show that the column contains the same information between tables, for a foreign key relationship, is to use the same name. Column_ID is used to indicate the order of the column within the table.

This view contains the descriptions and formats for the information you can store in your table. The Data_Type column defines the type of data that can be stored. Data_Types include VARCHAR2, CHAR, DATE, NUMBER, LONG, BLOB, CLOB, LOB, and user-defined data types. Each data type that can be stored also has an associated Data_Length. Dates are always stored in 7 bytes; numbers are stored in a maximum of 22 bytes. Data_Precision and Data_Scale contain information about numeric columns where you have defined the size of the column instead of accepting the Oracle default of 38 digits. Data_Precision is the maximum total length of data in that column, including the decimal places. Data_Scale is the number of decimal places to store for that numeric column. Why would you want to define numbers with precision and scale? If you know that the value in the column can never be larger than three digits, such as a person's age, you can ensure that no one enters a number larger than that by specifying the column as NUMBER(3). If users attempt to enter a four-digit number into that column, they will get an error. Data_Type_Mod and Data_Type_Owner contain information about the user-defined data type.

Columns can be defined as null or not null. Not null columns must either have data entered into them during an insert or update or have a default value assigned. The Nullable column in DBA_TAB_COLUMNS indicates whether the column can contain null values. Data_Default and Default_Length will only have data in them if you have assigned a default value to the column, and they contain the default value for the column and the length of the default. Why assign defaults? Let's suppose you are building a database for a veterinarian. One of the tables will contain information about the pet owners. One of the columns in this table is Number_Pets. Since pet owners come to the veterinarian because they have at least one pet, you can set a default of 1 for this column. That way, the doctor's staff only has to enter information in that column if the client has more than one pet.

The Num_Distinct, Low_Value, High_Value, and Density columns are filled when you analyze the table. This information is used by the Cost Based Optimizer to determine which query path to use when you access the table. The information in these columns is also stored in the DBA_TAB_COL_STATISTICS view, and these columns are kept in DBA_TAB_COLUMNS for backward compatibility to Oracle7. The User_Stats column, new in Oracle8i, indicates whether the statistical information has been entered by the user or generated by the **analyze** command as explained in the previous view.

There are four new columns in Oracle9i. The first two, Char_Length and Char_Used, are used mostly when you are using Unicode or multibyte character sets. For character columns, Char_Used will be B, and Char_Length will equal the Data_Length column, unless you are using NCHAR, NVARCHAR2, or NCLOB data types. The remaining two columns, V80_Fmt_Image and Data_Upgraded, are relevant for object tables or relational tables with object columns. They flag the table metadata as upgraded or not to the latest version of the referenced type.

Now let's look at a **create table** statement and see how the table definitions are stored within the view:

```
create table QC_USER.PRIMATES
(Code  varchar2(3) not null
     constraint Primates_PK
        primary key
,Description varchar2(250) not null
,Location  varchar2(30) not null
```

```
,Date_Of_Birth date  not null
,Status  varchar2(3)
,Name  varchar2(10) not null
,Date_Acquired date
,Cage_Num  number(8,2)
,Coloring  varchar2(3)
   constraint Chk_Color_Type
        check(Coloring in ('brn','blk','red','tan','bld'))
,Gender char(1) default 'U' not null
)
/

select Column_Name, Data_Type, Data_Length, Data_Precision,
       Data_Scale, Nullable, Column_ID, Default_Length
  from DBA_TAB_COLUMNS
 where Table_Name='PRIMATES'
   and Owner='QC_USER'
/

COLUMN_NAME          DATA_TYPE  LENGTH PRECISION SCALE NULL   ID DEF LENGTH
-------------------- ---------- ------ --------- ----- ---- ---- ----------
CODE                 VARCHAR2        3                 N       1
DESCRIPTION          VARCHAR2      250                 N       2
LOCATION             VARCHAR2       30                 N       3
DATE_OF_BIRTH        DATE            7                 N       4
STATUS               VARCHAR2        3                 Y       5
NAME                 VARCHAR2       10                 N       6
DATE_ACQUIRED        DATE            7                 Y       7
CAGE_NUM             NUMBER         22         8     2 Y       8
COLORING             VARCHAR2        3                 Y       9
GENDER               CHAR            1                 N      10          4
```

Hmm. The Cage_Num column was defined as NUMBER(8,2). Yet it shows with a Data_Length of 22. That is the maximum number of bytes that column can possibly take to store values. Like VARCHAR2 columns, the value of Data_Length is the maximum size of the column, not the actual number of bytes it will take up. LONG columns, which have no real length definition, will have a Data_Length of 0. The Gender column was created with a default, so there is a Default_Length for that column.

DBA_INDEXES

DBA_INDEXES contains descriptions for all indexes in the database. If you analyze the index or the table the index is on, the view will also contain statistics on the data distribution that the Cost Based Optimizer can use. Table 3-12 shows the columns in this view and what the columns represent.

Column	Description
OWNER	Username of the owner of the index
INDEX_NAME	Name of the index
INDEX_TYPE	Type of index (Normal, Bitmap, Function-based, Function-based Bitmap, or Domain)
TABLE_OWNER	Owner of the indexed object
TABLE_NAME	Name of the indexed object
TABLE_TYPE	Type of the indexed object
UNIQUENESS	Uniqueness status of the index: UNIQUE or NONUNIQUE
COMPRESSION	Enabled or disabled
PREFIX_LENGTH	Number of columns in the prefix of the key used for compression
TABLESPACE_NAME	Name of the tablespace containing the index
INI_TRANS	Initial number of transactions
MAX_TRANS	Maximum number of transactions
INITIAL_EXTENT	Size of initial extent
NEXT_EXTENT	Size of secondary extents
MIN_EXTENTS	Minimum number of extents allowed in the segment
MAX_EXTENTS	Maximum number of extents allowed in the segment
PCT_INCREASE	Percentage increase in extent size
PCT_THRESHOLD	Threshold percentage of block space allowed per index entry
INCLUDE_COLUMN	User column ID for last column to be included in index organized table top index
FREELISTS	Number of process freelists allocated to this segment
FREELIST_GROUPS	Number of freelist groups allocated to this segment

TABLE 3-12. *DBA_INDEXES View*

Column	Description
PCT_FREE	Minimum percentage of free space in a block
LOGGING	Logging attribute
BLEVEL	B-Tree level: depth of the index from its root block to its leaf blocks. A depth of 0 indicates that the root block and leaf block are the same.
LEAF_BLOCKS	Number of leaf blocks in the index
DISTINCT_KEYS	Number of distinct keys in the index
AVG_LEAF_BLOCKS_ PER_KEY	Average number of leaf blocks per key
AVG_DATA_BLOCKS_ PER_KEY	Average number of data blocks per key
CLUSTERING_FACTOR	A measurement of the amount of order of the rows in the table this index is for
STATUS	Whether a nonpartitioned index is UNUSABLE or VALID
NUM_ROWS	Number of rows in this index
SAMPLE_SIZE	Size of the sample used to analyze this index
LAST_ANALYZED	Timestamp for when this index was last analyzed
DEGREE	Number of threads per instance for scanning the index, NULL if PARTITIONED=NO
INSTANCES	Number of instances across which the indexes are to be scanned, NULL if PARTITIONED=NO
PARTITIONED	Indicates whether this index is partitioned; set to YES if it is partitioned
TEMPORARY	Is this index on a temporary table? (Y|N)
GENERATED	Was the name of this index system generated?
SECONDARY	Was this index created by the Oracle Data Cartridge?
BUFFER_POOL	Name of the default buffer pool for the index

TABLE 3-12. *DBA_INDEXES View* (continued)

Column	Description
USER_STATS	Were the statistics entered directly by the user?
DURATION	For an index on a temporary table, the duration (transaction or session) of the table
PCT_DIRECT_ACCESS	If index on IOT, then this is percentage of rows with VALID guess
ITYP_OWNER	Index Type owner; used with Oracle Data Cartridge Interface (domain index)
ITYP_NAME	Index Type name; used with Oracle Data Cartridge Interface
PARAMETERS	Parameter string used for domain indexes; used with Oracle Data Cartridge Interface
GLOBAL_STATS	For partitioned indexes, whether statistics were collected by analyzing the entire index or by estimates on the partitions
DOMIDX_STATUS	Reflects the status of the domain index. A NULL value means the specified index is not a domain index. A value of VALID means the index is a domain index and the index does not have any errors. If the value of this column is IDXTYP_INVLD, it means the index type corresponding to this domain index is invalid.
DOMIDX_OPSTATUS	Reflects the status of an operation that was performed on the domain index. A value of NULL indicates that the specified index is not a domain index. A value of VALID specifies that the index does not have any errors. A value of FAILED indicates that the operation performed on the domain index failed with an error.
FUNCIDX_STATUS	A value of NULL indicates a non-function-based index. ENABLED indicates the function-based index is enabled. DISABLED indicates the function-based index is disabled.
JOIN_INDEX	Indicates whether or not this index is a join index

TABLE 3-12. *DBA_INDEXES View* (continued)

The DBA_INDEXES view contains one row for every index on every table in the database. The Owner, Index_Name, Table_Owner, and Table_Name columns contain information about the ownership of the index and the table to which it refers. It is possible for a user who does not own the table to create an index on a table, if he has been given the **create any index** privilege. It is not possible for two different users to create an index with the same columns on the same table. Oracle ensures that only one index is created per combination of columns. Even though you can do it, it is not a good idea to have an index on a table owned by a user who is not the table owner. If another user attempts to access the table, she will not have access to that index. There is no way to create a synonym or grant select access for an index.

The Table_Type column distinguishes between tables that are simple tables and those that are parts of clustered tables. Index_Type contains information on the type of index. Indexes can be clustered indexes or normal indexes as well as bitmap or function-based indexes. *Bitmap indexes* store the rowids associated with a key value as a bitmap. The Uniqueness column indicates whether the index has been created as a unique index. *Unique indexes* are those where the only acceptable values in the columns are nulls or a unique combination of the columns making up the index.

Tablespace_Name, Ini_Trans, Max_Trans, Initial_Extent, Next_Extent, Min_Extents, Max_Extents, Pct_Increase, Pct_Free, Freelists, and Freelist_Groups all pertain to the storage allocation parameters for the index and have been discussed in detail in earlier sections.

Logging has to do with whether the creation of the index and subsequent direct-load changes to the index are logged to the redo logs. Although you can improve performance by not logging changes, you will have to rebuild the indexes if you need to do recovery. Thus, if you are going to disable logging of index information, you must be sure that you can re-create the index correctly should you need to do so.

Blevel, Leaf_Blocks, Distinct_Keys, Avg_Leaf_Blocks_Per_Key, Avg_Data_ Blocks_Per_Key, Clustering_Factor, Num_Rows, Sample_Size, and Last_Analyzed all contain information that can be used by the Cost Based Optimizer to determine whether this index should be used to improve the performance of a query. If you have not analyzed the index or the table that the index is built on, there will be no data in these columns. As of Oracle8i, you can insert your own statistics about the index into these views instead of analyzing the index, and this is flagged in the User_Stats column.

Buffer_Pool determines whether the data blocks of this index are retained in memory or flushed as they are no longer needed. Generated indicates whether the name of the index was created by the system or by the user.

With Oracle8i, users can create a function-based index. In earlier versions of the database, when you had an index on a character column, you could not be sure if the data in the column was stored in uppercase, lowercase, or some combination. You had to use a function on the column in the where clause to force it to a particular case. As soon as you used the function, Oracle would no longer use the index on that column. A *function-based index* is created with the function as part of the index, so you no longer have to add it to the where clause, and the index can be used for searches. If you use a function-based index, you must analyze the table and the index, or Oracle will not be able to use the index. The column Funcidx_Status indicates whether the index is a function-based index and the status of the index if it is.

Let's take a look at a table and the indexes on that table.

```
describe REGISTRATION

Name                            Null?    Type
------------------------------- -------- ----
USER_PK                                  NUMBER
USERNAME                                 VARCHAR2(32)
PASSWORD                                 VARCHAR2(32)
CREATED_DATE                             DATE
UPDATED_DATE                             DATE
FIRST_NAME                               VARCHAR2(40)
LAST_NAME                                VARCHAR2(40)
BIRTHDAY                                 DATE
GENDER                                   CHAR(1)
ZIP_CODE                                 VARCHAR2(20)
COUNTRY                                  VARCHAR2(40)
EMAIL                                    VARCHAR2(255)
STATE                                    VARCHAR2(32)

select Owner, Index_Name, Table_Owner, Table_Name, Table_Type,
       Uniqueness, Tablespace_Name, Funcidx_Status
  from DBA_INDEXES
 where Table_Name = 'REGISTRATION';

OWNER  INDEX_NAME        OWNER TABLE_NAME   TYPE  UNIQUENES TBS      FUNCIDX_
------ ----------------- ----- ------------ ----- --------- -------- --------
REG    REG_EMAIL_IDX     REG   REGISTRATION TABLE UNIQUE    REG_INDX ENABLED
REG    REG_PK            REG   REGISTRATION TABLE UNIQUE    REG_INDX
REG    REG_USERNAME_IDX  REG   REGISTRATION TABLE UNIQUE    REG_INDX
```

This table has three indexes, all of which are unique, but you cannot tell which columns are indexed by looking at this view, or what the function on the REG_EMAIL_IDX index is. We'll show you how to see the indexed columns in the next section on the DBA_IND_COLUMNS view.

DBA_IND_COLUMNS

Now that you know the indexes on the tables in your database, wouldn't it be helpful to know which columns in the table are indexed? You should know which columns are indexed and, for indexes with multiple columns, where the columns are in the column list. The optimizer will use an index for a query where possible, by checking the columns in the where clause to see if they are part of an index. You should examine the queries in your application that are either taking a long time to complete or doing full table scans to see if you can rewrite the query to take advantage of an existing index or add an index to improve the performance.

DBA_IND_COLUMNS contains descriptions of the columns composing the indexes on all tables and clusters in the database. Table 3-13 shows the columns in this view and what the columns represent.

The Index_Owner, Index_Name, Table_Owner, and Table_Name columns contain information about the ownership of the index and the table it refers to and can be linked back to the DBA_INDEXES view. Column_Name is the name of the column in the table, Column_Position is the position of the column in the column list for the index, and Column_Length is the default length of the column. With Oracle8i and later releases, you can now specify whether the column should be sorted in ascending or descending order.

Column	Description
INDEX_OWNER	Index owner
INDEX_NAME	Index name
TABLE_OWNER	Table or cluster owner
TABLE_NAME	Table or cluster name
COLUMN_NAME	Column name or attribute of the object type column
COLUMN_POSITION	Position of column or attribute within index
COLUMN_LENGTH	Indexed length of the column or attribute
DESCEND	Y/N; Y if this column is sorted in descending order

TABLE 3-13. *DBA_IND_COLUMNS View*

A sample of the indexes on a table and the columns in the indexes from an Oracle8.1.6 database is below.

```
select *
  from DBA_IND_COLUMNS
 where Table_Name = 'REGISTRATION'
 order by Index_Name, Column_Position
/

OWNER INDEX_NAME        TABLE_OWNER  TABLE_NAME COLUMN_NAME     POS  LENGTH DESC
----- ----------------- ------------ ---------- -------------- ---- ------- ----
REG   REG_EMAIL_IDX     RC           GM_REG     SYS_NC00022$      1     255 ASC
REG   REG_PK            UREG         GM_REG     USER_PK           1      22 ASC
REG   REG_USERNAME_IDX  UREG         GM_REG     USERNAME          1      32 ASC
```

Did you notice something interesting? The column indexed in the first index has an Oracle-generated name. If you remember from the prior section, that index is a function-based index. When you create a function-based index, Oracle isn't really indexing the column but is indexing the results of the function, so it "makes up" a name for the column. So how do you know what the index is really for? There's another DBA_ view called DBA_IND_EXPRESSIONS that has that information. If we join the DBA_INDEXES view with the DBA_IND_COLUMNS and DBA_IND_EXPRESSIONS views, we can find the index and the function:

```
select a.Index_Name, b.Column_Name, c.Column_Expression
  from DBA_INDEXES a, DBA_IND_COLUMNS b, DBA_IND_EXPRESSIONS c
 where a.Table_Name ='REGISTRATION'
   and a.Index_Name=b.Index_Name
   and b.Index_Name=c.Index_Name(+)
   and a.Funcidx_Status='ENABLED'
/

INDEX_NAME           COLUMN_NAME     COLUMN_EXPRESSION
-------------------- --------------- -------------------------------
REG_EMAIL_IDX        SYS_NC00022$    LOWER("EMAIL")
```

As you can see, the function forces the Email column to lowercase.

Don't create indexes just because the column is mentioned in a where clause. If the column does not have very discriminating data, such as a gender column, a regular index on that column will likely not be used by Oracle, although a gender column is an ideal candidate for a bitmapped index. While the more combinations of columns you have indexes for can help in querying data, remember that when you insert, update, or delete data, all the indexes on a table will also be modified. You can seriously degrade performance by having too many indexes. One of the authors had an application in which a query on the test database took 6 minutes, while the same query on the production database took 30 minutes. The test database had been refreshed from the production database, so the data being queried was identical. After some research, she found that there was an index on the production table that did not exist in the test database. She dropped the index, and the production query took 6 minutes! The additional index was not a very discriminating index, and Oracle was using it instead of one that had more unique characteristics. This is a perfect example of how an index can sometimes negatively impact performance. Always check the execution plan when you are having a performance problem to see which, if any, indexes are being used. We'll tell you how to create and read the execution plan in detail in Chapter 13.

Be cautious when deciding to add bitmap indexes. A bitmap index on a table that is very update intensive or on a column where new values are added frequently can actually hurt rather than help performance. You cannot do individual row-level locking with bitmap indexes, so the entire set of rows referred to by the bitmap index will be locked until the update, insert, or delete completes.

DBA_CONSTRAINTS

Constraints are restrictions on the contents of the columns of a table or view. DBA_CONSTRAINTS lists all constraints in the database. Table 3-14 shows the columns in this view and what the columns represent.

You can use *referential integrity constraints*—primary and foreign keys—as a means of ensuring that the data in your database is consistent across tables. A referential integrity constraint defines a relationship between columns in one or more tables. *Primary key constraints* require the data in that column or combination of columns to be a unique combination in the table and not be null. *Unique constraints* require that the data be a unique combination, but will allow you to insert null values. *Foreign key constraints* can only refer to columns defined as either primary key constraint columns or unique key constraint columns. When we refer to the tables in a referential integrity relationship, we call the primary/unique key table the *parent table* and the table with the foreign key defined on it the *child table*. Referential integrity guarantees that when you try to insert a value into the child table, the corresponding value already exists in the parent table.

At the XYZ Company, you would not want to be able to insert an order for a product not in your production line. A foreign key constraint on the orders table, referencing the product code column in the orders table back to the product code primary key column in the products table ensures that any product you list on the order is in the products table.

Oracle will automatically create indexes on the columns you define as unique or primary key constraint columns unless an index already exists, in which case the existing index will be used for the constraint and the index name and owner will be listed in the Index_Name and Index_Owner columns in the DBA_CONSTRAINTS view. However, indexes are not created on the columns in a foreign key constraint, and you should create those indexes yourself. If there is no index on the foreign key

Column	Description
OWNER	Owner of the table
CONSTRAINT_NAME	Name associated with constraint definition
CONSTRAINT_TYPE	C (check constraint on a table) P (primary key) U (unique key) R (referential integrity) V (with check option on a view) O (with read-only, on a view)
TABLE_NAME	Name associated with table with constraint definition
SEARCH_CONDITION	Text of search condition for table check
R_OWNER	Owner of table used in referential constraint
R_CONSTRAINT_NAME	Name of unique constraint definition for referenced table
DELETE_RULE	Delete rule for a referential constraint: CASCADE / NO ACTION
STATUS	Enforcement status of constraint: ENABLED or DISABLED
DEFERRABLE	Indicates whether the constraint is deferrable
DEFERRED	Indicates whether the constraint was initially deferred
VALIDATED	Indicates whether all data obeys the constraint: VALIDATED, NOT VALIDATED
GENERATED	Indicates whether the name is system generated
BAD	Creating this constraint should give ORA-02436
RELY	If set, this flag will be used in the optimizer
LAST_CHANGE	Indicates when the constraint was last enabled or disabled
INDEX_OWNER	The owner of the index used by this constraint
INDEX_NAME	The index used by this constraint
INVALID	
VIEW_RELATED	If this is a primary, unique, or foreign key constraint, is it on a view?

TABLE 3-14. *DBA_CONSTRAINTS View*

column, Oracle will lock the entire child table when you change the contents of the foreign key column in the parent table. Without an index, it is possible therefore to lock out all other users of the child table while one user updates a record in the parent table. This is not a terrific situation, especially if that user goes out to lunch before committing that update!

You can, if you want, write all the relationship checks into your application and not use the referential integrity constraints provided by Oracle. So why use the constraints? Although using the referential integrity constraints does make some maintenance difficult for a DBA, you still should use them. Without the constraints, it's possible for someone to bypass the application and insert inconsistent data into the tables. We'd rather spend a little extra time occasionally on maintenance than have to explain to an irate customer why we didn't ship the nonexistent product we let him order. And if the application is coded incorrectly, allowing you to insert data into the child table before the parent table insert is done, or delete from the parent table before the child rows have been deleted, the referential integrity constraint tells Oracle to return an error and protects the integrity of your data.

Check constraints ensure that the data being inserted into a column meets certain conditions. If you have a well-defined, limited set of possible values for the column, check constraints are a good idea. As an example, a gender column in an employee database is an excellent candidate for a check constraint. Any column that must have data in it can be defined with a special check constraint, the NOT NULL constraint.

You can also create constraints on views. A *read-only constraint* on a view flags that view as one that you cannot update, insert into, or delete from. A *check option constraint* on a view limits any inserts or updates to rows that the view itself can select. So if you create a view on an employee table that limits rows selected to those of the employee looking at the view, a check option constraint would prevent that employee from updating information about another employee. Let's create a view now, with a check option constraint.

```
create view UPD_EMP_INFO
as
select Empid, Last_Name, First_Name, Mid_Init,
       Address1, Address2, Address3, Zipcode
       Dependents, Marital_Status
  from Emp_Info
 where Empid=USER
  with check option constraint LIMIT_ACCESS
/
create public synonym UPD_EMP_INFO for QC_USER.UPD_EMP_INFO
/
grant select, update on UPD_EMP_INFO to PUBLIC
/
```

If we look in DBA_CONSTRAINTS, we can see the constraint there.

```
select Constraint_Name, Constraint_Type
  from DBA_CONSTRAINTS
 where Table_Name = 'UPD_EMP_INFO'
/

CONSTRAINT_NAME                C
------------------------------ -
LIMIT_ACCESS                   V
```

Now let's log on as one user and try to update the data for a different user.

```
connect 3456/3456
Connected.
update UPD_EMP_INFO set Dependents=5 where Empid=1234;

0 rows updated.
```

The check option constraint prevents any unauthorized updates. As of Oracle9i, you can create primary key, foreign key, and unique constraints on views, although they will not be enforced at the view level. You can check the View_Related column to see if the constraint is on a view or not.

The Owner of a constraint on a table will always be the table owner. The Constraint_Type column lists the type of constraint, as defined above. If the constraint is a check constraint, the Search_Condition column contains the conditions to evaluate. A foreign key constraint will have the R_Owner and R_Constraint_Name defined, indicating the primary or unique key constraint to which the foreign key constraint refers.

Delete_Rule defines what happens to the rows in the foreign key table when a row is deleted from the primary or unique key table. If the Delete_Rule column is CASCADE, then all rows in the child table with the foreign key column that matches the value being deleted from the parent table will also be deleted. If the Delete_Rule column is NO ACTION, Oracle will return an error message indicating that there are foreign key columns that depend on this value, and the delete of the row in the primary key table will fail.

The Deferrable and Deferred columns refer to a feature that allows you to delay the constraint checking to the end of the transaction, rather than have it checked as each row is inserted or updated. This allows you to insert a child record and then the parent record.

Let's look at the constraints for one user.

```
select Table_Name, Constraint_Name, Constraint_Type, Search_Condition,
       R_Owner, R_Constraint_Name
```

```
  from DBA_CONSTRAINTS
 where Owner='QC_USER'
/

TABLE      CONSTRAINT_NAME  C SEARCH_CONDITION     R_OWNER    REF CONSTR
---------- ---------------- - -------------------- ---------- -------------
PRIMATES   CHK_COLOR_TYPE   C Coloring in ('bro','
                              blk','red','tan','bl
                              d')
PRIMATES   PRIMATES_ANIM_FK R                      MY_SCHEMA  PRIMATES_PK
PRIMATES   PRIMATES_PK      P
PRIMATES   SYS_C00827       C CODE IS NOT NULL
PRIMATES   SYS_C00828       C DESCRIPTION IS NOT
                              NULL
PRIMATES   SYS_C00829       C LOCATION IS NOT NULL
PRIMATES   SYS_C00830       C DATE_OF_BIRTH IS NOT
                               NULL
```

This user has constraints on only one table. Four of the constraints are the special NOT NULL constraint. There is a check constraint on the column Coloring that limits the values to those listed in the Search_Condition. Trying to insert any other value will cause an error. The table has a primary key constraint defined and a foreign key constraint that refers to a table and constraint owned by another user. But what columns are these constraints defined on? For that information, we need to look at the DBA_CONS_COLUMNS view in the next section.

DBA_CONS_COLUMNS

In the prior section, we discussed the DBA_CONSTRAINTS view. Constraints are created against columns in a table or view. DBA_CONSTRAINTS gives you some information about the constraint, but it does not tell you which columns are part of the constraint itself and what order they are in. The data in the DBA_CONS_ COLUMNS view contains the information you need to fully understand the constraint.

DBA_CONS_COLUMNS contains information about the columns in the constraint definitions. Table 3-15 shows the columns in this view and what the columns represent.

Owner is the owner of the constraint, Constraint_Name is the name of the constraint, and Table_Name is the name of the table the constraint is defined on. All of these will match the corresponding columns in the DBA_CONSTRAINTS view. The Column_Name is the column the constraint is defined on, and Position refers to the position of the column within the constraint. For single column constraints, Position will always be 1.

DBA_CONS_COLUMNS will contain information on primary key constraints, foreign key constraints, and check constraints. However, for check constraints, the

Column	Description
OWNER	Owner of the constraint definition
CONSTRAINT_NAME	Name associated with the constraint definition
TABLE_NAME	Name associated with table with constraint definition
COLUMN_NAME	Name associated with column or attribute of the object type column specified in the constraint definition
POSITION	Original position of column or attribute in definition

TABLE 3-15. *DBA_CONS_COLUMNS View*

Search_Condition column in DBA_CONSTRAINTS will contain the column name, so the information in DBA_CONS_COLUMNS will not give you any more information.

Now, let's go back to the example from the previous section. We know that the owner of the constraint is QC_USER, the table the constraints are defined on is called PRIMATES, and there are several check constraints, as well as a primary key constraint and a foreign key constraint, defined on this table. Let's see what more we can find out. Because we know that we won't get any additional information about check constraints from this view, we're going to skip them by joining DBA_CONS_COLUMNS to DBA_CONSTRAINTS and eliminating any Constraint_Type of C.

```
select a.Owner, a.Constraint_Name, a.Table_Name,
        Constraint_Type, Column_Name, Position
  from DBA_CONS_COLUMNS a, DBA_CONSTRAINTS b
 where a.owner='QC_USER'
   and a.Table_Name ='PRIMATES'
   and b.Owner=a.Owner
   and b.Constraint_Name=a.Constraint_Name
   and b.Constraint_Type != 'C'
 order by a.Constraint_Name, Position
/

OWNER      CONSTRAINT_NAME   TABLE      C COLUMN_NAME     POSITION
---------- ----------------- ---------- - --------------- --------
QC_USER    PRIMATES_ANIM_FK  PRIMATES   R CODE                   1
QC_USER    PRIMATES_PK       PRIMATES   P CODE                   1
```

We have two constraints—one is a primary key constraint, the other is a foreign key constraint. Both of them are on the same column.

CHAPTER 4

How to Look at the Database Using the V$ Views

By now, you should be pretty comfortable with the concepts behind a view. You know that a view is like the difference between looking through a camera lens at a very narrowed scene or looking at an entire panorama. You have learned about how views are used to combine columns from more than one table and how they are used to hide columns, table names, and locations from users. In Chapter 3, you learned about the Oracle data dictionary views called the DBA_ views. The DBA_ views help you to monitor the contents of the database and the locations of objects.

In this chapter, you will learn about the views that Oracle has provided to help you see your database statistics—particularly the overall statistics. In Chapter 6, you will see the views that Oracle has provided to evaluate your database's performance. The views, commonly referred to as the V$ views (pronounced "Vee dollar"), are used to provide an organized view of the data in the Oracle dynamic tables providing you with a way to monitor your database and its performance.

Wait a minute. What's the difference between the DBA_ views and the V$ views? Aren't they basically the same? Well, no. The DBA _ views are referred to by Oracle documentation as "Static Data Dictionary" views, while the V$ views are referred to as "Dynamic Performance" views because they record real-time values that show the current state of the database. In other words, the DBA_ views show you the status and composition of the data dictionary, while the V$ views help you to see how your database is responding to information requests. V$ views can provide you with the following information:

- Insights into areas of database contention
- Amounts of data being read or written to or from disk
- Statistical information, such as the last time a datafile header or the summary information for the SGA was changed
- Values used for database recovery

There are some columns in a few of the V$ views that will not be populated with values unless the parameter **timed_statistics** is set equal to TRUE in the initialization parameter file. For the majority of operating systems, there is little performance impact in setting this parameter to TRUE, and in Oracle9i, Oracle enables this parameter by default in the starter database. However, generally, the parameter is initialized as FALSE. When you enable this parameter on your system for the first time, monitor the performance to ensure that there isn't any impact. If you notice an impact, enable the parameter only for short, controlled periods of time while you gather your database information. You can also change **timed_statistics** dynamically by using the **alter system** command. This way, the database does not have to be shut down and restarted. This is useful if you only want to have **timed_statistics** active for short periods of time.

Keep in mind, too, that the contents and descriptions of the V$ views can change from version to version, so do not rely on them to be the same when you change versions of the RDBMS. As we've said before, check the documentation that comes with the new release for changes between versions.

General V$ View Information

When you create a database, the first script you run after the database exists is the catalog.sql script. Here is a small section of the catalog.sql script for version 9.0.1:

```
rem Load PL/SQL Package STANDARD first, so views can depend upon it
@@standard
remark
remark      FAMILY "FIXED (VIRTUAL) VIEWS"
remark

create or replace view v_$sql_redirection as select * from v$sql_redirection;
drop public synonym v$sql_redirection;
create public synonym v$sql_redirection for v_$sql_redirection;
grant select on v_$sql_redirection to select_catalog_role;

create or replace view v_$sql_plan as select * from v$sql_plan;
drop public synonym v$sql_plan;
create public synonym v$sql_plan for v_$sql_plan;
grant select on v_$sql_plan to select_catalog_role;

create or replace view v_$sql_workarea as select * from v$sql_workarea;
drop public synonym v$sql_workarea;
create public synonym v$sql_workarea for v_$sql_workarea;
grant select on v_$sql_workarea to select_catalog_role;

create or replace view v_$sql_workarea_active as select * from v$sql_workarea_active;
drop public synonym v$sql_workarea_active;
create public synonym v$sql_workarea_active for v_$sql_workarea_active;
grant select on v_$sql_workarea_active to select_catalog_role;
```

From the comments in this snippet of the script, you can see that Oracle breaks the V$ views into families. There are 58 families listed in this version of the script. How many are in the catalog.sql script on your system? Should you care? You probably don't care, but a great way to become familiar with both the composition of the catalog.sql script and the different families of V$ views is to find out. We'll leave you to explore catalog.sql on your own. Just keep in mind that the script is the origin of the V$ views and the data dictionary views.

The V$ views act as a central repository of information and enable you to gather statistics over time about your database. They show the state of the database, objects, performance, backups, user processes, memory areas, and so on. New global views have been created to accommodate Oracle Real Application Clusters. They are basically the same as the V$ views but were created to ensure identification of parallel databases and multiple instances. For parallel databases, a column is added for the instance ID (Inst_ID) so that each instance connecting to a database can be tracked and identified.

A Look at the V$ Views

Now that you've had a chance to see where the V$ views come from, let's see what the DICTIONARY view has to say about them. Since the DICTIONARY view only shows the name and not much description, we'll only show a short piece of the listing here. You will find the complete list of V$ views and a brief description of each one in the Oracle Reference manual as well as in the view V$FIXED_TABLE.

There are 230 V$ views and 226 global GV$ views in version 9.0.1. Let's take a look at the first five V$ views listed in the DICTIONARY view:

```
set pagesize 999
column Table_Name format a29
column Comments format a49 wrap word
select Table_Name, Comments
  from DICTIONARY
 where Table_Name like 'V$%';

TABLE_NAME                    COMMENTS
----------------------------------------------------------------------
V$ACCESS                      Synonym for V_$ACCESS
V$ACTIVE_INSTANCES            Synonym for V_$ACTIVE_INSTANCES
V$ACTIVE_SESS_POOL_MTH        Synonym for V_$ACTIVE_SESS_POOL_MTH
V$AQ                          Synonym for V_$AQ
V$AQ1                         Synonym for V_$AQ1
```

As we said, the comments are not very helpful. The one interesting thing about the comments is that they give you a clue to the real names of each of the views. So, the V$ view names that you will be working with are really synonyms for slightly different views owned by SYS. Wow! Talk about hiding information!

In this chapter and in Chapter 6, we are going to present the V$ views that we use the most. As we did with the DBA_ views, we will list the views individually, explain them, and show some output from each. Where applicable, we will list the groups of views that you can join together to get more complete information and show you the output from the joined views.

NOTE
An account with the DBA role privileges is normally used to query the V$ views.

The Levels of V$ Views

There are two levels of V$ views: instance-level and session-level views. The instance-level views contain information about the instance as a whole. They record statistics from the time the database is started until it is shut down. We have further broken down the instance-level views into two categories: those that provide vital information but can't be influenced by changes in the initialization parameter file (referred to here as *static* V$ views) and those that can be influenced by changes (referred to here as *active* V$ views). Some of the active views have session-level counterparts. For example, there is a V$SYSSTAT view that lists basic information about the system statistics and a V$SESSTAT view that lists information about specific sessions. Some of the values in the active instance-level views are cumulative—they are collected from the time the database starts up. In Chapter 6, we'll tell you about the active V$ instance-level and associated session-level views that we use most.

Let's take a minute to look at some of the differences between a static and an active V$ view. When you want to look at the system global area (SGA) values, for example, there are two SGA views you can use. One of these views, V$SGA, records the summary information about the SGA. This information will remain constant until you shut down the database. If you dynamically change a value, such as **shared_pool_size**, the SGA space in memory will be a different size than it was previously. If you make changes dynamically to any of the dynamic parameters that affect the allocation of resources within the SGA, the summary information will remain the same, even though the allocation of resources within the SGA may have changed. So according to our definition, V$SGA would be a static view because the dynamic changes are not reflected in the data the view displays. The other view, V$SGASTAT, records the dynamic changes to SGA values as various resources are allocated or deallocated. If you change the value for the **shared_pool_size,** you'll see the change reflected in the V$SGASTAT view. Therefore, we would define V$SGASTAT as an active view. Are you beginning to get the picture? We hope so.

Lookup Tables or Views

Some of the V$ views are actually *lookup tables* that provide a translation of a number to a character value. For example, V$DBFILE contains the name of each datafile and its corresponding number. The file f:/ora9i/oradata/rbs01.dbf might have the number 6 assigned to it. In other views that reference this file (f:/ora9i/oradata/rbs01.dbf), only the number (6) will be used. Therefore, if you want to see the information about this datafile with its name—which is much more meaningful to us human beings—you will use the V$DBFILE view to look up the file number and provide the actual file name.

Just to make sure you understand how a lookup table works, let's say you work for a school that offers several different subjects, such as geometry, algebra, calculus, English, French, Spanish, biology, chemistry, history, geology, and so on. The school uses a computerized system to keep track of what courses each student is taking and the grade that each student earns for each course. You can use several different approaches to store the course names and grades. However, you've decided that the most efficient storage approach is to assign a number to each course and just store the course number each time a reference is needed. Good choice!

You could decide to use a scheme in which all courses will be assigned a three-digit number and each type of course will begin with a different number. All language courses will start with a 1, all mathematics courses will start with a 2, and so on. To take the example a step further, you've set up a table like Table 4-1 to keep track of what number is assigned to which course.

Table 4-1 does not reflect all of the courses that your school offers but should give you an idea of what we are trying to illustrate. Now, instead of having to list each course each time you need to reference it, you can just use the course number. If you are creating a report, you will want to list the course name to make the report more meaningful. At the time you create the report, you will use the course number to look up the translation for the course name. You've just created and used a lookup table! You will find several lookup tables within the DBA_ and V$ views.

The Static, Instance-Level V$ Views

The instance-level views that we use most often and have dubbed as static V$ views are shown in Table 4-2. We're going to explore these views thoroughly in this chapter. Do keep in mind that these are not all of the static V$ views but only the

Course	Number
English	110
Spanish	111
Latin	112
French	113
Geometry	210
Algebra	211
Trigonometry	213
Calculus	214
Biology	310
Chemistry	311

TABLE 4-1. *School Courses and Their Associated Numbers*

View	Description
V$DATABASE	Shows the database-specific information
V$DATAFILE	Displays datafile information from the control file
V$DATAFILE_HEADER	Shows the datafile header information
V$DBFILE	Contains the datafile number and datafile name
V$FIXED_TABLE	Lists the fixed objects: X$ tables, GV$ global views, and V$ views. In Oracle8i, there are 612 entries in this view, in Oracle9i there are 806.
V$INSTANCE	Shows the instance-specific information
V$PARAMETER	Lists each of the parameters in the database along with a description and information, such as whether it is modifiable or not
V$SGA	Contains summary information on the SGA
V$TEMPFILE	Contains information about the composition and status of temporary files

TABLE 4-2. *Instance-Level V$ Views*

ones we use frequently and are our favorites. You'll find a complete list, with a brief description of each view, in the Oracle Reference manual.

V$DATABASE

The V$DATABASE view provides general information about the database. Table 4-3 shows the columns in the V$DATABASE view and a brief description of each one.

Now let's look at the columns we tend to use most often. Until version 8, the database identification number was hidden in the control file and could not easily be seen. The Dbid column displays this value. The Name column is self-explanatory but vital. The Log_Mode column tells you whether archive logging has been enabled, while the Archive_Change# shows you the last archive log number that was used. The Open_Mode column shows whether the database is in READ WRITE mode or in READ ONLY mode. There are several new columns for Oracle9i that help you track whether the database is or has been in standby mode. You see, with Oracle9i, you have the ability to switch back and forth between a primary database and a standby one. We'll tell you more about standby databases in Chapter 11.

Column	Description
DBID	The database ID—calculated when the database is created and stored in all file headers
NAME	Name of the database
CREATED	Creation date
LOG_MODE	Archive log mode: NOARCHIVELOG or ARCHIVELOG
CHECKPOINT_ CHANGE#	Last System Change Number (SCN) checkpointed
ARCHIVE_CHANGE#	Last SCN archived
RESETLOGS_CHANGE#	Change number at open resetlogs
RESETLOGS_TIME	Timestamp of open resetlogs
PRIOR_RESETLOGS_CHANGE#	Change number at prior resetlogs
PRIOR_RESETLOGS_TIME	Timestamp of prior resetlogs
CONTROLFILE_TYPE	CURRENT/STANDBY/CLONE/BACKUP/CREATED: STANDBY indicates database is in standby mode, CLONE indicates a clone database, BACKUP/CREATED indicates database is being recovered using a backup or created control file. A **standby database activate** or **database open after recovery** changes the type to CURRENT.
CONTROLFILE_CREATED	Control file creation timestamp
CONTROLFILE_SEQUENCE#	Control file sequence number incremented by control file transactions
CONTROLFILE_CHANGE#	Last change number in backup control file. Set to NULL if the control file is not a backup.
CONTROLFILE_TIME	Last timestamp in backup control file. Set to NULL if the control file is not a backup.

TABLE 4-3. *V$DATABASE View*

Column	Description
OPEN_RESETLOGS	NOT ALLOWED/ALLOWED/REQUIRED: indicates whether the next database to be opened allows or requires the resetlogs option
VERSION_TIME	The version time
OPEN_MODE	Open mode information. Shows whether the database is set to READ WRITE or READ ONLY.
STANDBY_MODE	Shows whether the database has a standby database associated with it if it is a primary database. The options are either PROTECTED or UNPROTECTED mode.
REMOTE_ARCHIVE	Indicates whether or not redo logs can be archived to a remote destination
ACTIVATION#	Number assigned to the database instantiation and used with Data Guard
DATABASE_ROLE	Shows whether the database is a primary or standby database
ARCHIVELOG_CHANGE#	Last SCN of the redo log last archived. On the primary, it is the last archived log, and on the standby, it is the last archived log applied.
SWITCHOVER_STATUS	Shows whether the database can be switched over to standby mode or not

TABLE 4-3. *V$DATABASE View* (continued)

The control file information is important to you if you need to perform recovery on your database, since you can view the V$ information even if the database is started and mounted but not opened. The Open_Mode parameter shows you whether the data in the database can be modified (mode would be READ WRITE if it can be) or only queried or looked at (mode would be READ ONLY).

The output from this view looks like this:

```
select *
  from V$DATABASE;

DBID       NAME      CREATED   RESETLOGS_CHANGE# RESETLOGS
---------- --------- --------- ----------------- ---------
PRIOR_RESETLOGS_CHANGE# PRIOR_RES LOG_MODE     CHECKPOINT_CHANGE#
----------------------- --------- ------------ ------------------
ARCHIVE_CHANGE# CONTROL CONTROLFI CONTROLFILE_SEQUENCE# CONTROLFILE_CHANGE#
--------------- ------- --------- --------------------- -------------------
CONTROLFI OPEN_RESETL VERSION_T OPEN_MODE  STANDBY_MOD REMOTE_ARCH ACTIVATION#
--------- ----------- --------- ---------- ----------- ----------- -----------
DATABASE_ROLE    ARCHIVELOG_CHANGE# SWITCHOVER_STATUS
---------------- ------------------ -----------------
1433635648 MYDB9     23-AUG-01            253462 23-AUG-01
                      1 05-JUL-01 NOARCHIVELOG            603099
         562387 CURRENT 23-AUG-01                  8820              603099
28-DEC-01 NOT ALLOWED 23-AUG-01 READ WRITE UNPROTECTED ENABLED      1433613888
PRIMARY                              0 NOT ALLOWED
```

From this listing, you can see that the database was created on August 23, 2001. But the time set for Prior_Res (prior reset logs) is July 5, 2001. Huh? How could that be? Where did that date come from, and how can it be earlier than the date on which the database was created? Under normal circumstances, you would expect the database creation date to match or be earlier than the prior reset log date, and you'd be right. But the database we are looking at is the demonstration database that Oracle creates and then bundles to ship with their software. When you choose to create the demo database, Oracle unbundles this database and places the files on your system, opens the database, and runs the environment scripts (catalog.sql, catproc.sql, etc.). So, in reality, this database was created in July 2001 on an Oracle Corporation computer and then unbundled and placed on our computer in August 2001. If you look carefully at some of the listings in the following sections, you'll see this July 5 date again, because many of the datafiles associated with this database were created in the default database supplied with the Oracle software.

Now that we have the date straight, there seem to be a lot of columns dealing with something called resetlogs. What does the clause *resetlogs* mean? Resetlogs is a command clause used in several different commands. It or its counterpart *noresetlogs* can be used when you issue the command **alter database** to either **open** the database after recovery, create a standby control file, or **backup controlfile to trace**. Resetlogs resets the current log sequence number to 1 and discards any redo information that has not been applied during recovery of the database. By resetting the redo log sequence number, you ensure that any unapplied redo will never be used. Thus, any changes that are in the redo log but not in the database will be discarded. You will use this clause when you've performed an incomplete database recovery. For now, let's get back to the contents of the V$DATABASE view.

The database has been named mydb9, and archive log mode has not been enabled. The database is in read/write mode and was last opened on December 28, 2001. The next time the database is opened, the resetlogs clause cannot be used. The database we are looking at is a primary database and does not have a standby database associated with it. You can tell that by the fact that the STANDBY_MODE is UNPROTECTED and SWITCHOVER_STATUS is set to NOT ALLOWED.

V$DATAFILE

Looking at the columns of the V$DATAFILE view, you might be tempted to ask, "What do I need to look at in this view that isn't in the DBA_DATA_FILES view?" That's a great question, and the answer is, "Quite a bit." When you look at the DBA_DATA_FILES view, you are looking at the datafile information from the database's perspective. When you look at the V$DATAFILE view, you are seeing information from the control file's perspective. The V$DATAFILE information in some ways overlaps the DBA_DATA_FILES data.

There are several columns that you might find of interest in this V$ view. Before we start looking at the columns individually, let's look at all of the columns to see what they contain. Table 4-4 shows the columns and a very brief description of each one.

Column	Description
FILE#	File identification number
STATUS	Type of file (system or user) and its status. Values: OFFLINE, ONLINE, SYSTEM, RECOVER, SYSOFF (an offline file from the SYSTEM tablespace)
ENABLED	Describes how accessible the file is from SQL. The values can be DISABLED, READ ONLY, READ WRITE, and UNKNOWN.
CHECKPOINT_CHANGE#	SCN at last checkpoint
CHECKPOINT_TIME	Timestamp of the checkpoint number
UNRECOVERABLE _CHANGE#	Last unrecoverable change number made to this datafile. This column is always updated when an unrecoverable operation completes.
UNRECOVERABLE_TIME	Timestamp of the last unrecoverable change

TABLE 4-4. *V$DATAFILE View*

Column	Description
BYTES	Current size in bytes; 0 if inaccessible
CREATE_BYTES	Size when created, in bytes
NAME	Name of the file
CREATION_CHANGE#	Change number at which the datafile was created
CREATION_TIME	Timestamp of the datafile creation
TS#	Tablespace number
RFILE#	Tablespace relative datafile number
LAST_CHANGE#	Last change number made to this datafile. Set to NULL if the datafile is being changed.
LAST_TIME	Timestamp of the last change
OFFLINE_CHANGE#	Offline change number of the last offline range. This column is updated only when the datafile is brought online.
ONLINE_CHANGE#	Online change number of the last offline range
ONLINE_TIME	Online timestamp of the last offline range
BLOCKS	Current datafile size in blocks; 0 if inaccessible
BLOCK_SIZE	Block size of the datafile
PLUGGED_IN	Describes whether the tablespace is plugged in. The value is 1 if the tablespace is plugged in and has not been made read/write, 0 if not.
BLOCK1_OFFSET	The offset from the beginning of the file to where the Oracle generic information begins
AUX_NAME	The auxiliary name that has been set for this file via the **configure auxname** command

TABLE 4-4. *V$DATAFILE View* (continued)

There are several "last number" values with timestamps that you may need to know if you are trying to determine the last time a datafile was changed. Two different forms of status values tell the status of the datafile: the Status column and the Enabled column. The Status column values are offline, online, system, recover, sysoff (an offline file from the SYSTEM tablespace). The Enabled column tells whether you can perform the following tasks through SQL commands: write to the datafile, read from it; or it tells you whether SQL interaction has been disabled or the SQL interaction availability is unknown.

You can see the size, in bytes, when the datafile was originally created. This value is meaningful if you've enabled autoextend and want to get a feel for how quickly or slowly the file is growing. You can compare the original datafile size with the current size by multiplying the Blocks column by the database block size. Using the BLOCK1_OFFSET value, the exact length of the file can be computed as follows: BYTES + BLOCK1_OFFSET.

```
column File# format 999
column Ts# format 999
column Rfile# format 99999
column Checkpoint_Change# heading 'CHKPNT_CHG#' format 99999999
column Creation_Change# heading 'CREATE_CHG#' format 999999999
column Name format a35
column Aux_Name format a35
select *
  from V$DATAFILE;

FILE# CREATE_CHG# CREATION_  TS# RFILE# STATUS  ENABLED     CHKPNT_CHG# CHECKPOIN
----- ----------- --------- ---- ------ ------- ---------- ----------- ---------
UNRECOVERABLE_CHANGE# UNRECOVER LAST_CHANGE# LAST_TIME OFFLINE_CHANGE#
--------------------- --------- ------------ --------- ---------------
ONLINE_CHANGE# ONLINE_TI      BYTES     BLOCKS CREATE_BYTES BLOCK_SIZE
-------------- --------- ---------- ---------- ------------ ----------
NAME                                PLUGGED_IN BLOCK1_OFFSET
----------------------------------- ---------- -------------
AUX_NAME
-----------------------------------
    1           4 05-JUL-01    0      1 SYSTEM  READ WRITE      603099 28-DEC-01
                  0                                             253461
       253462 23-AUG-01  340787200      83200            0        4096
D:\ORACLE\ORA90\ORADATA\MYDB9\SYSTE          0          4096
M01.DBF
NONE

    2        6318 05-JUL-01    1      2 ONLINE  READ WRITE      603099 28-DEC-01
                  0                                             253461
       253462 23-AUG-01  220200960      53760            0        4096
D:\ORACLE\ORA90\ORADATA\MYDB9\UNDOT          0          4096
BS01.DBF
NONE

    3        7315 05-JUL-01    2      3 ONLINE  READ WRITE      603099 28-DEC-01
                  0                                             253461
       253462 23-AUG-01   20971520       5120            0        4096
D:\ORACLE\ORA90\ORADATA\MYDB9\CWMLI          0          4096
TE01.DBF
NONE
```

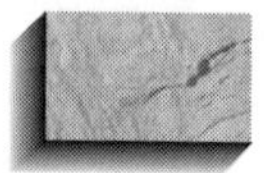

NOTE
Since there are 23 datafiles in this listing, only a few of the files are shown here to give you an idea of what the output looks like.

V$DATAFILE_HEADER

The V$DATAFILE_HEADER view has some interesting information about each of the datafiles in the database. Table 4-5 shows the columns and a brief description of each.

Column	Description
FILE#	Datafile number (from control file)
STATUS	ONLINE/OFFLINE (from control file)
ERROR	NULL if the datafile header read and validation were successful. If the read failed, the rest of the columns are NULL or may display invalid data. If there is an error, then usually the datafile must be restored from a backup before it can be recovered or used.
FORMAT	Indicates the format for the header block. The possible values are 6, for Oracle version 6 7, for Oracle version 7 8, for Oracle versions 8 and 9 0, which indicates the format could not be determined (for example, the header could not be read)
RECOVER	File needs media recovery: YES/NO
FUZZY	File is fuzzy: YES/NO
CREATION_CHANGE#	Datafile creation change number
CREATION_TIME	Datafile creation timestamp
TABLESPACE_NAME	Tablespace name
TS#	Tablespace number
RFILE#	Tablespace relative datafile number

TABLE 4-5. *V$DATAFILE_HEADER View*

Column	Description
RESETLOGS_CHANGE#	Resetlogs change number
RESETLOGS_TIME	Resetlogs timestamp
CHECKPOINT_CHANGE#	Datafile checkpoint change number
CHECKPOINT_TIME	Datafile checkpoint timestamp
CHECKPOINT_COUNT	Datafile checkpoint count
BYTES	Current datafile size in bytes
BLOCKS	Current datafile size in blocks
NAME	Datafile name

TABLE 4-5. *V$DATAFILE_HEADER View* (continued)

Until the inclusion of the V$DATAFILE_HEADER view, there was almost no way to successfully see any information about a datafile header. This view displays these important pieces of information:

- Status of the datafile (online or offline), in the Status column
- Whether any errors occurred when the datafile was brought online, in the Error column
- Whether the datafile needs recovery, in the Recover column
- The Oracle version of the header block (v6, v7, v8, v9, or unknown), in the Format column
- The current size of the datafile (in bytes and in blocks), in the Bytes or Blocks column

Here is an entry from the V$DATAFILE_HEADER view showing the information for the SYSTEM tablespace datafile:

```
col Error format a10
col Tablespace_Name format a15
select *
  from V$DATAFILE_HEADER
 where Tablespace_Name = 'SYSTEM';

FILE# STATUS  ERROR          FORMAT REC FUZ CREATE_CHG# CREATION_
----- ------- ---------- ---------- --- --- ----------- ---------
```

```
TABLESPACE_NAME  TS# RFILE# RESETLOGS_CHANGE# RESETLOGS CHKPNT_CHG# CHECKPOIN
--------------- ---- ------ ----------------- --------- ----------- ---------
CHECKPOINT_COUNT      BYTES     BLOCKS NAME
---------------- ---------- ---------- ----------------------------------
    1 ONLINE                         8 NO  YES            4 05-JUL-01
SYSTEM             0      1            253462 23-AUG-01      603099 28-DEC-01
             122  340787200      83200 D:\ORACLE\ORA90\ORADATA\MYDB9\SYSTE
                                       M01.DBF
```

Even if the query had not specified a name in the Tablespace_Name column, you can be sure the datafile listed here is for the SYSTEM tablespace (note the names of the datafile with the nomenclature system01.dbf) because a standard file-naming convention has been used in this database.

V$DBFILE

The V$DBFILE view is a lookup table (or view). As we talked about earlier in the section "Lookup Tables or Views," one column of the view is used to translate a value from a short representation, such as a number, to a much longer representation, such as a name.

In this case, the File# column is very short, while the Name column can be much longer. In all of the other views that need to reference the datafile, the File# will be used. When the actual file name is needed (for a report or other translation), you can use a lookup into this view to resolve the name. Table 4-6 shows the columns in the V$DBFILE view.

In our Oracle-supplied demonstration database for 9i, here are the values for the V$DBFILE view. We've again limited the amount of information returned to save space.

```
column Name format a44
column File# format 999
select File#, Name
  from V$DBFILE
 where File# < 6;

FILE# NAME
----- --------------------------------------------
    2 D:\ORACLE\ORA90\ORADATA\MYDB9\UNDOTBS01.DBF
    1 D:\ORACLE\ORA90\ORADATA\MYDB9\SYSTEM01.DBF
    5 G:\ORACLE\ORADATA\MYDB9\EXAMPLE01.DBF
    4 D:\ORACLE\ORA90\ORADATA\MYDB9\DRSYS01.DBF
    3 D:\ORACLE\ORA90\ORADATA\MYDB9\CWMLITE01.DBF
```

There's something different about the output from this query compared to the output from the V$DATAFILE and the V$DATAFILE_HEADER queries. Can you see what it is? In the other two queries, even though no **order by** qualifier is given, the file numbers are displayed in order. In the V$DBFILE query, no **order by** qualifier is given and the file numbers appear to be displayed out of order. There's a lesson to

Column	Description
FILE#	File identifier
NAME	Name of file

TABLE 4-6. *V$DBFILE View*

be learned here. If you want to be sure the numbers you are displaying will always be in a specific order, you must be sure to put in a clause to specify that order. People tend to get very upset when numbers are unexpectedly displayed out of sequence.

V$FIXED_TABLE

The V$FIXED_TABLE view displays all the names of the dynamic tables, views, and derived views that are contained in the database. The V$FIXED_TABLE view contains information on X$ tables, V$ views, and GV$ views and is the easiest way for you to find out the name of an X$ dynamic table. You will probably not need to use this view very often, but it's important that you can identify it and its contents. Table 4-7 shows the columns in this view.

Because there are 806 objects listed in this view and 352 of them are X$ tables, we are going to show you the output from a very limited subset of the X$ tables here.

```
select *
  from V$FIXED_TABLE
 where Type = 'TABLE'
   and Table_Num between 0 and 10;

NAME                                      OBJECT_ID TYPE   TABLE_NUM
---------------------------------------- ---------- ----- ---------
X$KQFTA                                  4294950912 TABLE         0
X$KQFVI                                  4294950913 TABLE         1
X$KQFVT                                  4294951149 TABLE         2
X$KQFDT                                  4294950914 TABLE         3
X$KQFCO                                  4294951036 TABLE         4
X$KSLLT                                  4294950993 TABLE         5
X$KSLLD                                  4294950994 TABLE         6
X$KSLED                                  4294951094 TABLE         7
X$KSLES                                  4294951095 TABLE         8
X$KSLEI                                  4294951102 TABLE         9
X$KSLLW                                  4294951183 TABLE        10
```

You can see that the names of the X$ tables listed here are not very meaningful or obvious. Although it's close to impossible to guess what each of the dynamic

Column	Description
NAME	Name of the object
OBJECT_ID	Identifier of the fixed object
TYPE	Object type: TABLE, VIEW
TABLE_NUM	Number that identifies the dynamic performance table if it is of type TABLE

TABLE 4-7. *V$FIXED_TABLE View*

tables listed here contains, many of the views have more meaningful names. We suggest you list the contents of the V$FIXED_TABLE view and explore the tables and views it contains. Remember that you must not in any way attempt to modify any of the dynamic tables or views. That would be a very quick way to compromise the integrity of your database!

If you try to use the **describe** command on an X$ table and you are not connected as "sys as sysdba," you will be told that the object does not exist. In other words, Oracle keeps the X$ tables well hidden. If you want to see the composition of an X$ table, first, you must be connected as sysdba, and if you know the name of an X$ table, you can select it and see its contents. A bit of caution is recommended when trying to view any of the X$ tables, as they can contain many thousands of rows (or more). We've found that doing a count of the number of rows contained in a table is a good practice to follow before selecting the data from that table. That's a great general rule to follow for any queries you do!

V$INSTANCE

The V$INSTANCE view provides general information about each instance that is connected to your database. This view has changed dramatically over time. There were originally only two columns: Key and Value. The Key column showed the name of the state variable, and the Value column showed the actual state value. As you can see from Table 4-8, the view has been modified to reflect much more information. Table 4-8 shows the columns for the most current version of the V$INSTANCE view.

There will be times when an application is coded with a detached process running. The detached process makes a connection to your database and maintains that connection indefinitely. There are many valid reasons to have an application process do this. However, a problem arises when you need to shut down your database. You won't be able to perform a normal shutdown because the application

Column	Description
INSTANCE_NUMBER	Instance number used for instance registration; corresponds to INSTANCE_NUMBER initialization parameter
INSTANCE_NAME	Instance name
HOST_NAME	Name of the host machine
VERSION	RDBMS version
STARTUP_TIME	Time when instance was started up
STATUS	Current status of the database; can be STARTED/MOUNTED/OPEN: STARTED after startup nomount; MOUNTED after startup mount or alter database close; OPEN after startup or after database open
PARALLEL	YES/NO in parallel server mode
THREAD#	Redo thread opened by the instance
ARCHIVER	STOPPED/STARTED/FAILED: FAILED means the archiver failed to archive a log last time but will try again within five minutes
LOG_SWITCH_WAIT	Event the log switch is waiting for; can be ARCHIVE LOG/CLEAR LOG/CHECKPOINT Note that if ALTER SYSTEM SWITCH LOGFILE is hung, but there is room in the current online redo log, then value is NULL.
LOGINS	ALLOWED/RESTRICTED
SHUTDOWN_PENDING	YES/NO
DATABASE_STATUS	The status of the database
INSTANCE_ROLE	Describes whether the instance is an active instance (PRIMARY_INSTANCE) or an inactive secondary instance (SECONDARY_INSTANCE), or UNKNOWN if the instance has been started but not mounted
ACTIVE_STATE	Describes the database states. The options are NORMAL, QUIESCING, and QUIESCED.

TABLE 4-8. *V$INSTANCE View*

process is running and the database will wait until all processes have disconnected before the shutdown is completed. There are two ways to solve this problem. You can make it a policy always to do a **shutdown immediate**, or you can have your developers use the V$INSTANCE view to determine whether your database is waiting to shut down by checking the Shutdown_Pending column. If this column value changes from NO to YES, the application can be coded to automatically disconnect from the database. You will, of course, have to give the application user the privilege to select from this view.

The new column Active_State can also help you identify the status of the instances. If the following command has been issued, the state will be QUIESCING and no new user transactions, queries, or PL/SQL statements will be processed in this instance.

```
alter system quiesce restricted;
```

Any user statements that were submitted before this statement was issued will be unaffected. Once the statement has completed, the Active_State will be set to QUIESCED and you can be sure that no new submitted queries will be processed. Keep in mind that this feature is only available if you are using Resource Manager.

```
column Instance_Number heading 'INST#' format 9999
column Host_Name format a12
column Version format a9
column Thread# format 9999999
select *
  from V$INSTANCE;

INST# INSTANCE_NAME    HOST_NAME    VERSION   STARTUP_T STATUS  PAR  THREAD#
----- ---------------- ------------ --------- --------- ------- --- --------
ARCHIVE LOG_SWITCH_ LOGINS     SHU DATABASE_STATUS   INSTANCE_ROLE
------- ----------- ---------- --- ----------------- ------------------
ACTIVE_ST
---------
    1 mydb9            MTHERIAULT   9.0.1.0.0 28-DEC-01 OPEN    NO         1
STOPPED             ALLOWED    NO  ACTIVE            PRIMARY_INSTANCE
NORMAL
```

If you are running Oracle9i Real Application Clusters (formerly the Parallel Server option), the instance name may not match your database name. Therefore, you can join the V$DATABASE and V$INSTANCE views together to view both the instance and database name, as follows:

```
select Instance_Name, Name
  from V$INSTANCE, V$DATABASE;

INSTANCE_NAME    NAME
---------------- ------------------------------------
mydb9            MYDB9
```

Did you notice something interesting about this query? Even though we did the select from two different views, we do not have a join clause. That's because we know there is only one row in each of these views. If you join two tables or views that have a single row in them, you do not have to provide a join clause.

Okay, so in this particular case, the names match. They may not always match, and this is a handy way to determine whether they do. Notice, though, that if a SQL statement was querying for a match of the two names, you would have to use either the **upper** or **lower** function to actually get the names to match, since one is stored in uppercase and the other is in lowercase. Very interesting!

V$PARAMETER

The V$PARAMETER view stores all of the database parameters. In earlier versions of Oracle, this view contained only the parameter number, parameter name, parameter type, and associated group. Now, as you can see in Table 4-9 which shows the

Column	Description
NUM	Parameter number
NAME	Parameter name
TYPE	Parameter type: 1 = Boolean; 2 = string; 3 = integer
VALUE	Parameter value
ISDEFAULT	Whether the parameter value is the default
ISSES_MODIFIABLE	TRUE/FALSE: TRUE indicates the parameter can be changed with **alter session**; FALSE indicates the parameter cannot be changed with **alter session**.
ISSYS_MODIFIABLE	IMMEDIATE/DEFERRED/FALSE: IMMEDIATE indicates the parameter can be changed with **alter system**; DEFERRED indicates the parameter cannot be changed until the next session; FALSE indicates the parameter cannot be changed with **alter system**.
ISMODIFIED	Indicates how the parameter was modified. If an **alter session** was performed, the value will be MODIFIED. If an **alter system** (which will cause all the currently logged-in sessions' values to be modified) was performed, the value will be SYS_MODIFIED.

TABLE 4-9. *V$PARAMETER View*

Column	Description
ISADJUSTED	Indicates that Oracle adjusted the input value to a more suitable value. (For example, the parameter value should be prime, but the user input a nonprime number, so Oracle adjusted the value to the next prime number.)
DESCRIPTION	A descriptive comment about the parameter
UPDATE_COMMENT	Comments associated with the most recent update

TABLE 4-9. *V$PARAMETER View* (continued)

columns for the V$PARAMETER view, there are many more columns with helpful information.

In our Oracle9i demonstration database, there are 250 parameters. We'll only look at the first few. You should take the time to do a select of all the parameters and look at what they do.

```
column Value format a7
column Description format a38
column Update_Comment format a30
select *
  from V$PARAMETER
 where Num < 12;
NUM        NAME                                                   TYPE VALUE
---------- --------------------------------------------- ---------- -------
ISDEFAULT ISSES ISSYS_MOD ISMODIFIED ISADJ
--------- ----- --------- ---------- -----
DESCRIPTION                            UPDATE_COMMENT
-------------------------------------- ------------------------------
         2 tracefile_identifier                                        2
TRUE      TRUE  FALSE     FALSE      FALSE
trace file custom identifier

         9 processes                                                   3 150
FALSE     FALSE FALSE     FALSE      FALSE
user processes

        10 sessions                                                    3 170
TRUE      FALSE FALSE     FALSE      FALSE
user and system sessions

        11 timed_statistics                                            1 TRUE
FALSE     TRUE  IMMEDIATE FALSE      FALSE
maintain internal timing statistics
```

This view is most valuable for letting you quickly see

- Which parameter values are still the default and which ones have been changed in the initialization parameter file
- Which parameters can be changed dynamically
- Which parameters have been changed
- Whether the parameter was changed by an **alter session** or **alter system** command

If the parameter was changed with the **alter session** command, the value will only be visible and usable by that specific session. If the parameter was changed using **alter system**, the value will be visible systemwide.

V$SGA

The V$SGA view displays the summary statistics for the allocation of space in the system global area. Table 4-10 shows the columns in the V$SGA view.

The V$SGA view gives you a feel for the total amount of memory that has been allocated to the SGA and how Oracle has divided that memory. Let's look at the memory allocation for the Oracle9i default demonstration database:

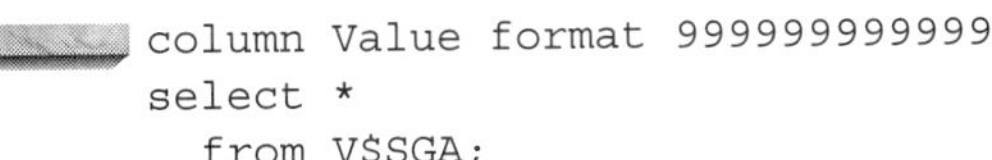

```
column Value format 999999999999
select *
  from V$SGA;

NAME                                                VALUE
--------------------------------------- ---------------
Fixed Size                                         282496
Variable Size                                    67108864
Database Buffers                                 33554432
Redo Buffers                                       532480
```

Column	Description
NAME	SGA component group
VALUE	Memory size in bytes

TABLE 4-10. *V$SGA View*

To see the total real memory allocation for the current SGA, you can select the sum of the Value column, as follows:

```
select sum(Value) from V$SGA;

SUM(VALUE)
----------
 101478272
```

From this listing, you can see that the total SGA for this instance is 100 megabytes. In Chapter 6, you'll see the counterpart view, V$SGASTAT, which shows the breakdown of the SGA by parameter instead of the summary values that V$SGA gives you. Both views are valuable.

V$TEMPFILE

The V$TEMPFILE view was new in Oracle8i and contains information about locally managed temporary tablespace files. Table 4-11 shows the columns for the V$TEMPFILE view.

FILE#	The absolute file number
CREATION_CHANGE#	The creation System Change Number (SCN)
CREATION_TIME	The creation time
TS#	The tablespace number
RFILE#	The relative file number in tablespace
STATUS	The status of the file (OFFLINE/ONLINE)
ENABLED	Enabled for read and/or write
BYTES	The size of the file in bytes (from file header)
BLOCKS	The size of the file in blocks (from file header)
CREATE_BYTES	The creation size of the file (in bytes)
BLOCK_SIZE	The block size for the file
NAME	The name of the file

TABLE 4-11. *V$TEMPFILE View*

By default in Oracle9i a locally managed temporary tablespace is used to support sort operations. Let's look at the output from a query examining this view.

```
select *
  from V$TEMPFILE;

FILE# CREATE_CHG# CREATION_  TS# RFILE# STATUS  ENABLED         BYTES     BLOCKS
----- ----------- --------- ---- ------ ------- ---------- ---------- ----------
CREATE_BYTES BLOCK_SIZE NAME
------------ ---------- ------------------------------------------
    1           0               6      1 ONLINE  READ WRITE   41943040      10240
    41943040       4096 D:\ORACLE\ORA90\ORADATA\MYDB9\TEMP01.DBF

    2           0              24      1 ONLINE  READ WRITE   20971520       5120
    20971520       4096 G:\ORACLE\ORADATA\MYDB9\MYTEMP01.DBF
```

Hmm. That's interesting. From this listing we can see that there are actually two temporary files within the database. Both files have a 4k block size and both are READ WRITE and ONLINE. Since we use a standard naming convention for our files, we can guess that there are two temporary tablespaces in the database: one with the name TEMP and the other with the name MYTEMP. A quick look at DBA_TEMP_FILES confirms this supposition.

```
select Tablespace_Name
  from DBA_TEMP_FILES;

TABLESPACE_NAME
---------------
TEMP
MY_TEMP
```

Like datafiles, you can turn autoextend on for tempfiles, so the Create_Bytes column tells you how big the tempfile was when you first created it, and Bytes tells you how big it is now.

One of the nice things about using tempfiles is that Oracle does not require you to back them up to have a complete backup, unlike setting a tablespace to **contents temporary** and using datafiles. In fact, RMAN, Oracle's Recovery Manager, will ignore tempfiles when you back up the database. If you have a very tight time window in which to complete your backups, this can save you significant time.

CHAPTER 5

How to Protect the Database

In the previous chapters, we described the data dictionary views that let you look at the database: the tablespaces and datafiles, the rollback and undo segments, the segments and extents, and the objects. While all this information is useful, you still need to know who can access your database and use the space in it. In this chapter we are going to examine how you can see the information about the users who have been created within your database and the privileges those users have been granted. As more and more people access the database, the potential for deliberate or accidental security breaches grows. So it's essential you manage and monitor access.

Views That Secure the Database

These views allow you to manage a user's *security domain*—the set of attributes that determine the limits of a user's actions, space quotas, and resources. Now, let's see who's been able to get into your database and what they can do once they've gotten in. Table 5-1 contains a list of the views we'll discuss in this chapter.

DBA_USERS

DBA_USERS contains the list of all users who can access your database. Table 5-2 shows the columns in this view and what the columns represent.

Let's take a look at the columns we use most often. Username is self-explanatory—that's the account name users will enter when they log on to the database. It can be made up of characters (letters of the alphabet), numbers, and these special

View	Description
DBA_PROFILES	Display all profiles and their limits
DBA_ROLES	All roles that exist in the database
DBA_ROLE_PRIVS	Roles granted to users and roles
DBA_SYS_PRIVS	System privileges granted to users and roles
DBA_TAB_PRIVS	All grants on objects in the database
DBA_TS_QUOTAS	Tablespace quotas for all users
DBA_USERS	Information about all users of the database
DBA_VIEWS	Information about all views in the database

TABLE 5-1. *DBA_ Database Protection Views*

Column	Description
USERNAME	Name of the user
USER_ID	ID number of the user
PASSWORD	Encrypted password
ACCOUNT_STATUS	Indicates whether the account is locked, expired, or unlocked
LOCK_DATE	Date the account was locked if account status was locked
EXPIRY_DATE	Date of expiration of the account
DEFAULT_TABLESPACE	Default tablespace for data
TEMPORARY_TABLESPACE	Default tablespace for temporary segments
CREATED	User creation date
PROFILE	User resource profile name
INITIAL_RSRC_CONSUMER_GROUP	The initial resource consumer group for the user
EXTERNAL_NAME	User external name

TABLE 5-2. *DBA_USERS View*

characters: underscore (_), dollar sign ($), or pound sign (#). The username must begin with an alphabetic character unless you surround the name with double quotation marks ("). In general, Oracle recommends that you do not use the pound or dollar sign in a username—and so do we. The "Schema Object Names and Qualifiers" section in the SQL Reference manual contains a complete set of the rules on choosing usernames.

User_ID is the unique identifier for that user and is made up of numbers. In addition to the unique identifier, the Username column must also contain a unique value. Why does Oracle have both columns, when each one is unique? Well, the underlying database tables on which these views are built have indexes on them so that Oracle can return the information to you quickly. In general, it's better to index a numeric column than it is to index a character column. So even though both columns are unique, and there is some extra space "wasted" to store the User_ID, Oracle includes that column to improve performance. Besides, it's much easier for your users to remember a name than a string of numbers.

When a user creates an object and doesn't specify a tablespace in which to create it, Oracle will create the object in the tablespace that you have assigned as the Default_Tablespace. Temporary_Tablespace contains the name of the tablespace for a user that Oracle uses when a SQL statement requires sorting. Statements that require sorting are index creation statements; **select** statements with **union**, **minus**, and **intersect** clauses; and statements with joins, group by clauses, order by clauses, and distinct clauses. These will use the temporary tablespace if they cannot be completed in memory. If you don't specify a default tablespace for a user when you create one, Oracle will use the SYSTEM tablespace. If you then grant that user the ability to create objects in his or her default tablespace, the user will be able to create objects in SYSTEM. If you have not specified a default temporary tablespace when you created the database, and if you then do not specify one when you create a user, Oracle will use the SYSTEM tablespace as the temporary tablespace as well. As we've said before, the SYSTEM tablespace should only contain objects that belong to the user SYS, to help keep it from getting fragmented and to ensure that there is always room for the data dictionary tables to grow. You should always specify a default and temporary tablespace for each new user you create, even when you know the user will never own any objects and even if you have specified a default temporary tablespace for the database. Over time, requirements have a habit of changing.

You can check to see if any users were created in the SYSTEM tablespace with the following query:

```
select Username, Default_Tablespace, Temporary_Tablespace
  from DBA_USERS
 where Default_Tablespace = 'SYSTEM'
    or Temporary_Tablespace = 'SYSTEM'
/
```

The results of that query are below.

```
USERNAME        DEFAULT_TABLESPACE   TEMPORARY_TABLESPACE
--------------- -------------------- --------------------
SYS             SYSTEM               SYSTEM
PROD_OWNER      SYSTEM               SYSTEM
```

In general, no user should have a temporary tablespace of SYSTEM, not even SYS. Sorting in the SYSTEM tablespace will fragment the tablespace, and when the data dictionary tables need to extend, Oracle may not be able to find an extent large enough. In addition, we've said that no user other than SYS should have a default tablespace of SYSTEM because of fragmentation issues. The user PROD_OWNER has SYSTEM as both the default and temporary tablespaces. You can change both of these tablespace values for a user while the database is up and active using the

alter user command. However, making the change will only affect the location of any new objects. Existing objects that were created in the SYSTEM tablespace will not be moved. If there are only a few objects, you can move them using the **alter table ... move** or **alter index .... rebuild** commands. If there are a large number of existing objects, you can relocate them by exporting the user's objects, changing the default tablespace, dropping the objects, creating an empty version of the object in the new default tablespace, and importing the user's objects, specifying the **ignore=y** parameter on the import command. A lengthy and tedious process! We recommend you make sure that all users are created with their default and temporary tablespaces declared properly from the beginning so that you do not have the extra work involved in correcting the tablespace declarations later.

The Password column contains the encrypted password for that account. Let's create a user called RACHEL and then see what the stored password for the RACHEL user entry looks like:

```
Create user RACHEL identified by TEST
default tablespace USERS
temporary tablespace TEMP;

User created.

select Username, Password
  from DBA_USERS
 where Username like 'RACHEL';

USERNAME                       PASSWORD
------------------------------ ------------------------------
RACHEL                         DE0E2C8587E4087E
```

When the user RACHEL was created, you used the password TEST. As you can see, the output from the Password column doesn't look anything like the word TEST!

In Oracle versions prior to 8.0 (when Oracle introduced password protection, history, and expiration), you could extract a user's encrypted password, change that password and log in, and then restore the original encrypted password using the "identified by values" clause of the **alter user** command. Why would you want to do that? Well, suppose you wanted to make absolutely sure that no one could access the userid that owned all your production tables, unless you wanted to make changes yourself. You could create the user with a password that could not be used:

```
create user prod_owner identified by values 'no access';
User created.

select Password
  from DBA_USERS
```

```
 where Username = 'PROD_OWNER';

PASSWORD
------------------------------
no access
```

Wow! The actual value that you told Oracle to store as the password is displayed instead of an encrypted one. Since the password is stored in the database exactly as you entered it and not as an encrypted value, there is no way for someone to figure out the unencrypted value of that password, and no one can log in as that user—not even you. Now, let's say you want to make changes to the objects in that schema. How are you going to get in if there is no unencrypted password for you to type? Well, you can either make changes from an account that has DBA privileges or has been granted the "any" privileges (**alter any table**, **create any table**, **create any index**, etc.). You can also change the password so that you can log in as the production user directly and then change it back when you are done. If you do not take advantage of Oracle's password expiration and history features, you can still use this method to protect your passwords—a very handy feature to know about. If you do use the history and expiration features, when you go to reset the password after using the account, you will not be able to, because the password has already been used once within the history and expiration times.

Okay, since we've begun talking about the new password features, let's discuss the Account_Status, Lock_Date, and Expiry_Date columns, which all pertain to the password features in Oracle8. Account_Status tells you whether users can access their accounts and if they can't, why they can't. Lock_Date is the date an account was locked, because the user failed to enter the correct password *x* number of times. (You can set the number of allowable attempts in the user's profile.) Expiry_Date is the date the account password expired. You can set a grace period during which users can log in with the old password before being forced to change it. Let's take a look at one of the users and see what her Account_Status is.

```
select Username, Account_Status, Lock_Date
  from DBA_USERS
 where Account_Status != 'OPEN'
/

USERNAME                       ACCOUNT_STATUS                   LOCK_DATE
------------------------------ -------------------------------- ---------
RACHEL                         LOCKED(TIMED)                    24-JAN-02
```

Oh dear, it looks like RACHEL is not going to be able to access her account. You can clear the locked status and allow her to access the database again using the command

```
 alter user RACHEL account unlock;
```

The remaining two columns in the DBA_USERS view are Created, which is the date you created this user account, and Profile, which is the Oracle user profile to use when checking the resource limits placed on this user. Hmm, we see a connection here to the next DBA_ view we'll talk about, DBA_PROFILES.

DBA_PROFILES

The DBA_PROFILES view contains information about all profiles that have been defined in the database. By default, when you create an Oracle database in versions 8 and 9, Oracle creates a profile named DEFAULT. Table 5-3 shows all the columns in this view and what they represent.

Why do we need profiles? Profiles define limits on groups of system resources (those with a Resource_Type of KERNEL) and define password restrictions (those limits with a Resource_Type of PASSWORD). So for different users, you can set up different limits. In order for Oracle to apply the KERNEL limits you set in the profiles you create, you must first set **resource_limit** to TRUE in your initialization parameter file.

Perhaps you want to limit the amount of time the payroll clerks can be connected without doing something that accesses the database. Or perhaps you want to limit the number of times a user can log in and open concurrent sessions. You can define the limit of IDLE_TIME or the limit SESSIONS_PER_USER in the default profile. But what if you want to give different types of users different limits? You may want to limit the idle time for a clerk, but you probably don't want to limit the idle time for the CEO of your company. Like the roles we discussed in Chapter 2, Oracle allows you to set up multiple profiles and assign each one to one or more users. By default, each new user created in your database is assigned the DEFAULT profile. If you want a user to be assigned a specific profile, you tell Oracle the profile to use when you issue the **create user** command. We'll talk more about assigning profiles a bit later in this section.

You can also define password limits with a profile. You can limit the number of times a user can try to log in before the account is locked, the number of password

Column	Description
PROFILE	Profile name
RESOURCE_NAME	Resource name
RESOURCE_TYPE	Resource type
LIMIT	Limit placed on this resource for this profile

TABLE 5-3. *DBA_PROFILES View*

changes that must occur before a password can be reused, along with a number of other password-specific limits.

So how do you create a profile and how do you use it? A sample profile create statement is

```
create profile CLERK_PROFILE limit
    sessions_per_user 2
            idle_time 10
failed_login_attempts 3
         connect_time 60;
```

In this example, the CLERK_PROFILE profile specifies limits for

- Number of sessions a user can have (2)
- Amount of time the process can be idle (10 minutes)
- Number of times a user can attempt to connect without the correct password (3)
- Total amount of time the user can be connected to the database (60 minutes)

You can then assign that profile to a user with the statement:

```
alter user RACHEL profile CLERK_PROFILE;
```

Now, let's see what happens when RACHEL logs in and enters the wrong password three times. On each of the first three attempts, an error message indicating an invalid username or password is returned. On the fourth try, it doesn't matter what password is entered; the account is now locked, and the DBA must unlock that account, unless the Password_Lock_Time has been set so that the account will automatically unlock after the specified amount of time has passed.

```
connect RACHEL/BADPSWD
ERROR:
ORA-01017: invalid username/password; logon denied
connect RACHEL/BADPSWD
ERROR:
ORA-01017: invalid username/password; logon denied
connect RACHEL/BADPSWD
ERROR:
ORA-01017: invalid username/password; logon denied
connect RACHEL/TEST
ERROR:
ORA-28000: the account is locked
```

Now that you've seen what the profiles are and what you can use them for, how do you see which profile limits are assigned to which user? Remember the Profile column in DBA_USERS? You're going to join the two views together and see what you get. Any limit that you have not specifically mentioned in your **create profile** statement will keep the same value as it has in the DEFAULT profile. Although you can change the values of the profile limits for the DEFAULT profile, we recommend you don't. Any value you change that is not specifically overridden in your other profiles will take on the new value in those other profiles as well.

```
select Username, Resource_Name, Limit
  from DBA_USERS, DBA_PROFILES
 where DBA_USERS.Profile != 'DEFAULT'
   and Limit != 'DEFAULT'
   and DBA_USERS.Profile = DBA_PROFILES.Profile
/

USERNAME   RESOURCE_NAME                    LIMIT
---------- -------------------------------- ----------
RACHEL     FAILED_LOGIN_ATTEMPTS            3
RACHEL     SESSIONS_PER_USER                2
RACHEL     IDLE_TIME                        10
RACHEL     CONNECT_TIME                     60
```

You've just managed to find the nondefault profile settings for a user! And you've seen how you can join two of the DBA_ views to extract and combine information. For a complete listing of the profile limits for your version of Oracle, you can check the SQL reference manual, in the "Create Profile" section.

DBA_ROLES

The DBA_ROLES view contains information about all the roles that have been defined in the database. When you create an Oracle database in versions 8 or 9, Oracle creates several default roles. Table 5-4 shows the columns in this view and what they represent.

Column	Description
ROLE	Role name
PASSWORD_ REQUIRED	Indicates whether the role requires a password to be enabled

TABLE 5-4. *DBA_ROLES View*

In versions of Oracle prior to Oracle6, there were only three roles available for assignment to users:

- **CONNECT** Gives the user the ability to access the database
- **RESOURCE** Gives the user the ability to create objects and use space in the database
- **DBA** Gives the user the ability to do anything in the database

In fact, these roles did not exist as roles, but were a set of privileges, defined and stored within the Oracle kernel, that you could grant to a user. With Oracle's version 6, true roles were introduced. By Oracle7, the DBA received the ability to combine groups of system and object privileges, and to create customized roles to fit the needs of the applications that resided in the database.

If you do a select from an Oracle9.0.1 database, you see the roles that have been created by default.

```
select * from DBA_ROLES;

ROLE                           PASSWORD
------------------------------ --------
CONNECT                        NO
RESOURCE                       NO
DBA                            NO
SELECT_CATALOG_ROLE            NO
EXECUTE_CATALOG_ROLE           NO
DELETE_CATALOG_ROLE            NO
EXP_FULL_DATABASE              NO
WM_ADMIN_ROLE                  NO
IMP_FULL_DATABASE              NO
RECOVERY_CATALOG_OWNER         NO
AQ_ADMINISTRATOR_ROLE          NO
AQ_USER_ROLE                   NO
GLOBAL_AQ_USER_ROLE            GLOBAL
OEM_MONITOR                    NO
HS_ADMIN_ROLE                  NO
```

Wow, there are 15 roles that get created! Depending on which products you install, you may see other default roles. If you install Oracle's JVM (Java Virtual Machine), you'll see another 6 roles created.

Notice that CONNECT, RESOURCE, and DBA still exist. Oracle retains these roles for backward compatibility but does not guarantee they will always be there. The predefined roles may change from version to version, and, as with the DBA_ views themselves, you should always check to see what new roles have been added and what roles have been removed.

One thing to remember is that the role RESOURCE grants the privilege **unlimited tablespace** to a user. With this privilege, users can create objects in tablespaces that are not their default tablespace and that they have no quota on. *Quota* is the amount of space a user can use in a tablespace. We'll discuss quota in more detail a bit later when we look at the DBA_TS_QUOTAS view.

The Password column indicates whether a password must be entered when a user or application enables a role. If a password is required, users will need to supply the password when they enable the role for their session via the **set role** command. There is one exception to this. If a role that requires a password is granted to a user as his default role, that role will be enabled when he logs on to the database, and he will not need to supply a password. You can have more than one default role, but they must all be assigned as part of the same SQL statement. You can see which roles are enabled for your session with the SQL statement:

```
select * from SESSION_ROLES;
```

You can create a role if you have been granted either the **create role** privilege or if you have been granted a role that has been granted this privilege. To create a role:

```
create role TESTROLE;
```

To add privileges to the role, you can grant each privilege to that role. Let's say you want the TESTROLE role to have the **create role** privilege. You'd just need to grant that privilege as follows:

```
grant CREATE ROLE to TESTROLE;
Grant succeeded.
```

Now, if you grant the TESTROLE to a user, that user will be able to create roles in the database.

DBA_ROLE_PRIVS

In the previous section you've seen how to find roles that exist in the database. The DBA_ROLE_PRIVS view tells you which users or roles have been granted these roles, and what administrative privileges have been granted for the role. Table 5-5 shows the columns in this view and what they represent.

Once a role has been created, it must be granted to a user or other role before it can be used. The DBA_ROLE_PRIVS view allows you to see what roles have been granted. The Grantee column is the username or role that has the ability to access this role. You cannot grant roles in a circular fashion. That means, if you create a

Column	Description
GRANTEE	Grantee Name, User, or Role receiving the grant
GRANTED_ROLE	Granted role name
ADMIN_OPTION	Grant was with the ADMIN option
DEFAULT_ROLE	Role is designated as a DEFAULT ROLE for the user

TABLE 5-5. *DBA_ROLE_PRIVS View*

role called CLERK and another role called MANAGER, you can grant the role CLERK to MANAGER, but once you have done that, you cannot grant MANAGER to CLERK, since that would have the MANAGER role referencing itself.

Granted_Role is the same as the Role column in the DBA_ROLES view, and Admin_Option means that the user who has been granted this role can grant it in turn to others. Default_Role means that when the user logs in to the database, this role will automatically be enabled.

To see which roles have been granted to a user and whether they are automatically enabled, you can type

```
select Grantee, Granted_Role, Default_Role
  from DBA_ROLE_PRIVS
 where Grantee not in ('SYS','SYSTEM')
 order by Grantee;

GRANTEE              GRANTED_ROLE                   DEF
-------------------- ------------------------------ ---
DBA                  DELETE_CATALOG_ROLE            YES
DBA                  EXECUTE_CATALOG_ROLE           YES
DBA                  EXP_FULL_DATABASE              YES
DBA                  IMP_FULL_DATABASE              YES
DBA                  SELECT_CATALOG_ROLE            YES
DBSNMP               CONNECT                        YES
DBSNMP               RESOURCE                       YES
DBSNMP               SNMPAGENT                      YES
EXP_FULL_DATABASE    EXECUTE_CATALOG_ROLE           YES
EXP_FULL_DATABASE    SELECT_CATALOG_ROLE            YES
IMP_FULL_DATABASE    EXECUTE_CATALOG_ROLE           YES
IMP_FULL_DATABASE    SELECT_CATALOG_ROLE            YES
JAMES                CONNECT                        YES
JAMES                RESOURCE                       YES
JAMES                TESTROLE                       YES
MY_SCHEMA            CONNECT                        YES
```

```
RACHEL                 CONNECT                        YES
RACHEL                 TESTROLE                       NO
```

Both RACHEL and JAMES have been granted the role TESTROLE, but RACHEL cannot use the privileges from that role until she enables the role for her session. JAMES will automatically inherit any privileges from that role when he logs on and will not have to enter a password if that role has a password.

If you want to see whether any roles that require passwords have been granted to anyone, you can join the DBA_ROLES and DBA_ROLE_PRIVS table as follows:

```
select Grantee, Granted_Role
  from DBA_ROLES a, DBA_ROLE_PRIVS b
 where a.Role = b.Granted_Role
   and a.Password_Required='YES';

GRANTEE                GRANTED_ROLE
-------------------- ------------------------------
RACHEL                 TESTROLE
JAMES                  TESTROLE
```

DBA_SYS_PRIVS

The next view, DBA_SYS_PRIVS, shows you which system-level privileges have been granted to which users or roles. System-level privileges are those that allow you to manipulate the database environment, either by creating, dropping, or altering objects within the database. Table 5-6 shows the columns in this view and what they represent.

Once again, we advise you to check the number and type of system privileges available in each new version of the database. As Oracle adds new features, new privileges are added to manage them. While you may not need to use all the new features and privileges available to you, a smart DBA will at least be aware that they exist and know how each one works. In Oracle8.1.6, there are 115 system privileges, while in Oracle9i, there are 127.

Column	Description
GRANTEE	Grantee Name, User, or Role receiving the grant
PRIVILEGE	System privilege
ADMIN_OPTION	Grant was with the ADMIN option

TABLE 5-6. *DBA_SYS_PRIVS View*

Okay. So how do you find out all the system privileges that a user has been granted? If you do a **select** from the view, you get the following:

```
select *
  from DBA_SYS_PRIVS
 where Grantee ='JAMES';

GRANTEE                   PRIVILEGE                                ADM
------------------------- ---------------------------------------- ---
JAMES                     UNLIMITED TABLESPACE                     NO
```

Hmm. That doesn't make sense. We saw earlier that JAMES has the CONNECT, RESOURCE, and TESTROLE roles granted to him. He should have some privileges associated with these roles, as well as the privilege **unlimited tablespace**. In fact, he does, but he inherits the rest of his privileges from the roles. So to truly see what privileges he has, you also have to look for the privileges that are granted to the roles he has been granted.

One thing to note, before we show you how to extract the privileges that have been granted to both JAMES and the roles, is that this user has been granted **unlimited tablespace**. As we've said before, this system privilege allows a user to create an object in *any* tablespace, including SYSTEM, even if he doesn't have quota on that tablespace. Oracle automatically grants this privilege when you grant RESOURCE to a user. If we are beginning to sound like a broken record about this, you must assume that we think it's a pretty important and dangerous situation. We do! In general, a much better idea is to create your own roles and assign the privileges you want them to have, rather than to use the predefined roles of CONNECT and RESOURCE. The CONNECT role allows the user to create tables, views, database links, sequences, and synonyms. That is a lot more power than the name of the role implies! If you only want a user to be able to log in to the database, but not create any objects, you should grant the **create session** privilege instead of the CONNECT role. We feel even more strongly about not assigning the DBA role to anyone who does not warrant having total control over your database.

Now, to see the privileges that have been granted to JAMES and the roles he has been granted, you can run the following:

```
select b.Grantee, b.Privilege
  from DBA_ROLE_PRIVS a, DBA_SYS_PRIVS b
 where a.Grantee=b.Grantee and a.Grantee='JAMES'
 union
select b.Grantee, b.Privilege
  from DBA_ROLE_PRIVS a, DBA_SYS_PRIVS b
 where a.Granted_Role=b.Grantee and a.Grantee='JAMES'
/
```

```
GRANTEE                  PRIVILEGE
------------------------ ---------------------------------------
CONNECT                  ALTER SESSION
CONNECT                  CREATE CLUSTER
CONNECT                  CREATE DATABASE LINK
CONNECT                  CREATE SEQUENCE
CONNECT                  CREATE SESSION
CONNECT                  CREATE SYNONYM
CONNECT                  CREATE TABLE
CONNECT                  CREATE VIEW
JAMES                    UNLIMITED TABLESPACE
RESOURCE                 CREATE CLUSTER
RESOURCE                 CREATE PROCEDURE
RESOURCE                 CREATE OPERATOR
RESOURCE                 CREATE INDEXTYPE
RESOURCE                 CREATE SEQUENCE
RESOURCE                 CREATE TABLE
RESOURCE                 CREATE TRIGGER
RESOURCE                 CREATE TYPE
TESTROLE                 CREATE ANY TABLE
```

That's better! The union of the two separate queries is necessary because you are trying to extract not just the privileges granted directly to JAMES but also the privileges granted to the roles he has been granted. This script will work only for the user and the roles that user has been directly granted. If any of the roles granted to the user have also had roles granted to them, the privileges from those roles will not appear in this listing. Huh? What does that really mean? Well, earlier, we said that a role can be assigned to another role. We used the example of the CLERK role being assigned to the MANAGER role. If JAMES is now granted the MANAGER role and the script is run, the privileges that the CLERK role contains will not show up in the listing because this script will not show the privileges of a role granted to a role. To find those privileges, you must run the script again and substitute one of the role names for JAMES.

There is something interesting in the output of this script though. While in older versions of Oracle the CONNECT privilege only allowed the user to connect to the database, it now gives the user privileges to create objects. So JAMES inherits the ability to create tables from both the CONNECT and RESOURCE roles. Of course, if JAMES does not have the RESOURCE role and its explicit grant of **unlimited tablespace**, he will not be able to create any tables unless he also has an allocation of quota on a tablespace in which his table will reside.

If you look closely, you'll see a privilege is "missing." Which one is it? Well, CONNECT and RESOURCE both give you the ability to create a table, but what about indexes? The **create table** privilege implicitly gives users the ability to create an index on any table they create, so it does not have to be explicitly granted. To create an index on a table in someone else's schema, you would need to have the **create any index** privilege granted.

DBA_TS_QUOTAS

The DBA_TS_QUOTAS view, described in Table 5-7, gives you information about each tablespace and the users that have the ability to allocate space within that tablespace.

We've talked a little about quota on tablespaces. Now it's time to explain what that really means. What is quota? It's the amount of physical space within a tablespace that a user can allocate for objects.

When you create a user, you define the default tablespace for that user. Unless you also assign quota on that tablespace to a user, she cannot create objects in the tablespace. You can also assign quota on tablespaces that are not the default tablespace for that user.

The columns Max_Bytes and Max_Blocks indicate the maximum amount of space the user can allocate in the tablespace. Bytes and Blocks are the already allocated space. Both Blocks and Max_Blocks are in Oracle blocks. A value of –1 in Max_Bytes and Max_Blocks means there is no limit to the space the user can allocate (up to the total available space in the tablespace).

Let's look at a couple of examples. In the first, you are going to see only what the quotas are for the various users in your database.

```
select Username, Tablespace_Name, Max_Bytes
  from DBA_TS_QUOTAS;

USERNAME   TABLESPACE_NAME MAX_BYTES
---------- --------------- ---------
QC_USER    USER_DATA         1048576
MY_SCHEMA  USER_DATA              -1
RACHEL     TESTTBS           2097152
JAMES      USER_DATA         2097152
```

Column	Description
TABLESPACE_NAME	Tablespace name
USERNAME	User with resource rights on the tablespace
BYTES	Number of bytes charged to the user
MAX_BYTES	User's quota in bytes, or –1 if no limit
BLOCKS	Number of Oracle blocks charged to the user
MAX_BLOCKS	User's quota in Oracle blocks, or –1 if no limit

TABLE 5-7. *DBA_TS_QUOTAS View*

Only one user can allocate as much space as is available in the tablespace. The others all have limits. Wait a minute. Doesn't JAMES have **unlimited tablespace**? Why does he show up in this list with a limit? JAMES has the ability to override any quota assignment because he has **unlimited tablespace**, but he will still show up in this list if he has been granted any quota on a specific tablespace. In other words, he has been granted quota on the USER_DATA tablespace but will actually be able to create objects beyond the amount of space that he's been given because the **unlimited tablespace** privilege will override the quota specified.

In the second example, we're going to use both the DBA_TS_QUOTAS view as well as the DBA_USERS view to find all the users who have quota on a tablespace that is not their default tablespace and see how much of that quota they've already used.

```
select a.Username, Tablespace_Name, Max_Bytes, Bytes
  from DBA_TS_QUOTAS a
 where Tablespace_Name not in (select Default_Tablespace
                                 from DBA_USERS b
                                where b.Username = a.Username)
/

USERNAME   TABLESPACE_NAME MAX_BYTES     BYTES
---------- --------------- --------- ---------
RACHEL     TESTTBS           2097152   2048000
```

It seems that RACHEL has quota of 2M on the tablespace TESTTBS and has already used 2,048,000 bytes of that quota. If she tries to allocate more than 49,152 bytes more in the TESTTBS tablespace, she will get an error. You can use this view to see who is using up the space within your tablespaces.

DBA_TAB_PRIVS

The DBA_TAB_PRIVS view, described in Table 5-8, gives you information on all grants on all objects in the database.

The DBA_TAB_PRIVS view sounds like it has information on the table privileges, right? Well, in this case, the "TAB" is a bit misleading, since this view actually contains access information on all objects in the database. What is an object? A simple answer is that an object is anything that a user can own. We've already seen the DBA_OBJECTS view in Chapter 3 and discussed how you can use it. Although you can grant privileges on most objects, there are several exceptions. Indexes, triggers, and synonyms are considered objects, but they are not accessible in and of themselves. If you are granted access to a table, you automatically have access to the indexes and triggers on that table. Oracle will execute a trigger if it applies to the action you are taking on the table, and will modify or access an index on that table if necessary. A synonym is just an alias and, as such, requires no privileges to use it.

Column	Description
GRANTEE	User to whom access was granted
OWNER	Owner of the object
TABLE_NAME	Name of the object
GRANTOR	Name of the user who performed the grant
PRIVILEGE	Table privilege
GRANTABLE	Privilege is grantable
HIERARCHY	Privilege is with hierarchy option

TABLE 5-8. *DBA_TAB_PRIVS*

As newer versions of Oracle are released, new types of objects may be added to the database. Once again, we stress that with each new release, you should read through the documentation and, if possible, build a test database to try things out. As an example, with Oracle9i, you can create a subview of a view, and the Hierarchy column indicates if the privilege is granted to every object within the view hierarchy.

The column Grantee refers to the user who has been given this privilege. Owner is the owner of the object itself. Table_Name refers to the object name, while Grantor is the user actually doing the grant. Privilege is the access being granted, and Grantable determines whether the user who has received this privilege can, in turn, grant it to someone else. Because Oracle allows the owner of an object to give another user the right also to grant access, this view needs both the Owner and Grantor columns to show who granted the access.

So, now that you know what objects are and what the columns in the view refer to, what kind of access can you grant? If you perform a query for privileges available in a 9.0.1 database, you get the following:

```
select distinct Privilege
  from DBA_TAB_PRIVS;

PRIVILEGE
----------------------------------------
ALTER
DEBUG
DELETE
DEQUEUE
ENQUEUE
```

```
EXECUTE
INDEX
INSERT
ON COMMIT REFRESH
QUERY REWRITE
READ
REFERENCES
SELECT
UNDER
UPDATE
WRITE
```

You can grant 16 different privileges to a user in Oracle9.0.1. In fact, the **read** privilege is a new privilege as of Oracle8.0, and it refers to the ability to read an operating system–level directory and the files within it. **Write**, introduced in Oracle9i, complements the **read** privilege and gives you the ability to write to an operating system-level directory and files.

What do the other privileges mean? The **execute** privilege refers to packages, procedures, functions, and libraries and allows the user who has this privilege to do exactly that—execute the object. This allows you, as the DBA, to maintain tighter security on your database. Rather than grant access to all the tables and views in the database, you can grant access only to the user who will create the packages and procedures that access the tables, and then that user can grant **execute** on her stored program to everyone else. While a user is executing a stored program, she has the access privileges that the owner of the stored program has and can access the tables through the program, without needing access in her own right.

Select, **insert**, **update**, and **delete** are the Data Manipulation Language (DML) privileges that allow a user to actually retrieve or affect the data in the database. **Alter**, **index**, and **references** are Data Definition Language (DDL) privileges that allow the user to alter the structure of the table, create an index on that table, or create a referential constraint on the table.

On commit refresh applies to materialized views, while **query rewrite** applies to both materialized views and function-based indexes. For a complete listing and explanation of the system and object privileges, check the section on the **grant** command in the SQL Reference manual for your version of the database.

We've seen in the section on DBA_SYS_PRIVS that roles can be granted privileges and that users can inherit these privileges when they are granted a role. The same holds true for table or object access privileges.

One of the best ways to protect your database is to spend a little time figuring out what privileges each set of users really needs and then build and grant roles that provide that access and no more. While it's certainly fast, it's not a good idea to **grant all to public** on every object.

Now let's see how we can use this view, along with the DBA_OBJECTS view, to see what privileges have been granted by a user. The select statement below looks for all the privileges that have been granted on all tables owned by the user RACHEL.

```
select *
  from DBA_TAB_PRIVS
 where Table_Name in (select Object_Name
                        from DBA_OBJECTS
                       where Owner = 'RACHEL'
                         and Object_Type = 'TABLE')
 order by Table_Name, Grantee;


GRANTEE    OWNER      TABLE_NAME GRANTOR    PRIVILEGE  GRA
---------- ---------- ---------- ---------- ---------- ---
JAMES      RACHEL     TESTTAB    RACHEL     ALTER      NO
JAMES      RACHEL     TESTTAB    RACHEL     INSERT     NO
JAMES      RACHEL     TESTTAB    RACHEL     REFERENCES NO
JAMES      RACHEL     TESTTAB    RACHEL     UPDATE     NO
JAMES      RACHEL     TESTTAB    RACHEL     SELECT     NO
JAMES      RACHEL     TESTTAB    RACHEL     DELETE     NO
JAMES      RACHEL     TESTTAB    RACHEL     INDEX      NO
MY_SCHEMA  RACHEL     TESTTAB    QC_USER    SELECT     NO
QC_USER    RACHEL     TESTTAB    RACHEL     SELECT     YES
MLT        RACHEL     TESTTAB    RACHEL     INSERT     NO
```

If we look at the output of that select statement, we see that RACHEL has granted all privileges on the table to JAMES, but has only granted **insert** on the table to MLT. In addition, QC_USER has been granted **select** on the table, along with the ability to pass that privilege on. MY_SCHEMA has been granted the **select** privilege on TESTTAB by QC_USER, not by RACHEL.

Let's see what happens when RACHEL revokes the **select** privilege from QC_USER.

```
revoke select on TESTTAB from qc_user;

select *
  from DBA_TAB_PRIVS
 where Table_Name in (select Object_Name
                        from DBA_OBJECTS
                       where Owner = 'RACHEL'
                         and Object_Type = 'TABLE')
 order by Table_Name, Grantee;


GRANTEE    OWNER      TABLE_NAME GRANTOR    PRIVILEGE  GRA
---------- ---------- ---------- ---------- ---------- ---
JAMES      RACHEL     TESTTAB    RACHEL     ALTER      NO
```

```
JAMES       RACHEL      TESTTAB     RACHEL      DELETE      NO
JAMES       RACHEL      TESTTAB     RACHEL      INSERT      NO
JAMES       RACHEL      TESTTAB     RACHEL      UPDATE      NO
JAMES       RACHEL      TESTTAB     RACHEL      INDEX       NO
JAMES       RACHEL      TESTTAB     RACHEL      SELECT      NO
JAMES       RACHEL      TESTTAB     RACHEL      REFERENCES NO
MLT         RACHEL      TESTTAB     RACHEL      INSERT      NO
```

Gee. Not only did QC_USER lose the ability to select from TESTTAB, but so did MY_SCHEMA!

A very important point to remember about granting a privilege to a user **with grant option** is that if the owner of the table later revokes the privilege from the first user, any other user who has received the privilege from the user will lose the privilege. Is that clear enough? Let's just walk through a quick example to make sure, since this is a really important point to remember.

To set the stage, you have three users: A, B, and C. User A owns a table named MYTAB and grants user B **insert** and **update** privileges on MYTAB with grant option. User B then grants the **insert** privilege on MYTAB to user C. Later, user B leaves the project, and, without thinking about the impacts, user A revokes the **insert** and **update** privileges on MYTAB from user B. User C is now out of luck, because the **insert** privilege to MYTAB is also removed from user C.

DBA_SYNONYMS

What is a synonym, and why or when would you want to use one? A *synonym* is a mask for another object—a way of referring to the object with the name of your choosing. If you need to select from a table owned by someone else, you could write the select statement as

```
select * from <other_owner>.<table_name>;
```

Of course, that starts to get annoying after a while, and what do you do if the owner of the table changes? Finding and correcting all references to this table in your code is time consuming, and we can almost guarantee that you will miss at least one.

Okay, now that we've discouraged you, how can you avoid this problem? Oracle provides a construct called a synonym, which allows you to mask the real name and owner of an object and refer to it by a constant, even if the owner or name of the object changes. Synonyms can be *private*, available only to the owner of the synonym, or *public*, available to any user in the database. To create a synonym, you use the following SQL:

```
create [public] synonym <synonym_name>
       for <owner>.<object_name>[@<database_link>];
```

If you include the word "public," you must have the **create public synonym** privilege, or you will get an error. You only need to include the database link clause if the object you want to reference is not in the local database.

DBA_SYNONYMS lists all synonyms in the database. Table 5-9 shows the columns in this view and what the columns represent.

So, what information does Oracle store about a synonym? The DBA_SYNONYMS view contains the Owner of the synonym and the Synonym_Name. If a synonym is a public synonym, the Owner column will contain the value PUBLIC. The columns named Table_Owner and Table_Name are misleading, as you can have a synonym for any object that you can access. So you can create synonyms for procedures, functions, views, packages, as well as tables. The Db_Link column contains the name of the database link if the synonym refers to an object in a remote database.

How does Oracle decide whether to use the synonym or use an object you own yourself? Oracle first checks to see if you own an object with the name you've used. If you do, then that object is the one Oracle will use. If not, Oracle then checks to see if you have a private synonym with that name, and if you do, the object referenced by your private synonym is used. Finally, if neither of these is true, Oracle checks to see if there is a public synonym with that name and accesses the object referenced by the public synonym if it exists. Only if none of these is true do you get an error that the object does not exist.

How can you make use of this hierarchy? Let's suppose you have a copy of your production database in your development database. One of your programmers wants to test changes to a stored procedure. Other people are working and testing, so they need the original version of this stored procedure. If you've set up synonyms for everyone for all the objects or, if you use roles, you've set up public synonyms for the objects, then the application can be coded to reference only the name of the stored procedure. The programmer who is testing can create a private synonym pointing to his version of the stored procedure. Any test he makes will use his stored procedure, but anyone else working in the database will use the original version.

Column	Description
OWNER	Username of the owner of the synonym
SYNONYM_NAME	Name of the synonym
TABLE_OWNER	Owner of the object referenced by the synonym
TABLE_NAME	Name of the object referenced by the synonym
DB_LINK	Name of the database link referenced in a remote synonym

TABLE 5-9. *DBA_SYNONYMS View*

Let's use an example to make this a bit clearer. We'll start out assuming the following:

1. The application schema owner is PROD_OWNER.
2. PROD_OWNER has a stored procedure named VALIDATE_HOLIDAY.
3. JAMES has his own version of VALIDATE_HOLIDAY.
4. MARLENE needs to use JAMES's new version of VALIDATE_HOLIDAY in her own testing.

When you set up the application in the database, you ran the following SQL:

```
create public synonym VALIDATE_HOLIDAY
   for PROD_OWNER.VALIDATE_HOLIDAY;
```

If you then select from DBA_SYNONYMS and DBA_OBJECTS, you see

```
select *
  from DBA_SYNONYMS
 where Table_Name = 'VALIDATE_HOLIDAY'
/

OWNER      SYNONYM_NAME       TABLE_OWNER     TABLE_NAME         DB_LINK
---------- ------------------ --------------- ------------------ ----------
PUBLIC     VALIDATE_HOLIDAY   PROD_OWNER      VALIDATE_HOLIDAY

select Owner, Object_Name, Object_Type
  from DBA_OBJECTS
 where Object_Name = 'VALIDATE_HOLIDAY'
/

OWNER      OBJECT_NAME          OBJECT_TYPE
---------- -------------------- ---------------
PUBLIC     VALIDATE_HOLIDAY     SYNONYM
JAMES      VALIDATE_HOLIDAY     PROCEDURE
PROD_OWNER VALIDATE_HOLIDAY     PROCEDURE
```

Now let's see who sees what. The hierarchy says that if you own an object, you will see your version of it, even if there is a public synonym for it. So JAMES sees his version of the stored procedure. Since there is a public synonym available for the version owned by PROD_OWNER, MARLENE sees the version owned by PROD_OWNER.

How can MARLENE test with the version owned by JAMES? Well, she can make a copy of JAMES's version in her own schema, and then she will see her own version. But if JAMES makes changes to his version, he's going to have to remember to tell MARLENE, and she's going to have to make another copy each time. Hmm, that doesn't sound like a good thing. Instead, if you run the statement

```
create synonym MARLENE.VALIDATE_HOLIDAY
   for JAMES.VALIDATE_HOLIDAY;
```

to create a synonym for MARLENE that points to JAMES's version, based on the hierarchy that private synonyms are resolved before public ones, MARLENE will see JAMES's version. Of course, JAMES will also have to give MARLENE permission to execute his stored procedure, or she won't be able to use the procedure.

```
select *
  from DBA_SYNONYMS
 where Table_Name = 'VALIDATE_HOLIDAY'
/

OWNER      SYNONYM_NAME       TABLE_OWNER     TABLE_NAME         DB_LINK
---------- ------------------ --------------- ------------------ ----------
PUBLIC     VALIDATE_HOLIDAY   PROD_OWNER      VALIDATE_HOLIDAY
MARLENE    VALIDATE_HOLIDAY   JAMES           VALIDATE_HOLIDAY
```

DBA_VIEWS

A view is a mask laid over a table or set of tables to define or restrict the columns users see when they access the database. Views can be on single tables or on joins of multiple tables.

Think of that ever-popular horse costume people wear at parties. It's actually made of two parts, the front half filled by one person, the back by another. Yet when it is put together, you see a single picture, a whole. Views can be used to create a single, simpler picture of the tables in your database and to make ad hoc queries and general coding easier for the end users and programmers. You can also use the view to restrict access to a subset of the underlying table data. We'll show you some examples a little later in this section.

DBA_VIEWS contains the text of all views in the database. Table 5-10 shows the columns in this view and what the columns represent.

Oracle stores a view as a select statement. Views can be owned by anyone who has been given the **create view** privilege and can be named anything that Oracle will accept as a valid object name. The Owner and View_Name columns contain this information and make up the unique identifier for a view. The Text column contains the actual SQL statement that will be executed when the view is accessed.

Column	Description
OWNER	Owner of the view
VIEW_NAME	Name of the view
TEXT_LENGTH	Length of the view text
TEXT	View text
TYPE_TEXT_LENGTH	Length of the type clause of the object view
TYPE_TEXT	Type clause of the object view
OID_TEXT_LENGTH	Length of the WITH OBJECT OID clause of the object view
OID_TEXT	WITH OBJECT OID clause of the object view
VIEW_TYPE_OWNER	Owner of the type of the view if the view is an object view
VIEW_TYPE	Type of the view if the view is an object view
SUPERVIEW_NAME	Name of the superview, if the view is a subview

TABLE 5-10. *DBA_VIEWS View*

This column is stored as a LONG data type, so the Text_Length column contains the true size of the select statement in bytes. With Oracle8, users were given the ability to create user-defined object types, and the remaining columns in the DBA_VIEWS view contain information about views created with user-defined object types.

Why use views? Why not just let the programmers write the complicated queries wherever they need them? Well, remember that if the SQL statement being executed is identical to one already stored in the SGA, Oracle will not have to develop a new execution plan, which improves performance. But if the statement is even slightly different, with an extra space or a column capitalized or lowercase, Oracle sees it as a different statement and will have to reprocess it. For very complicated queries, it's easy to code the query slightly differently and have it reprocessed.

Also, we believe strongly in modular programming and in making everyone's life easier when working on an application. If that complicated query changes, it's much simpler to change it in only one place, the view definition, than it is to go and find every program that contains that query and fix them all. Plan ahead and look like a hero!

There are other reasons to use views, even on single tables. Let's look at the XYZ Company. They have decided to implement a new system that allows employees to update some of their own personnel information. You can now log on to the system and change the number of dependents you want to list for your tax withholdings or change your address. The table that contains that information has the following structure:

```
desc EMP_INFO

Name                               Null?    Type
------------------------------- -------- ----
EMPID                                       NUMBER
LAST_NAME                                   VARCHAR2(30)
FIRST_NAME                                  VARCHAR2(30)
MID_INIT                                    VARCHAR2(1)
ADDRESS1                                    VARCHAR2(30)
ADDRESS2                                    VARCHAR2(30)
ADDRESS3                                    VARCHAR2(30)
ZIPCODE                                     VARCHAR2(9)
SALARY                                      NUMBER(9,2)
DEPENDENTS                                  NUMBER(2)
MARITAL_STATUS                              VARCHAR2(1)
```

What are the problems you can see if you give the employees access to the table itself? Hmm, we wouldn't want to let employees change their salary, or see someone else's salary, and we wouldn't want to let anyone change information for any other employee. So, how do you prevent them from doing this? If you said, "Use a view," congratulations, you've been paying attention! You can create the following view, and grant select and update access on the view to the employees.

```
create view UPD_EMP_INFO
as
select Empid, Last_Name, First_Name, Mid_Init,
       Address1, Address2, Address3, Zipcode,
       Dependents, Marital_Status
  from Emp_Info
 where Empid=USER;
```

The only column missing from this view is the Salary column. Notice the where clause. Oracle has built-in functions that return system values to you. The USER function returns the Oracle userid of the session currently logged on. This view assumes that employees log on to the system using their employee ID. Grant **select** and **update** to this view to PUBLIC, create a public synonym, and you are now ready to allow the employees to update everything but their salary.

First, let's look at what is in the table; then we'll take a look at what the view returns when we log on and select from it. We're going to attempt to update some of the information as well.

```
select *
  from EMP_INFO;
/

EMPID  LAST_NAME       FIRST_N M ADDRESS1           ADDRESS2
ADDRESS3            ZIPCODE      SALARY DEPENDENTS M
------ --------------- ------- - ------------------ ------------------
------------------ --------- --------- ---------- -
  1234 Carmichael      Rachel    1010 All Star Way  New York NY
                    10000        100000          0 W
  2345 Theriault       Marlene L 222 Dream Street   Washington, DC
                    20000        150000          0 D
  3456 Viscusi         James     1234 Racing Avenue Philadelphia PA
                    30000        125000          0 M

connect 3456/3456
Connected.

select *
  from UPD_EMP_INFO;


EMPID  LAST_NAME  FIRST_NAME M ADDRESS1            ADDRESS2
ADDRESS3 ZIPCODE   DEPENDENTS M
------ ---------- ---------- - -------------------- --------------
-------- --------- ---------- -
  3456 Viscusi    James        1234 Racing Avenue   Philadelphia PA
       30000               0 M

update UPD_EMP_INFO
   set Dependents=4;

1 row updated.

select *
  from UPD_EMP_INFO;

 EMPID LAST_NAME  FIRST_NAME M ADDRESS1            ADDRESS2
ADDRESS3 ZIPCODE   DEPENDENTS M
------ ---------- ---------- - -------------------- --------------
-------- --------- ---------- -
  3456 Viscusi    James        1234 Racing Avenue   Philadelphia PA
       30000               4 M
```

James can only see part of his own information, and he can update it. What happens when he tries to select information about another employee or attempts to update his salary?

```
select *
  from UPD_EMP_INFO
 where Empid=1234;

no rows selected

update UPD_EMP_INFO set Salary=200000;
update UPD_EMP_INFO set Salary=200000
                        *
ERROR at line 1:
ORA-00904: invalid column name
```

Perfect! You've protected the information you want to protect and allowed the employee to update only the information you wanted.

We've shown you how and why to use a view for a single table. Now let's take a look at an example of using a view to join multiple tables.

```
create or replace view ORDER_REPORT
as
select
       L.Order_Number Order_Number,
       L.Last_Name||', '||L.First_Name Customer,
       L.Order_Status Order_Status,
       L.Billto_State,
       L.Shipto_State,
       P.Orig_Order_Date Orig_Order_Date,
       P.Payment_Type
  from PAYMENT_INFO P,
       PURCHASE_LOG L
 where P.Order_Number = L.Order_Number
/
```

In this view, you are joining two tables together, selecting information from both, and joining them on the Order_Number column in each table. Views cannot be optimized, but you can include hints to direct the optimizer in the select statements that make up the view. Let's see what gets stored in DBA_VIEWS when we create a view with a hint.

```
select Text
  from DBA_VIEWS
 where View_Name = 'ORDER_REPORT'
/

TEXT
-----------------------------------------------------
select /*+ FIRST_ROWS */
       L.Order_Number Order_Number,
       L.Last_Name||', '||L.First_Name Customer,
```

```
       L.Order_Status Order_Status,
       L.Billto_State,
       L.Shipto_State,
       P.Orig_Order_Date Orig_Order_Date,
       P.Payment_Type
  from PAYMENT_INFO P,
       PURCHASE_LOG L
 where P.Order_Number = L.Order_Number
```

Looks familiar, doesn't it? Oracle will store the SQL statement that will be executed when you query the view. Now, since all the DBA_ views *are* views, they should also be in the DBA_VIEWS table, right? Let's see if we can find the underlying SQL statement for the DBA_VIEWS view itself.

```
select Text
  from DBA_VIEWS
 where View_Name='DBA_VIEWS'
/

TEXT
--------------------------------------------------------------------------
select u.name, o.name, v.textlength, v.text, t.typetextlength, t.typetext,
       t.oidtextlength, t.oidtext, t.typeowner, t.typename
from sys.obj$ o, sys.view$ v, sys.user$ u, sys.typed_view$ t
where o.obj# = v.obj#
  and o.obj# = t.obj#(+)
  and o.owner# = u.user#
```

Isn't it easier to type **select * from DBA_VIEWS** than all of the above? As we said, using views to hide multiple table joins makes life easier on your programmers and end users, and especially on you!

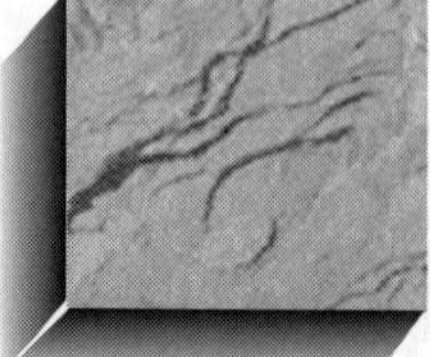

CHAPTER 6

How to Tune the Database

In Chapters 3, 4, and 5, you learned about the Oracle data dictionary views called the DBA_ views and the dynamic V$ (pronounced "Vee dollar") views. To review just a bit, the DBA_ views help you to monitor the contents of the database and the locations of objects, while the V$ views help you evaluate how well your database is performing.

In this chapter, you will learn about the views that Oracle has provided to help you see your database statistics—both the overall statistics and, more specifically, its performance. In Chapters 12 and 13, we'll tell you more about performance tuning and the Oracle-supplied tuning utility called STATSPACK. For now, we'll concentrate on telling you about the views that you can use to evaluate your database performance. Our goal is to help you understand the underlying views so that you know where to look for performance information. Remember that the DBA _ views are referred to by Oracle documentation as "Static Data Dictionary" views, while the V$ views are referred to as "Dynamic Performance" views because they record real-time values that show the current state of the database. Within the Oracle documentation, you'll see three different kinds of V$ views referenced: current state views, counter/accumulator views, and information views. The current state views give you a picture of what is going on within your system at the moment that you gather the statistics. As the name implies, the counter/accumulator views provide a look into how many times a specific event or action has occurred, while the informational views are less volatile and do not need to be monitored as often as the other views.

V$ views can provide you with the following information:

- Insights into areas of database contention
- Amounts of data being read or written to or from disks
- Statistical information, such as the last time a datafile header was changed or the summary information for the SGA
- Values used for database recovery

There are some columns in a few of the V$ views that will not be populated with values unless the parameter **timed_statistics** is set equal to TRUE in the initialization parameter file. For the majority of operating systems, there is little performance impact in setting this parameter to TRUE, and in Oracle9i, the value is set to TRUE by default. You can also change **timed_statistics** dynamically by using the **alter system** command. The database does not have to be shut down and restarted. This is useful if you only want to have **timed_statistics** active for short periods of time.

As we've said before, be sure to check the documentation that comes with each new Oracle RDBMS release for changes between versions.

Instance-Level Dynamic V$ Views Used for Tuning

When you decide to watch television, you can choose which program you want to watch, but you have no direct control over what programs are available for viewing. In the same vein, there are V$ views that you influence and others that you can't. In Chapter 4, you learned about the general information, instance-level views—the ones that are important but over which you have little noticeable effect. In this chapter, you will learn about the views Oracle has provided to help you see activity in the database that you can influence.

We are going to examine these instance-level views extensively. As we mentioned earlier, there are session-level counterparts to some of the V$ views. In the case where a session-level counterpart exists, we'll point it out and, in some cases, explain it as well.

Just as a coach monitors his ball team and has the players modify their actions to help improve how they play, you can use some of the V$ views to monitor your database to help give you insights into how to improve your database's performance.

In almost every case, poor database performance centers around the fact that there is some form of contention for resources on your system. Poor performance can almost always be tracked back to a process waiting for a resource that another process is using. The trick is to determine what resource is being waited for and see if you can find a way to eliminate contention for it. This is not always easy to do, but we'll try to help by showing you the areas you can monitor and suggesting actions you can take to help eliminate contentions on your system. Unfortunately, you can never totally eliminate contention from your system. Therefore, we recommend that you establish tuning goals and work toward accomplishing those goals. In that way, you'll know when to stop tuning and go on to other interesting tasks.

In order for you to use the V$ views, you will need some background knowledge about the structures you are looking at. Table 6-1 shows the views presented in this chapter. We have placed a notation after the view to show you whether the view is a current state (CS), counter/accumulator (C/A), or informational (I) view.

V$FILESTAT

The V$FILESTAT view provides information about activity on each file in the database. The columns are shown in Table 6-2. All columns whose names end in

View	Description
V$FILESTAT (C/A)	Lists the information on file read/write statistics
V$LATCH (C/A)	Lists statistics for nonparent latches and summary statistics for parent latches
V$LIBRARYCACHE (C/A)	Contains statistics about library cache performance and activity
V$LOCK (CS)	Lists the locks currently held by the Oracle server and outstanding requests for a lock or latch
V$LOCKED_OBJECT (CS)	Lists all locks acquired by every transaction on the system
V$PROCESS (I)	Contains information about the currently active processes
V$ROLLSTAT (C/A)	Lists the names of all online rollback segments
V$ROLLNAME (I)	Lists the rollback segment number and its corresponding name
V$ROWCACHE (C/A)	Shows statistics for data dictionary activity
V$SESSION (CS)	Contains information about each individual session within the database
V$SGASTAT (I)	Contains detailed information on the system global area
V$SYSSTAT (C/A)	Contains basic instance statistics
V$SYSTEM_EVENT (C/A)	Contains information on total waits for an event
V$UNDOSTAT (C/A)	Contains information about undo space usage, transaction concurrency, and query length
V$WAITSTAT (C/A)	Lists block contention statistics. Values are updated for this only when **timed_statistics** are enabled through the initialization parameter file.

TABLE 6-1. *Instance-Level V$ Views Used for Database Tuning*

TIM or TM will contain a zero if you have not set **timed_statistics** to TRUE in your initialization parameter file.

Column	Description
FILE#	Number of the file
PHYRDS	Number of physical reads done
PHYWRTS	Number of times DBWR is required to write
PHYBLKRD	Number of physical blocks read
PHYBLKWRT	Number of blocks written to disk; this may be the same as PHYWRTS if all writes are single blocks
SINGLEBLKRDS	Number of random I/O to this file
READTIM	Time (in hundredths of a second) spent doing reads
WRITETIM	Time (in hundredths of a second) spent doing writes
SINGLEBLKRDTIM	Total random I/O read time
AVGIOTIM	The average time (in hundredths of a second) spent on I/O
LSTIOTIM	The time (in hundredths of a second) spent doing the last I/O
MINIOTIM	The minimum time (in hundredths of a second) spent on a single I/O
MAXIOWTM	The maximum time (in hundredths of a second) spent doing a single write
MAXIORTM	The maximum time (in hundredths of a second) spent doing a single read

TABLE 6-2. *V$FILESTAT View*

This view is generally joined to the V$DBFILES view described in Chapter 3 as follows:

```
set pagesize 100;
set space 1
column pbr format 99999999 heading 'Physical|Blk Read'
column pbw format 999999 heading 'Physical|Blks Wrtn'
column pyr format 999999 heading 'Physical|Reads'
column readtim format 99999999 heading 'Read|Time'
column name format a38 heading 'DataFile Name'
column writetim format 99999999 heading 'Write|Time'
ttitle center 'Tablespace Report' skip 2
```

```
compute sum of f.Phyblkrd, f.Phyblkwrt on report
select fs.Name name,f.Phyblkrd pbr,f.Phyblkwrt pbw,f.Readtim,f.Writetim
  from V$FILESTAT f, V$DBFILE fs
 where f.File# = fs.File#
 order by fs.Name;

                              Tablespace Report

                                         Physical  Physical       Read    Write
DataFile Name                            Blk Read Blks Wrtn       Time     Time
---------------------------------------- --------- --------- --------- --------
/devora01/oradata/mydb/mydbev01.dbf        3064223     16382     49069    55495
/devora02/oradata/mydb/devtest01.dbf          1763         8        36       17
/qaora/oradata/mydb/pre_indexes01.dbf         1924        28       157       78
/qaora/oradata/mydb/pre_indexes02.dbf         7377      3368      2450     7204
/qaora/oradata/mydb/pre_sample_data01.dbf     1578         0        34        0
/qaora/oradata/mydb/pre_sample_data02.dbf    73340        51      2214      187
/qaora/oradata/mydb/pre_sample_data03.dbf     1784       695       270     1441
/qaora/oradata/mydb/des2000_01.dbf          215397         0      3341        0
/testora/oradata/mydb/rbs01.dbf                110    272553       133  1300607
/testora/oradata/mydb/system01.dbf          180180     30560      6716    83373
/testora/oradata/mydb/temp01.dbf                 0        18         0       83
/testora/oradata/mydb/tools01.dbf           104501     70036     13867   322179
/testora/oradata/mydb/users01.dbf           435678        31      6908       96
```

The output from this report shows the amount of activity on each datafile in the database. If there are several datafiles on the same disk with high read or write activity and performance is slow, you could move one or more of the datafiles to a different, less busy disk. The output above was obtained from a Unix system. If your output comes from a Windows system, file names may appear to be on different drives, but in reality, they could be on a partition of the same physical drive.

V$LATCH

At the back of one of the authors' houses is a fenced area with a lawn and a garden. The fence that surrounds the yard has a gate. The gate has a metal closure on it, commonly referred to as a latch. The latch on that gate helps to discourage people from coming into the garden to take any of the vegetables (except, of course, for the gardener, who always takes one or two tomatoes when he comes in to mow the grass). The latch on the gate is there to keep the gate shut and protect the garden, but people are periodically invited in to visit. While the gardener is bringing his (very large) lawn mower in and out of the garden, access to the garden is temporarily blocked. No one else can fit through the gate.

Latches in the database are used to prevent access to Oracle's internal memory structures while a process is accessing them. This action is necessary to ensure that the structure remains in a consistent state while it is being accessed. When a process needs to access an internal structure, it takes out a latch on that structure. Once a latch has been taken against a structure, like the lawn mower blocking the gate, no other process can interact with that structure until the current latch is released. Latches are generally held for a very brief amount of time, but if several processes are trying to access the same structure at the same time, contention will occur. Each process is contending for the same resource at the same time. Like the people we see waiting in line for refreshments at a movie theater, some processes will be willing to wait for the latch to become available, while others will be unwilling to wait and will go off to continue processing without having acquired what they initially came to get. Table 6-3 shows the columns that make up the V$LATCH view.

Column	Description
ADDR	Address of latch object
LATCH#	Latch number
LEVEL#	Latch level
NAME	Latch name
GETS	Number of times obtained a wait
MISSES	Number of times obtained a wait but failed on the first try
SLEEPS	Number of times slept when wanted a wait
IMMEDIATE_GETS	Number of times obtained without a wait
IMMEDIATE_MISSES	Number of times failed to get without a wait
WAITERS_WOKEN	How many times a wait was awakened
WAITS_HOLDING_LATCH	Number of waits while holding a different latch
SPIN_GETS	Gets that missed first try but succeeded on spin
SLEEP1	Waits that slept 1 time
SLEEP2	Waits that slept 2 times
SLEEP3	Waits that slept 3 times
SLEEP4	Waits that slept 4 times
SLEEP5	Waits that slept 5 times
SLEEP6	Waits that slept 6 times
SLEEP7	Waits that slept 7 times
SLEEP8	Waits that slept 8 times
SLEEP9	Waits that slept 9 times
SLEEP10	Waits that slept 10 times

TABLE 6-3. *V$LATCH View*

Column	Description
SLEEP11	Waits that slept 11 times
WAIT_TIME	Records the amount of time in milliseconds since the session began to wait for an event

TABLE 6-3. *V$LATCH View* (continued)

If the latch that is requested with a *willing-to-wait* state is not available, the requesting process will wait for a short time and try to obtain the latch again. The process will keep waiting and requesting over again until the latch becomes available and the process can obtain it. Each time a willing-to-wait latch request is successful, the Gets column value is incremented. If the process that is willing to wait does not get the latch on the initial attempt, the Misses column value is incremented. Once the process has made its initial request, the Sleeps column value will show how many times the process waited and requested the latch. Columns Sleep5 through Sleep11 contain no data in Oracle9i and are there for backward comptibility only.

When you look at the V$LATCH statistics, you want to look at both how often the latch has been requested and the ratio of misses/gets. You want to determine the percentage of waits that occurs due to spinning as well.

NOTE
Oracle tuning documentation recommends not to tune latches. When you see latch contention, look at the SGA area that is experiencing the contentious usage and work to tune it instead.

V$LIBRARYCACHE

When you walk into your local library (yep, just like Chapter 2, we're back in the library again!), you expect to find many different types of reading material. You'll see books, maps, newspapers, encyclopedias, and other reference materials, as well as videotapes, music CDs, and so forth. You can use the materials available in the library since they are there for everyone to share. Although they are all in one central building, the first time you go to get a specific book, it might take you a while to look up its location in the card or online catalog and locate the book on its shelf. Once you've found the book, you do not have to look up its location again or map your route to the shelf but can go straight to it if you want to use it again. Because you know where to look for it, you can access the book in question quickly.

Likewise, when a SQL statement is presented to Oracle for processing for the first time, Oracle must go through several steps to process the query. Since the beginning of version 7, SQL cursors can be shared; this means more than one process can execute the same SQL statement that is stored in memory. Note, however, that the Oracle parser must see the code as identical before it will reuse code stored in the library cache. Once Oracle has processed the statement and stored its execution plan for reuse, if the same statement is presented again, Oracle can execute the statement with much less processing. In other words, Oracle knows where the book is on the shelf and can go directly to it. SQL and PL/SQL statements are stored in the library cache. Remember, though, that the statement truly must be identical, down to spaces and upper- and lowercase letters, for Oracle to reuse it. Watch out for applications that use dynamic SQL. It's possible for an identical SQL statement to be reparsed every time because the statement is dynamically generated.

To aid in tuning the library cache, Oracle supplies the V$LIBRARYCACHE view. Table 6-4 shows the columns for this view.

Column	Description
NAMESPACE	The library cache namespace
GETS	The number of times a lock was requested for objects of this namespace
GETHITS	The number of times an object's handle was found in memory
GETHITRATIO	The ratio of GETHITS to GETS
PINS	The number of times a PIN was requested for objects of this namespace
PINHITS	The number of times all of the metadata pieces of the library object were found in memory
PINHITRATIO	The ratio of PINHITS to PINS
RELOADS	Any PIN of an object that is not the first PIN performed since the object handle was created, and which requires loading the object from disk
INVALIDATIONS	The total number of times objects in this namespace were marked invalid because a dependent object was modified
DLM_LOCK_REQUESTS	The number of GET requests lock instance locks

TABLE 6-4. *V$LIBRARYCACHE View*

Column	Description
DLM_PIN_REQUESTS	The number of PIN requests lock instance locks
DLM_PIN_RELEASES	The number of release requests PIN instance locks
DLM_INVALIDATION_REQUESTS	The number of GET requests for invalidation instance locks
DLM_INVALIDATIONS	The number of invalidation pings received from other instances

TABLE 6-4. *V$LIBRARYCACHE View* (continued)

To understand the values that the V$LIBRARYCACHE view is showing you, we must define some terms. *Gets* are the number of lookups for objects in the namespace. Each time a statement is presented to Oracle for execution, Oracle checks to see if the statement is already stored. That counts as one get. There are eight different types of items in the library cache for which statistics are kept: the SQL area, consisting of SQL statements and PL/SQL blocks; Table/Procedure; Body; Trigger; Index; Cluster; Object; and Pipe. Each row in the V$LIBRARYCACHE view reflects one of these item types, and the types are stored in the Namespace column. *Pins* reflect the number of executions for each of these areas. *Reloads* are the number of times statements had to be reparsed in order to be executed. If a statement was aged out of the cache, or an object referenced by the statements was invalidated (changed in some way), the statement must be reparsed to be reexecuted.

The V$SGASTAT view, described later in this chapter, can be used to show the way in which shared pool areas have been allocated. You can use this view to determine whether you have enough space allocated in the shared pool.

To see the values that pertain to performance in the V$LIBRARYCACHE view, you can use the following query:

```
column Namespace format a8
column Gets format 99999
column Pins format 999999
column Reloads format 99999
column Gethits format 9999999
select Namespace, Gets, Gethits, round((Gethitratio * 100),2) GetRatio,
       Pins, Pinhits, round((Pinhitratio * 100),2) PinRatio, Reloads relds
  from V$LIBRARYCACHE;
```

```
NAMESPAC   GETS   GETHITS  GETRATIO    PINS   PINHITS  PINRATIO  RELDS
-------- ------ --------- --------- ------- --------- --------- ------
SQL AREA   1414      1328     93.91    3824      3642     95.24      8
TABLE/PR    333       262     78.67     496       363     73.18      0
OCEDURE
BODY          4         2        50       4         2        50      0
TRIGGER       0         0       100       0         0       100      0
INDEX        29         0         0      29         0         0      0
CLUSTER     131       126     96.18     178       173     97.19      0
OBJECT        0         0       100       0         0       100      0
PIPE          0         0       100       0         0       100      0
```

The Gethitratio determines the percentage of parse calls that find a cursor to share. The value is derived from Gethits divided by Gets. This ratio should be in the high 90s. A lower Gethitratio indicates that there is room to tune the SQL code.

Now, let's look at reloads and pins. Reloads should never be more than 1 percent of pins. The ideal is to have zero reloads, but that's very difficult to achieve. Here's how to check the reloads to pins:

```
select sum(Pins) "Executions", sum(Reloads) "Cache Misses",
       sum(Reloads)/sum(Pins)
  from V$LIBRARYCACHE;

Executions Cache Misses SUM(RELOADS)/SUM(PINS)
---------- ------------ ----------------------
      8632            7              .00081094
```

If the Reloads to Pins ratio is greater than 1 percent, increase the initialization parameter **shared_pool_size**.

V$LOCK

There are locks everywhere we look. We use key locks for the doors in our houses, offices, and almost everywhere. We use combination locks with chains to protect our bicycles and padlocks to protect the contents of storage sheds. Different kinds of locks are everywhere we look, and the different types of locks offer different degrees of protection for the things we value. I might give you a copy of my house key so you can come in to water my plants while I am on vacation (thank you very much!), but I will probably not give you a copy of the key to my safe deposit box at my bank. Oracle uses the same locking concepts to protect your data in the database.

Earlier, we talked about the different types of latches in an Oracle system. Now, we're talking about locks. What's the difference? Well, a latch is a form of low-level locking used to protect a memory structure, while a lock is normally used to protect a data structure. A latch is usually held for a very brief amount of time, while a lock can be held continuously until a commit or rollback takes place.

The Oracle server automatically manages locks. Oracle's locking policy is to try to apply the least restrictive lock needed to protect data consistency while allowing the highest amount of data availability to all processes. If you are performing a query, Oracle will not place a lock on the structure you are looking at. If, however, you are inserting, updating, or deleting data, Oracle will use a lock to protect the structure from anyone else trying to do something to it while you're manipulating it.

There are several different kinds of locks. You can monitor them using the V$LOCK view. Let's look at the composition of the V$LOCK view, as seen in Table 6-5.

Lock Levels

There are three levels at which a structure may be locked (shown with their type): at a single row level (TX), at the partition level (TM), or at the table level (TM). There are Data Manipulation Language (DML) locks used to protect data at either the row, partition, or table level and Data Dictionary Language (DDL) locks used to protect the dictionary definition of an object such as a table or view. There are internal locks

Column	Description
ADDR	Address of lock state object
KADDR	Address of lock
SID	Identifier for session holding or acquiring the lock
TYPE	Type of lock. (See the section "Number and Types of Locks" for system lock types.)
ID1	Lock identifier number 1 (depends on type)
ID2	Lock identifier number 2 (depends on type)
LMODE	Lock mode in which the session holds the lock: 0 None, 1 Null (NULL), 2 Row-S (SS), 3 Row-X (SX), 4 Share (S), 5 S/Row-X (SSX), 6 Exclusive (X)
REQUEST	Lock mode in which the process requests the lock: 0 None, 1 Null (NULL), 2 Row-S (SS), 3 Row-X (SX), 4 Share (S), 5 S/Row-X (SSX), 6 Exclusive (X)
CTIME	Time since current mode was granted
BLOCK	The lock is blocking another lock.

TABLE 6-5. *V$LOCK View*

and latches used to protect memory structures (as you saw earlier). These locks are entirely automatic. There are distributed locks that are used to ensure that structures remain consistent across more than one instance. These are *instance-level* rather than transaction-level locks. And there are parallel cache management (PCM) locks used with shared server configurations. Used to lock one or more data blocks in the SGA, these locks are held at the memory, data-block level. They do not lock rows.

A lock can be either exclusive or shared. Queries are always allowed on a structure, even a locked one, but other activities may be prevented. In exclusive mode, the data structure remains locked, preventing the resource from being shared with any other transaction until the lock is released. If you are performing an update of a row in a table, no one else will be able to modify that specific row until you have issued either a rollback or commit command. Until you commit your change, Oracle will present a consistent view of that row as it appeared before you started to change it.

With shared locks, more than one transaction can hold a shared lock on a structure at the same time since shared locks are set at the table level for DML transactions. You issue the statement:

```
update EMPLOYEE
   set Salary = Salary * 2
 where Employee_Num = 123456;
```

Another user can issue the following statement, and you will both have a shared lock on the table, and will each have an exclusive lock on the individual row you are updating.

```
update EMPLOYEE
   set Salary = Salary * 2
 where Employee_Num = 654321;
```

Number and Types of Locks

As we said earlier in this section, there are three different levels of DML locks. A table-level lock (TM type) is set for any DML statement that modifies a table, such as **insert**, **update**, **delete**, **select...for update**, and **lock table**. The table lock protects the structure of the table from any DDL statement that would conflict with the transaction. A row-level lock (TX type) is automatically acquired for each row that is modified by a statement using **insert**, **update**, **delete**, and **select...for update**. This lock keeps anyone else from modifying the same row at the same time, as we illustrated.

A DML transaction will get at least two locks: a shared table lock (TM type) and an exclusive row-level lock (TX type). Internally, when a transaction goes to modify a row, Oracle turns a byte on in the row header pointing to the internal transaction lock (ITL) slot used by that transaction. At the row level, a lock mode can only be exclusive. If you are dealing with a partition table, the transaction will acquire a table partition lock for each required partition as well as a table lock.

The Enqueue Mechanism

Oracle maintains all locks as *enqueues.* The enqueue mechanism keeps track of users waiting for locks that are held by others and the lock mode these users require. The enqueue mechanism also keeps track of the order in which users requested the locks. Let's say there are three users (Marlene, Rachel, and Jim, in that order) who want to update the same row of a table at the same time. All three users will get the shared table lock, but only Marlene gets the row lock because Marlene made the first request. The table-locking mechanism keeps track of who holds the row lock and who is waiting for it. The initialization parameter file parameters **dml_locks** and **enqueue_resources** control the number of locks available for an instance.

Table-Level Lock Modes

There are five basic table lock modes within an Oracle system. For DML transactions, some lock modes are automatically assigned. Each lock mode has a different level of restrictiveness that will be used to determine the modes on the table that other transactions can obtain. Table 6-6 shows the five different lock modes. In some entries, you will see two different values used in parenthesis. This is because different Oracle documentation shows the notations for lock mode differently. We wanted you to see both versions.

Mode	Description
Row exclusive (RX or SX)	The least restrictive of the locks. Allows other transactions to **insert**, **update**, **delete**, or lock other rows in the same table. Prohibits **lock table...in exclusive mode**.
Row share (RS or SS)	Allows other transactions to **insert**, **update**, **delete**, or lock other rows in the same table. Prohibits **lock table** commands with the following options: **in share mode**, **in exclusive mode**, and **in share exclusive mode**.
Share (S)	Explicitly acquired through the **lock table...in...mode** command. Allows other transactions only to **select...for update**. Prohibits other modifications on the table.

TABLE 6-6. *Table-Level Lock Types*

Mode	Description
Share row exclusive (SRX or SSX)	Explicitly acquired; more restrictive than a share lock
Exclusive (X)	The most restrictive lock. Only a single transaction can lock a table in X mode.

TABLE 6-6. *Table-Level Lock Types* (continued)

Here's a sample output from V$LOCK:

```
column Sid format 99999
column Block format 9999999
select *
  from V$LOCK;

ADDR     KADDR      SID TY       ID1    ID2  LMODE   REQUEST     CTIME   BLOCK
-------- -------- ----- -- --------- ------ ------ --------- --------- -------
8C13807C 8C13808C     6 TS 1.342E+09      0      3         0    436120       0
8C1380B0 8C1380C0     4 RT         1      0      6         0    436476       0
8C1380E4 8C1380F4     2 MR        21      0      4         0    436476       0
8C138118 8C138128     2 MR        20      0      4         0    436476       0
8C13814C 8C13815C     2 MR        15      0      4         0    436476       0
8C138180 8C138190     2 MR        14      0      4         0    436476       0
8C138388 8C138398     2 MR         3      0      4         0    436476       0
8C1383BC 8C1383CC     2 MR         2      0      4         0    436476       0
8C1383F0 8C138400     2 MR         1      0      4         0    436476       0
0A0AD970 0A0ADA44    13 TX    196625    181      6         0         9       0
04CE2008 04CE201C    13 TM     10922      0      3         0         9       0
8B08F100 8B08F114    20 TM      2144      0      3         0         1       0
8B08F16C 8B08F180    20 TM      2337      0      3         0         1       0
00860230 008602E0    20 TX    196624 135448      6         0         1       0
8C138458 8C138468    20 TM      2204      0      4         0         1       0
8B08F1D8 8B08F1EC    20 TM      2184      0      3         0         1       0
```

Let's see. We have five different types of locks displayed in this listing: TS, RT, MR, TM, and TX. The TS entry, which is a system lock, is a temporary segment enqueue lock. The RT is also a system lock and is a redo thread global enqueue. The MRs are all system media recovery locks, which are okay because this listing was taken while a database recovery was taking place. Finally, Sid numbers 13 and 20 are users using DML enqueue and transaction enqueue locks. For the user locks with TX mode, the ID1 column will show the rollback segment number and slot number, while for TM mode, the same column will show the Object_Id being modified. Pretty interesting! A quick way to detect whether one lock is blocking another is to check for a "1" in the block column.

DDL Locks

When you issue a statement like **drop table** or **alter table**, you are affecting the underlying structure of the table, and therefore, an exclusive DDL lock will be taken out during the period of time that your statement is processing. There are two other types of DDL locks: shared DDL locks used in **create procedure** and **audit** statements, and breakable parse locks, which are held on each object in the SQL shared pool. DDL locks rarely cause contention on the system because they are held and released so quickly. However, you should be aware that DDL locks exist, and for exclusive locks (used for **create**, **alter**, and **drop** commands), a user cannot get an exclusive lock on a table if any other user holds any level of lock. Thus, if a user has issued a statement that has not been committed or rolled back, and you go to alter that table, your command will fail.

Detecting Lock Contention

In the section above we saw the output from a **select...from** for the V$LOCK view. Once you have the table number from this listing, you can determine the table name by using the V$LOCK view and the DBA_OBJECTS view discussed in Chapter 3. Running the following script, you can see the user and table names.

```
column Object_Name format a20
column Owner format a10
select Owner, Object_Id, Object_Name, Object_Type, V$LOCK.Type
  from DBA_OBJECTS, V$LOCK
 where Id1=Object_Id;

OWNER      OBJECT_ID OBJECT_NAME          OBJECT_TYPE        TY
---------- --------- -------------------- ------------------ --
SYS               11 I_USER#              INDEX              MR
SYS               10 C_USER#              CLUSTER            MR
SYS                9 I_FILE#_BLOCK#       INDEX              MR
SYS                8 C_FILE#_BLOCK#       CLUSTER            MR
SYS                7 I_TS#                INDEX              MR
SYS                6 C_TS#                CLUSTER            MR
SYS                5 CLU$                 TABLE              MR
SYS                4 TAB$                 TABLE              MR
SYS                3 I_OBJ#               INDEX              MR
SYS                2 C_OBJ#               CLUSTER            MR
SYS               12 FET$                 TABLE              MR
RACHEL         10922 EMPLOYEE             TABLE              TM
```

There is another, Oracle-provided way that you can check for lock contention on your system. If you suspect that lock contention is a problem, you can use the script utllockt.sql in the ORACLE_HOME/rdbms/admin directory and run it as SYSTEM. The script creates a list in tree order of the session holding a lock and the users who are waiting for that lock. From the comments section of the script, here is a sample of the script output:

```
WAITING_SESSION   TYPE MODE REQUESTED    MODE HELD          LOCK ID1 LOCK ID2
----------------- ---- ----------------- ----------------- -------- --------
8                 NONE None              None              0        0
   9              TX   Share (S)         Exclusive (X)     65547    16
      7           RW   Exclusive (X)     S/Row-X (SSX)     33554440 2
      10          RW   Exclusive (X)     S/Row-X (SSX)     33554440 2
```

You should run ORACLE_HOME/rdbms/admin/catblock.sql prior to running the utllockt.sql script since catblock.sql is not called from catproc.sql.

There are some problems with this script. For one thing, you can't easily tell who is holding the lock and blocking others. Also, if you look at the script for utllockt.sql, you will see that a table is created each time the script is run and then dropped at the end of the script. Since locks are taken out when you create a table, the script may get caught in the lock contention problem and add to it. To solve this problem, you can create the table and modify the utllockt.sql script so it will not create or drop this table when the script is run. You will, instead, need to change the code in the script to truncate the table before the next insert is performed so that old data will be removed.

Well, that solves problem two. What about problem one—the fact that we can't tell who owns the process that is blocking? There is an easy way to solve this problem. You can use the V$LOCKED_OBJECT view, which we are going to talk about next.

V$LOCKED_OBJECT

In the previous section, we looked at locks and the V$LOCK view. To get more information about the processes that are holding locks, Oracle has provided a view called V$LOCKED_OBJECTS. This view has remained unchanged from Oracle7.3 forward. Table 6-7 shows the columns for V$LOCKED_OBJECT.

The most valuable information is the Oracle_Username and the operating system username (Os_User_Name). The Locked_Mode tells us what type of lock is

Column	Description
XIDUSN	Undo segment number
XIDSLOT	Slot number

TABLE 6-7. *V$LOCKED_OBJECT View*

Column	Description
XIDSQN	Sequence number
OBJECT_ID	Object ID being locked
SESSION_ID	Session ID
ORACLE_USERNAME	Oracle username
OS_USER_NAME	OS username
PROCESS	OS process ID
LOCKED_MODE	Lock mode

TABLE 6-7. *V$LOCKED_OBJECT View* (continued)

being held currently or being requested. Let's run utllockt.sql and look at a locking situation on our system.

```
WAITING_SESSION      LOCK_TYPE         MODE_REQUESTED MODE_HELD      ID1     ID2
-------------------- ----------------- -------------- -------------- ------- ---
11                   None              None           None           0       0
   12                Transaction       Exclusive      Exclusive      196612 181
```

In this example, we've created a *deadlock* contention situation (which Oracle cleared out itself over time by killing off process 12, the requestor who caused the lock problem). A deadlock occurs when two or more users wait for data that is locked by each other. Oracle will kill the first server process that detects the deadlock, so you should always look for and fix code that can cause deadlocks.

Let's see what V$LOCKED_OBJECT shows under these circumstances.

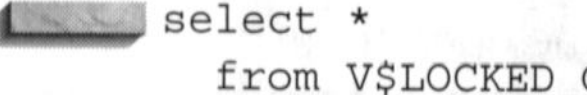

```
select *
  from V$LOCKED_OBJECT;

   XIDUSN    XIDSLOT     XIDSQN OBJECT_ID SESSION_ID ORACLE_USERNAM
--------- --------- --------- --------- ---------- -----------------
OS_USER_NAME                   PROCESS   LOCKED_MODE
------------------------------ --------- ----------
        3         4         0     19762         11 MARLENE
MYMACHINE-PC\marlene1          301:298          3

        0         0       181    196612         12 RACHEL
OTMACHINE-PC\rachel1           295:257          3
```

Looking back at the output from the utllockt.sql script in this section and comparing it to the output from this query, you can see that MARLENE has not acquired a lock yet, and RACHEL is holding an exclusive lock.

More importantly, if there is contention due to locking on your system, you now have the information you need to call the person who is holding the lock and ask her either to commit or rollback her session. As a last resort, you will need to kill the blocking session. You will need to determine both the Sid and the Serial# of the blocking process. You already have the Sid, but you still need the Serial#. To obtain the Serial#, you can query V$SESSION. Although we'll talk more about V$SESSION later, let's finish this conversation by performing the query to obtain the Sid and Serial# and kill off RACHEL. The query you need to execute to obtain the Sid and Serial# is

```
select Sid, Serial#, Username
  from V$SESSION
 where Username = 'RACHEL';

      SID   SERIAL# USERNAME
--------- --------- ------------------------------
       12        43 RACHEL
```

Because users can have multiple sessions in the database, verify that the SID is the same as the one you have from V$LOCKED_OBJECT. Here is the command you can use to kill a session:

```
REM alter system kill session 'Sid, Serial#';
REM
alter system kill session '12,43';
```

V$PROCESS

By itself, V$PROCESS provides some interesting information about each process that is active in an Oracle database. The columns that compose the V$PROCESS view are shown in Table 6-8.

NOTE
The TRACEID column is filled in if you set the initialization parameter TRACEFILE_IDENTIFIER or change it via the ***alter session set tracefile_identifier*** *command.*

Oracle9i enables you to dynamically tune the process global area and supplies three parameters for you to view the statistics for this area: PGA_USED_MEM,

Column	Description
ADDR	Address of process state object
PID	Oracle process identifier
SPID	Operating system process identifier
USERNAME	Operating system process username. Any Two-Task user coming across the network has -T appended to the username.
SERIAL#	Process serial number
TERMINAL	Operating system terminal identifier
PROGRAM	Program in progress
TRACEID	Enables easier identification of trace files
BACKGROUND	Value of 1 for a background process; NULL for a normal process
LATCHWAIT	Address of latch the process is waiting for; NULL if none
LATCHSPIN	Address of latch the process is being spun on; NULL if none
PGA_USED_MEM	PGA memory currently used by the process
PGA_ALLOC_MEM	PGA memory currently allocated to the process (includes free PGA memory that has not yet been returned to the system)
PGA_MAX_MEM	Maximum PGA memory ever allocated to the process

TABLE 6-8. *V$PROCESS View*

PGA_ALLOC_MEM, and PGA_MAX_MEM. You can use the parameters Pid, Spid, and Username to identify the process of interest and then look at the PGA values to help determine the amount of memory that the process is using.

Here are two queries that you can use to identify a specific process within the database and determine how much total memory is currently allocated, how much is in use, and the maximum amount of memory that has ever been allocated to the total group of processes:

```
select Pid, Spid, Username
  from V$PROCESS;

      PID SPID      USERNAME
--------- --------- ------------
        1
        2 110       SYSTEM
```

```
        3 237       SYSTEM
        4 163       SYSTEM
        5 85        SYSTEM
        6 44        SYSTEM
        7 189       SYSTEM
        8 255       SYSTEM
        9 271       SYSTEM

select sum(Pga_Used_Mem), sum (Pga_Alloc_Mem), sum (Pga_Max_Mem)
  from V$PROCESS;

SUM(PGA_USED_MEM) SUM(PGA_ALLOC_MEM) SUM(PGA_MAX_MEM)
----------------- ------------------ ----------------
          7570329           18726761         19009769
```

So, from the second output, we can see that the current amount of total memory being used by processes on our system is about 7.5 megabytes, while the total amount that's been allocated is almost 18 megabytes, with a total maximum allocation of about 19 megabytes. Therefore, we're currently using much less memory than we have allocated.

Is this a good situation or a bad one? Well, that depends on a great many variables. How many processes were active in the database at the time the statistics were measured? How many transactions were being processed? By evaluating the conditions within your database and the amount of processing that is going on when you look at the statistics, you can determine whether you are allocating too little, enough, or too much memory for each process.

V$SESSION

Remember we said at the beginning of this chapter that we would show you session-level views as seemed appropriate? Well, here comes one of those times. The V$PROCESS view, coupled with the V$SESSION view, can help you determine what's going on in the sessions in your database. Therefore, let's take a look at the V$SESSION view now.

Table 6-9 shows you more than you probably would ever want to know about each session on your system.

Column	Description
SADDR	Session address
SID	Session identifier

TABLE 6-9. *V$SESSION View*

Column	Description
SERIAL#	Session serial number. Used to identify uniquely a session's objects. Guarantees that session-level commands are applied to the correct session objects if the session ends and another session begins with the same session ID.
AUDSID	Auditing session ID
PADDR	Address of the process that owns this session
USER#	Oracle user identifier
USERNAME	Oracle username
COMMAND	Command in progress (last statement parsed)
OWNERID	The column contents are invalid if the value is 2147483644. Otherwise, this column contains the identifier of the user who owns the migratable session. For operations using Parallel Slaves, interpret this value as a four-byte value, the low-order two bytes of which represent the session number and the high-order bytes, the instance ID of the query coordinator.
TADDR	Address of transaction state object
LOCKWAIT	Address of lock waiting for; NULL if none
STATUS	Status of the session: ACTIVE (currently executing SQL), INACTIVE, KILLED (marked to be killed), CACHED (temporarily cached for use by Oracle*XA), SNIPED (session inactive, waiting on the client)
SERVER	Server type: DEDICATED, SHARED, PSEUDO, NONE
SCHEMA#	Schema user identifier
SCHEMANAME	Schema username
OSUSER	Operating system client username
PROCESS	Operating system client process ID
MACHINE	Operating system machine name
TERMINAL	Operating system terminal name
PROGRAM	Operating system program name

TABLE 6-9. *V$SESSION View* (continued)

Column	Description
TYPE	Session type
SQL_ADDRESS	Used with SQL_HASH_VALUE to identify the SQL statement currently being executed
SQL_HASH_VALUE	Used with SQL_ADDRESS to identify the SQL statement currently being executed
MODULE	Contains the name of the currently executing module as set by calling the DBMS_APPLICATION_INFO.SET_MODULE procedure
MODULE_HASH	The hash value of the above MODULE
ACTION	Contains the name of the currently executing action as set by calling the DBMS_APPLICATION_INFO.SET_ACTION procedure
ACTION_HASH	The hash value of the above action name
CLIENT_INFO	Information set by the DBMS_APPLICATION_INFO.SET_CLIENT_INFO procedure
FIXED_TABLE_SEQUENCE	This contains a number that increases every time the session completes a call to the database and there has been an intervening select from a dynamic performance table. This column can be used by performance monitors to monitor statistics in the database. Each time the performance monitor looks at the database, it only needs to look at sessions that are currently active or have a higher value in this column than the highest value that the performance monitor saw the last time. All the other sessions have been idle since the last time the performance monitor looked at the database.
ROW_WAIT_OBJ#	Object ID for the table containing the ROWID specified in ROW_WAIT_ROW#
ROW_WAIT_FILE#	Identifier for the datafile containing the ROWID specified in ROW_WAIT_ROW#. This column is valid only if the session is currently waiting for another transaction to commit and the value of ROW_WAIT_OBJ# is not -1.

TABLE 6-9. *V$SESSION View* (continued)

Column	Description
ROW_WAIT_BLOCK#	Identifier for the block containing the ROWID specified in ROW_WAIT_ROW#. This column is valid only if the session is currently waiting for another transaction to commit and the value of ROW_WAIT_OBJ# is not -1.
ROW_WAIT_ROW#	The current ROWID being locked. This column is valid only if the session is currently waiting for another transaction to commit and the value of ROW_WAIT_OBJ# is not -1.
LOGON_TIME	Time of logon
LAST_CALL_ET	The last call
PDML_STATUS	If ENABLED, the session is in a PARALLEL DML enabled mode. If DISABLED, PARALLEL DML enabled mode is not supported for the session. If FORCED, the session has been altered to force PARALLEL DML.
PDDL_STATUS	If ENABLED, the session is in a PARALLEL DDL enabled mode. If DISABLED, PARALLEL DDL enabled mode is not supported for the session. If FORCED, the session has been altered to force PARALLEL DDL.
PDML_ENABLED	This column has been replaced by PDML_STATUS. See above.
FAILOVER_TYPE	NONE if failover is disabled for this session, SESSION if client is able to failover its session following a disconnect, and SELECT if client is able to failover selects in progress as well
FAILOVER_METHOD	NONE if failover is disabled for this session, BASIC if client reconnects following a disconnect, PRECONNECT if the backup instance is able to support all connections from every instance that it is backup for
FAILED_OVER	TRUE if running in failover mode and have failed over, otherwise FALSE
PREV_SQL_ADDRESS	Used with PREV_HASH_VALUE to show the address of the previous SQL statement that was executed

TABLE 6-9. *V$SESSION View* (continued)

Column	Description
PREV_HASH_VALUE	Used with PREV_SQL_ADDRESS to show the address of the SQL statement that was previously executed
RESOURCE_CONSUMER_GROUP	Name of the session's current resource consumer group
PQ_STATUS	If ENABLED, the session is in a parallel query enabled mode. If DISABLED, parallel query enabled mode is not supported for the session. If FORCED, the session has been altered to force parallel query.
CURRENT_QUEUE_DURATION	Used to identify the amount of time in seconds that a session is waiting to become active. Used with the Active Session Pool directive in Resource Manager.
CLIENT_IDENTIFIER	Information set by the DBMS_APPLICATION_INFO.SET_CLIENT_INFO procedure

TABLE 6-9. *V$SESSION View* (continued)

Now, let's join V$SESSION with V$PROCESS and see what additional information you can obtain. We'll just look at a few specific sessions for this query, but you can remove the line **and Spid between 280 and 320** to view all of the session information for your database.

```
set linesize 80
set pagesize 999
column Username heading "Oracle Uname" format a12
column Osuser heading "Rmt Username" format a20 wrap
column Process heading "Rmt PID"
column Machine heading "Rmt System" format a18
column Program heading "Remote Program" format a20
column Spid heading "Local PID"
column Sid format 99999
column Serial# format 99999
select b.Username, b.Osuser, b.Process, b.Machine, a.Spid, b.Program,
       b.Sid, b.Serial#
  from V$PROCESS a,V$SESSION b
 where a.Addr = b.Paddr
   and Spid between 280 and 320
/
```

```
Oracle Uname Rmt Username          Rmt PID   Rmt System         Local PID
------------ -------------------- --------- ------------------ ---------
Remote Program        SID SERIAL#
-------------------- ------ -------
RACHEL       MYSYSTEM\myuseracct  310:314   MYNET1\MYSYSTEM    316
SQLPLUSW.EXE               9    1602
MARLENE      MYSYSTEM\myuseracct  317:133   MYNET1\MYSYSTEM    300
SQLPLUSW.EXE              11    1398
JAMES        MYSYSTEM\myuseracct  299:278   MYNET1\MYSYSTEM    282
SQLPLUSW.EXE              13    1563
```

If you want to shut down your database normally (not using the **immediate** or **abort** option), you can use the above query to gain the information you need to remove active sessions other than the detached processes and your own session from the database. Armed with this information, you can contact the people who are active in your database, issue a **kill** command from the database level, and also be able to kill the process at the operating system level should you need to. (Sometimes, just killing a session does not automatically stop the associated process at the operating system level, and you must interactively kill the OS process as well.)

We talked about lock contention earlier in the V$LOCK section. V$SESSION provides information on the row and table participating in a lock contention. Let's see how. In this example, we've created a lock contention situation. You can use the following query to determine the Owner and Object_Name by joining the V$SESSION view with the DBA_OBJECTS view described earlier in this book. Here's the query you can use:

```
column Object_Name format a20
column Object_Type format a10
column Owner format a15
select Row_Wait_Obj# obj#, Row_Wait_File# file#, Row_Wait_Block# block#,
       Row_Wait_Row# row#, Sid, Object_Name, Owner, Object_Type
  from V$SESSION, DBA_OBJECTS
 where Row_Wait_Obj# = Object_Id
   and Row_Wait_Obj# > 0;

OBJ#       FILE#      BLOCK#     ROW#       SID        OBJECT_NAME
---------- ---------- ---------- ---------- ---------- ---------------
OWNER      OBJECT_TYP
---------- ----------
    10922          2        263          0         12 EMPLOYEE
RACHEL     TABLE
```

The Row_Wait_Obj# is the object number in the database that uniquely identifies the table (in this case) where contention is occurring. You can easily see who owns the table and that it is, indeed, a table.

We'll leave the other contents of the V$SESSION view as an exercise for you to explore yourself.

V$ROLLSTAT

As we said in Chapter 4, rollback segments are used to store undo or before-change information. If a transaction must be rolled back to its content before the change, the information stored in the rollback segment will be used for this purpose. Transactions are assigned to rollback segments in a circular manner, and the faster a user acquires the rollback header and rollback data block, the better. Table 6-10 shows the columns of the V$ROLLSTAT view.

Column	Description
USN	Rollback segment number
EXTENTS	Number of extents in rollback segment
RSSIZE	Size in bytes of rollback segment
WRITES	Number of bytes written to rollback segment
XACTS	Number of active transactions
GETS	Number of header gets
WAITS	Number of header waits
OPTSIZE	Optimal size of rollback segment
HWMSIZE	High-water mark of rollback segment size
SHRINKS	Number of times the size of a rollback segment decreases
WRAPS	Number of times rollback segment is wrapped
EXTENDS	Number of times rollback segment size is extended
AVESHRINK	Average shrink size
AVEACTIVE	Current size of active extents, averaged over time
STATUS	Rollback segment status
CUREXT	Current extent
CURBLK	Current block

TABLE 6-10. *V$ROLLSTAT View*

There are many different areas of information contained in this view that you will find interesting. To see how your rollback segments are performing (how much traffic they are getting and how often they are extending and shrinking), you can use the following script:

```
column Name format a7
column Extents format 999 heading 'Extents'
column Rssize format 999,999,999 heading 'Size in|Bytes'
column Optsize format 999,999,999 heading 'Optimal|Size'
column Hwmsize format 99,999,999 heading 'High Water|Mark'
column Shrinks format 9,999 heading 'Number of|Shrinks'
column Wraps format 9,999 heading 'Number of|Wraps'
column Extends format 999,999 heading 'Number of|Extends'
column Rownum noprint
select Name, Rssize, Optsize, Hwmsize, Shrinks, Wraps, Extends
  from V$ROLLSTAT, V$ROLLNAME
 where V$ROLLSTAT.Usn = V$ROLLNAME.Usn
 order by Rownum;

                Size in      Optimal  High Water Number of Number of Number of
Name              Bytes         Size        Mark   Shrinks     Wraps   Extends
------- ------------ ------------ ----------- --------- --------- ---------
SYSTEM        733,184                 733,184         0         0         0
R01        21,295,104   20,971,520  64,958,464         5        63        41
R02        21,295,104   20,971,520  21,295,104         0        19         0
R03        21,295,104   20,971,520  21,295,104         0         5         0
R04        21,295,104   20,971,520  21,295,104         0        16         0
R05        21,295,104   20,971,520  21,295,104         0        13         0
R06        21,295,104   20,971,520  21,295,104         0         8         0
R07        21,295,104   20,971,520  21,295,104         0         5         0
```

Each time a rollback segment adds another extent (Extends), wraps around to the first extent (Wraps), or returns to its optimal size (Shrinks), Oracle has to perform the work of tracking the action. The overhead involved in extends, wraps, and shrinks can impact system performance. You will use the V$ROLLSTAT view (joined to the V$ROLLNAME view to resolve the rollback segment names) to see the value for **optimal** that's been established for the rollback segments (stored in the Optsize column) by performing the query:

```
select Name, Optsize
  from V$ROLLSTAT s, V$ROLLNAME n
 where s.Usn = n.Usn;

NAME                              OPTSIZE
------------------------------ ---------
SYSTEM
RB1                                512000
```

```
RB2                               512000
RB3                               512000
RB4                               512000
RB5                               512000
RB6                               512000
RB7                               512000
RB8                               512000
RB9                               512000
```

You can also derive the average of Waits to Gets by using the following query:

```
set head off;
select 'The average of Waits to Gets is '||
       round((sum(Waits) / sum(Gets)) * 100,2)||'%'
  from V$ROLLSTAT;

The average of Waits to Gets is 0%
```

If the ratio of Waits to Gets is more than 1 to 2 percent, consider creating more rollback segments. If you have enough disks and controllers and you are seeing high rollback segment activity, you can increase the rollback segment tablespaces to two or more sets on different disks using separate controllers with several rollback segments spread evenly over them.

V$ROLLNAME

In the previous query under V$ROLLSTAT, the view was joined to the V$ROLLNAME view to resolve the rollback segments' names. V$ROLLNAME is a lookup view and contains the columns shown in Table 6-11.

In both views, the column you use to join the views to resolve the rollback segment name is called Usn. Therefore, you must distinguish the names by fully qualifying the value, using the view name coupled with the column name, as in: V$ROLLSTAT.Usn. If you don't use this form of qualification, Oracle will return an error about being unable to resolve the column name.

Column	Description
USN	Rollback (undo) segment number
NAME	Rollback segment name

TABLE 6-11. *V$ROLLNAME View*

V$UNDOSTAT

While we're on the subject of monitoring rollback segments, let's take a look at a new view for Oracle9i that enables us to monitor undo segments—V$UNDOSTAT. The composition of this view is shown is Table 6-12.

Column	Description
BEGIN_TIME	Beginning time for each time interval
END_TIME	Ending time for each time interval
UNDOTSN	Tablespace ID number of the last active tablespace in use during the time frame
UNDOBLKS	Number of undo blocks used during the interval
TXNCOUNT	Contains the total number of transactions executed within the interval
MAXQUERYLEN	Maximum length of the longest query, in seconds, executed in the instance
MAXCONCURRENCY	Highest number of concurrently executed transactions within the interval
UNXPSTEALCNT	Number of attempts to obtain undo space by stealing extents that have not expired from other transactions
UNXPBLKRELCNT	Number of unexpired blocks that have been removed from undo segments to be used by other transactions
UNXPBLKREUCNT	Number of unexpired undo blocks that have been reused by transactions
EXPSTEALCNT	Number of attempts to steal expired undo blocks from other undo segments
EXPBLKRELCNT	Number of expired undo blocks stolen from other undo segments
EXPBLKREUCNT	Number of expired undo blocks reused within the same undo segment
SSOLDERRCNT	Number of OER errors that have occurred during an interval
NOSPACEERRCNT	Number of OER errors reported in the current instance

TABLE 6-12. *V$UNDOSTAT View*

One of the really interesting things about this view is that it stores the undo information in 10-minute increments throughout each 24-hour period. Therefore, there are 144 rows in this view after a day's cycle has been completed; six rows per hour times 24 hours. The first row in the view displays the current time interval's statistics.

Now, let's look at the columns that offer the most meaningful information for monitoring undo segment performance. The Undoblks value helps you determine the rate at which undo blocks are being consumed. You can, therefore, estimate the size of the undo tablespace that you need to handle the workload by examining the values in this column and looking for the maximum value that has been used.

Since the Maxquerylen column indicates the length of the longest query in seconds, you can use this value to help determine the proper setting for the UNDO_RETENTION parameter. By watching for increases in the Ssolderrcnt, you decide whether or not UNDO_RETENTION is set properly based on the size of the undo tablespace. If you see a high number of OER errors based on the values within the Ssolderrcnt column, you may want to lower the value of UNDO_RETENTION to reduce the error count. Likewise, if you see a value in the Nospaceerrcnt column, the indication is that the undo tablespace needs more space. Therefore, you want to increase the parameter UNDO_RETENTION.

Here is a script you can use to determine the amount of undo that's generated for simple DML:

```
select to_char(Begin_Time, 'HH24:MI:SS'),to_char(End_Time,'HH24:MI:SS'),
       Undoblks
  from V$UNDOSTAT;
```

V$ROWCACHE

V$ROWCACHE provides you with insights into the performance of the dictionary cache. Each user who connects to the database, and every data request that user makes, references the data dictionary. The data dictionary cache is an area of the shared pool that contains data dictionary information in memory. Table 6-13 shows the columns of this view.

Column	Description
CACHE#	Row cache ID number
TYPE	Parent or subordinate row cache type
SUBORDINATE#	Subordinate set number

TABLE 6-13. *V$ROWCACHE View*

Column	Description
PARAMETER	Name of the initialization parameter that determines the number of entries in the data dictionary cache
COUNT	Total number of entries in the cache
USAGE	Number of cache entries that contain valid data
FIXED	Number of fixed entries in the cache
GETS	Total number of requests for information on the data object
GETMISSES	Number of data requests resulting in cache misses
SCANS	Number of scan requests
SCANMISSES	Number of times a scan failed to find the data in the cache
SCANCOMPLETES	For a list of subordinate entries, the number of times the list was scanned completely
MODIFICATIONS	Number of inserts, updates, and deletions
FLUSHES	Number of times flushed to disk
DLM_REQUESTS	Number of DLM requests
DLM_CONFLICTS	Number of DLM conflicts
DLM_RELEASES	Number of DLM releases

TABLE 6-13. *V$ROWCACHE View* (continued)

The values stored in the V$ROWCACHE view reflect activity since the database was started. Therefore, a database that was just started will have values that do not reflect the true activity of the system. You will want to wait at least an hour or two after starting the database to look at this view's contents.

When an Oracle database starts, Oracle loads definitions into the cache. Therefore, the Getmisses column should never be equal to 0. However, the Gets column, which shows the total number of requests for an item, could be 0. We have taken this into account by adding a really small value to the Gets column when performing the ratio computation. Here's a look at a way to determine the hit ratio of each data dictionary cache item using the V$ROWCACHE view. The sample query was performed on a very quiet system. Normally, you want the percentage of misses to be below 15 percent.

```
column Parameter format a30
select Parameter, Gets,
      Getmisses, round(Getmisses / (Gets+0.000000000001) * 100,2) pctmisses
from V$ROWCACHE;

PARAMETER                            GETS GETMISSES PCTMISSES
------------------------ ------ --------- ---------
dc_free_extents                      1550        96      6.19
dc_used_extents                        40        20        50
dc_segments                            65        37     56.92
dc_tablespaces                        109         3      2.75
dc_tablespace_quotas                    0         0         0
dc_files                                0         0         0
dc_users                               55        15     27.27
dc_rollback_segments                 1707        28      1.64
dc_objects                            426        73     17.14
dc_global_oids                          0         0         0
dc_constraints                          0         0         0
dc_object_ids                         231        33     14.29
dc_sequences                            3         2     66.67
dc_usernames                           80         4         5
dc_database_links                       0         0         0
dc_histogram_defs                       0         0         0
table_scns                              0         0         0
dc_outlines                             0         0         0
dc_profiles                             3         1     33.33
encrypted_object_row_cache              0         0         0
encrytion_profile_row_cache             0         0         0
ifs_acl_cache_entries                   0         0         0
dc_users                                0         0         0
dc_histogram_data                       0         0         0
dc_histogram_data_values                0         0         0
partition_scns                          0         0         0
dc_user_grants                         28        13     46.43
dc_app_role                             0         0         0
```

V$SGASTAT

The system global area (SGA), which is sometimes referred to as the shared global area, is a memory structure that is highly tunable. The SGA is composed of three memory structures: database buffers, shared pool, and redo log buffers. The shared pool also consists of three structures: the library cache, data dictionary cache, and user global area (UGA). A cache miss (not finding the needed information in memory) on the data dictionary or library cache is much more expensive than a database buffer cache miss. If the cache is too small, Oracle must dedicate resources to managing the limited space (like a juggler who must keep at least one of many balls constantly in the air because he does not have enough space in his hands to hold all of them at once). If there is not enough space, CPU resource is consumed, and you see contention on the system for resources.

Column	Description
NAME	SGA component name
BYTES	Memory size in bytes
POOL	Designates the pool in which the memory in the NAME column resides. Value can be **large pool**, meaning memory is allocated from the large pool, or **shared pool**, meaning memory is allocated from the shared pool.

TABLE 6-14. *V$SGASTAT View*

V$SGASTAT is used to display information about the sizes of all the structures in the SGA. Table 6-14 shows the columns for V$SGASTAT.

Here's a list of the values in our sample database:

```
select *
  from V$SGASTAT;

POOL        NAME                           BYTES
----------- -------------------------- ----------
            fixed_sga                     282576
            db_block_buffers            33554432
            log_buffer                    524288
shared pool 1M buffer                    1049088
shared pool Checkpoint queue              141152
shared pool DML lock                      100408
shared pool FileIdentificatonBlock        323292
shared pool FileOpenBlock                 695504
shared pool KGK heap                        3756
shared pool KGLS heap                     172836
shared pool KSXR pending messages que     226636
shared pool KSXR pending reply queue       90292
shared pool KSXR receive buffers         1060000
shared pool PL/SQL DIANA                  499276
shared pool PL/SQL MPCODE                  89524
shared pool PLS non-lib hp                  2068
shared pool VIRTUAL CIRCUITS              266120
shared pool character set object         315704
shared pool db_handles                     93000
shared pool dictionary cache              580792
shared pool enqueue                       171860
shared pool errors                         37864
shared pool event statistics per sess    1356600
shared pool fixed allocation callback         60
```

```
shared pool free memory                   31255900
shared pool joxlod: in ehe                  311404
shared pool joxlod: in phe                  114732
shared pool joxs heap init                    4220
shared pool ksm_file2sga region             148652
shared pool library cache                  2342072
shared pool message pool freequeue          772672
shared pool miscellaneous                  2218096
shared pool parameters                        2088
shared pool processes                       127800
shared pool sessions                        395760
shared pool simulator trace entries          98304
shared pool sql area                        885032
shared pool transaction                     182376
shared pool trigger defini                    1352
shared pool trigger inform                     992
shared pool trigger source                      60
java pool   free memory                   28131328
java pool   memory in use                  5423104
```

To obtain the total allocated size of the SGA, you can do a sum of the Bytes column:

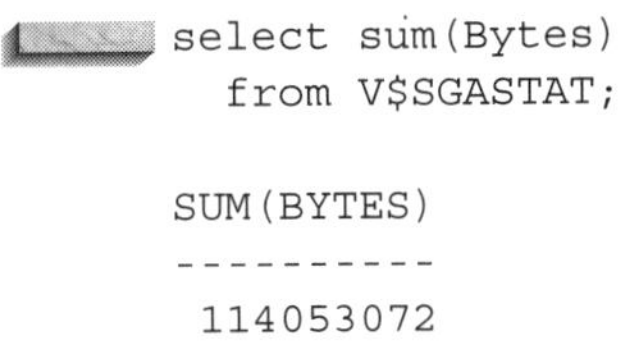

```
select sum(Bytes)
  from V$SGASTAT;

SUM(BYTES)
----------
 114053072
```

Sizing the SGA correctly is an important step in tuning your system. V$SGASTAT can help you determine the amount of space being used currently and how that space is allocated. If you increase any of the following initialization parameter file parameters, you will change the size of the SGA: **shared_pool_size, log_buffers**, **db_block_buffers** (**db_cache_size** in Oracle9i**)**, **processes**, **open_cursors**, **java_pool_size**, **large_pool_size**. Also, be aware that changes you make to one parameter may have a "ripple" effect and influence the size of another parameter.

V$STATNAME

A fundamental question must be asked when you examine both the V$STATNAME view and the V$SYSSTAT view. That question is, Why does the V$STATNAME view exist at all? That's a great question! Looking at the two column listings (Tables 6-15 and 6-16), the only difference between the two views is that the V$SYSSTAT view contains a value for each entry. Take a moment to look at the two tables and ponder the existence of the V$STATNAME view.

Column	Description
STATISTIC#	Statistic number
NAME	Statistic name
CLASS	Statistic class: 1 (User), 2 (Redo), 4 (Enqueue), 8 (Cache), 16 (OS), 32 (Parallel Server), 64 (SQL), 128 (Debug)

TABLE 6-15. *V$STATNAME View*

Okay, we won't keep you in suspense any longer. There is a third view, V$SESSTAT, that still relies on V$STATNAME to provide the resolution of each statistic's name. The only columns in the V$SESSTAT view are Sid, Statistic#, and Value. Thus, V$STATNAME still serves an important function (and we've very sneakily slipped a bit of discussion about a V$ session view into this section).

Notice the Class column and the values listed in its description. The eight different classes of statistics provide a wonderful map for you. You can use the Class column to see exactly which statistics are valuable for different areas of tuning. For instance, there are 24 statistics in the Oracle9i version of the view that pertain to users and 12 that pertain to redo. We'll look more at the values in the next section, but let's just take a quick, preview peek at the statistic names for the redo statistics.

```
column Name format a30
select *
  from V$STATNAME
 where Class = 2

STATISTIC# NAME                                CLASS
---------- ------------------------------ ----------
       114 redo entries                            2
       115 redo size                               2
       116 redo buffer allocation retries          2
       117 redo wastage                            2
       118 redo writer latching time               2
       119 redo writes                             2
       120 redo blocks written                     2
       121 redo write time                         2
       122 redo log space requests                 2
       123 redo log space wait time                2
       124 redo log switch interrupts              2
       125 redo ordering marks                     2
```

In this case, the statistic numbers for each member of the Class are all consecutive. However, that is rarely the case. Most of the statistic classes are mixed together.

Well, guess we've beaten this view to death! Let's go on to a really interesting view packed full of fascinating information.

V$SYSSTAT

V$SYSSTAT provides a wealth of information about the performance of your database. Before we begin to examine all of the statistics that you can obtain from this view, we'll look at the composition of it. Table 6-16 shows the V$SYSSTAT columns.

As we said in the previous section on V$STATNAME, the only difference between the two views is the Value column. Let's perform the same query that we did earlier and see what the values are for the redo statistics (Class 2).

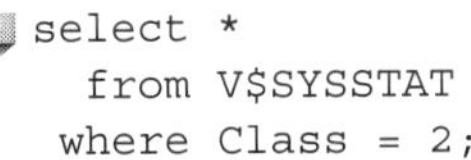

```
select *
  from V$SYSSTAT
 where Class = 2;

STATISTIC# NAME                                       CLASS      VALUE
---------- ------------------------------ ---------          --------
       114 redo entries                                   2        176
       115 redo size                                      2      42620
       116 redo buffer allocation retries                 2          0
       117 redo wastage                                   2      23348
       118 redo writer latching time                      2          0
       119 redo writes                                    2         75
       120 redo blocks written                            2        133
       121 redo write time                                2         79
       122 redo log space requests                        2          0
       123 redo log space wait time                       2          0
       124 redo log switch interrupts                     2          0
       125 redo ordering marks                            2          0
```

Column	Description
STATISTIC#	Statistic number
NAME	Statistic name
CLASS	Statistic class: 1 (User), 2 (Redo), 4 (Enqueue), 8 (Cache), 16 (OS), 32 (Parallel Server), 64 (SQL), 128 (Debug)
VALUE	Statistic value

TABLE 6-16. *V$SYSSTAT View*

A valuable area of information that you can gain from V$SYSSTAT is the volume of sorts that Oracle is performing in memory as opposed to having to sort to disk. Ideally, all sorting operations will be performed in memory, because the overhead of having to place sort values on disk and then retrieve them into memory is costly.

Normally, sort operations (**order by**, **group by**, etc.) are performed in the user's process global area (PGA). However, if there is not enough memory available in this area to hold the sort values, Oracle will shift the sorting operation into the area designated as the user's temporary tablespace. The sorts performed in this area will be done to disk. You can see how many sorts are being performed, how many are in memory, and how many are to disk by executing the query:

```
column Name format a30
select Name, Value
  from V$SYSSTAT
 where Name like 'sort%';

NAME                                         VALUE
---------------------------------------- ---------
sorts (memory)                              168700
sorts (disk)                                    25
sorts (rows)                               1077000
```

In this database, the ratio of sorts performed in memory to sorts performed to disk is

ratio of sorts = round((25 / 168700) * 100,3)
ratio of sorts = 0.015%

V$SYSTEM_EVENT

We've said that contention--users waiting for resources on your system--is at the center of performance tuning. The V$SYSTEM_EVENT view gives you a tool to help quickly identify those areas of contention. Before we show you how to use this view, look at Table 6-17 to see the view's composition.

Column	Description
EVENT	The name of the wait event
TOTAL_WAITS	The total number of waits for this event
TOTAL_TIMEOUTS	The total number of timeouts for this event

TABLE 6-17. *V$SYSTEM_EVENT View*

Column	Description
TIME_WAITED	The total amount of time waited for this event, in hundredths of a second
TIME_WAITED_MICRO	The total amount of time waited for this event, in microseconds.
AVERAGE_WAIT	The average amount of time waited for this event, in hundredths of a second

TABLE 6-17. *V$SYSTEM_EVENT View* (continued)

Here is a script that you can use to look at the system wait events in order of impact:

```
col Event format a37 heading 'Event'
col Total_Waits format 99999999 heading 'Total|Waits'
col Time_Waited format 9999999999 heading 'Time Waitd|In Hndrds'
col Total_Timeouts format 999999 heading 'Timeout'
col Average_Wait heading 'Average|Time' format 999999.999
set pages 999
select *
  from V$SYSTEM_EVENT
 where Time_Waited > 0
   and Event not in('pmon timer','smon timer','rdbms ipc message',
       'parallel dequeue wait','virtual circuit','SQL*Net message from client',
       'client message','Null event','dispatcher timer')
 order by Time_Waited desc
/
                                          Total         Time Waitd     Average
Event                                     Waits Timeout  In Hndrds        Time
------------------------------------- --------- ------- ----------- -----------
db file sequential read                 1368816       0      875970        .640
db file scattered read                   479104       0      609420       1.272
db file parallel write                    27857       1      104577       3.754
log file switch (checkpoint incomplet      1024     645       81086      79.186
ed)
log file parallel write                   23377       1       46002       1.968
log file sync                             18733       1       35011       1.869
buffer busy waits                         28200      30       12315        .437
enqueue                                     194      14       11178      57.619
control file sequential read                128       0         843       6.586
library cache pin                             7       2         784     112.000
control file parallel write                1855       0         455        .245
file identify                                30       0         317      10.567
direct path read                             48       0          89       1.854
```

```
db file single write                    12        0        78      6.500
log file single write                   10        0        38      3.800
refresh controlfile command              1        0        27     27.000
process startup                          1        0        23     23.000
file open                               84        0        18       .214
checkpoint completed                     1        0        16     16.000
direct path write                       24        0         9       .375
instance state change                    1        0         6      6.000
db file parallel read                    1        0         5      5.000
```

Looking at the output above, you would probably want to look at disk file access and log file switches that are not completing in a timely manner before you examined free buffer waits or enqueue. One thing to note is that "db file sequential read" actually refers to index accesses, while "db file scattered read" refers to full table scans.

Once you have examined the overall system, you can use the V$SESSION_EVENT view to drilldown to a finer-grain level to identify the session or sessions that might be experiencing resource contention.

```
col Sid format 9999 heading 'Sess|ID'
col Event format a30 heading 'Event'
col Total_Waits format 99999999 heading 'Total|Waits'
col Time_Waited format 9999999999 heading 'Time (ms)|Waited'
col Total_Timeouts format 999999 heading 'Total|Timeout'
col Average_Wait heading 'Ave (ms)|Time' format 999999.999
set pages 999
select Sid, Event, Total_Waits, Time_Waited, Average_Wait
  from V$SESSION_EVENT
 where Sid = &Sid
 order by Time_Waited desc, Event
/

 Sess                                       Total   Time (ms)     Ave (ms)
   ID Event                                 Waits      Waited         Time
----- ------------------------------ --------- ----------- -----------
    8 SQL*Net message from client        20964     4127008      196.862
    8 log file switch (checkpoint in       269       21496       79.911
      complete)
    8 log file sync                       4149        7778        1.875
    8 enqueue                               15        1246       83.067
    8 buffer busy waits                      6         854      142.333
    8 log file switch completion            21         752       35.810
    8 db file sequential read              789         596         .755
```

```
    8 write complete waits                11          26       2.364
    8 latch free                         168          12        .071
    8 free buffer waits                    1          10      10.000
    8 log buffer space                     3          10       3.333
    8 SQL*Net message to client        20965           0        .000
    8 SQL*Net more data to client         16           0        .000
    8 control file sequential read         2           0        .000
```

V$WAITSTAT

Earlier in this chapter, we looked at V$ROLLSTAT to determine the rate at which rollback segments are extending and shrinking. V$WAITSTAT can be used to help monitor for rollback segment contention. Table 6-18 shows the V$WAITSTAT columns.

In the case of rollback segments, the V$WAITSTAT view will give you a much clearer picture of whether you have enough rollback segments and whether they are large enough to support the transaction activity for your system. Let's take a look at the output from the V$WAITSTAT view and see what it can tell you.

```
select *
  from V$WAITSTAT;

CLASS                  COUNT      TIME
------------------ --------- ---------
data block               218       176
sort block                 0         0
save undo block            0         0
segment header             0         0
save undo header           0         0
free list                  0         0
extent_map                 0         0
1st level bmb              0         0
2nd level bmb              0         0
3rd level bmb              0         0
bitmap_block               0         0
bitmpa index block         0         0
file header block          0         0
unused                     0         0
system undo header         0         0
system undo block          0         0
undo header              126        82
undo block                 0         0
```

Column	Description
CLASS	Class of block
COUNT	Number of waits by this OPERATION for this CLASS of block
TIME	Sum of all wait times for all the waits by this OPERATION for this CLASS of block

TABLE 6-18. *V$WAITSTAT View*

In this output, you see that there is contention for undo header in our sample database. If you see contention for undo header, you generally do not have enough rollback segments to support the workload on your system. If you see contention on the undo blocks, increase the size of the rollback segments or use larger extents.

PART II

Managing Your World

CHAPTER 7

Oracle Installation, Configuration, and Build

In an ideal world, you would begin employment as an Oracle DBA in a company with a fresh system and a clean slate. There would be no Oracle software installed, no databases built, no decisions already made about how your world would look or run. Of course, there is no ideal world; so, when you start a new job as a DBA, you usually inherit a system that may or may not be set up in the most effective way to promote optimal performance or ensure ease of manageability.

In this chapter, we will start from the very beginning and show you how the Oracle software can be installed and a database can be created and configured to make your life easier and the database work better. We'll look at the steps you can take from the time you receive your new CD-ROM software disk from Oracle to make your installation go more smoothly. As you explore this chapter, you will find information that will help you recognize areas of your current database that may need reconfiguration or reorganization to improve performance or manageability. You'll find scripts and tips to help you learn to be more effective as a DBA.

About Software Installation

Before we dive into the steps you should take when you receive your Oracle software CD-ROM disks (yes, there are now several disks provided for your software installation and documentation), let's talk for a minute about the differences between an installation, an upgrade, and a migration. You will hear these words all used interchangeably, but they really have very different actions and meanings associated with them.

When you take the disks that you receive from Oracle and put the first one in your CD-ROM drive and, through the Oracle installation routines, move the files into directories on your system, you are performing an installation. During the installation session, you usually have the option of letting Oracle install a basic demonstration database. We'll talk a little later about why you should accept this offer. During the installation, Oracle also offers other configuration and installation options that we'll talk about later as well.

Upgrade vs. Migration

The words "upgrade" and "migration" have two different connotations. We'll look first at what is meant by the terms *software upgrade* versus *software migration*. After exploring these terms, we'll examine the differences between a database upgrade and database migration.

Software Upgrade vs. Migration

In earlier versions of Oracle, it was not uncommon for a DBA to receive a disk (or in those days, a nine-track tape or TK50 tape) and just install the new software on top of the old software. When you overwrite the old Oracle software with the new files, you are performing a *software upgrade*. By placing the software files in the same directory structure in which the old software resided, you will be overwriting and deleting any files that have the same name as the original files. Any files that have different names will be left behind. Therefore, you will be left with a complete set of files from the new version and some old files from previous versions. That can get very messy and confusing, especially if you have a problem down the road and need to look at files in a specific directory.

The second approach that you can use and that we heartily recommend—called a *software migration* or fresh installation—is to create a separate directory structure under a different ORACLE_HOME location for the new software version. You will have two (or more) copies of different Oracle software versions on your system at one time in completely separate directories. Unless space is a critical issue, we recommend that you always keep separate versions of the software in different directory locations on your system for the following reasons:

- If you overwrite your current version, you will be running your applications in an untested environment.
- Overwriting the old version with a new one may leave behind a mix of old and new files.
- You will not have a chance to verify the new database features delivered with your new software.
- Your developers will not be able to pretest their applications with the new software or incorporate new features that may improve their applications.
- You may have customized some of the files in one of the directories that will be overwritten by the new installation.
- If anything goes wrong, you will have to back out the installation and restore your old environment. Having to stop users from working while you upgrade the software and, again, while you back out the upgrade can be both time consuming and frustrating for them and for you.

If you perform a software migration or fresh installation, you will be able to accomplish the following:

- Verify the new software.
- Be sure the version of software you are working with is untainted by previous software.
- Determine what is different between the old version and the new one.
- Test all the new features thoroughly before you put the new version into production.

- Allow developers to test new features and adapt them to their applications.
- Make the change without disturbing your users.
- Allow for easy migration—when you have finished testing, your migration can be as simple as changing the path for ORACLE_HOME.

In today's fast-paced, "got to get it done *now*" environment, fresh installations are the approach that makes the most sense.

Going One Step Further

In today's computing environment, it's not unusual to find that companies are using more than one computer with a full complement of disks to provide a development environment that is separate from their production system. If you have separate environments, you will be able to "field" the new version of Oracle software to your development system, test it, enhance the applications, and then carry the new version to production. This approach gives you the best of both worlds. You'll have a protected place in which to work with the new version while maintaining your old environment.

Bringing Your Database to a New Version

Another use of the word "upgrade" applies to upgrading a database. Until recently, if you had a database at version 9.0.1 Release 1 and you wanted it to be a 9.0.1 Release 2 database, you would be doing an upgrade. If you were moving your database from version 8.1.6 to version 9.0.1, you would be doing a migration.

When doing an upgrade, you have two choices, as follows:

1. You can shut down your current database under the old version, start it up under the new version, and immediately run some configuration scripts to convert the database to the new version.
2. You can create a new database under the new version, make a copy of your old database, and put that copy into your new database. This approach is used more frequently in a database migration but can be appropriate in a database upgrade as well.

Just as keeping software versions separate makes a lot of sense, keeping database versions separate can also provide you with the same kinds of benefits. You'll be able to test the performance of your new version while the old database is still available to your users. If there are changes in the way features work between versions, or if new features are available, you will be able to modify your application to handle the change or take advantage of the new feature. Oracle also fixes bugs between releases. We've had occasions when programmers took advantage of one of the quirks of a bug, and when the upgrade was done, suddenly the application stopped working. Separate database versions would have allowed us to catch this problem and correct the application before end users were hurt by the change.

A Suggested Configuration

In many shops, the approach that has proven to be the most sound and productive is to have two different machines (also referred to as platforms or boxes)—one for development and preproduction, or quality assurance (QA), and one for production. The development box will have at least two copies of the database that reflect the production database. One database will be used for the developers to create and debug their enhancements to the current application, while the second database will be kept as a mirror of the production database. The second database will be used for preproduction and quality assurance testing to ensure that any new features scheduled for release into production will work correctly and not cause unexpected problems in the production environment. Figure 7-1 shows this configuration.

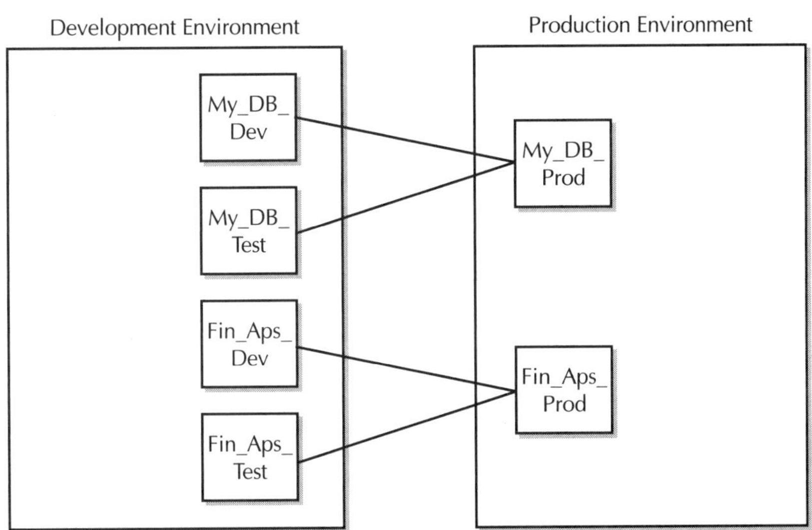

My_DB_Dev - Development database for My_DB application
My_DB_Test - exact copy of current production database for test
Fin_Aps_Dev - Development database for Fin_Aps application
Fin_Aps_Test - exact copy of current production database for test

FIGURE 7-1. *Two systems with associated databases*

In Figure 7-1, we show more than one database on each system. One database is used for tracking the company's property, and another database is used for personnel information. On the production box, there are two databases—one for each application. On the development box, there are four databases—one for each application's development and one for each application's preproduction work. If at all possible, we recommend that you use this approach.

Keep in mind that the production database may be too large to move to a development box in a cost-effective manner. In one shop, the DBA creates a copy of the production database on development. He then loads the data and uses a set of routines generated in-house to pare down the database to a manageable, usable size while still retaining enough test data for the developers to be able to work effectively. You may need to use the same approach in your area.

In many shops, the disk space allocated for development is not large enough to make a full copy of the production database before resizing. In a case like that, you'll need to be a bit more creative in providing a development environment. One approach is to do a full database export with no data and use this to create scripts that can be modified to resize the tables and indexes. Then create the smaller test database, tablespaces, and tables; use SQL*Plus or PL/SQL to extract a subset of the data and generate files that can be used as input to SQL*Loader (Oracle's data load utility program); and load these files into development. This is a time-consuming process, but it may be the only means you will have to generate a useful development database. A third alternative would be to build a smaller database and do a DBLINK load over the network of a subset of data. This would be slow if the network is slow but could be a valid approach.

Software Installation Steps

Although specific information about installing the Oracle-supplied software is beyond the scope of this book, we will briefly cover the steps that you normally follow when you receive the Oracle software CD-ROM disks and any generic documentation. Unfortunately, Oracle has, of late, ceased to ship any hard-copy documentation with their software releases, so you must rely on reading the documentation set online.

Initial Actions to Take

Although making copies of software for distribution to unlicensed people is illegal, making copies of the software for your own protection and use is okay. Therefore, if you have a CD-ROM copier, the very first thing you should do is make at least three copies of the CD-ROM disks—one set for your documentation room, one as your private set of disks, and one set to keep for group access. Once you have made your copies, insert the first CD-ROM and look for any files with "readme" or "installation" in their names. This may be all of the installation documentation that you are going to receive, and these files can contain very important information that you need to know *before* you begin to install the Oracle software. If your company has purchased a support contract from Oracle, you can log on to MetaLink (metalink.oracle.com) and verify if there are any known problems with the version you received and any associated patches for that version that you will want to obtain.

If you have not received a platform-specific version of the installation manual with your software, you should check with Oracle to see if a copy exists. Each platform has its own peculiarities when it comes to software installations, and an installation guide should be available for your specific machine.

When you log on to the support pages, verify that the operating system you are using is the version—with all associated operating system patches installed—that is required for the specific version of the Oracle server software you have received. Do not assume anything! It's very easy to believe you are on version 4.0.d of an operating system and find out later that you are actually on version 4.0.b. You may find that you need operating system patch number XXXXXXX in order to run Oracle's version X.X on your Unix, OpenVMS, or Windows system. And, yes, this just recently happened to one of us. Marlene was asked to help a group installing Oracle version 8.1.7 on a Compaq Unix box. The link kept failing, with two undefined symbols. After several hours, it was finally determined that the operating system level that was installed was not the correct version required for this Oracle installation. Everyone assumed the system administrator had upgraded the operating system. She had upgraded all of the other machines to the correct operating system version but not the machine on which the installation was being performed. Making sure you have the right operating system and operating system patches can save you a lot of time in the long run.

Once you have verified that the operating system versions and patches are correct, read through the installation instructions to verify that your system memory and disk resources are adequate for the Oracle version you are going to use. Be sure to read through all of the instructions so you have the appropriate answers for each question for which you will be prompted. Decide before you begin the installation process whether you will want the Oracle installation to create a default database. Based on the installation version you are licensed for, the database may automatically be built without your accepting that option.

In some later versions of the software installation, you will have to decide whether you want Oracle to link the appropriate software; install, configure, and start up your Listener and Intelligent Agent; and install and configure the Oracle Internet Directory Server.

About the Demonstration Database

We recommend letting Oracle create a small default database during your software installation for the following reasons:

- If the database creation succeeds, you will have verified your installation as well as proven that a database can be built.
- You can "poke around" in the default database to see what roles, role composition, and default users (along with their privileges) are being created by Oracle.
- In some versions, Oracle creates default users with easily guessed passwords and DBA privileges! In Oracle9i, the majority of accounts are locked and their passwords are expired, but you need to know which accounts are supplied and evaluate which ones you need to unlock and change passwords for and which accounts you can safely remove.
- You will have a model of the naming conventions and files that Oracle feels are important, although the sizing of these files may be unrealistic for your development or production needs.
- You will have a small test database that you can use as a "sandbox" to perform practice scenarios for disaster recovery and sanity checks if things fail to work correctly in another database.

Some Installation Decisions

Based on the version of Oracle you are installing, you may be asked whether you would like the installation to perform any of the following tasks:

- Link the application software, which is the Oracle-supplied code
- Configure the Oracle Net Listener, which is used to support client connections to the database either in dedicated or shared mode
- Configure the Intelligent Agent, which is used to communicate between the database and the Oracle Enterprise Manager (the Oracle-supplied, remote database administration tool)
- Add your newly created database to an existing Oracle Internet Directory structure

If these options are presented to you, we recommend that you allow Oracle to link the application software and configure the Listener and Intelligent Agent so that you will be able to see how Oracle performed these tasks. Configuring these tools can be a very confusing task, so letting Oracle perform the work for you can be a great starting point to ensure that you will be able to add your site-specific databases successfully by following the default examples. If you already have a version of Oracle on your system with Net8 or Oracle Net running and you are going to use the same directory structure to install the new version of Oracle, we recommend that you make a copy of your current tnsnames.ora, sqlnet.ora, and listener.ora files (used by the Oracle Net Listener). By making a copy of these files, you ensure that you will retain the correctly configured files for your system. If the same directory structure is used, these files will be overwritten with sample files and your current configuration will be lost.

In versions earlier than Oracle9i, installing and configuring the Oracle Names Server was another option about which you could be asked to make a decision. The Names Server is a mechanism that you used to enable SQL*Net or Net8 clients to look up the correct IP address of the machine and database to which they want to connect. With a Names Server, you would not need to maintain a tnsnames.ora file on each client machine, and centralized connection information is easy to obtain. In Oracle9i and later, the emphasis is on the Oracle Internet Directory Server, which uses directory lookups to resolve the IP address of the machine and database for client connections. The OID also provides a way to identify the password and privileges of each user. Therefore, the OID can serve several different purposes in one central structure. Since the Oracle Names Server is going to be desupported in the future, if you do not currently have a directory server installed and configured, you should look into doing so.

Installation Options

During the installation, you are prompted about whether you want the Oracle installation to create a demonstration database (discussed in the previous section) or whether you want to perform a customized database build or customized installation (only install a selected subset of software instead of installing the complete default configuration).

We're going to describe the various options that you have available to you during the Oracle software installation. You'll need to decide what options you are licensed to use and which ones you want installed before you begin your installation.

There are three different options to choose from when you install the Oracle9i software based on what option your company has purchased:

- **Enterprise Edition** Includes the installation of the following: a preconfigured seed database; networking services; licensable Oracle Options; database environment tools; the Oracle Enterprise Manager framework of management tools, including Console, Management Server, and Intelligent Agent; Oracle utilities; and online documentation. Products most commonly used for data warehousing and transaction processing are also included.

- **Standard Edition** Includes the installation of the following: a preconfigured seed database, networking services, Oracle Enterprise Manager Console, and Oracle utilities.
- **Personal Edition** Includes the installation of the following: a preconfigured seed database that supports a single-user development and deployment environment. The environment requires full compatibility with Oracle9i Enterprise Edition and Oracle9i Standard Edition and contains features found in the Enterprise Edition but not found in the Standard Edition.

You can use the Custom option to install or reinstall individual products. Notice that in both the Standard and Enterprise Editions, a preconfigured seed database is automatically included during the installation. There's a Database Configuration Assistant that you can use to help walk you through the database configuration and creation steps. The DBCA will run automatically after your Oracle software has been installed if you choose the Enterprise or Standard Edition options.

There is also a front-end database application available to support Oracle networking and client interaction with a database located on a separate server. The Client installation types available are as follows:

- **Administrator** Includes the installation of the following: the Oracle Enterprise Manager Console, including enterprise management tools, networking services, utilities, basic client software, and online documentation.
- **Runtime** Includes the installation of the following: networking services and support files.

Again, you can use the Custom option to install or reinstall individual components available in the Administrator and Runtime options.

There are three management installation types available as follows:

- **Oracle Management Server** Consists of the following: the Oracle Management Server, which processes all system management tasks and administers the distribution of these tasks to Intelligent Agents on managed nodes across the enterprise, as well as basic client software and online documentation.
- **Oracle Internet Directory** Consists of the following: a Lightweight Directory Access Protocol (LDAP)–enabled Oracle Internet Directory Server, LDAP-enabled client tools, and the Oracle Internet Directory database schema.
- **Oracle Integration Server** Consists of the following: XML-enabled components, including Oracle9i JVM, a workflow engine, and advanced queuing.

Again, you can use the Custom option to install or reinstall individual products.

Although you can actually install the management software during the regular Enterprise Edition software installation, you should install the database product set with the preconfigured database first and then rerun the installation disks to install the management products. You see, during the Enterprise Edition installation, the framework for the management server software is installed. The management software requires a database for its support, and if you install the software and create a database first, you can use the preconfigured database as the location rather then letting the management software installation create an additional database for each of the management options. You'll have to determine how much space and resources you have available for support databases as part of the process you go through to map out the software and database creations.

Separately Licensed Options

Along with the products delivered on the Oracle9i distribution disks, you can choose to install other Oracle software options. These options are included on your disks, but your company must pay an additional amount to use the features. Here's the current list of added-cost options that were available as of this writing:

- Oracle Advanced Security
- Oracle Change Management Pack
- Oracle Data Mining
- Oracle Diagnostics Pack
- Oracle Label Security
- Oracle Management Pack for SAP
- Oracle Management Pack for Oracle Applications
- Oracle OLAP
- Oracle Partitioning
- Oracle Real Application Cluster (formerly Oracle Parallel Server)
- Oracle Spatial
- Oracle Tuning Pack

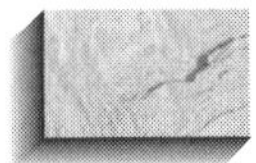

NOTE

Some of these products may be installed on your system during software installation. If you have not paid an additional amount for these products, verify with your Oracle salesperson that you have been licensed to use them.

Creating a Database

Based on the Oracle software installation type you have selected, you are given the opportunity to create a preconfigured database. As we mentioned earlier, we strongly urge you to allow Oracle to create a preconfigured database.

After the Oracle software has been installed, the Oracle Database Configuration Assistant is automatically run to gather the necessary information to create a database. Once you've created the first database, how will you create additional databases? Although the DBCA runs automatically during installation, you can run it interactively afterwards any time you want to. Therefore, you'll be able to use it whenever you need to create a database on your system.

Because you can run the DBCA after the software has been installed, the database creation steps we're going to show you here will reflect the postinstallation database creation steps and descriptions. We'll point out the difference in the steps that you see during the installation run as opposed to postinstallation runs.

Using the Oracle Database Configuration Assistant

When you run the Oracle Database Configuration Assistant, a welcome screen is presented first, followed by a screen that prompts for the operation you want to perform. Your choices are as follows:

- Create a Database—create a new database.
- Configure Database Options in a Database—change the configuration from a dedicated server to a shared server or to add options that were not previously included in your database creation, such as the added-cost options listed earlier in this chapter.
- Delete a Database—delete the database and all of its associated operating system files.
- Manage Templates—modify existing database templates or create new ones.

The Oracle Database Assistant has three "canned" templates that are sized and configured to represent the most commonly used database configurations. The advantage of having database creation templates is that you can quickly and easily create duplicate databases without having to specify the necessary parameters more than once.

Within the template management option, you can create a template from an existing one, create a template based on an existing local or remote database structure, or create a template from an existing database, including the data within the database. The last option is wonderful for creating a new database that mirrors a production one as an application development environment or as the basis for a standby database. We'll tell you much more about standby databases in Chapter 11.

Choosing a Database Template

When you choose to create a new database, the next screen displays the Oracle-supplied database templates based on a projected pattern of user interaction within the new database, including

- Data Warehousing or Decision Support System (DSS)—numerous complex queries are performed processing large quantities of data requiring high availability, excellent response time, and accuracy. In a DSS environment, the queries range from simple queries returning a small number of records to complex queries that sort many thousands of records over several tables.
- General Purpose—a variety of database tasks are performed, including simple transactions as well as complex queries.
- New Database—this option enables you to create a database customized for your users' processing environment. This option is not available during the Oracle postinstallation database creation activities.
- Transaction Processing—each transaction, either reading, writing, or deleting data from the database, is a relatively simple operation that processes a small amount of information, but there are many users performing a large number of concurrent transactions.

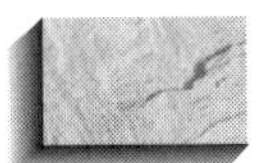

NOTE
Oracle recommends that you create at least one seed database to serve as a template for future database creations.

Figure 7-2 shows the Oracle Database Configuration Assistant, Database Templates screen with the Transaction Processing database option selected. A button at the bottom of the screen enables you to show the details of the database configuration. You can examine the proposed options but cannot, at this point in the database configuration steps, modify any of the values. The options shown are common options, including some unlicensed product installations, initialization parameters, datafile, control file, and redo log file locations.

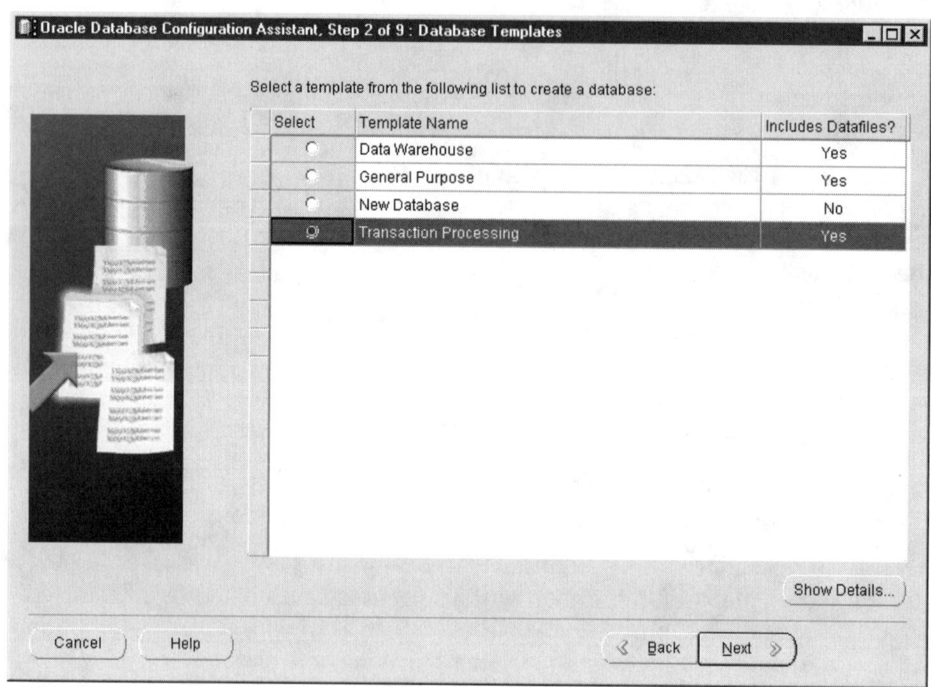

FIGURE 7-2. *Database Templates screen*

Declaring the Database Name and Registering the Database

You will be prompted to supply both a global database name and an instance (SID) name for the new database. The standard global database extension is .world, and you can supply this value unless your company has an established domain name to use. Check with your system administrator to verify whether there is a specific domain name you must use instead of the .world extension. When you type in the global database name, the same value up to the "." will be automatically placed in the SID field. For example, if you enter the global database name DB9I.world in the Global Database name field, the value DB9I will automatically be written in the SID field. Figure 7-3 shows the Database Identification screen with the value DB9I.world entered.

The next option deals with network configuration for the new database and lets you register the database within a directory service. If you or your network

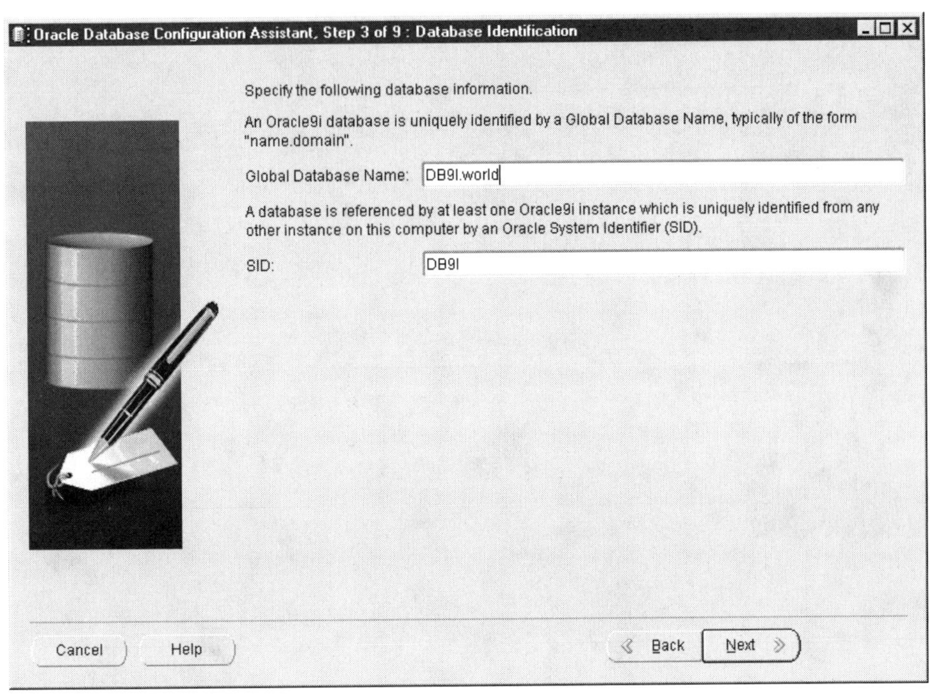

FIGURE 7-3. *Database Identification screen*

administrator has already configured a directory server such as Oracle Internet Directory or Microsoft Access, you can opt to register the new database within that server. The default value, as shown in Figure 7-4, is not to register the database. You can check with your system administrator or network administrator to verify whether there is already a directory available. We recommend that you verify this feature before you begin your database creation.

Dedicated vs. Shared Server Option

The Database Connection Options screen, as shown in Figure 7-5, enables you to specify the way each client will connect to the database. If your new database is going to support a low number of clients or the clients are going to remain connected to the database for long periods of time, select the Dedicated Server Mode. Figure 7-5 shows the Dedicated Server Mode selected.

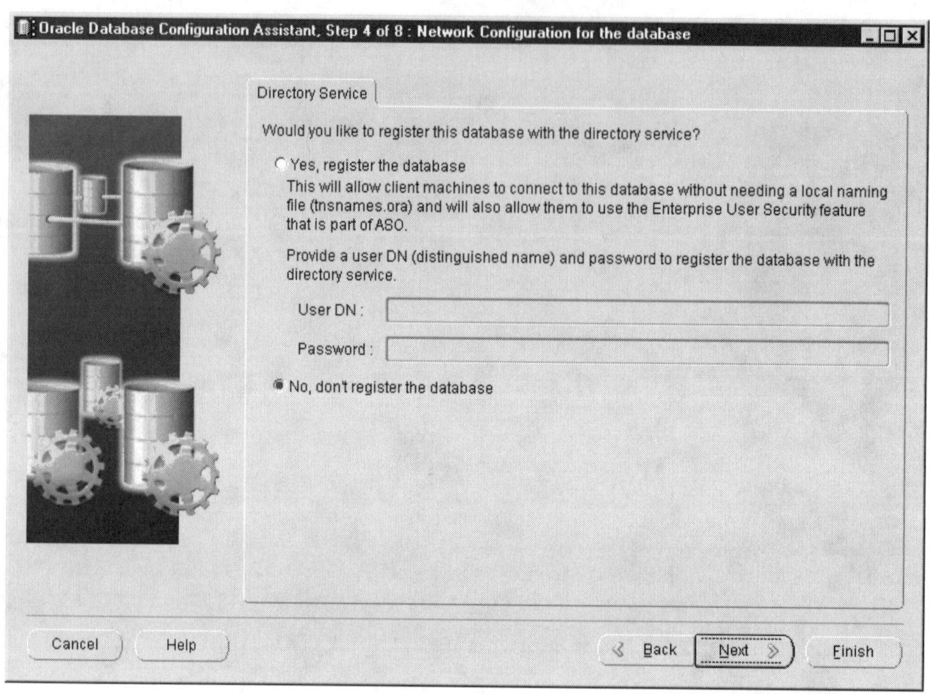

FIGURE 7-4. *Network Configuration for the Database screen*

If, however, your database is going to support a high volume of clients, you can enable the clients to share a pool of resources by selecting the Shared Server Mode. Hmm, what's a "high volume of clients," you might ask. Great question! On a Unix system, you might consider thousands of users as being a high volume, while in a Windows environment, several hundred might qualify as a high traffic value. Therefore, you are left to decide for yourself whether the volume of traffic on your system is high enough to enable the Shared Server Mode.

When you select the Shared Server Mode, you are given the opportunity to modify the default Shared Server configuration by clicking the Edit Shared Connections Parameters button. The Shared Server Mode Basic/Advanced configuration tabs are presented, as shown in Figure 7-6. You can modify the connection protocol from

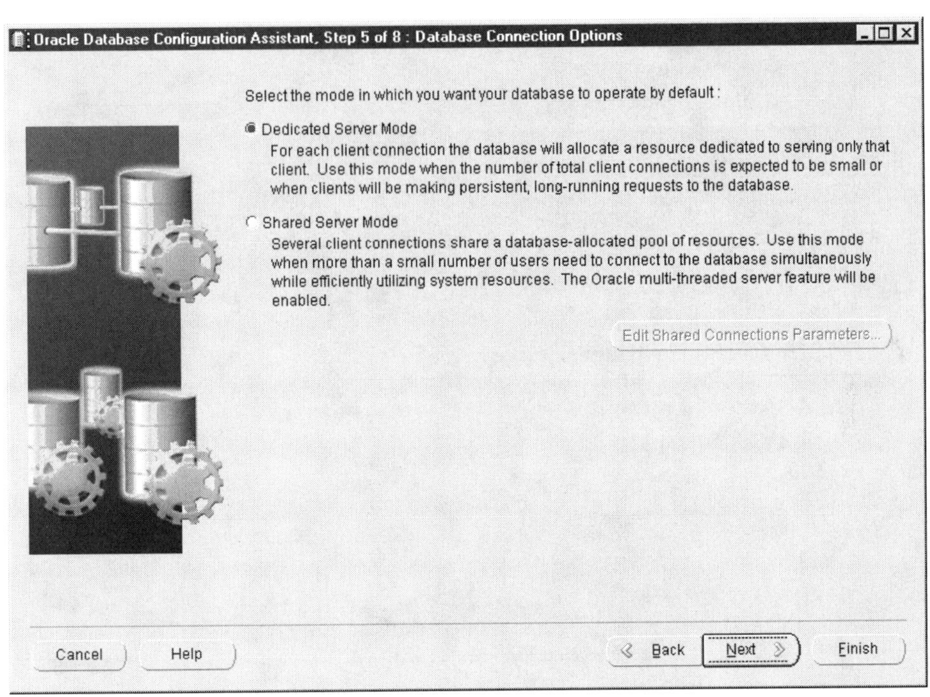

FIGURE 7-5. *Database Connection Options screen*

its default of TCP to SPX, NMP, TCPS (the secure TCP option), or IPC, as well as modifying the following:

- Number of Dispatchers—used as messengers to pass the queries to the database and return the responses to the clients. The default is 1 dispatcher.
- Maximum Number of Connections per Dispatcher—the maximum number of network connections to allow for each dispatcher.
- Maximum Number of Dispatchers—a static value. You must reboot the database to modify the value once it is set. The value defaults to whichever is higher: 5 or the value you set.

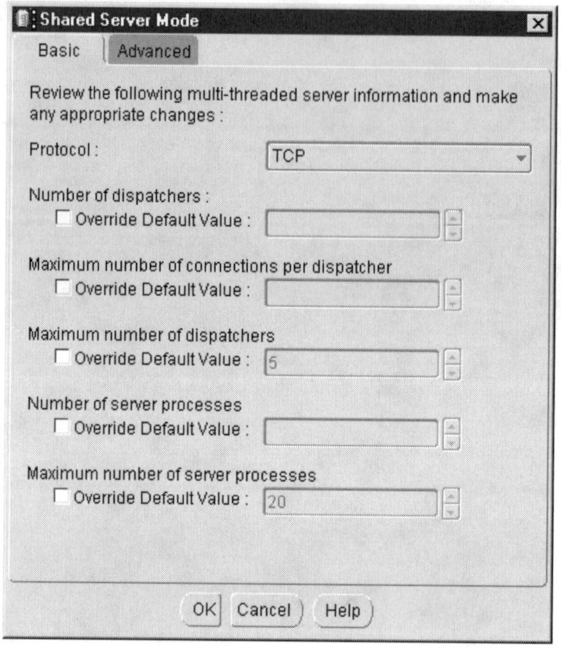

Shared Server Mode

Basic | Advanced

Review the following multi-threaded server information and make any appropriate changes :

Protocol : TCP

Number of dispatchers :
Override Default Value :

Maximum number of connections per dispatcher
Override Default Value :

Maximum number of dispatchers
Override Default Value : 5

Number of server processes
Override Default Value :

Maximum number of server processes
Override Default Value : 20

OK | Cancel | Help

FIGURE 7-6. *Shared Server Mode, Basic screen*

- Number of Server Processes—a dynamic parameter that defines how many server processes will be created when an instance is started. The value varies based on the system activity but will never go below the maximum number of server processes that have been defined.
- Maximum Number of Server Processes—a static parameter that defaults to whichever is greater: 20 or two times the value of MAX_SERVERS.

The Advanced Shared Server Mode tab includes the options shown in Figure 7-7. The advanced options include the ability to enable multiplexing of shared server connections. Multiplexing allows the Oracle Connection Manager Connection Concentration feature in which multiple client network sessions are funneled through a single transport protocol connection. You can define the mode in which you want the connection concentration to be enabled. The options are

- Off—disables the feature for both incoming and outgoing connections
- On—enables the feature for all connections

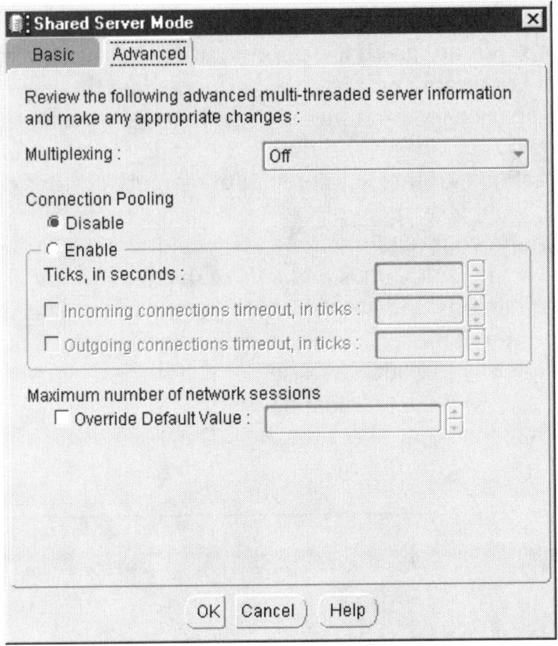

FIGURE 7-7. *Shared Server Mode, Advanced screen*

- Incoming Connections—enables the feature for incoming connections only
- Outgoing Connections—enables the feature for outgoing connections only

Using Connection Pooling, you can maximize the number of physical network connections to a shared server. You have the choice of specifying the following options:

- Disable—Connection Pooling is disabled for both incoming and outgoing network connections.
- Enable—Connection Pooling is enabled for both incoming and outgoing network connections.

If you enable Connection Pooling, you must specify the size of the network measure known as a *tick*. You specify the value for the size of a tick in seconds. After establishing the size of a tick, you specify the amount of time, in ticks, that an incoming connection should wait before timing out. You also specify the amount of time, in ticks, that an outgoing connection should wait before timing out.

The final value in the Advanced Shared Server Mode configuration tab is the maximum number of network sessions to allow for each dispatcher.

In the next step, you are given the opportunity to modify the memory parameters, enable or disable archive log mode, declare the maximum amount of memory that can be used for each process's sort area size, select the character sets to be used within your database, and define the basic file locations. Figure 7-8 shows the Initialization Parameters screen with memory options displayed.

In Chapter 12, we'll look more closely at memory parameters and how to adjust them to help fine-tune your database performance. For now, we recommend that you accept the basic, default values and ensure that you do not activate archive log mode for your first demonstration database. If you find later that you are beginning to use this database for more serious information storage, you can enable archive log mode. We'll talk more about database protection in Chapter 10. Since this is the first created database, we've let Oracle determine the file locations to be used. In later database creations, if you select the New Database option, you'll be able to

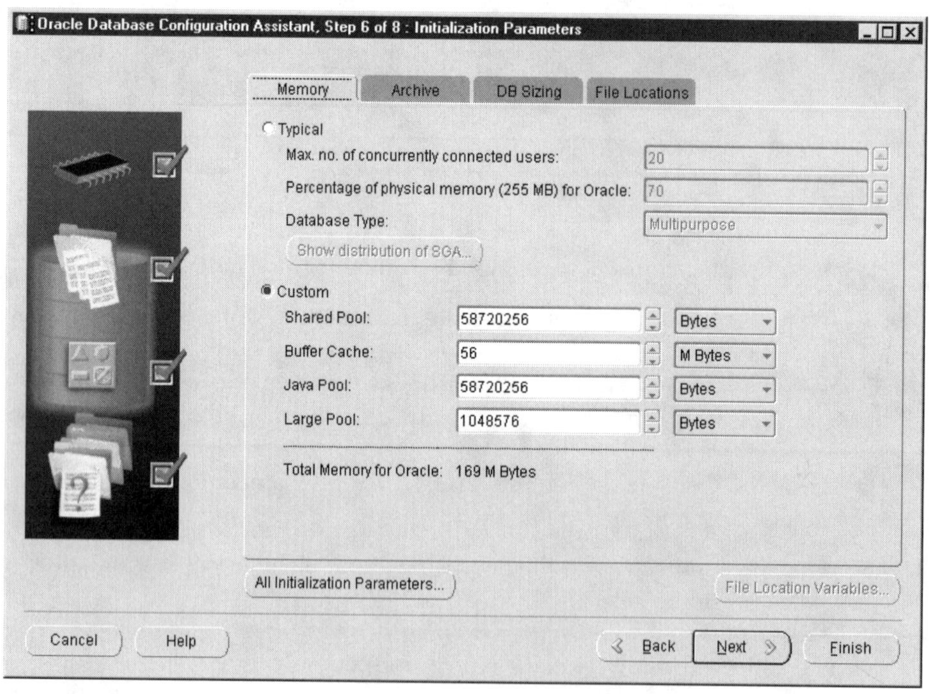

FIGURE 7-8. *Initialization Parameters screen*

save a script of the database creation commands and modify the file locations within the scripts to accommodate the locations you want to use.

Speaking of scripting, we strongly suggest that you script everything you do, as you do it, so you will be able to re-create your actions later. We can almost guarantee that you will repeat these actions, either because you are creating yet another database or because there was a problem, as simple as a typo, the first time. Scripting lets you see what you did and either repeat it or correct it. Besides which, who wants to keep typing in the same commands over and over and over again? We sure don't!

In addition to scripting, you should keep a spool file of the results of running your scripts. Often, error messages scroll so fast on the screen that you miss them. With a spooled log file, you can review what went wrong and fix it.

In Step 7, you can define the locations and sizes of your control files, redo log files and groups, and datafiles. Figure 7-9 shows the initial Database Storage screen. Notice the tree structure on the left side of the screen. You can click on each of the

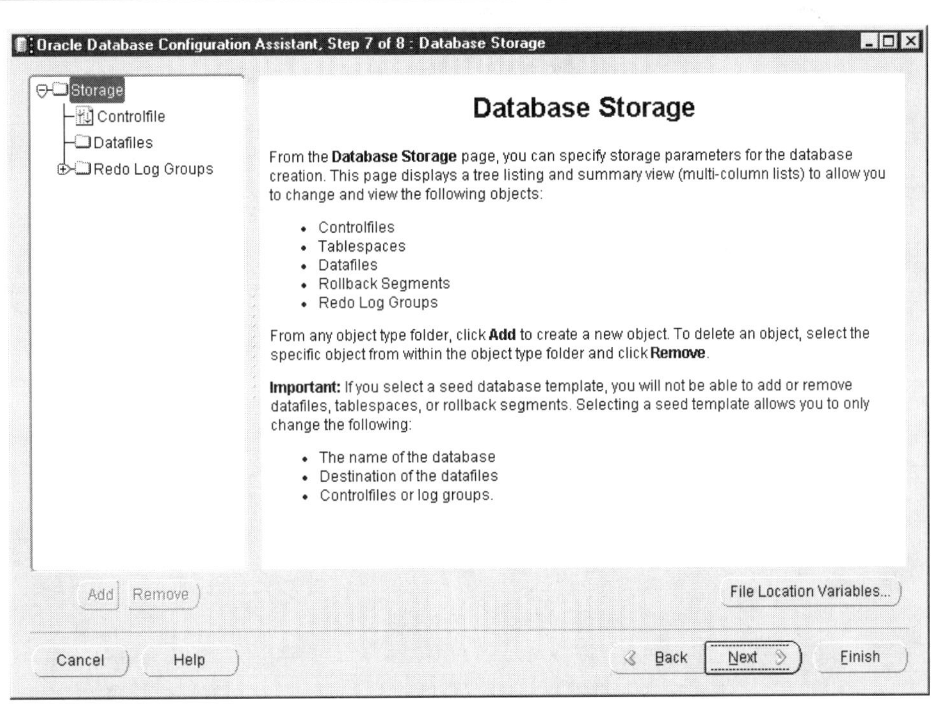

FIGURE 7-9. *Initial Database Storage screen*

options, and the information for that option is displayed. Once you have displayed the information, you can modify it if you so desire.

Since we are using an Oracle-defined template, when we get to Step 8, the only options presented are to create the database, save the database template in another name (without saving the datafile information), or both. There is no option given to enable you to create scripts of the database creation. As we mentioned before, the only time that you are given an opportunity to create and save scripts is if you select the New Database option. Figure 7-10 shows the creation options with Create Database selected.

Oh, by the way, did you notice that from Step 4 on, you have the option to Finish at any time? The reason you are given this option throughout the latter part of the configuration is so that if you decide you want to change something but don't want to "walk forward" through the rest of the screens again, you can backtrack, make your modification, and select Finish to get to the last screen quickly. Pretty cool, no?

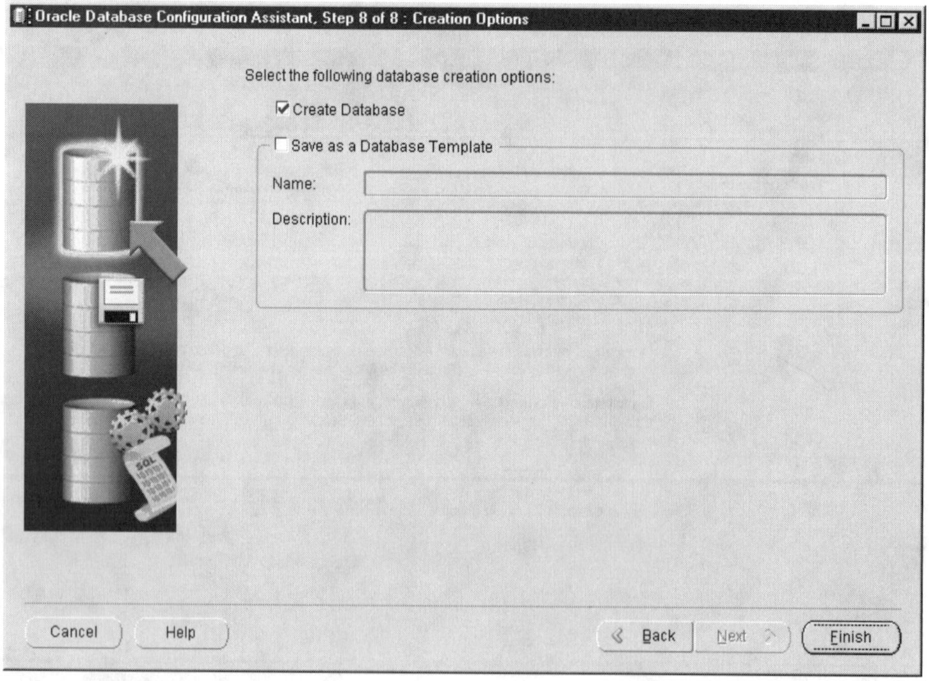

FIGURE 7-10. *Creation Options screen*

After Installation

After the software has been installed and proven to work correctly (by creating a default database, etc.), you want to create your own *real* database. Before you create your first database, you need to make decisions about the following:

- How many copies of the control file you will want and where they will be located
- How many redo log files you will want and if you want to have Oracle mirror them
- The database block size for your database

As you learned in Chapter 2, the control files are used to map the physical files to the logical database objects. If you had only one control file on your system and something damaged it, you would have major problems recovering your database. Therefore, Oracle recommends at least two control files. The control files take up very little space. We recommend that you create and keep three copies of the control file on your system—in different directories on different disks on different controllers—to ensure recoverability. After all, if you have all of your control files on different disks but on the same controller and the controller fails, you still will be unable to get to the control files.

Redo log files contain enough information to allow Oracle to reconstruct or back out transactions. If you are creating a database with which a few developers will be working and very little load will be placed on the system, you will probably only need a few redo log files for your database. You must have at least two redo log files in order for Oracle to operate correctly. We recommend that you have at least three to five. We'll talk more about redo log files and how to monitor them in Chapter 9.

The default block size that Oracle uses to create a database is based on the form of transactions and the database template that you select when you use the Oracle Database Configuration Assistant. Historically, Oracle used a 2k (2048 bytes) block size that is generally just too small to be practical in anything other than a very small test database! If you are working on a Windows system, you will probably want to make your database block size 4k, or 4096 bytes. On Unix and Compaq OpenVMS systems, you can size your database block size as large as 16k or 32k. For a database just beginning to be developed, we recommend that you begin with a 4k or 8k block size. Remember too that, as of Oracle9i, your database can support both a basic block size and up to four other block sizes on a tablespace by tablespace basis. We'll talk more about database block sizes a bit later in this chapter.

Once Your Database Is Created

Once you have created your database, you will need to perform several tasks. Smart DBAs write a script to perform these tasks automatically. Writing a script gives you a chance to review what tasks you want to do and the order in which you want to do them; and, as we mentioned before, most DBAs create databases over and over again. Why retype when you don't have to? Another benefit of scripting is that the output can be captured in an output file. Having the output captured is very useful—especially if you are running a database creation script and want to verify that all of the tablespaces were created successfully.

Before we look at the tasks you must complete after building your database, let's take a few minutes to look at the users SYS and SYSTEM.

About SYS and SYSTEM

When a new database is created, Oracle populates the database with some default users. The following two users will always be created:

- **SYS** The most powerful user in the database, owns all of the internal objects that make up the database
- **SYSTEM** The original account from which you do most of your object creation

You can access the SYS and SYSTEM accounts through SQL*Plus, either through the GUI interface, through the Oracle Enterprise Manager, or from the operating system level. Regardless of the approach you use, to perform major database administration tasks you must connect to the database "as sysdba." If you are connecting to the SYS account, you must always connect with the "as sysdba" phrase. Figure 7-11 shows the correct syntax you use to connect to SYSTEM or SYS as sysdba.

NOTE
The notation "as sysdba" comes after the network connection string.

To connect using the Oracle Enterprise Manager, you can specify the phrase "as sysdba" from the OEM login screen pull-down menu. We'll tell you more about OEM in Chapter 13.

To connect to the database from the operating system prompt, you can issue the following command:

```
sqlplus "system/manager@db9i.world as sysdba"
```

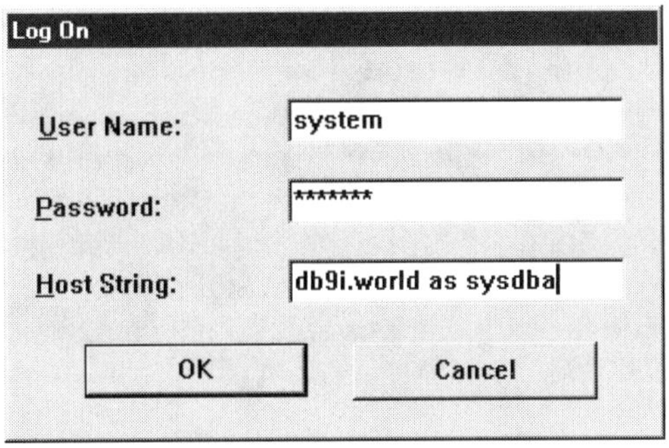

FIGURE 7-11. *Connecting to SYSTEM as sysdba through the GUI interface*

Look at the quotation marks surrounding the majority of the statement. They are necessary because there is a space between the words "as" and "sysdba." Without the quotation marks, the SQL*Plus utility won't know that there is more to the statement than the first phrase.

The default password for SYSTEM is "manager," while SYS has a default password of "change_on_install." These default passwords are widely known, and you are given the opportunity to change them as soon as you finish creating the database. You should change them as soon as possible, or you will leave a security hole. We know of an application manager who insisted that his database was totally secure. When called in to help fix a problem, we were able to log on to this "secure" system using the password "manager" for SYSTEM.

Okay, so what's the difference between these two accounts, and how do you know when to log on as one or the other? Up until version 8i, the only way you could create, start up, or shut down a database was through the Server Manager utility, using a special login that had four different forms, as follows:

- Connect internal or connect internal as sysdba
- Connect / as sysdba
- Connect internal as sysoper
- Connect / as sysoper

When you logged in to the database using the svrmgr and connect as "/" or "internal," you were really connecting to the SYS account with the highest privileges available. You can do great harm to a database using this account, so approach it with caution. As of Oracle9i, both the Server Manager utility and "connect internal" have been desupported and removed. Now, the only way that you can create, start, or stop the database is through either SQL*Plus or OEM. As mentioned earlier, to connect to the SYS account you must use the phrase "as sysdba," or Oracle will issue an error message and not let you connect.

When you need to create tablespaces, rollback segments, redo logs, and other objects, you can log on to the database either through SQL*Plus or OEM as SYS or SYSTEM, or another account with these specific DBA privileges. We feel that the safest approach is to create these objects from SQL*Plus as an account with the specific privileges to do these operations and do only the tasks that absolutely must be done through the SYS, or SYSTEM, account.

The "CAT" Scripts

Some scripts can only be run from SQL*Plus as SYS connected "as sysdba." The "cat" scripts are an example of the scripts that must usually be run as SYS. You will find these scripts in the following directories:

- On Windows, look in ORACLE_HOME\rdbms\admin.
- On OpenVMS, look in $ora_root:[rdbms].
- On Unix, look in $ORACLE_HOME/rdbms/admin.

Take the time to look at these scripts and review them so you know what they are doing. They are used to establish the data dictionary for the database and create and load many internal tables, views, and procedures.

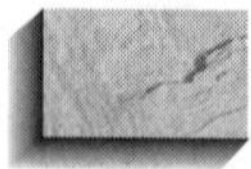

NOTE
*In Oracle 8i, these scripts can be run from SQL*Plus connected as the user "internal," while in Oracle9i, you must run these scripts from SYS as sysdba.*

When you have completed creating your database, you need to run the "cat" scripts (catalog.sql, catproc.sql, catexp.sql, etc.). Be sure always to run catalog.sql first, catproc.sql second, and then any of the other "cat" scripts in whatever order you want. You will find, if you look at these scripts, that they each call other scripts. If you have already run catalog.sql and catproc.sql, you do not have to run them again to run any of the other "cat" scripts.

Your next step is to create one small rollback segment in the SYSTEM tablespace if it has not, by default, been created for you. You cannot create any other objects or segments in the database until this rollback segment exists and is brought online. Once the SYSTEM rollback segment has been created, you can create the other tablespaces, rollback segments, and so on, that you want in your database.

In the next section, we will look at how to determine what your base tablespace configuration should look like. Keep in mind that if you use the Oracle database creation templates, several tablespaces will automatically be created for you.

On the Number of Tablespaces and Their Layout

At the 1991 International Oracle User Week conference, Cary Millsap presented a paper on a standardized approach to the naming of Oracle directories, placement of files on a system, and the amount and type of tablespaces that a basic database should have. The approach was developed to improve Oracle performance in earlier versions of the RDBMS and to enable consistency in database file location. Cary called his approach the Optimal Flexible Architecture (OFA).

Over time, Cary's concepts have proven to be an invaluable approach to configuring a database for optimal performance. Although his approach to directory structure and file-naming conventions is excellent, we'll concentrate more on his recommendations for database architecture. While performing research as he developed his concepts, Cary found that a database with at least seven initial, basic tablespaces located on different disks—preferably on different controllers—will yield better performance. Table 7-1 shows the recommended minimum tablespaces that should be created for a database and a proposed naming convention for each of them.

Now, let's take a look at these tablespaces and see what type of segments should be stored in each.

The SYSTEM Tablespace

At first glance, it would seem that the SYSTEM tablespace is self-explanatory—a tablespace to be used to store the objects that belong to the user SYSTEM. However, the SYSTEM tablespace should be used to store only those objects that belong to the user SYS. Once you have created the first five tablespaces listed in Table 7-1, we suggest you alter the SYSTEM user to use the TOOLS tablespace as its default tablespace and the TEMP tablespace as the temporary tablespace. We also suggest you alter the SYS user to point to the TEMP tablespace as its temporary tablespace for sort operations. The commands you will use are as follows:

```
alter user SYSTEM default tablespace TOOLS temporary tablespace TEMP;
alter user SYS temporary tablespace TEMP;
```

Why would you want to do this? To ensure that the only user who will be using the SYSTEM tablespace is SYS and that the SYSTEM tablespace will not be used to store temporary segments during sorting operations. Up until Oracle9i, by default, Oracle creates users with their default tablespace as SYSTEM and their temporary

Tablespace Name	File Name
SYSTEM	SYSTEM01.DBF
RBS or UNDO	RBS01.DBF or UNDO01.DBF
TEMP or TEMPORARY	TEMP01.DBF
TOOLS	TOOLS01.DBF
USERS	USER01.DBF
DATA	DATA01.DBF
INDEX	INDEX01.DBF

TABLE 7-1. *Seven Basic Tablespaces*

tablespace as SYSTEM. In Oracle9i, you can specify a default tablespace to be used for each new user in your database as you create them, to ensure that you assign the user a specific default tablespace and temporary tablespace. If you do not ensure that SYS is the only user assigned to the SYSTEM tablespace, that tablespace will

- Tend to get very fragmented
- Have potentially severe contention against it and affect performance

Because you cannot alter the SYSTEM tablespace offline, there is no way to rebuild this tablespace without rebuilding the entire database, and this can be very time consuming. If you are scripting everything as we've suggested, you will already have your create_user script. It's easy to build the script to prompt you for a username and temporary tablespace name, and rely on Oracle to assign the default user tablespace to ensure that these values are set properly.

Okay, so the only user in the SYSTEM tablespace is SYS.

The Rollback Tablespace or Undo Tablespace

The rollback tablespace is conventionally called RBS. You can create more than one rollback segment tablespace, each with a unique name, placed on different disks to improve performance. The rollback tablespace is used specifically to store rollback segments. If you have enough disks and controllers and find that you have high rollback segment contention, you might even want to have two or more sets of rollback segment tablespaces with the rollback segments spread evenly over them.

As of Oracle9i, you can have Oracle manage the rollback or undo information automatically by enabling the Undo tablespace feature to allow all change tracking to be done automatically within the database in an Undo Tablespace. With automatic undo segment management, you no longer have to create, drop, or alter rollback segments. You still do have the ability to use rollback segments instead of the new Undo Tablespace if you want to do so.

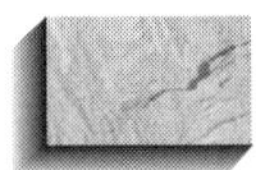

NOTE
When you use undo management, you can implement it using either manual or automatic.

To enable Undo Tablespace management, you set the parameter UNDO_MANAGEMENT in the initialization file to AUTO; otherwise set the value to MANUAL to use rollback segments. If you opt to use the automatic Undo Tablespace approach, there will be one tablespace created in the database called UNDOTBS. You cannot have more than one "active" Undo Tablespace within a database at a time. If you have enough space, you could have an extra large file available but offline.

Let's look at the Automatic Undo Management design. There will always be one SYSTEM undo segment within the SYSTEM tablespace whether you use automatic or manual segments. With rollback segments, you create several static segments of a specific size. With undo segments, Oracle creates and maintains the undo segments automatically and internally as they are needed. The only allocation that you do is to tell Oracle the size to make the overall Undo Tablespace.

To create an Undo Tablespace when you create your database, you use the following syntax:

```
create database DB9I
. . .
undo tablespace <tablespace_name>
datafile 'D:\oracle\ora90\oradata\db9i\undotbl01.dbf'
size 200M;
```

If you do not specify an Undo Tablespace clause in your database creation statement and UNDO_MANAGEMENT is set to AUTO, the system will create a tablespace called UNDOTBS, and AUTOEXTEND will be set to ON with an initial size of 10M. We recommend that if you are going to enable Undo Tablespace, you specify a tablespace name, include the DATAFILE description (the only argument allowed), and set a specific limiting size instead of letting Oracle do things for you.

To create an Undo Tablespace after database creation, create the tablespace and then put the UNDO_TABLESPACE parameter in the initialization file to specify the name of the tablespace to use on database startup; just as you would use ROLLBACK SEGMENTS= for rollback segments brought online at database startup.

```
create undo tablespace UNDO_TBLSP
datafile 'D:\oracle\ora90\oradata\db9i\undotbl01.dbf'
size 200M;
```

Once the tablespace is created, you can shut down the database, put the UNDO_TABLESPACE parameter in the initialization file, and restart the database.

You can alter an Undo Tablespace to add a datafile, rename the tablespace, bring the datafile online/offline, or begin or end backup. In order to drop an Undo Tablespace, the tablespace cannot be currently in use. This means that there cannot be any uncommitted transactions. You can use the V$TRANSACTION view to verify whether any transactions are active.

There is also an UNDO_RETENTION parameter that you can set to tell Oracle the amount of undo to retain (in seconds). The default value is 900 seconds. If you do not specify sufficient space in the Undo Tablespace to support all of the transactions, you can end up with Oracle overwriting data, which could lead to an ORA-1555 "Snapshot too old" error. You can use the V$UNDOSTAT view to produce a histogram of how well the system is performing. You can take the information you gain from V$UNDOSTAT to determine the size for UNDO_RETENTION as follows:

```
Undo space = UNDO_RETENTION value in seconds * Undo blocks per second
  * DB_BLOCK_SIZE + DB_BLOCK_SIZE
```

If UNDO_RETENTION is set to 3600 seconds (one hour) and the transaction rate is 20 undo blocks per second with a 4k block size, the required undo space would be

```
Undo space = 3600 * 20 * 4096 + 4096 = 2.95 GB
```

You can switch from one Undo Tablespace to another by using

```
alter system set UNDO_TABLESPACE=<new_tablespace_name>;
```

Once you've switched from one tablespace to the other, you can drop the old tablespace when all transactions using it have completed.

The TEMP or TEMPORARY Tablespace

The next tablespace on the list is TEMP or TEMPORARY. As the name implies, this tablespace is assigned to each user as the temporary tablespace that is used each time a sort operation is performed. What causes a sort operation? Any time a SQL statement includes a clause with "order by," "group by," or "union," for example, a sort is performed. When you create an index, a sort is also performed.

We want these sorts to be performed in a separate tablespace used specifically to store temporary segments so that other tablespaces are not fragmented. We find that it is a really good policy to store *only* temporary segments in a TEMP tablespace. Oracle agrees, and in Oracle9i, you must create this tablespace specifically as a temporary tablespace. You will not be able to put any other objects in there, even if they are viewed as temporary objects. You can also have more than one temporary tablespace, but each one should have a unique name that will help indicate with which application it is associated. If you have a payroll application in your database in which there is a great deal of sort activity, you might create an additional temporary tablespace named TEMP_PAYROLL and assign it as the temporary tablespace for the PAYROLL_USER schema. We'll talk more about temporary segments and tablespaces in Chapter 8.

The TOOLS Tablespace

The fourth tablespace on our list is the TOOLS tablespace. As we mentioned earlier, it is a good policy to alter the SYSTEM user's default tablespace to point to the TOOLS tablespace. If you are licensed to use the Oracle Developer, Oracle Discoverer, Oracle Portals software, or another Oracle product, you should install the base tables for these products either in their own schema area tablespaces or in the TOOLS tablespace. You can also use this tablespace for third-party products that require a tablespace in which to house their objects.

The USERS Tablespace

Our fifth tablespace is USERS. You can use this tablespace to provide an area where a user can create and store small objects such as test tables or the prototype of a new application under development. If the application seems to be turning into a "real" application, you want to move it from the USERS tablespace to an area of its own—a set of DATA and INDEX tablespaces. In a production database, users should not be creating objects, so you may not need this tablespace when you create a database that will be used for production.

As of Oracle8i, true temporary tables can be created, so the USERS tablespace might be a good place to create them on production, although a more fitting name would be TEMP_TABLES for such a tablespace.

The DATA and INDEX Tablespaces

If your database is going to be used for one very small application, you can assign your schema developer to the DATA tablespace and request that the developer use the INDEX tablespace to store indexes for the application. If you are going to house many applications or one large application in the database, you might want to create several tablespaces for data and indexes. The developer will have to name the specific index tablespace to be used in the index creation script because, by default, Oracle will place all objects created by a user in his or her default tablespace. In general, it is a good idea for developers to specify the tablespace for each table or index they create, even if they want it in their default tablespace. The DBA may decide to change the default tablespace of a user at any time, and the object may not end up where it was intended to go.

How the Default Tablespace Assignment Works

To better understand how the designation of a default tablespace works, we'll look at the following example. Let's say you are the PAYROLL application developer and you are working in the PAYROLL schema. The schema was created with the following statement:

```
create user PAYROLL
identified by payme
default tablespace PAYROLL_DATA
temporary tablespace TEMP_PAYROLL
quota unlimited on PAYROLL_DATA
quota unlimited on PAYROLL_INDEX
/
```

You could grant the schema the Oracle-defined CONNECT role using the statement

```
grant connect to PAYROLL
/
```

Next, you could create a basic table for the PAYROLL application using a statement like this:

```
create table PAY_SALARY (
       Empname              VARCHAR2(20),
       Empnum               NUMBER,
       Job_Title            VARCHAR2(10),
       Salary               NUMBER(9,2))
/
```

Now, you'll need to create a basic unique index for the PAYROLL application. The statement you'll use to create this index might look like the following:

```
create unique index PAY_SALARY_IDX
on PAY_SALARY (Empname, Empnum)
tablespace PAYROLL_INDEX
/
```

Notice that the table creation statement does not have a tablespace explicitly named, while the index does. By default, since the PAYROLL user was created pointing to the default tablespace PAYROLL_DATA, any objects that the PAYROLL user creates with no tablespace clause will be created in that tablespace. Notice also the granting of an amount of quota on each of the tablespaces to which the user will have access. Even though the user has been granted the ability to create tables through the CONNECT role, without quota being granted on a tablespace, the user could not create objects—he or she would not be allowed to use any physical space in the tablespace. Quota is granted either as a specific amount of physical space (for example, 10M) or as "unlimited." If you grant a specific amount of space, the user will be able to create and extend objects until the total amount of space used by these objects reaches that specific limit. If you grant quota as unlimited, the objects belonging to that user can grow to use up all available space in the tablespace.

Sizing Your Tablespaces

You deal with sizing issues every day, but you don't think about them very much. When you go into a grocery store, you make one sizing decision after another—what size can of corn to buy or how much meat is enough to feed you and your dinner guests. Will the economy-size package of ice cream be too big to be eaten in a reasonable amount of time? By now, you can make these decisions almost automatically because you've been shopping for a while. But how do you know, if you've never sized a tablespace, how big, or small, to make it? When you start out as a DBA, you will be called upon to size not only tablespaces but also the objects that will go into them.

There are several ways to determine the size that you can make your database tablespaces. Let's look at some possible scenarios to see the different approaches you can use in determining the sizes your tablespaces need to be.

A Development Database Moving into Production

If an existing database is moving from development into production, you can look at the volume of existing space currently being used. Once you have the current usage, you can meet with the developers and try to estimate how large each object in the database is projected to grow within the next year or two. You will have to consider how much disk space is available to you for establishing your new database. One goal you could have is to try to ensure that each tablespace will be large enough for each object to grow within it without running out of space for at least six months to a year. Sizing of production tablespaces becomes much more critical if you are supporting a database that will be available 24 hours a day, 7 days a week, 365 days a year (referred to as a 24 x 7 x 365 shop). As more electronic commerce sites come into being, there will be more and more demand for these types of shops.

A Copy of an Existing Database

If you are building a new database that will be a copy of an existing database, your job in sizing the tablespaces becomes much easier. You can perform the following steps:

1. Copy the scripts that were used to create the original database into the new database's directory structure.
2. Modify the creation scripts to contain the new database's tablespace names and directory locations.

3. Consider any changes to the new database that will increase its tablespace size requirements.
4. Build the new database.

Wow, that was easy! Once you've established an initial database on your system and scripted everything about the database build, things can get to be almost that simple.

Vendor-Supplied Products

If you are using an Oracle-supplied product, Oracle will generally tell you just how much space you need to build the database to support that product. We recommend adding extra space to Oracle's suggested values; they sometimes underestimate the amount of space you really need. Most third-party vendors will provide guidelines for their products' space requirements. Reading the documentation for any product that will be going into your database will help you determine the space requirements more accurately.

The Tablespace Default Storage Clause

Once you've decided on the size of each of your tablespaces, you'll need to look at a sizing clause that's available when you create each tablespace. This clause is very confusing at first, so we'll go slowly and see if we can make it easier to understand. This clause, called the tablespace default storage clause, is like a safety net beneath a trapeze artist. It is used when someone creates a segment—such as a table, index, cluster, temporary segment, or rollback segment—in a tablespace and doesn't tell Oracle what size to make the segment. For example, let's say you issue the following table creation statement with no storage clause:

```
create table MY_TAB
(My_Name  VARCHAR2(40))
/
```

Since no sizing is listed anywhere in the statement, Oracle will look at the tablespace default storage clause on the tablespace that is declared as your default tablespace to see what sizing parameters to use.

Storage Parameters

The storage parameters available for a segment are as follows:

- **initial extent** How big the segment's first extent will be
- **next extent** The segment's second extent size

- **pctincrease** A factor by which each successive extent will exponentially grow
- **minextents** Minimum number of extents the segment can have
- **maxextents** Maximum number of extents the segment can have

After the segment has been created, the initial and minextents values can be changed without dropping and rebuilding the segment using the **alter** command. However, the changes will not take effect until the segment is rebuilt.

But what happens if you do not provide Oracle with a tablespace default storage clause? Well, Oracle has a predetermined (very small) storage clause that it will use if you do not provide one when you create the tablespace. You are always better off providing a default storage clause for each tablespace that you create.

If you are not sure what values have been assigned to the default parameters for a tablespace, you can see the sizes in the DBA_TABLESPACES and USER_TABLESPACES views. Remember, these parameters are only used when a segment is created with no storage clause.

How Extents Work

When a segment is created, it will acquire at least one or more extents based on the value you put in for minextents. Let's say you've specified minextents equal to one. The initial extent will be used to store data until it no longer has any free space available. Will the extent be completely filled up? Well, that depends on the size established in the **pctfree** clause. This clause tells Oracle the percentage of each block in each extent to reserve for updates of existing rows. In other words, if you are inserting data into a row of a table but you don't know all the values for the row, the **pctfree** clause will tell Oracle how much space to save so you can come back later and expand the row without having to move it to a new block.

There is also a **pctused** clause, which informs Oracle that no new inserts can be placed into the block unless the block is less than the value of **pctused** full. For example, suppose **pctfree** is 10% and **pctused** is 40% (the defaults). Inserts will be placed into the block until the block becomes 90 percent full, which is 100 percent of the **pctfree** value. Since you have the minimum amount of space free (as determined by the **pctfree** value), a new insert cannot be placed into the block, so a new block will be allocated and the row will be placed there. Updates to existing rows within the block will use the 10 percent of free space. If, or when, space in the block is freed via data being removed, inserts will not take place into the block until the block becomes less than 40 percent full—the **pctused** value. Once the block becomes less than 40 percent full, inserts will be written into the block until it becomes 90 percent full again.

When additional data is added to the segment, the segment will extend by obtaining a second extent of the size specified by the **next** parameter. There is no guarantee that the second extent will be stored physically next to (or contiguous to) the first extent.

You can use the **pctincrease** parameter to minimize the number of extents to which a table will grow. If you set the **pctincrease** value to zero, each extent will be exactly the same size as the last extent in the table. If you set the **pctincrease** parameter to a value greater than zero, you might be letting yourself in for some trouble. You see, a non-zero value for this parameter can be dangerous because it causes the size of each successive extent to increase geometrically by the **pctincrease** factor that you have specified. For example, say you create a data table with an initial extent of 20 database blocks. You have declared the next extent to be 20 database blocks. You have also declared that the **pctincrease** will be 50%. Table 7-2 maps out the size that the fifth extent will be.

Gee, did that table get big fast. And the table will continue to grow even bigger at a much faster rate as the extents grow. In just ten extents, the table's size will be increased by 7700 percent! Keep in mind that the 185 database blocks mentioned in Table 7-2 could represent a large number of bytes. If the database block size is set to 8k (8192 bytes), the actual bytes needed for this extent would be 8192 * 185, or 1,515,520 bytes, or 1.5M of space. Imagine what the size of the next extent will be after 20 more extents!

Look again at Table 7-2. Notice that each extent after the initial one is based on the value that is given in the **next** extent parameter and not the size of the current extent. If you change the **pctincrease** parameter value, be sure to reevaluate what the **next** value should now be. For example, if you change the value of **pctincrease** to zero after the fifth extent, the sixth extent would be 20 database blocks and not 290 database blocks. Figure 7-12 graphs the growth of a table with **pctincrease** set to a number greater than zero. Figure 7-13 graphs the growth of a table with **pctincrease** set to a value of zero.

Extent	Extent Size	Total Blocks	The Math
Initial extent	20	20	Initial
Next extent	20	40	Next
Third extent	30	70	Next*1.5
Fourth extent	45	115	Next*1.5*1.5
Fifth extent	70	185	Next*1.5*1.5*1.5

TABLE 7-2. *Effects of Percent Increase*

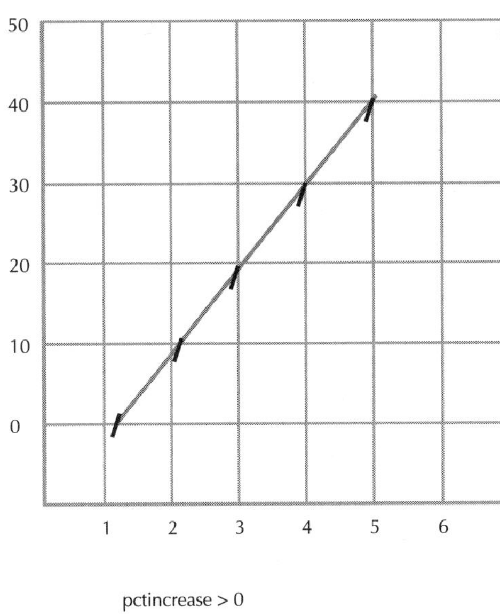

FIGURE 7-12. *Growth of a table with* ***pctincrease*** *greater than zero*

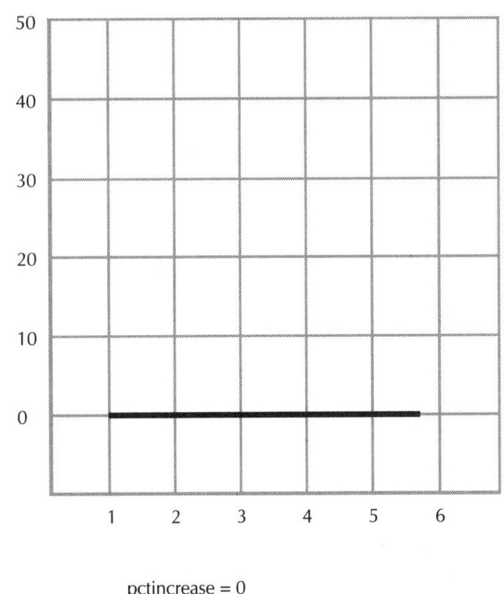

FIGURE 7-13. *Growth of a table with* ***pctincrease*** *set to zero*

Oracle9i provides an automatic segment space management option, but you must create your tablespaces as locally managed to take advantage of having Oracle manage the space. We'll talk more about locally managed tablespaces in Chapter 8.

Init.ora vs. SPFILE.ora

Historically, most nondefault configuration parameters have been placed in either the init.ora or config.ora files for Oracle's use when the database is started. One of the ongoing problems with having a static initialization file is that if you change configuration parameters dynamically (as you've been able to do since version 7), the changes are only in effect until the database is shut down. Once the database is restarted, unless you manually filter the changes back to the initialization file, you lose your modifications.

Examining the SPFILE Contents

Oracle now provides a new approach and new file, known as the SPFILE (Server Parameter file), to store the server parameters. The physical file is stored by default in the $ORACLE_HOME/dbs directory on some Unix systems and in ORACLE_HOME\databases on a Windows system and is named using the convention SPFILE<database_name>.ora. For example, the SPFILE for the DB9I database would be called SPFILEDB9I.ora.

If you attempt to edit this file, you will see a line of binary code at the top and bottom of the file and the rest of the file appears to be plaintext format. In reality, if you do edit this file, you will corrupt it! We believe that the line of code at either the top or bottom of the file contains a checksum of the file, and any modifications prevent the checksum of the modified file from matching the checksum stored in the binary line. The file will become unusable. Therefore, **do not modify this file interactively!**

Here are the contents of the SPFILE from our demo database:

```
*.compatible='9.0.0'
*.control_files='D:\oracle\oradata\mydb9\CONTROL01.CTL',
'D:\oracle\oradata\mydb9\CONTROL02.CTL',
'D:\oracle\oradata\mydb9\CONTROL03.CTL'
*.core_dump_dest='D:\oracle\admin\mydb9\cdump'
*.db_block_size=4096
*.db_cache_size=58720256
*.db_domain='world'
*.db_name='db9i
*.dispatchers='(PROTOCOL=TCP)(SER=MODOSE)','(PROTOCOL=TCP)
(PRE=oracle.aurora.server.GiopServer)','(PROTOCOL=TCP)
(PRE=oracle.aurora.server.SGiopServer)'
```

```
*.fast_start_mttr_target=300
*.instance_name='mydb9'
*.java_pool_size='58720256'
*.large_pool_size='1048576'
*.open_cursors=300
*.processes=150
*.remote_login_passwordfile='EXCLUSIVE'
*.shared_pool_size=58720256
*.sort_area_size=524288
*.timed_statistics=TRUE
*.undo_management='AUTO'
*.undo_tablespace='UNDOTBS'
*.user_dump_dest='D:\oracle\admin\mydb9\udump'
```

Note that there are values for both the Java pool and large pool and that the number of OPEN_CURSORS and PROCESSES is much larger than the values in previous releases. Also note that, by default, TIMED_STATISTICS are enabled (finally!) and the Undo Tablespace approach is used instead of rollback segments. The parameter FAST_START_MTTR_TARGET enables you to specify the number of seconds that it should take for database crash recovery. The range of values is between 0 and 3600. In this example, the recovery rate is set to 5 minutes.

Working with an SPFILE

If an SPFILE is present in the ORACLE_HOME\databases directory, Oracle will use it for database startup. If the file is not present, Oracle will look for the init.ora file. If none is available, Oracle will error, and you will then have to specify the initialization parameter file location using "pfile=".

The beauty of using an SPFILE is that when you issue **alter system** statements, you can specify whether you want the changes retained permanently, just used for the current session, or both. Also, you can use the same parameter file for all members of a Real Application Cluster (formerly known as Parallel Server). Using an SPFILE enables you to use the Recovery Manager to back up the initialization parameters automatically when performing backups. The SPFILE only resides on the server, and once created, the Oracle server maintains it.

To create an SPFILE from your current init.ora file, you issue the statement:

```
create SPFILE [=<spfile_name>]
  from PFILE[=<pfile_name>]
```

In later versions, you should not have to enter the SPFILE name. You must have SYSDBA or SYSOPER privileges to execute this command.

To create an init.ora file from a current SPFILE, you issue the statement:

```
create PFILE [=<pfile_name>]
  from SPFILE[=<spfile_name>]
```

Therefore, if you want to interactively modify an SPFILE, you can convert it to init.ora, modify it, and then convert it back. To view the contents of the SPFILE, you can use the V$SPPARAMETER view.

When you modify a system parameter, you can specify whether to retain the value until the database is shut down (Memory-resident), permanent (SPFILE), or both by using the SCOPE clause as follows:

```
alter system set SORT_AREA_SIZE=1048576 scope=both;
```

The SCOPE clause options are MEMORY, SPFILE, BOTH. Therefore, if you are changing a parameter that is not dynamic but you want it to be written to the SPFILE, you can list the SCOPE as SPFILE. You can also use the keyword DEFERRED for dynamic parameters, which makes them available only for future sessions. If you have started the database using an init.ora file, the changes to the SPFILE will not be in use. You can enable using the SPFILE from a location other than the default by specifying "spfile=<location_of_the_SPFILE_file>".

As we mentioned earlier, you can share the same SPFILE among different instances. To enable one SPFILE to support different instances, the parameters within the SPFILE must each contain an individual SID. For example, if the instances were named DB1I, DB2I, and DB3I, the INSTANCE_NAME parameter entries would be

```
db1i.instance_name=db1i
db2i.instance_name=db2i
db3i.instance_name=db3i
```

Each instance would contain an instance-specific initialization parameter file with just one entry: the designation SPFILE=<location_of_the_actual_SPFILE>. For example, if the SPFILE were located in /dev/rdisk3/spfile, the location specified in the instance init.ora file would be SPFILE=/dev/rdisk3/spfile.

Instance vs. Database

What constitutes an instance, and what makes up a database? Although the terms are often used interchangeably, "instance" and "database" in the Oracle world have very specific meanings. Since nomenclature is often important, let's take a quick look at the meanings of each of these words.

At a minimum, an Oracle instance is made up of the following background processes:

- **SMON** System monitor
- **PMON** Process monitor

- **DBWR** Database writer
- **LGWR** Log writer
- **CKPT** Checkpoint writer

It may also include other processes, such as:

- **RECO** Recovery manager for distributed databases
- **ARCH** Archive log writer
- **SNP#** Job queue processes
- **Other processes** Any other detached processes used to support parallel servers or multithreaded servers

Although the system global area (SGA), which is a reserved shared memory area, is not a process, it is included with the detached processes as part of the instance. So the detached processes, coupled with the SGA, make up the instance. In the next section, we'll look more closely at the SGA and its composition.

As we explained in Chapter 2, the database is the set of physical files in which all of the objects (tables, indexes, views, synonyms, procedures, programs, etc.) and all of the metadata (data dictionary information) are stored. There is often a mix of logical and physical references when we talk about a database. The logical entities are the tablespaces, tables, indexes, views, and other objects, while the physical entities are the actual datafiles that reside at the operating system level and the blocks allocated within those datafiles. Table 7-3 shows the relationship between the logical constructs and the physical objects that make up an Oracle database.

Logical Construct	Physical Implementation
Instance	Database
Tablespace	Datafiles
Tables/indexes/rollback and temporary segments	Segments
Extents	Blocks

TABLE 7-3. *Relationship of Logical to Physical Database Constructs*

Composition of the SGA

Let's take a moment to think about your office or work area at your place of business. You probably have a desk in which to store things like office supplies. You may have your personal computer sitting on your desk or on a table next to or attached to your desk. Regardless of your profession, you have books in either a bookshelf or cupboard so that you can easily use them for references. In other words, you have a specific area in which you do your work and store your documents or reference materials. Oracle is the same way except that Oracle uses a part of the computer's memory as its work place.

Now, what happens if someone comes in and rummages through your desk to look for something or takes books from your shelf without telling you? Chances are, your area will be disrupted and you will not be able to find the information you need when you need it. So, what do you do? Well, if you are in an office with a door, you install a lock, and whenever you are away from your office, you lock the door so no one else can get in and disturb your possessions. Oracle locks an area of the computer's memory and performs its work there. This area is called the system global area, or SGA.

From a different perspective, Oracle uses the SGA to enable processes to share information and resources. When you run a SQL script, the first time the script is presented, Oracle performs several tasks to process the code before it is run. If you run the same piece of code over again and Oracle still has the information available in the SGA, Oracle can use the information that is already stored about the code to reduce the amount of processing time. If many users run the same code, Oracle's reuse of the stored information can substantially reduce the amount of processing time for each execution of the code.

Defining the SGA

So, what is the SGA really, and why do you care what's in it? Remember that the SGA plus the processes described earlier make up an Oracle instance. Oracle uses the SGA to manage interaction between all the user processes and the database itself. By compartmentalizing the SGA, multiple users can share data within memory, avoiding the need to physically access data from disks repeatedly—a time-consuming process.

The SGA may enable the sharing of data blocks, rollback segment blocks, SQL statements, and multithreaded server information. If you get the SGA tuned well for your application, you will be able to eliminate the database's memory usage as a potential performance problem. We'll talk more about performance in Chapter 12.

Controlling the Size of the SGA

Historically, the SGA has always been a static allocation of memory shared across all threads of execution. The memory size is calculated based on the values of parameters in the init.ora file, and once allocated, the memory area cannot grow or shrink. To change the size of any of the values on which the SGA is based, you must first shut the database down, change the value of the parameter in the init.ora file, and then restart the database. Shutting a 24 x 7 x 365 database down to change a parameter can impact production systems.

To solve this problem, Oracle has introduced a dynamic SQL area in Oracle9i. The SGA configuration can now be changed while the database is running so you can modify buffer cache, shared pool, and large pool values on the fly without shutting the database down. You can also impose limits at database startup on how much physical memory is used for the SGA. In this way, you could underallocate memory for the buffer cache, shared pool, and large pool at startup, and then they could grow and shrink as they need to based on their workloads.

To perform this work, Oracle has provided a new unit of allocation for the SGA called a *granule* that represents an amount of contiguous virtual memory and is based on the size of the parameter SGA_MAX_SIZE. To determine a granule's size, you take the total size of the SGA. If the SGA total size is less than 128M, each granule will be 4M. If the SGA is larger than 128M, the granule size will be 16M.

You can use the V$BUFFER_POOL view to determine the allocated granules for the components of the buffer cache that owns granules. The buffer cache can grow and shrink based on the granule boundaries. Initially, the minimum amount of granules to be allocated is three: one for the fixed SGA (including redo buffers), one for the buffer cache, and one for the shared pool. V$BUFFER_POOL displays the number of granules allocated to each component, any pending operations (like allocation or freeing of granules when you use the **alter system** command, or the corresponding self-tuning), and the target size in granules. Unfortunately, you can't easily find or see the granule size that's being used. Here's an example query for the V$BUFFER_POOL:

```
select Block_Size, Current_Size, Buffers, Target_Size, Prev_Size
  from V$BUFFER_POOL
 where BUFFER != 0;

BLOCK_SIZE CURRENT_SIZE    BUFFERS TARGET_SIZE  PREV_SIZE
---------- ------------ ---------- ----------- ----------
      4096           56      13769          56          0

where:
BLOCK_SIZE - Block size for buffers in this component
```

```
PREV_SIZE - Primary block size (Y or N)
CURRENT_SIZE - Present size of the component in Mb
BUFFERS - Present number of buffers in this component
TARGET_SIZE - The new target size if a resize is in progress, otherwise null
```

You can dynamically alter the SHARED_POOL_SIZE and LARGE_POOL_SIZE using **alter system** command, but the restrictions are that the value you use must be an integer multiple of the granule size and the total SGA size cannot exceed the SGA_MAX_SIZE value. Note that you cannot change the Java pool size dynamically.

In the case of the DB_CACHE_SIZE, the two rules apply as well as the restriction that the DB_CACHE_SIZE cannot be set to zero.

Let's look at some examples to see how changing the size plays out.

```
Init.ora parameter values:
SGA_MAX_AREA = 128M
DB_CACHE_SIZE = 96M
SHARED_POOL_SIZE = 48M
```

What will happen? Since the combined size of the DB_CACHE_SIZE + SHARED_POOL_SIZE exceeds the SGA_MAX_AREA, the database will not come up.

```
alter system set SHARED_POOL_SIZE = 64M;
(insufficient memory error message)
. . .
alter system set DB_CACHE_SIZE = 64M;
alter system set SHARED_POOL_SIZE = 64M;
(insufficient memory error message, check V$BUFFER_POOL to see when the shrink has completed)
alter system set SHARED_POOL_SIZE = 64M;
```

What we see in this example is that there is a lag between issuing the alter command and the command to shrink completing. Once the two parameters have been adjusted not to exceed the SGA_MAX_AREA, the database will come up.

When a DBA increases the memory allocation, the system takes reserved granules (as specified in the init.ora parameter file) and adds or subtracts granules to the component by rounding the required size up to the nearest multiple of 16M. Increasing a component's size by adding reserved granules is known as "growing a component's SGA memory area."

How to See the Size of the SGA Using a V$ View

You can query the V$ view V$SGA to see the size of the SGA, as shown in the following listing:

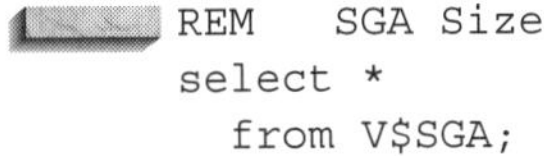

```
REM   SGA Size
select *
  from V$SGA;
```

Sample output from V$SGA is shown below. The output shows the size of the different areas within the SGA.

```
NAME                        VALUE
-------------------- ------------
Fixed Size                  38904
Variable Size            10313056
Database Buffers         10240000
Redo Buffers                16384
```

As shown in the V$SGA query output, the database has 10,240,000 bytes dedicated to its database block buffer cache (the "Database Buffers" line). The redo log buffer cache (the "Redo Buffers" line) is 16,384 bytes in size. The shared SQL area is the chief component of the "Variable Size" of the SGA, which accounts for 10,313,056 bytes in the example.

In general, increasing the size of the SGA will improve the performance of your database environment. You should ensure that the SGA is not so large that it causes swapping and paging to occur at the operating system level. (Swapping and paging are mechanisms that the operating system and Oracle use to move information in and out of the computer's memory. Each time a chunk of information is moved into or out of a computer's memory, there is a set amount of "cost" for the operation in time lost from doing the actual work of processing. Therefore, each time a paging or swapping operation occurs, system and database performance can be affected.)

About the Demo Tables

When you create a database, several scripts are run—either by Oracle or by you. If you accept Oracle's offer to build a default database (and even if you don't), you'll find that Oracle creates several default users within the database based on what template or approach you use to create the database. The majority of these users will be locked with their passwords preexpired. As you find a need to enable these users, you can unlock the accounts and alter the passwords. You can look at the users within the database and their account status (thereby determining what accounts have preexpired passwords) by issuing the following command:

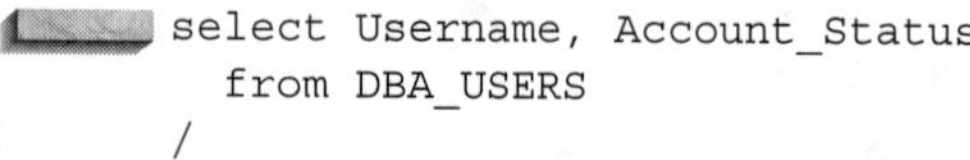

```
select Username, Account_Status
  from DBA_USERS
/
```

The results from a modified default database created in version 9.0.1 on a Windows system are

```
USERNAME                       ACCOUNT_STATUS
------------------------------ ------------------
SYS                            OPEN
SYSTEM                         OPEN
DBSNMP                         OPEN
AURORA$JIS$UTILITY$            OPEN
...
MDSYS                          EXPIRED & LOCKED
ORDPLUGINS                     EXPIRED & LOCKED
ORDSYS                         EXPIRED & LOCKED

30 rows selected.
```

You can unlock an account and change the password at the same time by issuing the following command:

```
alter user <USERNAME> identified by <NEW_PASSWORD> account unlock;
```

CHAPTER 8

General Database Considerations

To paraphrase an old adage, an Oracle DBA's work is never done. As a DBA, you will never lack for things to do. However, there are many ways in which you can do your tasks, and some approaches may prove to be easier or quicker than others.

In this chapter, we'll look at some of the general database considerations and tasks that you can perform to help you maintain your database effectively. Since every object in your database is housed in a tablespace, we're going to spend quite a bit of time looking at tablespaces and the actions you can take to make them function optimally. We'll also cover the parameters you use the most for creating tables, indexes, and users, as well as some considerations for sizing those objects. We'll talk more about privileges, grants, roles, synonyms, and views in Chapter 10 when we talk about securing your database.

The Care and Feeding of Tablespaces

To get things rolling, let's pack a picnic lunch and go off to the zoo for a while. My, isn't the weather glorious? The sun is shining and the birds are singing—if not outside your window, then somewhere in the world! Ah. Here we are at the zoo. As we enter the zoo, there are wide expanses of land with fences around each one. Oh, look! There's Monkey Island with its moat of water around the outside and piles of rocks and trees for the monkeys to climb. The monkey over there is smiling at the guy with the camera as he takes his picture. How funny! To our right is the Feline House with the lions and tigers and panthers and other big cats. Let's walk in there for a minute. Wow! Look at how large that male lion is. Isn't he ferocious? The female looks almost playful sitting next to him. There's a panther in the cage next to them. Look at that tiger prowling around his cage. He's so sleek looking. It sure is a good thing they didn't put the lions and tigers together, isn't it? We suspect they would not get along well at all. Well, let's move on to the other areas. There's a mountain goat sitting on top of a huge rock near the top of that mountain to our left. There are antelope and giraffes and a reptile house, as well as seals and bears and an Amazon rain forest. Gee! Look at the size of that elephant. There is just too much to see in one day here, and our time to visit is just about up.

Wasn't that fun? Now, what in the world do animals in a zoo have to do with objects in tablespaces? So glad you asked! Let's review what we saw in the zoo. In some areas, there were wide expanses of land with several kinds of animals living happily together, while in other areas, there were cages with only one kind of animal in each cage. Antelope can live happily with giraffes and elephants, but lions would probably enjoy an antelope meal or two. The ideal would be to house each kind of animal in its own area with all of the space it needed to live safely and happily. In the next section, we'll apply these ideas to a database and show you how you can effectively place your objects.

Creating and Dropping a Tablespace

There are three actions that you can take in regard to a tablespace: create, alter, and drop. Before we begin talking about maintaining and modifying tablespaces, we need to look at how you go about creating and removing a tablespace.

There are actually two different types of tablespaces: data dictionary managed ones and locally managed ones. As the name implies, the tablespaces that are data dictionary managed have their information stored within the data dictionary. This means that every time an extent is allocated in the tablespace, information must be modified in both the SYS free extents table (FET$) and used extents table (UET$). Picture, if you will, a person keeping score. Each time an extent is allocated, the person must run over to the FET$ table and remove an extent. The scorekeeper must then run over to the UET$ table and add the extent information there. If a large number of extents are allocated and deallocated frequently, imagine our poor scorekeeper madly running from one table to the other and back again. There could certainly be a lot of overhead activity for Oracle just to keep track of the tablespaces' space usage.

To help reduce the overhead of volatile tablespaces and reduce fragmentation within the tablespaces, Oracle created another approach to tablespace space usage called the locally managed tablespace. When you create a locally managed tablespace, Oracle stores the extent information in a bitmap within the datafile header itself and not within the data dictionary. As extents are allocated and deallocated, the space usage is tracked within the header—a much more efficient way to track the information.

Although you have the option with data dictionary managed tablespaces to create extents that can be increased in size using the **pctincrease** parameter, we strongly urge you to use a **pctincrease** of zero. With locally managed tablespaces you can declare that each extent will be of a uniform size, and you can describe what that size is to be. By using uniform extent sizes, you ensure that when an extent is dropped, the space can easily be reused the next time an extent is needed. You can accomplish the same thing with data dictionary managed tablespaces, but you have to enforce uniform extent sizes yourself by ensuring that your initial and next extent values are the same and that you have set the **pctincrease** value to zero instead of allowing Oracle to handle the allocations itself.

Creating a Tablespace

The command syntax to create or drop a tablespace is mapped out in the Oracle-supplied documentation, but the parameters may seem a bit confusing, so let's take a look at them now. Table 8-1 shows the parameters you can use in the **create tablespace** command.

Parameter	**Definition**
Tablespace Name	The name assigned to the tablespace—should reflect the tablespace's functionality
Datafile specifications:	
File location	The fully qualified directory path and file name
Size	The total initial allocated size of the datafile
Reuse	If the datafile exists, reuse the file instead of giving an error. The datafile must be the same size as defined in the **size** parameter.
Autoextend	Enable/disable Oracle's ability to automatically increase the size of the datafile—can either be **off** or **on**. If **on**, the additional parameters are **next**: number of bytes by which to increase file each time it extends **maxsize**: largest size to which the datafile can grow—can be **unlimited**
Minimum extent	Used to control fragmentation—all extents must be this size or a multiple of it
Blocksize	An integer value used to specify a nondefault block size in bytes or kilobytes
Logging/Nologging	Specifies whether redo log information is to be kept on objects in the tablespace
Default storage	The amount of space to allocate for an object if no storage clause is supplied—use with the following additional parameters:
Initial	The amount of space to allocate for the first extent
Next	The amount of space to allocate for the second and successive extents
Minextents	The minimum number of extents to allocate
Maxextents	The maximum number of extents to allocate—can be set to **unlimited**
Pctincrease	The percentage by which to enlarge successive extents—based on the value of **next**

TABLE 8-1. *Create Tablespace Parameters*

Parameter	Definition
Freelist groups	Used with the RAC option to specify the number of freelists for objects created in this tablespace without storage clauses
Freelists	Specifies the number of freelists for objects created in this tablespace without storage clauses
Optimal	Used only for rollback segments—shows the minimum amount of space to automatically shrink rollback segments after they have extended beyond the optimal value
Online/Offline	Specifies the state in which the tablespace should initially be placed
Permanent/Temporary	Specifies whether the tablespace will hold objects or be used for temporary segments
Extent management	Used with the following additional parameters:
Dictionary	Specifies that the extent management will be performed in the data dictionary
Local	Specifies that some part of the datafile has been set aside for a bitmap. The extent management choices for local are either **autoallocate**, where the space will be automatically allocated as needed, or **uniform**. If **uniform**, the additional parameter is an integer **size** specified in either kilobytes or megabytes.
Segment space management	Specify **manual** to have Oracle manage the free space of segments in the tablespace using freelists or **auto** to have Oracle manage the space using a bitmap. This applies only to locally managed tablespaces.

TABLE 8-1. *Create Tablespace Parameters* (continued)

Within the datafile parameters is the qualifier **reuse**. This qualifier can be used in place of a size specification in a tablespace creation statement. Here are a few rules associated with the **reuse** qualifier:

- If the file already exists, its size must match that of the **size** parameter. If no **size** parameter is specified, the size is assumed to be that of the existing datafile.

- If the file does not exist, Oracle ignores this clause and creates the file.
- You can omit this clause only if the file does not already exist. If you omit this clause, Oracle creates the file.

Now that you've seen the parameters, let's see if you can put them together and create a tablespace. First, to see what Oracle will supply as default values, create a tablespace without specifying anything but the required parameters:

```
create tablespace MYTAB
  datafile 'G:\oracle\oradata\mydb9\mytab01.dbf'
  size 1M;
```

Now, you can use the DBA_TABLESPACES view we told you about in Chapter 3 to see what default values Oracle supplies.

```
select *
  from DBA_TABLESPACES
 where Tablespace_Name = 'MYTAB';

TABLESPACE_NAME                BLOCK_SIZE INITIAL_EXTENT NEXT_EXTENT MIN_EXTENTS
------------------------------ ---------- -------------- ----------- -----------
MAX_EXTENTS PCT_INCREASE MIN_EXTLEN STATUS    CONTENTS  LOGGING   EXTENT_MAN
----------- ------------ ---------- --------- --------- --------- ----------
ALLOCATIO PLU SEGMEN
--------- --- ------
MYTAB                                4096          65536                       1
 2147483645                   65536 ONLINE    PERMANENT LOGGING   LOCAL
SYSTEM    NO  MANUAL
```

In this example, Oracle has made the initial extent 16 database blocks in size. There is no listed next extent size. The minimum extents are set to 1, while the maximum extents value is set to 2 gigabytes. The percent increase is not listed, and the tablespace is placed online, is permanent, and available with logging enabled. The tablespace is created as locally managed with manual segment management. Now, because the tablespace is locally managed, you can't specify default storage parameters nor can you specify a MINIMUM_EXTENT value. If AUTOALLOCATE is specified, the tablespace is system managed with the smallest extent size being 64K. If UNIFORM SIZE is specified, then the tablespace is managed with uniform size extents of the specified SIZE value you put in. By default, if you do not specify a value for SIZE, 1M is used.

Dropping a Tablespace

To permanently remove a tablespace from your database, you can use the **drop tablespace** command. However, to really drop a tablespace, the tablespace must first be placed offline to ensure that no transactions are being performed while you are trying to remove the tablespace from the system. You must remember, too, that when you drop the tablespace from your database, you are only removing the entry information from the data dictionary; you are not removing the datafile from the operating system directory structure unless you include the phrase **and datafiles**. To drop the tablespace and ensure that the underlying datafiles are also removed, follow these steps:

1. Alter the tablespace offline.
2. Issue the **drop tablespace** command. You must include the command phrase **including contents and datafiles** to ensure that the underlying files are removed from the operating system directory.

You can drop the MYTAB tablespace by issuing the following commands:

```
alter tablespace MYTAB offline;
drop tablespace MYTAB including contents and datafiles;
```

Note that if there has never been any data stored in the tablespace, you do not have to specify **including contents** for the tablespace to be dropped. However, if you want to remove the underlying datafiles from the operating system, you must include the entire phrase **including contents and datafiles** when you issue the **drop** command, even if the tablespace has never been used.

Placing Objects in Tablespaces

Let's take what you've seen at the zoo and apply the concepts to your database and tablespaces. All the objects in your tablespaces (tables, views, indexes, sequences, packages, procedures, etc.) would be most "happy" if each one was in its own tablespace. However, as with the zoo, that's not always possible in the real world. Imagine the waste of resources if you placed a 200-byte table alone on a 9-gigabyte disk. My, wouldn't your management like that? No! You are encouraged by your management to house objects together, with as little wasted space as possible.

Just as you would not put lions and tigers in the same confined area because they would attempt to dominate each other, you should not put table segments and index segments in the same tablespace. They could "fight" each other and cause disk contention. What else will you want to keep separate? You will want to house rollback segments and temporary segments in separate tablespaces on separate disks. You will also want to place your control files, redo log files, and archive log files on separate disks.

Wouldn't it be wonderful to be able to start with a totally fresh and new database and begin to place objects and tablespaces from the beginning exactly where they should go? Unfortunately, you don't always have this luxury. More often than not, you will inherit a database that's already laid out, and not necessarily in the best manner. What can you do about a database whose objects are placed badly? Why, you can change it, of course.

Changing Your Tablespace Configuration

If you have inherited a database, how will you know whether it is laid out well or not? The first thing you can do is look at the current configuration. We've talked extensively about the DBA_ (pronounced "DBA underscore") views in Chapters 3 and 5. Let's review just a bit.

The first view you can look at is the DBA_TABLESPACES view. This view will show you the overall information about the tablespaces that are currently in your database and whether they are online and available or offline and unavailable. You can select parts of the view to gain information about the tablespaces in your database. You can look at the Tablespace_Name and the Status of each tablespace by performing the following query:

```
select Tablespace_Name, Status
  from DBA_TABLESPACES;

TABLESPACE_NAME                STATUS
------------------------------ ---------
SYSTEM                         ONLINE
UNDOTBS                        ONLINE
USERS                          ONLINE
TEMP                           ONLINE
OEM_REPOSITORY                 ONLINE
INDX                           ONLINE
DATA                           ONLINE
TOOLS                          ONLINE

8 rows selected.
```

So, in this database, there are eight tablespaces, and all of them are online and available. It's really great to know how many tablespaces you have and their names, but, looking at this report, you still don't have a clear picture of the location of each of the tablespaces on disks in your system.

You can use the DBA_DATA_FILES view, which shows you the names of the tablespaces that exist in your database, the datafiles that make up the tablespaces and their locations on disks, and the initial amount of space that's been allocated for each datafile. This view does not give you the status of each tablespace or the storage values assigned to the tablespace. Thus, both views are important and provide different pieces to help you build a complete picture of your tablespace configuration and composition. For now, you are interested in getting the location of each of the datafiles in each of the tablespaces. Here are both the script to use to see this information and the output from the command:

```
set pagesize 999
column Tablespace_Name format a15
column File_Name format a50
select Tablespace_Name, File_Name
  from DBA_DATA_FILES;

TABLESPACE_NAME FILE_NAME
--------------- --------------------------------------------------
SYSTEM          C:\ORACLE\ORA90\ORADATA\MYDB9\SYSTEM01.DBF
UNDOTBS         E:\ORACLE\ORA90\ORADATA\MYDB9\UNDOTBS01.DBF
USERS           F:\ORACLE\ORA90\ORADATA\MYDB9\USERS01.DBF
TEMP            G:\ORACLE\ORA90\ORADATA\MYDB9\TEMP1_.DBF
OEM_REPOSITORY  F:\ORACLE\ORA90\ORADATA\MYDB9\OEMREP01.DBF
INDX            F:\ORACLE\ORA90\ORADATA\MYDB9\INDX01.DBF
DATA            G:\ORACLE\ORA90\ORADATA\MYDB9\DATA01.DBF
TOOLS           F:\ORACLE\ORA90\ORADATA\MYDB9\TOOLS01.DBF

8 rows selected.
```

The output shows that the tablespaces are on four different disks but with the same directory naming convention. Using the same naming convention for each database for each disk makes maintaining the database much easier. Under normal circumstances—that is, in a shop that follows a set of standards—if you know the name of one directory location for one of your files, you will be able to find the rest of the database files by a quick check of each disk for the same directory name. In an area where standards have not been followed, all bets are off. Datafiles may have been placed anywhere on the system. In that case, the only way you will be able to find the locations of the datafiles for your database is to query the DBA_DATA_FILES view, as shown above, and add an **order by** qualifier on the Tablespace_Name column to make it easier to find all the files for a single tablespace.

Note that if you installed and are looking at the Oracle-supplied demonstration database, the tablespaces, as well as all of the other files associated with the database, may be on the same disk in the same directory. You should not be surprised to see this form of configuration for the demo database since Oracle doesn't know what disks you have available on your particular system. If, however, you see this layout (all of the tablespaces and support files on one disk) on your production system, you know you are in trouble.

Moving the Contents of a Tablespace

A tablespace can have one or more datafiles, so you want to be sure you know where all of the datafiles for a tablespace are located. There are several approaches that you can use, including using the Oracle Enterprise Manager (OEM) tools, to move a tablespace's datafile(s) from one disk to another. Right now, we'll concentrate on the manual steps so that you can learn them.

To move a tablespace from one disk to another, the tablespace must first be placed offline. By placing the tablespace offline, you will ensure that no one is performing any transactions in the tablespace while you are trying to move it. However, while the tablespace is offline, no one can access any of its contents. Isn't that a dual-edged sword! Make sure you have let everyone who needs to know that the tablespace and its contents will be unavailable during the time you are moving it.

Here are the steps you will perform to move the tablespace from one disk to another:

1. From SQL*Plus, take the tablespace offline by issuing the command:

   ```
   alter tablespace <tablespace_name> offline;
   ```

2. From the operating system level, copy the tablespace's datafile(s) to its new location.

3. From SQL*Plus, rename the datafile to modify the location in the data dictionary:

   ```
   alter tablespace <tablespace_name>
   rename datafile '<directory_name><file_name>' to
   '<new_directory_name><file_name>';
   ```

4. From SQL*Plus, put the tablespace online:

   ```
   alter tablespace <tablespace_name> online;
   ```

5. From the operating system level, remove the datafile(s) from the old directory.

On some operating systems, you can reverse steps 2 and 3, but on others, you cannot rename the datafile until an actual file exists in the new directory location. Therefore, we recommend that you make sure the file exists in its new location before you do the logical rename for the datafile. Also, you can eliminate step 5 if you move the datafile in step 2 instead of copying it. We recommend copying it though, just in case there is a problem with the move.

Using these steps, you can move the datafiles that make up the DATA tablespace from one disk to another. The same steps are given next, without the step numbers, with the actual values filled in to move the DATA tablespace.

```
alter tablespace DATA offline;
Tablespace altered.
```

From the operating system, you can now copy the datafile(s) for the DATA tablespace from one disk to another. On a Unix system, the command would look like the following:

```
cp /ora9i/oradata1/mydb9/data01.dbf /ora9i/oradata/mydb9/data01.dbf
```

From a Windows NT system, you can copy and paste the file from one directory to the other or, at the DOS prompt, issue the **copy** command as follows:

```
copy G:\ora9i\oradata\mydb9\data01.dbf C:\ora9i\oradata\mydb9\data01.dbf
```

After the copy of the datafile(s) has been completed, from SQL*Plus, type the following commands to modify the data dictionary and put the tablespace back online:

```
alter tablespace DATA
rename datafile 'G:\ORA9I\ORADATA\MYDB9\DATA01.DBF' to 'C:\ORA9I\ORADATA\MYDB9\DATA01.DBF';
Tablespace altered.
alter tablespace DATA online;
Tablespace altered.
```

That was easy! The only step left is to go back to the operating system level and delete the datafile from the G disk. On a Windows NT system, you can use Microsoft Windows Explorer to select the file and delete it. From a Unix system, you would use the following command:

```
rm /ora9i/oradata1/mydb9/data01.dbf
```

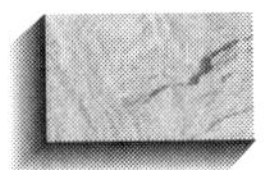

NOTE
Because you cannot take the SYSTEM tablespace offline, you can't relocate the datafiles for the SYSTEM tablespace to another disk without rebuilding the database.

Resizing a Tablespace

Some of the authors love to go on cruises, and some of us have been on several different ones. The cruise lines seem to be in a contest to see who can entice you to eat more by offering food service 24 hours a day and making each food offering look incredibly delectable. By the end of a cruise, the salt air seems to have shrunk the clothes you brought, and you notice that they've become snugger (more snug? Okay, just plain tight!) than they were when you boarded the ship.

Marlene has a law about the expansion of things in general. Her law states that "given the opportunity, anything will expand to exceed any allocated amount of space." Actually, on thinking about it, Oracle may have written that law, since everything in an Oracle database seems, over time, to expand to exceed the given amount of space available. Therefore, one thing you must carefully monitor in your database is the amount of space each object is using. As objects grow, the amount of free space available in their tablespace decreases. Eventually, if you do not take any action, a tablespace can fill to a point where there is not enough room to allocate another extent. Later in this chapter we'll show you a method for monitoring your tablespace growth. We'll show you how to add a datafile to your tablespace if there is not enough space available to support the extension of the object of interest.

There are several different actions you can take to help avoid this situation:

- Add one or more datafiles to the tablespace.
- Enable a mechanism called autoextend. (We'll discuss the advantages and disadvantages of using autoextend in a later section.)

Under what circumstances would you want to add a datafile to a tablespace? Let's say you have a production database with a table that has grown much faster than had been predicted. The tablespace that houses the table is rapidly running out of space, but it's the middle of a very busy workday and you cannot take the tablespace offline and rebuild it with more space right now. You can add a datafile to the tablespace to enable the table to continue to grow. If you do not take some kind of action before the tablespace reaches a point where it is unable to find any more usable space, the user who needs the space to perform work in the database will not be able to perform that work. Anything that delays work in a database can be costly to a company. In cases where a company relies on electronic commerce—customers being able to buy things from an Internet Web site—the loss of revenue while a database or table is unavailable for any length of time can run into tens of thousands of dollars.

Adding Space to a Tablespace

To add a datafile to a tablespace, you must first determine where the current datafile(s) for the tablespace are and how much room is available on the disk where you will be placing the new datafile. You can use the script we gave you earlier in this chapter to display the tablespace names and datafile locations. To see how much space is available on the disk of interest, for a Unix system, you can use the command:

```
df -k
```

NOTE

*The **df –k** command may report that there is only a small amount of space available within a file system. There may be unallocated space on a disk. You should check with the system administrator or system group to see if there is any unallocated space. You may find that your Unix administrator does not place file systems on all drives; space is sometimes reserved for emergency use. This reserved space will not be shown via a **df** command.*

For a Windows system, from the Windows Explorer, click on the disk of interest, and the amount of used and free space will be displayed at the bottom of the screen. You can also click the right mouse button while the disk is highlighted. Select the Properties option, and a graph of the used and available disk space will be displayed.

Once you know the amount of available space on the disk, you must decide how big you should make the datafile to add to the tablespace. In reality, how big you can make your datafile may depend more on how much space is available for your use and less on the ideal size to which you would like to be able to expand the tablespace. If you have a tablespace that is filling rapidly, you may want to increase its size by a much larger amount than if your tablespace has been filling very slowly over a long period of time.

Let's say you have a tablespace that currently has 300 megabytes of space allocated to it. Your reports show you that 260 megabytes are currently being used. That leaves you 40 megabytes of free space in which to grow. That sounds like a lot of space, but it may not be. Your disk has over 3 gigabytes of space free. As you spend more time working with your database and applications, you begin to get a feel for what the "right" amount of space to allocate should be. Some of the questions that you will ask both yourself and your developers to determine how much space to add are as follows:

- How much space is available on the disk of interest?
- Is this disk dedicated to your Oracle database, or is it shared with other applications and shared for other uses?
- How fast have the objects in the tablespace been expanding?

- Has there recently been a new object added that is growing rapidly?
- How many other tablespaces are located on the same disk?
- Are there tables that can have data either purged or removed to a history table?
- How much more space is needed to accommodate newly added objects?
- Should additional disk space be purchased to accommodate the addition of future objects?

In our scenario, we already have the first answer: 3 gigabytes of space are left. We'll fill in the rest of the answers by saying that the disk is a dedicated Oracle disk with only one other, very slow growing tablespace that has a great deal of growth room. The tablespace of interest has only just recently started to grow rapidly because a new table was added that is a huge data entry table. You have two choices under these circumstances. You can either add a large datafile to the tablespace or move the new table to its own tablespace and size the new tablespace to match the table's growth pattern. Since this section is devoted to enlarging a tablespace, we'll show you the steps to perform this task.

To keep round numbers, we'll arbitrarily choose to add another 400 megabytes of space to the tablespace to support the expansion of the new table. For this example, the tablespace name is USER_DATA, and the directory that the tablespace datafile is in is F:\ora9i\oradata\mydb9\. The name of the original datafile is user01.dbf. To make it easier to recognize that the new datafile is associated with the USER_DATA tablespace and the user01.dbf datafile, you will want to name the new datafile user02.dbf. To add the space, all you need to do is submit the following command:

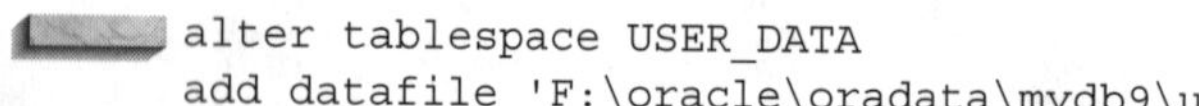

```
alter tablespace USER_DATA
add datafile 'F:\oracle\oradata\mydb9\user02.dbf' size 400M;
```

NOTE
Notice that no storage clause is specified. This is because we are just adding space to the existing tablespace. The storage parameters used at tablespace creation still apply. It would have been possible to specify autoextend parameters to the added datafile.

If, as in this case, the datafile is being added to support a fast-growing table, you will want to monitor the tablespace to gauge how fast the new table is expanding.

Reducing the Size of a Tablespace

Now, let's look at the other side of the tablespace sizing coin—reducing the size of a tablespace. Why in the world would you ever want to "give space back"? Perhaps you initially sized a tablespace very large to accommodate a table for a data warehouse. The table is supposed to be very large. All of the other tables in the tablespace are very static tables and they will remain about the same size from now on. After all of the tables have been loaded, you find that the tablespace is only half full. There is a lot of space in the tablespace that will never be used—space that could be used by another tablespace or other object on the system. What can you do?

You can either move the table to another smaller tablespace, or you can rebuild the tablespace. We'll look at both options and let you decide which one you want to use. (Isn't it nice to have options to choose from and the knowledge to make a choice?)

If there are only a few tables in the tablespace, you can easily move them to a smaller tablespace using the **alter table** command. The syntax for this command is

```
alter table <tablename> move <tablespacename>;
```

You can also change the storage parameters for the table if you have determined that they are incorrect. A word of warning—while the table is being moved, no user can access it; it will be locked in exclusive mode. If you are moving a very big table, this can take a while. So be sure to do this at a time when very few people are accessing the database.

In addition to tables, a tablespace can contain indexes. The syntax to move an index is slightly different from the one to move a table:

```
alter index <indexname> rebuild tablespace <tablespacename>;
```

Just as with tables, you can also alter the storage parameters for the index while you rebuild it. Once you have moved all the tables and indexes from the tablespace that is too large, you can now drop the original tablespace as we described earlier in this chapter.

But what if you don't have enough disk space on your server to create a second tablespace while you do this? That brings us to the next alternative for resizing tablespaces—rebuilding the entire tablespace.

In order to completely rebuild a tablespace, you first need to identify and export all the objects in that tablespace. You can do this using the DBA_SEGMENTS view as follows:

```
select Segment_Name, Segment_Type
  from DBA_SEGMENTS
where Tablespace_Name = <tablespacename>;
```

This will give you the list of tables to export, as well as a list of indexes that will need to be rebuilt once the new tablespace has been created. Using DBA_INDEXES and DBA_IND_COLUMNS (aren't you glad we discussed these earlier?), you can extract the information you will need to re-create the indexes. Once you have all this information, what do you do with it? These are the steps you will take to (finally!) resize the tablespace:

1. Export all the tables from the tablespace.
2. Alter the tablespace offline and drop it, along with the datafiles.
3. Re-create the tablespace with the smaller datafiles.
4. Import the tables back into the tablespace.
5. Rebuild any indexes that were in the old tablespace.

Phew! That's a lot of work. And while you are doing all of that, no user can access any of that data. As you can tell from all of this, it's really important to properly size your tablespaces.

A Neat Tablespace Status Script

We realize that the current accepted approach to tablespace management is to use locally managed tablespaces with uniform extent sizes. However, you may have inherited a database in which the tablespaces are data dictionary managed with fragmentation. Thus, there may be times when you want to see the general status of all of your tablespaces:

- How much space was allocated
- How much space (generally) has been used
- How much space is remaining
- The smallest and largest available, contiguous amount of space in each tablespace
- The number of extents in each tablespace that have been allocated

Here's a really neat script to show you this information:

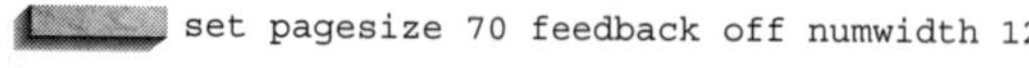

```
set pagesize 70 feedback off numwidth 12

compute sum of Bytes on report
compute sum of Bytes on Tablespace_Name
break on Tablespace_Name skip 2
```

```
column One noprint
column Two heading 'Space type' format a20
column Bytes format 9,999,999,990
column Tablespace_Name format a18
set termout off echo off heading on

spool ts_space.txt
select 1 One, Tablespace_Name, 'Max available: ' Two, sum(Bytes) Bytes
  from DBA_DATA_FILES
 group by Tablespace_Name
 union
select 2 Two, Tablespace_Name, 'Allocated: ',
       nvl(((sum(Bytes) + decode(Tablespace_Name, 'SYSTEM',2048,1024)) * -1),0)
  from DBA_EXTENTS
 group by Tablespace_Name
 order by 2, 1;
clear computes
clear breaks
column Tb heading 'Frag' format 9,990
column Sm heading 'Small' format 9,999,999,990
column Lg heading 'Large' format 9,999,999,990
rem
select Tablespace_Name, sum(Bytes) Bytes, count(Blocks) Tb, min(Bytes) Sm,
       max(Bytes) Lg
  from DBA_FREE_SPACE
 group by Tablespace_Name;
spool off
```

A shortened version of the output from this script, found in the ts_space.txt file, follows:

```
TABLESPACE_NAME    Space type                    BYTES
------------------ -------------------- --------------
INDX               Max available:            2,097,152
******************                      --------------
sum                                          2,097,152

OEM_REPOSITORY     Max available:            5,242,880
                   Allocated:               -1,895,424
******************                      --------------
sum                                          3,347,456
...
USERS              Max available:            3,145,728
                   Allocated:               -1,547,264
******************                      --------------
sum                                          1,598,464

TABLESPACE_NAME             BYTES   Frag          Small          Large
------------------ -------------- ------ -------------- --------------
INDX                    2,095,104      1      2,095,104      2,095,104
OEM_REPOSITORY          3,346,432      1      3,346,432      3,346,432
...
USERS                   1,597,440      1      1,597,440      1,597,440
```

The first portion of the output shows the amount of allocated space in each tablespace in the database, the amount of used space, and the amount of space remaining. The second portion of the output shows the amount of available space, the number of allocated extents, the smallest amount (or chunk) of contiguous space, and the largest amount (or chunk) of contiguous space left in that tablespace. If you ever have a tablespace fail to extend when you know there is still more than enough space left in the tablespace, run this set of scripts to verify that the largest available chunk of space is large enough to handle the next extent size for the tablespace. Chances are, you will find that although there is enough "space" in the tablespace, there is not enough contiguous space to support the next extent size.

Enabling Autoextend for a Tablespace

At the beginning of this chapter in the "Creating a Tablespace" section, we showed the parameters for the autoextend option. When we talked about resizing a tablespace later in this chapter, we again mentioned this option. We said then that we would talk more about this parameter later. Well, "later" has finally arrived!

What Autoextend Is

Before we look at how to enable or disable this feature, let's talk a bit about what the feature actually does. When you enable autoextend, you are telling Oracle that you want the datafile to be able to allocate more space if it is running too low on space to be able to allocate a next extent for an object. Gee, that sounds wonderful, doesn't it? You can enable autoextend on a datafile and never have to worry about the tablespace running out of room. In theory, this feature really *is* wonderful. However, there is a potential problem associated with letting a tablespace's datafile(s) grow unbounded. A problem that you can encounter deals with the actual space available on the disk. Let's say autoextend is enabled with no upper limit placed on the amount of space that the tablespace can consume. There is a very real probability that, eventually, the tablespace or combination of tablespaces on a disk will "devour" all of the available space—just as that lion we saw at the zoo would probably, eventually, devour the antelope. As a proactive DBA, you want to monitor and have control over the growth of tablespaces on your system. The last thing you want is to have a process or multiple processes fail because a disk runs completely out of space.

Now, let's look at a situation where autoextend can be used to your advantage. One of the authors was supporting a database during the time that a worldwide promotion was being offered by her company. There was no way to predict how many transactions would be received on a daily basis during the promotion. The normal activity for the database was no more than 8,000 records added per day. The possible number of records expected during the promotion could be as high as 800,000 per day. How could she ensure that the tablespaces supporting the increased traffic would not run out of space in the middle of the night? She enabled autoextend for the tablespaces in which the data was being loaded. This solution worked very well.

To see if autoextend has been enabled for a tablespace datafile, you can look in the DBA_DATA_FILES view.

Autoextend Parameters

The **autoextend** clause can be specified for a datafile either when you issue the command **create tablespace** or by using the **alter database datafile…** command. As shown earlier in Table 8-1, the parameters for the **autoextend** clause are **off** or **on**, with additional parameters for the **on** option. The parameter **on** enables autoextending, while the parameter **off** disables the automatic extension of a datafile. By default, if you do not specify this clause, **autoextend** is set to **off**. If you use either **create tablespace… autoextend off** or **alter database datafile… autoextend off**, you disable **autoextend** if it is turned on. When **off** is specified, the parameters **next** and **maxsize** are automatically set to zero. When you use either **create tablespace… autoextend on** or **alter database datafile… autoextend on**, values for **next** and **maxsize** must be specified. The **next** parameter specifies, in bytes, the size of the next increment of disk space to be automatically allocated to the datafile when more extents are required. You can use **K** for kilobytes or **M** for megabytes to specify the size. The default is one data block, which is pretty small. If you let the size for the next extent default to one database block, you could run out of extents really quickly, especially if the block size is small (2K) and **maxextents** is set to 121 (the default for a 2K database block size). The parameter **maxsize** is used to define how large the datafile can grow, that is, how much total disk space the datafile can use. You have the choice of specifying a number or the parameter **unlimited**. In a case like the worldwide promotion described earlier, when you do not know how large the datafile needs to grow, the **unlimited** parameter can be used.

We do recommend caution if you use the autoextend feature at all. Our recommendation is not to use this feature unless you have a really good business reason to do so.

Temporary vs. Permanent Tablespaces

Within Oracle, you can define a tablespace as either temporary or permanent. By default, all tablespaces are created as permanent. A tablespace that is defined as temporary can be used only for sort operations. Objects such as tables and indexes cannot be stored in a tablespace that has been defined as temporary.

Why would you want to create a tablespace designated as temporary instead of permanent? Remember when we were talking about locally managed tablespaces instead of data dictionary managed ones? We talked about a referee who was keeping track of each free extent and used extent. Let's say that Oracle has allocated an extent in a permanent tablespace while performing a sort operation. When the sort completes, Oracle deallocates the extent. Thus, you have the overhead of physically extending and then deallocating extents. If there are a large number of sorts being done and each sort does a lot of allocating and deallocating extents, performance can really suffer. When you create and use a temporary tablespace, as extents are needed, they are allocated. However, when the sort completes, the extents are not deallocated, but merely reused, so you save all of the overhead of allocating and deallocating extents. Performance should be better!

When you create a user in your database, you designate a default tablespace where the user's objects will be stored if he or she does not specify a tablespace name in the create statement. You also designate a temporary tablespace that will be used for the user's sort operations. As of Oracle9i, to assign a user to a temporary tablespace, the tablespace must actually be created as temporary. In other words, let's say that you have created a permanent tablespace called TEMP. You cannot successfully issue the command:

```
alter user NELSON temporary tablespace TEMP;
```

This command will fail because the tablespace you are referencing is not a temporary tablespace.

If you have an application in which a great many sorts are being performed, you might consider creating a separate tablespace for that application and modifying the application schema to point to that tablespace for sort operations. You will gain performance benefits from placing the tablespace on a different controller and defining the tablespace as temporary.

All operations that use sorts, such as joins, index builds, ordering (**order by**), computations of aggregates (**group by**), and the **analyze** command will be performed using a temporary tablespace if there isn't enough free space in memory to do them there. You see, Oracle processes its management operations differently against these tablespaces than it does against the ones that are permanent.

To create a temporary tablespace, you can issue the **create temporary tablespace** command instead of **create tablespace**.

Transportable Tablespaces

Here's an interesting question for you to ponder: is there ever a situation in which you will want to move a tablespace or subset of tablespaces from one database to another? The wise DBA will, of course, answer, "Yes." If you're not feeling particularly wise today, that's okay, because we'll explain some of the situations in which you might want to perform this task.

Rationales for Moving a Subset of a Database

One situation that you might already have thought about is when you want to move a subset of the database from your production environment back to a development or test/quality assurance area. In the case of a test/QA database, you start out with an exact replica of your production system. Some application code testing has been done, and a subset of the database has been damaged or radically changed by the test. You have very limited time to return the database to its prior configuration. A database rebuild is too time consuming, and you are absolutely sure that the subset of tablespaces from production can be moved to the test database without leaving the test database in a questionable state.

Another situation in which you might want to move one tablespace or a subset of tablespaces is if you have multiple development activities taking place at the same time and each one requires a separate, but identical, environment. You could create several separate schemas in several databases and populate them all by moving the same tablespace from one schema to another.

A third scenario would be one in which you want to remove a tablespace from one database entirely and place it in another database. For this situation, you might have an application that was originally placed with one or more other applications in a database. This new application is not "getting along well" with the other applications. Perhaps the new application is growing much more rapidly than expected, or the availability requirements for the new application have changed and it must either remain up for longer periods of time or be shut down intermittently. The new requirements might dictate that this application be moved to a separate, isolated database.

Possible Approaches

If you want to move part of a database to another database, how are you going to do it? Think for a moment about the possible problems involved and the amount of work you might have to perform to accomplish this task. There could be more than one schema in a given tablespace, so you can't export a specific user schema and import it to move the tablespace. It would be cumbersome and time consuming to rebuild the entire database just to move one tablespace. Well, before you give yourself a brain cramp thinking about the problems involved, we'll tell you that, as of version 8i, Oracle supplies a facility to make this job fairly easy.

The transportable tablespace feature enables you to move a subset of an Oracle database from one database to another. You can clone (make an exact copy of) a tablespace and "plug it into" another database, or you can "unplug" (remove) a tablespace from one database and relocate the tablespace or database subset to another database.

In the first situation mentioned earlier, you did not have much time to clone the tablespace(s) from the production database back to the test/QA database. Moving data using the transportable tablespace facility can be substantially faster than exporting and importing or unloading and reloading the data. Why is this approach so much faster? When you export and import data, you must first drop and rebuild the tablespace(s) involved, which can be very time consuming. Moving the indexes associated with the tables in the tablespace(s) can also take time as well. By using the transportable tablespace feature, you need only copy the datafiles that are associated with the tablespace(s) and move the tablespace metadata. The indexes can be moved as well, saving the rebuild time that you would normally have to use after importing or data loading.

In Oracle8i, there are rules that you must follow to use the transportable tablespace feature:

- The databases must have the same data block size.
- The databases must have the same character set.
- The databases must be on compatible platforms from the same hardware vendor.
- A tablespace cannot be transported to a target database in which a tablespace with the same name already exists.

In Oracle9i, you can have up to five different block sizes within the same database, so the block size rule no longer applies. The other rules still apply though.

In both Oracle8i and 9i, transportable tablespaces do not support

- Snapshot/replication
- Function-based indexes
- Scoped REFs
- Domain indexes
- Advanced queues with multiple recipients

How Transportable Tablespaces Work

The whole idea behind transportable tablespaces is to quickly move the tablespace datafiles and the tablespace metadata from one database to another. In order to copy or move a tablespace, you must first declare the tablespace as read-only and then export the tablespace metadata. You import the metadata to the target database and copy the tablespace's datafile(s) over to the new location.

Oracle provides some parameters that you can use to perform the tablespace metadata operations. In the Export utility, the parameters **transport_tablespace** and **tablespaces** are used; the first designates that the transportable tablespace facility is to be used, and the second provides a list of one or more tablespaces to be moved. You must first set the tablespace(s) to read-only:

```
alter tablespace MYTAB read only;
alter tablespace USERS read only;
```

Next, you perform an export of the tablespace metadata by using the following parameters for the export:

```
transport_tablespace=y
tablespaces=(MYTAB,USERS)
```

In this example, the **transport_tablespace** parameter is set from its default of "n" to "y" to indicate that the tablespace metadata is to be exported. The **tablespaces** parameter indicates that the metadata for the tablespaces MYTAB and USERS is to be captured.

Once the tablespaces' datafile(s) are copied to their new location, the Import utility is run to move the tablespace metadata into the new database. The parameters that you use to move the tablespace metadata into the new databases match the Export utility parameters with the following additional parameters:

- The **datafiles** parameter to tell Oracle the names and locations of the datafiles for the tablespaces
- The **tts_owners** parameter to tell Oracle the names of the users/schemas that own the data

The Import utility parameters could look like the following:

```
transport_tablespace=y
tablespaces=(MYTAB,USERS)
datafiles=(d:\ora9i\oradata\newdb\mytab01.dbf,d:\ora9i\oradata\newdb\
users01.dbf)
tts_owners=(MYAPP,USER01)
```

In this example, the parameters tell the Import utility that the locations for the tablespaces specified will be in the NEWDB directory and that the owners of the schema areas are to be MYAPP and USER01 in that order.

Documenting Your Database

If a disaster were to occur today, would you know where every one of your files in each of your databases was? Could you be sure that the list of files you have today will be current and valid next week? Here is a script that you can run from a nightly batch or cron job that will produce a report of the location of all your database files. You can set it up to run for each of your databases. We recommend that you set up the job and have it print the results so you will have a hard-copy document of your file locations on a daily basis. You can use this for disaster recovery and database documentation.

```
set pages 999
col File_Name format a45
col Tablespace_Name format a20
col Bytes format 9999999999
col Blocks format 9999999999
col Member format a38
col Group# format 99999
set head off feedback off termout off
col Name format a10
col Dbname new_value xdb noprint
col Today new_value tdy noprint
select substr(Sysdate,1,9) Today
  from DUAL
/
select Value Dbname
  from V$PARAMETER
 where Name = 'db_name'
;
spool &tdy..&xdb
select 'Datafile Information for '||Name||' - '||Sysdate
  from V$DATABASE, DUAL;
prompt
prompt
set head on feedback on termout on
select *
  from V$DATABASE;
prompt
prompt
select a.Group#, a.Member, b.Bytes
  from V$LOGFILE a, V$LOG b
 where a.Group# = b.Group#;
prompt
prompt
col Value heading 'CONTROL FILE INFO'
select Value
  from V$PARAMETER
 where Name like '%control%';
prompt
prompt
select Tablespace_Name, File_Name, Bytes
```

```
  from DBA_DATA_FILES
 order by 2,1;
spool off
exit
```

This script creates a file with a name in the form of DD-MON-YY.<database_name>, such as 10-APR-02.MYDB, and produces a report like the following:

```
Datafile Information for MYDB - 09-APR-02
NAME       CREATED           LOG_MODE     CHECKPOINT_CHANGE# ARCHIVE_CHANGE#
---------- ----------------- ------------ ------------------ ---------------
MYDB       11/21/01 08:22:17 NOARCHIVELOG              14274           14144
1 row selected.
GROUP# MEMBER                                   BYTES
------ -------------------------------------- -----------
     1 MYDISK01:[ORACLE.MYDB]ORA_LOG1.RDO        3145728
     2 MYDISK01:[ORACLE.MYDB]ORA_LOG2.RDO        3145728
     3 MYDISK01:[ORACLE.MYDB]ORA_LOG3.RDO        3145728
3 rows selected.
CONTROL FILE INFO
-----------------------------------------
MYDISK38:[ORACLE.MYDB]ORA_CONTROL1.CON, MYDISK39:[ORACLE.MYDB]ORA_CONTROL2.CON,
MYDISK40:[ORACLE.MYDB]ORA_CONTROL3.CON
1 row selected.
TABLESPACE_NAME     FILE_NAME                                     BYTES
------------------- --------------------------------------------- -----------
MY_TS               MYDISK41:[ORACLE.MYDB]MY_TS01.DBF               10485760
SYSTEM              MYDISK01:[ORACLE.MYDB]ORA_SYSTEM.DBF           629145600
RBS                 MYDISK702:[ORACLE.MYDB]RBS01.DBF               314572800
TEMP                MYDISK703:[ORACLE.MYDB]TEMP01.DBF              314572800
TOOLS               MYDISK704:[ORACLE.MYDB]TOOLS01.DBF             157286400
USERS               MYDISK704:[ORACLE.MYDB]USERS01.DBF             157286400
6 rows selected.
```

You will also want to include the location of archive logs (if archive logging is used) and the location of the initialization parameter file. The alert log will include any nondefault initialization parameter settings that were enabled at database startup. You will want to capture them as well.

Creating Objects in a Database

At the beginning of this chapter, you saw the parameters that you can use when you create a tablespace. In this section, you will see the parameters that you use the most for the objects you will be called upon most often to create—tables, indexes, views, roles, synonyms, and users.

Creating Tables

There are two schools of thought about the duties of a DBA when it comes to dealing with the creation of objects. One school of thought goes by these general principles:

- The developers create all of the objects as they are needed for the new application.
- The DBA creates all public synonyms, as required, for the new application.
- The DBA gives the developer privileges on the development system only as each privilege is required.
- For production, the DBA creates the new database and the required schemas for the new application.
- For production, the developers create all of the objects for the new application and populate the new database.
- Optionally, for production, the new database is created by the DBA and populated by an export from the development database.

The other school of thought goes by these principles:

- The DBA is handed the object creation requirements for each object during the development phase of the project.
- The DBA creates scripts for each object's creation.
- The DBA runs the scripts to create all of the objects in both the development and production environments.
- The DBA controls the creation of all objects, roles, and grants, and assists with all data loading.

In the second scenario, the DBA has much more control of the development and production environments, as well as much more work and responsibility for object sizing and creation. Both schools of thought are valid for different company cultures. Since you may end up working in a company whose approach to application development requires you to be deeply involved in object creation, we are going to show you the parameters available and explain how each works for the objects that you will most likely be called upon to create.

Let's start with tables since every form of data is stored in one kind of table or another, and there are several different kinds of tables to deal with. The list of table types for Oracle9i consists of the following:

- **Relational table** The basic, most common table in a database, which can now be global and/or temporary as well as permanent
- **Partitioned tables** Used to spread a large table over a set of smaller tables for ease of maintainability and more efficient data retrieval
- **Advanced Queue tables** Used to integrate a message-queuing system within the database
- **Index-Organized tables** Used to store index columns as a table to aid in faster data retrieval
- **Nested tables** Used to store multiple columns of data within one column of a table
- **Object tables** Used to enable the creation of object types that more closely represent their composition in the real world
- **Temporary tables** Used to store either session-specific or transaction-specific data on a temporary basis

Since this is a basic book, we are going to concentrate on the basic table creation parameters.

Relational Table Creation Parameters

In Chapter 2, we talked about creating a simple table, but we didn't show you the parameters available for table creation. Let's look at the more basic ones now. Table 8-2 shows the list of basic table creation parameters, a brief description of each one, and, where applicable, the default value for the parameter. A complete list of table creation parameters can be found in the Oracle9i SQL Reference.

In order to create a table in your own schema, you must have the **create table** privilege and quota on the tablespace in which you are creating the table. If, as is usually the case for a DBA, you need to create a table in another schema, you will need to have the **create any table** privilege and either quota on the tablespace in which the table will be created or the **tablespace unlimited** privilege. The **tablespace unlimited** privilege enables you to create objects in any tablespace in the database without having any quota granted explicitly to you.

Parameter	Description	Default Value
Table	Name of the table	n/a
Column	Name of the column	n/a
Default	Specifies a default value for the column if no value is supplied during data insertion	n/a
Column Ref Constraint	Specifies a reference to another table's column constraint to apply to this column	n/a
Column Constraint	Specifies an integrity constraint as part of the column definition	n/a
Datatype	Specifies the type of data—number, character, large object type, etc.	n/a
Table Constraint	Specifies a constraint definition for the entire table	n/a
Table Ref Constraint	Specifies a reference to another table's constraint to apply to this table	n/a
Tablespace	The tablespace in which the table is to be placed	The owner's specified default tablespace
Logging/Nologging	Specifies whether the object information is to be tracked in the redo log file	Logging
Pctfree	Specifies the percentage of free space to be retained in each data block of the table for future updates to the table's rows	Range is 1–99, default is 10%
Pctused	Specifies the minimum amount of used space that Oracle maintains for each data block of the table	Range is 1–100, default is 40%
Initrans	Specifies the initial number of transaction entries allocated within each data block allocated to the table	Range is 1–255, default is 1 (for cluster, or index is 2)

TABLE 8-2. *Basic Table Creation Parameters*

Parameter	Description	Default Value
Maxtrans	Specifies the maximum number of concurrent transactions that can update a data block allocated to a table—does not apply to queries	Range is 1–255, default is a function of the data block size
Storage clause	Same parameters as for a tablespace	

TABLE 8-2. *Basic Table Creation Parameters* (continued)

Creating a Complex Table

Now that you have all of the basic parameters for creating a table, let's see how many of them you can use in one table creation statement—just for practice. Here's the assignment. You need to create a table that will hold information about the primates in the zoo we visited earlier in this chapter.

```
create table ZOO.PRIMATES
(Code              varchar2(3) not null
     constraint Primates_PK primary key
,Description       varchar2(250)    not null
,Location          varchar2(30)     not null
,Date_of_birth     date        not null
,Status            varchar2(3)
,Name              varchar2(10)    not null
,Date_Acquired     date
,Cage_Num          number(8,2)
,Coloring          varchar2(3)
    constraint Chk_Color_Type
         check(Coloring in ('brn','blk','red','tan','bld'))
)
 tablespace ZOO_DATA
   parallel (degree 1 instances 1)
    pctfree 10
    pctused 40
   initrans 1
   maxtrans 255
    logging
    storage
(   initial 73728
       next 73728
 minextents 1
 maxextents 500
pctincrease 0
```

```
freelists 1
 freelist groups 1);
```

Well, you certainly used most of the basic parameters. Good job! Of course, in the real world, your goal is not to see how many parameters you can use but to make sure the creation script is as thorough as it needs to be so the table is created clearly and effectively. You do not have to list the parameters anywhere that the default values will be used. We do, however, recommend that you try to use a consistent approach to coding your creation scripts. Therefore, you may decide to include all of the basic parameters in each script—even the default ones—to ensure that you do not accidentally miss a parameter that you need.

Now, let's see what you've got in the table creation script. You are creating a table in the ZOO schema called PRIMATES. The primary key is the Code column. There are several informational columns and a check constraint on the color of the animal. The animal's color can only be black, brown, red, tan, or blonde. No other color will be permitted. The tablespace is ZOO_DATA. For the next several parameters listed, the default values are used. The storage clause has been filled in with **initial** and **next** values. The **minextents** value is the default, while the **maxextents** value has been set to 500. The **pctincrease** has been set to 0, and the rest of the parameters are default values.

Creating Indexes

An index is used to help retrieve data quickly from the database. As we said in Chapter 2 in the "Indexes" section, without indexes, each time you wanted to retrieve information, Oracle would have to perform a full table scan of the data and look at each and every row in each table of interest. How time consuming!

If you have a commonly used query that just retrieves two columns of a table containing a large volume of information, you can create an index on those two columns. Oracle will look in the index for the information you want instead of walking through every complete row of the table. Much quicker!

As with tables, you can create different forms of indexes on each of the different table types. For this chapter, we will look at the basic index creation parameters that you will use the most.

Index Creation Parameters

Table 8-3 shows the basic parameters that you can use to create an index on a relational table.

To create an index, you will need either the **create index** or **create any index** privilege and quota on the tablespace in which the index will be created or the **tablespace unlimited** privilege.

Parameter	Description	Default Value
Unique	Specifies that the value of the column(s) in the index must be unique	Non-unique
Bitmap	Specifies that the index will be a bitmap rather than a B-Tree index—used with low cardinality columns	B-Tree
Schema	Specifies the name of the index owner	The creator's schema
Index_name	Specifies the name of the index	n/a
Cluster index clause	Specifies that the index is to be built on a cluster and lists the cluster attributes	n/a
Table index clause	Specifies the table on which the index is to be built, includes any alias for the table name, index_expression_list, whether the index is local or global (for partitioned indexes)	Defaults are the index creator's schema, no alias, and global
Index expression list	Specifies either the column(s) on which the index is based or an expression list to create a function-based index	For a regular index, 32 columns max; for a bitmap index, 30
ASC/DESC	Specifies whether the index is to be created in ascending or descending order	Ascending
Physical attribute list	Same as for a table: **pctfree**, **pctused**, **initrans**, **maxtrans**, **storage_clause**	
Logging/ Nologging	Specifies whether the object information is to be tracked in the redo log file	Logging
Online	Specifies whether the index is to be made immediately available	Online
Compute statistics	Specifies whether statistics are to be generated for the index	
Tablespace	Specifies the tablespace in which the index is to be stored	Default tablespace of the index creator
Compress/ Nocompress	Used to eliminate repeated occurrences of key values	Nocompress

TABLE 8-3. *Index Creation Parameters*

Parameter	Description	Default Value
Nosort	Specifies that the values are to be inserted in ascending order—Oracle does not have to sort the rows on insertion	n/a
Reverse	Stores the bytes of the index in reverse order, excluding the row ID—cannot be used with Nosort	n/a

TABLE 8-3. *Index Creation Parameters* (continued)

Creating an Index on the PRIMATES Table

Now that you have the parameters, let's see if you can use them to create an index on the PRIMATES table you created earlier in the table creation section. It turns out that the animal's name, date of birth, and status have been heavily queried lately, and the query response time has been really slow because a full table scan is being used. To help speed up the query, you need to add an index to these columns. The order in which the information is being queried is Status, Date_Of_Birth, and Name. Although the status (living or dead) and the date of birth are not unique by themselves (since many different animals could have been born on the same date), if you add the animal's name—which will never be the same as that given to any other animal born the same day—the combination of columns becomes unique. Thus, you can create a unique index on the combination of the three columns, even though you could not create a unique index on any one of the columns by itself.

```
create unique index PRIMATES_IDX1
         on ZOO.PRIMATES(Status,Date_Of_Birth,Name)
 tablespace ZOO_INDEX
    logging
    pctfree 10
   initrans 2
   maxtrans 255
    storage
(   initial 52630
       next 52630
 minextents 1
 maxextents 350
pctincrease 0
);
```

In this example, a unique index PRIMATES_IDX1 is created on the ZOO.PRIMATES table using the ZOO_INDEX tablespace. As you can see, the storage and other parameters are used in the same basic manner as the table creation parameters. However, for an index creation, **initrans** must be set to a value of at least 2 instead of 1.

Creating Users

One task you'll be called upon to perform most frequently is creating users in your database. There are really two connotations to the term "users." The connotation you are probably most familiar with is the term applied to a person who logs on to your database to perform work. The other connotation is the reference to an application schema area where the objects for an application are housed. Either way, you will be creating users on your system.

As we have done with the other objects, we will show the parameters first, and then you will have a chance to try your hand at creating a few different users.

User Creation Parameters

Table 8-4 shows the parameters for creating a user.

To create a user, you must have the **create user** privilege. In order for a user to connect to a database, the user must have the **create session** privilege.

Now, let's see if you can create a user or two.

Creating a User with Roles and Privileges

The first user for you to create will be yourself! How generous will you be with your roles and other parameters? Take a minute to think about what you would like to

Parameter	Description	Default
User name	Specifies the name of the user	n/a
By password	Specifies the password for the account	n/a
Externally	Specifies that operating system authentication is to be used	n/a
Globally as	Specifies that the user is to be a "global" user and specifies the name to identify the user	n/a
Default tablespace	Specifies where objects created by the user are to be stored if no tablespace value is given	SYSTEM
Temporary tablespace	Specifies the temporary tablespace for the user's sort operations	SYSTEM
Quota <amount> on <tablespace>	Specifies the quota a user is to have in an integer amount (K or M) and the tablespace on which the quota is applied	No quota assigned
Profile	Specifies the name of a profile for the user	Default profile

TABLE 8-4. *User Creation Parameters*

Parameter	Description	Default
Password expire	Specifies that the password is to expire at a certain time	Not expired
Account lock/Unlock	Specifies whether the account is to be initially locked and inaccessible or unlocked	Unlocked

TABLE 8-4. *User Creation Parameters* (continued)

have as your default tablespace, your temporary tablespace, and so on, and then start coding.

```
create user <Put_Your_Name_Here>
identified by <Put_Your_Password_Here>
   default tablespace USERS
 temporary tablespace TEMP
   profile DBA_PROFILE;
```

For security purposes, Oracle will store passwords in an encrypted form. If you select the Password column from DBA_USERS, you will see an encrypted password.

To give yourself roles, you use a separate command. Okay, go ahead and give yourself the Oracle-supplied roles CONNECT, RESOURCE, and DBA.

```
grant CONNECT,RESOURCE,DBA
   to <Put_Your_Name_Here>;
```

Can't you just feel the power? Of course, you can also implicitly create a user by writing a **grant** statement with the following syntax:

```
grant CONNECT,RESOURCE,DBA
   to NEW_USER
identified by PASS1;
```

The problem with using this syntax is that you will then have to perform an **alter user** command in order to assign a default tablespace and all of the other parameters that you want the user to have. We do not recommend that you use the implicit form of user creation since it's too easy to miss modifying a default parameter that you really want changed. In Oracle9i, you can declare a temporary tablespace using the parameter **default_temp_tablespace** when you create the database. If you create a user and do not declare a temporary tablespace, Oracle will use the value you declared in the **default_temp_tablespace** for the user's temporary tablespace.

CHAPTER 9

What We Do Daily

hink about the routines in your life. Every weekday, you get up at the same time, brush your teeth, take a shower, make and eat breakfast. On your way to work you stop off and get a newspaper and a cup of coffee. You take the same train or bus into work. If you are still in school, you have a schedule of classes you attend. Once a week you go grocery shopping or do laundry. Once a month you might get a haircut. Every year you visit your doctor and dentist and have your car inspected. Okay, so maybe your life isn't quite that orderly, but human beings tend to be creatures of habit, so chances are that if you have a steady job, you tend to follow some kind of a schedule or routine.

We believe that, just as you have routines in your daily life, you should have routines in your work as a DBA. Following procedures and processes helps to make your job easier by letting you know about potential problems and trends so that you can take action before things go wrong. Becoming a proactive DBA is a wonderful goal to have. Not only will you increase your chances of having a smooth-running database, but you will decrease the number of weekends you have to spend at work. You will help ensure that molehills do not grow into overwhelming mountains.

Throughout this chapter, we will include scripts to help you implement new "routines" in your life. To run each of the scripts described in this chapter, you will need to be logged on to the database as a privileged user. You can use the SYS or SYSTEM account with the Oracle-supplied DBA role or create a user with the DBA role or the equivalent privileges. We recommend that you create a specific account for monitoring your database.

General Monitoring

Why monitor your database on a regular basis instead of just setting up processes to notify you of errors? Looking at your database daily can give you a feel for many of the following elements:

- What is normal
- Growth patterns of space usage
- Timing of log switches
- Number of users connecting

Once you have a feel for the normal functioning of your database, anything unusual will catch your eye immediately, and you can fix the problem before it actually becomes one. It's much better to say to your management, "I noticed we were running low on space for the application master table so I added a datafile," than to have an entire department's work grind to a halt because there is no room for a table to grow.

That said, let's take a look at what kinds of things you should be monitoring.

Alert Logs

When your database is created, Oracle also creates a log, known as the *alert log*, in which it writes information about

- Each time the database is started.
- Any recovery that was performed on database startup.
- Each time the database is shut down.
- Each time a log switch occurs (referred to as a *thread switch*).
- What parameters (from the initialization parameter file) were used within the database at startup and are not default parameters.
- Any DDL commands that change the structure of the database, such as "alter tablespace PAYROLL_TS add datafile..."
- Space allocation errors that have occurred (ORA-1650 through ORA-1659).
- Errors that occur and the location and name of the error file (called *trace files* because they have the extension .trc). Oracle creates these files to more fully document the error and provide Oracle Support with information to help them help you resolve the cause of the error.

As you can see, the alert log, which is given the following names in different systems, contains a good deal of important information and, oddly enough, is never reduced in size automatically.

- alert_<SID>.log on a Unix system
- <SID>alrt.log on a Windows 2000 system

In other words, the alert log is created when the database is created, and information is appended to the file each time one of the actions listed above occurs. As you can imagine, this file can grow very large, especially if your database has been around for a long time. If you have an alert log that's been around for, say, a year, and you need to look at an entry from last week, you may have a huge amount of data to wade through just to get to the information in which you are interested. So, what can you do?

Here is an interesting fact for you: Oracle will create a new alert log, with the default name, if it can't find one when it wants to write an entry to the log. That means you can rename the file daily and back up the old ones and remove them from your disk on a regular basis. This does two things: keeps your current alert log relatively small so that you don't run out of disk space and lets you keep old alert logs to review for trends. We have a batch job that runs nightly and renames each of our database alert log files by adding the current date as the extension. The routine then emails the log to our email account so we can quickly scan the file to see if anything looks like a problem area—for example, a 600 error occurring or too frequent thread switches. An Oracle error that ends with a number in the 600 range is referred to as "an ORA-600 error." Although not always a signal for database disaster, these errors can be a very serious form of internal database error and should be given strict attention. Unless you are familiar with the specific ORA-600 error that you have received, you will want to check Metalink to verify what, if any, actions you should take to correct the error.

If you have many databases, you may not be able to read through all the alert logs on a daily basis and still get anything else done. Or you may work in an environment that can't wait until the next day for you to see problems. Some DBAs have created routines that check for errors and email notification only if an error is found. If you work in an environment where any errors or downtime is unacceptable, you might want to develop or purchase software that will constantly monitor for errors and page you if one occurs. Generally speaking, it takes only a few minutes daily to scan through a day's worth of alerts from your database. Some of us have routines that email the alert logs from our production databases to our own email accounts. If you send the alert log to yourself daily, you can check it for entries that will enable you to do the following:

- Quickly see any problems
- Manually check the files to ensure that your redo logs are not switching too frequently
- Verify that the log writer is not being overwhelmed, which would indicate that there are not enough and/or large enough redo logs on your system

The Oracle Enterprise Manager has a service, the Event Monitoring service, which will also help you to monitor the database. We'll talk more about OEM and its features and functions in Chapter 13.

If you set the initialization parameter **log_checkpoints_to_alert** to TRUE, Oracle will add more information to the alert log about your log switches. While this will increase the size of your alert log, it will also give you more information about what is going on in your database. Below is a sample section of an alert log from an Oracle9i database with **log_checkpoints_to_alert** set to TRUE.

```
Wed Mar 06 15:14:32 2002
Beginning log switch checkpoint up to RBA [0x33.2.10], SCN: 0x0000.000f9792
Thread 1 advanced to log sequence 51
  Current log# 3 seq# 51 mem# 0: C:\ORACLE\ORADATA\DB901\REDO03.LOG
Wed Mar 06 15:14:32 2002
ARC0: Beginning to archive log 2 thread 1 sequence 50
ARC0: Completed archiving  log 2 thread 1 sequence 50
Wed Mar 06 15:14:33 2002
Beginning log switch checkpoint up to RBA [0x34.2.10], SCN: 0x0000.000f9793
Thread 1 advanced to log sequence 52
  Current log# 1 seq# 52 mem# 0: C:\ORACLE\ORADATA\DB901\REDO01.LOG
Wed Mar 06 15:14:33 2002
ARC0: Beginning to archive log 3 thread 1 sequence 51
ARC0: Completed archiving  log 3 thread 1 sequence 51
Wed Mar 06 15:14:35 2002
Completed checkpoint up to RBA [0x34.2.10], SCN: 0x0000.000f9793
Completed checkpoint up to RBA [0x33.2.10], SCN: 0x0000.000f9792
Wed Mar 06 15:14:37 2002
Beginning log switch checkpoint up to RBA [0x35.2.10], SCN: 0x0000.000f9795
Thread 1 advanced to log sequence 53
  Current log# 2 seq# 53 mem# 0: C:\ORACLE\ORADATA\DB901\REDO02.LOG
Wed Mar 06 15:14:37 2002
ARC0: Beginning to archive log 1 thread 1 sequence 52
ARC0: Completed archiving  log 1 thread 1 sequence 52
Wed Mar 06 15:14:40 2002
Completed checkpoint up to RBA [0x35.2.10], SCN: 0x0000.000f9795
Wed Mar 06 15:16:49 2002
Beginning global checkpoint up to RBA [0x35.4.10], SCN: 0x0000.000f9798
Completed checkpoint up to RBA [0x35.4.10], SCN: 0x0000.000f9798
Wed Mar 06 15:18:32 2002
Wed Mar 06 20:27:22 2002
ORA-1653: unable to extend table RACHEL.LRGTABLE by 640 in tablespace LRGDATA
```

Oops. It looks like the DB901 database had a space problem at 8:27 p.m. on Wednesday, March 6, 2002. Assuming that there were no users on the system that late at night, you might conclude that a nonstandard batch job was running and loading the LRGTABLE table. Unfortunately, the tablespace for that table did not have enough contiguous space to allocate an extent. An error was written to the alert log, and the process trying to load the table failed. If you have a process constantly monitoring the alert log and paging you with errors, you will get the message right after the problem occurs and will be able to add the necessary space immediately, contact the user to restart the job, and send out a follow-up email to everyone involved with that data load (and your boss—just to keep her informed), letting them know the problem has been addressed and resolved.

Later in the chapter, we will give you a script that lets you see if there are any objects in the database that will not be able to extend the next time they need to because of lack of space. You will then be able to add space before a problem occurs in any of your application's normally scheduled jobs. If you see that a particular batch job is failing frequently, you can use Oracle's new resumable space allocation feature to pause the job until you can take appropriate action and then resume the job where it left off so that it can run to completion. We'll talk about that in more detail in Chapter 11.

LISTENER.LOG

The Oracle Net listener (called Net8 in all versions of Oracle8 and SQL*Net in earlier versions) generates a log when it is started and writes to the log—either with a great deal of information or minimally, depending on what level of logging has been enabled. With minimal messaging enabled on a listener, the information that is provided

- Shows when the listener was started
- Lists the ports being listened on
- Shows the machine on which the listener is running
- Contains a notation for every connection made through this listener

A sample entry looks like this:

```
TNSLSNR for 32-bit Windows: Version 9.0.1.1.1 - Production on 13-JAN-2002 11:43:43

Copyright (c) 1991, 2001, Oracle Corporation.  All rights reserved.

System parameter file is C:\oracle\ora90\network\admin\listener.ora
Log messages written to C:\oracle\ora90\network\log\listener.log
Trace information written to C:\oracle\ora90\network\trace\listener.trc
Trace level is currently 0

Started with pid=1192
Listening on: (DESCRIPTION=(ADDRESS=(PROTOCOL=tcp)(HOST=DRAGONFLY_LAPTOP)(PORT=1521)))
Listening on: (DESCRIPTION=(ADDRESS=(PROTOCOL=ipc)(PIPENAME=\\.\pipe\EXTPROC0ipc)))

TIMESTAMP * CONNECT DATA [* PROTOCOL INFO] * EVENT [* SID] * RETURN CODE
```

If you enable logging at a more intensive level, more information will be written to the log, but more overhead traffic will be incurred. We recommend you periodically check your listener.log for errors. If you seem to be encountering Oracle Net problems, turn on more trace information at that time. Note that earlier versions will give different log information. One way to remove a listener log file that has become too large is to stop the listener process, delete the log file, and restart the listener process. Unlike the alert log, if you rename the listener log file, Oracle will continue to write to the renamed file. When you stop the listener process, you do not lose any existing connections to the database, but no new connections can be made until you restart the process. For that reason, we normally start at least two listener processes for each instance and put both ports into all the TNSNAMES.ORA files on our clients. When Oracle Net attempts to connect to a listener from the client, it tries the first port listed in the TNSNAMES.ORA file. If there is no listener active on that port, it will attempt to connect to the next port in the TNSNAMES entry. So you can take your listeners down one at a time, delete or rename the log files, and then restart them, and not interfere with your users' ability to connect to the database.

The only overhead to having multiple listeners is in the management of the listeners and the additional server process that will be created for each new listener. Multiple listeners allow you to spread network traffic over multiple NICs (Network Interface Cards), which will allow you to load-balance connections to your database server. For more detailed information on networking, check the Net Services Administrator's Guide and the Net Services Reference Guide in the Oracle documentation set.

Redo Log Status

Why check on the status of your redo logs? Well, you may want to change the size of your redo logs because you are switching too frequently. If you want to retain the names of your redo logs, you'll need to drop them before re-creating them at the new size. You need to know the status of the redo log you want to drop before you drop it. Dropping the current redo log is not good practice, unless you are testing recovery scenarios!

Information about the online redo logs is kept in two of the V$ views, V$LOG and V$LOGFILE. The views can be joined on the column Group# to get information from both. Redo logs can be part of a redo log group, which allows you to mirror your redo logs using an Oracle software feature and provides yet another layer of protection against the loss of a redo log. If you lose a single online redo log, you will have to perform recovery on your database, while if you have redo log groups and lose a single log in the group, Oracle will write a message to that effect in the alert log and then continue on, using the remaining members of the group. You will have a chance to drop and replace that log from the group without database downtime.

The script below selects information about the redo logs in a test database. A SYSTEM-like account is used to run this script.

```
col Member format a40
col Logstat format a10 heading 'Use Status'
select Member,
       a.Group#,
       b.Status,
       a.Status Logstat
  from V$LOGFILE a, V$LOG b
```

```
 where a.Group#=b.Group#
/

MEMBER                                   GROUP# STATUS           USE STATUS
------------------------------ -------------- ---------------- ----------
/ORADATA6/TEST/TEST_redo1.rdo                 1 ACTIVE
/ORADATA7/TEST/TEST_redo2.rdo                 2 CURRENT
/ORADATA6/TEST/TEST_redo3.rdo                 3 INACTIVE
/ORADATA7/TEST/TEST_redo4.rdo                 4 INACTIVE
```

Looking at the output of this script, you can tell certain things about this database. For instance, you can gain the following facts from looking at the report above:

- The DBA for this database has decided not to take advantage of Oracle's log mirroring, because there is only one redo log (member) per group#.
- There are four redo logs, and all are part of the database.
- The USE STATUS column, which is the Status column from V$LOGFILE, is blank if the redo log is in use by the database.
- The redo logs are placed on two different disks, and the DBA has attempted to improve performance by alternating the placement of the redo logs on these disks. Since Oracle will read the prior log to archive it, you can have disk head contention if the two logs are on the same disk. By placing them on different disks, one disk can be read while the other is being written to. If possible, you should always put your redo logs on disks that have nothing else on them (or at least files that are accessed very infrequently).
- The current and in-use redo log is redo2 (Status column is CURRENT).
- The redo log that was last used is redo1 (Status is ACTIVE).
- It is possible that the file redo1 is either being archived or is still needed for instance recovery if the database should crash. A status of INACTIVE means the redo log is not needed for instance recovery.

Other values for the Status column of V$LOG can be found in the Oracle documentation.

Fragmentation

Why do you want to check on the level of fragmentation in your tablespaces? Think of your tablespace as a puzzle that you are trying to piece together. As you find spots for more and more puzzle pieces, the empty spaces become more and more difficult to fill with just any piece. You have to have precisely the right size space for the next piece you want to use, or you can't make it fit.

Finding space in your tablespace to add another extent works in a similar way. If you're lucky, you have either built or inherited a database where the tables in each tablespace use the default storage parameters for that tablespace, so every extent is the same size or a multiple and you have no chunks of space that are too small to use. Unfortunately, not all of us are that lucky. You may have a large amount of free space left in a tablespace, but none of it is in a large enough chunk to fill the request for the extent. While the extents in an object do not have to be contiguous (one right after another on disk), the blocks within an extent must be. So you need to monitor your tablespaces to make sure you have large enough chunks of free blocks to fill the requests you get.

The PL/SQL script below will display the extents available within your tablespace and the size of each extent. To run the script, you first have to create a table to hold the intermediate results, using the **create table** script. You will use an account with SYSTEM-like privileges to run the fragmentation script.

```
create table FREESP (
Fname  VARCHAR2(513),
Tspace VARCHAR2(30),
First  NUMBER(10),
Blocks NUMBER(10),
Last   NUMBER(10))
/
```

Rather than create this table each time the PL/SQL script is run (and further fragment the tablespace), FREESP is created once and the **truncate** command is used to empty it before each use in the fragment.sql script.

```
set feedback off term off verify off pagesize 60 newpage 0 linesize 66
truncate table FREESP;
declare
  Fileid    NUMBER(9);
  Filename  VARCHAR2(513);
  Tsname    VARCHAR2(30);
  Cursor Tablespaces is
     select File_Name, File_ID, Tablespace_Name
       from DBA_DATA_FILES
      where Tablespace_Name = upper('&1');
begin
open Tablespaces;
loop
  fetch Tablespaces into Filename, Fileid, Tsname;
  exit when Tablespaces%NOTFOUND;
```

```
declare
  First   NUMBER(10);
  Blocks  NUMBER(10);
  Last    NUMBER(10);
  Tfirst  NUMBER(10);
  Tblocks NUMBER(10);
  Tlast   NUMBER(10);
  Cursor Free is
    select Block_ID a, Blocks b, Block_ID+Blocks c
      from DBA_FREE_SPACE
     where File_ID = Fileid
     order by Block_ID;
begin
  open Free;
  fetch Free into First, Blocks, Last;
  if Free%NOTFOUND
   then
       goto close_free;
  end if;
  loop
    fetch Free into Tfirst, Tblocks, Tlast;
    exit when Free%NOTFOUND;
    if Tfirst = Last
      then
        Blocks := Blocks + Tblocks;
        Last := Tlast;
      else
        insert into FREESP
          values (Filename, Tsname, First, Blocks, Last-1);
        commit;
        First := Tfirst;
        Blocks := Tblocks;
        Last := Tlast;
    end if;
  end loop;
      insert into FREESP
         values (Filename, Tsname, First, Blocks, Last-1);
  commit;
<<<close_free>>>
  close Free;
end;
end loop;
commit;
close Tablespaces;
end;
/
set term off echo off
 ttitle center ' TABLESPACE FRAGMENTATION REPORT'
```

```
col Tspace heading 'TABLESPACE|NAME' format a10 trunc
col Fname heading 'FILE' format A30 trunc
col First heading 'START|BLOCK' format 999,999
col Blocks heading 'SIZE(BLKS)' format 99,999,999
break on report on Tspace skip 1 on Fname skip 1
compute sum of Blocks on Fname
compute sum of Blocks on report

spool fragmentation.rpt
select Tspace, Fname, First, Blocks
  from FREESP
 order by Tspace,Fname,First;

spool off
```

The script runs for a single tablespace and expects the tablespace name as input. Let's take a look at the output of the script.

```
                  TABLESPACE FRAGMENTATION REPORT

                                                    START
TABLESPACE                                          BLOCK  SIZE(BLKS)
NAME       FILE                                  --------  -----------
---------- ------------------------------
USR1       /home01/oracle/user_1                    3,215           3
                                                    4,065          40
                                                    5,586          75
                                                    8,475         145
                                                   10,080         110
                                                   10,545         100
                                                   21,832       3,215
                                                   50,563          85
                                                   61,054         111
                                                   85,045       1,420
                                                   95,996           7
                                                  108,526          70
                                                  121,503         121
                                                  125,689         275
                                                  127,250         450
                                                  131,418          58
                                                  151,903         895
                                                  159,394          50
                                                  171,876         325
                                                  270,022         665
                                                  292,477          18
                                                  328,862          50
                                                  328,922          85
                                                  334,617         110
                                                  344,614         285
```

```
                                    359,493          670
                                    360,328          675
                                    365,297          125
                                    366,197          325
                                    366,567          435
                                    369,117           33
                                    371,945           13
                                    372,033          220
                                    372,833          155
                                    375,651          150
                                    423,382          195
                                    425,657          100
                                    431,110           72
                                    434,692        1,905
                                    481,830           40
******************************                -----------
sum                                               13,881


**********                                    -----------
sum                                               13,881
```

Yikes! This tablespace is badly fragmented. There are 40 extents making up the 13,881 free blocks—an average of less than 350 blocks per extent. If all you did was add up the number of blocks available in the DBA_FREE_SPACE view for this tablespace, it would look like you had tons of space left. Too many inexperienced DBAs fall into the trap of checking total space available and thinking they have enough space, when in reality, the space is so fragmented that there really is not enough contiguous space to allocate another extent. When you look closely at the space in the tablespace in the report above, most of the extents are less than 500 blocks. Unless this tablespace is either read-only or contains tables that are updated infrequently, you're going to have problems allocating space in here.

Oracle does not merge contiguous free extents unless there is no other alternative; so your tablespace becomes more and more fragmented as Oracle first allocates space from the largest free extent it encounters in the tablespace before reusing and coalescing the smaller free extents that are created as objects are dropped. Figure 9-1 illustrates available extents within a tablespace before and after a request for an extent has been allocated.

The DBA_FREE_SPACE data dictionary view contains information about every free extent in the datafiles that make up the database. Oracle does not go through the view to see if any of the extents are contiguous. So you can have information about two extents that are right next to each other (as they are in Figure 9-1a), but you will see them as two separate rows in this view. This is not too efficient, and

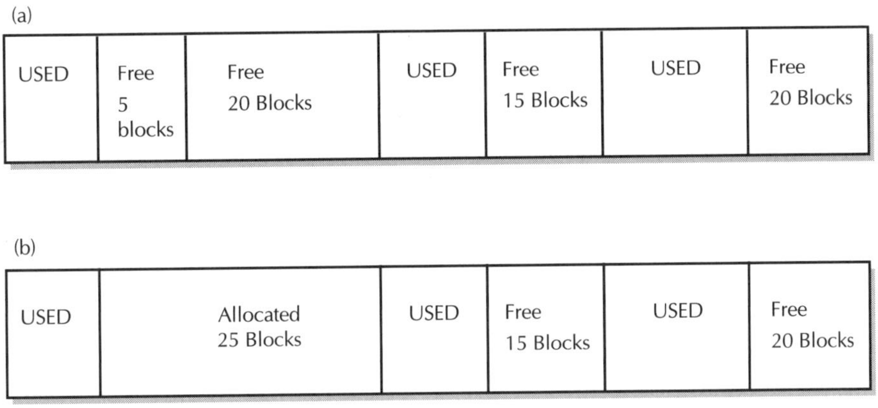

(a)

USED	Free 5 blocks	Free 20 Blocks	USED	Free 15 Blocks	USED	Free 20 Blocks

(b)

USED	Allocated 25 Blocks	USED	Free 15 Blocks	USED	Free 20 Blocks

FIGURE 9-1. *Contiguous extents coalesced: (a) Fragmentation with two contiguous extents before a 25-block extent request (b) Fragmentation after the extents are coalesced and allocated*

not too useful, since it's not a true picture of the free space available in your datafiles! The fragment.sql script reads the DBA_FREE_SPACE data dictionary view, looks for extents that are contiguous, adds up the number of blocks in the contiguous extents (or just reports the number if the extents are not contiguous), stores the results in a temporary table, and reports, by datafile, on the fragmentation in your tablespace. By saving prior days' versions of this report, you can see how your tablespace is being used and fragmented and how frequently fragmentation is occurring.

If you are using locally managed tablespaces, you will not have to worry about coalescing free extents. For dictionary managed tablespaces, you can manually coalesce the tablespace using the command

```
alter tablespace <tablespace name> coalesce;
```

Rollback Segments

Have you ever had to write a poem? You start with an idea and, maybe, a first line or theme. You might write several lines and then decide the poem is just awful, and you start over again. You get halfway through and decide that most of what you've written is wonderful, but a line here or there needs to be changed. Finally, you get to the end of the poem and realize that a line you took out should have been left in. Now, you have to scramble to try to remember exactly what that line said (which, by now, you are convinced will make the poem spectacular and must be recaptured). If you carefully wrote each line and started out fresh—recopying everything you wanted to keep—each time you began to rewrite the poem, you would have a copy of exactly what the poem looked like through each phase of the writing. You could easily go back and see what that one, wonderful line said. Once you completed each version of the poem and made a clean copy of it (committed it), you could hand off that clean copy to someone else to read while you continued to revise the poem. Oracle uses rollback segments, just like you use that clean copy, to keep track of exactly how data looked before it was modified—called *before images.*

Why store the before image of data? Oracle promises that "readers won't block writers, and writers won't block readers." What does this mean? Suppose you start to look at the payroll table and are reporting on salaries. Now someone else comes along and changes some of the salaries. Without the rollback segment, your report would show inconsistent data—some from before the change and some from after the change. Oracle ensures that you won't see a mix of unmodified and modified data by using the rollback segments to give you a consistent picture of the data, even if someone is making changes to it.

With Oracle9i, Oracle introduced the concept of automatic undo management. Basically, this means that you create a special tablespace called an "Undo Tablespace" and set the initialization parameter **undo_management** to AUTO, and then Oracle takes over and allocates and deallocates undo extents as needed.

When a user begins to do work, such as generate a report or modify rows of a table, a rollback segment is assigned to the user's process. In Chapter 2, we talked about how rollback segments are allocated and how they are extended. But what happens if a rollback segment runs out of space? If a large transaction requires more space than the rollback segment has already allocated, the rollback segment will extend into the free space remaining in the tablespace, just as a table extends when you add more data to it. If the rollback segment requires more space than is available in the tablespace, then the transaction causing the rollback segment to extend will fail. If the transaction fails, you can probably expect a call from an irate user! So, what can you do about ensuring that there is enough space in the rollback segment tablespace to support the volume of data transactions that are occurring? Why, you can monitor the number of times the rollback segments have to extend to support the load.

If the extents within the rollback segment are too small, then the transaction will "wrap" from one extent to another within the rollback segment. Each time a rollback segment wraps, Oracle has to perform internal space management tasks. These tasks take time and performance resources away from processing time. So, ideally, you want to size a transaction's rollback segment entry to fit entirely within one extent of the rollback segment, thus minimizing the performance and internal space management issues associated with wraps.

You can monitor the number of times the rollback segment entries wrap from one extent to another within the rollback segment. We'll show you how in the next section.

Monitoring Rollback Segment Size

Rollback segments are assigned to processes in a circular manner, and all transactions, regardless of their size, compete for the same available rollback segments. Unless you specifically use the **set transaction use rollback segment** command as the first statement after every **commit** to allocate a specific rollback segment to your next transaction, you have no control over which rollback segment will be used during your transaction processing. The **set transaction use rollback segment** statement, if you are going to use it, must be the first statement in the transaction, and the **commit** or **rollback** statement is the last statement of the transaction.

If you use the **set transaction use rollback segment** command to support a large transaction, you should create a rollback segment that is specially sized for the transaction. If you do not use the **set transaction use rollback segment** command, a rollback segment will be assigned to your transaction in a round-robin fashion. Since most rollback segment assignments for transactions are random, you should use a standard size for all of your rollback segments (except for those that specifically support large transactions). There is no guarantee that the large rollback segment you have placed online to be used just for your large transaction will not be allocated to other processes before your process is started. Although many transactions can and do share rollback segments, you cannot ever be 100 percent sure that yours will be the only transaction in your large rollback segment unless there are no other users on the system while your process is running.

As we said, a single rollback segment can store the data from multiple transactions. Any of the entries within the rollback segment can force the rollback segment to extend. Therefore, if you have a lot of small transactions in a rollback segment, you are just as likely to have extension occur as you would with a single large transaction.

The Rollback Segment Optimal Parameter

Now, let's say that a rollback segment has been extending and now reaches a point where it has used up all of the available space in the rollback segment tablespace. What will happen next? The transaction that is attempting to extend will fail. As other rollback segments attempt to extend, since there is no available space left to extend into, more transactions will fail. What are your options at this point? Well, there is really only one thing you can do: add a datafile to the rollback segment tablespace to make more space available.

However, before things ever get that critical, there is something you can do to help ensure that you will not run out of space in the rollback segment tablespace. To control the extension of rollback segments, you can rebuild the rollback segments (one at a time, if necessary) and set an optimal size for each of the rollback segments. You can use the optimal parameter of the **storage** clause to set an optimal value when you are performing a **create rollback segment** or **alter rollback segment** command. You can find the value of the rollback segment's optimal parameter setting, along with other rollback segment statistics, in the V$ROLLSTAT view, which records cumulative statistics about all rollback segment usage since the database was last started, as explained in Chapter 6.

If you have set an optimal size for your rollback segments, then rollback segments that have extended beyond their optimal size can shrink. The optimal size should be set to minimize the number of extensions and shrinks required for the rollback segment to support the size and volume of transactions. Shrinking rollback segments back to optimal size can have a performance impact, so it's always best to size the rollback segments so that they don't extend. However, for those infrequent large transactions that force an extension, optimal will allow you to recover that space.

Looking at the Optimal Value, Shrinks, and Extends

The following script queries V$ROLLSTAT along with V$ROLLNAME. The V$ROLLNAME view shows the names of the online rollback segments, while in V$ROLLSTAT, the rollback segments are identified only by their USN (Undo Segment Number) value. The query in the following listing will show the optimal size, number of shrinks, average size per shrink, and number of extensions per rollback segment.

```
REM  Rollback Segment Extensions
REM
column Name format A20
select Name, Optsize, Shrinks, Aveshrink, Extends
  from V$ROLLSTAT, V$ROLLNAME
 where V$ROLLSTAT.Usn=V$ROLLNAME.Usn;
```

Sample output for the V$ROLLSTAT query is shown in the following listing:

```
NAME                    OPTSIZE    SHRINKS  AVESHRINK     EXTENDS
-------------------- ---------- ---------- ----------  ----------
SYSTEM                                   0          0           0
R01                    10485760          4   41943040          32
R02                    10485760          2   44564480          17
```

Let's take a look at the report and see what we have. There are three active rollback segments in the database. The SYSTEM rollback segment is used for data dictionary transactions. Users' transactions are assigned to either the R01 or R02 rollback segment. Each of the user rollback segments has an optimal size of 10M (10,485,760 bytes). Each user rollback segment has extended beyond its optimal value and has been forced to shrink back to its optimal size two or more times.

The rollback segments have shrunk by an average of almost 40M each time they have shrunk. If you think carefully about the report output, you will realize that the R01 and R02 rollback segments are not properly sized for the transactions they are supporting. They are frequently extending (49 times since the last database startup) and extend, on average, to five times their optimal size. If a rollback segment has to constantly extend beyond its optimal setting and then shrink back to its optimal setting, Oracle is performing a great deal of unnecessary space management work. To reduce the number of rollback segment extensions, you should modify the rollback segments' optimal settings, increasing them to at least 40M. After modifying the rollback segments' storage settings, you can periodically execute the script to determine the impact of the changes. You might also want to consider adding more rollback segments to the database to help accommodate the transaction load.

When a rollback segment extends beyond its optimal setting the first time, the rollback segment will not shrink. The second time the rollback segment extends beyond its optimal setting, the rollback segment will shrink—provided the second transaction forced the rollback segment to allocate a new extent. Although setting a value for the optimal parameter will not completely prevent you from having any rollback segment space management issues, it can help you limit the number and kind of space management issues you have.

Because of the manner in which rollback segments extend and shrink, the number of "Extends" in the previous script's output should always be more than the number of "Shrinks." For example, if the rollback segment started with a size less than its optimal setting, acquiring new extents would increment the "Extends" statistic value, but no "Shrinks" would be necessary. Once a rollback exceeds its optimal setting in size, it only shrinks at the end of a transaction—and that transaction may have forced multiple extensions.

You can use the **alter rollback segment** command to shrink rollback segments to a size of your choosing and at a time of your choosing. The rollback segments must always have a minimum of two extents. If you do not specify a size to shrink to, the rollback segment will shrink to its optimal size. In the following listing, the R01 rollback segment is shrunk back to its optimal size.

```
alter rollback segment R01 shrink;
```

Monitoring Rollback Segment Extent Size

To simplify the management of multiple rollback segment entries within a rollback segment, you should try to size the rollback segment so that each of its extents is large enough to support a typical transaction.

When a transaction's rollback segment entry cannot be stored within a single extent, the entry wraps into a second extent within the rollback segment. The extents within a rollback segment are assigned circularly, so a rollback segment entry can wrap from the last extent of the rollback segment to its first extent—as long as there is not an active rollback segment entry already in the first extent. If there is already an active rollback segment entry in the first extent, the rollback segment will extend.

You can query the V$ROLLSTAT view to see the number of wraps that have occurred in each rollback segment since the last time the database was started. If there have been no wraps in the rollback segment, then its extents are properly sized for the transactions it supports. If there is a non-zero value for the number of wraps, then you should re-create the rollback segments with larger extent sizes. We'll look at two different outputs from this query and tell you how to interpret what you see. First, here's the query:

```
REM   Rollback Segment Wraps Check
REM
column Name format A20
select Name, Optsize, Shrinks, Aveshrink, Wraps, Extends
  from V$ROLLSTAT, V$ROLLNAME
 where V$ROLLSTAT.Usn=V$ROLLNAME.Usn;
```

Like the query for rollback segment extension, the script in the preceding listing queries statistics from V$ROLLSTAT along with the rollback segment names from V$ROLLNAME. The first sample output we'll look at from the query is shown in the following listing:

```
NAME                    OPTSIZE    SHRINKS  AVESHRINK      WRAPS    EXTENDS
-------------------- ---------- ---------- ---------- ---------- ----------
SYSTEM                                   0          0          0          0
R01                    10485760          4   41943040         41         32
R02                    10485760          2   44564480         26         17
```

As you can see, the sample query output shows that 67 wraps have occurred since the last time the database was started. Given the number of extensions that have occurred, the number of wraps is not surprising (because extensions usually require wraps). The extensions indicate that the rollback segments are handling larger transactions than they were designed for; and if the entire rollback segment cannot handle a transaction's rollback information, a single extent will not be able to hold it either. Thus, rollback segments that extend will frequently have high numbers of wraps.

The second sample output is shown in the following listing. This output is slightly modified from the preceding output. Notice that there are no extensions, but there are wraps.

```
NAME                    OPTSIZE    SHRINKS  AVESHRINK      WRAPS    EXTENDS
-------------------- ---------- ---------- ---------- ---------- ----------
SYSTEM                                   0          0          0          0
R01                    10485760          0          0         41          0
R02                    10485760          0          0         26          0
```

If there are wraps but no extensions, as shown in the preceding listing, the rollback segment has the proper optimal setting, but its extent sizes are too small. That is, the rollback segment is large enough to support its transactions without extending; however, the transaction entries require multiple extents within the rollback segment. If you have wraps with no extensions, then you should re-create your rollback segments using the same optimal setting but larger extent sizes.

Monitoring Extents

Because the software was modified to enable the header block to extend, you can actually have as many extents as your operating system will support, and you can create your table with **maxextents unlimited** or any number you choose. **maxextents unlimited** is not actually unlimited. If you look at the Max_Extents column of DBA_TABLES for a table created with **maxextents unlimited**, you will see that it actually translates to 2,147,483,645, which for all intents and purposes *is* unlimited. If the tablespace does not have maxextents defined, and you do not specify a maxextents value on the storage clause when you create a table, the maxextents value on that table will be the default maximum extent limit based on the block size for that database. For example, let's create a tablespace in an 8K-block size database as follows:

```
create tablespace MY_TS
datafile 'mydisk1:[Oracle.mydb]my_ts01.dbf' size 10M
default storage(initial 500k
                next 500k
                minextents 1)
online;
Tablespace created.
```

We have not specified a maxextents value. Now, let's create a table and see what the default value for maxextents will be.

```
create table MY_TAB (Ename varchar2(20), Empno number);
Table created.
```

Next, we'll select the values from USER_TABLES and see what our maxextents value is by default.

```
select Table_Name, Initial_Extent, Max_Extents
  from USER_TABLES
 where Table_Name = 'MY_TAB';
```

```
TABLE_NAME                     INITIAL_EXTENT MAX_EXTENTS
------------------------------ -------------- -----------
MY_TAB                                 524288         505
```

We see that the value for maxextents is equal to the default value for an 8K-block size database.

To monitor the growth of tables in a database, you can use the following script:

```
prompt CHECKING FOR FRAGMENTED DATABASE OBJECTS:
prompt
column Owner noprint new_value Owner_Var
column Segment_Name format a30 heading 'Object Name'
column Segment_Type format a9 heading 'Table/Indx'
column Bytes format 999,999,999 heading 'Bytes Used'
column Extents format 999 heading 'No.'
break on Owner skip page 2
ttitle center 'Table Fragmentation Report' skip 2 -
  left 'creator: ' Owner_Var skip 2
select Owner,
       Segment_Name,
       Segment_Type,
       Bytes,
       Max_Extents,
       Extents
  from DBA_SEGMENTS
 where Extents > 50
   and Segment_Type = 'TABLE'
 order by Owner, Segment_Name, Segment_Type, Max_Extents
/
ttitle center 'Index Fragmentation Report' skip 2 -
  left 'creator: ' Owner_Var skip 2
select Owner,
       Segment_Name,
       Segment_Type,
       Bytes,
       Max_Extents,
       Extents
  from DBA_SEGMENTS
 where Extents > 50
   and Segment_Type = 'INDEX'
   and Owner not in ('SYS','SYSTEM')
 order by Owner, Segment_Name, Segment_Type, Max_Extents
/
```

In this script, we check for any table or index with a number of extents exceeding 50. You can, of course, set your threshold to whatever value makes sense for your environment. The idea is to keep track of those tables that are growing and may reach a point where they will exceed the amount of extents allocated for them. The results of running this script against a sample database are shown here:

```
CHECKING FOR FRAGMENTED DATABASE OBJECTS:

                                    Table Fragmentation Report

creator: TEST

Object Name                     Table/Ind   Bytes Used MAX_EXTENTS  No.
------------------------------ --------- ------------ ----------- ----
REG_IN                          TABLE      105,881,600        1000  584
REG_OUT                         TABLE       38,666,240        1000  211

                                    Index Fragmentation Report

creator: TEST

Object Name                     Table/Ind   Bytes Used MAX_EXTENTS  No.
------------------------------ --------- ------------ ----------- ----
IDX_REG_IN                      INDEX        2,867,200         505   67
IDX_REG_OUT                     INDEX        1,925,120         505   43
IDX_REG_OUT_2                   INDEX        3,072,000         505   71
SYS_C005595                     INDEX        1,269,760         505   30
SYS_C005598                     INDEX        1,720,320         505   40
```

As you can see, the tables REG_IN and REG_OUT have maxextents set to a number larger than the default. When we look at the index portion of the report, we see two indexes whose names begin with SYS_C. When you create an index without specifying a name, Oracle will assign a name beginning with SYS_C followed by a number. While there is nothing wrong with allowing Oracle to name your index for you, it does make it difficult to quickly relate an index to the table to which it applies. In general, we recommend that you explicitly name all indexes when you create them and use some sort of naming convention that will allow you to quickly relate the index to its associated table.

As an alternative, you can run the following script:

```
set feedback off;
set term off
set pagesize 60;
set newpage 0;
set linesize 80;
col Db_Name new_value instance
select 'INSTANCE NAME' Description, Value Db_Name from V$PARAMETER
```

```
   where upper(Name) = 'DB_NAME'
/
ttitle center instance ' TABLESPACE/FILE/EXTENTS REPORT'
column Tablespace_Name format a15 heading 'TABLESPACE|NAME'
column Segment_Name format a20 heading 'TABLE|NAME'
column Extents format 99999 heading 'EXTENTS'
column Max_Extents format 99999 heading 'MAXEXTENTS'
column Owner format a10
column Segment_Type format a7 heading 'TABLE|TYPE'
break on Tablespace_Name skip 2 on report
spool check_extents.log
select Tablespace_Name,Segment_Name,Segment_Type, Owner, Extents, Max_Extents
  from DBA_SEGMENTS
 where Segment_Type not in ('CACHE','ROLLBACK','DEFERRED ROLLBACK')
   and ((Extents/decode(Max_Extents,0,1,Max_Extents))*100 > 25
    or (Extents > 250 and Max_Extents = 2147483645))
order by Tablespace_Name,Owner,Segment_Name
/
spool off
exit
```

This version of the script will report on all segments (tables, indexes, temporary segments) with more than 25 percent of their maxextents already allocated or where the maxextents are set to unlimited and the number of extents allocated is over 250. The **decode** statement in the where clause is used to make sure the equation does not do a divide by zero. This report output looks like the sample shown here:

```
                     TEST TABLESPACE/FILE/EXTENTS REPORT
TABLESPACE      TABLE                TABLE
NAME            NAME                 TYPE    OWNER      EXTENTS MAXEXTENTS
--------------- -------------------- ------- ---------- ------- ----------
USERS           REG_IN               TABLE   TEST           533       1000
DICTMGMT        OVERMAX              TABLE   RACHEL         278 2147483645
```

In addition to monitoring for objects that are approaching their maxextents limit, we want to know which objects will not be able to extend at all. The following script will identify all the objects whose next extent is larger than the available free space in the tablespace.

```
column "OBJECT" format a20
column "TABLESPACE" format a20
column "TYPE" format a6
column "NEXT (M)" format 99999
column "EXTENTS" format 999
set pages 60
ttitle 'NEXT EXTENT BLOWUP REPORT'

select Segment_Name "OBJECT", Segment_Type "TYPE", Extents "EXTENTS",
       round(Next_Extent/1024/1024) "NEXT (M)",
```

```
      ds.Tablespace_Name "TABLESPACE", round(df.Lrgstext/1024/1024) "LRGSTEXT"
  from DBA_SEGMENTS ds,
      (select Tablespace_Name "TABLESPACE", max(Bytes) "LRGSTEXT"
         from DBA_FREE_SPACE
         group by Tablespace_Name) df
 where ds.Tablespace_Name = df."TABLESPACE"
   and Next_Extent > "LRGSTEXT"
   and ds.Segment_Type not in ('ROLLBACK','DEFERRED ROLLBACK','TEMPORARY')
/

Mon Mar 11                                                        page    1
                          NEXT EXTENT BLOWUP REPORT

OBJECT               TYPE   EXTENTS NEXT (M) TABLESPACE           LRGSTEXT
-------------------- ------ ------- -------- -------------------- ----------
TAXRETURN            TABLE        1        5 SMALLTBL                      4
```

This report shows that the next extent for the TAXRETURN table is 5M but that the largest extent available in the SMALLTBL tablespace is only 4M. If the TAXRETURN table needs to extend, the transaction will fail because there is not enough space in the tablespace. If the number of already allocated extents was large, you might consider rebuilding the table with a larger initial and next extent size and, if you have arranged the tablespaces in your database with small, medium and large default extent sizes, changing the tablespace that the table is in as well.

Okay, so you now know that if the table needs to extend it will fail, but how do you know when this table is likely to extend? We're going to tell you that right now.

Space Remaining

Although the scripts in the previous section will tell you how fragmented your tables and indexes are, and you can compare the outputs over several days or weeks to track how often your objects are extending, they won't tell you when your objects are likely to extend.

Why do you want to track the used space in your objects? Well, suppose all the objects in your tablespace were to extend at once. Do you have enough space free in the tablespace for this to happen, or will you run out of room and have your users running to you with space problems? Do you have a large enough extent free in your tablespace to hold the largest next extent in that tablespace?

One way to track all of this is to create a table to hold historical information about the objects and their storage characteristics. You can use this table for trending analysis, and you can run a daily report against it to warn you of objects close to extending. We use the following script to create a historical information table. We then initially fill the table with information about our largest, most frequently updated objects. We use the remaining scripts in this section to continue filling the table with daily statistics about the objects we want to track and to report on the contents. Oracle provides a package, DBMS_SPACE, which can be found in the /rdbms/admin directory under ORACLE_HOME. This package contains a procedure, UNUSED_SPACE, which reports on the amount of allocated space that has not yet been used for data. Before you can use the package, you must first log in to your database and then load the DBMS_SPACE package as follows (this example is for a Unix system):

```
sqlplus "/ as sysdba"
@$ORACLE_HOME/rdbms/admin/dbmsutil.sql
@$ORACLE_HOME/rdbms/admin/prvtutil.plb
```

Once you have run these scripts, you will be able to use the DBMS_SPACE package.

```
create table EXTGROW
(Segname      VARCHAR2(81)    NOT NULL
,Segown       VARCHAR2(30)    NOT NULL
,Growdate     DATE            NOT NULL
,Segtype      VARCHAR2(17)
,Segtbs       VARCHAR2(30)
,Exts         NUMBER
,Nextext      NUMBER
,Tbsfree      NUMBER
,Hwm          NUMBER
,Totbytes     NUMBER
,Usedbytes    NUMBER
,Contigfree   NUMBER
,Freepct      NUMBER
,Tbsexts      NUMBER
)
tablespace TOOLS
storage (initial      819200
         next         819200
         minextents   10
         maxextents   505
         pctincrease  0
)
/
alter table EXTGROW add constraint EXTGROW_PK
      primary key (Segname, Segown, Growdate)
      using index tablespace TOOLS_IDX
      storage (initial     81920
               next        81920
               minextents  10
               maxextents  505
               pctincrease 0);
```

The rate at which this table will grow will depend on how many tables and indexes you want to track. Some of the information being stored is data about the tablespace the object resides in; the remainder is information about the object itself.

To fill the table initially, you can use the following script. It will prompt you for the name of the table and index owner. You can run the script multiple times if you have more than one user in your database that owns objects you want to track.

```
insert into EXTGROW (Segname, Segown, Growdate, Segtype, Segtbs, Exts,
                     Nextext, Tbsfree, Hwm, Totbytes, Usedbytes,
                     Contigfree, Freepct, Tbsexts)
       select   Segment_Name,Owner,
                to_date(to_char(sysdate-1,'YYYYMMDD'),'YYYYMMDD'),
                Segment_Type, Tablespace_Name,0,0,0,0,0,0,0,0,0
         from DBA_SEGMENTS
        where Owner = upper('&1')
          and Segment_Type in ('TABLE','INDEX')
/
```

To fill the table on a daily basis, run the script below. The script expects a date in YYYYMMDD format as input. This date is the date you are running the script, and the procedure assumes that there is data in the EXTGROW table for the prior day.

```
declare
   Total_Blocks         NUMBER;
   Total_Bytes          NUMBER;
   Unused_Blocks        NUMBER;
   Unused_Bytes         NUMBER;
   Lue_File_Id          NUMBER;
   Lue_Block_Id         NUMBER;
   Last_Used_Block      NUMBER;
   T_Name               EXTGROW.Segname%TYPE;
   Ts_Name              EXTGROW.Segtbs%TYPE;
   Hwm                  NUMBER;
   T_Exts               NUMBER;
   T_Own                EXTGROW.Segown%TYPE;
   N_Exts               NUMBER;
   T_Free               NUMBER;
   N_Ext_Bytes          NUMBER;
   L_Chunk              NUMBER;
   Db_Blk_Size          NUMBER;

cursor TABSPACE is
       select Table_Name,
              dt.Owner,
              dt.Tablespace_Name,
              dt.Next_Extent,
```

```
                Extents,
                dt.Blocks
           from DBA_TABLES dt, EXTGROW eg, DBA_SEGMENTS ds
          where Table_Name = Segname
            and dt.Owner=Segown
            and ds.Owner=Segown
            and Segment_Name = Segname
            and Growdate=to_date('&1','YYYYMMDD')-1;

cursor INDSPACE is
       select Index_Name,
              di.Owner,
              di.Tablespace_Name,
              di.Next_Extent,
              Extents
         from DBA_INDEXES di, EXTGROW eg, DBA_SEGMENTS ds
        where Index_Name = Segname
          and di.Owner=Segown
          and ds.Owner=Segown
          and Segment_Name=Segname
          and Growdate=to_date('&1','YYYYMMDD')-1;

begin

select Value
  into Db_Blk_Size
  from SYS.V_$PARAMETER
 where upper(Name) = 'DB_BLOCK_SIZE';

open TABSPACE;

loop
   fetch TABSPACE
    into T_Name,
         T_Own,
         Ts_Name,
         N_Ext_Bytes,
         T_Exts,
         Hwm;

    exit when TABSPACE%NOTFOUND;

DBMS_SPACE.UNUSED_SPACE(T_Own,T_Name,'TABLE',Total_Blocks, Total_Bytes,
Unused_Blocks, Unused_Bytes, Lue_File_Id, Lue_Block_Id, Last_Used_Block);

Hwm := Hwm*Db_Blk_Size;

select count(*),
```

```
       sum(Bytes),
       max(Bytes)
  into N_Exts, T_Free, L_Chunk
  from DBA_FREE_SPACE
 where Tablespace_Name = Ts_Name;

insert into EXTGROW (Segname, Segown, Growdate, Segtype, Segtbs, Exts,
                     Nextext, Tbsfree, Hwm, Totbytes, Usedbytes,
                     Contigfree,  Freepct, Tbsexts)
     values (T_Name, T_Own, to_date('&1','YYYYMMDD'), 'TABLE',Ts_Name,
             T_Exts, N_Ext_Bytes, T_Free, Hwm, Total_Bytes,
             (Total_Bytes-Unused_Bytes), L_Chunk,
             (Unused_Bytes/Total_Bytes)*100, N_Exts);

commit;

end loop;
close TABSPACE;

open INDSPACE;

loop
   fetch INDSPACE
    into T_Name,
         T_Own,
         Ts_Name,
         N_Ext_Bytes,
         T_Exts;
exit when INDSPACE%NOTFOUND;

DBMS_SPACE.UNUSED_SPACE(T_Own,T_Name,'INDEX',Total_Blocks, Total_Bytes,
                        Unused_Blocks, Unused_Bytes, Lue_File_Id,
                        Lue_Block_Id, Last_Used_Block);

select count(*),
       sum(Bytes),
       max(Bytes)
  into N_Exts, T_Free, L_Chunk
  from DBA_FREE_SPACE
 where Tablespace_Name = Ts_Name;

insert into EXTGROW (Segname, Segown, Growdate, Segtype, Segtbs, Exts,
                     Nextext, Tbsfree, Hwm, Totbytes, Usedbytes,
                     Contigfree,  Freepct, Tbsexts)
     values (T_Name, T_Own, to_date('&1','YYYYMMDD'), 'INDEX',Ts_Name,
             T_Exts, N_Ext_Bytes, T_Free, NULL, Total_Bytes,
             (Total_Bytes-Unused_Bytes), L_Chunk,
             (Unused_Bytes/Total_Bytes)*100, N_Exts);
```

```
commit;

end loop;
close INDSPACE;
end;
/
```

This script is used to fill the EXTGROW table with the information about the allocated and used space in each object named in the table for a date that you pass in as a parameter. PL/SQL code that is not stored in the database as a procedure or package is called an *anonymous PL/SQL block* and is recompiled each time it is run. If you are going to run this script more than once a day, it's a good idea to turn it into a stored procedure, so that Oracle can take advantage of the fact that the code in a stored procedure is already compiled and can be executed faster.

Now that we've collected the information, we need to extract it in a readable form. The following SQL script will extract rows and format them, based on the criteria you pass in. Save the output into a file called spacerpt.sql.

```
set pagesize 50 trimspool on linesize 250 verify off feedback off
set echo off term off
col Segname format a20 heading 'OBJECT'
col Segown format a10 heading 'OWNER'
col Segtype format a5 heading 'TYPE'
col Segtbs format a15 heading 'TABLESPACE'
col Exts format 9999 heading 'OBJEXTS'
col Nextext format 9,999,999,999 heading 'NEXT EXTENT'
col Tbsfree format 9,999,999,999 heading 'TOTAL TBS FREE'
col Hwm format 9,999,999,999 heading 'HIGHWATER MARK'
col Totbytes format 9,999,999,999 heading 'TOT ALLOC SPC'
col Usedbytes format 9,999,999,999 heading 'USED SPACE'
col Contigfree format 9,999,999,999 heading 'LARGEST FREE'
col Freepct format 999.99 heading '% FREE'
col Tbsexts format 9999 heading 'TBSEXTS'
compute sum of Nextext on Segtbs
break on report on Segtbs skip 1 on Tbsfree on Contigfree on Tbsexts on Segown
select Segtbs,
       Tbsfree,
       Contigfree,
       Tbsexts,
       Segown,
       Segname,
       Segtype,
       Hwm,
       Totbytes,
       Usedbytes,Exts,
       Nextext,
       Freepct
  from EXTGROW
 where Freepct < &1 and Growdate = to_date('&2','YYYYMMDD')
```

```
   and Segtbs like upper('%&3%')
 order by Segtbs, Segown, Segname

set concat +
spool spacerpt_&2.log
/
exit
```

When you run this script, you will need to provide it with three parameters: the percentage of remaining free space to report on, the date you want to view (in YYYYMMDD format), and the tablespace you want to look at. If you want to see the data for all objects with 10 percent or less free space remaining, for March 10, 2002, and for all tablespaces, at the SQL*Plus command line you would type

```
@@spacerpt 10 20020310 "%"
```

Sample output of this script is below. The amount of information being extracted is large, and the listing will wrap over several lines.

```
TABLESPACE       TOTAL TBS FREE   LARGEST FREE TBSEXTS OWNER      OBJECT                  TYPE
HIGHWATER MARK   TOT ALLOC SPC     USED SPACE OBJEXTS    NEXT EXTENT  % FREE
--------------- -------------- -------------- ------- ---------- -----------------------
-------------- -------------- -------------- ------- -------------- - -----
USERS              603,635,712     66,314,240     327  TEST      IDX REG_IN             INDEX
                       327,680        327,680       8          40,960      .00
                                                                 IDX_REG_OUT            INDEX
                     2,621,440      2,621,440      60          40,960      .00
                                                                 REG_IN                 TABLE
    44,998,656      14,049,280     14,049,280     332          40,960      .00
                                                                 REG_OUT                TABLE
    15,351,808      52,510,720     52,428,800     224       1,048,576      .16
*************** ************** ************** ******* *************
                                                       --------------
sum                                                         1,171,456
```

The **select** statement uses substitution variables instead of hard-coding values so that you don't have to continually edit the script when the date changes or when you want to see different percentages or tablespaces. We are firm believers in coding with parameters so that you only have to write the script once, and not go back and change it every time you, or the end user, needs to see something slightly differently.

If you pass in 100 for the first substitution variable (&1), you can see every table and index in the tablespaces you select for the date you select. The second variable is the date, and the script expects it in the format of YYYYMMDD, and concatenates the date to the name of the output log. By using this format, the output files will sort in date order. So that Oracle does not use the period to signify the end of the substitution variable, the script changes the concatenation character to a + before referencing the variable in the spool file name.

Oracle uses % as a wildcard, to match any value. By framing the &3 with %, you are telling Oracle to select any tablespace name that has the value of the third substitution variable anywhere in it. By passing in % as the third variable, you can select data for every tablespace.

Okay, now that we've shown you the script and the output, let's look a little more closely at what the output of this script tells us. There is a good deal of information on each line of the report, and each output line wraps onto two lines so it's pretty hard to read without some initial guidance.

```
TABLESPACE      TOTAL TBS FREE   LARGEST FREE TBSEXTS OWNER       OBJECT                    TYPE
HIGHWATER MARK  TOT ALLOC SPC     USED SPACE OBJEXTS      NEXT EXTENT  % FREE
--------------- -------------- -------------- ------- ---------- --------------------------
-------------- -------------- -------------- ------- -------------- - -----
USERS                 603,635,712     66,314,240     327 TEST          IDX REG_IN             INDEX
                         327,680        327,680        8          40,960      .00
                                                                       IDX_REG_OUT            INDEX
                       2,621,440      2,621,440       60          40,960      .00
                                                                       REG_IN                 TABLE
    44,998,656        14,049,280     14,049,280      332          40,960      .00
                                                                       REG_OUT                TABLE
    15,351,808        52,510,720     52,428,800      224       1,048,576      .16
*************** ************** ************** ******* *************
                                                            --------------
sum                                                            1,171,456
```

What can we tell from this report? The USERS tablespace has 603,635,712 bytes free, with the largest contiguous extent sized at 66,314,240. The tablespace is pretty fragmented, since the total free space is in 327 extents. This information is printed only on the first line because of the break commands we set, so it is easier to tell when there is a change.

None of the objects on this listing has a next extent larger than the largest free extent in the tablespace. The sum of the next extents for the percentage of free space remaining is 1,171,456 bytes, which will easily fit into both the total tablespace free space and the largest free extent in the tablespace. All of the objects show a very small percentage free, making them all likely to extend in the near future. This list may or may not show all the objects in the tablespace. The only way to make absolutely sure that you have enough space is to run the report and pass in 100 for the first substitution variable so that you see every object with 100 percent or less free space remaining.

Trace Files

When you have an internal error in a user session or background process, Oracle will create a trace file, to help in debugging and resolving the error. As the DBA, you can define where the trace files should be created and their maximum size, using the following initialization parameters:

- **MAX_DUMP_FILE_SIZE** Maximum size the trace file can become
- **BACKGROUND_DUMP_DEST** Location for trace files created by the Oracle background processes
- **USER_DUMP_DEST** Location for trace files created out of user sessions

Trace files created by the background processes will have the name of the background process that generated the trace file as part of the trace file name; those created by user processes will have the user process ID in the name of the trace file.

In general, it is a good idea to move the trace file directories from the default locations under the ORACLE_BASE directory tree to another disk. Trace files are not automatically purged and can grow quite large. You can end up with a large number of trace files that are old and of no value to you. Therefore, you should consider how long you need to retain trace files and how often you want to remove them from your directory. The only value of keeping trace files around for a long time is to help you to go back and determine when a problem first occurred.

When a trace file is created due to an internal error, a line will be written into the alert log, with the Oracle error number and the name and location of the trace file. Check the meaning of the Oracle error, and if it is not due to programming or user error, you should log on to Oracle's support site, MetaLink, and log an iTAR. You will generally be asked to send them the trace file for analysis.

We have included two sample trace files below. The first is from the user dump directory, and, based on the contents, looks like a user set her session to trace her SQL statements. It is therefore not a problem that would have to be called in to Support.

```
Dump file C:\oracle\admin\db901\udump\ORA00784.TRC
Mon Mar 11 13:14:18 2002
ORACLE V9.0.1.2.1 - Production vsnsta=0
vsnsql=10 vsnxtr=3
Windows 2000 Version 5.0 Service Pack 2, CPU type 586
Oracle9i Enterprise Edition Release 9.0.1.2.1 - Production
With the Partitioning option
JServer Release 9.0.1.2.0 - Production
Windows 2000 Version 5.0 Service Pack 2, CPU type 586
Instance name: db901

Redo thread mounted by this instance: 1

Oracle process number: 13

Windows thread id: 784, image: ORACLE.EXE


*** 2002-03-11 13:14:18.000
*** SESSION ID:(8.65) 2002-03-11 13:14:18.000
APPNAME mod='SQL*Plus' mh=3669949024 act='' ah=4029777240
=====================
PARSING IN CURSOR #1 len=32 dep=0 uid=21 oct=42 lid=21 tim=776580816 hv=1197935484 ad='66a43df8'
```

```
alter session set sql_trace=true
END OF STMT
EXEC #1:c=0,e=0,p=0,cr=0,cu=0,mis=0,r=0,dep=0,og=4,tim=776569816
*** 2002-03-11 13:14:42.000
=====================
PARSING IN CURSOR #1 len=51 dep=0 uid=21 oct=3 lid=21 tim=800264816 hv=3203075711 ad='66cac340'
select loan_id, total_due, remaining_bal from loans
END OF STMT
PARSE #1:c=0,e=0,p=0,cr=0,cu=0,mis=1,r=0,dep=0,og=4,tim=800264816
EXEC #1:c=0,e=0,p=0,cr=0,cu=0,mis=0,r=0,dep=0,og=4,tim=800264816\
FETCH #1:c=0,e=0,p=0,cr=3,cu=0,mis=0,r=1,dep=0,og=4,tim=800264816
FETCH #1:c=0,e=0,p=0,cr=1,cu=0,mis=0,r=3,dep=0,og=4,tim=800264816
STAT #1 id=1 cnt=4 pid=0 pos=0 obj=5279 op='TABLE ACCESS FULL LOANS '
```

The second trace file shows a small section of a trace file from the background dump destination. This file shows a portion of an ORA-600 error that should be called in to Support for them to confirm whether this is a serious error.

```
/u03/home/oracle/product/8.0.5/rdbms/log/prod_ora_10760.trc
Oracle8 Enterprise Edition Release 8.0.5.0.0 - Production
PL/SQL Release 8.0.5.0.0 - Production
ORACLE_HOME = /u03/home/oracle/product/8.0.5
System name:      SunOS
Node name:  x2
Release:    5.7
Version:    Generic_106541-08
Machine:    sun4u
Instance name: PROD
Redo thread mounted by this instance: 0 <none>
Oracle process number: 0
Unix process pid: 10760, image: oraclePROD

*** 2002.01.23.23.32.22.000
ksedmp: internal or fatal error
ORA-00600: internal error code, arguments: [SKGMBUSY], [1], [0], [0], [0], [], [], []

Current SQL information unavailable - no session.
```

As we saw in the first trace file, you can generate trace files for tuning purposes. To do this, set **sql_trace** = TRUE, either in the initialization parameter file or in the user session itself. These trace files are used by TKPROF to analyze the SQL statements. However, a severe performance impact comes along with setting **sql_trace** equal to TRUE for more than just a specific session on your system. We recommend that you either set this variable to TRUE only in a specific, monitored SQL session or set it to TRUE for the entire database for a very limited and controlled amount of time. You have to shut down and restart the database to set this variable to TRUE for the entire database, so you have double the impact. First, you have the impact of setting the variable to TRUE, and second, you have the impact of shutting down and restarting the database twice—once to enable **sql_trace** and the second time to turn it back off. You will definitely not want to run your database for an extended period of time with this variable set to TRUE. We discuss TKPROF in more detail in Chapter 13.

User Session Status

If you look in the V$SESSION view, you can tell the status of each user session in the database at that moment. The following script will return a count of sessions grouped by status in the database. Why do you want to check on these counts? You set an explicit or implicit limit to the number of sessions allowed in the database at any one time in your initialization parameter file by setting the parameter **sessions** to a value. If there are a large number of "KILLED" or "SNIPED" sessions in the database and that number does not go down over time, you are wasting the number of allowable sessions that you can have. The only way you can clear the number of sessions that are being counted is to shut down and restart the database.

```
select Status,count(*)
  from V$SESSION
 group by Status
/
```

The following listing is returned:

```
STATUS           COUNT(*)
-------- --------------
ACTIVE                 26
INACTIVE              160
KILLED                 30
CACHED                  5
SNIPED                  3
```

The Status column values can be misleading. A value of INACTIVE does not mean the user process is not doing anything; it merely means that at the moment the **select** was run, the process was not executing a SQL statement. ACTIVE sessions are executing SQL, KILLED sessions are marked by Oracle to be killed and removed from the database, and SNIPED sessions are inactive and waiting for the client to do something. CACHED sessions have to do with Oracle*XA, an external interface that allows global transactions to be handled by a transaction manager other than Oracle. If the numbers of KILLED, SNIPED, and CACHED sessions do not change, or continually increase, there is a problem in the database and session slots are being unnecessarily used. You will have to shut down and restart the database to resolve this problem.

Monitoring Object Modifications

You can check on changes to database objects using the data dictionary views USER_OBJECTS or DBA_OBJECTS. Why do you care when objects were last changed? If you are running a production system, you want to control when changes are made and who makes them. You can use auditing to monitor who has made use of a privilege that changes an object, but auditing won't tell you which object was changed. The DBA_OBJECTS and USER_OBJECTS views contain a column called Last_DDL_Time. This column contains the time that the object was last modified. However, Oracle considers adding grants or an index to be a modification to the object, so this field doesn't really reflect the last time the object itself was changed. To find out the actual time an object was changed, you can look in the Timestamp column of the DBA_OBJECTS or USER_OBJECTS view. This field is VARCHAR2(75), so you will need to convert it to a date. Set up a batch job to execute once a day that runs the following SQL script:

```
col Owner          format a20
col Object_Name    format a30
col Timestamp      format 220
select Owner, Object_Name, Object_Type, Status, Timestamp
  from DBA_OBJECTS
 where TO_CHAR(sysdate-1,'YYYY-MM-DD')
 order by Owner, Object_Name
/
```

This script will list all objects that have changed since the prior day, in owner order. The Status column is included because procedures, functions, and packages are objects and can become invalid when changed. Sample output from this report is shown here:

```
OBJECT_NAME                    OBJECT_TYPE  STATUS  TIMESTAMP
------------------------------ ------------ ------- -------------------
DBASE_TEMP                     TABLE        VALID   2002-05-08:15:20:42
TSPACE_TEMP                    TABLE        VALID   2002-05-08:15:15:12
IDX_REG_IN                     INDEX        VALID   2002-05-08:10:01:00
TEMP_IN                        PACKAGE      VALID   2002-05-08:09:12:47
TEMP_IN                        PACKAGE BODY INVALID 2002-05-08:09:32:59
```

Looking at the report above, you can see that the package TEMP_IN must either have had errors in the package body compilation or that one of the tables it references has changed, since the status is still INVALID. You can first attempt to revalidate it by recompiling it:

```
alter package temp_in recompile;
```

If recompiling still produces errors, you can then contact the programmer responsible for the package and have him investigate the problem.

PART III

Protecting Your World

CHAPTER 10

Oracle Security and You

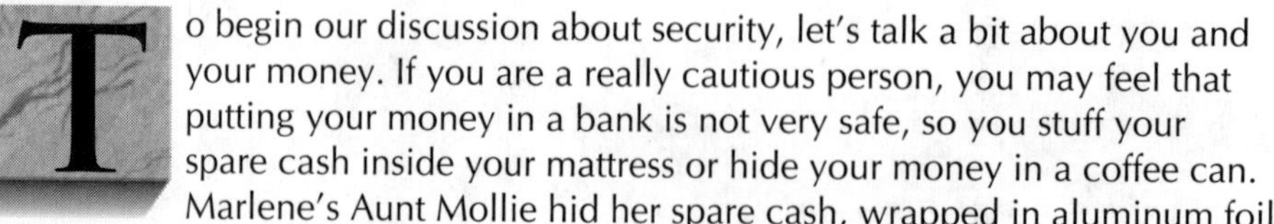

To begin our discussion about security, let's talk a bit about you and your money. If you are a really cautious person, you may feel that putting your money in a bank is not very safe, so you stuff your spare cash inside your mattress or hide your money in a coffee can. Marlene's Aunt Mollie hid her spare cash, wrapped in aluminum foil, in a book safe. The safe looked just like any other old, battered book on her shelf, but when you opened the cover, you found that the book was hollowed out and there was a covered compartment with a combination lock on the front. Of course, the combination to the lock was glued to the plate just below the lock, so it was very easy to open the safe and remove the money. Aunt Mollie felt safer keeping her money there, although she did have accounts at the local bank as well. Heaven only knows why she wrapped the money in aluminum foil though!

Like Aunt Mollie, you might have an account at the local bank and feel that your money is very secure because the bank has many safeguards to protect you and your assets. Let's think about the safeguards a bank uses. For one thing, at some banks, you must show picture identification to prove that you are the person entitled to take money out of one or more specific accounts. If you have a safe deposit box and want to access it, your signature must match the one on file, or you might have to present both a matching signature and a specific password. You cannot see information about accounts to which you have no privileges. There is an armed guard posted inside the door, and there are video cameras mounted in strategic places to record the faces and actions of everyone coming into and going out of the bank. There is a huge vault in which the money is kept, and the vault is locked at night to help protect your assets. Each teller has a silent alarm button that can be pressed to alert the police that a robbery is taking place if someone tries to rob the bank.

What does a bank's security approach have to do with Oracle databases? Glad you asked! Just as there are many different layers of security implemented within a bank to ensure that your money remains safe, there are many different layers of Oracle security that you can use to ensure that your company's data and your systems stay safe.

If you are starting out with a brand-new system, you should work with the system administrator to ensure that the operating system security has been enabled before you begin to install the Oracle software and build your system. Security should start from the operating system upward, from the network inward, and from within the database.

The realm of Oracle security is very broad, and we have a limited number of pages that we can devote to this vital topic within our book. Therefore, in this chapter, we are going to show you the steps you can take to secure your Oracle database, from the internal database security, to the application level, and out to the world at large via Oracle's networking mechanism, Oracle Net. We recommend that you look at the *Oracle Security Handbook,* by Marlene Theriault and Aaron Newman (Osborne/McGraw-Hill, 2001), for more complete coverage of this topic.

Internal Database Security

There are many mechanisms that you can create to help secure your data within the database. Among the useful things that you can use are privileges, grants, roles, synonyms, and views. We've talked about all of these mechanisms in Chapter 2 but want to examine them here from a security perspective. Please bear with us if we repeat ourselves a bit.

There are several steps like the ones listed here that you can take to ensure that your database is secure:

- Create user and developer accounts, and distribute appropriate privileges as needed to approved people by authority of approved people, and document same.
- Establish and protect the DBA privileged accounts and passwords.
- Ensure that the user accounts are all password protected, and create procedures to advise employees of the penalties for sharing their passwords and accounts with others.
- When appropriate, use Oracle's auditing facilities to monitor table/user activities.
- Write your own set of auditing procedures if Oracle's are not granular enough.
- Develop, document, and maintain change control procedures to prevent unauthorized changes to database objects.

In the first bullet, we've emphasized using appropriate privileges. On the surface, privileges and grants may seem to be the same thing since they both enable you to interact with objects in the database. In the Oracle world, privileges are used to define the actions that you can take to perform work in the database, while grants are the syntax you use to convey the privileges to yourself and others. For example, if you need to insert information into the PRIMATES table that we created in Chapter 3, you must have been *grant*ed the **insert** *privilege* on the table. Does that make sense to you? Let's look more closely at each of these facilities to make things clearer.

Privileges

To review a bit from Chapter 2, Oracle has two different levels of privileges: those used to manipulate data and those used to perform actions. Privileges to manipulate data are called *object privileges,* and privileges to perform actions are called *system privileges.*

Object privileges include but are not limited to the following rights:

- Look at rows and columns in your tables and views (select).
- Add new rows (insert).
- Update existing rows (update).
- Delete information (delete).
- Execute stored programs (execute).

System privileges allow you to perform actions that affect the overall state or structure of the database, like creating or removing objects. A few simple privileges are as follows:

- Create a table, index, view, snapshot.
- Drop a table, index, view, snapshot.
- Create a session in the database to connect and perform work.

For a complete list of object and system privileges, look in the Oracle SQL Reference manual for your version.

A Closer Look at Privileges

As you can see from the first list above, there are different types of privileges that you can grant to a user. You can grant or, by not granting, restrict the access to both system and object privileges. Object privileges enable a user to manipulate data within a table or view, or execute a package, procedure, or function. Let's formalize the object privileges and put them in a tabular format. You can see a list of the Oracle9i object privileges and their descriptions in Table 10-1.

Many system privileges have both a specific form relating only to that particular object or user and a corresponding, more general form with a broader range. The general form is derived from the specific form by adding the word **any** to the privilege. For example, a user with the **create table** privilege can create tables within her own schema. Her specific system privilege, **create table,** gives her the right and ability to create tables within her own account or schema. Now, there is also a general, more powerful form of many of the system privileges that allows a user to operate on objects in other schemas. For example, the same user with the **create any table** privilege can create a table in any user's schema and in any tablespace that she has quota in, including the SYSTEM schema and SYSTEM tablespace. Likewise, a user with the **create any view** privilege can create a view on any table in the database that he has **select** privileges on, while a user with the **create view** privilege can only create views on tables that he owns.

Privilege	Action
Select	View information within a table or view.
Insert	Insert new rows of information into a table or view.
Update	Modify one or more columns of information within a table or view.
Delete	Remove one or more rows of information from a table or view.
Alter	Change an object's definition.
Execute	Compile, execute, or access a procedure or function referenced in a program.
Read	Read files in a directory.
Reference	Create a constraint that refers to a table.
Query rewrite	Rewrite queries and utilize materialized views.
Index	Create an index on a table.

TABLE 10-1. *Object Privileges*

Now let's look at some other system privileges, such as **create session** and **execute any procedure**. These privileges do not pertain to a specific schema but give users privileges that are systemwide. While there is an **execute any procedure** system privilege, there is no corresponding **execute procedure** system privilege. There is no **execute procedure** privilege because you are granted **execute** on procedures on a one-by-one basis.

Because granting general privileges, like the ones that include **any** within them, gives the user considerable control over the database, you should carefully consider to whom and why you are granting privileges before you do so. In addition, system privileges should not be granted to the pseudo-user PUBLIC unless absolutely necessary, because you leave a potential security hole that a malicious user could exploit.

Oh, by the way, there are 124 system-level privileges in the initial production release of Oracle9i and 125 in the 9.0.1.2 release. In Oracle8i, there were 117. We just thought the statisticians among you might want to know that.

Why Grant Privileges?

From a security perspective, let's consider why you need privileges on objects in your database or, more importantly, why you might not want to grant privileges on some objects. Imagine for a moment that your company manufactures a machine called the Amazing Fabroskravitz. Your database stores the inventory of parts necessary to make each Fabroskravitz and tracks the purchase information for all of your customers. Of course, you must keep the parts list and fabrication instructions out of the reach of your competitors, but you must protect your customer information as well—especially credit card numbers and expiration dates.

Who should be able to see the data in the inventory area? Certainly, your managers and fabrication specialists would need access to this area. Your order entry clerks must be able to enter newly received parts information, and as the stock is used, someone must update the inventory records so that buyers know when they need to place an order for replacement parts. Likewise, the operators must be able to enter order information into the system and verify whether the number of Fabroskravitzes ordered are available or need to be placed on back order and the customer notified of the situation.

Do the order entry people need to see the fabrication stock inventories? Do the fabrication people need to see the customer purchase information? Usually not! Thus, how you allocate privileges within your database helps you control how specific information is accessed and by whom. Careful evaluation should be performed to ensure that no one accessing your database can see more than he or she is entitled to see.

Granting Privileges

You can determine who needs access to your database by setting up a spreadsheet of the objects in the database and the work that must be accomplished. Next, you can set up the list of users who need access and the areas in which they need to work. Let's see how all of this plays out by continuing with our Fabroskravitz example.

We'll say that the following tables exist in the database:

Table Name	**Description**
FAB_PARTS	Parts lists used for fabricating the Fabroskravitzes
FAB_ITEMS	Items that are currently on order to replenish stock
FAB_ORDERS	Customer orders
FAB_CUSTOMERS	Customer information

Now that you know the objects involved, you need to establish who can see the information in each table. An employee who is on the assembly floor needs access to the FAB_PARTS table, while a supervisor needs to be able to look at the FAB_ITEMS and FAB_ORDERS tables. Order entry clerks must enter information into both the FAB_ORDERS and FAB_CUSTOMERS tables, while shipping clerks need to be able to access the same tables to determine where to send the orders and to update the orders table to show that products have been shipped. Of course, this is a very simplistic example just to give you an idea of how to establish your spreadsheet, so we won't go any further into the makeup of the database. Let's put a spreadsheet together. Table 10-2 shows the spreadsheet we've created.

Table	Employee	Required Privileges
FAB_PARTS	Assemblers	Select
	Supervisors	Select, update
	Purchase clerks	Select, insert, update
	Managers	Select, insert, update
FAB_ITEMS	Supervisors	Select, update
	Purchase clerks	Select, insert, update
	Managers	Select, insert, update
FAB_ORDERS	Order entry clerks	Select, insert, update
	Managers	Select, insert, update
FAB_CUSTOMERS	Order Entry Clerks	Select, insert, update
	Managers	Select, insert, update

TABLE 10-2. *Privileges Spreadsheet*

Oops! It doesn't look like anyone can ever remove any information from these tables. Please remind us to add **delete** to the managers' privileges when we actually create the scripts to grant them. Speaking of which, we haven't really identified any specific people to grant the privileges to. We've only identified groups of people at this point. In the next section, we'll be talking about roles and their use in securing your database. For now, we'll just arbitrarily say that Sue works in assembly, Roz is a purchase clerk, Cathy is a supervisor, Jean is an order entry clerk, and Nelson is a manager. Here is the script to grant each person the appropriate privileges based on the spreadsheet we've created:

```
grant select on FAB_PARTS to SUE;
grant select, update on FAB_PARTS to CATHY;
grant select, update on FAB_PARTS to ROZ;
grant select, insert, update, delete on FAB_PARTS to NELSON;
grant select, update on FAB_ITEMS to CATHY;
grant select, insert, update on FAB_ITEMS to ROZ;
grant select, insert, update, delete on FAB_ITEMS to NELSON;
grant select, insert, update on FAB_ORDERS to JEAN;
grant select, insert, update, delete on FAB_ORDERS to NELSON;
grant select, insert, update on FAB_CUSTOMERS to JEAN;
grant select, insert, update, delete on FAB_CUSTOMERS to NELSON;
```

After running the script, your various employees have the appropriate access to do their jobs effectively but do not hold more access than they are really entitled to possess or use. Always remember that controlling user access is one of the most effective ways to protect the contents of your database.

Who should have system privileges? Remember that system privileges give users access to create objects within your database. Thus, developers need system privileges to enable them to create and own objects. Some DBAs grant system privileges to developers within the development system but prefer to have the developers pass their scripts to the DBA to create the objects in the production environment. We recommend having only the DBA create objects in production because the production DBA must ensure that the objects are sized correctly and placed in the appropriate tablespaces. Here's the syntax you would use to grant a developer named Roz the ability to create tables within her own schema:

```
grant CREATE TABLE to ROZ;
```

By default, if the **any** keyword is not used, the grant is limited to the user's own schema. If you use this form,

```
grant CREATE ANY TABLE to ROZ;
```

Roz can create tables in any tablespace and under any schema name in the system. Be very careful to whom you grant privileges with the **any** keyword.

Just as important as knowing how to grant and control privileges is knowing how to remove privileges from users when necessary. To remove privileges from a user, you can issue the following command:

```
revoke <privilege> on <object_name>from <user_name>;
```

If you want to remove the **insert** privilege from Roz on the FAB_ITEMS table, you use this form:

```
revoke INSERT on FAB_ITEMS from ROZ;
```

It took us 11 statements to grant all the appropriate privileges to the users in our database. And we only had four tables and five users! Most databases have many more users and many more tables, and the number of **grant** and **revoke** statements you as DBA will have to run grows incrementally. Oracle provides a tool to simplify this and help ensure you don't miss anything. In the next section, we'll look at using roles instead of granting privileges to individual users.

Creating Roles

We talked at length about roles in Chapter 2, so we'll just remind you here that a role is a set of privileges that can be granted to one or more users. Roles make the administration of users much easier while helping to further secure your database objects. You can easily add or remove privileges from a role and affect every user who has been granted that role.

Role Creation Parameters

You only need to know a few parameters to create a role. Table 10-3 shows the parameters.

There are two forms of roles: those that are automatically enabled and accessible when a user connects to the database and those that are enabled and accessible through the command **set role**. The **set role** command is usually issued by an application on behalf of the user, and, generally, a password or external operating system authentication is required to enable the role.

To create a role, you need the **create role** privilege.

Creating Two Types of Roles

This time, your task is to create two roles—one that does not require identification and one that does. The syntax for the role creation statements should be pretty

Parameter	Description	Default
Role name	Specifies the name of the role	n/a
Not identified	Specifies that there is no password required for the role	Not identified
Identified	Specifies that the command **set role** must be used to enable and access the role	
Identified by password	Specifies a password to be used to enable and access the role	n/a
Identified externally	Specifies that operating system authentication is to be used to enable and access the role	n/a

TABLE 10-3. *Role Creation Parameters*

straightforward, so take a moment to think about it. First, create a role that requires no identification:

```
create role MY_ROLE;
```

Next, create a role that requires a password, and specify the password required:

```
create role MY_PWROLE identified by NEEDAPASSWORD;
```

In order to access the privileges assigned to the role MY_PWROLE, the user must use the **set role** command using the following syntax:

```
set role MY_PWROLE identified by NEEDAPASSWORD;
```

Oracle-Supplied Roles vs. DBA-Created Roles

You can use system-level roles to grant access to commands used to manage the database. You can either create customized system-level roles or use the ones that Oracle supplies with the database. You can find the existing roles on your system by issuing the following command:

```
select Role from DBA_ROLES;
```

In our demonstration database, there are 26 Oracle-supplied roles. Based on how you create your database, you may have more or fewer roles.

There is a clause that you can use to pass along to the grantee the ability to grant the privilege to other users. The clause is **with grant option**. If I write

```
grant Select on FAB_ITEMS to YOU with grant option;
```

then YOU can grant **select** to CATHY, and she will be able to see the contents of the FAB_ITEMS table.

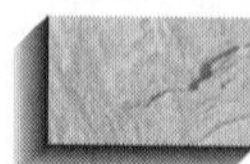

NOTE

*The **with grant option** clause is only used when granting object privileges and cannot be used with roles. To enable passing of grants with roles, use the **with admin option**.*

Table 10-4 lists a few of the most-used system-level roles and the privileges that each contains. These roles are provided with and by Oracle. You can use these Oracle-supplied roles to grant controlled access to users and other DBAs. In addition to the roles shown in Table 10-4, your database may include roles generated to support the Advanced Queuing Option (AQ_USER_ROLE,

GLOBAL_AQ_USER_ROLE, and AQ_ADMINISTRATOR_ROLE), Java development (JAVAUSERPRIV, JAVAIDPRIV, JAVASYSPRIV, JAVADEBUGPRIV, JAVA_ADMIN, and JAVA_DEPLOY), for Oracle Context Management (CTXSYS), and for use by the OEM Intelligent Agents (the OEM_MANAGER role).

NOTE
*In addition to the privileges listed in Table 10-4, users with the DBA and RESOURCE roles also receive the **unlimited tablespace** system privilege.*

Normally, if the Oracle-supplied roles are used, the CONNECT role is typically granted to end users. Although it does have some object creation abilities (including the **create table** privilege), it does not give users any space quotas on any tablespace.

Role Name	Privileges Granted to Role
CONNECT	**alter session**, **create cluster**, **create database link**, **create sequence**, **create session**, **create synonym**, **create table**, **create view**
RESOURCE	**create cluster**, **create procedure**, **create sequence**, **create table**, **create trigger**
DBA	All system privileges **with admin option**
EXP_FULL_DATABASE	**select any table**, **backup any table**, **insert**, **delete**, and **update** on the tables SYS.INCVID, SYS.INCFIL, and SYS.INCEXP
IMP_FULL_DATABASE	**become user**
DELETE_CATALOG_ROLE	**delete** on all dictionary packages
EXECUTE_CATALOG_ROLE	**execute** on all dictionary packages
SELECT_CATALOG_ROLE	**select** on all catalog tables and views
CREATE TYPE	**create type**, **execute**, **execute any type**, **admin option**, **grant option**
RECOVERY_CATALOG_OWNER	**drop role recovery_catalog_owner**, **create role recovery_catalog_owner**, **create trigger**, **create procedure to recovery_catalog_owner**

TABLE 10-4. *A Few System-Level Roles Provided in Oracle9i*

Users cannot really create objects unless they have quotas on at least one tablespace; so, unless you grant quotas on tablespaces to users, they will not be able to create tables.

The RESOURCE role is typically granted to developers. The RESOURCE role gives developers the most-used application development privileges. The DBA role includes all 124 system-level privileges, with the option to grant those privileges to other users. Because the RESOURCE role also grants **unlimited tablespace** (the ability to create objects in *any* tablespace), we recommend that if you grant RESOURCE, you also immediately revoke the **unlimited tablespace** privilege and grant specific quotas on tablespaces.

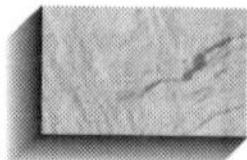

NOTE
Oracle Corporation recommends that you create your own roles rather than rely on these supplied roles. CONNECT, RESOURCE, and DBA may not be automatically created in future versions, and the composition of the roles can change from version to version.

The IMP_FULL_DATABASE and EXP_FULL_DATABASE roles are used during Import and Export, respectively, when you perform a full database Import or Export (see Chapter 11). These roles are part of the DBA role; you can use these roles to grant users limited database management privileges. The roles SELECT_CATALOG_ROLE, EXECUTE_CATALOG_ROLE, and DELETE_CATALOG_ROLE were introduced in Oracle8.

The SELECT_CATALOG_ROLE and EXECUTE_CATALOG_ROLE roles grant users privileges to select from data dictionary tables like DBA_TABLES or execute exportable data dictionary objects. That is, not every database object is exported during a full system export. For example, the dynamic performance views are not exported. Thus, SELECT_CATALOG_ROLE does not give the user the ability to select from the dynamic performance tables like V$ROLLSTAT; it does, however, give the user the ability to query from most of the data dictionary. Similarly, EXECUTE_CATALOG_ROLE grants users the ability to execute procedures and functions that are part of the data dictionary.

The CREATE TYPE role is enabled if you use the Objects option. Users who have the CREATE TYPE role enabled can create new abstract data types.

Since the Oracle-supplied DBA role is very powerful, we recommend that you consider the following suggestions:

- No one but the primary database administrator(s) should be granted the DBA role.

- No developers should ever be granted the DBA role.
- Any secondary database administrators should have a subset of the system-level privileges granted to them based on the tasks they perform.

Since DBA-level privileges are required to perform account creation, backup and recovery operations, and so on, you can and should select out a subset of privileges that are needed to create new users or back up/recover your system.

For example, you can create a new system-level role called USER_ACCT_CREATOR. This account will only be able to create users; it will not be able to perform any other DBA-level commands. Here are the commands that create this role:

```
create role USER_ACCT_CREATOR;
grant CREATE SESSION, CREATE USER, ALTER USER
   to USER_CREATOR;
```

The first command in this listing creates a role called USER_ACCT_CREATOR. The second command grants that role the ability to log in (**create session**) and create and alter accounts (**create user** and **alter user**). The USER_ACCT _CREATOR role can then be granted to a centralized help desk or specific people who need to create accounts. You can create this role using the OEM tool. We'll tell you more about OEM in Chapter 13.

By using centralized account creation, you ensure that proper authorization procedures are followed when accounts are requested. Creating a specific role to enable a user or set of users to perform a specific function ensures that the users can get the job done but can't see any data to which they should not have access. Of course, the person who is creating accounts will also need to be able to grant other privileges to the newly created accounts or will have to be able to grant one or more roles to the newly created accounts. You and the application managers would have to determine who grants access to the new accounts and then ensure that the person who needs to grant access has the rights to do so.

Many third-party packaged applications assume they will have full DBA authority in your database, when in fact they only need the ability to execute **create user** and **alter user** commands. By creating a USER_ACCT_CREATOR role, you can limit the package schema owner's privileges in the rest of your database.

By default, your roles are enabled each time you log in. You can alter the default role for a user via the **default role** clause of the **alter user** command. For example, you can alter a user to have no roles enabled by default:

```
alter user SUE default role NONE;
```

You can specify the roles to enable:

```
alter user SUE default role CONNECT;
```

And you can specify the roles that should not be enabled when the session starts:

```
alter user SUE default role all except ACCOUNT_CREATOR;
```

If you have not granted the specified roles to the user, then the **alter user** commands will fail. If the user has not been granted a specified system-level role such as CONNECT, then attempting to set that role as a default role for a user will result in the following error:

```
ORA-01919: role 'CONNECT' does not exist
```

Hmm, what if the specified role is one that you've created and is not an Oracle-supplied role that has not been granted to the user? In that case, the **alter user** command will fail with the following error:

```
ORA-01955: DEFAULT ROLE 'USER_ACCT_CREATOR' not granted to user
```

You must grant the roles to the users before establishing the users' default roles.

If you use the **default role all** clause, then all of a user's roles will be enabled when the user's session begins. If you plan to dynamically enable and disable roles at different parts of an application (via **set role** commands), then you should control which of the roles are enabled by default. Oh, by the way, a role is set as a default role automatically when it is granted to a user.

To revoke a privilege from a role, you use the same syntax as when you revoke privileges directly from a user. To revoke **create user** from the USER_ACCT_CREATOR role, you write

```
revoke CREATE USER from USER_ACCT_CREATOR;
```

The initialization parameter **max_enabled_roles** limits the number of roles that any user can have enabled at once. In Oracle9i, the default value for **max_enabled_roles** is 20. The range of values is from 0 to 148. Keep in mind that when you create a role, it is enabled for you by default. If you create many roles within your database, you may exceed the **max_enabled_roles** setting, even if you are not the user of those roles.

Creating Synonyms

Synonyms are often referred to as nicknames or shortcuts or alternatives for the syntax object_owner.object_name. Synonyms can be created for tables, views, procedures, packages, materialized views, sequences, stored functions, Java class schema objects, and even for other synonyms.

Synonyms are very powerful constructs because they let you reference an object without having to know exactly who owns the object or where the object is located in the database. For example, you could have a table named FAB_ITEMS owned by the schema FABROS. Every time you refer to the table, you need to use the construct FABROS.FAB_ITEMS so there will be no question of which table you are referencing. If you create a synonym for the table, you can reference the table FAB_ITEMS without using the qualifier FABROS.

To create a synonym in your own schema, you must have the **create synonym** privilege. You need **create any synonym** to create a synonym for another user's schema. To create a public synonym, you need the **create public synonym** privilege.

Let's take a look at the parameters available for synonym creation.

Synonym Creation Parameters

Table 10-5 shows the parameters you can use to create a synonym.

To create a synonym that is only available to someone connected directly to your schema—that is, a private synonym—you do not need to use **create private synonym** because a private synonym is the default.

Now, it's time to create a synonym or two.

Creating Private and Public Synonyms

The first synonym you will create is a very basic private synonym for the FABROS.FAB_ITEMS table. This should be easy, so take a moment to think of what your syntax will be.

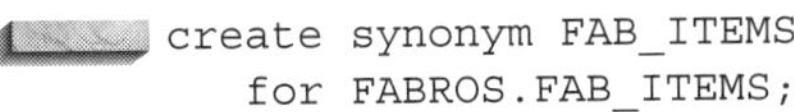

```
create synonym FAB_ITEMS
   for FABROS.FAB_ITEMS;
```

See? We told you that would be easy.

Parameter	**Description**	**Default**
Public	Specifies whether the synonym is to be seen by all users	Private
Synonym_name	Specifies the name of the synonym	n/a
For	Specifies the object for which the synonym is created	n/a
Dblink	Specifies the full or partial database link to create a synonym for an object on a remote database	n/a

TABLE 10-5. *Synonym Creation Parameters*

Now, you can get a bit more complex. Try to create a public synonym called ITEMS for the FABROS.FAB_ITEMS table:

```
create public synonym ITEMS
   for FABROS.FAB_ITEMS;
```

That wasn't too bad, now, was it? What have you learned from this exercise? The most important lesson in this creation statement is that the synonym name does not have to match the underlying object's name. If a user wanted to select item names from the FABROS.FAB_ITEMS table, he could just use the following syntax:

```
select Item_Name
  from ITEMS;
```

Isn't that much easier than the fully qualified **select** statement that follows?

```
select Item_Name
  from FABROS.FAB_ITEMS;
```

Also, it's a much more secure approach because the user does not know who owns the table or what the real table name is. However, keep in mind that privileges still need to be given on the base objects for users to access them, even if the synonym is public. For example, a user needs **select** privilege on the FABROS.FAB_ITEMS table to successfully select using the ITEMS synonym.

Creating Views

There are often times when you will need to create a view either to join parts of several tables together more rapidly or to hide information from one or more columns or one or more rows in a table. Hide information? Why would you want to do that? There will be times when you do not want specific column names to be known to the general users. Employment information is a good example of data you might need to hide. If users do not know there is a Salary column in the PAYROLL table, they will be much less likely to try to see the information or will have a much harder time seeing the data. You could have a table called PAYROLL with columns that all employees should be able to see, such as the number of hours they work each week or the number of vacation or sick leave hours they have accrued. You can create a view called PAYROLL_V that contains the columns you want them to see while excluding other columns.

To create a view in your own schema, you need the **create view** privilege; to create a view in another user's schema, you need the **create any view** privilege.

As we have done in the other creation sections, let's first look at the available basic parameters, and then you can create a view using them.

View Creation Parameters

Table 10-6 shows the parameters available for creating a basic view. Once you have the list of view creation parameters, you can create a view.

Creating a Basic View

For this exercise to be meaningful, you will create a view on the PAYROLL table called PAYROLL_EMP_V that will include the columns Employee_Name, Vacation_Accrued, and Sick_Accrued. You do not want the employee to be able to change anything, so you will enforce a read-only constraint. Okay, take a stab at it.

```
create or replace view PAYROLL_EMP_V
as select Employee_Name, Vacation_Accrued, Sick_Accrued
     from PAYROLL
with read only;
```

Parameter	Description	Default
Create or Replace	Specifies whether this is a new view creation or a modification to an already existing view	Create
Force/Noforce	Specifies whether to create the view, even if there are creation errors (such as an underlying column that does not currently exist)	Noforce
Schema	The name of the schema that will own the view	Creator's schema
View_name	Specifies the name of the view	n/a
Alias	Specifies the alias to use for each expression in the view—the number of aliases must match the number of expressions used in the view	Oracle will derive the alias from the expression name
As (subquery)	Specifies columns and rows on which the view is based	n/a
With clause	Specifies one or more constraints: "with read only," with "check option" constraint (name for check constraint)	n/a

TABLE 10-6. *View Creation Parameters*

Employees will see the information that you have made available without being able to modify the information. We'll talk about solving the problem of controlling who sees another person's information later in this chapter.

Application Security

One of the most common security problem areas is the application code that your developers and third-party vendors write. Poor programming practices can invariably lead to inadvertent security holes. Some programming techniques are now known to cause security problems. In this section, we'll talk about one of the major coding problems—buffer overflow. We'll show you how to help your developers avoid creating this problem. We'll also look at a way for you to implement controls to prevent users from accessing data they are not entitled to see. This mechanism is known as Virtual Private Database (VPD).

Application Protections

As your developers write their code, they must ensure that they consider all potential areas where a hacker could introduce a *buffer overflow*. A buffer overflow results from a program filling up a buffer of memory with more data than the buffer can hold. Once the program begins to write beyond the end of a buffer, the program's execution path can be changed.

When you connect to the database, you use a password, much like you provide a picture ID when you go to some banks to make a transaction, to prove that you are who you say you are. This action is referred to as user authentication. Once you've been authenticated, Oracle checks to see what privileges you have or what objects you have been authorized to see and interact with. Thus, you must usually go through both an authentication process and then an authorization process to access and manipulate data within the database.

Buffer overflows cause a real problem when they can be exploited remotely before authentication occurs. Here's an example of how a buffer overflow might work in a Web server. When you enter a request to search a Web site for the topic "oracle," your Web browser submits the request as

```
http://www.domainname.com/search.idc?search=oracle
```

This command says to submit the word "oracle" to the parameter **search** through the Web page search.idc. Code behind search.idc processes the parameter. This code sets up a variable, or buffer, to hold the value you passed in.

If the Web server software has been coded correctly, the code will check the length of the parameter and only copy a limited number of characters. If the programmer forgets to validate the length of the string, the code may copy the parameter passed in over other memory.

Now, a malicious user sends the following command:

```
http://www.domainname.com/search.idc?search=xxxxxxxxxxxxxxxxxxxxxxxxxxxxx0x
230x150x170x450x560x00
```

Notice the hexadecimal numbers embedded in the string just after the "search=" area. These numbers are placed there to overwrite specific places in memory with new machine language code to perform some kind of potentially harmful action. The Web server, which is probably running with escalated privileges, will execute this code instead of its own code.

To avoid this form of attack, make sure that your developers always check the size of the buffer being returned from a query, or verify that the data being received is in a valid format. In software development, it's easy to fall into the trap of knowing which parameters are expected to be returned and not considering the results if a user submits a different set of parameters to the program. Since you, as the DBA, are tasked with ensuring the security of the database, we want you to be aware of another way in which your database could become compromised.

Using the Virtual Private Database Feature

Imagine that you have an EMPLOYEE table within your database that contains information on each employee's address, home telephone number, current salary, job classification, amount of vacation time accrued and taken, and amount of sick time accrued and taken. You want the employees to be able to view and modify their personal information but only view their vacation and sick time data. Each employee should be able to see his or her own information but no other employee's information. How are you going to control and impose these access rules? If you create an application to control access to the data, the employee will only be restricted when accessing her records through the application. In other words, if she connects directly to the database and knows the name of the table, she can skirt the application controls and see all of the records in the table, as long as she has **select** privilege on that table.

In the first Oracle8i release, Oracle introduced the Virtual Private Database (VPD) to provide a solution to the problem we just described. VPD is designed to provide fine-grained access control coupled with a secure application context. Using VPD, you can establish policies to control what data each user sees. The policies are actually where clauses that are attached to every query that users present to the database. Instead of a user being able to select all of the information from the EMPLOYEE table, he would only be able to see the information that pertained exclusively to him. Since the security policies are attached to the data within the database instead of through the application, security rules are enforced at all times, regardless of how the user connects to the database. If you have an area like the Human Resources department, where employees must be able to view everyone's information, you code your policies to ensure that they will be able to perform their tasks. In other words, you can control both access and denial of access as you need to by how you code the VPD policies.

The most positive feature of VPD is that an organization needs to build a security structure only once in the data server. You don't have to keep building security into every individual application. The data presented from a query is identical regardless of the connection mode: from an application, SQL*Plus, or an ODBC driver.

Along with the Virtual Private Database, Oracle offers a Label Security option. Both of these features help to provide multiple layers of security mechanisms to create an environment where no single failure will result in a compromise of the entire system. This approach is referred to as "deep data protection." Label Security enables you to attach an access code to each row of data within the database and enable users to access only the information that corresponds to their specific access code. When you purchase and implement Label Security, Oracle provides a utility that you can use to create your VPD automatically.

Unfortunately, VPD without Label Security relies on several mechanisms to ensure data privacy for each user. To accomplish data separation, you must first ensure that your tables are designed to enable you to restrict data access according to the values in one or more columns. Let's look at the composition of our EMPLOYEE table to see if there are any columns that we can use to control how the data is accessed. Here is the code we used to create the EMPLOYEE table. Do you see any columns that we can use as unique identifiers for access control?

```
create table EMPLOYEE(
EMPLOYEE_NUMBER  number(7) primary key,
SOCIAL_SECURITY  number(9),
USERNAME         varchar2(8) not null,
LAST_NAME        varchar2(20),
FIRST_NAME       varchar2(15),
MIDDLE_NAME      varchar2(10),
ADDRESS1         varchar2(25),
ADDRESS2         varchar2(25),
CITY             varchar2(20),
STATE            varchar2(10),
ZIP_CODE         number(9),
COUNTRY          varchar2(15),
HOME_PHONE       number(10),
SALARY           number(9,2),
JOB_CLASS        varchar2(15),
VACATION_ACCRUED number(6,2),
VACATION_USED    number(6,2),
SICK_ACCRUED     number(6,2),
SICK_TAKEN       number(6,2))
/
```

There are three potentially good candidates that we can consider for our purposes here: EMPLOYEE_ID, SOCIAL_SECURITY, and USERNAME. We know that the EMPLOYEE_ID column is unique and not null because it is the primary key for the table. Although this should never happen, there is a possibility that the SOCIAL_SECURITY number can be the same for more than one person, thus, we can eliminate it from consideration. We must have a unique value on which to base our user access. We'll actually use the USERNAME column, as we'll show you later.

To see how our final VPD will work, let's consider the following statement:

```
select * from EMPLOYEE;
```

Issuing this statement will provide you with every entry in the table. However, if the EMPLOYEE table has a security policy associated with it that restricts employees from seeing any information other than their own, the query would be automatically rewritten as

```
select *
  from EMPLOYEE
 where EMPLOYEE_ID = sys_context('EMPLOYEE_CONTEXT','ALL_EMPLOYEE_ID')
/
```

In this example, the where clause that is automatically appended to the user's query by the policy ensures that users can only see their data no matter what data is in the table and how they construct their queries. The employee's ID is obtained from the user-defined application context, EMPLOYEE_CONTEXT. We'll show you how to build an application context soon. There is a system function called **sys_context** that returns the value for the attribute ALL_EMPLOYEE_ID in the EMPLOYEE_CONTEXT. That value is the unique identifier we've been talking about.

Within VPD, you must still grant users the appropriate privileges for each table, but you do not need to create views and procedures to prevent users from accessing other users' data. Thus, using VPD, you no longer have to worry about users accessing the database through SQL*Plus with different privileges than they have through an application.

Creating a VPD

Creating an Oracle VPD is very different from installing and configuring most Oracle tools. The VPD is not actually an application unto itself, but rather is installed with the database. To create a VPD, follow these steps:

1. Determine the database objects and their relationships.
2. Define your security policy objectives.
3. Create the application context.

4. Create a package that sets the context.
5. Create the policy function.
6. Associate the policy function with a table or view.

Wow! There is certainly a lot of work involved with creating a VPD, isn't there? There are different ways to perform several of the steps listed here. We present the approach that we believe will yield the most robust, scalable, and secure implementation.

Determine the Database Objects and Their Relationships

To begin creating your VPD, you must determine the database objects involved, their relationship to each other, and the keys on which the security approach will be built. For example, using the EMPLOYEE table, employees can view and obtain copies of their own information electronically but not access anyone else's information.

Keeping each employee's information secure and private is of major importance. The primary key that links employee information together is the employee's unique ID number. In our example (which is overly simplified), there is only one table in which data is stored: EMPLOYEE. You've already seen the composition of the EMPLOYEE table. The EMPLOYEE_ID uniquely identifies each record in the table.

Define Your Security Policy Objectives

The security policy for our example is simply stated as "Employees can only see their own information." Your policy objectives will generally be more complex, and you can have several security policies associated with a table or view. Be very clear on how you phrase your policies because each security policy that you define must be translated into PL/SQL function code that will be attached to the specified application table or view. You may need to enlist the aid of a developer to help you code the first function you create if you are unsure of how to effectively write the code.

Create the Application Context

An application context is a named set of attributes and values that you can set and then associate with the current user's session. An example of an attribute could be eyeColor with the set of values: BLUE, GREEN, BROWN, HAZEL, and BLACK. Notice how "eye color" is written. We've intentionally written the attribute name this way to follow the convention that is normally used for naming attributes.

Oracle provides the default context, USERENV, which contains system information about the current session such as the username, host, and program name. If you want to define other attributes for a user, such as EMPLOYEE_ID, you can do so using application contexts—code you write yourself.

Using the privilege **create any context**, you can create the application context. You supply a unique context name and then associate the name with the package that implements the context. Context names must be unique across the entire database. Therefore, if you attempt to create a context using a name that already exists, you will receive an error.

To create the context, you must have the **create any context** privilege granted to you. For this example, you will create a context called EMPLOYEE_SEC_CTX that will belong to our PL/SQL package stored in the FABROS schema and named EMPLOYEE_SEC. The syntax follows:

```
create context EMPLOYEE_SEC_CTX using FABROS.EMPLOYEE_SEC;
```

Create a Package that Sets the Context

Once the context is created, create the package and functions that set the context. The example below shows how you set the EMPLOYEE_ID context attributes using the current user's username obtained from the default context, USERENV. The function uses the username to look up the necessary attributes in the table.

```
create or replace package EMPLOYEE_SEC is
   procedure GET_EMPLOYEE_ID;
end EMPLOYEE_SEC;
/
create or replace package body EMPLOYEE_SEC is
   procedure GET_EMPLOYEE_ID
   is
   EMPLOYEE_ID_VAR number;
   begin
    select EMPLOYEE_ID
      into EMPLOYEE_ID_VAR from EMPLOYEE
     where EMPLOYEE_USERNAME = SYS_CONTEXT('USERENV','SESSION_USER');
    dbms_session.set_context('EMPLOYEE_SEC_CTX', 'EMPLOYEE_ID', EMPLOYEE_ID_VAR);
   end GET_EMPLOYEE_ID;
end EMPLOYEE_SEC;
/
```

Oracle supplies the predefined function SYS_CONTEXT and the built-in context USERENV so that you can return the name of the user executing the procedure. There are many other values that you can obtain from the SYS_CONTEXT function. Displayed in Table 10-7 are some of the more useful values for security.

Attribute	Value Returned
AUTHENTICATION_DATA	The data being used to authenticate the login user
AUTHENTICATION_TYPE	The method used to authenticate the user. The available values are Database—username/password authentication OS—operating system external user authentication Network—network protocol or ANO authentication Proxy—OCI proxy connection authentication
BG_JOB_ID	If an Oracle background process established the current session, the job ID of the job will be returned.
CLIENT_INFO	Used in conjunction with the DBMS_APPLICATION_INFO package to store information, this parameter returns up to 64 bytes of user session information.
CURRENT_SCHEMA	Name of the default schema being used as the current schema
CURRENT_USER	Name of the user whose privileges the current session is under
CURRENT_USERID	ID of the user whose privileges the current session is under
DB_DOMAIN	Database domain as specified in the DB_DOMAIN initialization parameter
DB_NAME	Database name as specified in the DB_NAME initialization parameter
ENTRYID	Available auditing entry identifier. Set if the AUDIT_TRAIL parameter is set to TRUE in the initialization parameter file.
EXTERNAL_NAME	External name of the database user. The distinctive name stored in the user certificate is returned for SSL authenticated sessions using v.503 certificates.
FG_JOB_ID	If an Oracle foreground process established the current session, the job ID of the job will be returned.
HOST	Name of the host machine the client connected from

TABLE 10-7. *SYS_CONTEXT Parameters*

INSTANCE	The instance identification number of the current instance
ISDBA	If you have the DBA role enabled, TRUE will be returned. If you do not, FALSE will be returned.
NETWORK_PROTOCOL	Network protocol being used for communication
OS_USER	Operating system username of the client process that initiated the database session
PROXY_USER	Name of the database user who opened the session on behalf of the SESSION_USER
PROXY_USERID	Identifier of the database user who opened the session on behalf of the SESSION_USER
SESSION_USER	Database username by which the current user is authenticated. This value remains the same throughout the session.
SESSION_USERID	Identifier of the database username by which the current user is authenticated
SESSIONID	Auditing session identifier
TERMINAL	Operating system identifier for the client of the current session

TABLE 10-7. *SYS_CONTEXT Parameters* (continued)

To set the context for a user session, call the function that was associated with the context when the context was created. You can do this from your application or, perhaps, by using a login trigger. Using a login trigger ensures that the context is set no matter how the user logs in to the database. To set a login trigger, use the **on logon** trigger, available in Oracle8i, version 8.1.5 and beyond.

Create the Security Policy Functions

Next, you need to create a PL/SQL function to implement the policy. The function will then be associated with the EMPLOYEE table.

Here is the process that occurs to impose fine-grained security on a query once the function is in place. By the way, the word "query" as used here means any form of information access from a table or view, including but not limited to **select**, **insert**, **delete**, **update**, and subquery statements. Once a security policy is associated with a table or view, when a user presents a query, the query processor calls the policy function, and the function returns a value in the form of an access control condition, or *predicate*.

In reality, the predicate is a where clause that is appended to the user's SQL statement to limit the rows that will be returned, updated, or deleted depending on the type of statement that is used and the access privileges the user holds.

Our goal is to enable employees to view only their own information based on their own EMPLOYEE_ID. Here's a sample PL/SQL procedure to accomplish that goal:

```
create or replace package EMPLOYEE_SEC as
 function EMPLOYEE_ID_SEC return varchar2;
 END EMPLOYEE_SEC;
/
create or replace package body EMPLOYEE_SEC as
/* LIMITS SELECT STATEMENTS BASED ON EMPLOYEE_ID VALUE */
 function EMPLOYEE_ID_SEC return varchar2
 is
   MY_PREDICATE varchar2 (2000);
   begin
     MY_PREDICATE := 'EMPLOYEE_ID=SYS_CONTEXT(''EMPLOYEE_SEC_CTX'',''EMPLOYEE_ID'')';
     return MY_PREDICATE;
    end EMPLOYEE_ID_SEC;
end EMPLOYEE_SEC;
/
```

To conserve space, no error handling is shown within the procedure.

In this code example, we retrieve the EMPLOYEE_ID from the application context EMPLOYEE_SEC_CTX and generate the predicate to be appended to a query on the EMPLOYEE table. To see how the predicate will look, let's say that the EMPLOYEE_ID is 234345675. The returned predicate will read

```
EMPLOYEE_ID = 234345675;
```

This predicate will be used in the where clause to ensure that the only information this employee will see is data that matches the correct EMPLOYEE_ID.

Associate the Policy Function with a Table or View

Oracle provides a PL/SQL package called DBMS_RLS (Row Level Security) to manage security policy administration. You find it in the $ORACLE_HOME/rdbms/admin directory in a Unix system and on a Windows system, in ORACLE_HOME\rdbms\admin. Anyone creating or administering policies must have **execute** granted for this package through the SYS user. Table 10-8 shows the four procedures available in the package.

You use the DBMS_RLS package to associate a policy function to a table or view. There are different arguments that you use with each of the procedures. Table 10-9 shows the arguments.

Procedure	Function
DBMS_RLS.ADD_POLICY	Add a policy to a table or view.
DBMS_RLS.DROP_POLICY	Remove a policy from a table or view.
DBMS_RLS.REFRESH_POLICY	Force a reparse of open cursors associated with a policy to immediately take advantage of a new or changed policy.
DBMS_RLS.ENABLE_POLICY	Enable or disable a policy that has been previously added to a table or view.

TABLE 10-8. *DBMS_RLS Package Procedures*

Parameter	Description
Object_schema	Name of the schema containing the table or view
Object_name	Name of the table or view
Policy_name	Name of the policy to be added or dropped; must be unique for the table or view
Function_schema	Schema of the policy function
Policy_function	Name of a function, which generates a predicate for the policy. If the function is defined within a package, the name of the package must be present.
Statement_types	Statement types to which the policy will apply. Can be any combination of **select**, **insert**, **update**, and **delete**. The default is to apply to all of these types.
Update_check	When set to TRUE, the value will be checked against security policies after insert or update (optional argument).
Enable	Indicates whether the policy is enabled when added; default is TRUE.

TABLE 10-9. *DBMS_RLS Parameters for ADD_POLICY*

The parameters **object_schema**, **object_name**, and **policy_name** are required for the DROP_POLICY, REFRESH_POLICY, and ENABLE_POLICY procedures. **Enable** is the only other required parameter for the ENABLE_POLICY procedure.

For this example, you can add the policy named EMPLOYEE_POLICY to the EMPLOYEE table as follows:

```
execute DBMS_RLS.ADD_POLICY
('FABROS','EMPLOYEE','EMPLOYEE_POLICY','FABROS','EMPLOYEE_SEC.EMPLOYEE_ID_SEC','SELECT
',FALSE,TRUE);
```

The statement creates the policy EMPLOYEE_POLICY that causes the EMPLOYEE_SEC.EMPLOYEE_ID_SEC function to be run when **select** statements are executed against the EMPLOYEE table in the FABROS schema.

Statements are parsed and placed in the shared pool for use by other users with the same access privileges.

In our example, the policy function is in the same schema as the actual application tables. In practice, you should keep your policy functions in a schema area owned by your company's security officer to prevent anyone from inadvertently or intentionally removing a policy from a table or view.

Create the Trigger

Once all of the pieces are in place, you must create a trigger to enforce the policy. We recommend that you use an **on logon** trigger to accomplish this task so that the policy will be activated regardless of the approach a user takes to connect to the database.

```
create or replace trigger logon_trigger1 after logon on database
when (USER in ('RACHEL' or 'FABROS_MGR')
declare
 begin
  if(user = 'RACHEL') then
     EXECUTE IMMEDIATE 'alter session set current schema=ADMINDBA';
  elsif(user = 'FABROS_MGR') then
     EXECUTE IMMEDIATE 'alter session set current_schema=FABROS';
  end if;
end;

/
```

This trigger ensures that when Rachel logs in to the database, she will see the ADMINDBA schema objects as if they were her own, while when the FABROS_MGR logs in, he will see the FABROS schema objects as if they were his.

One word of warning though: if your trigger does not function properly, you could end up in a situation where no one can log on to your database. In that case, you must connect as a user with **sysdba** privileges and remove the trigger until you can correct the error.

Encrypting Database Columns

Along with VPD and Label Security, Oracle9i also provides you with the ability to selectively encrypt data columns within the database. By encrypting sensitive data within columns in the database, you can ensure that even super-privileged users or users trying to view data through examination of database columns or the operating system files will not be able to see or compromise the secured information.

Encrypting Column Data

Oracle supplies a PL/SQL package, available since Oracle8i, release 8.1.6, called the DBMS_OBFUSCATION_TOOLKIT, to provide a mechanism for use in encrypting and decrypting stored data within the database. For example, you could apply this feature to the column that stores credit card information within the FAB_CUSTOMER table. Before we look at the DBMS_OBFUSCATION_TOOLKIT, we'd like to tell you a little about encryption and key protection.

In 1973, the National Institute of Science and Technology (NIST) started the selection process for a standard symmetrical algorithm to use in encryption. The algorithm had to be flexible, secure, fast, and royalty free. IBM's candidate algorithm, known as the Data Encryption Standard, or DES, was accepted. DES uses a 56K key length. To encrypt a piece of data using this algorithm, the data is input to a program that uses a randomly generated key to change each byte of data into another value. By the time the data is output, it's in a format that can't be easily decoded without the associated decryption key.

The data passed into the DBMS_OBFUSCATION_TOOLKIT must be either 8 bytes or a multiple of 8 bytes. Bulk data encryption is supported in Oracle8i and Oracle9i using the DES algorithm. The procedure DESEncrypt is used to encrypt data, while DESDecrypt is used for decryption. The encryption key used in the encryption and decryption must be provided programmatically. That is, a developer must create the code to provide an encryption key mechanism and create a secure method to store and retrieve keys. The method that is developed must ensure that the key is easy enough to retrieve to enable the user or application to decrypt the requested data without impacting the system performance. The key storage must also be strong enough to withstand malicious attacks. One suggested approach would be to use the wrap utility to obfuscate or hide the PL/SQL package body code that is used to perform the encryption. You could put the key in the PL/SQL package body and then wrap it, thereby making it unreadable to anyone attempting to compromise the database, including the most highly privileged DBA. To wrap a package body called HIDETHEKEY, you use the following syntax run from the operating system level:

```
wrap iname=/oracode/hidethekey.sql
```

Since wrapping is not 100 percent unbreakable, you could also break the key up within the package body and then have a separate routine to reassemble it prior to use. There are other approaches that you can develop to protect the keys effectively.

Using the OBFUSCATION_TOOLKIT

The DBMS_OBFUSCATION_TOOLKIT requires a 64-bit key, but the DES algorithm itself only provides a 56-bit key length. To get around this problem, Oracle supplies the procedure GetKey, which calls a secure random number generator. Remember that the goal here is to encrypt the sensitive information in a column within a table. You would not generally use this mechanism to encrypt all of the data within a table or the entire database because the encryption and decryption overhead could be too costly.

The DBMS_OBFUSCATION_TOOLKIT package contains four procedures—two procedures that encrypt varchar2 and raw data types and two procedures that decrypt varchar2 and raw data types. First, you must install the package in the database, so you need to log in to SQL*Plus with the SYS username and password "as sysdba."

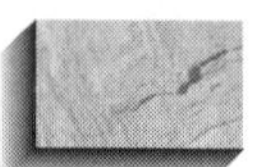

NOTE
If you don't include the phrase "as sysdba," you will be reminded to connect with the higher privileges.

The scripts that you must run to create the package are found in the $ORACLE_HOME/rdbms/admin directory on a Unix system and ORACLE_HOME\rdbms\admin on a Windows system. From SQL*Plus, run the scripts dbmsobtk.sql and prvtobtk.plb.

Next, you have to grant execute on DBMS_OBFUSCATION_TOOLKIT to PUBLIC:

```
grant execute on DBMS_OBFUSCATION_TOOLKIT to PUBLIC;
```

The procedures accept two parameters—the data to encrypt and the key used for the encryption or decryption algorithm.

Let's look at a simple call to the encryption procedure:

```
DBMS_OBFUSCATION_TOOLKIT.DES3Encrypt
(input_string => customer_encrypt.unencrypted_credit_card_no,
key_string => customer_encrypt.customer_key,
encrypted_string => encrypted_credit_card_no);
```

In this example, the customer's unencrypted credit card number is presented, along with the encryption key (customer_encrypt.customer_key). The output is the encrypted string called encrypted_credit_card_no.

About Auditing

Oracle has created the ability to audit all actions that take place within your database. Audit records may be written either to the operating system's audit trail or to the SYS.AUD$ table. However, your ability to use the operating system's audit trail as a destination for Oracle audit records is operating system dependent.

There are several different reasons why you might want to enable one or another form of auditing on your system. For example, you want to audit failed login attempts to help detect someone using brute-force password guessing to break into your database. You could audit access to a specific table to see if someone is making changes to a sensitive column like the Salary column in the EMPLOYEE table that we used in the VPD section earlier. If you don't have auditing enabled on a sensitive column and a damaging change is made, how will you know who made the change or when the change occurred?

There are three different types of actions that you can audit: login attempts, object accesses, and database actions. We'll look at each of these action types in the following sections. By default, the database functionality is to record both successful and unsuccessful commands. However, you may find that you do not need or want to track both actions. When you establish auditing, you can enable as much or as little auditing as will help you protect your database without too much impact on its performance.

To enable auditing in a database, the initialization file for the database must contain an entry for the **audit_trail** parameter. The **audit_trail** values are shown in Table 10-10.

The **audit** commands described in the following sections can be issued regardless of the setting of the **audit_trail** parameter. However, auditing will not be activated unless the database is started using an initialization parameter file setting for **audit_trail**.

If you decide to store the audit records within the database in the SYS.AUD$ table, you must remember that Oracle never removes entries from that table. Since it is in the data dictionary, this table is in the SYSTEM tablespace and may cause

Parameter	Description
None	Disables auditing
DB	Enables auditing, writing to the SYS.AUD$ table
OS	Enables auditing, writing to the operating system's audit trail (operating system dependent)

TABLE 10-10. *Audit Trail Options*

space problems if its records are not cleaned out occasionally. You should, therefore, periodically archive the table's records, and the table should then be **truncate**d. You can grant DELETE_CATALOG_ROLE to an administrator to give that user the ability to delete records from the SYS.AUD$ table.

NOTE
Oracle supports interactive deletion of records from the SYS.AUD$ data dictionary table only. Do not ever remove records from any other data dictionary tables.

Login Audits

Since malicious users can attempt to connect to a database by guessing the passwords for various accounts, every attempt to connect to the database can be audited. The command that you can use to begin auditing of all login attempts is

```
audit session;
```

In reality, you may be more interested in tracking only those login attempts that fail. To audit only connection attempts that are successful or that fail, use one of the commands shown in the following listing:

```
audit session whenever successful;
audit session whenever not successful;
```

You can use the DBA_AUDIT_SESSION view to audit records that are stored in the SYS.AUD$ table. The query shown in the following listing retrieves login audit records from the DBA_AUDIT_SESSION view. It lists the operating system account that was used, the Oracle account name, and the terminal ID that was used. The Returncode column is evaluated using the **decode** syntax that says

- If the return value is 0, the connection attempt succeeded.
- If the return value is 1005, a username was presented without a password.
- If the return value is 1017, an incorrect password was entered.

The login timestamp and logoff times are also displayed.

```
select OS_Username, Username, Terminal,
       DECODE(Returncode,'0','Connected',
              '1005','FailedNull',
              '1017','Failed',Returncode),
```

```
       TO_CHAR(Timestamp,'DD-MON-YY HH24:MI:SS'),
       TO_CHAR(Logoff_Time,'DD-MON-YY HH24:MI:SS')
  from DBA_AUDIT_SESSION;
```

If you opt to audit all successful connections to your database, please keep in mind that you may end up with a huge audit log very quickly—depending on how many connections are normal for your database per day. Enabling auditing can have both space and performance effects that can be detrimental to your system. Please give great thought to the areas that you really need to audit, and have a sound business basis to back up your decisions in case you need to defend your actions to upper management. If your business logic is sound, management will generally back your auditing decisions.

To disable session auditing, use the **noaudit** command, as shown in this example:

```
noaudit session;
```

Action Audits

You can audit any action that affects a database object—such as a table, database link, tablespace, synonym, rollback segment, user, or index. The possible actions—such as **create**, **alter**, and **drop**—that can affect those objects can be grouped together during auditing. Grouping commands helps reduce the amount of administrative effort necessary to establish and maintain the audit settings.

All of the system-level commands can be audited, and groups of commands are provided. For example, to audit all commands that affect roles, enter the command

```
audit role;
```

When you issue the **audit role** command, you tell Oracle to audit the **create role**, **alter role**, **drop role**, and **set role** commands.

To disable this setting, enter the command

```
noaudit role;
```

You may audit each individual command covered (such as **create table**). Oracle also provides the groups of statement options shown in Table 10-11.

Each action that can be audited is assigned a numeric code within the database. These codes are accessible via the AUDIT_ACTIONS view. The following query will display the available action codes for your database:

```
select Action, Name
  from AUDIT_ACTIONS;
```

Command	Description
Connect	Audits Oracle logons and logoffs
DBA	Audits commands that require DBA authority, such as **grant, revoke, audit, noaudit, create**, or **alter tablespace**; and **create** or **drop public synonym**
Resource	Audits **create** and **drop** for tables, clusters, views, indexes, tablespaces, types, and synonyms
All	Audits all of these commands
All privileges	All of the preceding commands plus **delete**s, **insert**s, **update**s, and several other commands

TABLE 10-11. *Groups of Audit Statement Options*

Once the action code is known, you can use the DBA_AUDIT_OBJECT view to determine how an object was affected by the action. The query shown in the following listing retrieves login audit records from the DBA_AUDIT_OBJECT view. It lists the operating system account that was used, the Oracle account name, and the terminal ID that was used. The object owner and name are selected, along with the action code for the action performed. The Returncode column is evaluated: if it is 0, then the connection attempt succeeded; otherwise, the error number is reported. The login and logoff times are also displayed.

```
select
  OS_Username,
  Username,
  Terminal,
  Owner,
  Obj_Name,
  Action_Name,
  DECODE(Returncode,'0','Success',Returncode),
  TO_CHAR(Timestamp,'DD-MON-YYYY HH24:MI:SS')
from DBA_AUDIT_OBJECT;
```

You can also specify particular users to audit, using the **by *username*** clause of the **audit** command, as shown in the following code. In this example, all **update** actions by the user NELSON will be audited.

```
audit update table by NELSON;
```

Object Audits

In addition to system-level actions on objects, data manipulation actions on objects can be audited. These may include auditing **select**, **insert**, **update**, and **delete** operations against tables. You audit actions of this type in a manner that is very similar to the action audits we described in the previous section. The only difference is the addition of a new clause in the **audit** command.

Audit by Session or by Access

The additional clause for object audits is the **by session** or **by access** clause. This clause specifies whether an audit record should be written once for each session (**by session**) or once for each time an object is accessed (**by access**). For example, if a user executed four different **update** statements against the same table, auditing **by access** would result in four audit records being written—one for each table access. Auditing the same situation **by session** would result in only one audit record being written.

Auditing **by access** can therefore dramatically increase the rate at which audit records are written but can quickly highlight a high-traffic object. The **by access** option is generally used on a limited basis to gauge the number of separate actions taking place during a specific time interval. Once you have completed testing and determined the number of transactions occurring within the given time span, auditing should be reverted to **by session** status.

Examples of these options are shown in the following listing. In the first command, all **insert** commands against the EMPLOYEE table are audited. In the second command, every command that affects the FAB_CUSTOMERS table is audited. In the third command, all **delete** operations against the FAB_ORDERS table are audited, on a per-session basis.

```
audit insert on FABROS.EMPLOYEE;
audit all on FABROS.FAB_CUSTOMERS;
audit delete on FABROS.FAB_ORDERS by session;
```

You can view the resulting audit records via the query that we showed in the previous section against the DBA_AUDIT_OBJECT view.

Fine-Grained Object Auditing

One of the problems with Oracle's implementation of object auditing has always been that although you can see that the object was accessed and see who accessed it, you cannot see what values were changed and what the old values were. Oracle9i provides a PL/SQL package to enable fine-grained object auditing that helps you track accessed information in your database and how the information has been modified.

Just as you did in creating the Virtual Private Database earlier in this chapter, to enable fine-grained object auditing, you create a SQL predicate (a where clause) to describe the conditions under which an audit record should be logged. The SQL predicate defines the data access conditions that should trigger an audit event. You use the PL/SQL package DBMS_FGA to administer the fine-grained audit policies. The actions you can take using DBMA_FGA are shown in Table 10-12.

Let's say that the bees over in hive number five want to audit anyone checking on the current amount of honey in stock. The bees have been having a problem with bears stealing their honey recently. The Hive5 bees would create a procedure to define how they want to be notified of anyone querying the HONEY_COMBS table and then create an audit policy to establish the audit criteria.

```
/* add the policy */
exec DBMS_FGA.ADD_POLICY(
object_schema => 'HIVE5',
object_name    => 'HONEY_COMBS',
policy_name    => 'CHK_HONEY_QUANTITY',
audit_condition => 'PRODUCT = ''HONEY'' ',
audit_column => 'QUANTITY',
handler_schema => 'SEC',
handler_module => 'LOG_ACTION',
enable                 =>  TRUE);
```

In this example, an audit policy is created to capture anyone who selects the quantity value associated with the HONEY entry from the PRODUCT table. You must also create an error handler, such as a trigger, to activate when the audit policy condition is met. In this case, the trigger LOG_ACTION in the SEC schema was used. The commands that were issued will be automatically captured and placed in the handler_module you have specified.

Package Action	Description
Add_policy	Add a fine-grained auditing policy to a table or view.
Drop_policy	Drop a fine-grained auditing policy from a table or view.
Enable_policy	Enable a security policy for a table or view.
Disable_ policy	Disable a security policy for a table or view.

TABLE 10-12. *DBMS_FGA Policy Action*

NOTE
Although we show the policy creation listing on separate lines for readability, you must enter the statement without any carriage returns. Carriage returns within the statement may result in command failure.

Protecting the Audit Trail

Since the database audit trail table, SYS.AUD$, is stored within the database, any audit records that are written there must be protected. Otherwise, a malicious user may attempt to delete his or her audit trail records after attempting unauthorized actions within the database.

The ability to write audit records to the operating system audit trail helps to get around this problem by storing the records external to the database. However, this option is not available for all operating systems. You can check with your system administrator to determine whether writing your audit trail to the operating system is feasible and doable.

If you must store the audit trail information in SYS.AUD$, then you *must* protect that table. Start with auditing actions against the table via the following command:

```
audit all on SYS.AUD$ by access;
```

If any actions are made against the SYS.AUD$ table (**insert**s generated via audits of other tables don't count), then those actions will be recorded in the audit trail. Not only that, but actions against SYS.AUD$ can only be deleted by users who have the ability to connect as SYSDBA or SYSOPER (they are in the DBA group). Any actions made while connected as a privileged user like SYSDBA are automatically written to the audit trail.

Wherever possible, coordinate your database auditing and your operating system auditing. This will make it easier to track problems and coordinate security policies across the two environments. Since the system managers will most likely not want to see reams of audit trail entries, it also forces the DBA to analyze exactly which actions are the most critical to audit. Your aim should be to have an audit trail in which every record is significant. If it is not, then use the commands given in this chapter to modify the auditing options to reflect the true actions of interest. Remember, too, that the audit trails won't do you any good if you don't take the time to examine them often. You should also evaluate your auditing position at least once every three to six months to ensure that the areas you are auditing are still valid areas of concern and to enable you to add new areas as needed.

External Database Security

Oracle Corporation provides a suite of tools to protect data integrity as information travels around the network. The tools, known as the Oracle Advanced Security Option (ASO) and available as an added-cost option, provide several different features. For example, to ensure that a message isn't tampered with in any way, Oracle Advanced Security features enable a cryptographically secure message digest to be generated and attached to the message. The message digest is generated using an algorithm known as MD5 to create a cryptographic checksum. This checksum is different from the normal, standard checksum that operating system hardware generates and is included with each packet that is sent across the network. If any of the packets are tampered with, the checksum won't match the packet contents.

Network Security

If your company's computers were never configured to interact with computers outside of your installation, you could still face data compromise because your users are distributed throughout your company and, therefore, access the company databases via a network. The problem is compounded when you connect to the outside world. Any companies that are connected at least in part to the Internet face the challenge of ensuring that malicious individuals cannot gain access to private data or damage the integrity of the computers on which corporate data resides. We've all heard about malicious users who have gained access to and defaced government and corporate Web sites. We're sure that you don't want your company to be the next target!

To help you secure your network traffic, we're going to look at basic Oracle Net security that you can use.

Oracle Net and the Oracle Advanced Security Option

When Oracle introduced the client-server architecture in the late version 4 and early version 5 of the RDBMS, the product was called SQL*Net. When Oracle8 was introduced, the name SQL*Net was changed to Net8. With the advent of Oracle9i, Oracle's networking functionality has undergone yet another name change, this time to Oracle Net.

With Oracle Net, the emphasis for network security has been enhanced to include stronger firewall access control through the Oracle Advanced Security Option. In an intranet environment, you can use the Oracle Connection Manager as a firewall for Oracle Net traffic. Using the Oracle Connection Manager, you can configure enabling or disabling of specific client access by establishing filtering rules based on the following criteria:

- Source host names or IP addresses for clients
- Destination host names or IP addresses for servers
- Destination database service name
- Whether the Oracle Advanced Security option is being used by the client

The Oracle Connection Manager is used to enhance your firewall security by filtering out client access based on one or more aspects of the filtering rules that you create.

To establish a firewall between the Internet and your application gateway and application Web server, and a second firewall between the gateway and server and your corporate intranet and databases, Oracle has worked with some firewall vendors to provide the Connection Manager software in a firewall-vendor solution.

In Oracle9i, the Oracle Connection Manager acts in the same way as the listener has in prior releases, using the Multi-Threaded Server (MTS) option. The Connection Manager accepts requests from the Web Application Server and passes the requests on to dispatchers. Just as with MTS, the dispatchers pass the requests on to the shared server processes for processing within the database. Figure 10-1

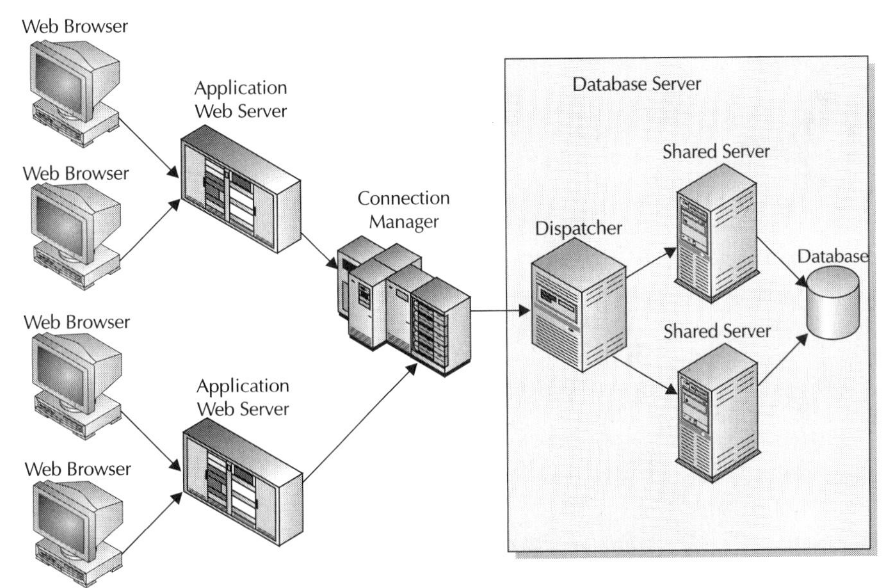

FIGURE 10-1. *Oracle Net Web-browser-to-database request flow*

shows the flow from Web browsers through the Web Application Servers to the Connection Managers and over to the dispatchers and shared server processes. In this way, Oracle Net supports connection load balancing for dedicated server configurations as well as across shared server configurations.

To support a large body of users, you can configure multiple Connection Managers to support the query load.

You can also use the sqlnet.ora file to specify configuration parameters describing the criteria that the software should use to determine whether a client will be able to connect to your databases. The parameters you can use are as follows:

- **tcp.excluded_nodes** to specify those nodes that are not to be allowed access
- **tcp.invited_nodes** to designate specific nodes that are to be allowed access
- **tcp.validnode_checking** to check for the values for **tcp.invited_nodes** and **tcp.excluded_nodes** to determine who is to be permitted or denied access

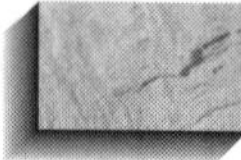

NOTE
The TCP parameters were originally in protocol.ora and now are in sqlnet.ora for version 9i.

CHAPTER 11

Availability

hat do we mean by availability? The dictionary defines availability as "the quality of being at hand when needed." So availability will mean different things to different people, depending on their needs. Hmm, just what does that really mean? Let's go back to the bank. If you are going out to dinner and you realize you don't have enough money in your wallet, you want the bank's ATM to be open and available so you can get cash. However, if you have a question about something on your latest bank statement, you probably can wait until morning to contact someone at the bank to get the answer. So the same bank can be available in different ways and at different times for you, depending on what you need.

Sit down next to a group of experienced DBAs at any user conference and listen for a while. Pretty soon the conversation will turn to "war stories"—disasters and the lengths they went to in order to recover from them. Almost every senior DBA will have such a story, sometimes two or three. There's a saying in the Oracle DBA world, "There are only two kinds of DBAs, those who have had a database crash and recovered it and those who will."

In this chapter we are going to talk about the ways you can make your database and the data within it available to your users and what is involved in working with each of those ways. We'll also talk a bit about the types of things that can go wrong and how you can deal with them.

Availability Concepts

One of the authors is fond of quoting a character in the children's book *Willie Wonka and the Chocolate Factory*: "I want it NOW, Daddy!" We sometimes think our users have heard her, because when we ask them what their requirements are for how quickly they want their database available, their response is, "I want it NOW!"

So how do we quantify "I want it now"? Does "now" mean five minutes? Is an hour of downtime acceptable? What about a day? Under what conditions does "now" change? Before you can begin to plan your strategy, you need to define your goals.

You should always be sure to have a *service-level agreement* (SLA) with your users, data center, operations staff, and programming staff. An SLA will, at minimum, define

- Normal availability time
- Performance requirements (response time for application and hardware)
- Regular maintenance schedule
- Backup schedule
- Response time for hardware and software problems

- Escalation procedures
- Contingency procedures

Oh yes, you will need to get senior management to sign off on the SLA, or you won't get the support you need to enforce it. Now let's look at each of these items more closely.

Normal availability time defines the hours when the application and database are available for users to access. As we develop more and more Internet-accessible databases and our operations go global, normal availability time tends to be 24 hours a day, 7 days a week, 365 days a year (24 x 7 x 365).

Performance requirements have several components to them. Though our users say, "I want it now," and are not concerned whether the delay is in the database, the network, or the hardware itself, we need to break down the response time and define it for each component. In general, the response time requirement for a report from a data warehouse will be longer than that for an online ordering application. But you will need to sit down with everyone, from hardware vendors to data center operations staff to programming staff, and figure out what the response time for each piece is, and what the best overall response time can be. Remember too, if users are happy with a six-second response time, there is really no need for you to try to cut it down to two seconds!

A regular maintenance schedule will allow you to plan for database upgrades, operating system upgrades, and any internal database reorganizations you need to do. With 9i, Oracle has made it easier to do most database internal maintenance online, while the database is accessible, but there are still some things that have to be done while the database is quiesced.

Backup schedules are vital in planning for another section of the SLA—the response time for problems. The more frequently you do a database backup, the shorter the recovery time will be, as there will be fewer archived redo logs to apply. If you are running with a standby database, the backup schedule should also include the timing for moving the archived redo logs to the standby server. We'll talk more about the kinds of backups you can do a little later in this chapter.

Response time for problems defines how quickly someone must be on-site (or dialed in) and fixing the problem. For hardware problems, it will define how long the vendor has between the time the call for support is placed and the time they are on-site working on the problem (not how long until it is fixed!). For the applications and database staff, it will define whether or not someone is on call, how he is contacted, and how quickly he must begin to work on defining and correcting the problem. Again, while it would be nice to be able to define how quickly the problem is fixed, you can't foresee every possible problem. Oracle has introduced some new features that help the DBA to get the database open and available as soon as possible.

Escalation procedures define when it's time to move on to the next step or person in the process. In general, this should be a list of people to call and when to call them. As an example, if a report fails, the first person to call might be the programmer. If the programmer does not respond after a certain amount of time, or if the programmer responds but determines that the problem is in the database, then the DBA might be the next one to call, Depending on how severe the problem is, the escalation procedures might list senior management contacts as well. One of the escalation procedures would be defining when you would need to go into contingency, which leads us to the next item in the SLA.

Contingency procedures detail what to do in case of a catastrophic occurrence. These procedures would be followed in the case of a major power outage, a flood, or anything that will cause an outage for longer than acceptable in the other sections of the SLA. They define where and how you would failover your system to your contingent system, and as importantly, they should define how you come back to your primary site.

The list above does not necessarily include everything that should be in your SLA. You should add and remove items as appropriate for your database and applications. The SLA must, however, be a joint effort among all business groups.

Now that we know our goals, we can begin to plan how to implement them.

Just What Are We Protecting Against?

If you own an automobile, you probably have a spare tire in the trunk. Why? Well, to ensure that, should you get a flat tire on a dark road in the middle of the night coming home from work, you'll be able to change that tire and continue home safely. (We won't even go into why you might be coming home late at night from work!) In other words, you have a contingency strategy. You have the tools you need to implement your strategy: a spare tire, a jack, a tire iron, and some lubricant to help loosen up the lug nuts. You know the basic procedures to change a tire, or you have a manual that can guide you through the process. You might never have that flat tire, but at least you are prepared in case of an emergency. And, of course, the probability is that if you were not prepared, disaster would surely strike.

In the same way, we're suggesting you prepare in advance for the possibility that your database will experience some problem that could cause a loss of data to your system. As cited in the *Oracle8i Backup and Recovery Handbook*, by Rama Velpuri and Anand Adkoli (Osborne/McGraw-Hill, 1998), the IEEE defines four different categories of outages that can occur on a system:

- Physical
- Environment
- Design (software bug)
- Operational

These break down into two general types of problems—physical, involving either hardware or the world around you, and logical, involving people. Let's think about what constitutes an outage of each type.

Physical Problems

Physical outages are hardware failures: a disk, controller, or CPU goes bad. Equipment ages. There's no way of getting around that fact. Each piece of equipment has an expected life span. Most computer equipment we've seen seems to fail well before the manufacturer's designated life span date. If a disk is beginning to go bad, signs of this problem may show up as corrupted blocks in your database. In that case, Oracle will give you ample warning that a problem is brewing by issuing an ORA-00600 error with an appropriate set of arguments. (Oracle Support, or the new ORA-600 Lookup facility on MetaLink, will be able to tell you what the arguments of a 600 error mean.) By letting your systems operations people know that you have found a corrupted block error in the database, they may be able to track down what's going wrong on the system—a disk or a controller going bad—before the problem reaches catastrophic proportions.

Most operating systems provide hardware error reporting tools. System administrators regularly check reports produced by these tools. The reports give details of both permanent and temporary errors. One sign of a disk going bad is a steady increase in the number of temporary errors. You can ask the system administrator to forward these reports to you so that you can monitor for temporary errors as well. Your alert logs, as discussed in Chapter 9, can also provide indications of disk access problems. Watch for errors that end with a number in the 600 range.

The other type of physical problems is environmental outages. Environmental outages are generally disasters caused by nature: lightning strikes, fires, floods, and so on. Having a storage area off-site that contains the most current backups and a hard-copy listing of what's in the backups could save your company huge volumes of downtime. If warranted, you can have a contract with your hardware vendor that states the equipment that will be replaced and the time frame in which the new hardware will be made available to you and your systems group. Having an off-site location where equipment can be placed that will allow you to connect to your network is also recommended. If your computer room burns to the ground, how fast will your company be able to recover its systems and be back in business?

Logical Problems

Logical problems are always the result of something a person does. Design outages occur when software code fails. We generally refer to these outages as software bugs and/or viruses. The problem code can come from your software vendor (Oracle-delivered executables, for example), from your in-house applications developers, or from shareware or freeware code downloaded from an Internet site.

Operational outages are always caused by a human being. For example, a person accidentally issues an incorrect command using a privileged account in your production database and truncates a table, or someone walks out to a machine in your computer room and pulls a disk out of a slot because she thinks the disk has failed. She inadvertently pulls out the wrong disk. Oops!

Any of these outages can strike your facility at any time. It's your job to be prepared for them beforehand. Remember, too, that there is no single correct answer to the question, "What should I do to protect *my* systems?" Only you and your management can determine the correct answer for your company.

Types of Recovery

Just as there are many different things that can go wrong with your database, there are several different ways that they can be fixed, or recovered. There are three basic types of recovery that can be done. We'll talk about each of them in the next few sections.

Data Recovery

Data recovery involves just that—recovering data that has been changed or deleted accidentally. There isn't much you can do to prevent the user errors that cause you to do recovery, but you can do some things to make them less likely to happen. Be very careful with the privileges you hand out to your users. Giving users the ability to drop tables or truncate them can have consequences that will involve some sleepless nights for the DBA.

Early in her career, one of the authors accidentally dropped a production tablespace. Fortunately, she had export files, and the tablespace contained static tables, so recovery was a matter of re-creating the tablespace and then importing the lost tables. If she hadn't had the export, the users would have had to manually reenter all the information from the missing tables. In the section "Logical Backups (export)," we'll tell you about all the different options you have when doing an export.

Instance Recovery

Instance recovery is needed whenever there is an instance failure. Instance failure can result from a hardware problem (such as a server crash) or a software problem (such as an operating system crash or a forced shutdown). Anytime you do not shut down the database with a **shutdown, shutdown transactional,** or **shutdown immediate**, you cause an instance failure.

Oracle will automatically detect instance failure when you next open the database and will attempt to recover the instance on its own. Depending on what was going on in the database when the instance failure occurred, it may take anywhere from a few seconds to hours to open the database. There are initialization parameters you can set to help make the database available as soon as possible after instance failure, and we will talk about those later in the chapter.

Media Recovery

Media recovery is necessary when you have a problem either reading from or writing to one of the database files on disk. You may need to recover files because of bad spots on the disk or because of a controller problem or a disk crash. Media recovery is usually associated with hardware problems. Any file associated with the database, including control files, online redo logs, archived redo logs and datafiles, is vulnerable to media failure.

How you recover from media failure will depend on how you have set up the database, how you are doing your backups, and the extent of the media failure. If you use Oracle mirroring of your online redo logs, and one log in the mirror group is lost, the database will remain open and available, and you will be able to drop the lost member of the group. If you lose a control file, it will also cause an instance failure, and you can either remove it from your initialization file or make a copy of it from one of the remaining control files before you restart the database.

However, if you lose a datafile from the database, your recovery strategy will depend on whether or not your database is in archivelog mode and how you have been doing backups. When DBAs talk about backup and recovery strategies, they are most often concerned with recovery from media failure.

Types of Backups

Now that we know what we may have to deal with in terms of recovery, how do we protect against all the possibilities? We're going to look into the two types of backups—physical and logical—and see how they complement each other and how they can help us. Since DBAs are most concerned with media failure and recovery, let's start with physical backups.

Physical Backups

There are two types of physical backups—those taken while the database is closed, called *offline database backups,* and those taken while the database is open, called *online database backups.* If you have your database in noarchivelog mode, where Oracle does not save the online redo logs before reusing them, the only valid backup you can take is an offline database backup. If you are running your database in archivelog mode, you can take either an online or an offline database backup and have a consistent backup. We're going to go into some detail about these two types of backups and also talk a bit about RMAN, Oracle's Recovery Manager, which you can use to help in making backups of your database.

Offline Database Backups

An offline database backup, also referred to at times as a *cold backup, image backup,* or *files-level backup,* derives its name from the fact that the database is shut down to perform this action. You must ensure that no processes are active within the database when you attempt to shut down the database. A good shutdown procedure will include verification that all processes have been stopped before a **shutdown normal** command is performed. With the use of Oracle Enterprise Manager (OEM) to enable remote database management, an Intelligent Agent is attached to your database at all times. If you are using OEM and have an active Intelligent Agent on your system, you will use a **shutdown immediate** command instead. If the **shutdown immediate** doesn't complete, there may be long-running SQL statements that Oracle is waiting to complete before finishing the shutdown. If you cannot wait for the shutdown immediate to complete, you can open another session and issue the **shutdown abort** command. However, since doing this can leave your database in an inconsistent state, you should always do a **startup** and **shutdown normal** after a **shutdown abort** before proceeding with anything else.

Performing an Offline Backup Once the database is shut down, each file that makes up the database is copied either to another disk or to tape. You should be sure to include all datafiles, redo logs, control files, and the initialization parameter file when you perform the files-level backup. There are many different system-dependent utilities that you can use to perform the actual backup of the files, and you can use any of the copy utilities available on your platform.

After the files-level copy process is completed, you can restart the database. Once the copy is completed, if a disaster occurs, the database can be recovered to the condition it was in when the copy was made. Thus, if you make your file copies at midnight on Monday and your database crashes at noon on Tuesday, all transactions that were performed in your database from Monday at midnight until Tuesday at noon will not be captured. Performing an offline backup by itself is like taking a photograph of your database as it is at one particular moment. The database condition is frozen at the point in time when the database was shut down. This is a very important factor to keep in mind as you begin to plan your backup strategies. If you are running in archivelog mode and you have the backup control file from a later point in time, as well as the archived logs since the time of the backup, you will be able to roll forward to a point in time past the time of the offline backup. However, if you are not running in archivelog mode, you can only recover to the time of the backup.

Online Database Backups

Online database backups are essential for a 24 x 7 environment. They derive their name from the fact that the database remains up and running while the backup is performed. Essentially, you perform the same files-level copies of the datafiles and control files, but you do not back up the redo log files. Archivelog mode must be enabled so that Oracle knows the database is recoverable. Online backups are also known as *hot backups*. For an online database backup to be valid, you must be running the database in archivelog mode.

While with an offline backup you must back up all the files of the database at once, with an online backup you can back up some or all of the files at any one time. The smallest unit you can back up is a datafile. To begin an online backup of a tablespace's datafile(s), you put the tablespace into backup mode by issuing the command

```
alter tablespace <ts_name> begin backup;
```

There are some procedures that you must follow after the backup completes if effective hot backups are to be made:

- Be sure to take the tablespace out of backup mode by issuing the command **alter tablespace <ts_name> end backup** once you complete the file copies of each tablespace's datafiles.
- Archive the current redo log file by completing a log switch. You will use the **alter system switch logfile;** command.
- Capture all archived redo logs that have been created from the time the backup was started through the time the backup is completed.
- Back up the control file using the **alter database backup controlfile to <filespec>;** command, where the **filespec** parameter is the complete directory path and file name of the location where you want the control file written.

Unlike offline backups when you are not in archivelog mode, the database can be recovered to a point in time or until you cancel the recovery. During normal database operations, only the changed information of a transaction is written to the redo log file and archived log files. However, during the time that the **alter tablespace begin backup** command is in effect, the entire block containing changed data is written to the log files. Thus, the volume of log files generated can become quite large if there are a lot of changes going on in your system while online backups are being performed. Therefore, Oracle recommends that you perform online backups during periods when less DML is occurring on the system.

As of Oracle8i, if you are using the Oracle-supplied Recovery Manager (RMAN), you will not have to manually place the tablespaces in and out of backup mode. Oracle will handle these actions automatically for you.

Enabling Archivelog Mode If you think about a video recorder, you know that you can record a message to your grandmother wishing her a happy birthday. You rewind the tape and send it off to her. She receives the tape and plays your message and is delighted to hear both your good wishes and see your face. In fact, she's so excited by your thoughtful recording that she calls in all of her neighbors and plays the tape over and over for anyone who will watch it. Keep Grandma and her tape recording in mind as we discuss the concepts behind enabling archivelog mode on your system.

We've mentioned the term archivelog mode in a few other chapters, but we haven't really talked about what that means or how to enable it. What better time to talk about this feature than now? We've talked about redo log files and their use in an Oracle database. When you enable archivelog mode, you tell Oracle that as each redo log file fills up, you want an exact copy of that filled redo log file to be copied to one or more disk locations.

Why would you want to copy redo log files? Well, Oracle writes to the redo log files in a circular fashion. When a redo log file fills up, Oracle switches over and begins writing to the next redo log file. Once Oracle has filled the entire set of redo log files, it starts over at the first one and overwrites the contents of that redo log file. If you save the contents of a redo log file by archiving it before Oracle begins to overwrite the old data, you can "roll forward" through the file, replaying the transactions, much like Grandma can rewind that tape of yours and bore her neighbors over and over again.

When you perform a database recovery and play through the archive logs on the system, you are actually said to be restoring the database to a point in the future. Hmm, what does that really mean? Well, the files that make up your database were copied at midnight on Monday. If you must perform a database recovery on Tuesday at noon, you are restoring your database to a point in time much later than Monday midnight, or to a point in time beyond when the original backup was made. But if you restore the files from last night, the redo log files and control files are from last night too. How will Oracle know that you want to restore to a time in the future? Great question!

Before you restore your files from last night's backup, you save the current redo log files and control files to a safe place where they will not be overwritten by last night's files. You can then restore the files from the backup and replace the older log files from your backup with the current saved ones. At this point, if you attempt to start the database, Oracle will look at the current control file and redo log files and see that their checksums do not match the information in the restored files. Oracle will tell you that your database needs recovery, and you can then tell Oracle to begin playing through the archived log files to recover the database.

An important factor to keep in mind if you are considering using backups that copy the physical datafiles as your only method of backups is that the entire database will be unavailable to users while you are performing database recovery.

Many different backup and recovery scenarios are discussed in the *Oracle8i Backup and Recovery Handbook* mentioned earlier. For a really complete picture of backup and recovery, we highly recommend this book.

Recovery Manager (RMAN)

Now that we understand the two types of physical backups, we can talk about a tool that Oracle provides for protecting your databases and ensuring successful recovery. Remember though that using Recovery Manager does not mean you no longer have backup planning issues. For example, what type of datafile backup will you use? What are the implications for your recovery procedures? What tapes and backup media will you need to have available in order to perform a recovery? Will you have the catalog data placed in your control file (the default in Oracle9i) or use a recovery catalog instead?

Starting with Oracle9i, Recovery Manager now stores its configuration parameters in the database control files, and you must allot adequate storage retention in the control file to ensure a complete backup history for database recovery. You can alternately decide to store the catalog information in a database repository. If you opt to store the catalog information within a database, you must ensure that the database holding the catalog is protected and backed up frequently.

But, the primary question for you to ask is, "Why should I use RMAN instead of user-management methods?" RMAN can do block-level backups, backing up only the changed blocks, while all other methods involve the entire file. In addition, RMAN provides you with a media management API (application programming interface) so that you can incorporate your third-party vendor media management software easily. As RMAN performs online backups, each fractured data block is reread to ensure data consistency. Fractured blocks are those where the database writer was writing the block to the disk as the operating system was reading it, and the block is not internally consistent in the backup. As backups are performed, RMAN calls the same kernel utilities that all other processes use to validate the integrity of Oracle data blocks.

Recovery Manager Architecture

The Recovery Manager is commonly known as RMAN, although technically that refers only to the actual executable. There are four components within the Recovery Manager: the RMAN executable, one or more target databases, the recovery catalog, and the media management software. A target database is the database you wish to back up. A recovery catalog is a separate schema used by RMAN to store and maintain information about the target databases and backups taken. It can be created in any existing database, or can have its own database, known as a *repository database*. We recommend you don't store the recovery catalog for the target database within the target database itself, since if you lose the target database, you will also lose the recovery catalog. The terms "recovery catalog" and "repository" are often used interchangeably.

Since RMAN automatically stores its metadata in the target database's control file, you do not have to have a recovery catalog. However, because there are so many additional benefits to having a recovery catalog, we recommend that you include one. Media management software is supplied by third-party vendors and will not be discussed here.

Another feature available through RMAN is the ability to perform automatic archived log failover if RMAN encounters a missing or corrupt log during a backup. If RMAN finds a missing or corrupt log, it will evaluate the other log copies listed in the repository as alternative candidates for the backup.

Using an RMAN Repository

If you choose to create and enable an RMAN repository, you will have a set of metadata in which information about the target database and its backup and recovery operations is stored. You can store information for multiple databases within one recovery catalog, although Oracle recommends a separate catalog be created for each target database. These don't have to be separate databases but can be separate schemas within a single database. Some of the information that RMAN stores is about image and proxy copies, backup sets and pieces, archived redo logs, target database schema, and persistent configuration settings.

With an RMAN repository, you can report information such as

- Which files need to be backed up
- Which files have not been backed up for a specific number of days
- Which backups can be deleted
- Current RMAN persistent settings

Creating a Recovery Catalog

A recovery catalog should be created in its own schema within its own tablespace in a database that is separate from all of the target databases you intend to back up. Installing the recovery catalog in a target database defeats the purpose of having a recovery catalog because if you lose the database, you lose not only your catalog but also the ability to restore the target database. Although you can use the SYSTEM tablespace to store the recovery catalog, we strongly recommend that you use a totally separate tablespace to help ensure less tablespace contention.

Storing Recovery Information in the Target Control Files

You can have RMAN store recovery information within a recovery catalog or completely within the target database control file. RMAN can perform all the necessary backup and recovery operations using just control file information, but you will not be able to take advantage of RMAN repository capabilities like the following:

- Store manually created scripts for backup, restore, or recovery
- Store copies of operating system backup files
- Restore and recover a target database if its control files become lost or damaged
- Generate reports on files that require backup, are unrecoverable, or are obsolete
- View metadata about backup sets, proxy copies, and image copies

Using RMAN

The most significant benefit to using RMAN is the ability to perform incremental physical backups of your datafiles. During a full (called a *level 0*) datafile backup, all of the blocks ever used in the datafile are backed up. During a cumulative (*level 1*) datafile backup, all of the blocks used since the last full datafile backup are backed up. An incremental (*level 2*) datafile backup backs up only those blocks that have changed since the most recent cumulative or full backup. You can define the levels used for incremental backups.

The ability to perform incremental and cumulative backups of datafiles may greatly improve the performance of your backups. The greatest performance improvements will be realized by very large databases in which only a small subset of a large tablespace changes. Using the traditional backup methods, you would need to back up all of the datafiles in the tablespace. Using Recovery Manager, you only back up the blocks that have changed since the last backup.

In pre-Oracle9i versions of RMAN, if a backup failed, you had to start from the beginning and re-back up all of the files of interest. With Oracle9i, you can restart an unsuccessful backup attempt where the backup left off; only missing or incomplete files will be backed up. RMAN bases its decision to back up a file on the backup time of the existing files.

A complete explanation of the commands can be found in the *Oracle9i Recovery Manager Reference* guide.

RMAN Recommendations

There are some commonsense things that you should be doing if you are using RMAN.

1. Ensure that you are backing up files that RMAN does not back up. Use conventional methods to back up these files:
   - Initialization parameter file (init.ora or spfile.ora)
   - Oracle Net and/or Net8 configuration files
   - oratab
   - crontab (or other schedule file)
   - Relevant scripts (backups, database DDL scripts, etc.)
2. MetaLink note 148138.1 has some useful Oracle9i RMAN information describing how you can use RMAN to clean up old archive log files. With conventional backups, cleanup must be performed manually.
3. RMAN can be used as a diagnostic tool. If you use RMAN to do your backups, RMAN checks for and reports block-level corruption. The time to catch corruption is during backup, not recovery.
4. When you use RMAN, you must resynchronize the recovery catalog from time to time. You should do this whenever there is a change to the file layout of the database.
5. The database storing your recovery catalog can be backed up by a third database containing another recovery catalog, or can be backed up using conventional means. Shutting down the recovery catalog database and taking a cold backup has no effect on the availability of the databases whose backup information is in the recovery catalog. The disadvantage of backing up the recovery catalog with conventional means is that you do not get the block corruption benefit of backing up with RMAN.
6. Avoid placing the recovery catalog database on the same server as the databases for which the catalog is storing backup information. If the catalog must be on the same server, the datafiles of the recovery catalog database should be on different physical disks than those of the target databases.
7. No matter what tool you use, make sure that your backups accurately reflect your recovery requirements. Once you have established your backup procedures and scripts, test them and document your recovery procedures and the performance you experienced. You will then be able to implement

the available procedures in a way that makes the most sense for your installation. The result should be a well-protected database and quick, efficient recoveries. And that, in turn, should lead to fewer calls to Oracle Support at 3:00 a.m.

Logical Backups (export)

Let's take a second to go back to Grandma and your tape recording. By now, she's played that tape so often that her friends and neighbors are avoiding her. Poor thing! The concept of making a copy of something that you can replay over and over again can be applied both to files-level backups and to an Oracle-supplied utility called *export*.

An export, like an offline backup, is actually a snapshot in time. Instead of making a copy of the datafiles that reside on your system, you make a binary copy of the objects and their data as they exist within your database. In other words, when you export your entire database, you make a copy of each individual table, index, view, synonym, package, procedure, trigger, and so on, that makes up your database. The export file can be read by another utility called *import* that enables you to restore your database to the point in time that the export was performed.

Unlike an online or offline backup with archivelog mode enabled, you cannot restore a database using the import utility to a time in the future. In other words, there is no way to apply archive log files to an import to bring it to another point in time beyond when the export was made.

One of the major advantages of making an export file of your database is that you can easily restore one or more tables or an entire schema if you need to. If you've been careful to keep each application's database structure in its own specific tablespace, you can recover only one schema without affecting other applications in your database.

Types of Exports

There are several types of exports that you can perform:

- **Full** A complete database export
- **Owner** A complete schema or user export
- **Tables** A single table or set of tables within one or more schemas
- **Tablespaces** All tables (and their associated indexes) in one or more tablespaces

In **full** mode, the complete database is exported. Here's what happens during a full database export: Oracle reads the entire data dictionary and writes the data dictionary language (DDL) commands needed to re-create the entire database to the export dump file. The export dump file, with a default name of expdat.dmp, includes definitions for all tablespaces, all users, and all of the objects, data, and privileges in their schemas. If you need to re-create the complete database, you can use the dump file from your full export to perform this task once you have built a skeleton database.

In **owner** mode, Oracle reads the data dictionary and exports the specified user's objects, as well as the data within those objects. Oracle will include all of the grants and indexes created by the user on the user's objects in the export file. However, if there are any grants and/or indexes that were created by users other than the owner, they are not included in a user mode export.

In **tables** mode, one or more tables are exported. You tell Oracle which table or tables you want exported, and Oracle places the table's structure, indexes, and grants in the export file along with its data, based on the parameters that you specify. You can use **tables** mode to export the full set of tables owned by a user (by specifying the schema owner, but no table names). You can also specify partitions of a table to export.

In **tablespaces** mode, new in Oracle9i, all the tables in a tablespace are exported, regardless of the table owner. In earlier versions of Oracle, you had to ensure that you had listed every owner who had a table in the tablespace, or you could lose data. With the **tablespaces** mode, you can simply include the tablespace name, or a list of tablespace names, and Oracle will ensure that all tables are exported. One thing you need to remember is that if you have an index in the tablespace, but the associated table exists in a different tablespace, the index will not be exported when you use **tablespaces** mode. So you still need to check that either all the indexes in the tablespace have their associated table in the same tablespace or that you have a valid script to re-create the index if necessary.

To see the full list of the available export parameters, you can issue the command **exp help=y** at the operating system command prompt. Before you can perform an export of a database, the database must be up and opened. Export files are very portable, and you can use them to move or copy a database from one system to another. However, the process of exporting an entire database can be very slow and may not be feasible for very large databases. An interesting point to keep in mind is that the export process will identify any data block corruption—it will do this by failing. Another way to identify data block corruption is to use the command **analyze table validate structure** on each table.

The **consistent** parameter tells Oracle whether to keep track of any changes that are occurring while the export is taking place. If you use **consistent=y**, you will need to make sure that you have a really large rollback segment available for the export to use. You see, while Oracle is performing the export, as each table is exported, a copy of the table is stored in the rollback segment. Now, as each additional table is exported, Oracle checks to see if any changes that would affect the current table have been made to the previously exported tables. Remember, we said earlier that Oracle exports the object information from the data dictionary. The data dictionary stores table names in alphabetical order:

```
select Table_Name
  from DBA_TABLES
 where Owner = 'ROSS';

TABLE_NAME
------------------------------
ACCOUNTING
BONUSES
DEPTMENT
EMPLOYEE
RECEIPTS
SALARY
```

In this schema, there is a dependency between the DEPTMENT and the EMPLOYEE tables. Because Oracle exports alphabetically, DEPTMENT will be exported before EMPLOYEE. Okay, so Oracle is exporting the EMPLOYEE table and someone makes a change to the DEPTMENT table. There's no problem in the current database, but if you must recover the tables from the export, they are now going to be inconsistent. If you use the parameter **consistent=y**, the change in the DEPTMENT table will be noticed during the export, and a correction will be made. Because Oracle has to be constantly checking the status of tables that depend on each other, the export will take much more time to perform and, as we said, could require a very large rollback segment. Therefore, we recommend that instead of using this parameter for a full database export, you break your export into two or more processes and just export specific tables that must be kept consistent in one export process.

For tables where data consistency is not an issue, you can then export them much more quickly with much less resource requirement.

One last parameter we'd like to talk about is the **where clause**. One of the problems with export has always been that you had to export the entire table each time. If you had a table and wanted to archive data a year or more old, you would have to create a temporary table and insert that data into it and then export the temporary table before deleting the old data. Then you would have to remember to drop the temporary table each time. With the **where clause**, you can now export only the data matching your criteria. The restriction is that all the tables being exported must be able to have that clause applied to them.

Database Features

In addition to the various backups you can do, Oracle provides you with some features in the database itself to help you keep your database as available as possible. In the next few sections, we are going to discuss several of these features.

Mean Time to Recovery (MTTR) Target

What do we mean by *mean time to recovery*? In mathematical terms, a mean is an average, the midpoint between two extremes. In database terms, mean time to recovery is the average time you would like it to take before your database is back up and available after instance recovery. Obviously, we would all prefer never to have a database fail, and if it does, to have it back up in under a second. While this is not realistic, Oracle has been working toward making the recovery time as short as possible.

Oracle will automatically delay the rollback phase of recovery to allow users into the database as soon as possible. This feature is called "fast-start on-demand rollback," and as soon as the roll forward of the information in the redo logs has completed, Oracle opens the database. At this point, Oracle will continue to do the rollback behind the scenes. If a transaction attempts to access a row that is still locked, Oracle will roll back only those changes necessary to complete the transaction.

In Oracle9i, there is a new initialization parameter, **fast_start_mttr_target**, which is used to limit the length of the redo log and the number of dirty data buffers in the cache. This parameter calculates internal system values for triggers and uses estimated times to read a redo block and to read and write a data block.

DBAs use this parameter to specify a target time (in seconds) to complete the roll forward part of instance recovery. The maximum value of this parameter is 3600, an hour. There is no minimum value, but you cannot just target the recovery time as low as you want. Crash recovery time is limited by other factors inside and outside the database, including the time it takes to open the database files.

Oracle will initially use internal defaults but will replace the defaults with execution time estimates taken during system operation. The best way to set these values is to take measurements from an actual instance recovery from failure. What does this imply? In order to effectively set the **fast_start_mttr_target** parameter, you should perform several instance recoveries to allow Oracle to accurately record the time it takes to read a redo block and to read and write a data block. You can then use the Target_Mttr column in V$INSTANCE_RECOVERY to see the effective MTTR. In other words, as we have said in various other places throughout this book, *test*!

Once these internal values have been calculated, Oracle will use them to automatically vary the incremental checkpoint writes and limit the redo buffer length. Setting the target too low can severely impact performance, as rollback will happen when the block is accessed rather than at startup.

Flashback Query

Flashback query allows you to view and repair historical data. It offers the ability to perform queries on the database as of a certain wall clock time (with certain limitations) or user-specified System Change Number (SCN). Once the errors are identified, undoing the updates is a straightforward process that can be done without intervention from the database administrator. More importantly, the restoration can be achieved with no database downtime. This is a good solution to logical error problems, where the data has been changed by accident and there is no valid export to use to recover. One of the authors worked in a shop where a programmer was fixing production data and entered the following SQL statement:

```
Update ORDER_TABLE
   set Order_Item = <newvalue>;
 where Order_No = <order number>;
```

Seems fine, right? Look again, carefully, at the second line. There's a semicolon at the end of it, which tells Oracle that the statement is ended and should be executed. So instead of just the one row being updated, *every* row in the table was changed. Then, the programmer ended his session, which automatically committed the change.

Ouch! This was a database that needed to be available at all times. So, what did the DBAs do? Without flashback query, it was a long process, involving restoring the backup to another server, applying archived logs until just before the bad SQL was run, creating a database link, and then updating the production table through the link—thousands of rows. All in all, it took about three hours. With flashback query, the steps would have been:

1. Enable flashback query to the point in time before the SQL was executed.
2. Open a cursor and select the data.
3. Disable flashback query and update the table with the old data.

Start to finish, less than 30 minutes.

Oh yes, step 4, done after the recovery is complete, is to appropriately discipline the guilty party. We'll leave the details of that step to your imagination!

Setting Up the Database for Flashback Query

Although you can use flashback query if you are running the database with manually managed rollback segments, if you plan to make frequent use of this option, you are better off running the database with Automatic Undo Management (AUM). Unlike manual rollback segment management, when you use AUM, Oracle does not overwrite the contents of the undo extents until the time limit you have set has passed. This allows flashback query to be more certain of finding the information needed to view and/or repair prior queries.

Set the initialization parameter **undo_retention** to a value that represents how far in the past you might want to query (the value is in seconds). If you only need to recover data immediately after a mistaken change is committed, the parameter can be set to a small value, say 360 (an hour). If you need to recover deleted data from days before, you might need to use 86400 × number of days (86400 is 60 × 60 × 24, or the number of seconds in a day). Keep in mind, if you tell Oracle to keep one day's worth of undo—that is, you set **undo_retention** to 86400—and the Undo Tablespace does not have enough room to keep that much undo information, Oracle will ignore the keep time you set and begin to reuse the space, starting with the oldest undo.

In addition to setting the **undo_retention** parameter, you must load the DBMS_FLASHBACK package to enable and disable flashback query. Logged into the database as "/ as sysdba" you run the dbmstran.sql script, located in the rdbms/admin directory under your ORACLE_HOME, and then grant execute on DBMS_FLASHBACK to anyone who needs it.

Use and Limitations of Flashback Query

Now that we have flashback query available in the database, what can we use it for? Have you ever had a batch report die in the middle of the night and by the time you found out, the data had changed and you could no longer generate your report? With flashback query, if you have set the retention times properly, you can now rerun that report the next morning, with the data from the middle of the night. Cool, huh? A few other potential uses are

- Recover lost data or undo incorrect changes, even after the changes are committed
- Compare current data against the data at some time in the past
- Check the state of transactional data at a particular time

As with everything in life, nothing is perfect, and there are always limitations. Flashback query does not undo anything in and of itself. If you want to back out a change, you would first enable flashback query, fetch the old data into a cursor, disable flashback query, and then issue the appropriate insert, update, or delete statements to undo the change.

Flashback query cannot do the following:

- Undo anything on its own
- Tell you what has been changed
- Work through DDL operations that alter the structure of a table
- Track changes farther back than five days server uptime (not wall clock time)
- Work in a nested fashion—you cannot set another flashback interval while one is still enabled

- Map the data dictionary tables back to the flashback time—the current state of the data dictionary is used
- Work on remote tables accessed through a database link

LogMiner

Have you ever realized that you were thinking about something totally different from what you had been thinking about just five minutes ago? Out of curiosity, you start to trace back the changes in what you had been thinking, and finally, you have all the steps that you went through to get from thought A to thought E.

Now think about your database. Wouldn't it be wonderful if you could trace back through the log files and see all the changes that had been made in the order they had been made? With the release of LogMiner in Oracle8i, you can.

The LogMiner utility allows you to read and query the online and archived redo logs through PL/SQL packages provided by Oracle. With the release of 9i, you can now also use a GUI interface, the LogMiner Viewer available through the Oracle Enterprise Manager, to view the log files. You can track DDL statements, limit the queries you see to only committed transactions (making the output much more readable), and query the logs based on actual data values. LogMiner can now support queries against

- Clustered tables
- Chained and migrated rows
- Direct loads
- LONGs and LOBs
- Data definition statements (DDL)

LogMiner can now also display the primary key and let you query the logs based on the content of the changes.

In order for LogMiner to read the log files, it has to have access to the database metadata. The metadata is used to translate the internal object IDs and data to a form readable by the DBA. If you do not have the metadata, LogMiner will return the data in hex bytes.

You can give LogMiner access in one of three ways:

- Extract the metadata to a flat file
- Extract the metadata to the redo log files
- Use the current database data dictionary

Prior to Oracle9i, you could only use a flat file to help LogMiner read the redo log files. If you are using the flat file option, it's important to keep that file in sync with the data dictionary of the database you want to mine. Using the flat file allows you to run LogMiner against a "foreign" database—that is, the redo log files do not belong to the database you are running LogMiner against. Let's go through what you need to do to work with LogMiner.

Setting Up LogMiner

The LogMiner packages are automatically built in the database when you create the database. They are run from the catproc.sql script. There are three scripts in the rdbms/admin directory that create the LogMiner packages—dbmslmd.sql, dbmslm.sql, and prvtlm.plb.

Four stored procedures (three in the DBMS_LOGMNR package and one in the DBMS_LOGMNR_D package) are used to create the metadata information and to mine the logs:

- **DBMS_LOGMNR_D.BUILD** This procedure builds the dictionary file used by the main LogMiner package to resolve object names and column data types. You should generate this file frequently, to ensure that all objects in the database are included in the metadata for LogMiner.
- **DBMS_LOGMNR.ADD_LOGFILE** This procedure must be called once for every log file you want to analyze and mine. It will add a row to the fixed table X$LOGMNR_LOGS(V$LOGMNR_LOGS) with a row for each log file you add.
- **DBMS_LOGMNR.START_LOGMNR** This procedure populates the fixed tables V$LOGMNR_DICTIONARY, V$LOGMNR_PARAMETERS, and V$LOGMNR_CONTENTS. You can pass in start and end SCN or start and end time to this procedure.
- **DBMS_LOGMNR.END_LOGMNR** This procedure must be called when you exit the session after completing the log mining. Failure to run this procedure will cause an ORA-600 error on logoff.

LogMiner Output

It's important to remember that the SQL output you will see from LogMiner will not be the exact syntax of the SQL statement that was actually run but instead a SQL statement (or statements) that would have the same effect. For example, if you ran a **delete** statement that deleted 1000 rows, you would expect to see a single **delete** statement in the LogMiner output. Instead, you will have 1000 **delete** statements, each deleting a single row.

Once you have executed DBMS_LOGMNR.START_LOGMNR, you will need to query the V$LOGMNR_CONTENTS table to see the actual mining results. This table is populated only for the life of the session, and is not visible to any other session in the database. The columns you will be most interested in are the Sql_Redo and Sql_Undo columns.

LogMiner Output Uses

The LogMiner output can be used to generate statements to undo logical changes, such as an erroneous delete. While you cannot generate SQL to undo anything that does not go into the redo logs (such as drop or truncate table statements), you can retrieve and undo deletes, inserts, and updates. For statements that are done with the **nologging** option, you will not be able to use LogMiner as a recovery tool. In those cases, flashback query may help.

Replication

Dictionary.com defines replication as "Creating and maintaining a duplicate copy of a database or file system on a different computer, typically a server. The term usually implies the intelligent copying of parts of the source database which have changed since the last replication with the destination." Please note the words "intelligent copying" in the second sentence of the definition. If you do not spend the time up front to plan and design your replication strategy and implementation, you are going to have problems later on.

Replication allows you to have multiple copies of your data in different databases at different sites. You can use the various copies as alternate access sites to improve response times, as backup copies for increased availability, or as reporting database sites. You can access the data locally, and each system can continue to function on its own, even if the other databases in the distributed environment are inaccessible.

Replication Types

Oracle implements basic replication using materialized views. A materialized view stores the results of a query against one or more base tables or views in a separate schema object. Unlike ordinary views, it takes up physical space within the database. This physical implementation is what allows users at the remote sites to continue processing, even if the network connection between the sites is broken.

There are three ways to replicate data in Oracle:

- **Read-only materialized views** There is one master site and one or more remote sites with full or partial copies of data from the master site. The copies (materialized views) are read-only in the remote databases. Data from the master table is refreshed in the materialized views at user-defined intervals.

- **Updatable materialized views** Again, there is one master site and one or more remote sites with full or partial copies of data from the master site. You can insert, update, and delete rows in the materialized views at the remote sites, and the changes are propagated back to the master site. Conflict resolution is defined at the master site.
- **N-way multimaster replication** Each site is considered a master site. Complete copies of all the data are stored on all sites, and the data can be modified at any site and will be propagated back to all the other master sites.

Replication can be done synchronously or asynchronously. When you use synchronous replication, the transaction must be propagated successfully to all sites, or it will be rolled back. Synchronous replication ensures that there will be no conflicts between sites. However, this requires a very stable environment and is best used in environments using read-only materialized views. With asynchronous replication, changes to each site are stored locally and forwarded to the other sites. Conflicts can result, and conflict resolution routines are required for updatable materialized views and multimaster replication.

Replication Uses

If replication is so complicated, why use it? We're going to go back to your bank again, and visit the ATM machine. Each time you access the machine, the bank's applications have to read information from the central database. If you are in New York City, and the central database is in San Francisco, there is going to be some lag time as the data flows across the network. As a customer, you want to complete your transaction as quickly as possible. To help ensure that you get in and get out quickly, the bank may replicate the information to local databases, set up with multimaster replication so that your account contains the same information no matter where you access it. Now you can get your account information quickly.

So replication can be used to improve performance across the network. If you have a database with a mix of online transactions and heavy reporting access, you can replicate the database to another database and use one database for online processing and the other for reporting, improving performance for both applications. Applications with large numbers of users can balance the load against the database and servers by implementing replication.

Data Guard/Standby Database

Data Guard is an extension of the standby database capability first introduced with Oracle 7.3. We've talked about the redo logs in earlier chapters, and described their purpose. The archive log is a copy of the redo log, taken before Oracle marks that redo log for reuse. If you are not running in archivelog mode, Oracle will simply reuse the redo logs in a circular fashion when the prior log is filled. If you run in archivelog mode, Oracle will first copy the redo log (via the ARCH process) to the location you have designated as the archive log destination when it switches to the next redo log. The archive log contains a record of all the committed transactions written to the database. When Oracle has written something to that log, it guarantees that you will be able to rebuild your database if you have a good backup and all the archived logs from the time of the backup forward to the place you want to be. If you think about it, Oracle is creating a perfect ordered list of all the changes made to your database.

At first, that log could only be applied to the database that created it, but from an availability standpoint, the next logical step was to devise a way to apply that log to another copy of that same database. This capability was first introduced in Oracle 7.3 as the *standby database*. A standby database could be created from a copy of the production database, and archive logs generated from the production database could be read and applied to the new copy. Now that list of transactions that Oracle had already taken the trouble to order and condense into a nice manageable format could be applied to a copy of the database. With that, the copy would now be able to stay in sync as a duplicate of the original because all committed DDL and DML would be read from the log and applied to the copy. This type of standby database is now called a *physical standby*. The database is not normally available for use like a normal database except under some special circumstances that we'll cover shortly.

To make the implementation of a standby database easier, the first version of Data Guard was released with Oracle8i. This tool managed the shipment and application of the archive logs and made some additional monitoring and recovery features available to the DBA. In Oracle9i, this capability was significantly improved, and the ability to maintain a standby database using a set of SQL statements derived from the log files (called a *logical standby*) was added. The great benefit here is that the database becomes more than just a high availability option. You can configure this type of database for online processing, allowing reporting activities that can be supported with additional indexes or views.

Architecture/Terminology

That first section had a lot of new terms and concepts! Let's try and summarize some of the more important ones before we talk about the benefits of this capability in a highly available environment.

Physical Standby

A standby database that is being kept current by the application of archive logs from the production (or primary) instance is known as a physical standby. The standby database is a perpetual state of database recovery similar to the process we discussed earlier in this chapter. Data Guard processes are constantly moving each completed archive log to the location of the standby and applying it. Since the database is in recovery, it cannot be accessed by any normal SQL commands. To make the standby database available, Data Guard completes the recovery with the log transactions it has and opens the database. In 9i, a new process has been added to manage the application of redo records on the standby side—the Managed Standby Process (MSP).

Logical Standby

A type of standby database called a logical standby is kept up-to-date using a process very similar to the LogMiner product that we reviewed above. Instead of using the completed archive log, Data Guard reconstructs a SQL statement from the records contained in the log file and applies them to the standby database. This has the advantage over physical standby because the standby database is open during the application of Data Guard's SQL statements. It allows reports and other activities that would read the production database to be done away from other production activity. There is also a new process here that is unique to Data Guard—the Logical Standby Process (LSP).

Other Processes

In addition to the processes directly required to manage the application of logs or SQL statements depending on the choice of standby, some background processes are required regardless of the type of standby. The Remote File Server Process (RFS) receives the redo for the standby database regardless of the type of standby. The Fetch Archive Log Process (FAL) runs on the primary side to make sure the synchronization of logs continues even after a network outage.

Data Guard Broker

The GUI framework that controls the setup and management of a Data Guard implementation is called the Data Guard Broker. The Broker is used to set up the primary and standby databases, monitor the performance of your standby by keeping track of how quickly log records are being applied, and control the switch between the primary and standby databases.

Failover

A switch to the standby from primary database that occurs as a result of a failure on the primary site is called a *failover*. The chief points to note here are that this is usually an unplanned activity, and something must be done to reactivate the primary database.

Switchover

A switch to the standby from primary database in a planned, orderly fashion is called a *switchover*. Of note here is that the roles of primary and standby can be considered reversed. The database is still projected with a standby site.

Data Guard Configuration Options

Data Guard allows you as the DBA to make the trade-off between overall performance of your production database and maximum recoverability. There are four levels of protection that you can configure.

- **Guaranteed protection** In this mode, the production database will shut down if the LGWR can't send redo information, guaranteeing no data loss (divergence) but potentially causing a "perceived" service outage (if the network is unavailable). This is a "no data loss" option.
- **Instant protection** Data Guard again uses the LGWR process to ship the redo information and will not commit the transaction until it has either shipped the redo to at least one standby or confirmed that it cannot do so. Redo transactions that cannot be shipped immediately are moved later when the connection is available. Data loss is possible for this (and any other option) if connectivity does not return before an outage on the primary database
- **Rapid protection** LGWR copies logs to the standby location as soon as possible without checking the connectivity to the standby. This method has the potential to be farther behind in shipping redo logs and could potentially lose more data in the event of an outage.
- **Delayed protection** Logs will be copied to the standby site by the ARCH process instead of LGWR. They will get there as long as the network is available, but the potential exposure for data loss is large, as redo information is not moved to the standby site until the log is processed by the archiver process.

Data Guard Benefits

Of course, the benefits from a high availability standpoint show themselves when you consider separating the copies of the database to different machines. (You don't necessarily have to do this, but this is the most common case in a highly available environment.) Assuming you have the network bandwidth available, your primary and standby databases could be anywhere in the world! The first benefit is obvious: with this functionality in place, Oracle provides a mechanism to keep a separate copy of your database available and up-to-date with the latest transactions. In the event of a disaster that renders your primary copy of the database unusable, you can failover to your standby copy. When all the outstanding logs have been applied, your users can then reconnect and continue processing. The process of moving to a standby database is almost the same as doing a database recovery. All of the outstanding log transactions have to be applied before the database can be opened.

This implies that a failover from primary to standby can be noticeably long to your users, perhaps on the order of half an hour or more, depending on how many logs you have to apply. To control this time somewhat, Oracle has introduced the initialization parameter we talked about earlier, **fast_start_mttr_target**. This parameter is expressed in seconds and gives Oracle some guidance on how long a recovery should take. Oracle then adjusts the behavior of DBWR and LGWR and flushes dirty blocks from the database cache and does additional log checkpoints to modify the recovery time.

Data Guard offers some additional advantages that are not obvious at first glance. We mentioned earlier that the logs have to be transported from the primary site to the standby site and then applied to the standby to keep in sync. Although the logs are shipped to the standby sites as quickly as possible, the amount of time between generation of the log and application to the standby is a parameter controlled by the DBA. As an additional level of protection, you as the DBA may choose to delay the application of those logs against the standby database for a few hours. While the recovery time in the event of a failover may be longer, the standby site is protected from any accidental human or software error.

For example, if a user were to accidentally drop a table in the production database, that table would still exist in the standby database until the logs had been applied. You as the DBA could then go to the standby database and quickly recover the user's lost data, without having to do any other type of recovery. This would be especially easy using the logical standby, as the database would already be open and available for processing.

Data Guard also offers an additional level of uptime by allowing you as a DBA the option to continue production processing without a significant outage for hardware upgrades. If you needed to add resources to a production database server, you could execute a switchover operation. Although this is not seamless, your users can continue processing on the standby node until the upgrade is complete, and then you can switch back to the primary.

Real Application Clusters (RAC)

There has been a lot of coverage of this topic from Oracle, as Real Application Clusters (RAC) and their underlying technology are key features in Oracle9i. RAC is the Oracle product that allows you to connect multiple instances of Oracle to each other and to the same set of shared files on disk. An explanation of the underlying technology is beyond the scope of this chapter, but we'll touch on a couple of the high points as we review the potential benefits of this solution when considering highly available solutions. The most important part of this solution is this: most of the complexity of building a multinode redundant database is handled by Oracle, not you!

RAC requires an underlying set of cluster management software to function. This type of software is available from many different operating system vendors, such as Sun, IBM, and HP/Compaq for Unix/Linux and Microsoft operating systems. In addition, the hardware configuration has to allow the different database servers to access a set of shared disks and a high-speed interconnect mechanism to transport messages between the servers. These different servers are usually called *nodes* in a cluster. These hardware features provide the underlying "plumbing" that allows the nodes to communicate with each other. To stretch the analogy a bit further, when working with plumbing, something needs to hold those pipes together. The cluster software provided by the operating system vendor allows the different nodes in the cluster to communicate and share messages between the operating systems as well as ensure that access to the shared disk is done in an orderly fashion and acts as the pipe fittings.

So a hardware cluster is two or more nodes sharing access to the same disk and messages between each other. What does Oracle add? Oracle RAC uses the plumbing created by the cluster as the vehicle to let the individual instances of the database coordinate with each other. The component that handles this work is called the Distributed Lock Manager (DLM). In past releases, clustered databases from Oracle were not able to take advantage of the memory interconnect for sharing information between the instances of Oracle on the different nodes. The ability to use this interconnect for instance-to-instance communication is called *cache fusion*. It refers to the fact that a changed database block and log information on one instance can be moved to another instance in the cluster through the memory interconnect without first writing the change to disk. This is the innovation that sets RAC apart from previous cluster database products provided by Oracle. It frees applications designers (and DBAs!) from worries about "partitioning" applications and sending certain work to one instance and subset of disks. Oracle manages this instead.

A key benefit of this technology is the scalability that RAC offers to system designers. Instead of large hardware boxes to handle large applications, a cluster of smaller servers can be used. If additional system resources are required due to the growth of the system, additional resources can be added to the cluster to share the workload without changing the application. And in most cases, tuning the application is done in the same fashion as described in Chapter 12.

From the standpoint of high availability, the idea of multiple nodes with Oracle RAC provides some excellent alternatives. Since users can connect to any node to do their work, the failure of any single node does not cause an application outage. Users working on other nodes are almost completely unaffected by the failure of a single node. While users of a node that fails will lose the contents of the transaction they are working on at the time of failure, committed work is still saved to the database. Users can reconnect (or, depending on your application, be automatically reconnected) to surviving nodes and continue processing. This is the architecture of choice for a system with stringent availability requirements, as users can be reconnected and running again within minutes.

Real Application Clusters Guard

Real Application Clusters Guard (RACG) is a specialized application of RAC. In a RACG environment, you still install all the plumbing required (the cluster hardware and software) and RAC. However, instead of running any number of nodes equally, you configure only two nodes. These two nodes are configured in a primary and standby configuration. With this product, users only connect to the primary node for production processing. In the event of a failure, RACG disconnects users from the primary node and reconnects them to the standby node.

The advantage to this solution over a Data Guard solution is the time of recovery. Instead of having to finish the application of archive logs before opening the database, the standby in this case is already open and available. The recovery is similar to that of the failure of a RAC node, in that users connected to the primary are reconnected to the secondary, and the database completes a special type of recovery (called a *crash recovery*) before work can begin. This can have the user reconnected to the database in minutes.

RACG is an additional service available with an Oracle RAC installation that comes complete with scripts that monitor the database and cluster and initiate failover automatically if a problem is detected.

Other Availability Features

In addition to the backup and recovery features, Oracle provides several other availability features.

TAF (Transparent Application Failover)

Transparent Application Failover addresses the problem of user session disconnects when a server in a RAC or RAC Guard cluster fails and the connections to the database are dropped. TAF will reestablish the application-to-database connections automatically and optionally allows the application to resume a **select** statement that was in progress.

Online Redefinition of Objects

Prior to Oracle9i, the only way DBAs could rebuild a table was to restrict access to the table and then do one of two things: they could either create a copy of the table with the new storage parameters, insert into it, drop the original table and rename the new one, and create all the associated indexes; or they could export the table data, drop the table, create an empty version, and import the data (and indexes) back in. Both options are messy, vulnerable to human error, and mean that the table is unavailable for DML operations while the reorganization is going on.

With Oracle9i, reorganization of the table and associated index can be done online while the table is available to users. The Oracle-supplied package

DBMS_REDEFINITION, found in the dbmshord.sql script in the rdbms/admin directory, can be used both to determine whether a table can be reorganized and to accomplish the reorganization if it can.

Here are the steps to reorganize a table using the DBMS_REDEFINITION package:

1. Determine if the table can be reorganized using the procedure DBMS_REDEFINITION.CAN_REDEF_TABLE.
2. Create an empty, interim table in the form you want the table to look like.
3. Start the redefinition using the procedure DBMS_REDEFINITION.START_REDEF_TABLE. This moves the data from the original table to the interim table, and Oracle will begin to track all changes made to the original table until the redefinition is completed.
4. Create all triggers, indexes, constraints, and grants on the interim table.
5. Finish the redefinition using the procedure DBMS_REDEFINITION.FINISH_REDEF_TABLE. This will sync up the two tables and complete the redefinition. Once you have run this procedure, you can drop the interim table.

In addition to online table redefinitions, you can also rebuild indexes online using the **alter index <indexname> rebuild online** command. You can rebuild the index with the existing storage parameters, or you can specify new ones as part of the command.

For details on rebuilding and reorganizing objects online, consult the Oracle9i documentation set.

Resumable Space Allocation

Have you ever had a large insert fail, when it was almost done, because you had run out of space in the tablespace? It's an incredibly frustrating experience and, prior to Oracle9i, one you had to suffer through without any way to recover the work you had nearly finished.

Now you can use resumable space allocation for queries, DML statements, export and import, and certain DDL statements. It will also work with dictionary-managed tablespaces, but the DDL statements will not be resumable unless the problem occurs in a locally managed tablespace. The correctable error conditions are "out of space in the tablespace," "maximum extents on the segment reached," or "space quota exceeded." If resumable space allocation has been enabled, the DBA can correct the problem, and the transaction (called a *resumable statement*) will automatically continue.

In order to use this feature, the DBA must have granted the user the RESUMABLE system privilege, and the session must have invoked resumable space allocation with the **alter session enable resumable** command.

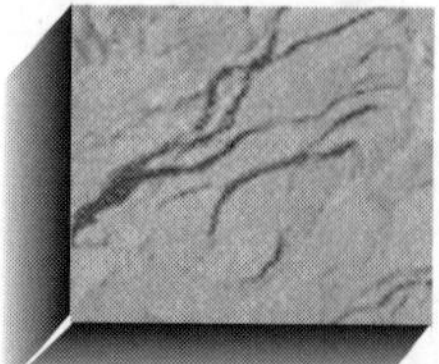

PART IV

Tuning Your World

CHAPTER 12

Server Performance

NOTE
The authors of this book owe a great deal of thanks to Anjo Kolk for the discussion of wait events tuning methods.

Years ago, one of the authors was involved in a theater group that put on four plays or musicals a year. The group was made up of volunteers who got together once or twice a week and rehearsed. When a new play was chosen and the group began to practice, things were pretty rough. The players didn't know their lines or cues, and they didn't know where to stand or where they were supposed to walk to, and so on. Over time, with lots of rehearsals, the performance became very polished, and on opening night, the group generally put on a pretty professional production within the appropriate time constraints. Well, okay, no one in the audience ever threw rotten tomatoes, so we guess the productions were a success.

Another of the authors was into motorcycle riding and racing. He spent a great deal of time and money modifying his hardware to produce motorcycles that ran just a fraction of a second faster than the competitors' bikes.

What do the people who participated in these two hobbies have in common? Well, they both dealt with improving performance. In the first example, members of the theater group worked steadily to improve the way they did things by keeping track of how smoothly their production was going. There was always room for improvement, and they were continuously trying to enhance their performance—trying to say their lines more smoothly, have their props in the correct places in a timely manner, and so on. They proactively took steps to make their product better each time they rehearsed. The motorcyclist was more reactive. During the course of each race, if he was winning, he just kept going and did not pay much attention to how the bike was running. However, if he was behind, he would be constantly making mental notes to himself. As soon as that particular race was over, he'd make adjustments to the bike that he hoped would give him that extra edge he needed to succeed—meet his performance requirements. He might even try to make minor adjustments during the race to help improve his position. In other words, the biker reacted to how the bike performed and either made changes or left the bike alone based on how the bike was running in each race.

Like the member of the theater group, your goal in performance management should be to work most of the time as a proactive DBA—taking measurements and making adjustments to help you tune your database effectively. However, there will be times when you will not be able to avoid having to react to a situation—becoming a reactive DBA. This chapter is intended to help you be as proactive as possible in the performance tuning arena while supplying the tools you need to react effectively to emergency situations.

Understanding Performance Management

Invariably, as a DBA you will at some point be faced with questions about the performance of your system. If you're lucky, the questions posed to you will be detailed and will give you a good basis for your investigation! For example, a user may come to you and say, "Yesterday, I ran my report and it took 4 minutes. Today, I ran my report and it took 20 minutes. What's going on?" Sometimes the questions are a little less specific. In fact, they could be as generic as "Why is the system so slow?" Inevitably, no matter how specific the question is, the next question is a constant: "What are you going to do to make it faster?" Using questions is a great approach to guiding you through performance tuning. The questions help you get a clear understanding of the problems your users are facing and give you objectives to fulfill. Of course, if you can figure out the answers before the questions are ever asked, you will be well ahead of the game.

In this chapter, you'll see the topic of performance tuning from several angles. First, we'll define what we mean by performance tuning and discuss some steps to prepare you and your users to answer the questions listed above—before they are asked. In case you have been forced to turn to this chapter because you already have a performance problem and you want some tips on how to fix it, we'll provide some questions that will help you isolate the problem. We'll finish with a discussion of commonly encountered performance problems and some tips for detecting and correcting them.

A common example will be used to illustrate some of the points we want to make in this chapter. So, for now, you are the brand-new Oracle DBA of the XYZ Company. Congratulations on your new job! XYZ has been producing widgets for years, with many aspects of production and distribution controlled by legacy code. (You can translate *legacy code* to mean that the software is old and does not perform well and should have been rewritten years ago.) XYZ has decided to migrate to a new application that will use Oracle as its engine. The new code will tie the manufacturing and product distribution directly to the reporting and planning applications. Your job is to manage the new Oracle database. Although there are many areas to consider in a scenario such as this, we will focus on the performance tuning aspects in this chapter. Good luck, and don't panic!

Although tuning a system is still considered more of an art than a science, our goal is to give you a systematic approach to use throughout the database and software development life cycle. This approach will help to minimize the effect of performance issues in your shop and provide some strategies for handling performance issues as they develop later, during day-to-day activities. Most importantly, a solid process that covers the fundamentals will improve your efficiency, thereby reducing your stress level when dealing with tuning issues. Let's take a look at some concepts that will be used often in this chapter.

The 80/20 Rule

In general, the suggestions here will follow a principle well known to you in everyday life. The 80/20 rule, conceived by Vilfredo Pareto, will be used as the basis for your approach to tuning a database. The 80/20 rule says that a minority of causes, inputs, or efforts usually produces a majority of the results, outputs, or rewards. In other words, you want to look for the things that take the least amount of effort but achieve significant tuning results.

If you are starting out with the development of a brand-new system, you can achieve the 80/20 rule by doing as much work as possible up front—in the design phase. By designing the application and database effectively from the start, much of the database performance will already be enhanced.

You must define and set realistic expectations between your management and your developers and users. There are times when expectation setting is the most effective performance tuning tool. If the absolutely fastest startup time your users can ever obtain is a three-second response time, then setting their expectation to the fact that they will have a three-second startup time is the way to go. If your management is not willing or able to enhance a system with enough resources to support the user requirements effectively, setting expectations may be your only real approach.

Just now, we mentioned response time as the amount of time that it might take for an application to be loaded into memory and an initial screen to be displayed for user interaction. In reality, the majority of your tuning efforts will be to try to help improve the response time of one area of the database or another. In the next sections, we'll take a closer look at what the term *response time* means and the actions you can take to improve it.

What Is Response Time?

In general terms, response time can be described by the following formula:

Response Time = Service (or Work) Time + Wait Time

Let's see if we can break this formula down into meaningful terms. By service (or work) time, we mean the amount of time it takes the database to respond to a request or perform an actual amount of work. By wait time, we mean the amount of time the user or process is waiting for an action or amount of work to be completed. Thus, if either service time or wait time is high, the total response time will be affected.

Okay, so now that you know the formula for computing response time, how do you get the figures you need to see your database's response time? By using the Oracle database dynamic views, you can calculate the total service time and the total wait time within the Oracle database. We'll show you exactly how to determine your database's response time during our discussion of reactive performance tuning later in this chapter. The response time that you determine will always be less than or equal to the actual response time that the end user will see. The difference is due to external forces—delays in other layers of the system, such as the network or other components or tiers in the application. While you should not ignore the other components of your system, you can begin your tuning efforts within your database and first make sure you eliminate any problems there.

You must realize that when you are asked to improve the response time, you are really being asked to tune a system. The system consists of all the components between the users and the database. These components include, but are in no way limited to

- The network
- The client (PC or browser)
- Any number of middle-tier servers
- The operating systems for the database server and any of their middle tiers

All of these pieces work together to satisfy a request to the database. Obviously, we are not going to cover all of these areas here, but it is important to be aware of these other considerations when tuning. Although our focus is primarily on the database server, you must realize that the best tuning gains can sometimes come from other areas.

Where's the Problem?

Even when focusing strictly on the database component, most performance issues do not originate directly from the database server, so the question you need to ask yourself is "Where *is* the problem?"

In reality, many performance problems originate from the application because of design issues or coding problems. Thus, most performance improvements can be achieved by making changes in the application. Given this reality, why is the main focus usually on the database? Generally, the database is a victim of its own capabilities. Administrators and users tend to focus on the database because it supplies easy access to a wealth of statistics on its performance. In addition, application tuning may not be simple or straightforward. Applications are designed around business rules and processes. It is sometimes impossible, or extremely difficult, to find algorithms that match both the business need and optimal performance on the database. However, information from the database can be used to pinpoint these types of issues.

Another reason for turning to the database instead of the application code for answers may relate more to cost than anything else. Finding out that a poorly designed application has already been implemented, either internally by a project team or externally through consultants, is not a discovery that most organizations will happily accept. Necessary changes will incur greater costs that will not be welcomed by the manager whose budget is going to be impacted.

If management is resistant to forcing application changes, what can you do? Here's where expectation setting comes in (again). Make sure your management realizes that you can do only so much to improve database performance when poor application design is at fault.

There are some areas in which you can try to improve performance, and we'll talk about them next.

Response Time vs. Throughput

When discussing performance and tuning problems, remember that the primary goal can be either one of the following (or both): improve response time, or improve throughput. We've already talked a bit about response time but haven't, as yet, mentioned throughput. *Throughput* is the number of transactions being processed within a given amount of time.

For example, if you have a pipe with a one-half inch diameter into which you are putting marbles (and, please, don't ask us why you might want to put marbles into a pipe), you might be able to get 12 marbles into the pipe. If, however, you have a pipe with a one and one-half inch diameter, you might be able to put 24 or more marbles into it. Your throughput has increased because you've increased the capacity of your pipe.

Okay. With this definition of throughput in mind, let's look at the two goals mentioned above.

Improving Response Times

Improving response times normally means you can either improve the service time or the wait time. Usually the improvement is driven by the need to have some individual transactions finish faster. The obvious way to begin to improve response time is by tuning the component with the largest time.

For example, if the service time (the time spent actually running on the CPU) is 20 percent of the total response time, then the remaining 80 percent of the response time must be due to some kind of delay in processing or wait time. (Total response time = 20 percent work time + 80 percent wait time.) If you spend all your efforts tuning elements that affect only the amount of CPU used by the transaction, you will not make much of a difference in the transaction's overall response time! Even if you reduce the amount of work done in this transaction by 50 percent, that would only translate to a 10 percent reduction in the overall response time (because you are only tuning 20 percent of the overall equation). However, if you focus your efforts on the delay time, which is a larger component of the response time in our example, the same 50 percent improvement would get you a 40 percent increase in response time and make your users that much happier.

Improving Throughput

Improving throughput can be a bit more complicated. Throughput improvement is usually driven by the need to complete more transactions in the same time frame and with the same system resources (like trying to stuff more marbles into that pipe without increasing the diameter). Looking at a database-oriented problem, if an application is running out of available CPU time on the system, you need to reduce the service time. A simple but expensive way to correct the problem would be to add more or faster components, for example, more disks or more or faster CPUs. Another possibility would be to have each batch process or user process do more work during each CPU cycle. You could achieve this goal by reducing the wait time of the process, thus improving the overall response time. By reducing the wait time and increasing the amount of work performed during each CPU cycle, each process will complete each transaction quicker. Over time, more transactions can actually be done without changing the available resource.

Determining the Performance Benefit

Whether you tackle response time or throughput, or both, you must identify the percentage of performance improvement desired. As an example, a user may require a 30 percent response time or throughput improvement. Your normal reaction when faced with the requirement is to look for any ratios that seem to be "bad." Trying to improve these so-called bad ratios without considering how much the change will contribute to the overall performance of the system will usually fail to improve things noticeably.

Although rewriting an application or purchasing hardware may be expensive, determining the performance benefit before weighing the cost is also important. So how can you use the concepts we've just discussed in order to proactively avoid performance problems? To understand your options, you must first understand the business or corporate objectives that your database supports. In the next section, you'll learn more about determining and supporting your corporation's objectives.

Understanding the Critical Business Transactions

We've already mentioned several areas in which you may need to set both management's and users' expectations about how the database or applications will perform. We've also mentioned throughput as the number of transactions completed over a specific amount of time. We've talked about some of the factors that influence both response time and throughput.

For you to be able to set realistic tuning goals, you must understand the composition of your critical business transactions, the underlying objectives of your company, and who the appropriate people to define the issues and objectives are.

Looking at Transactions

In our discussion of throughput, we've been a bit remiss about what we mean by a transaction. So, here goes. A *transaction* is defined in Oracle terms as the work done between two commit statements. This definition is a little narrow for our discussion. In our case, a transaction is any unit of work that is required as a part of the application. This could be as simple as a single SQL statement, or any series of statements, or the generation of a complete report. In fact, for the discussion here, any unit of work that needs to be executed against the database can be thought of as a transaction.

Busy databases will have millions of transactions executed against them during the course of a workday. The trick is to determine which of those transactions need to be completed within a certain period of time and which of them, if not completed in time, will have an impact on the business. Let's say your boss requests a report at XYZ, and the report runs a few minutes longer than it takes him to get a cup of coffee. He complains about the database being slow. Is this situation as critical as the shipping department not being able to fill orders and ship product on time? While both situations may be critical to your career as a DBA, the inability to ship a product is usually going to have a more lasting impact on your (and your company's) future than your boss having to wait a few seconds more for his report. Of course, if the report that your boss is waiting for is going to determine your company's entire future existence, the report may take precedence.

So we will define a *critical business transaction* as a consistent unit of work that when executed against the database, must be completed in a specific period of time under the expected workload. Further, there is some significant negative consequence or impact if the transaction does not complete in the specified time. These transactions and their day-to-day performance will become your yardstick for measuring the health of your system.

Tongue-in-cheek comments about bosses aside, defining the transactions that need to complete in a specific window should be the first step in tuning. As Stephen Covey states in his book *7 Habits of Highly Effective People*, one of the things we need to do is "Begin with the end in mind." In your case, that means you need to understand which transaction's performance is most important to your users. In addition, you need to set some goals with your users in terms of how fast they need the system to perform. Beware the answer, "As fast as it can!" That answer is an open-ended invitation to tune a database forever.

By understanding what criteria make your business successful, you can work with your users to understand and set a standard of performance for the database. Once you have achieved that performance, you can use those transactions as a benchmark to gauge the performance of your system over time.

The following sample interview dialogue should provide some guidance on how to isolate the critical business transactions in your system. We'll refer back to them when we look further at XYZ's new manufacturing system.

Examining the Application Flow

Let's return to your job at the XYZ Company. Yes, it's time to get back to work! The current legacy system is used on the manufacturing floor to keep track of the amount of raw material coming into the plant and the total number of widgets created. A different function in the system captures the customer's order and is used in the creation of a packing list and shipping labels. Purchasing uses the data from the order entry component to determine when they should reorder needed material to keep the widget manufacturing line running with minimal inventory in-house. Accounting uses the order data to generate sales reports and projections. Both departments use the same reports on a daily and weekly basis, with some additional reports run monthly, quarterly, and at the end of the year.

The new system will have some additional features. An analysis component for the planning and forecasting department to develop what-if scenarios is being included. The reports from the new component will be run on an as-needed basis, using queries designed by the users. The new system will now also keep track of the intermediate products that go into the manufacture of a widget and track those as separate inventory items. Figure 12-1 shows the various departments that depend on the database, with the legacy system's tasks identified by the letter *L*. The new system area is shown in Figure 12-1 with a designation of *N*.

Since the majority of the work in this system is being done in interactive, short processes, you would classify this as an online transaction processing (OLTP) system with some additional reporting components. From the above description, you can determine some transactions that are a part of this application, as follows:

- **Order entry** Completion of an order in the system.
- **Inventory management** Entry of raw inventory and completed products into the database. In the new system you have the added requirement of tracking a widget during its assembly process.
- **Shipping** Creation of a packing and shipping list from a completed order.
- **Analysis** Reports are run by the purchasing and sales departments, usually overnight in a specific batch window. In the new system, the planning department will need to run its own reports against the data.

Each of these areas contains critical business transactions.

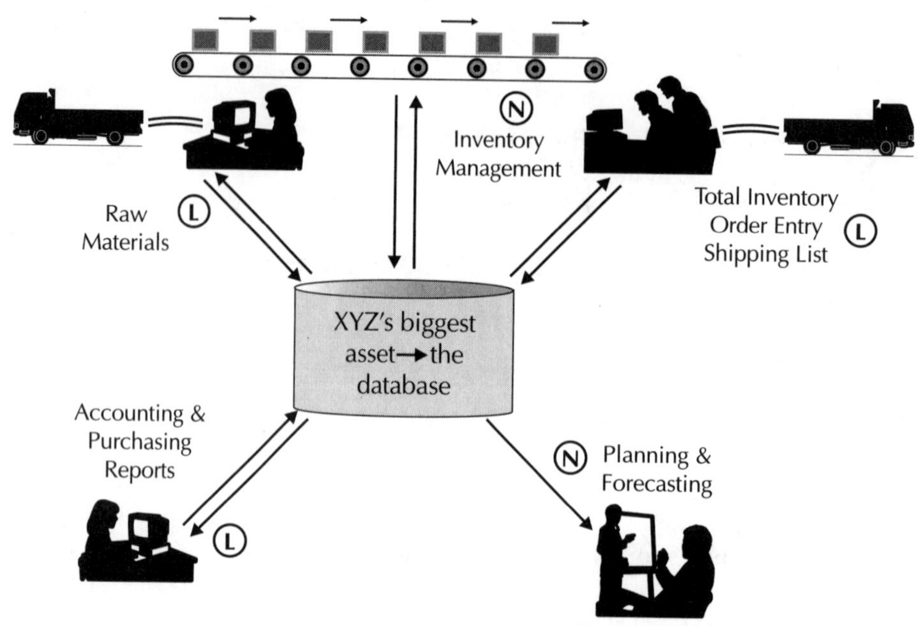

FIGURE 12-1. *Various departments of the XYZ Company. Transactions marked with an Ⓛ are from the legacy system, and new transactions are marked with an Ⓝ .*

Identifying Expected Response Times

The next step in the process of identifying the critical business transactions in the system is to determine the expected time in which these transactions should complete and the consequences if these transactions do not complete in the given amount of time. In an ideal world, this information will be available to you from design specifications or knowledge of the system, or perhaps even from your intuition. Since you live in the "real" world, it is more likely that you will have to go and find this information yourself! Surprisingly and unfortunately, the information you are trying to obtain can be difficult to get. At this point, your users become one of your most valuable resources.

For any system, old or new, the users will be able to provide you with a wealth of information on what areas or applications they perceive are running slowly. More to the point, they will be able to tell you about the transactions they do in the current system on a daily basis. This information will give you insights into where to focus your efforts. Fortunately, you have some other data available that will be very valuable to you as well.

Back at your job at XYZ, assuming things were running smoothly in the current application and system performance is acceptable, you have the baseline for the performance of the new system—at least for those functions that are currently implemented. For new systems and additions to existing systems, determining the baseline time will take you back to negotiating with the users.

In our example, the time it takes to enter an order into the system and the time it takes to create a shipping and packing list are critical transactions that you have been doing all along. The transactions required to create the documents must run fast enough to ensure they are not a bottleneck in the shipping process. You can determine a baseline value by examining the existing system.

An Online Transaction Processing Situation

You can also see that in the manufacturing environment, the new requirement of checking partially completed widgets in and out of inventory during the assembly process is a transaction that will occur many times throughout the day. This transaction will have to complete fast enough to ensure that no delays in the assembly process occur. From talking to the users and studying the systems, you can determine something about the transactions themselves. All of these transactions will be relatively short inserts or updates to the database and will be done interactively. As we mentioned earlier, these types of transactions describe an OLTP system.

The other transactions mentioned here could have an impact on the business as well. Cataloging the inventory used in the manufacturing process must be done in a timely fashion. However, this process will most likely not be done online (interactively) as part of the day-to-day work. You can verify this at XYZ with your users. Keep in mind that your realization that the cataloging of inventory is not an interactive process does not give you license to let the transaction run slowly, but it probably is not the first place to concentrate your tuning efforts. If this form of transaction processing runs so slowly that it starts to infringe on the time you need for backups or maintenance, you may want to start tuning here.

Another consideration is the human factor. At XYZ, users at terminals enter the inventory manually. You can see another facet of setting goals for tuning based on the users' interaction with the application. In reality, the inventory data entry may not require any more responsiveness than is required to keep the user productive. However, a user who sits for more than a few seconds waiting to perform a repetitive task is bound to be dissatisfied with the performance of the system, even if the responsiveness is meeting the business need. Keep the user's idle time in mind, since we'll discuss this more in the section "Defining a Service-Level Agreement" later in this chapter.

A Batch Processing Situation

The existing sales and marketing department reports will most likely not be time critical. You will, of course, need to verify this supposition with the users. In your system, the sales and marketing reports are static reports that are run the same way each month. The only change in each month's run is the value for each input variable. The reports are run overnight and away from the peak usage time of the system. Thus, you gain some advantages in your efforts to tune them. The reports can be written and tuned with supporting indexes and hints, as we will discuss in Chapter 13. The response time for running these reports is bounded only by the window of time it takes to run the reports in a batch mode. The only restriction you face is ensuring that the report runs do not interfere with any scheduled maintenance window. In other words, you must ensure that the reports are completed before you begin your nightly database maintenance tasks. At this point, your system behaves more like a decision support system, where you would be optimizing more for the long-running transactions.

Potentially Unbounded Queries

The planning department requirement is another matter entirely. Their expectation to allow their users to run ad hoc queries during the day can have serious consequences for the performance of the system. Because the queries will be undefined and, therefore, not tunable, you cannot predict their effect on the system. Unfortunately, this is another all-too-common problem when developing systems. You may not have enough data to determine the impact of a requirement on a new system or a design change on an existing system.

The inability to predetermine the effect of some kinds of queries on your system is one of the strongest arguments you can use for building a test system with live data, as close to the production data and production load as possible. As a DBA responsible for the performance of your system, you will want to make sure that time to test the impacts of various forms of queries is built into the development cycle of your project. If you can't build performance testing into the development cycle, you won't be able to accurately confirm that the system will meet its performance and design targets. This really is an example of the old adage "you can pay me now or pay me later." If you are not given the opportunity to test and verify the system up front, you may face major performance problems later. Some of these problems could be inherent in the system design and will not be easily corrected once the system "goes live."

Defining a Service-Level Agreement

In Chapter 11, we defined a *service-level agreement* in terms of availability. Earlier in this chapter, we talked about users' idle time and again mentioned the term. In our current context, we are talking in terms of performance rather than availability.

A service-level agreement is a set of expectations upon which you and your users agree regarding the performance of the system. The agreement should be for specific transactions in your system and should specify exactly how you are going to measure the result set. We have talked about setting expectations with your users on system performance in concrete terms. With the use of service-level agreements, you really are trying to move from the art of performance to a definable science.

Asking questions like "What are the expected transaction rates and completion rates for the critical business transactions on this system?" and "How do you measure performance?" (in terms the users can understand) not only gives you the starting point to make agreements with your users on how the system should perform, but also gives you concrete objectives to work toward when tuning.

Setting Up Measurement Generation

How the result set is measured is less important than agreeing on a way to implement the measurement process. One suggestion for measuring the performance of transactions that do not alter the data is to set up transactions in a script and execute that script at various times of the day during all kinds of system load. Collect statistics just before you start to run the script and just after the run so you can gauge the impact of the run on your system. You can then compare the results of each run and begin to get a feel for how your system is responding during specific periods of time and over time. The collection of measurement data will allow you to understand whether the system is meeting the users' performance expectations. Additionally, you can examine the statistical data for trends in performance.

For example, a trend toward longer response times could be correlated to an increase in the number of users on the system, allowing you to forecast when the system will no longer be able to meet the current expectations. The detailed statistics you collect can help you to justify to your management the building of a maintenance window for database reorganizations or table rebuilds. You can also use the statistics to predict when your well-tuned system will no longer be able to meet user requirements, justifying the purchase of additional hardware, network equipment, and so on.

Additionally, you can see sudden changes in performance (ideally, they will be positive ones due to your activities!). If the change is negative and the reason is unknown, the data approach will let you pinpoint a smaller range of time to examine the system and find the answer to the question "What changed?"

Data can be measured using the same type of methodology by having the users record the transaction completion times during their normal workday. Although having your users record their processing times is a little less automated and more prone to errors, this gets users involved in the process of performance tuning, which may help make them allies instead of adversaries.

One of the authors was receiving complaints from users that the system seemed to slow down noticeably during the day. She had the users write down the times during the day when they felt the system slowed down noticeably, and from their reports, she determined that a performance problem was occurring at about the same time every day. Investigation showed that a batch job was being run about that time daily. The batch job was rescheduled to run two hours later in the day (during lunchtime, when most of the data entry people were away from their terminals), and the performance improvement and the users' perception of the improved performance was dramatic.

Overall, the statistical data that you gather becomes the yardstick for measuring the performance of your system. One advantage of using this method is that you and your users have agreed on what you are measuring and what units you are using to do the measurements.

The following questions provide some guidance in constructing a service-level agreement if one does not exist:

- How many transactions should be completed per minute?
- How many users should be connected to the system at peak time?
- How many concurrent processes should be running at peak time?
- What times of day are considered for online usage only?
- What is the batch processing window?
- What is the expected response time for an online process?
- How much system resource should be available during peak time? Define the margin of error.

The Initial Steps Summarized

Let's look back on our XYZ example. In the first stage of performance analysis, before the system goes live, you have taken the time to meet with your users and understand the type of system and the transactions that will be most prevalent. You understand that your system is a mix of OLTP and decision support systems (DSS), with some ad hoc queries thrown in. You've discussed the most common transactions that will be run on the system and identified them as the critical business transactions (CBTs). After identifying the CBTs, you were able to work with your users and, for most of those transactions, identify how long each transaction should take and when it will normally be run. You were not really able to do this for your new ad hoc planning department transaction. You were also able to define the day-to-day workload characteristics of the system and define your maintenance and availability windows. Based on the CBT and the workload definition, you worked with the users to build a test system with representative data and test the response time. Also, you set up your test transactions in a script that will allow you to repeat the exact transactions over and over and to monitor the response time of the CBTs over time. This allows you to stop any trends in reduced response time before they become problems. You've really done a great job!

Diagnosing a Problem

Now that we have talked about the "right" way to design and build for performance, let's talk about the way it really happens! More often than not, the first time you are introduced to performance tuning is when there is a problem and the users are looking to you for help. In Chapter 13, we'll talk about the tuning of specific SQL statements for better performance. Here, we will look at the overall system and give you some steps to use in determining where your performance problem may be located. After that, we will discuss isolating a problem in the database using some of the Oracle V$ tables (explained more fully in Chapter 6).

Quick Hits: How to Spend the First Five Minutes

Let's return to your job as the DBA at XYZ. Let's assume for the moment that you came into the job well into the development cycle and were not able to set up any proactive measures in advance. Whether you put those measures in place or not, at some point, you will get a call from your user community telling you that the database is "slow." What you do in the first few minutes after that phone call will determine how much work (and stress) you will have to deal with to resolve the complaint. Yes, we're now going to talk about reactive performance tuning.

Talking to the Users

The first thing you need to do is define the problem clearly with the users. Defining the problem clearly, early in the process is a large step forward in finding the solution, much in the same way that we discussed using service-level agreements and critical business transactions during the proactive tuning process. Done correctly, your talk with the users will provide both of you a clear understanding of the goal to be accomplished, which helps both sides to stay focused and understand how to prioritize the steps that must be taken to solve the problem. You'll be asking questions that should provide some clues about which parts of your overall system are good candidates to investigate further. For this discussion, we'll assume that more than one user is reporting a problem.

When defining the problem, get the users to state the problem clearly. Ask them for specifics. First, get them to tell you what they mean by slow and what they are comparing that against. How are they measuring the response time? What were they running at the time? How were they running it? You need to move users from telling you about generic slowness in their workstations to a specific application (perhaps even a specific transaction) that is running slowly. Often, a generic complaint about slow response time can be refined to something more specific. If it can't, that tells you something as well. We'll discuss the implications of a vague complaint that can't be refined as we go.

Your discussion with the users should be kept open ended, but the desired outcome is to guide the users to an explanation of the specific issues. Your conversation might also start to provide clues to the location of the bottleneck that is causing the problem. For example, the users may feel that the entire system is slow or slower than it has been. This information is helpful because it may indicate that the problem is one that affects all transactions, such as a problem with the client interface or the network. Also, understanding the characteristics of the beginnings of the problem can provide some information. If the onset of the problem has been gradual, then either data fragmentation issues or an increase in system usage could cause the slowdown over time. A more sudden onset points to a specific environmental change such as a system upgrade or version change. The rate that the problem occurs can also provide some clues as to the true cause of the problem. A problem that occurs intermittently can perhaps be related to another environmental factor that changes with the same frequency. Often, the initial conversation alone is enough for you to determine exactly where the problem is occurring and to proceed directly to tuning.

At this point, users may present you with multiple problems, all of which are extremely urgent in their eyes. If this is the case, you must work with them to define which issue is the most critical and prioritize the work on that basis. Remember, all of the problems are important, but some are more important than others. Helping users to understand and build that prioritized list and then solving their problems in a systematic manner will give your users confidence that you are taking steps to get them back on track in a logical, well thought out manner and that you are taking their complaints seriously. Also, as you solve each problem on the list, your users will be able to share in that sense of accomplishment with you!

Asking the Right Questions

In this section, we'll look at a collection of questions you can use to help isolate the problem that is slowing down your system. For each problem presented to you, ask the questions given here. Understanding the environmental factors (time of occurrence, number of users affected) should also give more indications of the nature of the problem. But these questions will usually provide enough information to develop a hypothesis and possible cause, giving you some thoughts on where to start tuning.

What, specifically, is underperforming?

We touched on this a bit earlier, but by way of further explanation, this is where you need to understand exactly what the users were doing at the time performance degraded. What transaction were they running? What specific variables did they enter (if any)? At what time did the system start running slowly? Did they run the application/transaction any differently than they usually do? If so, what did they do differently?

This discussion alone may be enough to get users thinking about what is different now from what they have done in the past. Capturing this information now will be helpful later, when you need to test and see if you have corrected the problem.

What is the nature of the problem?

What is the system doing that it shouldn't be doing? What isn't the system doing that it should be doing? Here, you are trying to isolate the problem definition based on examining the expectation of performance, both positive and negative.

Is the problem occurring with specific users or at specific locations? (If yes, where is or isn't the problem occurring?)

These questions will help you determine whether physical location is a component of the problem. For example, you might find out that all the users in a particular remote site are having a sudden performance slowdown, but users in other remote sites or locally are not experiencing any problems. This not only defines the problem nicely, but also gives you good reason to believe that the problem is outside of the application (and database) entirely. This might also point you to a specific user who is having a problem. A user whose permissions and synonyms are set up incorrectly might be pointing to the wrong version of the data.

Can the problem be isolated to a specific component?

This question relates to the previous question. You are trying to determine whether a distinction can be drawn between a place where the problem is occurring and a place where it is not. One example of isolating the specific component that is a problem would be testing clients on a different part of the network or eliminating the network entirely. If the performance problem still occurs after running the application directly connected to the server, then you have eliminated the network as a possible suspect. Conversely, if the problem is reduced or eliminated when you run the application directly on the server, you have narrowed down your culprit. At this point, you as the DBA may need to be creative in thinking about other places or ways that you can run the application.

Are any third-party tools causing a load on the servers or network?

By the time you ask this question, you are beginning to look outside of your system to see if some other application's load has changed. This is not the question you would expect users to answer when you are doing your initial assessment. This question is one for you to file away in the back of your mind if the other questions do not produce any good starting points.

Are specific transactions slow? Are those transactions slow when they are run in an isolated environment?

Here, you are trying to isolate the application code as a potential cause for the problem. If users can point to a specific transaction as the problem and the transaction is always slow, regardless of the system load at the time of execution, then you may have found your culprit and can begin the exercise of tuning the SQL. You will need to make sure that when you are trying to isolate the transaction, you take into account any triggers or related events that might occur during the execution of a front-end process. If you have a SQL statement that responds quickly when run from SQL*Plus but runs slowly from inside the application, you will need to see if there are any triggers or functions that are being run as a result of the SQL. An underlying trigger or function may be slowing the process down.

Has this problem always occurred? If not, when did it start? Are there any correlated events?

Here, you need to make a distinction between *day-one* deviations and deviations over time. A day-one deviation is one that occurred the first time the transaction was executed. In other words, the process is slow and has always been slow! Before you begin any type of tuning, this is a time when examining the users' expectations is worthwhile. Assuming the expectations are realistic, you can then begin tuning. There is no magic formula for determining "realistic" expectations, nor are there any good general guidelines. Each system hardware configuration and application design will be different and will produce different results.

If a problem occurs after the system was performing in an acceptable manner, examining the time between when performance was acceptable and when it became unacceptable should help pinpoint some event that is related to the change. At least you will have narrowed down the search.

Does the problem occur consistently?

Problems that can be consistently reproduced are less likely to be related to some external event, while problems that do not occur consistently may be related to an external event.

If the problem is intermittent, is there a pattern?

Again, you are trying to establish some connection to another cause outside of the specific transaction that seems to be causing the problem.

Is the rate of the problem getting better, worse, or staying consistent?

This question will help isolate whether transaction volume or overall system load is influencing the problem. If the onset of the problem was gradual and measurements over time show that the problem is getting worse, you can try to map the deterioration to an increase in users or a need to do some maintenance on some objects that may have grown or become disorganized over time.

How many users or locations are affected?

Here, you are trying to draw some distinctions between where the problem is occurring and where it is not occurring. You might determine from this question that only a single user is affected (perhaps a workstation problem). You may find that a group of users are affected—perhaps an index was dropped on a table that is used by all sales department users in their reports; or all the users on the second floor are affected, but everything else is fine, indicating a potential network problem. Or you might find that all users are affected, and you will begin the search for the problem directly with a global component like the database itself.

How much functionality is affected?

This is another question that will help users to isolate whether a specific transaction is the problem. Here, if users tell you all the transactions are running slowly in the sales application, you might ask them to run something in the marketing application, if possible, to see if that application area is slow as well.

Evaluating the Answers for the XYZ Company

Well, back to work you go. In your conversations with the users reporting slow response time at XYZ, you found that all functions related to the new order entry, inventory, and shipping system were slow at points throughout the business day. You verified that all users were affected (no difference between sites on the LAN or WAN, most likely ruling out the network as a bottleneck).

You found that all transactions were slow at these times and that no specific transaction was involved. With this information, you ruled out any specific SQL as the cause and increased your suspicion that the problem is systemic in nature. The facts you have gathered give you a reason to check with the system administrators to see if there have been any changes on the system.

When you asked about the rate of the problem, you found out that it was intermittent and inconsistent. Also, the problem just started happening "a few days ago." An event that is happening outside of the users' application but still in the overall system may be the offender. You now have a time frame to narrow down your investigation of any changes or errors.

You have spoken to the users about how quickly the transactions should complete. Since you did not get the chance to build your baseline of critical business transactions (as we discussed in the proactive sections earlier in this chapter) and the slowdown is occurring in varying transactions, you do not have a baseline of performance to work toward. You could use this opportunity to ask the users to focus on a few transactions and record the times for the transactions when performance is good and bad. This gives you a chance to work with the users to determine critical business transactions. Gathering data about when the performance is bad will also give you information on the rate of the problem.

You tried to discuss the ordering of transactions to deal with first (prioritizing), but could not because of the intermittent nature of the problems and the transactions affected.

Where to Look First: Tuning Within the Database Server

You have now gone through the set of questions to try and isolate a possible cause. You have put in a call to the system administrator to see if there were any system changes that could have impacted performance. Now, you are ready to begin your investigation into the database. You will be investigating the database at the system level, although these techniques apply to the session level, too. Where appropriate, we will show you the session-level statements as well. How do you know whether to look at the system or session level?

Looking at the System/Instance Level

If sessions on your system log on or off the database frequently, you will want to perform your investigation at the instance or system level. You will obtain a general overview of what could be wrong with the instance. Use the V$SYSSTAT and V$SYSTEM_EVENT views, discussed briefly in Chapter 6, to look into what is occurring over the entire database.

Looking at the Session Level

If sessions stay connected to the database over a long period of time, looking at the session level is more beneficial. You will be able to perform direct measurement of response times by looking at the session level. Use the V$SESSTAT and V$SESSION_EVENT views, discussed briefly in Chapter 6, to drilldown into the activities of each user.

Setting the initialization Parameter timed_statistics

To properly analyze the performance within Oracle, you will want to set the initialization parameter **timed_statistics** to TRUE. On most platforms, this feature introduces a small (maximum of 2–3 percent) impact on performance, but returns the much greater benefit of more detailed statistics to use when diagnosing performance bottlenecks. Many sources of tuning information recommend disabling **timed_statistics** due to perceived overhead (which was larger on some older operating systems), but tuning a system without this information becomes an almost impossible task. Note that, as of Oracle7.3, you can dynamically change the setting of **timed_statistics** while the database is up by issuing one of the following two commands:

```
alter system set timed_statistics = TRUE (for all users. DBA privileges required)
alter session set timed_statistics = TRUE (for this session only)
```

Calculating the Total Response Time

Earlier in this chapter, we talked about what total response time is and mentioned that you can use the V$ views to determine your system's response time, but we didn't show you how to actually determine this value. In this section, we'll cover how to retrieve the relevant statistics that you need from the Oracle performance tables in order to calculate total response time.

To restate the original response time formula:

Response Time = Service (or Work) Time + Wait Time

Now let's look at how to determine each of the values needed.

Calculating Service (or Work) Time

The service time is equal to the statistic "CPU used by this session," which is shown through entries in the V$SYSSTAT or V$SESSTAT view. You select from these tables for this event. Use the lookup table V$STATNAME to help you find the correct statistic number for "CPU used by this session" for each platform and release. This event represents the total amount of CPU time used.

NOTE
V$SYSSTAT does not include CPU used by the Oracle background processes, and V$SESSTAT doesn't show the amount of CPU used per Oracle background process.

The SQL statement to run at either instance or session level is shown below. The first query is used to determine the instance-level service time value. This value is expressed in hundredths of a second.

```
select a.Value "Total CPU Time"
  from V$SYSSTAT a
 where a.Name = 'CPU used by this session';

Total CPU Time
--------------
        408153
```

For the session-level query shown next, you must join the view V$SESSTAT with V$STATNAME in order to obtain the value for the CPU.

```
select a.Sid, a.Value "Total CPU Time"
  from V$SESSTAT a, V$STATNAME b
 where a.Statistic# = b.Statistic#
   and b.Name = 'CPU used by this session'
 order by Sid;

      SID  Total CPU Time
--------- ---------------
        1             222
        2              25
        3              57
        4             155
        5             457
        6             296
        7            1443
        8              60
        9            1362
       11            2503

10 rows selected.
```

Now that you know the amount of service or work time, you will need to obtain the amount of wait time to complete the formula.

Calculating Wait Time

The wait time is recorded through entries in V$SYSTEM_EVENT or V$SESSION_EVENT by summing the time waited for all the events excluding those waited for due to the foreground process and all background waits. We can ignore the following wait events, as they have little impact on the overall performance or measure delays that are outside of the DBA's control:

- client message
- dispatcher timer
- KXFX: execution message dequeue - Slaves
- KXFX: Reply Message Dequeue - Query Coord
- Null event
- parallel query dequeue wait
- parallel query idle wait - Slaves

- pipe get
- PL/SQL lock timer
- pmon timer
- rdbms ipc message
- slave wait
- smon timer
- SQL*Net message from client
- virtual circuit status
- WMON goes to sleep

Here's the query you will use to collect the total wait time from the instance level. Note that this query excludes the entire list above.

```
select sum(Time_Waited) "Total Time Waited"
  from V$SYSTEM_EVENT
 where Event not in ('pmon  timer', 'smon  timer', 'rdbms ipc
message', 'parallel dequeue wait', 'virtual circuit', 'SQL*Net message
from client', 'client message', 'NULL event');

Total Time Waited
-----------------
          2771194
```

Like the query of V$SYSSTAT, this value is listed in hundredths of a second. For the session-level query, you would use the following:

```
select Sid, sum(Time_Waited) "Total Time waited"
  from V$SESSION_EVENT
 where Event != 'SQL*Net message from client'
 group by Sid;

      SID Total Time Waited
--------- -----------------
        1            218329
        2               104
        3               358
        4                72
        5               654
        6              2488
        9              3284
       11                80
8 rows selected.
```

Tuning to Change Overall Response Time

Now that you have the data for either the instance or session, you can decide how to best direct your tuning efforts by examining the area that is taking the highest percentage of time. The next step involves further examination of the largest component of the response time equation. Keep in mind that once all this data has been gathered, the problem may not be at the database level at all, but only manifesting itself there.

Decomposing CPU Time

If CPU usage contributes the most to total response time, you will need to break the value down further into detailed segments to properly understand the problem. CPU time basically falls into three categories:

- Parse time CPU
- Recursive CPU usage
- Other CPU

Let's look at each of these categories individually.

Parse Time CPU

This parameter reports the amount of CPU used for parsing SQL statements and consists of four components: parse count, execute count, session cursor cache count, and session cursor cache hits. We'll look at each of these components briefly.

Generally, parse time CPU should not exceed 10 percent to 20 percent of the total CPU. A high value for parse time CPU can be a strong indication that an application has not been well tuned. High parse time CPU usually indicates that the application is either spending too much time opening and closing cursors or is not using bind variables. Check the following statistics from V$SYSSTAT or V$SESSTAT:

- **Parse count** Total number of hard and soft parses. A *hard parse* occurs when a SQL statement has to be loaded into the shared pool. In this case, Oracle has to allocate memory in the shared pool and parse the statement that is more costly in terms of resources. A *soft parse* is recorded when Oracle checks the shared pool for a SQL statement and finds a version of the statement that can be reused. An application using dynamic SQL may have a high parse count. Dynamic SQL statements usually have a one-to-one ratio for the execute count (see next item).

The number of soft parses is available as a separate statistic. The total number of hard parses can be computed as hard parses = parse count – soft parses – session cursor cache hits.

- **Execute count** Total number of executions of Data Manipulation Language (DML) and Data Definition Language (DDL) statements.
- **Session cursor cache count** Total size of the session cursor cache for the session (in V$SESSTAT) or the total size for all sessions (in V$SYSSTAT).
- **Session cursor cache hits** Number of times a statement did not have to be reopened and reparsed, because it was still in the cursor cache for the session. This records the number of times a SQL parse can be satisfied from a previously executed statement.

From these statistics, the percentage of parses versus executes can be calculated (parse count / execute count). If this ratio is higher than 20 percent, consider the following:

- Ensure that the application is using bind variables. By using bind variables, it is unnecessary to reparse SQL statements with new values before reexecuting. It is significantly better to use bind variables and parse the SQL statement once in the program. It will also reduce resource contention within the shared pool. If you cannot change the application to use bind variables (3rd party application), consider setting the initialization parameter **cursor_sharing** to FORCE to have Oracle convert the statement to internal bind variables.
- If applications open/reparse the same SQL statements and the value of "session cursor cache hits" is low compared to the number of parses, it may be useful to increase the number of cursor cache hits for the session. Increasing the initialization parameter **session_cached_cursors** will set aside additional memory for this purpose and will reduce the number of hard parses by holding a copy of the parsed SQL statement in a cache. If no hit ratio improvement results, lower this number to conserve memory and reduce cache maintenance overhead.

Recursive CPU Usage

This value includes the amount of CPU used for executing row cache statements (data dictionary lookup) and PL/SQL programs. If recursive CPU usage is high relative to the total CPU, check for the following:

- Determine whether much PL/SQL code (triggers, functions, procedures, packages) is executed. Stored PL/SQL code always runs under a recursive session, so it is reflected in recursive CPU time and will skew this value.

Consider optimizing any SQL coded within those program units. This activity can be determined by querying V$SQL.

- Examine the size of the shared pool and its usage, and possibly, increase the SHARED_POOL_SIZE. This can be determined by monitoring V$SQL and V$SGASTAT.

In the next section, we'll show you a script to extract the different kinds of CPU values.

Other CPU

This last category is composed of CPU time that will be used for tasks such as looking up buffers, fetching rows or index keys, and so on. Generally, "other CPU" should represent the highest percentage of CPU time out of the total CPU time used. Also look in V$SQL to find SQL statements that have a high number of BUFFER_GETS per execution and/or a high number of physical reads per execution. These statements will be among the most costly in terms of disk and CPU resources on your system. Investigation of these "gets" (especially the first) will help to reduce the remaining, or other, CPU time. The following SQL statement will find the overall SQL usage:

```
select a.Value "Total CPU",
       b.Value "Parse CPU",
       c.Value "Recursive CPU",
       a.Value - b.Value - c.Value "Other"
  from V$SYSSTAT a, V$SYSSTAT b, V$SYSSTAT c
 where a.Name = 'CPU used by this session'
   and b.Name = 'parse cpu time'
   and c.Name = 'recursive cpu';
```

NOTE
The descriptors in V$SYSSTAT may change between versions.

In the next query, you'll be looking for the CPU usage per session. In that query, you're using the Statistic# column instead of a meaningful name. Before you run that query, you can use the following select statement to see the names of the values you'll be selecting when you look for the CPU usage per session. Since Oracle may change the Statistic# value associated with a statistic name from version to version, you should double-check the statistic names and Statistic# values for the version you are on before you run the query.

```
select Statistic#, Name
  from V$STATNAME
 where Statistic# in (12,162,8);

STATISTIC# NAME
---------- ----------------------------------------------------------------
         8 recursive cpu usage
        12 CPU used by this session
       162 parse time cpu
```

The following SQL statement will show the CPU usage per session. The most interesting thing about this query is that it is joining against the same V$ view several times. Therefore, you will see a separate set of values for each of the joins, with the same session ID (SID) shown many times. The results set can be very large depending on the number of sessions that are running when you perform the query. Therefore, we are going to narrow our select to one SID. We'll arbitrarily pick session ID number 11.

```
select distinct a.Sid, a.Value "Total CPU",
       b.Value "Parse CPU",
       c.Value "Recursive CPU",
       a.Value - b.Value - c.Value "Other CPU"
   from  V$SESSTAT a, V$SESSTAT b, V$SESSTAT c
 where a.Statistic# = 12
   and b.Statistic# = 162
   and c.Statistic# = 8
   and a.Sid = 11
/

      SID Total CPU Parse CPU Recursive CPU Other CPU
--------- --------- --------- ------------- --------
       11        27         0             0       27
       11        27         0             8       19
       11        27         1             0       26
       11        27         1             8       18
       11        27         2             0       25
       11        27         2             8       17
       11        27        17             0       10
       11        27        17             8        2
```

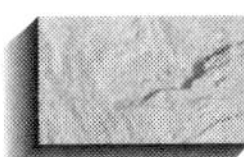

NOTE
The descriptors in V$SYSSTAT may change between versions.

Decomposing Wait Time

If wait time is the largest contributor to total response time, you can decompose it into detailed segments to further understand the problem. To correctly identify the events contributing the highest amounts of wait time, query the view V$SYSTEM_EVENT and order the events by Time_Waited in descending order:

```
col Event format a30
select *
  from V$SYSTEM_EVENT
 where Event not in ('pmon timer', 'smon timer', 'rdbms ipc message', 'parallel
   dequeue wait', 'virtual circuit', 'SQL*Net message from client', 'client message',
   'Null event')
 order by Time_Waited desc;
EVENT                          TOTAL_WAITS TOTAL_TIMEOUTS TIME_WAITED AVERAGE_WAIT
------------------------------ ----------- -------------- ----------- ------------
dispatcher timer                        36             36      221221    6145.0278
virtual circuit status                  72             72      221217    3072.4583
db file sequential read               1502              0        2461     1.638482
library cache pin                        5              1         589        117.8
db file scattered read                 359              0         578    1.6100279
rdbms ipc reply                          7              0         508    72.571429
file open                               83              0         367    4.4216867
control file sequential read           137              0         275    2.0072993
control file parallel write            754              0         169    .22413793
file identify                           29              0         131    4.5172414
log file parallel write                 43              0          73    1.6976744
log file sequential read                11              0          32    2.9090909
reliable message                         1              0          17           17
buffer busy waits                        1              0          14           14
refresh controlfile command              5              0           9          1.8
db file single write                    11              0           2    .18181818
db file parallel write                   2              0           2            1
log file single write                   10              0           1           .1
direct path read                        44              0           1    .02272727
log file sync                            3              0           1    .33333333
direct path write                       22              0           0            0
instance state change                    1              0           0            0
SQL*Net message to client              129              0           0            0
SQL*Net more data to client              1              0           0            0
SQL*Net break/reset to client            2              0           0            0
```

If you get all zeros in the Time_Waited and Average_Wait columns, check to see if the parameter **timed_statistics** is set to TRUE in your initialization parameter file.

The output from V$SYSTEM_EVENT has been ordered to show the events that are the greatest contributors to the amount of time waited. From the event descriptions, you can take appropriate actions to correct any performance problems that you've identified. However, for the purpose of this book, the following discussion covers the primary events that usually contribute the greatest amount of wait time.

Buffer Busy Waits

A high buffer busy waits event value can be caused by either of the following situations:

- Multiple sessions requesting the same block. (One or more sessions are waiting for a process to read the requested block into the buffer cache.)
- Multiple sessions waiting for a change to complete for the same block. (Only one process at a time can write to the block, so other processes have to wait for that buffer to become available.)

If buffer busy waits is high, determine which blocks are being accessed concurrently and whether the blocks are being read or changed. You can use the V$SESSION_WAIT and V$WAITSTAT views. V$SESSION_WAIT will show the file number, block number, and ID (where ID represents the status of the buffer busy wait event). V$WAITSTAT will show the block classes and the number of times waited for each. Different actions may be taken for each block class to alleviate contention. Tuning priorities should be oriented toward the classes that contribute the highest wait time percentage.

Segment Header Waits

Each segment has one segment header block. There are basically two types of segments: data and index. The following is a brief discussion on causes for segment header block contention based on the data structures they contain.

If you see a high insert rate on a table with insufficient transaction freelists that results in a bottleneck, the solution is to increase the number of freelists. On single-CPU machines, the CPU manages one process at a time, so the system may not benefit greatly from an increase in freelists. However, adding freelists on a single-CPU machine may ensure that the processor is used more efficiently. For databases running in exclusive mode, this recommendation may also circumvent the issue of a small block size constraining the number of available freelists.

If you observe Oracle constantly inserting new entries into the extent map within the segment header because extent sizes are too small, increase the size of each extent. Although Oracle7.3 and later versions allow an object to have unlimited extents, a small number of very large extents is better than a large number of small extents.

Data Block Waits

The data block class is used to store data (index or table data). Let's look at some reasons for data block waits:

- Multiple sessions could be requesting the same block from disk.

- Multiple sessions are going after rows in the same block because it contains so many rows.
- Multiple sessions are trying to insert into the same block because there is only one freelist (or insufficient freelists).

In the first case (this could actually happen for each block class), only one session will do the read from disk, and the other sessions will be waiting for the block to be placed into the buffer cache. The cause of this problem could be that the buffer cache is too small to keep the current working set in memory. Enlarging the buffer cache (**db_cache_size**) can help. Another option is to use buffer pools to reduce the number of buffers an object can occupy in the buffer cache. For example, you may effectively limit the number of buffers that a randomly accessed large table can occupy in the buffer cache by placing it in the recycle pool. Several new types of buffer pools were introduced in Oracle8.

If multiple sessions are going after rows in the same block because it contains too many rows, reduce the number of rows per block by modifying the pctfree/pctused settings. This is a "space for time" trade-off. The table will use more space, but buffer busy waits will be reduced.

Finally, adding multiple freelists to the object will increase the number of heads of freelists; thus the contention point can be distributed over the freelists, reducing the number of buffer busy waits. You can dynamically increase the freelists for an object; however, this will only affect new blocks, and you may still need to rebuild the object. In Oracle 9i, this rebuild can be done online either with the *alter index rebuild* command or the *alter table move* command.

Finding the Buffer Cache Size

The memory area referred to as the buffer cache or buffer pool is specified by several initialization parameters:

- **db_cache_size/db_nK_cache_size** Number of blocks
- **db_block_size** Block size

As a starting point, the buffer cache should be about 2.5 percent of the size of the database. Thus, if your total amount of data is 1GB and your block size is 4K, a good starting point would be to set the number of buffers to 5200. Please note that this is a generic starting point only, and you will need to adjust the buffer cache either up or down based on server memory availability, database size, and application needs. The main concept of the buffer cache is to hold data that has been read by previous queries. The assumption is that it's likely these blocks will be needed again.

When a query executes, Oracle will check to see if the data block is in the cache. If it is, that block will be used (a cache hit); if it's not, the query will have to fetch data from disk. The new blocks will be stored in the buffer cache. Eventually there will be no more room in the buffer cache to hold new blocks. When this happens, the DBWR background process will flush blocks out of the buffer cache to make room for the new blocks that must be brought into the cache from disk. A block that has been updated is marked as a dirty block and will be written to disk the next time DBWR is activated.

DBWR also uses an algorithm called LRU (least recently used) to clear some space in the cache. The LRU algorithm basically means the blocks in the cache that have not been accessed for the longest time will be removed. Blocks read into the cache via full table scans automatically get placed at the end of the LRU chain to avoid filling the entire cache with unnecessary data from one query. The flushing event is also triggered when a checkpoint occurs.

Cache hits are good for performance and are measured in terms of a hit ratio. Hit ratios can be measured at system or session level. Generally speaking, the higher the ratio the better. OLTP applications should aim for a hit ratio of better than 90 percent, while for batch applications, a cache hit ratio of around 60 percent to 70 percent is acceptable. These are, however, only guidelines to use when evaluating the system. If adding memory improves the cache hit ratio but does not have a corresponding increase in performance, it's time to look elsewhere for a solution.

To measure the hit ratio for the system, the following query can be used:

```
select trunc((1 -(sum(decode(Name,'physical reads',value,0)) /
        (sum(decode(Name,'consistent gets',value,0)) +
        (sum(decode(Name,'db block gets',value,0)))))
        ) * 100 ) "Buffer Hit Ratio"
  from V$SYSSTAT
 where Statistic# in (38,39,40);

Buffer Hit Ratio
----------------
              98
```

To get a breakdown of the buffer hit ratio at session level, execute the following query:

```
select a.Username,
       avg((b.Consistent_Gets + b.Block_Gets - b.Physical_Reads) *100 /
       (b.Consistent_Gets + b.Block_Gets)) "Buffer Hit Ratio"
  from V$SESSION a, V$SESS_IO b
 where a.Sid = b.Sid
   and (b.Consistent_Gets + b.Block_Gets) > 0
   and Username is not null
 group by Username;

USERNAME                       Buffer Hit Ratio
------------------------------ ----------------
AMRDEV                               99.9325682
```

```
AMRTEST                                  99.5589174
FWKDEV                                   89.1736861
FWKTEST                                  93.8428192
QDBA                                     99.0275177
SYSTEM                                   85.8736059
```

Freelist Block Waits

This statistic measures contention for "freelist group" blocks. Some documentation and tuning scripts claim that waits on this block class indicate that the number of freelists needs to be increased for some objects. Most databases that run in exclusive mode see zero waits on this block class because their DBAs do not create objects with freelist groups. Otherwise, the reasons and solutions for freelist block waits are similar to those of segment header waits. See that earlier section for details.

Db File Scattered Read

This wait event usually indicates some type of multiblock I/O operation (full table scans or fast full index scans). The number of data blocks read per I/O operation is determined by the initialization parameter **db_file_multiblock_read_count** (which can be changed dynamically).

Check V$FILESTAT to see which files have done scans:

```
select File#, Phyrds, Phyblkrd, Readtim
  from V$FILESTAT
 where Phyrds != Phyblkrd;

    FILE#    PHYRDS  PHYBLKRD   READTIM
--------- --------- --------- ---------
        1      1790      3850         0
        4        24       110         0
```

If phyrds is close to phyblkrd, then single block reads are occurring. If that is not the case, full scans or range scans are happening on that file. To reduce the cost of a db file scattered read, check the file placement on each disk, the number of disks, and the stripe size per disk. To reduce the amount of db file scattered reads, check for missing indexes on the object where the scan is happening, or check the SQL statement that is executing the scan.

Db File Sequential Read

This event occurs for single block reads (like index lookup). The normal way to reduce this event is to examine the amount and cost of the I/Os that are being performed. You can normally reduce the amount of I/Os and make each I/O faster by taking a combination of the following actions:

- Increase **db_cache_size**.
- Reduce physical reads per execute for SQL statements.

In the proactive tuning section, we discussed how tuning the application could have a big impact on the overall performance of the system. One of the biggest wait components of the SQL statement execution is the I/O. Finding the SQL statement with the highest number of disk reads per execution is a good start. Although you can use a SQL statement to "dump" all of the Sql_Text along with all of the Disk_Reads information, we recommend that you perform this search in two steps. First, determine the highest range of disk reads per execution that are being performed on your system, and then look at the SQL for those specific queries that are doing the high volume. Here's the first query to run:

```
select Disk_Reads, Executions, Disk_Reads/Executions
  from V$SQL
 where Executions != 0
 order by Disk_Reads desc;

DISK_READS EXECUTIONS DISK_READS/EXECUTIONS
---------- ---------- ---------------------
       969          4                242.25
       927          1                   927
       671          4                167.75
       487          1                   487
       216          1                   216
       137          2                  68.5
       114         12                   9.5
        58          1                    58
        53          1                    53
        44          1                    44
        30         84             .35714286
        26         18             1.4444444
        20         30             .66666667
        18         18                     1
        17         30             .56666667

15 rows selected.
```

Alternatively, you could order the query by the Disk_Reads/Executions column, since the row ordering shown here could potentially put a well-tuned query that is executed the most toward the top of the output list. In other words, you could have a situation where a well-tuned query does a small amount of disk I/O each time it's run, but it's run so frequently that it could show up with both a high execution count and a high disk I/O count. The way the output is currently shown, you would end up with this query very high on your list. If you order by reads per execution, you would have a very low count for the same query. Either approach in the query output order is fine as long as you pay primary attention to the reads per execution values.

The output you see here has been cut way back to conserve space but should give you an idea of what you are looking for from this query. Just for this example, let's look at the SQL statements that generated the three highest values for disk reads per execution.

```
select Disk_Reads, Executions, Disk_Reads/Executions, Sql_Text
  from V$SQL
 where Disk_Reads > 600;

DISK_READS EXECUTIONS DISK_READS/EXECUTIONS
---------- ---------- ---------------------
SQL_TEXT
----------------------------------------------------------------------------
       671          4                167.75
select i.obj#, i.flags, u.name, o.name from sys.ind$ i, sys.obj$ o,
sys.user$ u where
(bitand(i.flags, 256) = 256 or bitand(i.flags, 512) = 512) and
o.obj#=i.obj# and o.owner#=u.user#

       927          1                   927
select distinct i.obj# from sys.idl_ub1$ i where i.obj#>>=:1 and i.obj# not
in (select d.p_obj# from sys.dependency$ d)

       969          4                242.25
select i.obj#, i.flags, u.name, o.name     from sys.indpart$ i, sys.obj$ o,
sys.user$ u, ind$ idx where  bitand(i.flags, 512) = 512 and o.obj#=idx.obj#
ando.owner# = u.user# and idx.obj#=i.bo#
```

Once the SQL statement with the highest reads per execution has been identified, it is good to have a quick look at the number of executions (or the total number of reads that the SQL statement has done). You will want to verify that the SQL statement being tuned is significant to the application instead of being one that is executed only once or at night, for example, in a batch job. You can also use the same query to identify the SQL statements that are executed most:

```
select Disk_Reads, Executions, Disk_Reads/Executions, Sql_Text
  from V$SQL
 where Executions != 0
 order by 2;
```

Of the 112 rows displayed for this query, the highest two values are presented here:

```
DISK_READS EXECUTIONS DISK_READS/EXECUTIONS
---------- ---------- ---------------------
SQL_TEXT
-----------------------------------------------------------------------
        30         84            .35714286
select obj#,type#,ctime,mtime,stime,status,dataobj#,flags,oid$ from
obj$ where owner#=:1 and name=:2 and namespace=:3 and(remoteowner=:4 or
remoteowner is null and :4 is null)and(linkname=:5 or linkname is null
and :5 is null)and(subname=:6 or subname is null and :6 is null)

         7       2900            .00241379
select job from sys.job$  where next_date < sysdate <Nand (field1 = :1
or field1 = 0) order by next_date, job
```

By tuning the SQL, you can significantly improve the overall performance of your system. Tuning SQL statements is addressed in Chapter 13.

Reducing the Cost of I/Os

Each time Oracle has to process an I/O, there's a resource cost and wait time cost that must be paid. To help reduce the cost of I/Os, you can do the following:

- Increase the I/O speed.
- Check the wait time for each disk.

Faster disks can make a big difference. Also, using more disks to spread the I/O to different disks is the easiest and most consistent way to reduce I/O bottlenecks. The drawbacks are the cost of more or faster disks and the time it takes either to move datafiles from older, slower disks to newer, faster ones or to reconfigure the datafiles across the added disks.

You will be trying to find the disks with the highest wait time. Once you have identified them, check to see what objects reside on those disks. You may need to physically redistribute the data to reduce the wait times. In designing or redesigning an application's physical layout, a good approach to consider is the "Stripe and Mirror Everywhere" methodology. The idea is to stripe all of your application data and logs across all of the available disks on your system, spreading all the I/O operations evenly. This approach takes some of the guesswork out of designing a physical disk layout for your application. The full method is described in a paper available on Oracle's Technet Web site.

In order to determine which file may be causing a problem for I/O, you can use V$FILESTAT. Examine the ratio of Readtim (amount of time spent reading) and Phyrds (total number of reads) per file:

```
select File#, Readtim, Phyrds, Readtim/Phyrds
  from V$FILESTAT
 order by 4 desc;

FILE#      READTIM   PHYRDS     READTIM/PHYRDS
--------- --------- --------- --------------
        3        93        34      2.7352941
        1      2809      1757      1.5987479
        2        11        10            1.1
        4         0        24              0
        5         0         4              0
        6         0         4              0
        7         0         4              0

7 rows selected.
```

By showing the rows in descending order, the worst read time is always at the top of the list. To obtain the name of the file that has the worst read time, you can look it up in the V$DBFILE lookup table (explained in Chapter 4).

Look at the file with the highest read percentage out of the total reads and the highest read times. If the average cost per I/O is high, you may need to redistribute the I/O. If you are using a Windows system, be sure to check whether the drive numbers you are looking at are different drives or just logical drives representing partitions of the same disk. You can use the Disk Administrator tool to determine the physical drive on which each partition exists.

Free Buffer Waits

Free buffer waits may be caused by the session's scanning the buffer cache for a free buffer. If there are none available, a user process must wait for dirty buffers to be written to disk. Check for the following statistics in V$SYSSTAT and V$SESSTAT:

- **Free buffer inspected** The number of dirty and pinned buffers skipped before a free buffer is found
- **Free buffer requested** The number of buffers requested to store data by all sessions
- **Dirty buffers inspected** The number of dirty buffers (buffers that need to be flushed to disk before they can be reused by sessions)

The following formula will calculate the average number of buffers that a session is scanning at the end of an LRU to find a free buffer:

Average Number of Buffers Scanned = Free Buffer Inspected / Free Buffer Requested

This is, unfortunately, one of the areas in which you will have to make some manual calculations. You can select the values from V$SYSSTAT or V$SESSTAT, but then you will need to perform the math manually to get the average number of buffers that are being scanned. The query that you can use to obtain the values is as follows:

```
column Name format a30
select Statistic#, Name, Value
  from V$SYSSTAT
 where Name like 'free%'
    or Name like 'dirty%';

STATISTIC# NAME                                VALUE
---------- ------------------------------ ---------
        47 free buffer requested                3931
        48 dirty buffers inspected                 0
        51 free buffer inspected                   0
```

If the average number is close to zero, a process can find a buffer on average very quickly.

Latch Free Waits

With a high number of latch free waits, you will need to determine which latch is being requested the most. Two of the most highly contended latches are the shared pool latch and the library cache latch. Each of these latches can be held for a long time. There can also be a great deal of contention for the redo allocation latch. The redo allocation latch is used for allocating space in the log buffer when foregrounds need to write redo records.

All of these latches are potential points of contention. In the case of the library cache latches and shared pool latch, the number of "latch gets" occurring is influenced directly by the amount of activity in the shared pool, especially parse operations. Anything that can minimize the number of latch gets and, indeed, the amount of activity in the shared pool is helpful to both performance and scalability.

First, you can use V$LATCH to determine the latch with the highest sleep count:

```
select Name, Sleeps
  from V$LATCH
 where Sleeps > 0
 order by Sleeps
/
```

Since V$LATCH only shows the parent latch, check V$LATCH_CHILDREN to determine which child latch (if any) has the most contention:

```
select Name, Sleeps
  from V$LATCH_CHILDREN
 where Name = <latch name>
   and Sleeps > <minimum base>
 order by Sleeps
/
```

Depending on the latch type, you can make many different changes. Let's take a look at the type of latch and the changes that you can make.

Shared Pool Latch and Library Cache Latch Every time an application makes a parse call for a SQL statement and the parsed representation of the statement is not in the shared SQL area, Oracle parses and allocates space for the SQL in the library cache. The shared pool and library cache latches protect these operations. Once the SQL area becomes fragmented and available memory is reduced, the single-threaded shared pool latch may become a bottleneck. Contention for these latches can be achieved by increasing sharing of SQL and reducing parsing by keeping cursors open between executions.

Cache Buffer Hash Chain Latch Each hash chain latch protects a hash chain composed of a number of buffer headers, which, in turn, point to the buffer itself. This latch is acquired every time a buffer is queried or updated. The number of latches defaults to prime (**0.25 x db_block_buffers**). There could be a large number of latches, so you must add the clause "where sleeps > *<some number>*" to filter out most of the latches. Find the latch with the highest number of sleeps. Once you've found it, find the buffers that are protected by that latch. Here's the script to accomplish this task:

```
select Hladdr, Dbafil, Dbablk
  from X$BH b, V$LATCH_CHILDREN l
 where l.Name = (latch_name)
   and l.Addr = Hladdr
   and Sleeps >= <maxsleeps>;
```

NOTE
Use the column File# instead of Dbafil in Oracle8 and above.

When the Dbafil and Dbablk values are found, check DBA_EXTENTS to see what the object name and type is. Here is the code:

```
select Segment_Name, Segment_Type
  from DBA_EXTENTS
 where File = <file>
   and <block> between Block_Id and Block_Id + Blocks - 1;
```

Log File Sync

Log file sync happens at commit time when a foreground process is waiting for the LGWR to complete. If the LGWR process is too active, too much redo latch contention can occur. Another reason for a "small average redo write size" could be that LGWR is unable to piggyback many commits. The whole system may not be very busy, resulting in LGWR waking up immediately (when posted) and writing the redo for a session. Thus, the next session may have to wait for this write to complete before its redo will be written. The maximum I/O size for the redo writer is also operating system specific. The normal values can range from 64K to 128K.

Enqueue

V$SYSSTAT/V$SESSTAT will show some interesting information here:

- **Enqueue gets** The number of enqueue "get" operations that are performed. For example, getting the ST lock will count as an enqueue get.
- **Enqueue converts** The number of enqueue convert operations that are performed. For example, converting an enqueue from S (shared) mode to X (exclusive) mode.
- **Enqueue releases** Most enqueues that are obtained are then released. This means the number of conversions will be minimal or nonexistent on most systems.
- **Enqueue waits** The number of times a session tried to get an enqueue but could not get one right away (this is true for enqueue gets and enqueue conversions). Some tuning sources state that if the enqueue waits are high, **enqueue_resources** need to be increased. This is incorrect. Waits just indicate that an enqueue could not be granted. If **enqueue_resources** are depleted, an appropriate message indicating the need to increase resources is returned immediately.
- **Enqueue deadlocks** The number of deadlocks detected for the session or the number of ORA-60 errors returned to the session.
- **Enqueue timeouts** If an enqueue could not be granted, the session will have to wait (enqueue waits). Within this wait, there can be several timeouts.

Look in V$LOCK or V$SESSION_WAIT to see what the enqueue sessions are currently waiting on:

```
select *
  from V$SESSION_WAIT
 where Event = 'enqueue';
```

Join V$SESSION_WAIT with V$SESSION with V$SQL to find the current SQL statement and object for this session. Using the SID (session ID) from V$SESSION_WAIT, you can find the SQL statement waiting for an enqueue:

```
select a.Sid, a.Username, b.Sql_Text
  from V$SESSION a, V$SQL b
 where Sid = <sid value>
   and a.User# = b.Parsing_User_Id;
```

Write Complete Waits

When a buffer is being written, it cannot change until the buffer is flushed to disk. The most common reason for this is frequent checkpointing. Normally, a hot buffer will stay at the most recently used end of the LRU, and the chance that it will be written is small.

Frequent checkpointing usually occurs because of small redo log files or a low default setting for the **log_checkpoint_interval**.

SQL*Net More Data from Client/SQL*Net More Data to Client

When the application design is not judged a culprit, sometimes the network can be responsible for most of the wait time (or latency). *Network latency* is defined by the time it takes to gain access to a particular network device accompanied by the time it takes to transmit the data to the next device in the network. This latency can vary greatly based on the type of network, the opportunity to transmit on the network (bandwidth utilization), and distance traveled. Once the network has been created, however, the latency for each network packet that is being sent can vary. Thus, optimizing the performance of an application on a network can be done in two ways: by reducing the number of network packets or by reducing the latency (reducing the cost per packet).

To reduce the number of network packets:

- Bundle packages into bundled and/or deferred Oracle calls.
- Use array operations.
- Use a different session layer protocol (HTTP instead of Oracle Net or Net8 as in Web server–based applications).

To reduce the latency (reduce the cost per packet):

- Use Fiber Channel or Gigabit Ethernet in the backbone or data center.
- Use ATM or SONAT for the wide area network.

Solving the Problem at XYZ Company

Back at XYZ, you were able to run the queries to determine the components of your response time equation. You found that you were spending 85 percent of the time working and the remainder waiting for some resource. Further investigation showed that a majority of the CPU time was in the "other" category, related to application usage.

You then checked to see what SQL was running during one of the slowdown periods and found queries running related to the new planning department application. You have found the source of the problem! Good job! Now, your options are

- Work with the planning department to tune the queries and educate the staff on SQL tuning (reducing service time).
- If possible and the business requirements allow it, queue these queries for execution during off-peak hours or to another system specifically designed for their reporting needs.

Common Causes of Performance Problems

Some causes of performance problems that you will find when you are working either proactively or reactively on tuning will be design-time issues. You will have little control over these issues. There are other causes that you'll have more access to and control over, and we'll discuss some of these in the following sections.

Application and Database Design Faults

The designer may have designed the application with inherent bottlenecks, such as a sequence table that becomes a single-threaded choke point. You will see this design problem show up in many ways. In the sequence table example, you might see errors in the alert log signifying deadlocks or find that a particular block is being accessed frequently. You'd see this as a higher overall wait time in your transactions.

A bad design is difficult to correct the further you are in development of the system. Although we can provide you with tips, there is no easy way to see if your particular design will perform well. Thus, the best advice that we can give you is to test the system as heavily as possible during the development cycle.

Inefficient Datafile Layout and Storage Configuration

As the database grows in size, and when it is under high loads, I/O contention may indicate deficiencies in I/O distribution, striping, and object layout plans. In Chapter 8, we discussed the identification of deficiencies in I/O distribution. The problem is relatively easy to fix by moving the more frequently accessed datafiles to different, less busy disks if possible.

Inappropriate db_block_size for the Application

The block size determines how much information will be paged into memory with each read. Since physical reads are the most expensive operation, the size of the block can have a great deal of impact on the performance of the system. However, there is a balance to be struck. Bringing in too much information at one time can cause a problem by flushing other needed data out of the database block buffers too quickly. Therefore, you should put thought into your **db_block_size** decision before you build your database.

The default block size, 2K, is usually too small for all but the simplest of applications. A good rule of thumb is to make the block size either 4K or 8K for applications that are mostly OLTP, and 8K or higher for applications that are mostly batch. You can identify problems with a block size that is too small by delays in the application response time due to the need to read data into the buffers more frequently. You'll be able to identify problems with too large a block size by the amount of time it takes to read data into the buffer and by problems getting needed latches on block headers.

Oracle9i now gives the DBA the ability to create a tablespace with a nonstandard block size. As an example, if an application under design is mostly used for decision support, with the need to page in lots of data as quickly as possible, the logical choice would be to build the database with as large a block size as possible. But if the application had a series of small transactional tables, these could be contained in a tablespace with a smaller, more appropriate block size created using the new **blocksize** clause in the **create tablespace** command syntax.

Inappropriate Settings for Database Objects

Some values for the database objects, if set incorrectly, can impact performance. Let's look at them now.

Inittrans

The inittrans value controls the amount of space set aside in the Oracle block header for DML transactions to register the fact that they are modifying a particular block. The default value for inittrans is 1. Any other transactions that want to modify the block will have to allocate additional space for their control information during their transaction.

Maxtrans

The maxtrans header limits the total number of transactions that can access a block. The default value for maxtrans is usually 255, but it depends somewhat on the block size and space available in the block.

Freelists vs. Automatic Segment Space Management

In prior releases, space management on Oracle segments was handled using linked lists of blocks called freelists, which are the lists of free blocks within the segment. How a data block is determined to have available space is controlled by the pctfree and pctused settings, which are set during object creation. The pctfree parameter determines how much of the block is reserved for the growth of rows that are already in the data block. The pctused parameter determines at what threshold a block can be released back to the freelist.

The freelist can be a source of contention for systems that have a large amount of updates. Contention will show up in the V$SYSTEM_WAIT or V$SESSION_WAIT view. Careful choice of these parameters based on the type of application you are running is required to control the amount of activity on the freelist and the amount of unused storage in a block.

Oracle9i introduced the Automatic Segment Space Management feature. Instead of maintaining one or more freelists to manage available space in the segment, Oracle keeps track of the free space using a series of bitmaps. These bitmaps provide more efficient access to information on the available space of a data block and allow more concurrency in searching for free space overall. This feature is only available if the tablespace is defined initially as "locally managed," and if this feature is used it overrides all freelist, pctfree, and pctused settings set during the creation of an object when the target tablespace is managed in this fashion.

Unsuitable Sizing and Number of Rollback Segments

Contention for the rollback segments will show up in the V$SYSTEM_WAIT or V$SESSION_WAIT view for any of the following waits: undo header, undo block, system undo header, system undo block. If the values of these waits are greater than 1 percent of the total number of reads done in your system, consider adding more rollback segments.

In Oracle9i there is another alternative for solving this type of problem. Instead of using the traditional rollback segments, Oracle introduced the concept of automatic undo management. If this feature is used, Oracle keeps the information required to back out a transaction in a new type of tablespace called, appropriately enough, an Undo Tablespace. Now, the DBA has the option for new or existing databases to have Oracle assign all the rollback information to this tablespace and have the instance manage the amount of rollback using the **undo_retention** parameter. This value is expressed in seconds and controls how much data Oracle retains to rebuild a transaction, assuming there is storage available in the tablespace.

Poor Application Design

As we've said before, poorly designed applications are usually the major cause of performance issues on your system. Let's look more closely at some of the issues involved with poor application design.

Poorly Tuned Application Code

Nothing will reduce the overall performance of a system faster than bad application SQL! Monitor the V$SQL view for application code that is running overlong or requires many disk reads. Tips for detecting and tuning poorly written SQL are discussed in Chapter 13. A quick fix can sometimes be found in the statistics used to generate the query plan. Problems could be caused by out-of-date or nonexistent statistics with the Cost Based Optimizer (CBO). If the optimizer does not have the most up-to-date statistics, there is a greater chance that the plan will be less than optimal.

Shared Pool Issues

Performance will be improved by minimizing fragmentation in the shared pool and reducing the amount of time required to parse a SQL statement. Parsing is the work done by the database to validate the SQL statement and generate the query plan used for execution. One way to reduce parsing is to make sure you can reuse existing parsed statements as much as possible. Sharing SQL statements in the shared pool will help to ensure that Oracle will reuse existing parsed statements.

You can force more reuse of statements by making sure the statements are the same. For a SQL statement to be the same, everything about that SQL statement needs to be the same, including the capitalization and spacing. Sharing SQL cuts down on the time that any individual statement executes by reducing or eliminating the time needed to parse the statement, thus reducing the number of hard parses. (We discussed hard parses earlier in the section "Decomposing CPU Time.")

Bind variables are another factor that can influence SQL statement reuse. Bind variables allow parameters to be passed to the statement at execution time and make the statement more likely to be reused. There are some trade-offs when using bind variables though. The CBO will need to make assumptions that may be incorrect about data distribution. However, appropriate hints can help to overcome the CBO's incorrect assumptions.

Initialization Parameters

Some of the initialization parameters have great impact on the performance of your system. Let's take a look at them now.

Optimizer_mode The value for **optimizer_mode** in the initialization parameter file tells the database server which optimizer setting to use when generating an execution plan. The setting RULE invokes the Rule Based Optimizer, which will heavily favor the use of indexes. The setting CHOOSE will invoke the Cost Based Optimizer if statistics exist on any one of the tables involved in the SQL statement. FIRST_ROWS will invoke the CBO for any query, using default statistics for any table that does not have them. This setting will tend to produce plans that favor the return of rows quickly, even if the overall execution is a little longer than optimal. ALL_ROWS will behave the same as FIRST_ROWS with regard to the optimizer and statistics, but will favor producing the optimal plan.

The biggest "gotcha" here is the statistics when using the CBO. If the statistics are out of date and do not reflect the true distribution of data in the tables, the query plans will likely be suboptimal. These statistics are created and maintained by the **DBMS_STATS** command, which we will discuss in more detail in Chapter 13. You need to remember that session-level parameters and hints can override the optimizer mode setting.

Shared_pool_size The **shared_pool_size** variable controls the size of the memory area used for parsing and executing SQL statements. In general, a large number of hard parses indicates that you need more memory for your system (although sharing SQL statements, as noted above, also influences that value). As with all memory parameters, this value should not be increased to the point where swapping of memory pages occurs at the operating system level.

Sort_area_size This parameter controls the amount of memory allocated to each process in the Process Global Area (PGA) for any sorting activity. (For Multi-Threaded Server (MTS), this memory is allocated in the shared pool.) When a process needs more memory than is available for a sort operation, disk space must be allocated in the temporary tablespace. The **sort_area_size** is a value that will need to be tuned depending on the transaction mix of the application. An indicator that this memory might need to be increased (if available physical memory allows) would be a high ratio of sorts to disk, as seen in the V$SYSSTAT view. Changes to **sort_area_size** should be done cautiously, since this value impacts all sessions.

To see the values for sorts on your system, you can use the following query:

```
column Name format a30
column Value format 999999999999
select a.Name, Value
  from V$STATNAME a, V$SYSSTAT
```

```
 where a.Statistic# = V$SYSSTAT.Statistic#
   and a.Name in ('sorts (disk)','sorts (memory)','sorts (rows)')

NAME                                        VALUE
----------------------------------- ----------------
sorts (memory)                               6095
sorts (disk)                                    4
sorts (rows)                                15049
```

From this output, you can see that very few sorts are being performed to disk.

Sort_direct_writes Setting the correct value for this parameter can improve system performance of sorting, or overall performance if sorting is a large part of the system load. This parameter can be set to TRUE, which tells the server to allocate some additional memory for sorting outside the buffer cache. A process will gain the benefit of some additional memory if **sort_direct_writes** is set to TRUE because the process can use the additional memory for sorting but does not need to incur the cost of buffer cache management. Setting **sort_direct_writes** to TRUE stops pages from being flushed from the buffers that might be needed by another process.

Db_cache_size This parameter is expressed in database blocks and controls how much memory is available in the buffer cache for data blocks.

Db_file_multi_block_read_count This parameter controls the number of blocks read into the buffer cache in a single read during a full table scan. Oracle will read this many blocks into the cache from the first block needed, on the assumption that this read ahead to populate the buffer cache will be more efficient than single block reads (it usually is!). On most ports of Oracle, there is a limit of 64K total for **db_file_multi_block_read_count** times **db_block_size**, although on some ports, such as newer versions of Solaris, the maximum value is larger.

Redo Log Switching and Checkpoint Operations

Sometimes, you will see waits in the system due to a high redo log switch rate. Redo logs that are sized too small will cause frequent checkpoints, which cause a flush of all committed data buffers to disk from the data cache. A spike in writes to your datafiles and a delay in the processing of other statements while the checkpoint completes can occur. You can tune the number of checkpoints with the checkpoint_process variable. When Oracle comes to the physical end of any log, a log switch will occur, which will force a checkpoint.

There are trade-offs here as well. If you set the redo logs very large with an equally large checkpoint interval, when a thread switch does occur, Oracle will need a longer amount of time to write the redo information to disk. Also, the length of time between checkpoints has implications in the amount of time that you will need for recovery in the event of a database failure. The parameter **Fast_start_mttr_target** will also considerably influence the frequency of checkpoints. This parameter bounds the amount of recovery time it takes Oracle to do a database recovery. Oracle will increase the frequency of checkpoint operations to meet your recovery target. Your mission as a DBA is to balance the needs of your application if there are not enough system resources to achieve performance and recovery goals.

CHAPTER 13

Oracle-Supplied Tools

h no! The puppy was outside and it was raining, and now there are muddy paw prints all over the beige carpet. What can we do? There are several different approaches that we could take. We could use a sponge and soapy water or let the mud dry and use a vacuum cleaner to try to vacuum the dirt up. We could borrow or rent a rug shampoo machine, or we could hire someone with professional tools to come in and shampoo the rug.

As you can see, there are many different tools that you can use to "do the job." Some tools will provide you with a more elegant solution or make the job at hand easier to perform. This is all true of an Oracle database as well.

In this chapter, we are going to explore several different Oracle-supplied tools that you can use to see into your database. We looked at how to generate a report using SQL*Plus in Chapter 1. Now, we'll look at how to examine the SQL*Plus code that applications can use to evaluate the SQL code's performance. We'll discuss the tools Explain Plan and TKPROF and the information they provide to help you see how Oracle is going to execute the code. Next, we'll talk about the Oracle Cost Based Optimizer and how it works. We'll highlight the Oracle9i version of the Oracle Enterprise Manager (OEM) and what you can see using this tool. There are three additional tuning options associated with OEM that Oracle now bundles with the base product. We'll touch lightly on them. Oracle provides a utility called STATSPACK to examine how your database is performing. We'll tell you about this tool as well as a package called DBMS_STATS. Finally, we'll talk briefly about a facility that you can use, called stored outlines, to ensure that a piece of code you are running will always be evaluated and executed the same way.

So, let's get started with a look at how to tune SQL code.

Tuning SQL with Explain Plan, TKPROF, and Autotrace

Let's consider for a moment the impact on your database if your report query took several hours or days to run because a needed index or set of indices was missing. The probability is that your system would show an overall degradation in performance while this badly written query was running. Eventually, you'd probably have to interactively stop the query and try to figure out what was causing it to take so long. How would you go about your investigation to determine what was wrong with your query? Well, step right up lady or gentleman, we've got just the tool for you! However, before we can tell you about the tool you can use to determine your query's performance, we need to explain the tools Oracle uses to decide how your query will be executed. So, enter the optimizer.

The Optimizer

The part of Oracle that is responsible for determining how to retrieve the answer to your DML statement is called the *optimizer*. Oracle has two different optimizers that can be used to determine how to get the answer to any SQL statement, the Rule Based Optimizer (RBO) and the Cost Based Optimizer (CBO). The job of the optimizer is to break down a SQL statement into individual components and determine the fastest way to access the data and return the answer.

There are many steps that must be performed in preparation for Oracle to execute a SQL statement. First, the query syntax has to be checked for correctness. Then, Oracle must validate that the user submitting the query has the correct privileges to view the requested data. If the statement has already been processed and is stored in the shared pool memory area, Oracle will not have to take the time and overhead to create a new execution plan but can use the already stored plan, which can substantially improve performance.

If the statement has not been run before, Oracle must create an execution plan. An execution plan includes the access method for each table that the statement accesses and a join method if more than one table is involved. All this work must be done before Oracle actually starts to retrieve the data! It's a big job, and the CBO has only a limited amount of time to perform its tasks.

The CBO must understand which tables are involved in a SQL statement and find all the available access paths to that data. An *access path* is a fancy name for a method that Oracle can use to get to the data. Access paths break down into two general methods—either using an index or accessing the data directly from the table. If more than one table is involved, the optimizer has to figure out which join method to use. A *join method* is the name for the different algorithms the optimizer can call on to combine two different tables. What is important to remember is that the output of the optimizer is the *execution plan*—the set of instructions the optimizer puts together on how to access the data and, if necessary, join together multiple tables most efficiently.

Now, let's take a look at the two different approaches the Oracle optimizer can use to create its query plan.

Rule Based Optimizer

As the name implies, the Rule Based Optimizer is based on a fixed set of instructions that the optimizer can use as guidelines when building a query plan for a SQL statement. These rules tell the optimizer how to value one access path over another when trying to determine the quickest approach to get to or join your data. On the surface, this might look like the easiest way to create an optimizer. Unfortunately, Oracle has set up its optimizer to make some assumptions that can cause problems.

You see, the rules are determined by ranking the access paths to the data. That means Oracle has created an approach that says one method of access is always better than another method. The assumptions about which path is more efficient as built into the ranking of the rules do not take into account how much effort or resource it will take to use a particular access path. The RBO has not been enhanced since version 7.0 of Oracle. Currently, there are no plans to enhance the Rule Based Optimizer to include any new features.

Cost Based Optimizer

The Cost Based Optimizer (CBO) is as aptly named as the Rule Based Optimizer. In this case, the optimizer starts to take into account the relative resource "cost" of one access path over another when considering how to build the query plan. The best way to summarize the theory behind this approach is to say that the CBO attempts to take into account the relative effort of each table or index access and join operation when building the query plan. The cost calculation takes into account an estimate of CPU operations, network accesses, and disk accesses for any operation.

Using statistics kept in the data dictionary or default values in the optimizer code, the CBO is able to make the estimates for any table in the database. The CBO can then use this number when comparing different choices for accessing data from a table and, by comparing the relative costs, pick the operation with the lower cost, which should equate to creating the most efficient query plan.

To accomplish this cost calculation, the CBO first examines each table involved in a SQL statement and determines the least costly way to access each table. The access options can be through an index if one is available on the column or by a full table scan. The optimizer then computes a relative cost for each table access and saves the information. The cost of joining pairs of tables together using different join methods at its disposal is then computed. After finding the cheapest cost for the first pair, the CBO computes the cost of joining the next table to that result. When the cost of joining all the tables together is computed, the result is saved as a baseline and the CBO starts again, running through the tables in a different order. Obviously, the more complex the SQL statement, the more possible permutations the optimizer has to explore. In most cases, for a complex query, the optimizer is able to examine thousands of combinations in less than a second!

The CBO's success in picking a plan comes from its ability to evaluate the computed cost factor of each part of a SQL statement and use that cost as a gauge of the amount of resources that operation will take. But the CBO needs to understand more than just the types of access methods available to it when building a query plan. Information on the type and distribution of data in the tables or indexes is also required. Oracle provides the **analyze** command to gather statistics on objects within the database. **Analyze** gathers data by reading some or all of the data in an object and saving the information needed to understand the data distribution, such as the highest and lowest values in the column, the number of rows in the object, and the number of blocks in the object.

An abbreviated version of the **analyze** command syntax for a table is as follows. (The complete version is available in the Oracle SQL Reference Guide.)

```
analyze table <tablename> {estimate | compute} statistics
```

The interesting thing to note here is the end phrase about **estimate** or **compute statistics**. Rather than force the **analyze** command to review every row in each block of a table, you can allow the **analyze** command to sample some portion of the table to build its statistics. Since the optimizer is using statistical representations of the data to build its cost, a representative sample of the data may be all that is needed for a decision to be made.

NOTE
*Never run the **analyze** command directly against the SYS schema. When some of the tables in that schema are analyzed, performance problems can occur.*

In addition to the **analyze** command, which works on a single table or index at a time, Oracle has also provided the PL/SQL package DBMS_STATS to gather statistics on tables, indexes, or entire schemas. We'll tell you more about this package a little later in the chapter.

Setting the Optimizer in Your Environment

So, how do you set the optimizer for your instance? Since we're dealing with Oracle, there are several ways to do so, of course! Globally, the optimizer is set in the initialization parameter file using the **optimizer_mode** parameter. By default, the value is set to CHOOSE, which will default to the Cost Based Optimizer if statistics are available on at least one table in the query; but you can select several different values for this parameter: CHOOSE, FIRST_ROWS, ALL_ROWS, and RULE. Let's look at each of these value options more closely.

CHOOSE CHOOSE is the default setting, and the wording is significant. Above, we mentioned that the preferred optimizer is the CBO, but the optimizer will only use the cost-based method if certain conditions are met. First, if there are any statistics on at least one of the tables involved, Oracle will use the CBO. This fact is sometimes the cause of very poor SQL statement performance!

You see, if Oracle uses the CBO and does not have statistics for a table, it will substitute a set of default values to perform the cost calculations. As you can guess, the values are only placeholders and do not represent the actual data distribution in your table. Thus, it's often a case of "garbage in, garbage out," and the plan that the optimizer creates with these default values will most likely not be the best plan available. If you are going to use CHOOSE for the **optimizer_mode** parameter, plan to analyze all of the tables in your database frequently enough to capture the changes to data distribution. With this setting, if there are no statistics on any table involved in the SQL statement, Oracle will use the Rule Based Optimizer.

FIRST_ROWS This setting invokes the CBO, and, as such, all the guidance about statistics listed above still applies. However, this instruction biases the CBO to produce query plans that will produce the first set of data from a SQL statement as quickly as possible, even if it means producing a plan that would take a longer time overall. In other words, we are optimizing for best response time.

The FIRST_ROWS setting is good in environments where you are working with transactions that interface with users directly. In this case, we may want to get some data right to the users quickly (say to an Oracle Forms screen), where they can look at it, while the rest of the result set is built in the background.

In Oracle9i, you can even specify FIRST_ROWS_1, FIRST_ROWS_10, FIRST_ROWS_100, and FIRST_ROWS_1000 to tell the optimizer to consider the specified first number of rows. For example, using FIRST_ROWS_100, the optimizer will, as the name implies, consider the first 100 rows when developing its execution plan.

ALL_ROWS The opposite of FIRST_ROWS, this directs the optimizer to build the most efficient plan for returning all the data as quickly as possible. In this case, we are optimizing for best throughput. This is the default behavior of the optimizer with the CHOOSE setting.

RULE This is the setting for the Rule Based Optimizer, as we mentioned earlier in this section.

Tuning SQL

When you suspect a problem in the SQL code based on slow performance, you must first isolate the statements causing the problem. Oracle provides a V$ view, called V$SQL, that you can use to isolate a potentially poorly performing SQL statement. The output from the view can be sorted to show you how often a particular query is being run or how many resources are needed (in terms of database buffer reads). Two queries are illustrated below to show you how to use V$SQL. When deciding which query to tune, look at the output of both statements.

Tuning a query that uses a lot of resources but is only executed once a day may not be as profitable as tuning a query that uses only a few resources but is executed many thousands of times during the day. This incremental improvement can often provide more overall value to your system by reducing the amount of resources used through the entire day and making those resources available for other users.

Use the following queries on V$SQL to retrieve the SQL statements that have a number of disk accesses greater than some user-supplied number. The Sql_Text column shows the actual statement being executed.

```
select Disk_Reads, Executions, Disk_Reads/Executions, Sql_Text
  from V$SQL
 where Disk_Reads > {some number};
```

The second query on V$SQL that you can use follows. This time, we are looking for the most frequently executed statement by ordering on the Executions column.

```
select Disk_Reads, Executions, Disk_Reads/Executions, Sql_Text
  from V$SQL
 where Executions != 0
 order by 2;
```

The choices available for tuning are dependent on the optimizer you are using. Tuning SQL statements is an art unto itself, and many excellent books and courses are offered on the subject. Here, as a start, we will provide some basic tips for changing the access path of a query. With the Explain Plan facility to review the query plan chosen by the optimizer and **autotrace** and TKPROF to see how many resources a query is using, you can use these tips and see how they change the optimizer's access path decisions. As there are no hard-and-fast rules for getting to the optimal plan, the best advice is to experiment and see if you can change the plan in your favor.

When tuning SQL that has a query plan generated through the CBO, the first thing to review is the age and quality of the statistics. If the statistics are not up-to-date, the optimizer does not have the information it needs to create a proper query plan. The DBA_TABLES view has a column called Last_Analyzed that will show the last date statistics were gathered for this table. There is also a column, Num_Rows, that will show you how many rows were analyzed.

How much of a sample is needed depends in part on the distribution of the data in your database. Some studies have shown that a sampling rate of as little as 5 percent can give the optimizer enough information to compose an optimal plan. However, this is another case where "your mileage may vary"! We suggest you start by analyzing your data with an estimation factor of 5 percent. If the operation completes within a reasonable time frame and performance on your system is acceptable, then leave well enough alone. If you need to reduce the amount of time the **analyze** operation takes because of its overall impact on system performance, reduce the amount of information gathered.

One problem this shortage of time causes the CBO (and the DBA!) is that you cannot always guarantee that Oracle will process the statement in the most optimal fashion based on your testing. Oracle provides a facility in the optimizer known as "hints" to enable you to tell the optimizer that you want a specific index used or a statement to be handled a certain way. A *hint* is a direction that can be given to the Cost Based Optimizer to use a specific access method, join order, optimizer goal, or table order. In fact, RULE, ALL_ROWS, and FIRST_ROWS are all examples of hints. Hints are added to SQL statements using the comment syntax along with the + sign, as shown here:

```
select /*+ <hint> */
  from EMPLOYEE
 where <clause>;
```

The CBO will also be invoked if parallel operations are enabled in the instance by any means, either through the use of global parameters in the initialization file or by setting the default degree of parallelism for a table.

When dealing with the CBO, tuning is done primarily through the use of hints. One of the most common problems encountered with using hints is that Oracle does not report an error if the hint is used incorrectly. If the hint is syntactically incorrect, the optimizer will ignore it and create a query plan as normal. Of course, Oracle may ignore syntactically correct hints as well, and you'll be given no warning that your hint has been ignored.

Hints are a powerful tuning tool because you can use them to override the optimizer's choice of query plan with your own. This facility takes into account the fact that you, as the DBA or application developer, may know more about the tables or distribution of data than the optimizer can, based on the statistics available to it. While we cannot classify all the available hints here, they break down into the following categories:

- Hints to change the optimization approach for a SQL statement (RULE, CHOOSE, FIRST_ROWS, FIRST_ROWS(#), ALL_ROWS). These hints are general guidelines and will affect the construction of the entire query plan. The FIRST_ROWS(#) hint can be used (where # represents any number) to influence the number of rows returned quickly.
- Hints to change the access path for a table accessed by the statement. Here you can tell the optimizer to use or ignore specific indexes.
- Hints to change the join order for a join statement. For example, the ORDERED hint allows you to specify the exact order of table joins in the query plan.
- Hints to use a specific join operation. Here you can direct the optimizer to specific programmatic algorithms to use when joining two tables. As of Oracle8i, those methods include nested loop, sort-merge, hash join, semi-join, and anti-join.

Another factor that globally influences the optimizer is setting certain initialization parameters. Complete documentation of each of them is available in the Oracle Server Reference manual. When you are tuning the database, remember that changes to these parameters will change the query plan created by the Cost Based Optimizer. If you notice a sudden change in the plans created by the CBO, ensure that these values have not changed.

Explain Plan

Being able to "see" the execution plan that Oracle has created is most helpful in effectively tuning SQL statements. Oracle's **explain plan** command lets you display the path that the optimizer will use when the SQL is executed. **Explain plan** will evaluate the steps in a query plan and place one row for each step into a table called the PLAN_TABLE.

Although not required to use **explain plan**, the parameter **timed_statistics** can be set to TRUE to enable gathering more complete information. You can set the parameter dynamically using one of the following commands, based on whether you want to enable it for your current session only or for the entire system:

```
alter system set TIMED_STATISTICS = TRUE;
alter session set TIMED_STATISTICS = TRUE;
```

If you want the change to become permanent and you are using an SPFILE, you can use the following syntax:

```
alter system set TIMED_STATISTICS = TRUE
scope = BOTH;
```

In this command you are telling Oracle to set **timed_statistics** to TRUE right away and also write the change to the initialization file to make the change permanent. If you are not using the SPFILE approach, you can use the **alter** command and then, in the initialization parameter file, modify the **timed_statistics** parameter to TRUE. Note that enabling this tuning parameter has a minimal effect on the performance of the system.

Next, the PLAN_TABLE must be created. Oracle provides a script, utlxplan.sql, that you can use to create this table. It is located in the $ORACLE_HOME/rdbms/admin/ directory on a Unix system or %ORACLE_HOME%\rdbms\admin directory on a Windows system. You can create this table in all of your developers' schemas so that they can evaluate their SQL themselves.

To determine the execution plan of a query, preface the query with

```
explain plan set Statement_Id = <'your choice of identifier'> for
```

and then enter the SQL statement. The query will not actually be run but its execution plan will be written to the PLAN_TABLE. The same Statement_Id value can be used each time, as long as you empty the PLAN_TABLE before each use. To empty the table, use either **delete from** or **truncate**. If more than one developer is using a central PLAN_TABLE owned by SYSTEM, which we are opposed to, be careful to **delete from... where Statement_Id =** a specific value to ensure that you do not remove someone else's plan as well as your own.

Once the query has been executed, query the PLAN_TABLE to see the execution plan by using

```
 select lpad(' ',2*Level)||Operation||' '||Options||' '||Object_Name q_plan
   from PLAN_TABLE
  where Statement_Id = 'TEST'
connect by prior Id = Parent_Id
    and Statement_Id = 'TEST'
  start with Id = 1;
```

The plan is executed from inside out and from top to bottom, so you must read the plan using the same approach to understand how Oracle will process the statements. Items at the same level will be executed in the order that they appear in the execution plan. As a brief illustration of how Explain Plan works, the Oracle-supplied tables EMP and DEPT in the SCOTT schema will be used.

```
explain plan set Statement_Id = 'TEST' for
 select Ename, Empno, b.Deptno
   from EMP a, DEPT b
  where a.Deptno = b.Deptno;
```

The execution plan for this statement is

```
QPLAN
------------------------------
NESTED LOOPS
  TABLE ACCESS FULL EMP
  INDEX UNIQUE SCAN PK_DEPT
```

The entire EMP table will be read, but instead of also reading every row in the DEPT table and attempting to join the two (called a *Cartesian product*), a unique index scan will be performed on the primary key of the DEPT table, which should provide faster query processing. As queries are evaluated and tuned successfully, performance should improve. In some cases, just placing an index on a table to change a full table scan to an index scan can reduce query time from hours to minutes or even seconds.

The SQL Trace Facility (TKPROF)

Oracle provides the SQL trace facility known as TKPROF for gaining insight into SQL query processing. TKPROF is used to format output from a trace file into a more readable form. To activate the facility, you must

- Determine the location for USER_DUMP_DEST, where the output trace file will be located.
- Ensure that the parameter **max_dump_file_size** is set large enough to store the entire amount of output that will be generated.

As with Explain Plan, although not required, you can set the initialization parameter **timed_statistics** to TRUE to gather more complete information.

From the SQL*Plus user session, you can issue the following statement to let Oracle know that a trace file should be generated for the session.

```
alter session set SQL_TRACE = TRUE;
```

This will create a trace file that would give all but the most seasoned programmer eyestrain. Therefore, TKPROF was created to decode that trace into a more readable form. You can also use the procedure DBMS_SESSION.SET_SQL_TRACE to activate the SQL trace facility. If you wanted to enable the facility for the entire database (which we heartily suggest that you *not* do since it could degrade performance substantially for the system), the initialization parameter **sql_trace** can be set to TRUE and the database shut down and restarted.

NOTE
*Setting **timed_statistics** to TRUE will have little performance impact, but **sql_trace** set to TRUE for the system can have great negative impact.*

Like Explain Plan, TKPROF lets you see the execution plan for a statement or set of statements issued during a session in which **sql_trace** was set to TRUE. However, TKPROF also provides much more information, as you can see from the list of parameters displayed when just the command TKPROF is issued.

As an example, from the user DEMO_USER identified by DEMO, the following session was run:

```
alter session set SQL_TRACE = TRUE;
Session altered.
select Ename, Empno, b.Deptno
  from EMP a, DEPT b
 where a.Deptno = b.Deptno;
(output deleted to conserve space)
```

From the DOS prompt on a Windows system running Oracle 9.0.1 from the D:\ora9i\admin\mydb9\udump directory, TKPROF was run with the following command line:

```
tkprof ora01244.trc t.txt explain=demo_user/demo
```

The command follows the syntax: **tkprof** *inputfile outputfile* **explain**=*username/password*. The following output was produced (with all extra blank lines removed in order to conserve space). For readability, we have also removed some nonessential lines.

```
TKPROF: Release 9.0.1.2.1 - Production on Sat Mar 23 19:59:57 2002
 (c) Copyright 2001 Oracle Corporation. All rights reserved.
Trace file: ORA01244.TRC
Sort options: default
********************************************************************************
count    = number of times OCI procedure was executed
cpu      = cpu time in seconds executing
elapsed  = elapsed time in seconds executing
disk     = number of physical reads of buffers from disk
query    = number of buffers gotten for consistent read
current  = number of buffers gotten in current mode (usually for update)
rows     = number of rows processed by the fetch or execute call
********************************************************************************
********************************************************************************
select Ename, Empno, b.Deptno
  from EMP a, DEPT b
 where a.Deptno = b.Deptno
call     count       cpu    elapsed       disk      query    current        rows
------- ------  -------- ---------- ---------- ---------- ----------  ----------
Parse        1      0.00       0.03          0          0          0           0
Execute      1      0.00       0.00          0          0          0           0
Fetch        2      0.01       0.01          0          6          0          14
------- ------  -------- ---------- ---------- ---------- ----------  ----------
total        4      0.01       0.04          0          6          0          14
Misses in library cache during parse: 1
Optimizer goal: CHOOSE
Parsing user id: 28  (DEMO_USER)

Rows     Row Source Operatio
-------  ---------------------------------------------------
     14  MERGE JOIN
      4   SORT JOIN
      4    TABLE ACCESS FULL DEPT
     14   SORT JOIN
     14    TABLE ACCESS FULL EMP

Rows     Execution Plan
-------  ---------------------------------------------------
      0  SELECT STATEMENT   GOAL: CHOOSE
     14   MERGE JOIN
      4    SORT (JOIN)
      4     TABLE ACCESS (FULL) OF 'DEPT'
     14    SORT (JOIN)
     14     TABLE ACCESS (FULL) OF 'EMP'
********************************************************************************
```

```
OVERALL TOTALS FOR ALL NON-RECURSIVE STATEMENTS
call     count       cpu    elapsed       disk      query    current        rows
------- ------  -------- ---------- ---------- ---------- ----------  ----------
Parse        1      0.00       0.03          0          0          0           0
Execute      2      0.00       0.00          0          0          0           0
Fetch        2      0.01       0.01          0          6          0          14
------- ------  -------- ---------- ---------- ---------- ----------  ----------
total        5      0.01       0.04          0          6          0          14
Misses in library cache during parse: 1
Misses in library cache during execute: 1

OVERALL TOTALS FOR ALL RECURSIVE STATEMENTS

call     count       cpu    elapsed       disk      query    current        rows
------- ------  -------- ---------- ---------- ---------- ----------  ----------
Parse        0      0.00       0.00          0          0          0           0
Execute      0      0.00       0.00          0          0          0           0
Fetch        0      0.00       0.00          0          0          0           0
------- ------  -------- ---------- ---------- ---------- ----------  ----------
total        0      0.00       0.00          0          0          0           0

Misses in library cache during parse: 0
    2  user  SQL statements in session.
    0  internal SQL statements in session.
    2  SQL statements in session.
    1  statement EXPLAINed in this session.
********************************************************************************
Trace file: ORA01244.TRC
Trace file compatibility: 9.00.01
Sort options: default
       1  session in tracefile.
       2  user  SQL statements in trace file.
       0  internal SQL statements in trace file.
       2  SQL statements in trace file.
       2  unique SQL statements in trace file.
       1  SQL statements EXPLAINed using schema:
           DEMO_USER.prof$plan_table
             Default table was used.
             Table was created.
             Table was dropped.
      43  lines in trace file.
```

Demystifying the TKPROF Output

In the preceding example, we ran TKPROF with the **explain** option. This produces a copy of each SQL statement, the query plan, and the execution statistics for each statement. Reviewing the output, we see that the statistics for each SQL statement are decoded in a common fashion. For each statement, TKPROF creates a table of values from the trace file that gives some insight into how the statement was processed. In the points below, we cover some of the highlights most useful for SQL tuning.

- The Count column shows the number of times a statement was parsed, executed, or fetched in the time measured by the trace.
- The Cpu column records the CPU time in seconds for all parse, execute, or fetch calls attributed to it.
- The Elapsed column shows the elapsed time in seconds for all parse, execute, or fetch calls. Subtracting the CPU column from this value shows the amount of time the statement had to wait for some resource. When tuning, this gives you some insight into where to focus your efforts (on the work being done or the delays affecting the statement).
- The Disk column shows the number of data blocks physically read from disk for all parse, execute, or fetch calls.
- The Query column shows the number of buffers retrieved in consistent read mode for all parse, execute, or fetch calls. The sum of the Query and Current columns is the total number of buffers accessed by the statement.
- The Rows column is the number of output rows processed by the SQL statement. For **select** statements, the number of rows returned appears for the fetch step. For **update**, **delete**, and **insert** statements, the number of rows processed appears for the execute step.

As you can see from this example, you can obtain much more information about your session if you use TKPROF. If all you want is a quick insight into the execution plan of a query, Explain Plan is an excellent tool. For a more in-depth view of multiple queries, use TKPROF.

There's one other thing to consider when using TKPROF with the **explain** option. TKPROF will parse the query and report the plan back to you at the time TKPROF was run. It does not guarantee to show you the plan from the time the trace file was created. So it is possible that you are seeing a different plan than one that is in the trace file. If at all possible, make sure you are using the same session-level parameters and the same statistics when decoding a trace file with TKPROF. Also, remember that when you run the same statement a second time, your statement has already been stored in the library cache, so the processing time will be reduced. This can skew your statistics.

There are Oracle-supplied and third-party vendor tools available to assist you in analyzing explain plans. The tools are a great time-saver for both experienced and less experienced DBAs.

Autotrace

The **autotrace** command provides an easy way to explain the query path of a SQL statement. Using the options documented below, you can easily view the query plan chosen by the optimizer in a readable format. You can also use the trace function of this command to examine such information as the number of reads it took to resolve a query, or the number of sort operations that were required to return the data. This gives you a "quick and dirty" way to examine an individual SQL statement to see if it is perhaps the cause of a performance problem and worth some additional investigation. You use autotrace interactively from the SQL*Plus command line. Let's look at some examples of what you can do with the autotrace facility.

You must run the script plustrce.sql found in ORACLE_HOME/sqlplus/admin. After you have run the script, you can grant the PLUSTRACE role to anyone who will be using **autotrace**. Remember, too, that the SQL statement is always executed before Oracle produces and displays its explain plan and statistics, and that TIMED_STATISTICS must be set to TRUE.

In the first example, we use the **set autotrace** command to execute the query and view the explain plan.

```
set autotrace on explain
select count(*)
  from DEPT;

COUNT(*)
----------
         4

Execution Plan
----------------------------------------------------------
0      SELECT STATEMENT Optimizer=CHOOSE
1    0   SORT (AGGREGATE)
2    1     TABLE ACCESS (FULL) OF 'DEPT'
```

The first column of the output is basically a count of steps within the explain plan and is of little significance. The second column is helpful since it shows the order in which the steps of the explain plan are executed—the highest number is executed first. If two or more numbers of the same value are displayed, the order is from top to bottom.

In the above example, TABLE ACCESS (FULL) of 'DEPT' is the first step in the explain plan, followed by SORT (AGGREGATE). Thus, the above plan tells you that all of the rows from DEPT are read and then counted via the SORT AGGREGATE algorithm.

We can also look at the trace output for the same query. Notice how quickly you can tell how many reads, consistent reads, and sorts the SQL statement required. High values for the "reading" indicators or for sorting are sometimes clues that a query could be tuned further.

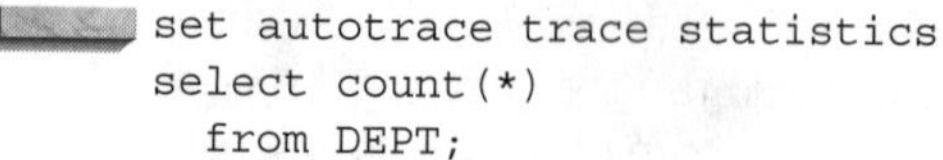

```
set autotrace trace statistics
select count(*)
  from DEPT;

Statistics
----------------------------------------------------
0         recursive calls
0         db block gets
0         consistent gets
0         physical reads
0         redo size
0         bytes sent via SQL*Net to client
0         bytes received via SQL*Net from client
0         SQL*Net roundtrips to/from client
0         sorts (memory)
0         sorts (disk)
1         rows processed
```

Using the Oracle Enterprise Manager (OEM)

Until now, we've shown you tools that you access from either SQL*Plus or your operating system command line. Now, it's time to look at a stand-alone GUI tool provided by Oracle that you can use to perform many different tasks. This tool set was introduced in version 7 and has been released for no extra cost, with a different version number, for each release of the Oracle RDBMS. For example, Oracle8i was released with OEM 2.0.4, and Oracle9i was released with OEM 9.0.1.0.0. For this book, we are going to focus on the features offered in the OEM version 9.0.1.0.0 release. Oracle9i's version is compatible with the earlier Oracle releases back to Oracle8.0 and offers the richest set of options currently available. Three tuning packages are bundled with the Oracle9i version of OEM. Until now, these packages were extra-cost options. They are now included at very small cost. We'll look very briefly at these packages as well.

The Oracle Enterprise Manager tool set offers you a way to manage your databases from one central PC. Several DBAs can connect to the same OEM repository. This important feature ensures that you and your fellow DBAs will be able to work in concert to manage databases remotely while not interfering with each other's jobs.

But, what is a repository, and what are the basic features that you can use with this tool set? Let's take a closer look at OEM. Since documentation of the installation, configuration, and management of the OEM could easily fill an entire book by itself and we have a limited number of pages available here, we are only going to give you a very brief overview of the tool set. We will tell you, though, that the installation of OEM is generally a two-step process. You must first install the underlying software when you install the rest of the Oracle software. Once you've built a database to house the OEM repository, you can go into the Configuration and Migration tools option and select the Oracle Enterprise Manager Configuration Assistant option to complete the installation and configuration of OEM. You will be asked either to designate a database to house the repository or choose to have the configuration assistant build a database specifically for the repository. We recommend that you either allow the assistant to build the database or build one yourself that will be dedicated to OEM. You see, there are two different ways to access OEM: in stand-alone mode and by logging in to the Oracle Management Server. Once you have designated a database to house the OEM repository, you will not see or be able to touch that database from the Oracle Management Server option. You will only be able to interact with it from stand-alone access.

Another idiosyncrasy of OEM is that in a Windows environment, the Management Server service must be started before you can access the Oracle Management Server. That doesn't sound like much of a problem, right? In reality, several other tasks must be performed before you can get the Management Server service started. The listener must be running, the database service must be started, and the database that housed the repository must be opened. If the Management Server service is not running and you attempt to connect to it, you receive an error message telling you to verify that you entered the correct connection information and the status of the Oracle Management Server.

By default, the Oracle Management Server service is set to start automatically. However, if the database is not already opened, the service attempt fails. If you have problems starting OEM in your environment, check for documentation on the MetaLink site for possible known problems and fixes.

OEM Basic Features

Several components make up the OEM. A set of screens, called the OEM *console*, let you manage databases. The OEM uses a set of tables that are stored in a database to hold information for the tool's use. These tables are referred to as the *repository*. There are many Java programs that you interact with to perform different areas of database administration. Some of these programs are referred to as *wizards* that guide you through an activity, such as creating a user or tablespace in your database.

When you initially access the OEM console, you are presented with the choice of launching the stand-alone mode or logging on to the Oracle Management Server.

OEM in Stand-Alone Mode

If you are going to be managing your databases locally, you can choose the Stand-alone option from the initial OEM startup screen. Choosing the Stand-alone option brings you to the Oracle Enterprise Manager screen shown in Figure 13-1. This option, as you can see by the list on the screen, enables you to perform any or all of the following tasks:

- Administer databases, iAS servers, applications, and services
- Diagnose, modify, and tune multiple databases
- Schedule tasks on multiple systems at varying time intervals
- Monitor database conditions throughout the network
- Administer multiple network nodes and services from many locations
- Share tasks with other administrators
- Group related services together to facilitate administration tasks
- Launch integrated Oracle and third-party tools

We've already expanded the database entry so that you can see the two databases we have available. The MYDB9 database is our repository database used to house the OEM metadata.

You can access options by either using the pull-down menus at the top of the screen or clicking on the icons on the left side of the screen. When you select a database, you can use the Object option of the pull-down menu to delete, connect, start up, or shut down the database. Because of the limited amount of pages we have here, we'll let you examine and play with the OEM stand-alone options yourself.

Oracle Management Server Option

When you choose the Oracle Management Server option, you are prompted to enter the appropriate username and password for your OEM session. Now, as a thinking DBA, you would assume that the username and password you need is the

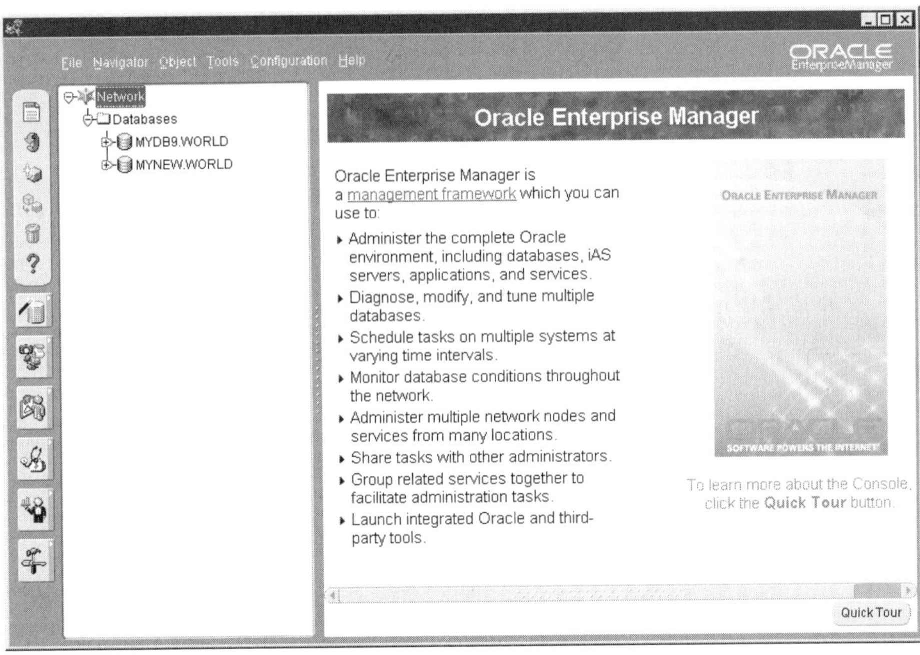

FIGURE 13-1. *Oracle Enterprise Manager Stand-alone Console screen*

SYSTEM user and its associated password. Unfortunately, you'd be wrong! If this is the first time that you are connecting to the Oracle Management Server console, the username is SYSMAN, and the password you must use is OEM_TEMP. Go figure!

Figure 13-2 shows the initial OEM Management Server screen. Again, we've expanded the database area to show you that the MYDB9 database is not available. As you can see, there are many more options in Management Server mode than in stand-alone mode and a much more extensive list of activities that you can perform.

Notice the entries between the Network option and the Databases option: Events, Jobs, and Report Definitions. Below the Databases option, there are listings for Groups, HTTP Servers, Listeners, and Nodes.

The Event Scheduler enables you to set up jobs that will test for specific problems or situations that may occur within your database. Oracle provides you with a very effective set of events that you can test for. By highlighting the Events option and then selecting Create from the pull-down menu, you can, under the

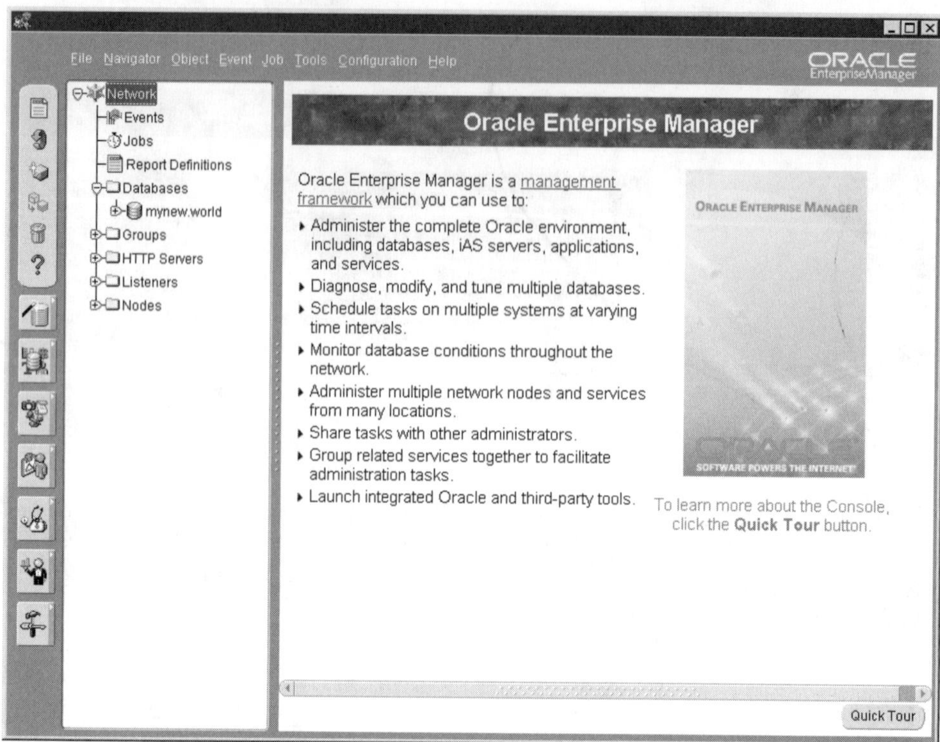

FIGURE 13-2. *Oracle Enterprise Manager Management Server initial screen*

Tests option, see the broad spectrum of events that you can monitor. Figure 13-3 shows some of the Event options provided by Oracle for your use.

Once you've selected an event to test for, you can select the Register option at the bottom of the screen to register the event. You can also add the event to the library to have it available to run on a periodic basis. Once you've registered the event, you can use the Schedule tab to establish a schedule, and even declare who can have access to monitor or be notified if an event you are testing for occurs.

Among the features within OEM is the Job Scheduler, which you can use to set up jobs to run either once immediately, once at a prescheduled time, or on a specific, recurring schedule. You could, for example, schedule your backup job to run on a nightly basis.

Using the Group option, you can create a view of several databases and perform tasks on all of the databases in the group at the same time. You can even scan in a background of your office or corporate layout and place the databases graphically

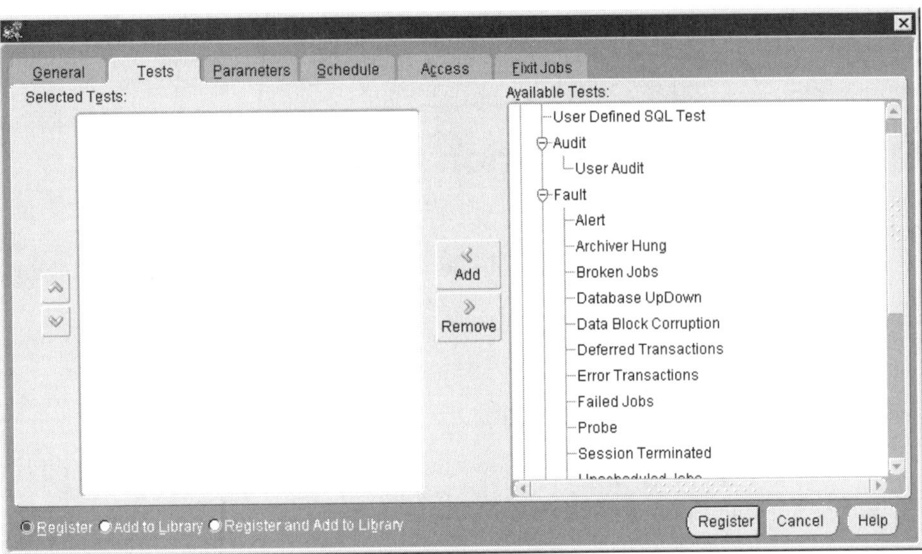

FIGURE 13-3. *OEM Create Event Tests screen*

on the background to show you where each database is located. Oracle supplies several geographical maps that you can use by default, such as a map of the United States and one of Europe.

You can manage the HTTP servers that have been discovered from the OEM console, administer listeners, and interact with known nodes on your system. Using the icons along the side of the screen, you can perform capacity planning, database management, performance evaluation and tuning, as well as access products like Data Guard and LogMiner. (See Chapter 11 for more about Data Guard and LogMiner.) OEM provides a graphical interface to the Recovery Manager (RMAN). In Oracle9i, this feature has been enhanced to work even better than it has in past versions. Chapter 11 also discusses RMAN more extensively.

If you want to perform prescheduled jobs or tasks other than looking at statistical information about your database, you will need to configure a process called the Intelligent Agent to run on each machine that has a database of interest. You can only configure one Intelligent Agent per machine, no matter how many different databases are available from that machine. The Intelligent Agent supports communication between the databases on that machine and the central OEM console. In earlier versions of OEM, the console had to be running and visible before scheduled jobs could be run correctly. In the latest version of OEM, the console can be closed and scheduled jobs will still run.

From the console, you can view the makeup of databases and administer different databases on one or more nodes at once. There are several database administration options that you can use from either the OEM console or as separate options from the Windows Start | Programs menu.

Database Administration OEM Options

There are several areas of interest available from OEM version 9.0.1.0.0 for database administrators.

Within the Instance options, you can perform the following tasks as explained in the Instance overview screen:

- Start up and shut down a database
- View and edit the values of instance parameters
- Manage users' sessions, and view currently running SQL and its Explain Plan
- Manage in-doubt transactions
- Monitor long-running operations
- Control processing resources via Resource Plans
- Manage stored configurations
- Administer locks and sessions consuming the highest amounts of resources (if the Diagnostics Pack is installed)

From the Schema option, you can create, alert, drop, and show dependencies for objects. The Security option enables you to create, alter, drop, or grant privileges and roles to users and profiles, while the Storage option provides you with a way to manage storage objects like tablespaces, datafiles, undo or rollback segments, and redo logs. As the name implies, the Replication Manager provides you with a way to manage distributed systems. The On-line Analytical Processing (OLAP) option enables you to provide data warehousing support, while the JVM (Java Virtual Machine) option helps you manage components authored in Java. Finally, the Workspace option helps you to manage a workspace environment. You can use the quick tours for each of these options to help you learn about and understand them better.

Other Available Packs

There are several additional OEM packs that Oracle has developed and made available in the base product. The packs are accessed using the icons along the left side of the OEM console screen below the task area. The first icon you see is the Database Wizard, which provides you with the tools to back up and recover your database. The rest of the icons provide access to the following packs: the Application Management pack, Change Management pack, the Database Applications pack, the Diagnostic pack, the Service Management pack, and the Performance Tuning pack.

Using the Application Management pack, you can access the Capacity Planner and evaluate the historic performance of your system to project disk space or I/O usage, and the Concurrent Processing Tuning Assistant for use with the Oracle Applications concurrent managers. You can use the Performance Manager to view the database performance using different forms of charts, and the Performance Overview tool to obtain an overview of the performance of a specific database.

With the Change Management pack, you can analyze the impact and complex dependencies associated with application change, and automatically perform upgrades. The Change Management pack enables you to investigate and track changes, define and plan changes, evaluate the impact a change has on the system, and then implement the change. You can keep a history of the changes and synchronize objects and schemas within different databases. Thus, you can perform a comparison of your production and development databases and synchronize the development database to match production. Seven change tools are provided with the Change Management pack: Create Baseline, Compare Database Objects, Find Database Objects, Change Manager, DB Quick Change, DB Alter, and DB Propagate.

The Database Application pack provides the ability to protect your database using Data Guard, Log Miner, Spatial Index Advisor, SQL Plus Worksheet, and Text Manager.

Using the Diagnostic pack, you can perform advanced database monitoring, diagnosis, and planning. You can track resource usage to help you plan your future resource needs. Oracle supplies a wide array of customized performance charts with this pack, and you can use the pack to identify and remove lock contention. The pack can be configured to perform many different event monitoring tasks that can be set up to send email, or even page you if a preestablished resource threshold is reached.

The Service Management pack provides a way to administer network components. There are two tools included with this pack: the Oracle Internet Directory Manager and the Oracle Net Manager.

With the Performance Tuning pack, you can identify and tune major database and application bottlenecks. The pack discovers tuning opportunities and generates the analysis and scripts necessary to help you tune your database. Using the Performance Tuning pack, you can obtain execution plans and tune your application's SQL statements as well as evaluate indexes, examine and create stored outlines, reorganize storage areas and rebuild fragmented objects like tables or indexes, and view the storage map of a tablespace.

Oracle is turning to the OEM Management Server more and more to provide a centralized place for DBAs to work with the latest tools as they are developed. We strongly recommend that you take the time to work through and become proficient in using all of the available options.

STATSPACK

In Chapter 12 we talked about server performance and some of the things you can do to correct problems. But how do you know when there are problems?

Well, you could, we suppose, just wait for your system administrator to run her reports or for your application users to complain that the system is slow or "Oracle is down." Of course, if you do that, you're not really going to be a proactive DBA and probably won't have a job for very long. So what can you do?

In earlier releases of the database, Oracle provided a set of SQL scripts to help look for problems. Known generally as "bstat/estat," they are actually named utlbstat.sql and utlestat.sql and reside in the rdbms/admin directory under your ORACLE_HOME. After setting TIMED_STATISTICS to TRUE in your initialization parameter file, you would run the utlbstat.sql script from an account with SYSTEM-like privileges at the beginning of the time period for which you wanted to collect statistics, and then run the utlestat.sql script at the end of the time period. The bstat script would drop a set of tables that were copies of some of the V$ views, re-create them, and take a snapshot of the database statistics at that moment by selecting from the V$ performance views. Later, after the amount of time you wanted to track had passed, you would run the estat script, which would take a second snapshot of the database statistics and create a report named report.txt about the average performance over that time period.

There were a number of problems with this approach:

- Since the scripts were SQL and not PL/SQL, the queries had to be reparsed every time you ran the scripts.
- The scripts dropped and re-created the tables every time they were run, increasing the possibility of fragmenting the tablespace they were in.
- The data collected was not saved, and no comparisons between different sets of time periods could be made.
- You could not automate the running of the scripts within the database itself.
- The report could only be generated when the utlestat.sql script was run and could never be re-created.
- If the database was shut down during the time period you were evaluating, the statistics reported would become erroneous.
- You didn't want to run them right after the database started up, otherwise the result set was skewed due to the startup.
- Not all of the pertinent ratios were precalculated, and the report.txt would only be formatted correctly using Server Manager.

Some DBAs would make copies of the scripts and modify them to permanently create the statistics tables and then truncate the data. Unfortunately, this only fixed one of the problems.

Oracle recognized the limitations of the bstat/estat scripts and, as of release 8.1.6, provided DBAs with a PL/SQL package called STATSPACK that addressed many of these issues as well as expanded on the statistical information collected and reported.

What STATSPACK Does

STATSPACK collects a variety of system statistical data and stores it in permanent tables. You can collect data at different levels of detail, at different times, and run reports over several time periods, changing the start and end dates to expand or contract the time period. Reports are generated separately from the data collection and have been significantly reformatted and expanded from the bstat/estat report.txt. There is now a high-level summary page, a section on high-resource SQL, and information on the following areas:

- Latching
- SGA memory
- Buffer ratio
- Wait events

We'll show you a sample of the new report a little later in this section. Before starting to work with STATSPACK, we suggest you read both the spdoc.txt file in the /rdbms/admin directory under ORACLE_HOME and the Oracle Performance Guide and Reference manual on STATSPACK.

How to Install STATSPACK

To install STATSPACK, you run a SQL script called spcreate.sql found in the rdbms/admin directory under your ORACLE_HOME. This script will run three additional scripts:

- Spcusr.sql—create the STATSPACK user PERFSTAT with the password PERFSTAT. We recommend that you change the known password as soon as the installation completes.
- Spctab.sql—create the permanent statistical tables owned by PERFSTAT.
- Spcpkg.sql—create the STATSPACK package owned by PERFSTAT.

Each of these scripts will create a log file (spcusr.lis, spctab.lis, and spcpkg.lis, respectively) that you should check to make sure the installation completes without errors.

Before running the spcreate.sql script, you will need to decide where you want the tables to reside. You can use the TOOLS tablespace, or create one specifically for the PERFSTAT user. In general, you will need a tablespace with at least 64M to 100M of free space for the PERFSTAT tables. If you plan on taking and saving a large number of STATSPACK snapshots, or if you want to save very detailed statistical information, you will probably need more space.

While running the spcreate.sql script, you will be prompted for the default and temporary tablespaces for the PERFSTAT user. The prompts, from a test database, are shown here:

```
Below are the list of online tablespaces in this database.
Decide which tablespace you wish to create the STATSPACK tables
and indexes. This will also be the PERFSTAT user's default tablespace.

Specifying the SYSTEM tablespace will result in the installation
FAILING, as using SYSTEM for performance data is not supported.

TABLESPACE_NAME                CONTENTS
------------------------------ ---------
DICTMGMT                       PERMANENT
DRSYS                          PERMANENT
INDX                           PERMANENT
TEMP                           TEMPORARY
TESTIT                         PERMANENT
TESTIT2                        PERMANENT
TOOLS                          PERMANENT
TOOSMALL                       PERMANENT
UNDOTBS                        UNDO
USERS                          PERMANENT

10 rows selected.

Specify PERFSTAT user's default   tablespace
Enter value for default_tablespace: tools
Using tools for the default tablespace

PL/SQL procedure successfully completed.

User altered.

User altered.

Choose the PERFSTAT user's temporary tablespace.

Specifying the SYSTEM tablespace will result in the installation
FAILING, as using SYSTEM for the temporary tablespace is not recommended.

Specify PERFSTAT user's temporary tablespace.
Enter value for temporary_tablespace: temp
Using temp for the temporary tablespace
```

Notice that the installation will not let you use the SYSTEM tablespace as the default temporary tablespace for the PERFSTAT user. You can find further details on installing STATSPACK in the Oracle Performance Guide and Reference manual.

Generating a STATSPACK Snapshot

Each time you collect the statistical data for STATSPACK to use, you are capturing, at that instant in time, the way that data looks. Thus, the data collection is called a *snapshot*. In order to generate a report, you will need two snapshots. You can generate and collect snapshots every hour, or generate snapshots when you are having performance problems. Each snapshot you generate is given a unique ID. In order to run STATSPACK in a Real Application Cluster (RAC) environment, the snapshot ID is actually a concatenated key, made up of a unique sequence number (snap_id), instance number (instance_number), and database identifier (dbid) in the PERFSTAT tables.

To generate a snapshot at the default level you have set, from the PERFSTAT user account, run

```
execute statspack.snap;
```

You can collect data at any one of several levels of detail. Table 13-1 shows the various levels and the information collected. Level 10 can be resource intensive, and you should only use it when advised by Oracle personnel.

To change the level of detail for the snapshot you are taking, you pass in the parameter **i_snap_level** to statspack.snap with the level at which you want to run. To permanently change the level so that all snapshots are taken at this new level, pass **i_snap_level** to statspack.statspack_modify_parameters. For a complete list of the parameters that can be set for STATSPACK, check the Performance Guide and Reference manual.

Generating the STATSPACK Report

Now that you know how to generate a snapshot and collect the data, it's time to move on to the next step and get to the "good stuff"—report generation. First, in order to generate a report, you need two snapshots, a beginning and ending collection so that you can analyze what's going on in that time period. Gee, that sounds a lot like doing a bstat/estat report doesn't it? So why bother with STATSPACK?

As we said before, STATSPACK is a bit more flexible than the bstat/estat report. Let's say you have taken several snapshots, as described in Table 13-2.

If you had been running the bstat/estat scripts, you would get a report for the time period of March 23, 2002, between midnight and 6:00 a.m., another one from 6:00 a.m. to noon, another from noon to 6:00 p.m., and so on. You could not look at any other combination of time periods.

Statistic Gathered	Level 0	Level 5	Level 6	Level 10
General performance statistics: wait statistics, system events, system statistics, rollback segment data, row cache, SGA, background events, session events, lock statistics, buffer pool statistics, parent latch statistics	Y	Y	Y	Y
High-resource SQL statements that exceed one of the following thresholds: number of executions, number of disk reads, number of parse calls, number of buffer gets, size of sharable memory used, version count	N	Y	Y	Y
SQL plans and plan usage data for each of the high resource usage SQL statements captured	N	N	Y	Y
Parent and child latch information	N	N	N	Y

TABLE 13-1. *STATSPACK Levels of Detail*

Snapshot ID	Time Taken
1	03/23/2002 00:00:00
2	03/23/2002 06:00:00
3	03/23/2002 12:00:00
4	03/23/2002 18:00:00
5	03/24/2002 00:00:00
6	03/24/2002 06:00:00

TABLE 13-2. *STATSPACK Snapshots Taken*

With the STATSPACK report, you tell Oracle the beginning and ending snapshot IDs to use for the report. So with the snapshots taken above, you could report on a daily basis (snapshot 1 to snapshot 5), or every 6 hours (snapshot 2 to snapshot 3), or every 12 hours (snapshot 4 to snapshot 6). How does this help you? Well, suppose you take a snapshot every two hours, but report only on a daily basis. Now suppose you see that the report from yesterday showed statistics that were very different from the previous few days. You can then run reports over smaller time periods, until you locate the two-hour interval when something changed. Once you've isolated the time frame in which a change occurred, you can check with the developers and end users to see if they were doing anything unusual at that time yesterday. If they weren't, you might decide to take extra snapshots at even shorter intervals today to see if you can locate exactly what is happening. Additionally, since STATSPACK also reports on the high-resource SQL for the time intervals, you can see which tables and indexes were being accessed and decide if you need to reorganize the table, add an index, or move an object to a different disk.

Now, how do you generate a report? Oracle provides a SQL script, spreport.sql, in the rdbms/admin directory under your ORACLE_HOME. You will run this script logged in as the PERFSTAT user. The script displays the snapshots available in your database, and prompts you for the beginning snapshot ID, the ending snapshot ID, and a report name. You cannot run a report across a database shutdown.

The summary page from a STATSPACK report on an Oracle9i database is shown here:

```
STATSPACK report for

DB Name         DB Id    Instance     Inst Num Release     Cluster Host
------------ ----------- ------------ -------- ----------- ------- ------------
SAND         2014984324 SAND                1 9.0.1.0.0   NO      laptop-jt

            Snap Id     Snap Time      Sessions Curs/Sess Comment
            ------- ------------------ -------- --------- -------------------
Begin Snap:       6 09-Mar-02 13:13:23        9       5.0
  End Snap:      10 09-Mar-02 13:18:09        9       5.2
   Elapsed:                4.77 (mins)

Cache Sizes (end)
~~~~~~~~~~~~~~~~~
               Buffer Cache:        20M      Std Block Size:          8K
           Shared Pool Size:        28M          Log Buffer:        512K

Load Profile
~~~~~~~~~~~~                            Per Second       Per Transaction
                                   ---------------       ---------------
                  Redo size:              4,653.57            332,730.00
              Logical reads:                 76.92              5,500.00
              Block changes:                  7.22                516.50
             Physical reads:                 32.24              2,305.00
            Physical writes:                  8.17                584.25
```

```
                User calls:                   3.20                229.00
                    Parses:                   0.73                 52.50
              Hard parses:                    0.03                  2.00
                     Sorts:                   1.08                 77.25
                    Logons:                   0.00                  0.00
                 Executes:                    1.42                101.25
             Transactions:                    0.01

  % Blocks changed per Read:    9.39    Recursive Call %:    82.42
 Rollback per transaction %:    0.00       Rows per Sort:    96.30

Instance Efficiency Percentages (Target 100%)
~~~~~~~~~~~~~~~~~~~~~~~~~~~~~~~~~~~~~~~~~~~~~
            Buffer Nowait %:  100.00       Redo NoWait %:  100.00
            Buffer  Hit   %:   58.09    In-memory Sort %:  100.00
            Library Hit   %:   96.08        Soft Parse %:   96.19
         Execute to Parse %:   48.15         Latch Hit %:  100.00
Parse CPU to Parse Elapsd %:   41.67     % Non-Parse CPU:   99.90

 Shared Pool Statistics        Begin   End
                               ------  ------
             Memory Usage %:   50.79   51.55
    % SQL with executions>1:   50.78   50.38
  % Memory for SQL w/exec>1:   73.39   72.98

Top 5 Wait Events
~~~~~~~~~~~~~~~~~                                             Wait     % Total
Event                                               Waits  Time (s)   Wt Time
-------------------------------------------- ------------ ----------- -------
db file scattered read                              1,190          22   78.56
db file sequential read                               244           2    8.01
control file parallel write                            92           2    5.52
log file parallel write                                29           1    4.22
resmgr:waiting in end wait                              8           0    1.25
          -------------------------------------------------------------
```

For specifics on how to interpret the summary page, and the additional pages of the report, check the Oracle Performance Guide and Reference manual.

Cleaning Up the STATSPACK Tables

The last time we looked through our closets, we realized that the things we were saving grew to fill all the space we had available. Biting the bullet, we dug through and threw out the clothes we hadn't used or needed for at least a year.

Just as we realized that we were packrats when it came to filling closet space, so you will realize that STATSPACK can consume all the space in the tablespace you've assigned to PERFSTAT, if you don't do something about it. Oracle provides several ways to clear out the PERFSTAT tables.

If you want to archive the older snapshots, you can export the tables and import them into another database before removing these snapshots. Oracle gives you a parameter file for the export, spuexp.par, located in the /rdbms/admin directory under your ORACLE_HOME. You run the export as follows:

```
exp userid=perfstat/<password> parfile=spuexp.par
```

Once you have exported the tables, you can import them into a historical database.

If you want to remove older snapshots, you can either remove all the snapshots by running sptrunc.sql (remember that you will need to take at least two snapshots before you can generate another report!) or some of them by running sppurge.sql, both of which are located in the /rdbms/admin directory under ORACLE_HOME. Sppurge.sql prompts you for a beginning and ending snapshot ID and removes all snapshots within the range you supply. Both of these scripts should be run while logged in as the PERFSTAT user.

Finally, what if you decide to remove STATSPACK completely? Well, while we don't suggest you do that, Oracle provides yet another script to remove all the PERFSTAT tables. To remove STATSPACK, log in to the database as "/ as sysdba", and then run spdrp.sql (again from the /rdbms/admin directory under ORACLE_HOME). Spdrp.sql runs spdtab.sql and spdusr.sql, which will remove the PERFSTAT tables, synonyms, packages, and finally, the PERFSTAT user.

DBMS_STATS

Wait a minute. Didn't we just talk about statistics? What's the difference between STATSPACK and DBMS_STATS? We're glad you asked, because we've found that many DBAs get the two confused. STATSPACK, as we said in the previous section, is used to gather and monitor the performance statistics of your database. DBMS_STATS is used to collect and view statistics for the Cost Based Optimizer. If you don't use DBMS_STATS, you may find that STATSPACK reports problems in many of your SQL statements that are using a poor execution plan because the statistics are bad or nonexistent. You can also use DBMS_STATS to store, change, or move statistics, based on what your database is being used for at any given time. We'll talk about that in more detail in a little while.

Installing and Running DBMS_STATS

To install DBMS_STATS (if the scripts have not already been run automatically during database creation), you need to run two scripts, logged in as "/ as sysdba". Both are located in the rdbms/admin directory under your ORACLE_HOME.

```
@dbmsstat.sql
@prvtstat.plb
```

The first script contains the package specification, with all the declarations of the procedures within the package that you can use. The script is commented so that you can get an understanding of what each of the procedures does. The second script contains the actual package body and all the procedure code. Access to the DBMS_STATS package is granted to PUBLIC, so that any user can execute it.

Now that we have DBMS_STATS loaded into our database, we need to run it. Table 13-3 contains a list of the procedures that affect tables that you can call from DBMS_STATS. The table procedures will collect or manipulate table, index, and column statistics.

So you will want to run DBMS_STATS.GATHER_TABLE_STATS if the data in your tables changes by any significant amount. You can also work with index or column statistics directly, by substituting the word INDEX or COLUMN for TABLE in the name of the procedure and using the appropriate parameters for those procedures. You cannot gather column statistics directly. You can work with the statistics for all objects in a schema by substituting SCHEMA for TABLE, and you can gather statistics for all objects in the database using the GATHER_DATABASE_STATS procedure. Finally, you can collect CPU and I/O statistics for the operating system by calling the GATHER_SYSTEM_STATS procedure. The Oracle9i Supplied PL/SQL Packages and Types Reference manual covers the DBMS_STATS package and procedures within it in detail.

Procedure	**Description**
GATHER_TABLE_STATS	Collects table, index, and column statistics. Gather attempts to collect in parallel.
SET_TABLE_STATS	Sets table-related information. This allows you to override the collected statistics and set them yourself.
GET_TABLE_STATS	Retrieves the table statistics so you can examine them for possible changes.
DELETE_TABLE_STATS	Deletes the table-related statistics.
EXPORT_TABLE_STATS	Retrieves statistics for a particular table from the data dictionary and stores them in the user stat table.
IMPORT_TABLE_STATS	Retrieves statistics for a particular table from the user stat table and stores them in the data dictionary.

TABLE 13-3. *DBMS_STATS Procedures for Tables*

Moving Statistics Using DBMS_STATS

Why would you want to move the statistics? If you are a proactive DBA, you want any code that goes into production to be properly tuned. You can accomplish this goal in several ways. If you have the disk space available, you can create an exact duplicate of your production database for testing, so that the statistics available really reflect the spread of the production data. Of course, if you are working with a database that is measured in terabytes of disk space, you're not likely to have that much available space for a test database.

You can also gather the statistics on the production database and move them to your test database. Now, you won't have the actual data, but the statistics will be accurate for the production database, and the Cost Based Optimizer uses the statistics, not the actual data, to determine the execution plan. Thus, you get the execution plan that Oracle will choose on production, and you can then tune the application SQL accurately and create indexes as necessary.

To move the statistics, you need to do the following:

1. Create a holding table in a user schema to hold the statistics (CREATE_STAT_TABLE procedure).
2. Copy the statistics from the data dictionary to the holding table (EXPORT_TABLE_STATS procedure).
3. Export/import the holding table into the second database.
4. Move the statistics from the holding table into the data dictionary (IMPORT_TABLE_STATS procedure).

You can also drop the holding table using the DROP_STAT_TABLE procedure.

There's one final point to remember: DBMS_STATS gathers statistics only for cost-based optimization. If you want to look at chained rows or the number of unused data blocks, you need to analyze the table using the **analyze table <tablename> compute statistics** SQL command.

Using Stored Outlines

Starting in Oracle8i, stored outlines have been provided as a way to ensure that a query will be processed and the same execution plan will be used at all times regardless of how the query is submitted. A stored outline stores a set of hints for a query. Those hints will be used every time the query is executed. Using the stored hints will increase the likelihood that the query will use the same execution path and execution plan each time. Although hints do not mandate an execution path (they're hints, not commands), they provide an essential benefit to a DBA faced with a common tuning problem when using the CBO. Oracle continues to modify the algorithms used to compute the costs of a query in each release. In fact, these changes can sometimes be implemented in a patch release for the current Oracle version. This change in costing a query can cause the performance to vary greatly. Hopefully, this is always for the better! However, there is always a chance that the changes could cause a suboptimal execution plan to be generated and your performance to degrade. By creating stored outlines for your SQL, you are giving yourself an insurance policy that performance will not change in any critical areas.

In addition, using stored outlines gives you a chance to tune third-party SQL statements, when you cannot otherwise touch the code.

Implementing Stored Outlines

For the stored outlines to be used by the optimizer, set the USE_STORED_OUTLINES initialization parameter to TRUE or to a category name (such as FAB_SALES in the earlier examples). Once the stored outline use is enabled, any query with a stored outline will use the hints generated when the outline was created. You can also enable USE_STORED_OUTLINES at the session level via the **alter session** command.

You must have the CREATE ANY OUTLINE system privilege in order to create an outline. Use the **create outline** command to create an outline for a query, as shown in the following listing:

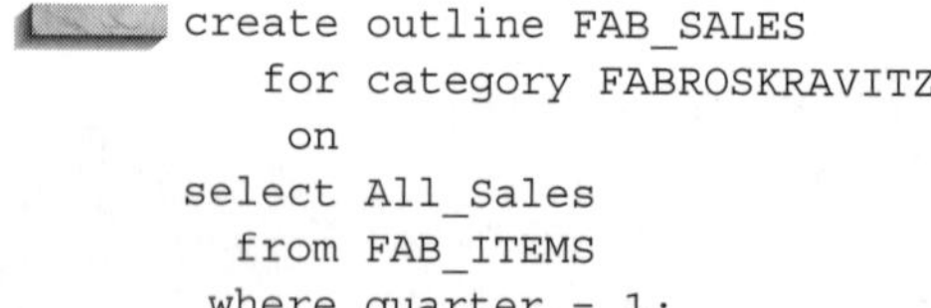

```
create outline FAB_SALES
   for category FABROSKRAVITZ
    on
select All_Sales
  from FAB_ITEMS
 where quarter = 1;
```

NOTE
If you do not specify a name for your outline, the outline will be given a system-generated name that may not be meaningful to human beings.

To start creating hints for all queries, set the CREATE_STORED_OUTLINES initialization parameter to TRUE. Once this is set, Oracle will then save an outline for every query executed. If you set CREATE_STORED_OUTLINES to TRUE, then all of the outlines will be saved under the DEFAULT category. As an alternative, you can create custom categories of outlines and use the category name as a value in the database initialization file, as shown in the following listing:

```
CREATE_STORED_OUTLINES = FAB_SALES
```

In this example, stored outlines will be stored for queries within the FAB_SALES category.

If you have set CREATE_STORED_OUTLINES to TRUE in your initialization file, Oracle will create stored outlines for your queries; using the **create outline** command gives you more control over the outlines that are created. You can create outlines for DML commands and for **create table as select** commands.

Once an outline has been created, you can alter it. You can use the **rebuild** clause of the **alter outline** command to regenerate the hints used during query execution, as shown here:

```
alter outline FAB_SALES rebuild;
```

You can also rename an outline via the **rename** clause of the **alter outline** command, as shown next:

```
alter outline FAB_SALES rename to FAB_SALES_BY_REGION;
```

You can change the category of an outline via the **change category** clause, as shown in the following example:

```
alter outline FAB_SALES_BY_REGION change category to DEFAULT;
```

You can verify that the outline is being used by looking at the V$SQL view. If the outline is being used, the Outline_Category column will display the name of the outline category for the SQL statement.

Two facilities are available for managing stored outlines: the OUTLN_PKG package and SQL statements, or Enterprise Manager. Using the OUTLN_PKG package, you can drop outlines that have never been used, or are within a specific category, and move outlines from one category to another. The OUTLN_PKG has three procedures: DROP_UNUSED, DROP_BY_CAT, and UPDATE_BY_CAT. To drop a specific outline, use the **drop outline** command. The Enterprise Manager Tuning pack also provides the same facility using a GUI front end.

You can view the outlines and related hints via the USER_OUTLINES and USER_OUTLINE_HINTS views. These views are based on the tables named OL$,

OL$HINTS, and OL$NODES owned by the user OUTLN and stored in the SYSTEM tablespace. A word of warning though—the password for OUTLN is the username, and this user does have DBA privileges!

As an added tuning benefit for the more advanced user, Oracle provides the ability to edit these stored outlines, either through a supplied stored procedure (DBMS_OUTLN_EDIT) or by using the Enterprise Manager Tuning Pack option Outline Editor.

PART V

Appendixes

APPENDIX A

Glossary

resented here is a set of brief definitions of the major terms you will encounter in this book. Every attempt has been made to ensure that all of the important terms have been included.

Access path The method that Oracle can use to get to the data. Access paths break down into two general methods—either using an index or accessing the data directly from the table. If more than one table is involved, the optimizer has to figure out which join method to use. *See also* Join method.

After image A copy of data after any changes have been made.

Alert log A file that is created when the database is created to track specific types of database interactions. The alert log contains information about each database startup and shutdown, each parameter that is not a default database value, each log thread switch, any database errors, and any data dictionary language commands that were used to alter the structure of the database.

Application One or more computer programs used to perform work on behalf of a business.

Applications DBA A DBA who works closely with application developers to assist in creating the structures within a database that are necessary to support an application.

ARCH (ARC0) The archiver background process. Used by Oracle to copy redo log files to one or more separate disks or tape drives to provide redundancy and help ensure database recovery. Required for online database backups and standby databases.

Architectural DBA A DBA whose primary function is to design and model the database structures for a system. This type of DBA should have a good understanding of the business processes to which the application is geared and the effect the processes have on both the flow and state of the data.

Archive log A file created by the archiver process that contains a copy of a redo log file. In Oracle8.0, archive logs can be copied to two locations, and in Oracle8i, they can be copied to up to five different locations on different disks and even to a remote site. As of Oracle9i, the number of different locations you may use has been increased to ten.

Archivelog mode A database state in which backups of the datafiles can be taken while the database is open. Databases must be in archivelog mode to be recoverable to a point in time past the time of the backup. When a database is in archivelog mode, the LGWR process cannot overwrite a redo log group until the group has been successfully archived.

Backup The process of copying one or more database files for protection of the data and recovery of the database; can be used in the database recovery process in the event of a failure/disaster. *See also* Backup, logical database and Backup, physical database.

Backup, logical database A method of storing database objects in an external file. The export (*see* Export) utility is used to perform this backup and can only be run when the database is up. The recovery process is performed via the import utility. *See also* Import.

Backup, physical database A method of directly copying Oracle datafiles to backup media. Physical backups can be either online or offline.

Backup plan A plan describing the procedures that will be used to back up and recover a database. Also known as a backup strategy.

Backup set Used in conjunction with the Recovery Manager; can contain either datafiles (a datafile backup set) or archive logs (an archive log backup set). Only one type of file can be stored in a backup set, but many files of the same type can be stored within each set. Often, the backup sets are written to tape.

Backup strategy *See* Backup plan.

Batch A group of rows returned in a single call to the database. Used with the **set arraysize** command; the maximum value is 5000. Setting the array size to greater than 100 usually has no additional effect on performance. The larger the array size setting, the more memory Oracle will need for each fetch.

Batch job *See* Batch process.

Batch process A procedure submitted to an operating system utility to perform work automatically. Can be scheduled to run immediately, once at a specified time, or repeatedly on a scheduled basis.

Before image A copy of data before any changes have been made.

Bit The smallest unit of data in a computer. A bit has a single binary value, either 0 or 1. *See also* byte.

Bit-mapped index Introduced in Oracle7.3, a bit-mapped index stores the rowids associated with a key value as a bitmap. These indexes should only be built on columns with a low number of different values. *See also* Low cardinality values.

Block Composed of bytes; the bytes are grouped together, usually in 512 bytes of operating system space per operating system block. *See also* Database block size.

Buckets Used in conjunction with a histogram to describe the distribution of data across a column in a table.

Byte Eight contiguous bits starting on any addressable boundary. A byte can be used to store one ASCII character. *See also* Bit.

Cache An amount of space reserved in memory in which data can be stored.

Check constraint Ensures that the data being inserted into a column meets certain conditions.

Check option constraint Placed on a view. Limits any inserts or updates to rows that the view itself can select.

Child table The table on which the foreign key is defined. *See also* Parent table.

Cold backup *See* Offline database backup.

Column An individual compartment in which a specific type of information is stored within a table. A column's definition will describe the type and size of the particular data that will be stored within it.

CONFIG.ORA A secondary configuration file used to store nondefault initialization parameters. Use the IFILE parameter in the init<sid>.ora file to include the contents of this file at startup.

Configuration files Used to store nondefault Oracle parameters. *See also* CONFIG.ORA, INIT.ORA, and SPFILE.ORA.

Constant A variable whose value is preassigned and retained throughout the execution of a software program.

Constraint A mechanism used to ensure that data is consistent within a table or across tables.

Cost Based Optimizer *See* Optimizer, Cost Based.

CPU A computer central processing unit.

Data DBA A person who determines the composition and management of data within a database. Often, this person is involved with data loading and data cleansing operations.

Data type The designation used to describe a specific data element.

Database A collection of information, electronically stored in one location, used to manipulate data in a logical way.

Database administrator (DBA) A person who creates, configures, and oversees the maintenance of a database.

Database block size The DBA-designated size of an Oracle block declared when creating a database and used for information storage. The default number of bytes in an Oracle database block in Oracle9i is 4096. *See also* Block.

Database migration The act of creating a new database under the new Oracle software version, making a copy of the old database, and putting that copy into the new database within the new version.

Database upgrade The act of shutting down the current database under the old Oracle software version, starting it up under the new Oracle software version, and immediately running configuration scripts to convert the database to the new Oracle software version.

Datafile The physical file used to store database information. Tablespaces are composed of datafiles.

DBWR (DBW0) The Oracle background process responsible for managing the contents of the data block buffer cache and the dictionary cache. The DBWR process reads blocks from datafiles and stores them in the SGA. The DBWR process also performs batch writes of changed blocks back to the datafiles.

Deadlock contention A situation that occurs when two or more users wait for data that is locked by each other. Oracle will kill the first server process that detects the deadlock.

Declaration (of variables) A mechanism used to describe the composition of a variable. *See also* Data type.

Detached processes The five or more processes that, along with the SGA, make up an Oracle instance. Each process has its own functionality and preassigned tasks.

Dictionary managed tablespace A tablespace whose free and used extents are tracked using the database data dictionary. *See also* Locally managed tablespace.

Directory The general area in which information is stored on a computer. There can be many different directories on a computer and several different levels of directories within a single directory.

Enqueue A mechanism that keeps track of users waiting for locks that are held by others and the lock mode these users require. The enqueue mechanism also keeps track of the order in which users requested the locks.

Export An Oracle-supplied utility that enables the capture of a table, set of tables, complete schema, set of schemas, or entire database as a snapshot in time. Instead of making a copy of the datafiles that reside on the system, a binary copy of the objects and their data as they exist within the database is made.

Extent A contiguous allocation of database blocks. An extent is dedicated to a specific table, cluster, index, temporary segment, or rollback segment. An extent is created whenever a segment is created or a current segment is not large enough to hold information that is being inserted.

File(s) The area in which information is stored within a directory.

File extension The ending names used to differentiate one form of file from another. Standard extensions are used for Oracle files, such as .ora to represent a parameter file, .exe to indicate an executable file, .dbf to designate a datafile.

File number, absolute The number identifying a datafile that is unique to the entire database.

File number, relative The number identifying a datafile that is unique within the tablespace.

Files-level backup *See* Offline database backup.

Foreign key constraint Refers only to columns defined as either primary key constraint columns or unique key constraint columns. Data values entered into these columns must already exist in the referenced columns. *See also* Referential integrity constraints.

Freelists Used to track the blocks that are available for inserts to the database.

Full table scan The action of examining every row in a table to gather information to fulfill a query.

Function A procedure that always returns a single value to the caller.

Function-based index Created with an expression (such as "upper") as part of the index.

Grant The action a DBA takes to assign a privilege to a user or role.

Header block The first of the extents allocated for a rollback segment. The header block is used by Oracle to store information that tracks the transactions accessing the specific rollback segment and the extents the transaction is using.

High availability (HA) Associated with backup and recovery. The methods and approaches used to ensure that a database and system are available 24 hours a day, 7 days a week.

Hint A direction that can be given to the Cost Based Optimizer to use a specific access method, join order, optimizer goal, or table order. *See also* Optimizer, Cost Based and Stored outline.

Histogram A set of statistics on a table that gives the optimizer additional information on the distribution of the data in the particular column of interest.

Hot backup *See* Online database backup.

Icon A symbol used to represent an object. On a Windows system, the directory indicators are file folder icons. Icons are frequently used in GUI applications.

Image backup *See* Offline database backup.

Image copy Used in conjunction with the Recovery Manager. An image copy is a copy of a single file (like a files-level backup); can be used either in a restore scenario or directly, by renaming a datafile within the database to the image copy.

Import An Oracle-supplied utility that enables the restoration of objects stored within an export file. Provides an easy way to restore one or more tables within a database.

Index A structure used to improve the speed of information retrieval in a database.

INIT.ORA A parameter file used by Oracle to define nondefault values for variables.

Installation *See* Software installation.

Instance Composed of a set of background processes and memory structures that access a set of database files. It is possible for a database to be accessed by multiple instances.

Join (tables or views) The act of combining parts of two or more tables or views to produce a complete picture of the information of interest.

Join method The name for the different algorithms the Oracle optimizer can call on to combine two different tables. Two of the different approaches available to join one set of data to another are nested loop and sort-merge. In a nested loop, one row of a table is selected, and then the process loops through the other table trying to find any matches. Using a sort-merge, both tables are sorted into the same order, and then the results are compared to find matches. *See also* Access path.

Latch A form of low-level locking used to protect a memory structure. A latch is usually held for a very brief amount of time.

Latches, immediate state A latch that is requested with an immediate state will try to obtain the latch once. If unsuccessful, the process will not wait but will continue on.

Latches, willing-to-wait state A latch that is requested with a willing-to-wait state will wait for a short time and try to obtain the latch again. The process will keep waiting and requesting over again until the latch becomes available and the process can obtain it.

LGWR A background process responsible for managing the writes of the contents of the redo log buffer to the online redo log files. The writes are performed in batches and contain the most up-to-date status of the data within the database.

LISTENER.ORA The primary file used to supply an Oracle Net or Net8 listener with configuration information.

Locally managed tablespace A tablespace whose header information contains a bitmap of all free and used extents within the tablespace. *See also* Dictionary managed tablespace.

Lock A mechanism normally used to protect a data structure. Can be held continuously until a commit or rollback occurs.

Locks, instance level Distributed locks used to ensure that structures remain consistent across more than one instance.

Locks, transaction level Used to ensure that a structure remains consistent while a transaction, such as an update, is performed.

Lookup table A table or view used to resolve a number into a meaningful name.

Low cardinality values In a table, a column that has a low number of different values, such as a gender column that has two different options—male and female. Bit-mapped indexes should be built only on low cardinality columns. *See also* Bit-mapped index.

Materialized view A refreshable, snapshot-like view that contains data for rapid query response. When used with query rewrite, provides a more performance rich environment.

Metadata Information about the database structure.

Mirroring The act of maintaining an exact copy of a file on a separate disk from the original file.

Net8 An Oracle-supplied utility to enable communication from a computer to a central database or from one database to another. *See also* Oracle Net and SQL*Net2.

Offline database backup A backup performed while the database is shut down to ensure that no processes are active within the database. Also known as cold backup, image backup, and files-level backup.

Online database backup Essential for an environment that operates 24 hours, 7 days a week. It derives its name from the fact that the database remains up and running while the backup is performed. The same files-level copies of the datafiles and control files are performed, but the redo log files are not backed up. Archivelog mode must be enabled so that Oracle knows the database is recoverable. Also known as hot backup.

Optimal (parameter for rollback segment) A value that is declared when a rollback segment is created to provide Oracle with a specific minimum size to which a rollback segment can be reduced.

Optimal Flexible Architecture (OFA) An approach, created by Cary Millsap, that describes the optimal way to locate files of an Oracle database on disks, defines the naming conventions to be used for files, and identifies the names and contents of directories used to house an Oracle database and software system.

Optimizer The part of Oracle responsible for determining how to retrieve the answer to a DML statement. The optimizer is used to break down a SQL statement into individual components and determine the fastest way to access the data and return the answer. It does this by first understanding which tables are involved in a SQL statement and choosing the best available access path to that data.

Optimizer, Cost Based Takes into account the relative resource "cost" of one access path over another when considering how to build the query plan. *See also* Access path, Hint, and Query plan.

Optimizer, Rule Based Uses a fixed set of instructions as guidelines when building a query plan for a SQL statement. These rules tell the optimizer how to value one access path over another when trying to determine the quickest approach to get to or join data.

Oracle Certified Professional (OCP-DBA) program The prescribed course of study and set of tests created by Oracle Education and administered by Prometrics to establish a DBA's basic knowledge of the Oracle products. There are three levels to the OCP program: Oracle Certified Associate (OCA), Professional (OCP), and Master (OCM).

Oracle Enterprise Manager (OEM) A graphical user interface (GUI) tool that enables management of remote databases from one central personal computer.

Oracle Enterprise Manager console An application that enables interface with the OEM tool set.

Oracle Enterprise Manager repository A set of tables stored in a database to hold information for the OEM tool.

Oracle Net An Oracle-supplied utility to enable communication from a computer to a central database or from one database to another. *See also* Net8 and SQL*Net2.

Oracle software A group of programs designed to enable the creation and interaction with an Oracle relational database.

Package Made up of combinations of procedures and functions, packages allow the grouping of related functions, procedures, and cursors as a single program unit.

Parent table The primary/unique key table. The table with the foreign key defined on it. *See also* Child table.

Parse The Oracle-performed act of examining a SQL statement to enable an execution plan to be created.

Personal Digital Assistant (PDA) A handheld device used for personal information storage.

Physical I/O The act of reading information from or writing information to a physical disk.

PMON The background process that cleans up behind failed user processes. PMON (process monitor) is responsible for releasing the lock and making it available to other users.

Primary key constraint Requires that the data in a particular column or combination of columns be a unique combination in the table and not be null.

Private synonym A synonym that is available only to the owner of the synonym.

Privilege The ability to perform a specific action within a database; granted to a user or role.

Procedures Several forms of stored programs, all of which are written either in PL/SQL, JAVA, or C (stored externally) and stored within the database. Each type of program can take input and return output. Functions always return a single value to the caller, while procedures can return none, one, or more values.

Process A job started by the operating system that can be used to run one or more computer programs.

Process freelist Also known as a freelist, this is a list of free data blocks within the extents within the segment.

Program A collection of computer commands assembled in one file that enables work to be performed on a computer.

Public synonym A synonym that is available to any user in the database. *See also* Synonym.

Query A statement presented to a database to obtain information. The query will always begin with the command word **select**.

Query plan The set of instructions the optimizer puts together on how to access the data and, if necessary, join multiple tables most efficiently.

Query rewrite The facility Oracle uses to automatically rewrite a query so that it uses a materialized view instead of the underlying tables to improve query response times. *See also* Materialized view.

Quota An allotment of space assigned to a user or process on a computer system.

RAID A redundant array of inexpensive disks used to enable the storage of data in a protected fashion.

Readme documentation One or more files supplied with computer software to provide additional information that may have been written after the official documentation was published.

Read-only constraint Placed on a view to flag that view as one you cannot update, insert into, or delete from.

RECO The background process used to resolve failures in distributed databases.

Recovery The act of replacing damaged or deleted database files with backed up copies.

Recovery Manager (RMAN) An Oracle-supplied utility to enable backup and recovery of a database in an easy, automatic manner.

Recovery plan A defined approach containing procedures to be used when a database recovery must be performed. *See also* Backup plan.

Redo log A collection of the changes made to a database.

Referential integrity constraints Primary and foreign keys. A referential integrity constraint defines a relationship between columns in one or more tables.

Relational database management system (RDBMS) A set of programs designed to manage and manipulate data in the fastest, most efficient manner.

Reloads The number of times statements are reparsed in order to be executed. If a statement is aged out of the cache, or an object referenced by the statements is invalidated (changed in some way), the statement must be reparsed to be reexecuted. The action of reparsing a statement is counted as a reload.

Repository A schema in the database used to store information to support a specific application. Used specifically with the Oracle Enterprise Manager tool and RMAN.

Revoke The action a DBA takes to remove a privilege from a user or role.

Rollback segment Used to capture the image of data before it is changed to provide read integrity. Queries, performed against the data while it is being changed, will return the before-image version of the data.

Rollback segment, private Explicitly acquired when a database is opened, these rollback segments are available only to the first instance that acquires them.

Rollback segment, public Available for use by any instance, these rollback segments can be acquired for a pool of rollback segments, if available.

Row An area of a table that stores one complete, individual set of information. A row can comprise one or more columns of information and is identified by a unique identification number within a table and within the database. In Oracle versions earlier than Oracle8 and later versions, the row identification number contains 6 bytes; in Oracle8 and later versions, the row identification number contains 10 bytes.

Rule Based Optimizer *See* Optimizer, Rule Based.

Schema An area designated within a database in which an application's objects are stored.

Segment A collection of extents that make up a single table, index, temporary segment, or rollback segment. *See also* Extent.

Self-referring constraint A constraint in which the parent and child tables are the same table.

Session A connection to the database including the memory area as well as the access privileges allocated to a specific user.

Shared pool or shared SQL pool Used to store the data dictionary cache and the library cache. Within the library cache is information about statements that have been run against the database. The shared pool contains the execution plans and parse trees for SQL statements run against the database. The second time an exact replica of a SQL statement is presented, the statement can be run much more quickly because the execution plan is already stored and available.

SMON The system monitor background process. Used to perform system tasks for an Oracle database, such as conducting instance recovery as needed, eliminating transactional objects that are no longer needed, coalescing adjacent tablespace free space.

Snapshot A picture of a table or set of tables that is captured at a point in time. Snapshots are copies of data in one database that have been copied to another database.

Snapshot, complex Created by selecting information from multiple tables with subqueries or "group by" clauses. *See also* Snapshot, simple.

Snapshot fast refresh A simple snapshot can be refreshed with changes to the data only.

Snapshot full refresh The data in a complex snapshot has to be completely copied to the remote database.

Snapshot refresh The act of updating a snapshot with the most current information available.

Snapshot, simple Created by selecting information from a single table or a simple set of tables that are joined together. *See also* Snapshot, complex.

Software A collection of computer programs designed to enable a user to accomplish a specific set of tasks.

Software installation The act of placing a complete set of software in a directory structure.

Software migration The act of creating a separate directory structure for the new Oracle software version's files. There will be two (or more) copies of Oracle software on the system at one time in completely separate directories.

Software upgrade The act of overwriting the old Oracle software version's files with the new version's files.

SPFILE.ORA System initialization parameter file that can be changed dynamically while the database is online and available. Replaces the INIT.ORA initialization parameter file.

SQL*Net2 An Oracle-supplied communications package that enables a remote client to communicate with a central Oracle database.

SQL*Plus An Oracle-supplied utility to enable a user to insert, update, remove, or view information in a database.

Standby database A separate database located on a remote node that mirrors the production database. Starting in Oracle8i, it can be used as a read-only database and switched over to a standby database to resynchronize the data. The ability to use the database in read-only mode provides the option of using the standby for decision support system types of activities.

Stored outline A collection of hints for a SQL statement saved in the data dictionary. *See also* Hint.

Stored program or procedure One or more PL/SQL scripts stored directly in the database for ease of access.

Striping The act of combining two or more disks into a logical, single disk for data storage and information protection.

Structured Query Language (SQL) An ANSI standard language used to interact with a database.

Synonym Sometimes referred to as an alias, a synonym masks or hides the real name and owner of an object.

System global area (SGA) Holds the most commonly requested structural information about the database and facilitates the transfer of information between users. The SGA comprises the data block buffer cache and the dictionary cache, the redo log buffer, and the shared SQL pool, which is made up of a context area and a program global area.

System identification number (SID) Generally, a name used to differentiate between instances and to ensure that the correct processes, and in turn the correct data, are being manipulated.

Systems DBA A DBA who oversees and performs database administration for a set of databases on a system.

Table The logical unit of storage for a specific collection of data. Made up of columns, a table is used to store rows of information.

Tablespace The logical storage area for one or more objects in a database.

Technical Assistance Request (TAR) An identification number assigned by Oracle Support, describing a problem that has been encountered with an Oracle product or database.

Temporary table A table specifically used for temporary data storage. The temporary table can be made available for one session or globally.

Temporary tablespace A tablespace specifically used for sort and aggregate operations such as sum, order by, group by, and so on. Objects cannot be created in a temporary tablespace. The temporary segments are retained after a sort operation completes and are made available for the next sort operation.

TNSNAMES.ORA A file that contains connection information describing the locations of databases. Configured to be used with the Oracle Net or Net8 listener.

Transportable tablespaces A mechanism that enables a tablespace to be relocated to another database.

Trigger Used to capture or verify information or load other tables with data as needed.

Undo segments Oracle-managed rollback segments stored in an Undo Tablespace.

Undo Tablespace Storage area for Oracle-managed rollback segments.

Unique constraint Requires that the data be a unique combination, but will allow you to insert null values.

Unique index An index in which the only acceptable values are nulls or a unique combination of one or more columns.

Unix A form of operating system available through several different hardware vendors. There are many different "flavors" of Unix, including SCO, Linux, HP-UX, Compaq, and AIX. Each flavor of Unix will require slightly different database installation and configuration procedures and Oracle software.

Unix process ID A unique identification number assigned to a Unix operating system process.

Upgrade *See* Software upgrade.

User A person who performs work on a system or database.

View A combination of columns from one or more tables that enable a user to see selected portions of database information while preventing access to other sensitive areas.

Willing-to-wait state *See* Latches, willing-to-wait state.

Wizard A Java program that guides the user through performing a task. In Oracle9i, many Java wizards are used to assist the DBA in performing various database administration tasks, such as database backup and recovery, and network configuration.

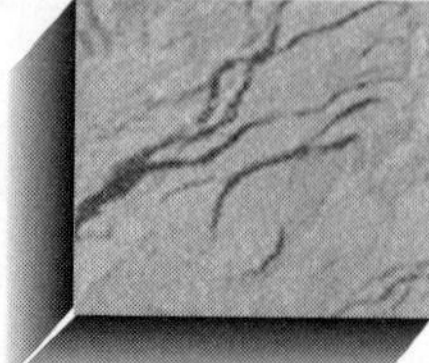

APPENDIX B

Resources

In the original Oracle DBA 101 book, in Chapter 1, we offered information on how to become a DBA. When we decided to update the book for Oracle9i, we reviewed the original manuscript to see what we could do to make the information more meaningful. After some consideration, we realized that although the information on becoming a DBA is very important, there are other resources that we did not cover in enough detail. Rather than have a section of the book with only one chapter, titled "Beyond Your World," we decided to present the material to you in an appendix. Thus, here is information on how to become a DBA, including the new approach Oracle is using for Oracle certification, and information on MetaLink and Oracle Technical Network (Technet), which enable you to interact with Oracle through the Internet.

On Becoming a DBA

As recently as ten years ago, the only actions you could take to become an Oracle DBA were these:

- Experiment with your database and hope you did not corrupt it beyond recoverability
- Read the Oracle documentation (a very daunting task indeed)
- Go to Oracle-supplied education classes
- Attend Oracle user group meetings and beat the information out of your fellow DBAs (which tended to make you a very unpopular attendee)

Today, there are many opportunities to gain Oracle database administration training. In this section, we're going to overview ways that you can train to become a DBA and the certification programs that Oracle now offers to help you prove that you have moved beyond just being able to spell Oracle.

About Training

As Oracle products have become more mature and gained in popularity, we have seen a shortage of Oracle DBAs in industry. Because of the high demand for trained DBAs, more and more companies have been created to supply Oracle-based training. Oracle Corporation has expanded its training offerings and, with each new release of its product set, has introduced a new set of training opportunities as well as a new set of certification examinations. Many colleges, universities, and some community adult continuing education venues offer Oracle training opportunities.

College, University, and Community Continuing Adult Education Classes

More and more colleges are offering classes not only in computer science or information technology but also in database administration. These classes are usually generic, teaching you the principles behind database administration. You will need a grounding in data modeling—the practice of taking the real-world information flow and turning it into entities and relationships that can then be translated into the physical world, the database structures, and objects. You will learn how to write and tune SQL, the Structured Query Language that is used to access most databases, Oracle included.

Some schools offer degree programs in Oracle database administration specifically. How do you go about finding these schools? The best place to start is with your local colleges and universities. Get a catalog and look through it. Call college bookstores and ask which books are part of the computer curriculum. The Oracle Academic Initiative (OAI) has a Web site that lists colleges that provide classes using the Oracle University curriculum.

If your local schools don't offer the classes you need, the Internet is the next place to go. Do a search on "database administration." Look for the schools that offer classes, in Oracle in particular, but in general database principles as well.

What if you already have a degree and want to change what you do? Going back to college for a four-year degree isn't always an option. That's when you have to be a bit more creative. Take classes from Oracle Corporation, or take the certification classes. (We'll discuss those in more detail in a little while.) Join your local Oracle users group. You will find people and companies there who offer training courses designed to teach you the specifics of administering a database.

Ask your company for training. Many companies will pay for classes that make you more valuable to them. It's often easier and less expensive for companies to train an employee in the new technology than to hire someone proficient in the technology who doesn't know their business. So don't be afraid to ask your current employer about opportunities to be trained as an Oracle DBA. Your manager may not be able to take immediate action in helping you get training, but if you don't speak up, how will anyone know that you want to become a DBA?

Search the Internet (try a search on "Oracle education") for companies that offer training classes on a variety of specific Oracle topics. Use several search engines, as you can often get hits from one engine that don't appear on a second engine's search results list.

Train Yourself

When all else fails, start training yourself. Oracle often offers free trial software. You can even purchase a one-user license and receive automatic software upgrades as new products are released for your platform of choice. Download the software from the Web—we'll tell you more about how to obtain the software in the section on Technet—if you have a fast enough Internet connection, or order the software to be shipped to you on CD-ROM disks. Install the Oracle software, and start playing.

Read the Oracle documentation (yes, all of it!). Or, at least read the Concepts manual and the "New Features" sections. Build yourself a test database and begin to work with it. Look for and read the many and varied technical books available at your local or Internet bookstores. Join an Oracle-based newsgroup or list server (listserv). There are several excellent ones out there, populated by all levels of DBAs who are willing to answer questions from the novice. A word of caution though: many of the listservs are very active, and you might receive as many as 100 to 200 emails per day from them. This can be an overwhelming amount of electronic mail and can easily flood some email storage allowances. However, the volume of educational information you can receive may be worth the amount of email traffic generated from some of these groups.

Before you post any questions to any of the groups, though, we recommend that you read the Oracle documentation. Often, the answers to your questions are in the documentation set. With Oracle9i, a very helpful and effective search engine is delivered with the documentation set. You can search by keyword or just look at the list of books included in the set and decide what books might cover the question you have.

Performing a Job Search

The need for trained Oracle professionals has been increasing rapidly over the last several years. Even with the recession in the United States, DBAs are still very much in demand. But where do you begin to look for the position that is right for you? What qualifications should you emphasize on a resume to help you get an entry-level position?

First, look in your local newspaper listings. Be creative in your search; database jobs can and will be listed under "Computers," "Database," "Oracle," and "Programmers." Join the local users group, and start networking. Talk to people who are presenting or who are running the meetings. Introduce yourself to other DBAs and talk to them. These are the people who will hear about jobs or know recruiters who are looking for DBAs. Look through the internal job listings at your current company. Many companies would rather promote or train someone from within.

Again, search the Internet. Just as you can find Oracle courses on the Web to train yourself, you will see companies, like Monster.com, OraPeople.com, or HotJobs.com, that specialize in job placements. Look on the Web sites of the companies that make third-party products to help DBAs monitor and maintain their databases. Often these companies will have an email address to which you can send your resume.

That said, what should you put on your resume to make a company want to hire you? The reality is, entry-level jobs are hard to find. Most companies want someone who already has experience as an Oracle DBA. Highlight the projects you have done in school. Include jobs and projects that are not directly related to database work, but that do reflect your strengths in planning and implementing projects.

About the Oracle Certified Professional Program

"Are you certifiable?" reads an advertisement from Oracle Education about their Oracle Certified Professional program. What's this certification about? What does it cover? Is it worthwhile?

For many years when someone applied for a job as an Oracle DBA, an employer had only the applicant's resume and the interviewer's skills to evaluate a prospective employee. This combination was not always enough to ensure that the person who was hired could perform the expected tasks effectively. To solve this problem, Oracle Education created and arranged for Prometric Testing Centers to proxy an Oracle database administrator certification program, although you can now take some of the tests at Oracle University Training Centers as well. The idea behind the program is to help the industry easily recognize a trained DBA from an untrained one. Over time, Oracle has enhanced the certification program and, with Oracle9i, has introduced three levels of database administration certification. In the next section, we'll tell you about these new programs and what's required to obtain each of the certifications in the database arena.

Oracle Certified Professional (OCA/OCP/OCM) Test

In 1997 at the Oracle Open World Conference in Los Angeles, Oracle Education unveiled a new version 7.3 certification program. As new versions of the database are released, Oracle Education releases matching versions of the tests to allow you to maintain and upgrade your certification level. Although the Oracle 7.3 Database Administrator certification has been desupported, Oracle Education offers certification for database administrators in the following areas:

- Three different levels of certification in Oracle9i: Oracle Certified Associate (OCA), Oracle Certified Professional (OCP), and Oracle Certified Master (OCM)
- Oracle Database Administrator certification in Oracle8 and Oracle8i (OCP)
- Oracle Database Operator certification in a subset of the database administration functions

Table B-1, taken from the Oracle Certification Web site, shows the Oracle9i database testing information.

Exam Number	Exam Title	Questions Required to Pass	Total Questions	Passing %	Duration
1Z0-001	Introduction to Oracle: SQL and PL/SQL	39	57	68%	2 hours
1Z0-007	Introduction to Oracle9i: SQL	45	60	75%	2 hours
1Z0-031	Oracle9i Database: Fundamentals I (Basic Section)	25	35	71%	1.5 hours
	Oracle9i Database: Fundamentals I (Mastery Section)	14	25	56%	
1Z0-032	Oracle9i Database: Fundamentals II	41	63	65%	1.5 hours
1Z0-033	Oracle9i Database: Performance Tuning (Coming 2002)	Not Available			
1Z0-030	Oracle9i Database: New Features for Administrators	38	56	67%	1.5 hours

TABLE B-1. *Oracle9i Certification Testing Requirements*

NOTE
Although the Basic and Mastery sections show the same test title and number, there are actually two sections to the exam. Questions in both the Basic and Mastery sections on the exam cover the fundamental concepts taught in the Oracle University courses. Questions in the Mastery section are somewhat more difficult than the questions in the Basic section, and may draw more extensively on your practice or experience. You must pass both sections in order to pass the exam.

Bear in mind that passing scores can vary from test to test and version to version, and the information is provided here just as a gauge of what Oracle is using at the time of this writing. Values could change tomorrow. Times and test numbers may change as well.

In the "Oracle9i Certified Professional" section a little later in the chapter, we'll concentrate on what's involved in becoming a certified Oracle9i database administrator.

Oracle9i Certified Associate

The initial set of tests for a DBA using Oracle9i, dubbed the Oracle Certified Associate exam, consists of two parts:

- Test 1: Introduction to Oracle9i: SQL (administered online)
- Test 2: Oracle9i Database: Fundamentals I (a proctored exam)

The goal of the Associate certification is to show that you have the foundation of knowledge to enable you to act as a junior team member working with database administrators or application developers. This certification will differentiate you from those without any credentials, and can help you obtain that first, entry-level position. Here are the topics you need to know to pass each of the tests. For the Introduction to Oracle9i SQL, you must be able to perform the tasks shown in Table B-2. The tasks you must be able to perform to pass the Fundamentals I test are shown in Table B-3.

Topic	Task
Writing Basic SQL Select Statements	List the capabilities of SQL SELECT statements
	Execute a basic SELECT statement
	Differentiate between SQL statements and iSQLPlus commands
Restricting and Sorting Data	Limit the rows retrieved by a query
	Sort the rows retrieved by a query
Single-Row Functions	Describe various types of functions available in SQL
	Use character, number, and date functions in SELECT statements
	Use conversion functions

TABLE B-2. *Requirements for Oracle9i SQL Test*

Topic	Task
Displaying Data from Multiple Tables	Write SELECT statements to access data from more than one table using equality and nonequality joins
	View data that generally does not meet a join condition by using outer joins
	Join a table to itself using a self-join
Aggregating Data Using Group Functions	Identify the available group functions
	Use group functions
	Group data using the GROUP BY clause
	Include or exclude grouped rows by using the HAVING clause

TABLE B-2. *Requirements for Oracle9i SQL Test* (continued)

Topic	Task
Oracle Architectural Components	Describe the Oracle architecture and its main components
	Describe the structures involved in connecting a user to an Oracle instance
Getting Started with the Oracle Server	Identify common database administrative tools available to a DBA
	Identify the features of the Oracle Universal Installer
	Explain the benefits of Optimal Flexible Architecture
	Set up password file authentication
	List the main components of the Oracle Enterprise Manager and their uses

TABLE B-3. *Requirements for Oracle9i Fundamentals I Test*

Topic	Task
Managing an Oracle Instance	Create and manage initialization parameter files
	Configure OMF
	Start up and shut down an instance
	Monitor the use of diagnostic files
Creating a Database	Describe the prerequisites necessary for database creation
	Create a database using Oracle Database Configuration Assistant
	Create a database manually

TABLE B-3. *Requirements for Oracle9i Fundamentals I Test* (continued)

You can find details and sample tests on the Oracle Education Web site using the link http://www.oracle.com/education/certification/index.htm. There is a fee to download the Oracle-supplied sample tests.

Oracle9i Certified Professional

To obtain the Oracle Certified Professional level, you must demonstrate skills managing a large-scale database or developing robust applications that are deployed enterprisewide. The Oracle certification program assumes that you will first pass your OCA and then take the OCP tests after a period of time working in the field and studying. To become an Oracle Certified Professional, you must pass all of the required exams. Having the OCP shows that you have attained a more senior level of knowledge.

You must pass the following two exams to obtain the OCP certification:

- Oracle9i Database: Fundamentals II (#1Z0-032)
- Oracle9i Database: Performance Tuning (#1Z1-033)

Let's take a look at the areas in which you must be knowledgeable. Table B-4 shows the requirements for the Oracle9i Fundamentals II test, and Table B-5 shows the requirements for the Oracle9i Performance Tuning test.

NOTE
The information provided here is based on information on the Oracle Education Web site and may not be complete.

Topic	Task
Networking Overview	Explain solutions included with Oracle9i for managing complex networks
	Describe Oracle networking add-on solutions
Basic Oracle Net Architecture	Explain the key components of the Oracle Net layered architecture
	Explain Oracle Net Services role in client server connections
	Describe how Web client connections are established through Oracle networking products
Basic Net Server-Side Configuration	Identify how the listener responds to incoming connections
	Configure the listener using Oracle Net Manager
	Control the listener using the listener control utility (lsnrctl)
	Describe Dynamic Service Registration
	Configure the listener for IIOP and HTTP connections
Basic Oracle Net Services Client-Side Configuration	Describe the difference between host naming and local service name resolution
	Use Oracle Net Configuration Assistant to configure the following: host naming, local naming method, Net service names
	Perform simple connection troubleshooting
Usage and Configuration of the Oracle Shared Server	Identify the components of the Oracle Shared Server
	Describe the Oracle Shared Server architecture
	Configure the Oracle Shared Server
	Identify and explain the usefulness of related dictionary views

TABLE B-4. *Requirements for Oracle9i Fundamentals II Test*

Topic	Task
Backup and Recovery Overview	Describe the basics of database backup, restore, and recovery
	List the types of failures that may occur in an Oracle environment
	Define a backup and recovery strategy
Instance and Media Recovery Structures	Describe the Oracle processes, memory structures, and files relating to recovery
	Identify the importance of checkpoints, redo log files, and archived log files
	Describe ways to tune instance recovery
Configuration of the Database Archiving Mode	Configure noarchivelog and archivelog mode
	Automatic and manual archiving of redo log files
	Multiple archival destinations and processes
Oracle Recovery Manager (RMAN) Overview and Configuration	Identify the features and components of RMAN
	Describe the RMAN repository and control file usage
	Describe channel allocation
	Describe Media Management Library interface
	Connect to Recovery Manager
	Configure the RMAN environment
User-Managed Backups	Describe user-managed backup and recovery operations
	Perform open and closed database backups
	Clean up after a failed online backup
	Back up the control file
	Discuss backup issues associated with "read-only" tablespaces

TABLE B-4. *Requirements for Oracle9i Fundamentals II Test* (continued)

Topic	Task
	Identify the backup implications of operations with NOLOGGING options
	Use DBVerify to check for block corruption
RMAN Backups	Identify RMAN-specific backups
	Use the RMAN BACKUP command to create backup sets
	Back up the control file
	Back up the archived redo log files
	Use the RMAN COPY command to create image copies
User-Managed Complete Recovery	Describe media recovery
	Perform recovery in noarchivelog and archivelog mode
	Perform read-only tablespace recovery
	Relocate and recover a tablespace
RMAN Complete Recovery	Describe the use of RMAN for restoration and recovery
	Perform complete recovery in noarchivelog and archivelog mode
	Restore data files to a different location
	Relocate and recover a tablespace
User-Managed Incomplete Recovery	Describe the steps of incomplete recovery
	Identify the situations that require incomplete recovery
	Perform an incomplete recovery
	Recover from the loss of current online redo logs
RMAN Incomplete Recovery	Perform incomplete recovery using UNTIL TIME
	Perform incomplete recovery using UNTIL SEQUENCE

TABLE B-4. *Requirements for Oracle9i Fundamentals II Test* (continued)

Topic	Task
RMAN Repository Maintenance	Perform cross-checking of backups and copies
	Update the repository when backups have been deleted
	Change the availability status of backups and copies
	Make a backup or copy exempt from the retention policy
	Catalogue backups made with operating system commands
RMAN Catalog Creation and Usage	Describe the contents of the recovery catalog
	List the RMAN features that require the recovery catalog
	Create the recovery catalog
	Maintain the recovery catalog by using RMAN commands
	Use RMAN to register, resynchronize, and reset a database
	Query the recovery catalog to generate reports and lists
	Create, store, and execute scripts
	Describe methods for backing up and recovering the recovery catalog
Transporting Data Between Databases	Export
	Import
	Guidelines for using export and import
Loading Data in the Database	SQLLoader--conventional and direct loads
	Uses of SQLLoader
	Direct inserts
	Guidelines for using SQLLoader and direct inserts

TABLE B-4. *Requirements for Oracle9i Fundamentals II Test* (continued)

Topic	Task
Oracle Performance Tuning Methodology	Describe the roles associated with the database tuning process
	Describe the dependency between tuning in different development phases
	Describe service level agreements
	Describe the tuning goals
	Describe the most common tuning problems
	Describe tuning goals associated with different types of applications
Diagnostic and Tuning Tools	Describe the data dictionary and dynamic performance views related to tuning
	Describe the statistics in the dynamic performance views
	Describe how STATSPACK collects statistics
	Collect statistics using STATSPACK
	List and describe how other tools can be used for tuning
	Describe uses of the ANALYZE command
	Describe the use of alert log and trace files
Sizing the Shared Pool	Measure and tune the library cache hit ratio
	Measure and tune the dictionary cache hit ratio
	Size and pin objects in the shared pool
	Tune the shared pool reserve space
	Describe UGA and session memory considerations
	Describe other tuning issues related to the shared pool

TABLE B-5. *Requirements for Oracle9i Performance Tuning Test*

Oracle9i Certified Master

New with version 9i is the Oracle9i Certified Master program. To become an Oracle Certified Master, the DBA should be a member of the senior IT staff, responsible for handling mission-critical database systems and applications. Master DBAs will have proven Oracle skills and be looked upon as experts within their organization. Generally speaking, people who qualify as Master DBAs will command the highest salaries in the industry. You must first hold an OCP to become an OCM, you must attend two advanced-level Oracle University courses, and you must take and pass the required examination.

Table B-6 lists the courses that you can choose from to qualify to take the Master's practicum exam. This list is from the Oracle Web site. We recommend that you check the Oracle Web site to confirm test availability dates.

Database Applications
Oracle9i: Program with PL/SQL
Oracle9i: Advanced PL/SQL
Oracle9i: SQL Tuning Workshop
High Availability
Oracle9i: High Availability in an Internet Environment
Data Warehouse and Large-Scale Databases
Oracle9i: Database: Implement Partitioning
Oracle9i: Real Application Clusters Implementation
Oracle9i: Data Warehouse Administration
Networking and Distributed Systems
Oracle9i: Advanced Replication
Systems Management
Oracle9i: Enterprise Manager

TABLE B-6. *Oracle9i Certified Masters Courses*

MetaLink

If you or your company has purchased Oracle support, you can connect to the Oracle Web site and join the MetaLink support service. The link is metalink.oracle.com. Through MetaLink, you can access public Oracle papers and bulletins and the technical forums, where you can post questions or read about problems and questions that other DBAs have had. These forums are monitored by Oracle technical support staff members who are quick to investigate and post responses. In addition, you will find that most DBAs who read these forums will post answers to others' questions.

NOTE
Some companies do not allow their employees to create their own accounts on MetaLink. They have a MetaLink Administrator who is responsible for logging TARs. The administrator can assign privileges to users within the company.

MetaLink also provides a place where you can check on known problems with Oracle software. You can search the bug database and see if someone else has logged a problem matching one that you have. You can also see recommended solutions for problems that have been reported and repaired.

Technet

Imagine connecting to one place on the Internet that offers its membership for free and supplies you with the ability to download all of the new Oracle products as they are released. The link for this site is technet.oracle.com, and it's a site you'll want to access often.

Referred to as the Oracle Technical Network, Technet is a members-only Web site that provides some wonderful information and guidance on product installation and Oracle white papers written by Oracle employees. You can find security alerts and sample code as well as trial product downloads, discussion groups, event highlights, and links to user groups, among other features. There's even an Oracle online store from which you can purchase your own copy of the Oracle9i Enterprise Edition software. We recommend that you bookmark the Technet home page and visit it often.

A Few Useful Links

The problem with listing "useful links" in a book is that the links may disappear tomorrow. Now, having said that, here's a list of links that have been around for quite a while that should remain available (hopefully) for a long time to come.

The Web site www.ioug.org is the home of the International Oracle User Group–Americas that represents Oracle professionals in the United States and South America. There are links on this site to most of the Oracle user groups in the United States. For European groups, you can start at www.eoug.com and www.ukoug.com. These sites provide information about user groups and activities for most of Europe, the Middle East, and Africa.

We've mentioned joining listservs, so here are a few that we like. Although Virginia Oracle User Group sounds like a local organization, members from all over the world submit questions and supply answers. Membership is free, and you can join by going to www.voug.com. A few others are

- www.nyoug.org—the New York Oracle Users Group site posts presentations and papers that have been given at various meetings, as well as a collection of older papers.
- Oracle-l listserv—this is an email group of Oracle DBAs and developers who post and answer questions for one another. To join this group, send an email to ListGuru@fatcity.com with the words SUBSCRIBE ORACLE-L and your name in the message body.
- www.lazydba.com—this site hosts an email group as well as downloads of SQL and shell scripts to help the DBA.
- www.orafaq.com—this site is a collection of links to other Oracle sites and FAQs about Oracle.

Index

A

D

E

F

G

H

I

J

K

L

M

N

O

P

Q

R

S

T

W

INTERNATIONAL CONTACT INFORMATION

AUSTRALIA
McGraw-Hill Book Company Australia Pty. Ltd.
TEL +61-2-9417-9899
FAX +61-2-9417-5687
http://www.mcgraw-hill.com.au
books-it_sydney@mcgraw-hill.com

CANADA
McGraw-Hill Ryerson Ltd.
TEL +905-430-5000
FAX +905-430-5020
http://www.mcgrawhill.ca

GREECE, MIDDLE EAST, NORTHERN AFRICA
McGraw-Hill Hellas
TEL +30-1-656-0990-3-4
FAX +30-1-654-5525

MEXICO (Also serving Latin America)
McGraw-Hill Interamericana Editores S.A. de C.V.
TEL +525-117-1583
FAX +525-117-1589
http://www.mcgraw-hill.com.mx
fernando_castellanos@mcgraw-hill.com

SINGAPORE (Serving Asia)
McGraw-Hill Book Company
TEL +65-863-1580
FAX +65-862-3354
http://www.mcgraw-hill.com.sg
mghasia@mcgraw-hill.com

SOUTH AFRICA
McGraw-Hill South Africa
TEL +27-11-622-7512
FAX +27-11-622-9045
robyn_swanepoel@mcgraw-hill.com

UNITED KINGDOM & EUROPE (Excluding Southern Europe)
McGraw-Hill Education Europe
TEL +44-1-628-502500
FAX +44-1-628-770224
http://www.mcgraw-hill.co.uk
computing_neurope@mcgraw-hill.com

ALL OTHER INQUIRIES Contact:
Osborne/McGraw-Hill
TEL +1-510-549-6600
FAX +1-510-883-7600
http://www.osborne.com
omg_international@mcgraw-hill.com